G000152711

PROGRAMMING THE OS/2 PRESENTATION MANAGER

PROGRAMMING THE OS/2 PRESENTATION MANAGER

The Microsoft® Guide to Writing Applications for the OS/2 Graphical Windowing Environment

PUBLISHED BY

Microsoft Press
A Division of Microsoft Corporation
16011 NE 36th Way, Box 97017, Redmond, Washington 98073-9717

Copyright © 1989 by Charles Petzold
All rights reserved. No part of the contents of this book may
be reproduced or transmitted in any form or by any means without
the written permission of the publisher.

Library of Congress Cataloging in Publication Data

Petzold, Charles, 1953-
Programming the OS/2 Presentation Manager.
Includes index.
1. OS/2 (Computer operating system)   2. Presentation Manager (Computer program)
3. Computer graphics.   4. C (Computer program language)   I. Title.
QA76.76.063P53   1989   005.4'469   88-27368
ISBN 1-55615-170-5

Printed and bound in the United States of America.

1 2 3 4 5 6 7 8 9   MLML   5 4 3 2 1 0 9

Distributed to the book trade in the United States
by Harper & Row.

Distributed to the book trade in Canada by General
Publishing Company, Ltd.

Distributed to the book trade outside the United States
and Canada by Penguin Books Ltd.

Penguin Books Ltd., Harmondsworth, Middlesex, England
Penguin Books Australia Ltd., Ringwood, Victoria, Australia
Penguin Books N.Z. Ltd., 182-190 Wairau Road, Auckland 10, New Zealand

British Cataloging in Publication Data available

Microsoft® and MS-DOS® are registered trademarks of Microsoft Corporation.
IBM® and PC/AT® are registered trademarks of International Business Machines Corporation.

Project Editor: Megan E. Sheppard   **Technical Editor:** Mary B. Ottaway

---

Contents

Preface

This book covers the basics of programming in C for the Presentation Manager, the graphical windowing environment included in OS/2 version 1.1. The Presentation Manager combines a powerful protected mode multitasking operating system (OS/2) with the application architecture and user interface of Microsoft Windows version 2 and a sophisticated graphics system from IBM.

The OS/2 Presentation Manager runs on IBM (and compatible) PCs and PS/2s that are based on the Intel 80286 and 80386 microprocessors. Although the Presentation Manager was designed for OS/2, IBM intends to port it to its minicomputers and mainframes, and Microsoft has announced plans to help port the Presentation Manager to run under UNIX.

I'm writing this preface just 37 days after OS/2 1.1 was officially released. Yet it already seems likely that the Presentation Manager will be the dominant application environment for small computers in the 1990s. Programmers, of course, will be responsible for writing these applications. The purpose of this book is to help aspiring Presentation Manager programmers get started in that job.

My Assumptions About You

I assume that you know how to program in C. If you don't, programming for the OS/2 Presentation Manager is probably not a good place to begin. I suggest you learn C programming for a more conventional environment such as the OS/2 kernel or DOS. You should have a comfortable familiarity with C pointers and structures, as well as an understanding of the concepts of ''near'' and ''far'' as they apply to the segmented-memory architecture of the Intel microprocessors.

I'm also assuming that you have some experience *using* the Presentation Manager. If not, take some time and play around with it.

I do not assume that you have any experience with programming for other graphical windowing environments such as the Apple Macintosh or Microsoft Windows. Experience with these environments might help with some of the initial conceptual hurdles, but it's not necessary.

What You'll Need

To compile and run the programs in this book, you need the following software installed on your hard disk:

- IBM OS/2 1.1 (if you have an IBM PC or PS/2) or a version of MS OS/2 1.1 available from the manufacturer of your computer

- The Microsoft OS/2 Software Development Kit, *or* The Microsoft OS/2 Programmer's Toolkit 1.1, *or* The Microsoft OS/2 Presentation Manager Softset

- The Microsoft C Compiler, version 5.1 (or later)

In addition, two of the programs shown in this book require the Microsoft Macro Assembler, version 5.1, but you can skip these programs if you want.

Both the Microsoft OS/2 Software Development Kit and the Microsoft OS/2 Programmer's Toolkit 1.1 have the header files you'll need for Presentation Manager programming, as well as the OS2.LIB import library, the resource compiler, development utilities such as ICONEDIT and DLGBOX, and technical documentation. Although *Programming the OS/2 Presentation Manager* shows you how to use many of the Presentation Manager function calls, it is not a replacement for the official technical documentation. (Note that the Microsoft OS/2 Presentation Manager Softset does *not* contain technical documentation. You might want to take this into consideration when deciding which package to purchase.)

You should be able to write and compile programs using the IBM OS/2 Programmer's Toolkit 1.1, the IBM C/2 Compiler 1.1, and the IBM OS/2 Technical Reference 1.1, but having not seen these packages, I can't verify this. Eventually, C compilers from other manufacturers will be suitable for compiling Presentation Manager programs. Check with the compiler manufacturer.

The hardware you'll need to run these programs is the same hardware you need to run OS/2 1.1. In addition, you should have a mouse. Although the Presentation Manager does not require a mouse, some of the programs in this book do.

Installing the C Compiler

The sample programs in this book generally use small model (that is, the .EXE files are compiled and linked to contain one code segment and one data segment). The "make files" for these sample programs assume that the OS/2 C run-time library for small model is named SLIBCE.LIB.

If You've Already Installed the Compiler

If you have already installed Microsoft C 5.1 for both OS/2 and DOS, the installed run-time libraries might be named SLIBCEP.LIB (for OS/2 protected mode) and SLIBCER.LIB (for real mode DOS). This is the default when you install the compiler for both OS/2 and DOS. In this case, rename SLIBCEP.LIB to SLIBCE.LIB.

It's also conceivable that when you installed Microsoft C 5.1 for OS/2 and DOS, you specified that you wanted to use the default library names for DOS. In this case, the installed run-time libraries are named SLIBCEP.LIB (for OS/2) and SLIBCE.LIB (for DOS). Rename SLIBCE.LIB to SLIBCER.LIB, and rename SLIBCEP.LIB to SLIBCE.LIB.

If you have already installed Microsoft C 5.1 and you know that your SLIBCE.LIB file is the OS/2 run-time library (rather than the DOS run-time library), you're in good shape.

If You're Installing for the First Time

If you are installing Microsoft C 5.1 for the first time, run the SETUP program included with the compiler. The second screen you see will ask you to make a number of decisions. You can choose the minimum configuration of Microsoft C 5.1 required to compile the programs in this book by accepting the defaults of five of the lines on this screen. You can handle the others as you wish. The important defaults are

- Build combined libraries.

- OS/2 Protect Mode libraries only.

- Emulator math library.

- Small memory model.

- Use default library names for the OS/2 libraries.

This configuration builds a small-model C run-time library for OS/2 named SLIBCE.LIB. Another question you're asked during the setup procedure is whether or not to delete the library components. You can answer "Yes."

If you prefer to install Microsoft C 5.1 for both OS/2 and DOS, you can do so. You should specify that you want to use the default library names for the OS/2 libraries but do *not* want to use the default library names for the DOS libraries. In this case, the OS/2 run-time library is named SLIBCE.LIB, and the DOS run-time library is named SLIBCER.LIB.

Some programs and dynamic link libraries in the last two chapters of this book do not use small model. These programs use special large-model libraries that are designed for multithread programs and dynamic link libraries. These libraries are always installed when you install Microsoft C 5.1 for OS/2, so you needn't do anything special to get them.

Other Books of Interest

The OS/2 Presentation Manager is a very large system that includes about 500 function calls in addition to the 240 functions in OS/2 1.0. I cannot pretend to cover them all in this book. In particular, my coverage of the Graphics Programming Interface (GPI) component of the Presentation Manager is restricted to the basics. A second book has been planned, and it will be dedicated to an in-depth discussion of GPI.

Before OS/2 1.1 there was OS/2 1.0, which is sometimes called the OS/2 kernel. Some of the programs in this book use OS/2 kernel functions. Although I discuss these functions when necessary, you can find much more information about the OS/2 kernel in Ray Duncan's *Advanced OS/2 Programming* (Microsoft Press, 1989).

Inter-Programmer Communication

If you'd like to get in touch with me, I can be reached through CompuServe (72241,56) or MCI Mail (CPETZOLD or 143-6815).

I can also frequently be found in the Programming forum of PC MagNet, *PC Magazine*'s information service available on CompuServe. To use this service, just type *go pcmagnet* at a CompuServe prompt and follow the menus to the Programming forum.

And Many Thanks

Programming the OS/2 Presentation Manager was begun in August 1987 (at a time when the Presentation Manager was barely functional) and was finished in early December 1988, about five weeks after the product had been officially released.

This book would have been impossible to produce without the help of some very fine people. I want to thank everyone at Microsoft Press who worked on the book during these 16 months, all of whom bore with me as the chapters and sample programs went through several series of revisions.

A number of people at Microsoft also helped in various ways, by answering questions, tracking down problems, offering suggestions and encouragement, pointing out the existence of a very useful function call that I had overlooked, or telling me I was doing something completely wrong. In alphabetic order, they are Steve Ballmer, Larry Barello, Mark Cliggett, Lori Hoerth, Doug Hogarth, Michael Hyman, Lionel Job, Neil Konzen, Jonathan Lazarus, Mike Leu, Mark Mackaman, Ron Murray, Tony Rizzo, Manny Vellon, and Ralph Walden. Thank you all very much.

I'd also like to congratulate everyone else at IBM and Microsoft involved in the design, development, and programming of the OS/2 Presentation Manager. You did a great job, and you did it by October 1988.

And many thanks to Jan and the Friday evenings that were my only refuge from the world of windows, messages, and presentation spaces.

Charles Petzold
December 7, 1988

Special Offer

Companion Disk to

PROGRAMMING THE OS/2 PRESENTATION MANAGER

Microsoft Press has created companion disks for PROGRAMMING THE OS/2 PRESENTATION MANAGER: 5.25-inch format (one high density disk) and 3.5-inch format (two low density disks). The disk(s) contain over 300 files from the book, which consist of the C source files, the MAKE files for compiling and linking the programs, as well as the other necessary support files. They also include the executable files for all programs in the book. And, the use of code fragments from the companion disks used for commercial or personal use does not infringe on the copyright of the book. So, save time, avoid those inevitable typing errors, and start using the source code in your programs right away!

If you have questions about the files on the disk, you can contact Charles Petzold via CompuServe (user ID 72241,56) or MCI Mail (user name CPETZOLD or 143-6815).

The Companion Disk to PROGRAMMING THE OS/2 PRESENTATION MANAGER is available only from Microsoft Press.

Domestic Ordering Information:

To order, use the special reply card bound in the back of the book. If the card has already been used please send $29.95, plus sales tax if applicable (CA residents 5% plus local option tax, CT 7.5%, FL 6%, MA 5%, MN 6%, MO 4.225%, NY 4% plus local option tax, WA state 7.8%), and domestic postage and handling charges: $5.00 per disk set. Send your order to: Microsoft Press, Attn: Companion Disk Offer, 21919 20th Ave S.E., Box 3011, Bothell, WA 98041-3011. Please specify 5.25-inch or 3.5-inch format. Payment must be in U.S. funds. You may pay by check or money order (payable to Microsoft Press) or by American Express, VISA, or MasterCard; please include both your credit card number and the expiration date. Please allow 2 – 3 weeks for delivery.

Foreign Ordering Information (within the U.K., see below):

Please follow ordering procedures for domestic order and add $6.00 for foreign postage and handling.

U.K. Ordering Information:

Send your order in writing along with £27.95 (including VAT) to: Microsoft Press, 27 Wrights Lane, London W8 5TZ. You may pay by check or money order (payable to Microsoft Press) or by American Express, VISA, MasterCard, or Diners Club; please include both your credit card number and the expiration date. Please specify 5.25-inch format or 3.5-inch format.

If any of these disks prove defective, please send them along with your packing slip to: Microsoft Press, Consumer Sales, 16011 NE 36th Way, Box 97017, Redmond, WA 98073-9717.

BASIC CONCEPTS

## CHAPTER ONE

OS/2 AND THE PRESENTATION MANAGER

The Presentation Manager is the primary application environment under OS/2. Programs designed to run under the OS/2 Presentation Manager share the video display with other programs in a graphical windowing environment. Presentation Manager programs are characterized by a consistent user interface involving menus, dialog boxes, scroll bars, and other visual devices that are accessible through either the keyboard or a pointing device such as a mouse. Users generally find such an interface to be easily learned and even mastered. Figure 1-1 on the following page shows several programs from this book running under the Presentation Manager.

The Presentation Manager user environment is reminiscent of systems developed at the Xerox Palo Alto Research Center (PARC) in the 1970s and early 1980s. In recent years, windowing environments have been popularized by the Apple Macintosh and, under MS-DOS, by Microsoft Windows. The user interface of the OS/2 Presentation Manager is the same interface used in Windows 2.0, Windows/286, and Windows/386.

For the program developer, the Presentation Manager has an extensive application program interface (API) that includes many high-level functions for creating windows and implementing the user interface. This API is largely derived from Microsoft Windows; although the two systems aren't exactly the same, they have many structural and conceptual similarities. The OS/2 Presentation Manager also includes the Graphics Programming Interface (GPI), a sophisticated graphics system adapted from IBM's Graphics Data Display Manager (GDDM) and the 3270 Graphics Control Program (GCP), with some elements inherited from the Windows Graphics

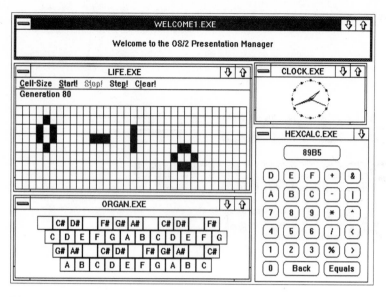

Figure 1-1. *An OS/2 Presentation Manager screen.*

Device Interface (GDI). Because the Presentation Manager runs under OS/2, programs designed for the environment can also take advantage of preemptive, priority-based multitasking, 16 megabytes of physical memory, virtual memory management, and interprocess communication.

This book shows you how to write programs for the OS/2 Presentation Manager. If you have some experience programming for Microsoft Windows or the Apple Macintosh, you're in good shape. But if your programming experience is limited to more conventional operating systems (such as MS-DOS, the OS/2 kernel, or UNIX), you need to put aside your preconceptions of how programs work and brace yourself for some strange ideas. We're off on a voyage to a new world.

The Big Picture

Developed by Microsoft and IBM as a successor to MS-DOS, OS/2 is an operating system for small computers based on the Intel 80286 and 80386 microprocessors. OS/2 uses the protected mode of the 80286 microprocessor to unleash the 16 MB address space of the 80286 and implement efficient and safe multitasking.

The introduction of OS/2 is a critical turning point for the entire industry that has grown up around the IBM PC. MS-DOS has proved unable to satisfy the growing needs of users and program developers. To be tolerable,

MS-DOS now requires various add-on kludges such as bank-switched memory or control programs based on the virtual-8086 mode of the 80386 microprocessor. OS/2 and the Presentation Manager give the IBM PC industry the opportunity to pull free of the MS-DOS quagmire and take a major step forward. Some people at Microsoft say that OS/2 will establish the foundations of PC operating systems for the next decade. That's a gutsy prediction. But considering that MS-DOS has lasted seven years already, it's really not so difficult to believe.

The OS/2 Kernel

The initial version of OS/2 (OS/2 1.0), often called the OS/2 kernel, has been available to programmers since June 1987. Microsoft released version 1.0 to original equipment manufacturers (OEMs) in December 1987, and IBM released it for retail sale the same month.

The OS/2 kernel is a traditional environment for both users and programmers. The command line interface and most internal and external commands have been inherited from MS-DOS. From the programmer's perspective, the functionality of the kernel resembles MS-DOS, UNIX, and traditional minicomputer operating systems. The kernel handles file I/O, memory management, and multitasking. The API includes facilities for keyboard and mouse input and a fast full-screen character-mode video I/O (VIO) system.

The OS/2 kernel supports multiple full-screen sessions (sometimes also called "screen groups"). Each session runs one or more processes that use the video display in either a teletype or full-screen fashion. A user can switch between sessions by pressing the Alt-Esc key combination. One session is the MS-DOS compatibility mode session, which uses the real mode of the 80286 microprocessor to run most existing programs written for MS-DOS.

The OS/2 Presentation Manager

The Presentation Manager is part of OS/2 version 1.1, released in the last quarter of 1988. In OS/2 1.1, one session runs in a graphics mode and is devoted to the Presentation Manager. All Presentation Manager applications (as well as a Task Manager and Start Programs window that are part of the Presentation Manager shell) run in this session. The addition of the Presentation Manager to OS/2 requires little in the way of changes to the OS/2 kernel. Instead, the Presentation Manager is basically a collection of dynamic link libraries (.DLL files) that extend the functionality of OS/2 to include window management and graphics.

Although the Presentation Manager session is primarily for Presentation Manager programs, many programs written for the OS/2 kernel can also run in "text windows" in this session. However, these programs can't use graphics or take advantage of menus, dialog boxes, and other aspects of the user interface. OS/2 kernel programs that write directly to the video display or that install video, keyboard, or mouse subsystems are prohibited from running under the Presentation Manager. These programs must continue to run in their own sessions.

Freedom of Choice

Programmers have a choice of developing applications for either the OS/2 kernel or the OS/2 Presentation Manager. Each environment has distinct advantages and disadvantages.

For some applications, the OS/2 kernel is obviously preferable. For example, an existing MS-DOS character-mode text editor or word processor that is known for its speed should probably be ported to the OS/2 kernel rather than to the Presentation Manager. Because the Presentation Manager runs in a graphics mode, a Presentation Manager version of the program will run more slowly with existing video display adapters. The kernel is also a better choice for developers who have designed a unique and well-known user interface for their MS-DOS programs and feel reluctant to abandon it.

Developers who want to port their MS-DOS programs to OS/2 as quickly as possible will find the kernel to be an easier path. Presentation Manager programs are more difficult to develop and debug than traditionally structured programs. Porting an existing MS-DOS program to the Presentation Manager often requires turning the program inside out to accommodate the Presentation Manager architecture.

But for many sophisticated applications — particularly those that use graphics — the Presentation Manager is clearly the better environment. Let's see why.

The Graphical Environment

The proof is in the programs. Two of the more interesting MS-DOS applications released in the past couple of years are Microsoft Excel and Aldus PageMaker, both of which run under Microsoft Windows. That both of these programs were originally developed for the Apple Macintosh indicates how a graphical windowing environment can inspire program developers to create a radically new and exciting variation of an older concept (in the case of Microsoft Excel) and even to create a whole new class of software (in the case of PageMaker). The graphical environment of the Presentation Manager is rich in functionality—programs can use graphics and formatted text to convey a high density of information to the user.

A traditional program gets user input from the keyboard and displays output to the screen. But with the addition of a mouse, the screen itself becomes a potential source of user input. Logic within the Presentation Manager assists the application in obtaining user input from various controls on the screen, such as menus, scroll bars, buttons, and dialog boxes. The interaction between the mouse and the screen narrows the gap between user and program.

The Consistent User Interface

Because the menu and dialog box interface is built into the Presentation Manager rather than into each individual application, the interface is consistent across applications. This means that a user with experience with one Presentation Manager program (or with Microsoft Windows) can easily learn a new Presentation Manager program. For example, the first time I saw a beta version of Microsoft Excel for Windows, I had no documentation, no help files, and no experience with the Macintosh version of Microsoft Excel. But I did have experience with other Windows programs. I knew how the menus and dialog boxes worked, and I was able to quickly learn much of Microsoft Excel solely by experimentation.

Some people fear that a system such as the Presentation Manager will lead to an undesirable uniformity of programs. Every program will look like every other program, they say, and designer creativity will be inhibited. To counter this view, the best examples are, again, PageMaker and Microsoft Excel. Although the menus and dialog boxes are certainly the most obvious aspects of the user interface, much more important interaction between the user and program occurs within the window itself. The programmer is liberated from worrying about the mundane aspects of the user interface and is free to spend more time where it really counts.

Device-independent Graphics

The IBM PC was designed around the principle of open architecture. Third-party manufacturers have responded to this fact by developing many different—and often incompatible—graphics output devices. Under MS-DOS, program developers have faced the problem of writing their own device drivers for the CGA, the Hercules Graphics Card, the EGA, and the VGA, as well as for a number of high-resolution video adapters. The problem of printers is even worse: Some MS-DOS word-processing packages include one or two disks containing nothing but small files, each supporting a different printer.

With the Presentation Manager, this all goes away. The Graphics Programming Interface (GPI) of the Presentation Manager is device independent. An application need not identify the output device in order to use it. If a Presentation Manager driver exists for the output device, then all Presentation Manager programs can use the device. This also helps to protect programs from obsolescence. Video technology is advancing very quickly, but Presentation Manager programs written today will run without change on the video adapters of the future.

The SAA Future

Aside from their important role in OS/2, the Presentation Manager user interface and API are also part of IBM's ambitious Systems Application Architecture (SAA). SAA attempts to correct a historical weakness in IBM's line of computers and operating systems by setting user interface and API standards. The Presentation Manager is one of the first products to be a part of SAA. If the goals of SAA come to pass, then the Presentation Manager user interface will become a common sight on IBM minicomputer and mainframe terminals. Just as important for the program developer, it may one day be possible to write a Presentation Manager program in a high-level language and compile it to run on a variety of computers from the IBM AT to the IBM 370.

Of course, this isn't going to happen next month or even the month after that. Porting Presentation Manager programs to other operating systems involves problems that PC programmers usually don't need to worry about (such as filenames over 12 characters in length) and problems PC programmers usually wish they didn't need to worry about (such as the segmented architecture of Intel microprocessors). Nonetheless, SAA indicates the potential importance of the Presentation Manager in the future of the personal computer and the not-quite-personal computers as well.

Presentation Manager Programming

At first glance, a typical Presentation Manager program seems to be written in an unfamiliar programming language. The programs are full of upper-case identifiers and variable types, strange-looking variable names, nested *switch* statements, and many calls to Presentation Manager functions. Those odd-looking Presentation Manager programs are usually written in C. Although it is possible to use other languages, C will probably remain the preferred language for Presentation Manager programming, largely because of its flexibility in pointer and structure manipulation. If you don't know C, programming for the Presentation Manager is probably not a good place to start learning the language. I recommend you learn C by programming for a more traditional environment, such as the OS/2 kernel. If your C is a little rusty, brushing up on structures and pointers is a must.

The Header Files

C programs for the Presentation Manager require the use of header files supplied with the Microsoft OS/2 Programmer's Toolkit. These are the header files used in OS/2 kernel and Presentation Manager programs:

Header File	Description
OS2.H	Includes OS2DEF.H, BSE.H, and PM.H
OS2DEF.H	Common type and macro definitions
BSE.H	Includes BSEDOS.H, BSESUB.H, and BSEERR.H
BSEDOS.H	*Dos* functions and structures
BSESUB.H	*Vio, Mou,* and *Kbd* functions and structures
BSEERR.H	*Dos, Vio, Mou,* and *Kbd* error codes
PM.H	Includes PMWIN.H, PMGPI.H, PMDEV.H, PMAVIO.H, and PMSPL.H
PMWIN.H	Most *Win* functions and structures; and includes PMSHL.H
PMSHL.H	*Win* functions for session manager shell
PMGPI.H	*Gpi* functions and structures
PMDEV.H	*Dev* functions and structures
PMAVIO.H	*Vio* functions for Advanced VIO interface
PMSPL.H	*Spl* functions and structures

These header files are an important part of Presentation Manager documentation. You'll want to print out a copy for reference.

Many Presentation Manager functions require numeric constants as parameters. You rarely need to remember the actual values of these constants, because the header files contain hundreds of *#define* statements that define identifiers for the constants. These identifiers are in uppercase letters. Most begin with a two-letter, three-letter, or four-letter prefix that indicates a general group of identifiers. The header files also define identifiers for most of the data types you use in your Presentation Manager programs, as well as numerous data structures used in passing information between the application and the Presentation Manager. I'll discuss these as we encounter them in the chapters ahead.

Programmers working with the Presentation Manager often find helpful a convention for naming variables that is known as "Hungarian notation," in honor of its inventor, the legendary Microsoft programmer Charles Simonyi. This convention adds a lowercase abbreviation of the data type to the beginning of the variable name. Again, I'll discuss this system in context as we begin writing Presentation Manager programs.

All OS/2 and Presentation Manager functions available to an application are declared in the header files. These function declarations provide type checking during compilation. In some cases, the function templates also help with pointer conversions. For example, whenever a pointer is passed as a parameter to an OS/2 function, it must be a far (or long) 32-bit pointer. However, you usually don't need to explicitly cast near (or short) 16-bit pointers to far pointers. The function template in the header file lets the compiler do this for you.

The OS/2 functions always begin with a three-letter prefix that identifies a large group of functions. The header files are generally organized around these groups of functions:

Prefix	Function Group
Dos	Kernel file I/O, memory management, and tasking
Vio	Video I/O
Kbd	Keyboard input in kernel programs
Mou	Mouse input in kernel programs
Win	Presentation Manager windowing and user interface
Gpi	Presentation Manager Graphics Programming Interface
Dev	Presentation Manager device context interface
Spl	Presentation Manager print spooler

The *Kbd* and *Mou* functions aren't used at all in Presentation Manager programs. *Vio* functions are used only in a Presentation Manager output system called "Advanced VIO," which I discuss in Chapter 7.

Message-based Architecture

Most traditional operating systems provide a set of functions that a program calls for various system services. That is still the case in the Presentation Manager, but a Presentation Manager program also gets information from the operating system in a very different way—through "messages." For example, in an OS/2 kernel program you use *Kbd* and *Mou* functions to obtain keyboard and mouse input. In the Presentation Manager, a program obtains keyboard and mouse input through messages that the Presentation Manager sends to the program.

But it's not only simple keyboard and mouse input that is delivered to a program in the form of messages. Messages also inform a program when a user has selected an item from a menu, when the program's window has been resized, and even when the program should repaint part of its window. In fact, Presentation Manager programs are largely message-driven. A program remains dormant most of the time until it receives a message; it thus does little but process messages. Coming to terms with this message architecture is a major hurdle of learning to program for the Presentation Manager. But don't worry about understanding this architecture right off the bat. We'll spend most of this book learning how to process messages.

A Note to Windows Programmers

If you have experience with programming for Microsoft Windows, you're already several steps ahead of everybody else in mastering the Presentation Manager. But don't feel too complacent. The major concepts are the same, but the details are different. For example, right now you're familiar with a program's "client area." In the Presentation Manager we speak instead of a "client window." All parts of the window that are "nonclient areas" under Windows are separate windows in the Presentation Manager.

I found it relatively easy to go from Windows programming to Presentation Manager programming. I also found it easy (in most cases) to convert existing Windows programs to the Presentation Manager API. The best news for Windows programmers, however, is that OS/2 is a more hospitable environment for a windowing and multitasking system. Under MS-DOS, Windows outclasses the operating system and has to compensate for the weaknesses in MS-DOS. Windows is like stained-glass artwork in the wall of a log cabin. Under OS/2, Windows (in the form of the Presentation Manager) has finally found its proper home.

Easy or Hard?

Microsoft Windows has the reputation of being a difficult system for programmers to learn, and it's likely that the Presentation Manager will gain the same reputation. I've already spoken of the hurdle of moving from a traditional operating system to a message-based architecture. That's part of the problem. The steep learning curve also results from the sheer bulk of Presentation Manager function calls (about 500 of them). But what's the alternative? Would you rather learn how to use the menu logic built into the Presentation Manager, or would you prefer to write your own menu routines? Would you rather learn how to draw circles using GPI functions, or would you prefer to write your own circle-drawing routines and adapt them for every video adapter and printer your program may encounter?

Out of necessity, application programs have become more complex in the past few years, because the programs have been made easier to operate for naive users and, at the same time, more powerful for sophisticated users. As the user base expands to encompass less sophisticated users, the applications, application program interfaces, and programmers must become more sophisticated. Program developers can no longer require users to spend many hours reading manuals before they begin to use an application. The application's interface must be obvious and intuitively clear. By programming for the Presentation Manager, you begin with an interface that is already familiar to the user. In short, learning to program for the Presentation Manager may be hard, but it's easier than the alternative.

So enough of this. Let's start pounding out some code.

## CHAPTER TWO

WELCOME TO PRESENTATION MANAGER PROGRAMMING

Books that teach you how to program in C often begin with a "do-nothing" program and proceed quickly to the traditional "Hello world" program. The Presentation Manager analogue of the "Hello world" program isn't quite as straightforward, so we'll spend this entire chapter creating it. We'll begin with a "do-nothing" program called W and progressively build it into a program called WELCOME1 that creates a window, displays a message in it, and (as a bonus) plays a little music.

W—The Do-Nothing Program

A Presentation Manager program is usually constructed from several files. Figure 2-1 on the following page shows the three files that make up the W program:

- W (a make file)
- W.C (a program source code file)
- W.DEF (a module definition file)

As you will see, these three types of files are normal for all Presentation Manager programs.

Because the W program itself does nothing interesting, we'll instead take a moment to examine the mechanics of compiling and linking a Presentation Manager program.

The W File

```
#-------------
# W make file
#-------------

w.obj : w.c
     cl -c -G2 -W3 w.c

w.exe : w.obj w.def
     link w, /align:16, NUL, os2, w
```

The W.C File

```
/*----------------------------
   W.C -- A Do-Nothing Program
----------------------------*/

int main (void)
     {
     return 0 ;
     }
```

The W.DEF File

```
;----------------------------
; W.DEF module definition file
;----------------------------

NAME          W          WINDOWCOMPAT

DESCRIPTION   'Welcome to PM -- Program No. 1 (C) Charles Petzold, 1988'
PROTMODE
HEAPSIZE      1024
STACKSIZE     2048
```

Figure 2-1. *The W program.*

The Make File

The first file is a "make file" named W. A make file is a text file that contains a series of commands to create a .EXE (executable) file from one or more source code files.

By convention, a make file is given the same name as the program it creates but with no extension. The MAKE.EXE program that is included with the

Microsoft C compiler reads this file and compares the date and time of the "target" file (to the left of a colon) with the date and time of the "dependent" file or files (to the right of the colon). If any dependent file has been changed more recently than the target file, the indented commands that follow are run. In the W make file, the C compiler (CL — the .EXE extension is assumed) is run if the W.C source code file is more recent than the W.OBJ object file. The linker (LINK — the .EXE extension is assumed) is run if W.OBJ or W.DEF is more recent than W.EXE. Besides simplifying the creation of .EXE files, the make file also serves as a form of documentation about the program. It shows the various modules that contribute to the program and how they are combined into an executable file.

Assuming you have the OS/2 C compiler and associated files properly installed, you can create W.EXE from W, W.C, and W.DEF by running the MAKE program on the OS/2 CMD.EXE command line (either in a full-screen character-mode session or running in a window in the Presentation Manager):

```
MAKE W
```

If MAKE, CL, or LINK reports errors, your system is probably not set up correctly. You should have the OS/2 C compiler, LINK, and MAKE accessible through a directory listed in your PATH environment variable and the C and OS/2 .LIB files in a directory listed in your LIB environment variable. In particular, LINK needs to find the SLIBCE.LIB library file. (I explain in the preface how to install Microsoft C 5.1 so that this file exists.)

Compiling

The following command line in the W make file compiles the W.C source code file, creating the W.OBJ object code file:

```
cl -c -G2 -W3 w.c
```

The switches used in this compilation are as follows:

The -c switch causes the C compiler to compile the program but not to link it. The link is the second step in the make file.

The -G2 switch generates 80286 code during the compilation. Because the OS/2 Presentation Manager runs only on an Intel 80286 or 80386 microprocessor, you should always use this switch. It creates smaller and faster programs.

The -*W3* switch stands for "warning level 3" and causes the C compiler to display additional warning messages about potential problems in your programs. This becomes particularly important when the program makes calls to OS/2 or Presentation Manager functions. You should set as a goal that all your Presentation Manager programs compile without any warning messages when the -*W3* switch is used.

Linking

If the compilation is successful, the following command in W links the W.OBJ file to create an executable W.EXE file:

```
link w, /align:16, NUL, os2, w
```

The first parameter to LINK.EXE is the name of the W.OBJ object code file. The .OBJ extension is assumed.

The second parameter is the name of the .EXE file. If this name isn't explicitly listed (as it isn't here), LINK uses the name of the first .OBJ file and adds a .EXE extension. The */align:16* switch aligns segments in the .EXE file on 16-byte boundaries. By default, LINK aligns segments on 512-byte boundaries. For programs with small code and data segments, this switch can appreciably reduce the size of the .EXE file.

The third parameter to LINK is the name of a map file. Specifying NUL prevents the map file from being created.

The fourth parameter lists the names of the libraries to be linked with the .OBJ file. (LINK also uses the C run-time library SLIBCE.LIB, but because the C compiler embeds this name in the .OBJ file, you don't have to list it in the LINK step.) OS2.LIB is an "import library" for OS/2 functions. This file allows LINK to construct the .EXE file so that it contains dynamic link information. When you run an OS/2 program, OS/2 uses this information in the .EXE files to link calls to OS/2 functions within the program with the functions themselves. Although W doesn't seem to make any OS/2 function calls, the start-up code makes a few. The presence of these imported functions causes LINK to create a .EXE file in the "New Executable" format, which is the OS/2 .EXE format.

The fifth parameter to LINK is the name of the program's "module definition file," W.DEF. The .DEF extension is assumed.

The Module Definition File

Although it isn't strictly required for this simple do-nothing program, Presentation Manager applications usually require a "module definition file." This is a simple text file that LINK uses when constructing the program's .EXE file. The module definition file commonly has the same name as the program, but with a .DEF extension.

The W.DEF file shown in Figure 2-1 begins with a NAME statement. This identifies the module as a program (rather than a dynamic link library) and gives it a module name of W. This should be the same name as the program's .EXE file. The keyword WINDOWCOMPAT causes LINK to set a flag in the W.EXE file. This flag tells OS/2 that although the program is *not* a Presentation Manager program, it *can* be run in a text window within the Presentation Manager session.

The text in the DESCRIPTION line is embedded by LINK in the header section of the .EXE file. This is an excellent place for a copyright notice or other information about the program.

The PROTMODE keyword indicates that the program will be run only in OS/2 protected mode. This often allows LINK to shorten the .EXE file.

The HEAPSIZE statement specifies an initial size of memory to be used for a local heap. The local heap is located in the program's automatic data segment. C library functions (such as *malloc*) and some Presentation Manager functions let you allocate memory from this heap.

The STACKSIZE statement specifies the size of the program's stack. The recommended minimum stack size for OS/2 programs is 2 KB. The stack size for Presentation Manager programs that create windows is 8 KB, so we'll use a larger STACKSIZE later in this chapter.

We'll add another line to the module definition file before this chapter is completed, but the general information shown in the W.DEF file will remain about the same for most programs in this book.

Running W.EXE

After creating W.EXE, you can run the program in a variety of ways, most easily by executing it from the OS/2 CMD.EXE prompt, either in a full-screen character-mode session or in a Presentation Manager window. You can also run the program from the File System or install it to be run from the Start Programs window. When installing it in the Start Programs window, specify that it is *not* a Presentation Manager program. If you run W.EXE from the File System or Start Programs window, a text window is briefly created for it and then destroyed as the program terminates.

WE — Obtaining an Anchor Block Handle

A Presentation Manager program makes many calls to Presentation Manager functions. But the very first Presentation Manager function that the program must call is *WinInitialize*. This function registers the program with the system and returns the "anchor block handle." (The term "anchor block" has origins in the mainframe world but has no significant meaning in the context of OS/2 or the Presentation Manager.) Before the program terminates, it should call *WinTerminate* to free the anchor block handle. The WE program in Figure 2-2 shows how this is done. WE is still basically a do-nothing program, but it's now a do-nothing program that can use some Presentation Manager functions.

The WE File

```
#--------------
# WE make file
#--------------

we.obj : we.c
     cl -c -G2 -W3 we.c

we.exe : we.obj we.def
     link we, /align:16, NUL, os2, we
```

The WE.C File

```
/*------------------------------------------------------------
    WE.C -- A Program that Obtains an Anchor Block Handle
  ------------------------------------------------------------*/

#include <os2.h>

int main (void)
    {
    HAB   hab ;

    hab = WinInitialize (0) ;

    WinTerminate (hab) ;
    return 0 ;
    }
```

The WE.DEF File

```
;-------------------------------------
; WE.DEF module definition file
;-------------------------------------

NAME            WE        WINDOWCOMPAT

DESCRIPTION     'Welcome to PM -- Program No. 2 (C) Charles Petzold, 1988'
PROTMODE
HEAPSIZE        1024
STACKSIZE       2048
```

Figure 2-2. *The WE program.*

You can create WE.EXE from the three files by executing

```
MAKE WE
```

You can run WE.EXE in the same way you run W.EXE. The program still doesn't do much of anything.

In going from W to WE, the changes made to the three standard files at first look innocuous. But you'll find when creating WE.EXE that the compilation takes a little longer than it did previously. It's almost as if the compiler has to digest several other files in addition to WE.C. As you'll see in the following discussion, that's exactly the case.

The Header Files

Near the top of WE.C is the preprocessor statement:

```
#include <os2.h>
```

OS2.H is a master header file that contains other *#include* statements for all other OS/2 and Presentation Manager header files. All of these header files should be located in a subdirectory listed in your INCLUDE environment string. These header files are extremely important, and you should treat them as primary documentation for the Presentation Manager, as I mentioned in Chapter 1. Even for a program as simple as WE, these header files supply function declarations and definitions of identifiers used in the program. Let's examine how the header files affect the compilation of WE.C.

The WE.C program defines one variable (*hab*) and calls two Presentation Manager functions, *WinInitialize* and *WinTerminate*. These two functions are located in the PMWIN.DLL dynamic link library that OS/2 links your program with when you run the program. The *hab* variable is defined within the *main* function of WE.C:

```
HAB  hab ;
```

The data type of *hab* is HAB, which stands for "handle to an anchor block." (I'll discuss what a handle is shortly.) This HAB type is defined by a *typedef* statement in OS2DEF.H:

```
typedef LHANDLE HAB
```

The LHANDLE data type is defined like this:

```
typedef void far *LHANDLE ;
```

Thus the C compiler will treat the variable *hab* as a 32-bit far pointer.

The *WinInitialize* and *WinTerminate* functions are declared in PMWIN.H:

```
HAB  APIENTRY WinInitialize (USHORT) ;
BOOL APIENTRY WinTerminate (HAB hab) ;
```

BOOL and USHORT are data types defined in OS2DEF.H:

```
typedef unsigned short BOOL ;
typedef unsigned short USHORT
```

Thus the *WinInitialize* function takes an *unsigned short* parameter and returns a 32-bit value of type HAB, a handle to an anchor block. The *WinTerminate* function accepts an anchor block handle as a parameter and returns an *unsigned short*. The program treats this return value as a BOOL, which is a data type that is either 0 or 1.

The APIENTRY identifier is also defined in OS2DEF.H:

```
#define APIENTRY pascal far
```

This indicates that the two functions are far functions (that is, the compiler must generate a far, or intersegment, call to these functions when compiling the program) and that they have a "Pascal" calling sequence. Using the

Pascal calling sequence tells the C compiler two important facts about the function:

- The parameters to the function are pushed on the stack from left to right, rather than from right to left as is normal with C functions.

- The function itself adjusts the stack to remove the parameters. When the function returns to the program, the parameters have already been removed.

For the Intel 8086 family of microprocessors, the Pascal calling sequence is slightly faster and more efficient than the C calling sequence. Because all Presentation Manager functions are far functions that use the Pascal calling sequence, they are all declared in the header files with the APIENTRY identifier.

If you were to write WE.C without using the header files or any *#define* or *typedef* statements, it would look like this:

```
void far * pascal far WinInitialize (unsigned short) ;
unsigned short pascal far WinTerminate (void far *) ;

int main (void)
    {
    void far *hab ;

    hab = WinInitialize (0) ;

    WinTerminate (hab) ;
    return 0 ;
    }
```

In one sense, this is easier to read, because it uses only data types that are understood by the Microsoft C Compiler. However, in many ways this version is much more obscure than the version that uses the Presentation Manager header files.

For example, the *WinTerminate* function is declared in PMWIN.H as returning a BOOL (Boolean value), indicating that the function returns a 0 if the function fails and a 1 if it succeeds. This fact could be important, and yet it's not at all intuitive if the *WinTerminate* function is declared as returning an *unsigned short*. Likewise, the return value of *WinInitialize* isn't just any old far pointer—it's a handle to an anchor block. It's not even important for you to know that an anchor block handle is really a far pointer. All you need to know is that it's an anchor block handle. You should use this value only in other functions that accept an anchor block handle as a parameter, such as *WinTerminate*.

Although the *far* and *pascal* keywords are supported in Microsoft C, you should keep in the back of your mind the possibility of one day recompiling your Presentation Manager programs to run on systems other than the PC. Because the *far* keyword is necessary only because of the segmented architecture of the 8086 family of microprocessors, this keyword probably isn't supported in C compilers on other systems. For this reason, many of the more machine-specific keywords in Microsoft C are redefined with uppercase names, like this:

```
#define FAR     far
#define PASCAL pascal
```

If you need to use the *far* or *pascal* keywords in your program, use these uppercase identifiers instead. This allows you to more easily port your programs to another system, because you'll recompile the program with different header files that define the identifiers as appropriate for the system.

The Proper Handling of Handles

When you program for the Presentation Manager, you're really engaged in a form of "object-oriented programming." Many Presentation Manager functions obtain information about an object, act on an object, or cause an object to act on itself. A "handle" is a number that refers to an object. Almost every Presentation Manager function call—one exception is *WinInitialize*—requires a handle as the first parameter.

> **NOTE:** *Although this requirement implies that every Presentation Manager function acts on an object, this is really not the case. Presentation Manager function calls require a handle as the first parameter because of the requirements of IBM's Systems Application Architecture (SAA), of which the Presentation Manager is a part. As you'll see, some functions really don't need a handle to anything. These functions sometimes require the anchor block handle as the first parameter.*

The concept of a handle shouldn't be new to you. If you've done assembly-language programming under MS-DOS or the OS/2 kernel, or if you've ever used the C file I/O functions *open*, *read*, *write*, and *close*, you're familiar with file handles. Under the OS/2 kernel, a program can obtain a file handle from the *DosOpen* function call. The open file is an object. The file handle refers to this object. You use the handle when calling *DosRead*, *DosWrite*, or other functions that act on the open file. You eventually close the file using *DosClose*. After the *DosClose* call, the file handle is invalid. Although the file handle is a number, the actual value of the handle returned from *DosOpen* isn't important to your program. The value of the file handle is meaningful only to the OS/2 kernel. Obviously, the OS/2 kernel maintains a table of open files, and the file handle somehow references that table. But your program doesn't need to know this. OS/2 hides this data from your program.

The handles you use in the Presentation Manager are similar to file handles. But in the Presentation Manager almost everything has a handle. Before we're finished with this chapter, we'll have encountered a number of them:

- Anchor block handles
- Message queue handles
- Window handles
- System mouse pointer handles
- Presentation space handles

Every handle is obtained from a Presentation Manager function. You save the handle in a variable. You then use this handle in other Presentation Manager functions. At some point, you usually call a function that destroys the resources connected with the handle. At that time the handle becomes invalid.

Most handles are 32 bits long, but some are 16 bits long. Often, handles are actually addresses to structures that are maintained internally by the Presentation Manager. But your program doesn't access these structures directly. You don't even have to know which handles are 32 bits long and which are 16 bits long, because you use the data types defined in the header files (such as HAB) to define variables to store the handles.

A handle with a value of 0 is called a NULL handle. (NULL is defined in OS2DEF.H as 0.) Just as in C programming, where a NULL pointer is often an invalid pointer, in Presentation Manager programming a NULL handle returned from a function is usually an indication of an error. In some cases, however, you can use a NULL handle as a default parameter to a function that requires a handle. We'll examine these cases as they arise.

The anchor block handle is a peculiar handle. I've already mentioned that handles refer to objects. The object to which the anchor block handle refers is the program itself—the program that calls *WinInitialize*. Let's be more precise. What we call a program is usually the .EXE file. But the program can be run multiple times. While a particular instance of a program is running, it is called a process. The anchor block handle refers to the particular process that calls *WinInitialize*.

Usually, a Presentation Manager program calls *WinInitialize* when it begins execution, so the program can then call other Presentation Manager functions. Right before the program is ready to terminate, it pulls up its anchor with *WinTerminate* and departs.

Running WE.EXE

I have some bad news for you. Although we are gathered here to write Presentation Manager programs, we're not there yet. You might think that calling the magic function *WinInitialize* turns an ordinary OS/2 program into a Presentation Manager program, but it's not so. Like W.EXE, WE.EXE is an OS/2 kernel program. Although a call to *WinInitialize* is necessary in a Presentation Manager program, it isn't sufficient. You can call *WinInitialize* from an old-fashioned character-mode OS/2 program also. Getting that anchor block handle lets you access some functions within the Presentation Manager—the heap management and atom management functions—that are not directly connected with the windowing or graphics facilities of the Presentation Manager. But don't fret: Although we're not quite there yet, the next step will get us there.

WEL—Creating a Message Queue

Calling *WinInitialize* to get an anchor block handle is like getting a pass to the pool. The next step—creating a message queue—is like jumping in. (We'll soon be swimming laps.) As you know, OS/2 supports multiple sessions, one being the Presentation Manager session. A program that creates a message queue is always run in the Presentation Manager session along with other Presentation Manager programs. The WEL program in Figure 2-3 shows how to create this message queue.

The WEL File

```
#- - - - - - - - - - - - - - -
# WEL make file
#- - - - - - - - - - - - - - -

wel.obj : wel.c
     cl -c -G2s -W3 wel.c

wel.exe : wel.obj wel.def
     link wel, /align:16, NUL, os2, wel
```

The WEL.C File

```
/*-------------------------------------------------
    WEL.C -- A Program that Creates a Message Queue
  ------------------------------------------------*/

#include <os2.h>

int main (void)
    {
    HAB   hab ;
    HMQ   hmq ;

    hab = WinInitialize (0) ;
    hmq = WinCreateMsgQueue (hab, 0) ;

    WinDestroyMsgQueue (hmq) ;
    WinTerminate (hab) ;
    return 0 ;
    }
```

The WEL.DEF File

```
;---------------------------------
; WEL.DEF module definition file
;---------------------------------

NAME          WEL       WINDOWAPI

DESCRIPTION   'Welcome to PM -- Program No. 3 (C) Charles Petzold, 1988'
PROTMODE
HEAPSIZE      1024
STACKSIZE     2048
```

Figure 2-3. *The WEL program.*

The Message Queue Difference

As you'll see, Presentation Manager programs are based on a message-driven input model. Programs receive all input in the form of messages. We're not quite ready to look at this message system in detail, but after working with it, you'll probably realize that this input model is almost a necessary part of a windowing environment like the Presentation Manager.

Many messages that a program receives from the Presentation Manager are stored in a message queue. This message queue must be created explicitly by the program with a call to the Presentation Manager. This call establishes the program as a Presentation Manager application.

Following the *WinInitialize* call, WEL.C makes this call:

```
hmq = WinCreateMsgQueue (hab, 0) ;
```

This call (as the name implies) creates a message queue. Like most Presentation Manager functions, *WinCreateMsgQueue* requires a handle as the first parameter. This is the anchor block handle, which is the only handle we have so far. The second parameter indicates the size of the queue, where 0 means a default size sufficient for most programs. The value returned from the function is the handle to the message queue. This is stored in a variable named *hmq* of type HMQ. The program destroys the queue like this:

```
WinDestroyMsgQueue (hmq) ;
```

Following this call, the *hmq* handle is invalid.

Message queues get a little more complex for programs with multiple threads of execution. A message queue is always associated with a particular thread — the thread that creates it. A thread can have only one message queue. In a multithread program, some threads can create message queues, but others don't have to.

When OS/2 is booted, the first program that calls *WinCreateMsgQueue* (normally, the Presentation Manager shell) establishes a session as the Presentation Manager session. It is during the *WinCreateMsgQueue* call that the screen display is switched from character mode to graphics mode. Later programs that call *WinCreateMsgQueue* — even if executed from the CMD.EXE prompt in a character-mode session — are run in this same session.

Notice also that the WINDOWCOMPAT keyword in W.DEF and WE.DEF has been changed to WINDOWAPI in WEL.DEF. This causes LINK to set a flag in the WEL.EXE file to inform OS/2 that this is truly a Presentation Manager program.

Inhibiting Stack Checks

Yet another switch, *-Gs*, has been added to the compile step. This switch is combined with the *-G2* switch and written as *-G2s*.

Normally, the C compiler inserts a call to the *_chkstk* function in the prologue section of every function in your program. This *_chkstk* function determines if the amount of space necessary for local variables in the function will cause a stack overflow. If so, the function displays a message to the standard error output device (the screen) using *DosWrite* and terminates the program. In the Presentation Manager, however, this approach is ineffective, because the Presentation Manager ignores output written to the display through *DosWrite*. The *-Gs* switch removes the checks for stack overflow. You should instead be sure that the stack size specified in the module definition file is sufficient for the program's needs.

WELC—Creating a Standard Window

A program running in the Presentation Manager session occupies one or more windows. In simple terms, a window is a rectangular area of the screen that the program uses to receive input and display its output. A window is like a virtual terminal. A user can move and resize the windows on the screen and select one window (and hence one program) as the active, or foreground, window. A Presentation Manager program must create the window that the program uses. The WELC program in Figure 2-4 shows how this is done.

The WELC File

```
#----------------
# WELC make file
#----------------

welc.obj : welc.c
    cl -c -G2s -W3 welc.c

welc.exe : welc.obj welc.def
    link welc, /align:16, NUL, os2, welc
```

The WELC.C File

```
/*-----------------------------------------------------------
    WELC.C -- A Program that Creates a Standard Frame Window
-------------------------------------------------------------*/

#include <os2.h>

int main (void)
    {
    static ULONG flFrameFlags = FCF_TITLEBAR       | FCF_SYSMENU  |
                                FCF_SIZEBORDER     | FCF_MINMAX   |
                                FCF_SHELLPOSITION  | FCF_TASKLIST ;
```

(continued)

Figure 2-4. The WELC.C File. *continued*

```
    HAB          hab ;
    HMQ          hmq ;
    HWND         hwndFrame ;

    hab = WinInitialize (0) ;
    hmq = WinCreateMsgQueue (hab, 0) ;

    hwndFrame = WinCreateStdWindow (
                    HWND_DESKTOP,       // Parent window handle
                    WS_VISIBLE,         // Style of frame window
                    &flFrameFlags,      // Pointer to control data
                    NULL,               // Client window class name
                    NULL,               // Title bar text
                    0L,                 // Style of client window
                    NULL,               // Module handle for resources
                    0,                  // ID of resources
                    NULL) ;             // Pointer to client window handle

    WinDestroyWindow (hwndFrame) ;
    WinDestroyMsgQueue (hmq) ;
    WinTerminate (hab) ;
    return 0 ;
    }
```

The WELC.DEF File

```
;------------------------------------
; WELC.DEF module definition file
;------------------------------------


NAME         WELC       WINDOWAPI

DESCRIPTION  'Welcome to PM -- Program No. 4 (C) Charles Petzold, 1988'
PROTMODE
HEAPSIZE     1024
STACKSIZE    8192
```

Figure 2-4. *The WELC program.*

WELC.EXE is the first version of the program that has a substantial, visible result. When you run WELC, a window appears that looks much like the windows of other programs running under the Presentation Manager. The window contains a thick resizing border, a system menu box in the upper-left corner, a minimize and maximize box in the upper-right corner, and a title bar across the top containing the name of the program, WELC.EXE. Not bad—but not perfect. The problem is that this window disappears almost immediately after it's created. We'll fix that problem in the next version of our program, but first, let's examine what we've done to get this far.

The *WinCreateStdWindow* Function

WELC.C calls two Presentation Manager functions in addition to those introduced earlier: *WinCreateStdWindow* creates a window, and *WinDestroyWindow* destroys it. *WinCreateStdWindow* is the function normally used to create a main window for a Presentation Manager application. This isn't the only way to create an application window, but it's certainly the easiest. The *WinCreateStdWindow* function requires nine parameters, which are identified with comments in WELC.C. (The double slashes are recognized by the Microsoft C Compiler as setting off single-line comments.) Six of the parameters are set to 0 or NULL in this example. Certainly, we're not yet taking advantage of *WinCreateStdWindow*'s full potential.

WinCreateStdWindow creates a type of window known as a "frame window." We'll examine what this means a little later. The function returns a handle to the frame window. In WELC.C this handle is stored in a variable named *hwndFrame* and defined as type HWND ("handle to a window"). This handle must be used in other Presentation Manager functions to refer to the window. For example, in WELC.C this window handle is passed to *WinDestroyWindow* to destroy the window, which means that the Presentation Manager frees all the resources associated with the window and removes it from the screen. The window handle then becomes invalid.

The first parameter to *WinCreateStdWindow* is the identifier known as HWND_DESKTOP (defined in PMWIN.H as 1), which specifies the "parent" of the frame window. This concept will be explored in more detail in the next chapter.

The second parameter specifies the style of the window. The parameter is the identifier WS_VISIBLE (which is defined in PMWIN.H as the value 0x80000000L). The WS prefix stands for "window style." This value instructs the *WinCreateStdWindow* function to make the window visible when it is created.

The third parameter is a pointer to the variable *flFrameFlags*. The "fl" prefix is an example of "Hungarian notation," which I alluded to in Chapter 1. The "f" indicates that the variable is a series of flags, and the "l" indicates that the flags are encoded in a 32-bit *long* data type. The *flFrameFlags* variable is defined as a ULONG (*unsigned long*). This "control data" parameter tells *WinCreateStdWindow* what the standard window should include. I've initialized *flFrameFlags* like this:

```
static ULONG flFrameFlags = FCF_TITLEBAR      | FCF_SYSMENU |
                            FCF_SIZEBORDER    | FCF_MINMAX  |
                            FCF_SHELLPOSITION | FCF_TASKLIST ;
```

The FCF ("frame creation flags") identifiers are defined in PMWIN.H. Some of these identifiers are almost self-explanatory: FCF_TITLEBAR means that we want a title bar across the top of the window; FCF_SYSMENU, a system menu box to the left of the title bar; FCF_SIZEBORDER, a thick sizing border around the window; and FCF_MINMAX, a minimize and maximize box to the right of the title bar. FCF_SHELLPOSITION instructs the Presentation Manager shell to give the window a default size and position on the screen. FCF_TASKLIST installs the program on the Task Manager.

Here's how these six identifiers are defined in PMWIN.H:

```
#define FCF_TITLEBAR       0x00000001L
#define FCF_SYSMENU        0x00000002L
#define FCF_SIZEBORDER     0x00000008L
#define FCF_MINMAX         0x00000030L
#define FCF_SHELLPOSITION  0x00000400L
#define FCF_TASKLIST       0x00000800L
```

Each identifier is a 32-bit constant with one or two bits set to 1 and the other bits set to 0. These identifiers are combined into one 32-bit number using the C bitwise OR operator (¦). Many identifiers defined in the header files work this way.

A Larger Stack

You'll notice that the WELC.DEF file specifies a STACKSIZE value of 8192. The earlier programs have a 2 KB stack. The 8 KB stack is required for any program that creates a window, even if the window is displayed only momentarily.

Of course, most windows created by Presentation Manager programs remain on the screen longer than the window in WELC. Our first priority is to fix that problem.

WELCO—Looping Through the Messages

The problem with WELC is that we don't have a chance to enjoy the wonderful window we've created. The program calls *WinCreateStdWindow* to create the frame window but then calls *WinDestroyWindow* to blow it away. Obviously, we have to insert some code between those two function calls to keep the window up on the screen a little longer. If this were a conventional OS/2 program, you might set up a little loop to call *KbdCharIn* and then wait for a keystroke before destroying the window. But the *KbdCharIn* function isn't allowed in Presentation Manager programs. Nor are any of the other keyboard functions provided by the OS/2 kernel. What we can do instead is add a "message loop." This message loop is something like a loop that reads the keyboard, but it is much, much more. A program with a message loop—WELCO—is shown in Figure 2-5.

The WELCO File

```
#-----------------
# WELCO make file
#-----------------

welco.obj : welco.c
    cl -c -G2s -W3 welco.c

welco.exe : welco.obj welco.def
    link welco, /align:16, NUL, os2, welco
```

The WELCO.C File

```
/*-------------------------------------------
   WELCO.C -- A Program with a Message Loop
  -----------------------------------------*/

#include <os2.h>

int main (void)
    {
```

(continued)

Figure 2-5. The WELCO.C File. *continued*

```
        static ULONG flFrameFlags = FCF_TITLEBAR      | FCF_SYSMENU  |
                                    FCF_SIZEBORDER    | FCF_MINMAX   |
                                    FCF_SHELLPOSITION | FCF_TASKLIST ;
HAB         hab ;
HMQ         hmq ;
HWND        hwndFrame ;
QMSG        qmsg ;

hab = WinInitialize (0) ;
hmq = WinCreateMsgQueue (hab, 0) ;

hwndFrame = WinCreateStdWindow (
            HWND_DESKTOP,       // Parent window handle
            WS_VISIBLE,         // Style of frame window
            &flFrameFlags,      // Pointer to control data
            NULL,               // Client window class name
            NULL,               // Title bar text
            0L,                 // Style of client window
            NULL,               // Module handle for resources
            0,                  // ID of resources
            NULL) ;             // Pointer to client window handle

while (WinGetMsg (hab, &qmsg, NULL, 0, 0))
    WinDispatchMsg (hab, &qmsg) ;

WinDestroyWindow (hwndFrame) ;
WinDestroyMsgQueue (hmq) ;
WinTerminate (hab) ;
return 0 ;
}
```

The WELCO.DEF File

```
;-----------------------------------
; WELCO.DEF module definition file
;-----------------------------------

NAME        WELCO       WINDOWAPI

DESCRIPTION     'Welcome to PM -- Program No. 5 (C) Charles Petzold, 1988'
PROTMODE
HEAPSIZE    1024
STACKSIZE   8192
```

Figure 2-5. *The WELCO program.*

When you run WELCO.EXE under the Presentation Manager, you'll be treated to a real Presentation Manager window, as shown in Figure 2-6. With this window you can

- Press the mouse button when the pointer is positioned over the title bar and drag the window around the screen.

- Drag the sizing border to change the size of the window.

- Click on the maximize arrow and expand the window to full screen.

- Click on the minimize arrow and compress the window into a little square.

- Use the mouse or keyboard to invoke the system menu.

- Size or move the window with the keyboard.

- Use Alt with a function key to invoke system menu options.

- Close the window, removing it from the screen.

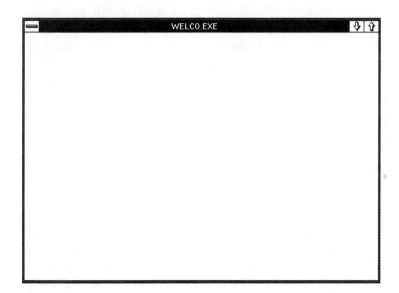

Figure 2-6. *A Presentation Manager window.*

That's a considerable improvement, considering that only three lines were added to the program.

Anatomy of a Window

As we develop a Presentation Manager program in this chapter, we will encounter three major concepts that are central to Presentation Manager programming:

- Windows

- Messages

- Presentation spaces

These three concepts are closely related: A window receives input in the form of messages and displays output to a presentation space. This entire book is about receiving messages and writing to presentation spaces. The window is at the center of it all.

Earlier I said that a window is a rectangular area on the screen. That's too easy. Sure, a window occupies an area on the screen, but that's what the window looks like, not what it is. As you start programming for the Presentation Manager, windows seem to take on life. You will use anthropomorphic language when thinking and talking about windows. You will say a window does something, a window responds in a certain way, and a window has a style. A window has a parent and can also have children; a window can talk to another window. And yes, a window occupies a rectangular area on the screen.

You'll find it helpful to think of windows in terms common in object-oriented programming. For example, you might now believe that some code someplace in the Presentation Manager draws the sizing border, system menu box, title bar, and minimize/maximize box so that they look the way they do. Yes, but no — you're closer to reality if you think of the window as drawing itself. The window itself determines how it will look.

This may become clearer if I discuss the *WinCreateStdWindow* function more. I've been speaking about the window that *WinCreateStdWindow* creates as if it were a single window. Actually, *WinCreateStdWindow* is a high-level function that does the work of several other functions. As used in WELC, *WinCreateStdWindow* causes four windows to be created:

- A frame window

- A title bar window

- A system menu window

- A minimize/maximize window

(A fifth window — the drop-down menu displayed from the system menu — is also created. But let's ignore that for this discussion.)

These are separate windows. They are certainly bound together into one tidy unit, and they certainly have some relationship among themselves, but in other ways these windows are distinct and independent.

The *WinCreateStdWindow* function creates the frame window, and the frame window creates the other three windows. These three windows correspond to the FCF_TITLEBAR, FCF_SYSMENU, and FCF_MINMAX flags set in the *flFrameFlags* parameter that is passed to *WinCreateStdWindow*. Each of these four windows has its own window handle. *WinCreateStdWindow* returns only the window handle of the frame window, but the other handles are available if you need them.

The frame window is like a base on which the other three windows are arranged. Each of these four windows draws itself. The frame window draws itself as a solid background surrounded by a sizing border. The title bar window, system menu window, and minimize/maximize window are relatively small windows that sit on top of the frame window.

Each of these four windows is distinct in appearance because each window draws itself in a unique way. Each window responds to input in a distinct way because each window processes its own input. This input takes the form of "messages."

Messages

In a conventional operating system, you must always ask for information. In the Presentation Manager, information is delivered to your program in the form of "messages." For example, in a conventional OS/2 kernel program, you can determine the size of the screen display in units of characters or pixels by calling the *VioGetMode* function. In a Presentation Manager program, the size of the screen is less important than the size of one of your program's windows. The size of these windows can change. The window is notified of such a change through messages. Messages are notifications of user input and everything else that affects the program's windows.

A Presentation Manager program works by processing messages. In fact, it does little else except process messages. We say that a Presentation Manager program is "message-driven."

A message is a data structure of type QMSG (queue message), which is defined in PMWIN.H as shown on the following page.

```
typedef struct _QMSG
    {
    HWND    hwnd ;
    USHORT msg ;
    MPARAM mp1 ;
    MPARAM mp2 ;
    ULONG  time ;
    POINTL ptl ;
    }
    QMSG ;
```

A message is usually directed to a particular window. The handle of the intended recipient of a message is given in the *hwnd* field of the structure.

The *msg* field (defined as type USHORT, or unsigned short) identifies the message. All messages have identifiers defined in PMWIN.H. Many of them begin with the letters WM ("window message"). Examples of these identifiers are WM_CREATE, WM_SIZE, WM_CHAR, WM_MOUSEMOVE, WM_PAINT, WM_DESTROY, and WM_QUIT. The *mp1* and *mp2* fields (defined as type MPARAM, which is a 32-bit far pointer) are "message parameters." They contain information connected with the particular message; The *time* field is the time the message was sent, and *ptl* (a POINTL structure) indicates the position of the mouse pointer at the time the message was sent. The following table summarizes this information:

THE MESSAGE STRUCTURE

The message is addressed to	*hwnd*
The message is	*msg*
More detailed information is found in	*mp1* and *mp2*
The time of the message is	*time*
The mouse pointer was positioned at	*ptl*

When a message is addressed to a particular window (the usual case), the window processes the message. Everything a window does is the result of processing messages.

The message queue is a place where messages are stored. After a thread creates a message queue by calling *WinCreateMsgQueue*, the Presentation Manager uses this queue to store messages to all windows created in that thread. Not all messages are stored in the message queue (a distinction I'll discuss a little later), but most messages relating directly to user input are stored there. The message queue created by WELCO stores messages for the frame window, the title bar window, the system menu window, and the minimize/maximize window.

The Message Loop

After a thread creates a message queue, it can create windows. Messages for the windows created in the thread are stored in the thread's message queue. Messages are retrieved from the message queue in a two-line piece of code called the "message loop." The program first must define a variable of type QMSG, the message structure:

```
QMSG  qmsg ;
```

After creating its windows, the program enters the message loop:

```
while (WinGetMsg (hab, &qmsg, NULL, 0, 0))
    WinDispatchMsg (hab, &qmsg) ;
```

Note that the last three parameters in the *WinGetMsg* call are set to NULL or 0. This is normal: It indicates that *WinGetMsg* should retrieve all messages to all windows created in that thread.

WinGetMsg passes to the Presentation Manager a pointer to the QMSG message structure. The Presentation Manager fills the fields of the structure with the next message from the queue and returns control to the program. When *WinGetMsg* returns, the QMSG structure holds a valid message from the message queue. The program then "dispatches" the message by calling *WinDispatchMsg*. When *WinDispatchMsg* returns, the program again calls *WinGetMsg*. If there are no messages in the queue, *WinGetMsg* waits until one is available. For all messages except WM_QUIT, *WinGetMsg* returns a nonzero value. WM_QUIT is a very special message. It causes *WinGetMsg* to return a 0 value and fall out of the *while* loop. (The WM_QUIT message is put into the queue when you select Close from the system menu.) The program then makes calls to *WinDestroyWindow*, *WinDestroyMsgQueue*, and *WinTerminate* and exits *main*, ending the program.

Do you find this message loop code a little peculiar? The program fetches a message from the queue with *WinGetMsg*. That's OK. But the program is seemingly not doing anything with the message. It's simply throwing the message away by calling *WinDispatchMsg*. If the message is actually being dispatched somewhere, who's getting it? Where does the message go? Well, the message is addressed to a particular window, so obviously that window gets the message. *WinDispatchMsg* sends a message to a window.

Perhaps this is still bothering you. Perhaps you're not quite comfortable with the concept of a window getting messages — it's too abstract. Would it make more sense if I said that *WinDispatchMsg* causes a function to be called? And that the message being dispatched takes the form of parameters to the function? And that this function interprets these parameters and does something to process the message? Would you be more comfortable with the idea that this function — in a very real sense — *is* the window?

The Window Procedure

Every window has an associated window procedure, which processes messages for the window. The window procedure determines how the window responds to input (in the form of messages) and what the window looks like.

WinGetMsg retrieves messages addressed to all windows that have been created in the thread of the process. During the *WinDispatchMsg* call, the Presentation Manager determines the address of the window procedure for the window whose handle is in the *hwnd* field of the message structure. It then calls this window procedure. The window procedure processes the message and returns control to the Presentation Manager, which then returns control to the program that called *WinDispatchMsg*.

The window procedures for the four windows created in WELCO are located in PMWIN.DLL, one of the dynamic link library modules that constitute the Presentation Manager. For example, PMWIN.DLL contains a function called *WinTitlebarWndProc*. This function is the window procedure that processes messages for all title bars created by all programs currently running under the Presentation Manager. The title bar window displays text because that happens to be the way the window procedure draws the window. The title bar changes color to indicate that the program (or more precisely, the frame window) is active because the frame window sends the title bar window a message telling it to change the color. The title bar window responds to mouse input in its own specialized way to allow the window to be repositioned on the screen, and it then sends a message to the frame window informing it of the new position.

A typical window procedure is shown in Figure 2-7. Note that the four parameters to the window procedure are the first four fields of the message structure — the window handle, the message identifier, and the two MPARAM values that provide message-specific information. When the *WinDispatchMsg* function calls the window procedure, it extracts these four fields from the structure to pass to the window procedure.

A window procedure generally processes messages using a *switch* and *case* construction. For each type of message, the *mp1* and *mp2* parameters provide additional information about the message.

```
MRESULT EXPENTRY DoodadWndProc (HWND hwnd, USHORT msg, MPARAM mp1, MPARAM mp2)
    {
        [definitions of local variables]
    switch (msg)
        {
        case WM_CREATE:
                [do initialization]
            return 0 ;

        case WM_PAINT:
                [paint the window]
            return 0 ;

        case WM_CHAR:
                [process keyboard messages]
            return 0 ;

        case WM_MOUSEMOVE:
                [process mouse movement messages]
            return 0 ;

        case WM_DESTROY:
                [clean up]
            return 0 ;
        }
    return WinDefWindowProc (hwnd, msg, mp1, mp2) ;
    }
```

Figure 2-7. *A typical window procedure.*

The value the window procedure returns depends on the message. Usually it's a 0. Any message the window doesn't process must be passed on to a function called *WinDefWindowProc*. This function does default processing of all messages that a window procedure chooses to ignore.

Why are we spending time looking at the structure of window procedures that are internal to the Presentation Manager? Because not all window procedures are inside the Presentation Manager. Presentation Manager programs can also contain window procedures. In fact, they almost always do. And that's why we will soon add a window procedure—and a new window—to our program.

WELCOM—Adding a Standard Icon

Before we add a new window to the program, let's address a little problem in WELCO.

If you minimize WELCO, you'll see the program displayed at the bottom of the screen as a small nondescript white rectangle. It should look more like a normal Presentation Manager icon.

We can add a standard application icon to the program with a few lines of code. The new version, called WELCOM, is shown in Figure 2-8.

The WELCOM File

```
#------------------
# WELCOM make file
#------------------

welcom.obj : welcom.c
    cl -c -G2sw -W3 welcom.c

welcom.exe : welcom.obj welcom.def
    link welcom, /align:16, NUL, os2, welcom
```

The WELCOM.C File

```
/*-------------------------------------------------
    WELCOM.C -- A Program that has a Standard Icon
  ------------------------------------------------*/

#define INCL_WIN
#include <os2.h>

int main (void)
    {
    static ULONG flFrameFlags = FCF_TITLEBAR      | FCF_SYSMENU |
                                FCF_SIZEBORDER     | FCF_MINMAX  |
                                FCF_SHELLPOSITION  | FCF_TASKLIST ;
    HAB        hab ;
    HMQ        hmq ;
    HWND       hwndFrame ;
    QMSG       qmsg ;

    hab = WinInitialize (0) ;
    hmq = WinCreateMsgQueue (hab, 0) ;
```

(continued)

Figure 2-8. The WELCOM.C File. *continued*

```
    hwndFrame = WinCreateStdWindow (
                    HWND_DESKTOP,        // Parent window handle
                    WS_VISIBLE,          // Style of frame window
                    &flFrameFlags,       // Pointer to control data
                    NULL,                // Client window class name
                    NULL,                // Title bar text
                    OL,                  // Style of client window
                    NULL,                // Module handle for resources
                    0,                   // ID of resources
                    NULL) ;              // Pointer to client window handle

    WinSendMsg (hwndFrame, WM_SETICON,
                WinQuerySysPointer (HWND_DESKTOP, SPTR_APPICON, FALSE),
                NULL) ;

    while (WinGetMsg (hab, &qmsg, NULL, 0, 0))
        WinDispatchMsg (hab, &qmsg) ;

    WinDestroyWindow (hwndFrame) ;
    WinDestroyMsgQueue (hmq) ;
    WinTerminate (hab) ;
    return 0 ;
    }
```

The WELCOM.DEF File

```
;-------------------------------------
; WELCOM.DEF module definition file
;-------------------------------------


NAME            WELCOM    WINDOWAPI

DESCRIPTION     'Welcome to PM -- Program No. 6 (C) Charles Petzold, 1988'
PROTMODE
HEAPSIZE        1024
STACKSIZE       8192
```

Figure 2-8. *The WELCOM program.*

Many Presentation Manager programs use customized icons to identify the program when it is minimized and displayed at the bottom of the screen. We'll begin doing this in Chapter 12. Until then, we'll use a standard icon that is defined within the Presentation Manager.

The frame window must display an icon when the window is minimized. We have to tell the frame window what icon to use for this. I've been discussing messages, and here we can see an example of one. A program can tell the frame window which icon to use by sending the frame window a WM_SETICON message. You do this by calling the *WinSendMsg* function:

```
WinSendMsg (hwndFrame, WM_SETICON,
        WinQuerySysPointer (HWND_DESKTOP, SPTR_APPICON, FALSE),
        NULL) ;
```

You'll recall that a window procedure has four parameters: the window handle, the message identifier, and two message parameters. *WinSendMsg* has these same four parameters. The first is *hwndFrame*, the handle of the window to which we're sending the message. The second parameter, WM_SETICON, identifies the message. The last two parameters to *WinSendMsg* correspond to the *mp1* and *mp2* parameters of the window procedure. These provide information unique to the WM_SETICON message.

For WM_SETICON, *mp2* is not used and can be set to NULL. The *mp1* parameter is a handle to a pointer. (The word "pointer," as used here, generally refers to the mouse pointer that you move on the screen using your mouse. But as you'll discover in Chapter 12, icons and mouse pointers are closely related and interchangeable in many cases.) This handle is obtained from the *WinQuerySysPointer* function call. The first parameter of this handle is HWND_DESKTOP, which is required for this function. The SPTR_APPICON identifier (the SPTR prefix stands for "system pointer") refers to a simple icon that looks like a little window if you use your imagination.

The last parameter to *WinQuerySysPointer* is set to FALSE to indicate that we do *not* want the Presentation Manager to make a copy of this icon. All we want is the handle to it. This is one case where you don't call a function to destroy the resources connected with the handle. You don't need to save the handle returned from *WinQuerySysPointer*; you just pass it to the *WinSendMsg* function.

You'll notice that I've added the following line to the top of WELCOM.C:

```
#define INCL_WIN
```

This line appears before the *#include* statement for OS2.H. The declaration for the *WinQuerySysPointer* function and the definition of the SPTR_APPICON identifier in PMWIN.H (as well as a number of other functions and identifiers) are not included by default. Defining INCL_WIN causes them to be included.

WELCOME—Creating a Client Window

The four windows in WELCOM seem to get along OK. But it's like a party taking place in your house to which you weren't invited. After WELCOM creates the four windows, all it does is retrieve messages from the message queue and dispatch them to window procedures located somewhere in PMWIN.DLL. Let's get in on this action. In the WELCOME version of our program, shown in Figure 2-9, I've changed the *WinCreateStdWindow* call slightly so that it creates a fifth window. This window will fill that large area between the title bar and the visible parts of the sizing border, covering the still-visible part of the frame window. This fifth window is our window—we process the messages to it.

The WELCOME File

```
#-------------------
# WELCOME make file
#-------------------

welcome.obj : welcome.c
    cl -c -G2sw -W3 welcome.c

welcome.exe : welcome.obj welcome.def
    link welcome, /align:16, NUL, os2, welcome
```

The WELCOME.C File

```
/*-------------------------------------------------------
   WELCOME.C -- A Program that Creates a Client Window
   -----------------------------------------------------*/

#define INCL_WIN
#include <os2.h>

MRESULT EXPENTRY ClientWndProc (HWND, USHORT, MPARAM, MPARAM) ;

int main (void)
    {
    static CHAR  szClientClass [] = "Welcome" ;
    static ULONG flFrameFlags = FCF_TITLEBAR      | FCF_SYSMENU |
                                FCF_SIZEBORDER     | FCF_MINMAX  |
                                FCF_SHELLPOSITION  | FCF_TASKLIST ;
```

(continued)

Figure 2-9. The WELCOME.C File. *continued*

```
    HAB         hab ;
    HMQ         hmq ;
    HWND        hwndFrame, hwndClient ;
    QMSG        qmsg ;

    hab = WinInitialize (0) ;
    hmq = WinCreateMsgQueue (hab, 0) ;

    WinRegisterClass (
                hab,                // Anchor block handle
                szClientClass,      // Name of class being registered
                ClientWndProc,      // Window procedure for class
                OL,                 // Class style
                0) ;                // Extra bytes to reserve

    hwndFrame = WinCreateStdWindow (
                HWND_DESKTOP,       // Parent window handle
                WS_VISIBLE,         // Style of frame window
                &flFrameFlags,      // Pointer to control data
                szClientClass,      // Client window class name
                NULL,               // Title bar text
                OL,                 // Style of client window
                NULL,               // Module handle for resources
                0,                  // ID of resources
                &hwndClient) ;      // Pointer to client window handle

    WinSendMsg (hwndFrame, WM_SETICON,
                WinQuerySysPointer (HWND_DESKTOP, SPTR_APPICON, FALSE),
                NULL) ;

    while (WinGetMsg (hab, &qmsg, NULL, 0, 0))
        WinDispatchMsg (hab, &qmsg) ;

    WinDestroyWindow (hwndFrame) ;
    WinDestroyMsgQueue (hmq) ;
    WinTerminate (hab) ;
    return 0 ;
    }

MRESULT EXPENTRY ClientWndProc (HWND hwnd, USHORT msg, MPARAM mp1, MPARAM mp2)
    {
    return WinDefWindowProc (hwnd, msg, mp1, mp2) ;
    }
```

The WELCOME.DEF File

```
;------------------------------------
; WELCOME.DEF module definition file
;------------------------------------

NAME            WELCOME   WINDOWAPI

DESCRIPTION     'Welcome to PM -- Program No. 7 (C) Charles Petzold, 1988'
PROTMODE
HEAPSIZE        1024
STACKSIZE       8192
EXPORTS         ClientWndProc
```

Figure 2-9. *The WELCOME program.*

This new window is called a "client window." Messages for this client window are stored in the message queue just like messages for the other four windows created in *WinCreateStdWindow*. The messages are retrieved from the queue with *WinGetMsg* and dispatched to the appropriate window procedure with *WinDispatchMsg*. But the window procedure for the client window is not in PMWIN.DLL. This window procedure is located in WELCOME itself.

Registering a Window Class

Every window has an associated window procedure. More precisely, every window is based on a particular "window class." It's the window class that defines the window procedure used to process messages for all windows created based on that class.

The Presentation Manager has nine predefined window classes. (One of them, for example, is the class called WC_TITLEBAR, using the PMWIN.H identifier.) Each of these window classes has a window procedure located in PMWIN.DLL. (The window procedure for the WC_TITLEBAR class is *WinTitlebarWndProc*.) When *WinCreateStdWindow* was called in previous versions of the program, it created four windows based on four of these predefined window classes. Messages to these windows go to the window procedure for the window class.

If you want *WinCreateStdWindow* to create a client window with a window procedure in your own program, you must first register a new window class that identifies this window procedure. You do this by calling *WinRegisterClass*, as shown in the WELCOME.C program. The second and third parameters to *WinRegisterClass* are the most important: They specify the name of the window class and the address of the window procedure for that class. The window procedure processes messages to all windows that are based on that class.

The predefined window classes in PMWIN.DLL are "public" window classes: They can be used by all programs running under the Presentation Manager. When your program contains a window procedure and you register a class for it, that is a "private" class that can be used only by your program.

The name of a private window class registered in a program is generally a character string that either is the name of the program or is derived from the name of the program, but it can really be anything you want. In WELCOME, the class name is the character string "Welcome" stored in the array *szClientClass*. (The *sz* prefix indicates that the variable is a string terminated by a zero byte.) The window procedure is the function named *ClientWndProc*, which in WELCOME is located after the *main* function. You can name the window procedure whatever you like. The window procedure is declared near the top of the program with the following statement:

```
MRESULT EXPENTRY ClientWndProc (HWND, USHORT, MPARAM, MPARAM) ;
```

Declaring *ClientWndProc* before *main* is mandatory: This lets the C compiler recognize *ClientWndProc* as a function when compiling code for the *WinRegisterClass* call.

The EXPENTRY identifier stands for "exported entry point" and indicates that the function is called from outside the program. It is defined in OS2DEF.H in the same way as APIENTRY:

```
#define EXPENTRY far pascal
```

All window procedures must be defined as EXPENTRY functions.

The New *WinCreateStdWindow* Call

The next step is to change some of the parameters to *WinCreateStdWindow* so that it creates a client window in addition to the other five windows. The fourth parameter to *WinCreateStdWindow* (previously set to NULL) is now set to the name of the client window class, which is the character array *szClientClass*. The last parameter to *WinCreateStdWindow* is a pointer to a variable that will receive the handle of the client window when *WinCreateStdWindow* creates it. This variable is named *hwndClient* and defined as type HWND.

WinCreateStdWindow now creates five windows, four of them based on pre-defined window classes and the fifth — the client window — based on the "Welcome" class. *WinCreateStdWindow* returns the window handle of the frame window, but it also stores the window handle of the client window in the variable pointed to by its last parameter.

Processing the Messages

The *ClientWndProc* window procedure in WELCOME is called only from the Presentation Manager, from outside the program's code segment, using the Pascal calling sequence, which is why it's defined as an EXPENTRY function. The window procedure returns an MRESULT (a 32-bit far pointer) to the Presentation Manager. *ClientWndProc* receives messages only for the client window. Whenever *ClientWndProc* is called, the *hwnd* parameter is the window handle of the client window. This is the same window handle stored in the *hwndClient* variable in *main*.

ClientWndProc doesn't yet process any messages itself. Any message a window procedure doesn't process must be passed on to the *WinDefWindowProc* function in the Presentation Manager. The value returned from *WinDefWindowProc* is then returned from the window procedure.

> NOTE: *That* ClientWndProc *doesn't process any messages causes a little problem: The client window isn't painted. If you experiment with* WELCOME *in the Presentation Manager, you'll find that the client window displays whatever was underneath it when it is created or resized! Of course, we'll fix this problem shortly.*

The Stream of Processing

With the client window procedure in place, you can now get a good sense of how Presentation Manager programs are structured and how they operate. The *main* function first performs initialization. At the very least, this involves calls to *WinInitialize*, *WinCreateMsgQueue*, *WinRegisterClass*, and *WinCreateStdWindow*. It then enters the message loop. When it exits the message loop, it cleans up with *WinDestroyWindow*, *WinDestroyMsgQueue*, and *WinTerminate* and exits *main*, terminating the program.

In the message loop, the program calls *WinGetMsg*, which retrieves the next message from the program's message queue. These messages include user input from the keyboard and mouse. The program passes the message back to the Presentation Manager by calling *WinDispatchMsg*. The Presentation Manager determines the address of the window procedure for the particular window that must receive the message, and it then calls the window procedure. This is either a predefined window procedure within the Presentation Manager or a window procedure within the program (such as *ClientWndProc*).

The window procedure either processes the message or calls *WinDefWindowProc*. The window procedure then returns control to the Presentation Manager (still in the *WinDispatchMsg* call), which returns control to the program's message loop.

This is a considerably more complex interaction between a program and an operating system than is typical in a more conventional operating system such as the OS/2 kernel. In the Presentation Manager, programs have a more intimate connection with the operating system and (potentially) other programs running under the Presentation Manager. It's the use of messages that makes the difference. Messages are the means of communication between the Presentation Manager and windows, and between windows themselves.

Queued and Nonqueued Messages

I've been discussing how messages get from the message queue to a window procedure. However, not all messages originate in the message queue. Window procedures can also be called directly from the Presentation Manager.

When a message is placed in a program's message queue, retrieved with *WinGetMsg*, and dispatched to the window procedure with *WinDispatchMsg*, that message is said to be a "queued message." Many of the messages relating to user input (such as the WM_CHAR keyboard message and the WM_MOUSEMOVE mouse message) are "queued" messages. Timer messages are queued, as are menu messages (which signal a window procedure that a menu item has been chosen). But many other messages are sent to the window procedure directly without first being placed in the message queue. For example, the WM_CREATE message — which is the first message that a window procedure receives — is sent to the window at the same time the Presentation Manager is executing the *WinCreateStdWindow* function. The WM_DESTROY message is sent to a window procedure as part of the Presentation Manager's processing of the *WinDestroyWindow* call. These are "nonqueued" messages.

Whether a message is sent directly to a window procedure or dispatched to the window procedure after being retrieved from the message queue is generally not very important. The window procedure is "message central"—it gets all messages to the window. It usually doesn't matter what route the messages took to get to the window procedure.

A window can also "post" or "send" messages to other windows. The *WinPostMsg* function places a message in the message queue associated with a particular window and returns immediately. The *WinSendMsg* function (which I used to send the frame window a WM_SETICON message) causes the Presentation Manager to call the window procedure directly. *WinSendMsg* returns after the window procedure has processed the message. (The *WinDispatchMsg* call used in the message loop is similar to the *WinSendMsg* call.)

In short, *post* means to put the message in the mail box; *send* means to hand-deliver the message to the recipient. A message that is posted becomes a queued message; a message that is sent becomes a nonqueued message. As I said, from the perspective of the window procedure, the distinction is usually not very important. When speaking about messages, the term *send* is often used for convenience even when the message is actually posted. In the chapters ahead, I'll discuss whether a message is queued or nonqueued when necessary, but otherwise I'll tend to use this convenient terminology.

Messages sometimes generate other messages. This can happen when a window procedure declines to process a message and passes the message to *WinDefWindowProc*. *WinDefWindowProc* sometimes does default processing of a message by sending the window procedure another message. Calling Presentation Manager functions also sometimes results in the window procedure being sent a message.

This means that the window procedure must be recursive. Generally, this fact doesn't cause any problems, but you should keep it in the back of your mind. If you encounter a strange bug (a static local variable in your window procedure changing when you call a Presentation Manager function, for example), perhaps your window procedure is changing the variable itself while processing another message generated by the call to the Presentation Manager function. You should also keep at a reasonable level the size of local automatic variables in *main* and in the window procedures. The recursive use of window procedures is the primary reason for the minimum recommended 8 KB stack size in Presentation Manager programs. Feel free to increase it if you use large automatic variables in a window procedure.

Special Treatment of Window Procedures

Window procedures require some special attention when you compile and link the program. First, for any program that contains a window procedure, the compiler requires yet another switch: *-Gw*. (The *w* stands for "window.") This switch is combined with the *-G2* and *-Gs* switches to make the *-G2sw* switch. Second, the window procedure must be mentioned in an EXPORTS statement in the module definition file:

```
EXPORTS    ClientWndProc
```

With this statement you're "exporting" the window procedure so that it can be called from another module (specifically, from the Presentation Manager).

The *-Gw* compiler switch and the EXPORTS statement are very closely related and involve some manipulation on the machine-code level when control passes between the Presentation Manager and your program. When a program calls a Presentation Manager function (such as *WinDispatchMsg*), that function generally uses its own data area, which is a data segment associated with the dynamic link library that contains the function. In assembly-language terms, the function must push the current DS register (which points to the data segment of the program making the function call) on the stack and set DS to its own data segment. Before returning to the program, it pops the original DS off the stack. However, in the course of the *WinDispatchMsg* function call, the dynamic link library might need to call the program's window procedure. The DS value associated with the window procedure isn't directly available. Thus the window procedure would be unable to access its own data segment.

The *-Gw* switch adds a special prologue and epilogue to the window procedure to save the value of DS (the dynamic link library's DS) on entry to the window procedure and restore it on exit. Exporting the window procedure directs OS/2 to add some code to this prologue to set DS to the program's data segment. Thus the window procedure can be called from the dynamic link library without problems.

WELCOME1—Painting the Client Window

Now that we have a client window with its very own window procedure that processes messages to the window, we are ready to process a few messages and paint the client window. The final WELCOME program in this chapter, WELCOME1, is shown in Figure 2-10.

The WELCOME1 File

```
#-------------------
# WELCOME1 make file
#-------------------

welcome1.obj : welcome1.c
    cl -c -G2sw -W3 welcome1.c

welcome1.exe : welcome1.obj welcome1.def
    link welcome1, /align:16, NUL, os2, welcome1
```

The WELCOME1.C File

```c
/*-----------------------------------------------------------
    WELCOME1.C -- A Program that Writes to its Client Window
   ------------------------------------------------------*/

#define INCL_WIN
#include <os2.h>

MRESULT EXPENTRY ClientWndProc (HWND, USHORT, MPARAM, MPARAM) ;

int main (void)
    {
    static CHAR  szClientClass [] = "Welcome1" ;
    static ULONG flFrameFlags = FCF_TITLEBAR      | FCF_SYSMENU |
                                FCF_SIZEBORDER     | FCF_MINMAX  |
                                FCF_SHELLPOSITION  | FCF_TASKLIST ;

    HAB          hab ;
    HMQ          hmq ;
    HWND         hwndFrame, hwndClient ;
    QMSG         qmsg ;

    hab = WinInitialize (0) ;
    hmq = WinCreateMsgQueue (hab, 0) ;

    WinRegisterClass (
                hab,             // Anchor block handle
                szClientClass,   // Name of class being registered
                ClientWndProc,   // Window procedure for class
                CS_SIZEREDRAW,   // Class style
                0) ;             // Extra bytes to reserve
```

(continued)

Figure 2-10. The WELCOME1.C File. *continued*

```
    hwndFrame = WinCreateStdWindow (
                    HWND_DESKTOP,       // Parent window handle
                    WS_VISIBLE,         // Style of frame window
                    &flFrameFlags,      // Pointer to control data
                    szClientClass,      // Client window class name
                    NULL,               // Title bar text
                    0L,                 // Style of client window
                    NULL,               // Module handle for resources
                    0,                  // ID of resources
                    &hwndClient) ;      // Pointer to client window handle

    WinSendMsg (hwndFrame, WM_SETICON,
                WinQuerySysPointer (HWND_DESKTOP, SPTR_APPICON, FALSE),
                NULL) ;

    while (WinGetMsg (hab, &qmsg, NULL, 0, 0))
        WinDispatchMsg (hab, &qmsg) ;

    WinDestroyWindow (hwndFrame) ;
    WinDestroyMsgQueue (hmq) ;
    WinTerminate (hab) ;
    return 0 ;
    }

MRESULT EXPENTRY ClientWndProc (HWND hwnd, USHORT msg, MPARAM mp1, MPARAM mp2)
    {
    static CHAR szText [] = "Welcome to the OS/2 Presentation Manager" ;
    HPS        hps;
    RECTL      rcl ;

    switch (msg)
        {
        case WM_CREATE:
            DosBeep (261, 100) ;
            DosBeep (330, 100) ;
            DosBeep (392, 100) ;
            DosBeep (523, 500) ;
            return 0 ;

        case WM_PAINT:
            hps = WinBeginPaint (hwnd, NULL, NULL) ;
```

(continued)

Figure 2-10. The WELCOME1.C File. *continued*

```
                  WinQueryWindowRect (hwnd, &rcl) ;

                  WinDrawText (hps, -1, szText, &rcl, CLR_NEUTRAL, CLR_BACKGROUND,
                               DT_CENTER | DT_VCENTER | DT_ERASERECT) ;

                  WinEndPaint (hps) ;
                  return 0 ;

             case WM_DESTROY:
                  DosBeep (523, 100) ;
                  DosBeep (392, 100) ;
                  DosBeep (330, 100) ;
                  DosBeep (261, 500) ;
                  return 0 ;
             }
        return WinDefWindowProc (hwnd, msg, mp1, mp2) ;
        }
```

The WELCOME1.DEF File

```
;-------------------------------------
; WELCOME1.DEF module definition file
;-------------------------------------

NAME         WELCOME1  WINDOWAPI

DESCRIPTION  'Welcome to PM -- Program No. 8 (C) Charles Petzold, 1988'
PROTMODE
HEAPSIZE     1024
STACKSIZE    8192
EXPORTS      ClientWndProc
```

Figure 2-10. *The WELCOME1 program.*

WELCOME1.EXE displays the text "Welcome to the OS/2 Presentation Manager" in the center of its client window as shown in Figure 2-11 on the following page.

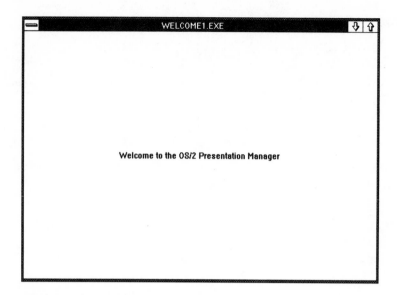

Figure 2-11. *The WELCOME1 display.*

Processing Messages

The *ClientWndProc* window procedure in WELCOME1 shows the typical *switch* and *case* construction used to process messages. The *msg* parameter to the window procedure identifies the message. *ClientWndProc* processes three messages: WM_CREATE, WM_PAINT, and WM_DESTROY. In most cases, a window procedure returns 0L when it processes a message. Any message not processed must be passed on to *WinDefWindowProc*, and the value returned from *WinDefWindowProc* must be returned from the window procedure.

The WM_CREATE message is the first message that a window procedure receives. It is sent directly to the window procedure during the *WinCreateStdWindow* call. A window procedure can perform some window initialization during the WM_CREATE message. In WELCOME1, *ClientWndProc* calls the OS/2 *DosBeep* function to play the notes of a C-major chord to indicate that the client window has arrived.

The WM_DESTROY message is the last message a window procedure receives. The Presentation Manager sends this message to the window procedure during the *WinDestroyWindow* call. Although window procedures can do some "cleanup" during the WM_DESTROY message, *ClientWndProc* again calls *DosBeep* a few times as a swan song to indicate that the client window is being destroyed.

The WM_PAINT Message

One of the most important messages that a window procedure receives is WM_PAINT, which tells the window procedure when to display something on the window. "What?" you say. "The Presentation Manager is telling *me* when I can display something on *my* window? I have to be given permission? What kind of fascist operating system is this?" Cool down. The WM_PAINT message is simply the Presentation Manager's way of telling you that a portion of your window is "invalid"—that is, that part of the window's visible area contains garbage or perhaps nothing at all. The WM_PAINT message tells the window function that the window is due for a paint job.

How does the window become invalid? When a window is first created, the entire window is invalid. In fact, one of the first queued messages the client window receives is WM_PAINT. The window function can take this opportunity to display something in the window. Now suppose you minimize the window and then restore it to the original size. The Presentation Manager doesn't save the contents of the window when the window is minimized. In a graphical environment it's simply too much data. Thus when the window is restored after being minimized, the window is invalid, and a WM_PAINT message is placed in the message queue. If you start rearranging several windows on the display, a window may overlap others. The Presentation Manager generally won't save the area of a window covered by another window. When the window is uncovered, the previously hidden area is invalid, and a WM_PAINT message goes into the message queue.

This is probably quite different from the way you usually think about using the video display. Under a conventional operating system, your program can display something on the screen whenever it wants and not worry about something on the screen mysteriously disappearing. Under the Presentation Manager, you can still—if you want—display something on a window whenever you want. But it makes more sense to do painting only when the window function receives the WM_PAINT message. The program must retain what it needs to recreate the appearance of the window, because it can receive a WM_PAINT message at almost any time. If the window function displays something on the window while processing a message other than WM_PAINT, it must also execute the same painting code when it gets a WM_PAINT message.

Normally, if you resize a window to make it smaller, the window procedure doesn't receive a WM_PAINT message. The Presentation Manager simply cuts off the edges of the window that previously extended past the new size. You'll note, however, that in WELCOME1 the fourth parameter to *WinRegisterClass* is set to CS_SIZEREDRAW. This is a class style. It causes the Presentation Manager to invalidate the entire window and post a WM_PAINT message to the client window whenever the size of the window changes.

When you get a WM_PAINT message, you can obtain the coordinates of the invalid area of the window. You need update only that part of the window. We'll explore this and other aspects of the WM_PAINT message more in upcoming chapters. Right now all you have to know is that WM_PAINT informs the window procedure that it's time to update the appearance of the window.

Processing WM_PAINT

The code that processes the WM_PAINT message in a window function must begin with a call to *WinBeginPaint* and end with a call to *WinEndPaint*. When *WinEndPaint* is called, the Presentation Manager validates the entire area of the window. Using a simple form of the *WinBeginPaint* call, the code looks like this:

```
case WM_PAINT:
    hps = WinBeginPaint (hwnd, NULL, NULL) ;
        [paint the window]
    WinEndPaint (hps) ;
    return 0 ;
```

If your program doesn't process WM_PAINT messages (as WELCOME doesn't), they are passed to *WinDefWindowProc*. *WinDefWindowProc* simply calls *WinBeginPaint* and *WinEndPaint* (with nothing in between) to validate the entire area of the client window. This is a good example of how *WinDefWindowProc* takes care of chores a program chooses to ignore. If *WinBeginPaint* and *WinEndPaint* aren't called during a WM_PAINT message, an area of the window remains invalid, and the WM_PAINT message isn't removed from the message queue.

The handle returned from the *WinBeginPaint* call is a handle to a presentation space. The handle is stored in a variable named *hps* of type HPS. You need this handle to the presentation space to draw on the surface of the client window. The presentation space handle is the first parameter to all the Graphics Programming Interface (GPI) drawing functions.

The presentation space is essentially a data structure that defines an abstract display surface. The presentation space is associated with a "device context," which defines a particular physical display medium. In the form of the *WinBeginPaint* call used here, the presentation space for which we get a handle is associated with a device context for the video display—in particular, the part of the display that the client window occupies. This form of the *WinBeginPaint* call (with the second parameter set to NULL) implies that we're using a subset of GPI that is called the "cached micro-PS."

Painting WELCOME1's Client Window

After the *WinBeginPaint* call, WELCOME1 obtains the dimensions of the client window by using this function:

```
WinQueryWindowRect (hwnd, &rcl) ;
```

The first parameter is *hwnd*, the handle to the client window. The *rcl* variable is a structure of type RECTL (rectangle). The RECTL structure has four fields: *xLeft*, *yBottom*, *xRight*, and *yTop*. *WinQueryWindowRect* fills the fields of the *rcl* structure with the current coordinates of the client window. These coordinates are relative to the lower-left corner of the window; hence the *xLeft* and *yBottom* fields are set to 0. The *xRight* field is actually the width of the window in pixels, and *yTop* is the height of the window in pixels.

The *WinDrawText* function is used to display the string "Welcome to the OS/2 Presentation Manager" in the center of the client window. It uses the *rcl* rectangle structure and the parameter DT_CENTER | DT_VCENTER | DT_ERASERECT to specify that the string is to be horizontally and vertically centered within the rectangle and that the rectangle (the entire window) is to be erased before the text is displayed. The CLR_NEUTRAL and CLR_BACKGROUND parameters specify the text color and background color. I'll discuss these two "colors" in Chapter 5.

Too Much Overhead?

This has been a long journey to write a simple program that displays some text and plays a tune. But we've basically covered all the facets of the Presentation Manager. You've learned about windows. You've learned about messages. You've learned about presentation spaces. That's it. Everything that follows is just detail.

## CHAPTER THREE

MORE FUN WITH WINDOWS

In Chapter 2, our rush to create a functional window required that we ignore some details and finer points of the art of window creation. Here we'll explore variations on the basic theme.

Exploring the Standard Window

The *WinCreateStdWindow* function creates one or more windows. In the final version of WELCOME1, shown in Chapter 2, *WinCreateStdWindow* creates five windows — the frame, title bar, system menu, minimize/maximize window, and the client window. The term "standard window" refers to this collection of windows organized around the frame window. All but one of the windows that make up the standard window are created based on window classes already registered by the Presentation Manager. Messages to these windows come through the program's message queue but are dispatched to the particular window procedure in PMWIN.DLL that is defined by the window class. The client window, on the other hand, is generally based on a window class that the program itself registers, and it uses a window procedure within the program (called *ClientWndProc* in WELCOME1) to process its messages.

The windows that make up the standard window receive messages from the Presentation Manager (often initiated by user input) but can also send messages to one another. They essentially carry on a family conversation.

The Family of Windows

Windows created in the Presentation Manager usually have a parent-child relationship. In the standard window, the frame window is the parent, and the other windows (including the client window) are the children of the frame window. Thus we can define the term *standard window* as "a frame window and its children." Windows with a common parent are called "sibling windows." A window can have many children but only one parent. A window's children, its children's children, and so forth are called the window's "descendants."

The grand matriarch of Presentation Manager windows is the "desktop window." The desktop window occupies the entire screen. Although it appears to be simply a background color, the desktop window is a real window with a window procedure in PMWIN.DLL named *WinDesktopWndProc* that processes its messages. Every other window is a descendant of the desktop window. (This isn't quite true. Some windows, called "object windows," have no parent. Like other windows, an object window can send and receive messages, but an object window isn't visible on the screen and doesn't receive user input. When I discuss windows in this book I'm usually talking about nonobject windows.)

A child of the desktop window is called a "top-level window." Virtually every program that runs under the Presentation Manager creates at least one top-level window. When a program such as WELCOME1 calls *WinCreateStdWindow* to create the application's main window, the frame window is a top-level window. The other windows created by the function are children of the frame window and are not top-level windows. The family tree for the WELCOME1 program is shown in Figure 3-1.

A child window is affected by its parent in several ways:

- A child window is always displayed within the area of the screen occupied by its parent. We say that the child is "clipped" on the area of its parent. This is fairly obvious in the case of the desktop window and the frame window because the desktop window encompasses the entire screen. The children of the frame window also appear within the area occupied by the frame. If the frame window tried to position part of the title bar window outside of the area that is occupied by the frame, the part of the title bar outside the frame window would not be visible.

- Child windows remain in the same position relative to the parent unless explicitly moved. When you move the frame window around the screen, the children follow. This happens automatically: When the frame window wants to move itself (usually because it has received a message from the title bar window that the user has moved the window), it need only tell the Presentation Manager to move the frame. The Presentation Manager takes care of moving the children.

- When a parent window is hidden, minimized, or destroyed, all of its children (and, by extension, all its descendants) are also hidden, minimized, or destroyed. This should be partly obvious in WELCOME1. If you minimize the frame window, all the children of the frame window are also removed from the screen. When the frame window is destroyed by the call to *WinDestroyWindow* after WELCOME1 leaves the message loop, all the children of the frame window (including the client window) are also destroyed. *ClientWndProc* receives a WM_DESTROY message at that time.

- Sibling windows can overlap on the screen. We'll see examples of overlapping siblings in the WELCOME2 and WELCOME3 programs in this chapter.

The Presentation Manager includes a function, *WinQueryWindow*, that you can use to determine a window's parent:

```
hwndParent = WinQueryWindow (hwnd, QW_PARENT, FALSE) ;
```

The variable *hwndParent* is set to the handle of the parent window of *hwnd*. For example, after the *WinCreateStdWindow* function returns control to your program, the following call obtains the frame window handle:

```
hwndFrame = WinQueryWindow (hwndClient, QW_PARENT, FALSE) ;
```

This will be the same window handle returned from *WinCreateStdWindow*.

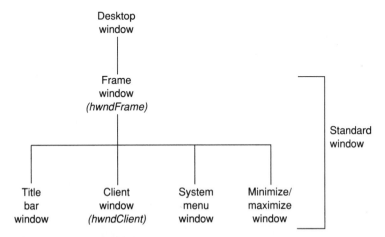

Figure 3-1. *The WELCOME1 family tree.*

If *hwndFrame* is a top-level window, you can obtain the desktop window handle by calling

```
hwndDesktop = WinQueryWindow (hwndFrame, QW_PARENT, FALSE) ;
```

Or you can use the function specifically designed for this purpose:

```
hwndDesktop = WinQueryDesktopWindow (hab, NULL) ;
```

In many Presentation Manager functions, the HWND_DESKTOP identifier is used to refer to the desktop window. Usually you pass HWND_DESKTOP as the first parameter to *WinCreateStdWindow*. This makes the frame a top-level window. The application often has no choice but to do this: The frame window must have a parent, but the application doesn't know about any other windows except the desktop window. The desktop is thus the only possible parent.

If the program calls *WinCreateStdWindow* a second time, it has a choice: The second frame window could be another top-level window, or it could be a child of one of the windows created in the first *WinCreateStdWindow* call (most likely a child of the first client window). Let's look at an example of the first approach.

Creating Multiple Top-Level Windows

The WELCOME2 program, shown in Figure 3-2, creates two top-level standard windows. The program contains two window procedures (*Client1WndProc* and *Client2WndProc*), registers two window classes ("Welcome2.1" and "Welcome2.2"), and calls *WinCreateStdWindow* twice. Note that the EXPORTS section of WELCOME2.DEF lists both window procedures.

The WELCOME2 File

```
#--------------------
# WELCOME2 make file
#--------------------

welcome2.obj : welcome2.c
    cl -c -G2sw -W3 welcome2.c

welcome2.exe : welcome2.obj welcome2.def
    link welcome2, /align:16, NUL, os2, welcome2
```

The WELCOME2.C File

```
/*-------------------------------------------------------------
   WELCOME2.C -- A Program that Creates Two Top-Level Windows
   ----------------------------------------------------------*/

#define INCL_WIN
#include <os2.h>

MRESULT EXPENTRY Client1WndProc (HWND, USHORT, MPARAM, MPARAM) ;
MRESULT EXPENTRY Client2WndProc (HWND, USHORT, MPARAM, MPARAM) ;

int main (void)
    {
    static CHAR  szClientClass1 [] = "Welcome2.1",
                 szClientClass2 [] = "Welcome2.2" ;
    static ULONG flFrameFlags = FCF_TITLEBAR      | FCF_SYSMENU |
                                FCF_SIZEBORDER     | FCF_MINMAX  |
                                FCF_SHELLPOSITION  | FCF_TASKLIST ;

    HAB         hab ;
    HMQ         hmq ;
    HWND        hwndFrame1, hwndFrame2, hwndClient1, hwndClient2 ;
    QMSG        qmsg ;

    hab = WinInitialize (0) ;
    hmq = WinCreateMsgQueue (hab, 0) ;

    WinRegisterClass (
                hab,            // Anchor block handle
                szClientClass1, // Name of class being registered
                Client1WndProc, // Window procedure for class
                CS_SIZEREDRAW,  // Class style
                0) ;            // Extra bytes to reserve

    WinRegisterClass (
                hab,            // Anchor block handle
                szClientClass2, // Name of class being registered
                Client2WndProc, // Window procedure for class
                CS_SIZEREDRAW,  // Class style
                0) ;            // Extra bytes to reserve

    hwndFrame1 = WinCreateStdWindow (
                HWND_DESKTOP,   // Parent window handle
                WS_VISIBLE,     // Style of frame window
                &flFrameFlags,  // Pointer to control data
```

(continued)

Figure 3-2. The WELCOME2.C File. *continued*

```
                  szClientClass1,      // Client window class name
                  NULL,                // Title bar text
                  OL,                  // Style of client window
                  NULL,                // Module handle for resources
                  0,                   // ID of resources
                  &hwndClient1) ;      // Pointer to client window handle

     hwndFrame2 = WinCreateStdWindow (
                  HWND_DESKTOP,        // Parent window handle
                  WS_VISIBLE,          // Style of frame window
                  &flFrameFlags,       // Pointer to control data
                  szClientClass2,      // Client window class name
                  " - Window No. 2",   // Title bar text
                  OL,                  // Style of client window
                  NULL,                // Module handle for resources
                  0,                   // ID of resources
                  &hwndClient2) ;      // Pointer to client window handle


     WinSendMsg (hwndFrame1, WM_SETICON,
                 WinQuerySysPointer (HWND_DESKTOP, SPTR_APPICON, FALSE),
                 NULL) ;

     WinSendMsg (hwndFrame2, WM_SETICON,
                 WinQuerySysPointer (HWND_DESKTOP, SPTR_APPICON, FALSE),
                 NULL) ;

     while (WinGetMsg (hab, &qmsg, NULL, 0, 0))
          WinDispatchMsg (hab, &qmsg) ;

     WinDestroyWindow (hwndFrame1) ;
     WinDestroyWindow (hwndFrame2) ;
     WinDestroyMsgQueue (hmq) ;
     WinTerminate (hab) ;
     return 0 ;
     }

MRESULT EXPENTRY Client1WndProc (HWND hwnd, USHORT msg, MPARAM mp1, MPARAM mp2)
     {
     static CHAR szText [] = "Welcome to Window No. 1" ;
     HPS         hps ;
     RECTL       rcl ;

     switch (msg)
          {
          case WM_PAINT:
               hps = WinBeginPaint (hwnd, NULL, NULL) ;
```

(continued)

Figure 3-2. The WELCOME2.C File. *continued*

```
                    WinQueryWindowRect (hwnd, &rcl) ;

                    WinDrawText (hps, -1, szText, &rcl, CLR_NEUTRAL, CLR_BACKGROUND,
                              DT_CENTER ¦ DT_VCENTER ¦ DT_ERASERECT) ;

                    WinEndPaint (hps) ;
                    return 0 ;
            }
      return WinDefWindowProc (hwnd, msg, mp1, mp2) ;
      }

MRESULT EXPENTRY Client2WndProc (HWND hwnd, USHORT msg, MPARAM mp1, MPARAM mp2)
      {
      static CHAR szText [] = "Welcome to Window No. 2" ;
      HPS        hps ;
      RECTL      rcl ;

      switch (msg)
            {
            case WM_PAINT:
                    hps = WinBeginPaint (hwnd, NULL, NULL) ;

                    WinQueryWindowRect (hwnd, &rcl) ;

                    WinDrawText (hps, -1, szText, &rcl, CLR_NEUTRAL, CLR_BACKGROUND,
                              DT_CENTER ¦ DT_VCENTER ¦ DT_ERASERECT) ;

                    WinEndPaint (hps) ;
                    return 0 ;

            case WM_CLOSE:
                    return 0 ;
            }
      return WinDefWindowProc (hwnd, msg, mp1, mp2) ;
      }
```

The WELCOME2.DEF File

```
;-------------------------------------
; WELCOME2.DEF module definition file
;-------------------------------------

NAME          WELCOME2   WINDOWAPI
```

(continued)

Figure 3-2. The WELCOME2.DEF File. *continued*

```
DESCRIPTION      'Creates Two Top-Level Windows (C) Charles Petzold, 1988'
PROTMODE
HEAPSIZE         1024
STACKSIZE        8192
EXPORTS          Client1WndProc
                 Client2WndProc
```

Figure 3-2. *The WELCOME2 program.*

The first parameter in the *WinCreateStdWindow* call is the parent of the frame window. In both function calls, this parameter is set to HWND-_DESKTOP. The two frame windows in WELCOME2 share the same parent and are thus siblings. The WELCOME2 family tree is shown in Figure 3-3.

When you run WELCOME2 (as shown in Figure 3-4), you'll find that the two top-level windows function independently, almost as if they were created in different programs. Both windows are listed on the Task Manager. Because all top-level windows are siblings, top-level windows overlap. Only one top-level window is "active" at any time. You can switch between the two windows (as you can switch among all top-level windows listed on the Task Manager) using the Alt-Esc or Alt-Tab key combinations.

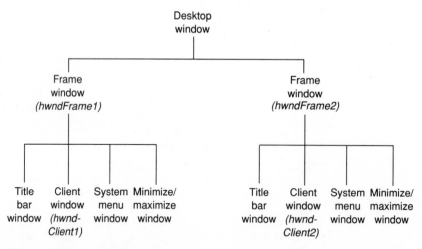

Figure 3-3. *The WELCOME2 family tree.*

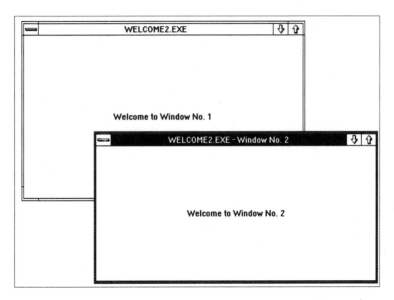

Figure 3-4. *The WELCOME2 display.*

To simplify this demonstration, I have both window functions in
WELCOME2 perform approximately the same task (display some text in the
client window). However, the two window functions could perform entirely
different tasks from one another. For example, it's not difficult to imagine a
Presentation Manager CAD (computer-assisted design) program organized
into two top-level windows. One window could be an ASCII text editor and
allow you to enter and edit a series of drawing commands. The other window could display the graphical representation of these commands. When
you change one of the commands in the editor window, the change could be
reflected in the graphics window; likewise, if you change the drawing itself
(perhaps using the mouse), the change could be reflected in the corresponding text command in the editor window. The two client window procedures
would communicate these changes to each other with messages. You would
store the two client window handles returned from the *WinCreateStdWindow*
calls in global variables so that they could be accessed by both window
procedures.

What messages would the two client windows send to each other? That's up
to you. PMWIN.H defines the identifier WM_USER specifically for the purpose of creating your own messages. Within a program, you can define private messages that use values of WM_USER or above.

```
#define WM_MYMESSAGE0  (WM_USER + 0)
#define WM_MYMESSAGE1  (WM_USER + 1)
#define WM_MYMESSAGE2  (WM_USER + 2)
```

If *Client1WndProc* needs to send a WM_MYMESSAGE1 message to *Client2WndProc*, it can do so:

```
WinSendMsg (hwndClient2, WM_MYMESSAGE1, MPFROMLONG (lData1),
            MPFROMLONG (lData2)) ;
```

lData1 and *lData2* are long integers with message-specific data. The MPFROMLONG macros convert a long integer to an MPARAM data type. The message would be processed within *Client2WndProc* like this:

```
case WM_MYMESSAGE1:
        [process message]
    return 0 ;
```

Keep in mind that the two MPARAM values that accompany messages can be far pointers to structures or to big blocks of memory, so the amount of data passed in the message can be very large. The value returned from *WinSendMsg* is the value that the window procedure returns once it has processed the message. This is defined as an MRESULT, which is also a far pointer.

Title Bar Text

Notice that in Figure 3-4 the first window's title bar contained the text "WELCOME2.EXE" and the second had "WELCOME2.EXE—Window No. 2." This is what you'll see when you run the program from the CMD.EXE prompt or the Presentation Manager File System. If you install WELCOME2 in the Start Programs window and run the program that way, you'll see the program title specified in Start Programs in place of "WELCOME2.EXE" on the title bar of each of the windows.

This is part of what the FCF_TASKLIST flag does. The title bar text (and the Task Manager entry) is the name under which the program was started, concatenated with the title bar text specified in the *WinCreateStdWindow* function. For most programs in this book, I use NULL for the *WinCreateStdWindow* parameter that indicates the title bar text. This causes the title bar to display only the .EXE filename or the program title from Start Programs. For the second window in WELCOME2, however, I used "—Window No. 2" in *WinCreateStdWindow*, so this text also appears in the title bar and on the Task Manager.

Terminating a Presentation Manager Program

I've written WELCOME2 so that you cannot terminate the program by selecting "Close" from the second window's system menu. This requires a little explanation of how Presentation Manager programs terminate. When you select Close from the system menu, the client window procedure receives a WM_CLOSE message. If the window procedure passes WM_CLOSE to *WinDefWindowProc*, the Presentation Manager posts a WM_QUIT message to the message queue. This causes *WinGetMsg* to return 0 when the WM_QUIT message is retrieved from the queue, and the program exits the message loop. If a window procedure simply traps WM_CLOSE messages and returns from the window procedure without calling *WinDefWindowProc*, then nothing happens. This is how *Client2WndProc* essentially disables the Close option on its system menu. (However, you can terminate the program by closing either of the two windows from the Task Manager. The Task Manager simply posts a WM_QUIT message to the message queue. I describe how to process this WM_QUIT message in Chapter 13.)

WELCOME2 is somewhat unorthodox. A Presentation Manager program usually creates only one top-level main window. Any other top-level windows created in the program (such as dialog boxes) exist for only short periods of time.

Creating Children of the Client

A more common approach to creating multiple standard windows is demonstrated in the WELCOME3 program, shown in Figure 3-5.

The WELCOME3 File

```
#--------------------
# WELCOME3 make file
#--------------------

welcome3.obj : welcome3.c
    cl -c -G2sw -W3 welcome3.c

welcome3.exe : welcome3.obj welcome3.def
    link welcome3, /align:16, NUL, os2, welcome3
```

The WELCOME3.C File

```
/*-------------------------------------------------------------
   WELCOME3.C -- Creates a Top-Level Window and Two Children
   -----------------------------------------------------------*/

#define INCL_WIN
#include <os2.h>

MRESULT EXPENTRY ClientWndProc (HWND, USHORT, MPARAM, MPARAM) ;
MRESULT EXPENTRY ChildWndProc  (HWND, USHORT, MPARAM, MPARAM) ;

int main (void)
    {
    static CHAR  szClientClass [] = "Welcome3",
                 szChildClass  [] = "Welcome3.Child" ;
    static ULONG flFrameFlags = FCF_TITLEBAR     | FCF_SYSMENU  |
                                FCF_SIZEBORDER    | FCF_MINMAX   |
                                FCF_SHELLPOSITION | FCF_TASKLIST ;
    HAB          hab ;
    HMQ          hmq ;
    HWND         hwndFrame, hwndChildFrame1, hwndChildFrame2,
                 hwndClient, hwndChildClient1, hwndChildClient2 ;
    QMSG         qmsg ;

    hab = WinInitialize (0) ;
    hmq = WinCreateMsgQueue (hab, 0) ;

    WinRegisterClass (
                hab,                // Anchor block handle
                szClientClass,      // Name of class being registered
                ClientWndProc,      // Window procedure for class
                CS_SIZEREDRAW,      // Class style
                0) ;                // Extra bytes to reserve

    WinRegisterClass (
                hab,                // Anchor block handle
                szChildClass,       // Name of class being registered
                ChildWndProc,       // Window procedure for class
                CS_SIZEREDRAW,      // Class style
                sizeof (PVOID)) ;   // Extra bytes to reserve
```

(continued)

Figure 3-5. The WELCOME3.C File. *continued*

```
            /*-------------------------
            Create top-level window
            -------------------------*/

hwndFrame = WinCreateStdWindow (
                HWND_DESKTOP,          // Parent window handle
                WS_VISIBLE,            // Style of frame window
                &flFrameFlags,         // Pointer to control data
                szClientClass,         // Client window class name
                NULL,                  // Title bar text
                0L,                    // Style of client window
                NULL,                  // Module handle for resources
                0,                     // ID of resources
                &hwndClient) ;         // Pointer to client window handle

WinSendMsg (hwndFrame, WM_SETICON,
                WinQuerySysPointer (HWND_DESKTOP, SPTR_APPICON, FALSE),
                NULL) ;


            /*-------------------------
            . Create two child windows
            -------------------------*/

flFrameFlags &= ~FCF_TASKLIST ;

hwndChildFrame1 = WinCreateStdWindow (
                hwndClient,            // Parent window handle
                WS_VISIBLE,            // Style of frame window
                &flFrameFlags,         // Pointer to control data
                szChildClass,          // Client window class name
                "Child No. 1",         // Title bar text
                0L,                    // Style of client window
                NULL,                  // Module handle for resources
                0,                     // ID of resources
                &hwndChildClient1) ;// Pointer to client window handle

hwndChildFrame2 = WinCreateStdWindow (
                hwndClient,            // Parent window handle
                WS_VISIBLE,            // Style of frame window
                &flFrameFlags,         // Pointer to control data
                szChildClass,          // Client window class name
                "Child No. 2",         // Title bar text
                0L,                    // Style of client window
                NULL,                  // Module handle for resources
                0,                     // ID of resources
                &hwndChildClient2) ;// Pointer to client window handle
```

(continued)

Figure 3-5. The WELCOME3.C File. *continued*

```
      WinSendMsg (hwndChildFrame1, WM_SETICON,
                  WinQuerySysPointer (HWND_DESKTOP, SPTR_APPICON, FALSE),
                  NULL) ;

      WinSendMsg (hwndChildFrame2, WM_SETICON,
                  WinQuerySysPointer (HWND_DESKTOP, SPTR_APPICON, FALSE),
                  NULL) ;

          /*-------------------------------------------------------
              Set reserved area of window to text string pointers
          -------------------------------------------------------*/

      WinSetWindowPtr (hwndChildClient1, QWL_USER, "I'm a child ...") ;
      WinSetWindowPtr (hwndChildClient2, QWL_USER, "... Me too!") ;

      while (WinGetMsg (hab, &qmsg, NULL, 0, 0))
          WinDispatchMsg (hab, &qmsg) ;

      WinDestroyWindow (hwndFrame) ;
      WinDestroyMsgQueue (hmq) ;
      WinTerminate (hab) ;
      return 0 ;
      }

MRESULT EXPENTRY ClientWndProc (HWND hwnd, USHORT msg, MPARAM mp1, MPARAM mp2)
      {
      static CHAR szText [] = "I'm the parent of two children" ;
      HPS       hps ;
      RECTL     rcl ;

      switch (msg)
          {
          case WM_PAINT:
              hps = WinBeginPaint (hwnd, NULL, NULL) ;

              WinQueryWindowRect (hwnd, &rcl) ;

              WinDrawText (hps, -1, szText, &rcl, CLR_NEUTRAL, CLR_BACKGROUND,
                          DT_CENTER | DT_VCENTER | DT_ERASERECT) ;

              WinEndPaint (hps) ;
              return 0 ;
          }
      return WinDefWindowProc (hwnd, msg, mp1, mp2) ;
      }
```

(continued)

Figure 3-5. The WELCOME3.C File. *continued*

```
MRESULT EXPENTRY ChildWndProc (HWND hwnd, USHORT msg, MPARAM mp1, MPARAM mp2)
    {
    HPS   hps ;
    RECTL rcl ;

    switch (msg)
        {
        case WM_PAINT:
            hps = WinBeginPaint (hwnd, NULL, NULL) ;

            WinQueryWindowRect (hwnd, &rcl) ;

            WinDrawText (hps, -1, WinQueryWindowPtr (hwnd, QWL_USER), &rcl,
                    CLR_NEUTRAL, CLR_BACKGROUND,
                    DT_CENTER | DT_VCENTER | DT_ERASERECT) ;

            WinEndPaint (hps) ;
            return 0 ;

        case WM_CLOSE:
            WinDestroyWindow (WinQueryWindow (hwnd, QW_PARENT, FALSE)) ;
            return 0 ;
        }
    return WinDefWindowProc (hwnd, msg, mp1, mp2) ;
    }
```

The WELCOME3.DEF File

```
;-------------------------------------
; WELCOME3.DEF module definition file
;-------------------------------------

NAME          WELCOME3  WINDOWAPI

DESCRIPTION   'Creates Top-Level and Two Children (C) Charles Petzold, 1988'
PROTMODE
HEAPSIZE      1024
STACKSIZE     8192
EXPORTS       ClientWndProc
              ChildWndProc
```

Figure 3-5. *The WELCOME3 program.*

WELCOME3 makes three calls to *WinCreateStdWindow*. The first call creates a top-level window. The second and third calls create child standard windows of the first client window. For these children, the first parameter to *WinCreateStdWindow* is *hwndClient*—the client window handle returned from the first call. The second and third standard windows are siblings. Both client windows of these children are based on the same window class (''Welcome3.Child'') and thus share the same window procedure, *ChildWndProc*, but they could easily be based on different window classes. Figure 3-6 shows the WELCOME3 family tree, and Figure 3-7 shows the program running under the Presentation Manager.

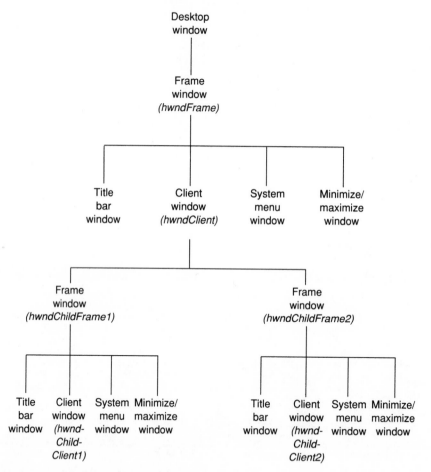

Figure 3-6. *The WELCOME3 family tree.*

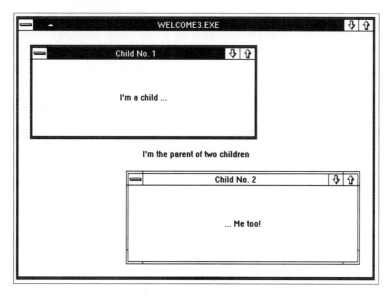

Figure 3-7. *The WELCOME3 display.*

This is the more common technique for creating multiple windows within a program and is the basis for the Multiple Document Interface (MDI) convention used by the File System program. The top-level window is the application's main window. The client window of this top-level standard window is the application's work space. Several other child windows can exist within this work space.

You'll notice that the two child standard windows obey the rules for child windows discussed earlier: They can be displayed only within the area occupied by their parent; because they are siblings, they can overlap; they follow the parent when the parent is moved around the screen; and they are minimized when the parent is minimized. You can also independently minimize these two children — their windows will still appear within the area of the parent. This is analogous to the organization and display of top-level windows relative to the desktop window.

Although you can use the Alt-Esc or Alt-Tab key combination to move between the top-level windows in the Presentation Manger, there is no automatic keyboard interface for moving between windows that are not top-level windows. The program would have to provide this keyboard interface. However, you can bring a particular child standard window to the top by clicking on its window with the mouse.

The two child windows are not listed on the Task Manager. Only top-level windows can be listed there. Before creating these child windows, WELCOME3 removes the FCF_TASKLIST flag from *flFrameFlags*:

```
flFrameFlags & = ~FCF_TASKLIST ;
```

This also causes the title bar text for the child windows to be exactly what is specified in the *WinCreateStdWindow* function.

WELCOME3 uses a little trick that allows the two child standard windows to display different text in their client windows. When the program registers the "Welcome3.Child" window class, it specifies that 4 bytes (the size of a PVOID or far pointer) are to be reserved for use by the program for every window created based on this class. This is indicated by the fifth parameter to *WinRegisterClass*:

```
WinRegisterClass (
          hab,                // Anchor block handle
          szChildClass,       // Name of class being registered
          ChildWndProc,       // Window procedure for class
          CS_SIZEREDRAW,      // Class style
          sizeof (PVOID);     // Extra bytes to reserve
```

After the two child standard windows are created, WELCOME3 uses *WinSetWindowPtr* to store something in that area:

```
WinSetWindowPtr (hwndChildClient1, QWL_USER, "I'm a child ...") ;
WinSetWindowPtr (hwndChildClient2, QWL_USER, "... Me too!") ;
```

What is stored in this space is actually the long (or far) address of the static text strings "I'm a child ..." and "... Me too!" In *ChildWndProc*, these addresses are retrieved during processing of the WM_PAINT message and passed to the *WinDrawText* function:

```
WinDrawText (hPS, -1, WinQueryWindowPtr (hwnd, QWL_USER), &rcl,
          CLR_NEUTRAL, CLR_BACKGROUND,
          DT_CENTER | DT_VCENTER | DT_ERASERECT) ;
```

Thus the window procedure doesn't have to figure out which child window is receiving the WM_PAINT message. Although this is a somewhat unusual application of the technique, storing window-specific data in the reserved area is often quite handy when two or more windows share the same window procedure.

The processing of the WM_CLOSE message in *ChildWndProc* destroys the window being closed but doesn't terminate the program:

```
case WM_CLOSE:
     WinDestroyWindow (WinQueryWindow (hwnd, QW_PARENT, FALSE)) ;
     return 0 ;
```

WinQueryWindow obtains the parent of the client window (which is its frame window); destroying that frame window also destroys the client window.

The program can be terminated only from the main window. After leaving the message loop, WELCOME3 destroys the program's top-level frame window as usual:

```
WinDestroyWindow (hwndFrame) ;
```

If one or both of the two child standard windows still exist, they, too, will be destroyed as a result. All windows in WELCOME3 are descendants of *hwndFrame*, so the one *WinDestroyWindow* call destroys all the windows in the program.

Controls and Their Owners

The frame window is the parent of all other windows created in the *WinCreateStdWindow* function. The frame window is also the "owner" of these other windows. A window is always displayed to the foreground of its owner (if it has one). However, it is not clipped to the surface of its owner. As with the parent/child relationship, when a window is hidden, minimized, or destroyed, the windows it owns are also hidden, minimized, or destroyed.

The owner relationship also affects how messages are sent between the windows. The title bar, system menu, and minimize/maximize windows are often called "control windows." Control windows usually have a relatively simple appearance and function. The primary job of a control window is to receive user input (keystrokes and mouse activity) in the form of messages and then send notification messages to the window's owner. The owner of the control window (which in all the examples so far is a frame window) then acts on the notification message.

For example, when you click on the maximize icon with the mouse, the minimize/maximize window sends a WM_SYSCOMMAND message to its owner—the frame window. The frame window then begins the process of maximizing the window. Likewise, the title bar window notifies the frame window of a new window position.

Although every window (except object windows and the desktop window itself) has a parent, windows do not need owners. The frame window created in *WinCreateStdWindow* has no owner. The frame window is the owner of the client window, but the client window doesn't really need an owner either.

You can determine the owner of a window by calling *WinQueryWindow*:

```
hwndOwner = WinQueryWindow (hwnd, QW_OWNER, FALSE) ;
```

A window can be assigned a new owner:

```
WinSetOwner (hwnd, hwndNewOwner) ;
```

The *hwndNewOwner* parameter can be set to NULL. This causes the window whose handle is *hwnd* to have no owner.

Registering the Window Class

Let's back up a little and examine in more detail some of the functions involved in creating a standard window. The standard window usually includes a client window. A preliminary step in creating a client window is the registering of a class for that window. The call to *WinRegisterClass* in WELCOME1.C from Chapter 2 looks like this:

```
WinRegisterClass (
            hab,                // Anchor block handle
            szClientClass,      // Name of class being registered
            ClientWndProc,      // Window procedure for class
            CS_SIZEREDRAW,      // Class style
            0;                  // Extra bytes to reserve
```

Of these five parameters, the second and third are the most important. The second parameter is the name of the window class being registered. The name is a zero-terminated character string generally derived from the name of the program. In WELCOME1 the class name is "Welcome1." The third parameter is the address of the window procedure for the class. This window procedure processes all messages to all windows that are later created based on this class.

The class style parameter is a 32-bit unsigned long integer that sets certain characteristics of all windows later created based on the class. You can set the class style parameter to 0L for a default class style. Or you can use one or more identifiers beginning with the letters CS ("class style") defined in PMWIN.H to specify a nondefault class style. You combine these identifiers with the C bitwise OR operator (¦). Each identifier sets one bit in the class style. For this reason, the identifiers are sometimes called "class style bits." Ten class style bits are defined in PMWIN.H and are shown in Figure 3-8 in a diagram that indicates how each identifier contributes to the resultant 32-bit window style.

These class styles are described in the documentation that accompanies the Microsoft OS/2 Programmer's Toolkit. Most of them are not commonly used. For the programs in this book, I use only CS_SIZEREDRAW and CS_SIZEREPAINT. The CS_SIZEREDRAW bit affects how the Presentation Manager should invalidate a window (and hence cause the window to receive a WM_PAINT message) when it is resized by the user. If the CS_SIZEREDRAW bit is *not* set and the window is reduced in size, the Presentation Manager does not need to invalidate the window. The part of the window outside the new size can be simply erased. When the CS_SIZEREDRAW bit is set, the entire window is invalidated when it is resized. CS_SIZEREDRAW should be used for all windows whose appearance depends on the size of the window. Because we have been displaying centered text in our client windows, CS_SIZEREDRAW is proper for the window class.

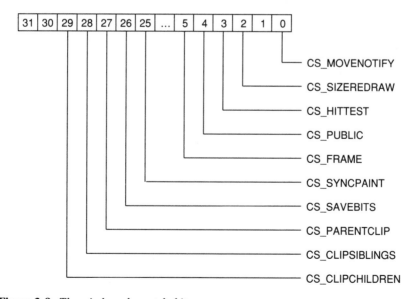

Figure 3-8. *The window class style bits.*

When CS_SYNCPAINT is set, WM_PAINT messages are sent directly to a window procedure when part of the window becomes invalid. When this bit is *not* set, WM_PAINT messages are posted to the message queue and retrieved later. The CS_SYNCPAINT bit is used mostly with small control windows that must be repainted immediately.

The parameter to *WinRegisterClass* labeled ''extra bytes to reserve'' reserves a block of memory associated with each window created based on this class. You put data into this area using *WinSetWindowUShort*, *WinSetWindowULong*, and *WinSetWindowPtr*; you retrieve it by using *WinQueryWindowUShort*, *WinQueryWindowULong*, and *WinQueryWindowPtr*. You can do whatever you want with this memory. As you saw in WELCOME3, it's a handy place to store data unique to each window. Here's the general rule: When a variable defined in a window procedure is needed only during the processing of a message, use an automatic variable. To retain information from message to message, use static variables. However, if two or more windows share the same window procedure, use static variables only for data that can be shared among all windows. Use the reserved area for data unique to each window.

Creating the Standard Window

The *WinCreateStdWindow* call from last chapter's WELCOME1 program looks like this:

```
hwndFrame = WinCreateStdWindow (
          HWND_DESKTOP,        // Parent window handle
          WS_VISIBLE           // Style of frame window
          &flFrameFlags,       // Pointer to control data
          szClientClass,       // Client window class name
          NULL,                // Title bar text
          0L,                  // Style of client window
          NULL,                // Module handle for resources
          0,                   // ID of resources
          &hwndClient) ;       // Pointer to client window handle
```

Two parameters in the *WinCreateStdWindow* function are ''window styles'': The second parameter is the window style of the frame window, and the sixth parameter is the window style of the client window. A window style is a 32-bit unsigned long integer. Like the class style discussed previously, the window style sets certain characteristics of the window. But although the class style applies to all windows based on the class, the window style applies only to the particular window being created.

The PMWIN.H header file contains identifiers (sometimes called "window style bits") to set bits in the window style when the identifiers are combined with the C bitwise OR operator (|).

The high 16 bits of the window style are defined in the same way for all window classes. The identifiers begin with WS ("window style"). These are shown in Figure 3-9.

Like the control style flags, many of these are rather rare. The WS_SYNC-PAINT, WS_SAVEBITS, WS_PARENTCLIP, WS_CLIPSIBLINGS, and WS_CLIPCHILDREN bits have the same purpose as the equivalent class style bits. Thus you can create a window class without these styles but then create windows based on that class that use these styles. The only window style from Figure 3-9 that we've used so far for the frame window is the WS_VISIBLE bit. By default, a window is invisible when it's created. Specifying WS_VISIBLE overrides that default. Alternatively, you can exclude WS_VISIBLE from the frame window style when creating the window and later call *WinSetWindowPos* and *WinShowWindow*. The WS_VISIBLE bit isn't required for the client window style, because the Presentation Manager specifically makes the client window visible.

The WS_GROUP and WS_TABSTOP style bits are used only for control windows (such as buttons) within dialog boxes. (Chapter 14 is devoted to dialog boxes.)

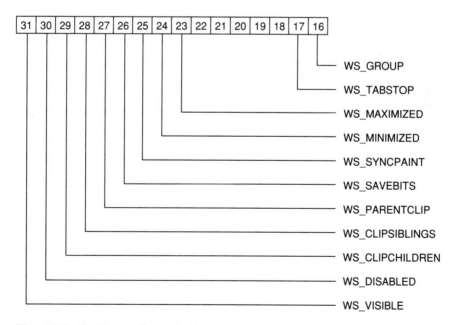

Figure 3-9. *The high window style bits.*

The WS_MAXIMIZED bit causes a window to be maximized when the window is first displayed. Similarly, the WS_MINIMIZED bit causes the window to be initially displayed as an icon.

If the WS_DISABLED bit is set, the window can't receive mouse input and is generally inert. The window can be subsequently enabled by a call to *WinEnableWindow*.

The low 16 bits of the window style have different meanings, depending on the window class. The window procedure for the class interprets these bits. We'll see examples of this in the WELCOME4 program coming up shortly.

The Frame Creation Flags

The third parameter to *WinCreateStdWindow* is a pointer to a ULONG that indicates what child windows should be created in the standard window. The frame creation flags you use for this are shown in Figure 3-10. The PMWIN.H header file also defines FCF_STANDARD to be the same as

```
FCF_TITLEBAR | FCF_SYSMENU | FCF_MENU |
FCF_SIZEBORDER | FCF_MINMAX | FCF_ICON |
FCF_ACCELTABLE | FCF_SHELLPOSITION | FCF_TASKLIST
```

The FCF_MINMAX identifier is the same as

```
FCF_MINBUTTON | FCF_MAXBUTTON
```

You can experiment with the WELCOME1, WELCOME2, or WELCOME3 program (within limits) by removing some of the frame creation flags and putting in others. For example, you can exclude FCF_SYSMENU by using

```
flFrame Flags = FCF_TITLEBAR | FCF_SIZEBORDER |
                FCF_MINMAX | FCF_SHELLPOSITION |
                FCF_TASKLIST ;
```

In this case, the system menu window isn't created, and the title bar extends to the left to fill the space. You'll have to exit the program from the Task Manager. If you exclude FCF_MINMAX, then the minimize/maximize window isn't created, and the title bar again fills the space. The Minimize and Maximize options are also disabled on the system menu. You can use FCF_MINBUTTON or FCF_MAXBUTTON to include one option but not the other.

If you exclude FCF_TITLEBAR, the title bar isn't created, and the Presentation Manager ignores the "title bar text" parameter of *WinCreateStdWindow*. The system menu and minimize/maximize box are created (if

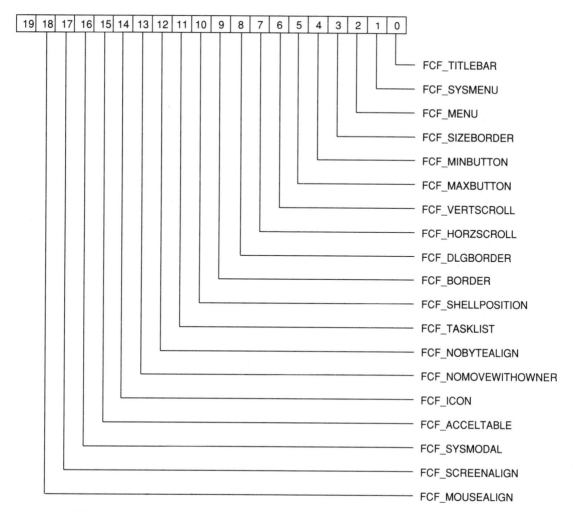

Figure 3-10. *The frame creation flag bits.*

FCF_SYSMENU and FCF_MINMAX are specified) and displayed in the normal places. But the area normally occupied by the title bar is not part of the client window. You can't move the window, because that is a function of the title bar.

If you exclude FCF_SIZEBORDER, the sizing border window isn't created. Without the sizing border, the window not only looks a little naked, but the user can change the size of the window only by minimizing or maximizing it from the system menu or from the minimize/maximize box. You'll probably want to use FCF_BORDER to draw a thin black border around the naked window. If you use both FCF_SIZEBORDER and FCF_BORDER, FCF_BORDER is ignored.

The FCF_DLGBORDER frame creation flag bit causes a wide border to be drawn. This is more commonly seen on dialog boxes. Like the title bar, the dialog border uses color to indicate if the window is active. If you use both FCF_DLGBORDER and FCF_SIZEBORDER for the window, FCF_DLGBORDER is ignored.

You can include FCF_VERTSCROLL or FCF_HORZSCROLL or both in the frame creation flags. The window will then include scroll bars. The vertical scroll bar appears to the right of the client window, and the horizontal scroll bar is on the bottom. We'll start using scroll bars in the next chapter.

At the moment you can't use the FCF_MENU, FCF_ICON, or FCF_ACCEL-TABLE bits in the frame creation flags. These bits cause the Presentation Manager to attempt to load a menu, icon, or keyboard accelerator table from the module (a .EXE or .DLL file) whose module handle is indicated in the seventh parameter of the *WinCreateStdWindow* function. Menus, icons, and accelerator tables are known as "resources." Every resource has an ID number. The ID number for all three of these resources must be the same and is specified as the eighth parameter in *WinCreateStdWindow*.

Note that some frame creation flags — specifically the FCF_TITLEBAR, FCF_SYSMENU, FCF_MENU, FCF_MINBUTTON, FCF_MAXBUTTON, FCF_VERTSCROLL, and FCF_HORISCROLL flags — cause windows to be created; others (such as FCF_SIZEBORDER, FCF_BORDER, and FCF_DLG-BORDER) affect only the appearance and functionality of the frame window.

The *WinCreateWindow* Function

The *WinCreateStdWindow* function creates several windows organized around a frame window. Within the Presentation Manager, each window is created by a call to *WinCreateWindow*. This function is available for use by your programs also. It looks like this:

```
hwnd = WinCreateWindow (
            hwndParent,        // Parent window handle
            szClassName,       // Window class
            szText,            // Window text
            WS_...,            // Window style
            xStart, yStart,    // Initial position of window
            xSize, ySize,      // Initial size of window
            hwndOwner,         // Owner window handle
            hwndOrder,         // Placement window handle
            idChild,           // Child window ID
            pControlData,      // Control data
            pPresParams) ;     // Presentation parameters
```

The parameters to this function indicate the full array of information required to create a window, and they show how *WinCreateStdWindow* makes the job of creating a standard window in your program a whole lot simpler.

You'll note here that each window has a "window text." But many control windows (such as the system menu window, sizing border window, and minimize/maximize window) don't display this text. The Presentation Manager uses the "title bar text" parameter to *WinCreateStdWindow* (concatenated to the name under which the program was started) as the "window text" parameter to *WinCreateWindow* only when it is creating the title bar window. The title bar window procedure displays that text in its window.

Each window also has a position and size. The position is relative to the lower-left corner of the window's parent. We haven't been worrying about this. The Presentation Manager gives the frame window a default position and size and then organizes the other windows within that.

The Predefined Window Classes

In the *WinCreateStdWindow* call, only one window class parameter is required—the window class of the client window. However, the Presentation Manager needs to specify a window class in each *WinCreateWindow* call it makes when creating the standard window. For the windows other than the client window, the Presentation Manager uses predefined window classes. These have identifiers in PMWIN.H and are shown in the following table:

Predefined Window Class	Type of Window
WC_FRAME	Standard frame window (including dialog boxes)
WC_BUTTON	Push button, check box, and so on
WC_MENU	Menu (including system menu & minimize/maximize window)
WC_STATIC	Text field, static rectangle
WC_ENTRYFIELD	Text editing field
WC_LISTBOX	List box
WC_SCROLLBAR	Scroll bar
WC_TITLEBAR	Standard title bar

Each of these window classes has a corresponding window procedure in PMWIN.DLL.

In the *WinCreateStdWindow* calls made in the various WELCOME programs, the Presentation Manager creates windows based on the WC_FRAME, WC_MENU, and WC_TITLEBAR styles. Perhaps it will be instructive to call *WinCreateWindow* ourselves in a program and see how this works.

Creating Child Control Windows

The WELCOME4 program, shown in Figure 3-11, creates one standard window and three control windows as children of the client window. These three control windows are created using *WinCreateWindow* and are based on the predefined window classes of WC_BUTTON, WC_SCROLLBAR, and WC_ENTRYFIELD.

The WELCOME4 File

```
#--------------------
# WELCOME4 make file
#--------------------

welcome4.obj : welcome4.c
    cl -c -G2sw -W3 welcome4.c

welcome4.exe : welcome4.obj welcome4.def
    link welcome4, /align:16, NUL, os2, welcome4
```

The WELCOME4.C File

```
/*------------------------------------------------------------
   WELCOME4.C -- Creates a Top-Level Window and Three Children
   ---------------------------------------------------------*/

#define INCL_WIN
#include <os2.h>

#define ID_BUTTON 1
#define ID_SCROLL 2
#define ID_ENTRY  3

MRESULT EXPENTRY ClientWndProc (HWND, USHORT, MPARAM, MPARAM) ;

int main (void)
    {
    static CHAR  szClientClass [] = "Welcome4" ;
    static ULONG flFrameFlags = FCF_TITLEBAR       | FCF_SYSMENU   |
                                FCF_BORDER         | FCF_MINBUTTON |
                                FCF_SHELLPOSITION  | FCF_TASKLIST ;

    HAB          hab ;
    HMQ          hmq ;
    HWND         hwndFrame,  hwndClient ;
    QMSG         qmsg ;
    RECTL        rcl ;
```

(continued)

Figure 3-11. The WELCOME4.C File. *continued*

```
        hab = WinInitialize (0) ;
        hmq = WinCreateMsgQueue (hab, 0) ;

        WinRegisterClass (
                    hab,                  // Anchor block handle
                    szClientClass,        // Name of class being registered
                    ClientWndProc,        // Window procedure for class
                    CS_SIZEREDRAW,        // Class style
                    0) ;                  // Extra bytes to reserve

        hwndFrame = WinCreateStdWindow (
                    HWND_DESKTOP,         // Parent window handle
                    WS_VISIBLE,           // Style of frame window
                    &flFrameFlags,        // Pointer to control data
                    szClientClass,        // Client window class name
                    NULL,                 // Title bar text
                    0L,                   // Style of client window
                    NULL,                 // Module handle for resources
                    0,                    // ID of resources
                    &hwndClient) ;        // Pointer to client window handle

        WinSendMsg (hwndFrame, WM_SETICON,
                    WinQuerySysPointer (HWND_DESKTOP, SPTR_APPICON, FALSE),
                    NULL) ;

            /*-----------------------------------------------------------
                Find dimensions of client window for sizes of children
              -----------------------------------------------------------*/

        WinQueryWindowRect (hwndClient, &rcl) ;
        rcl.xRight /= 3 ;                          // Divide width in thirds

            /*------------------------------
                Create push button window
              --------------------------*/

        WinCreateWindow (
                    hwndClient,           // Parent window handle
                    WC_BUTTON,            // Window class
                    "Big Button",         // Window text
                    WS_VISIBLE            // Window style
                        | BS_PUSHBUTTON,
                    10,                   // Window position
```

(continued)

Figure 3-11. The WELCOME4.C File. *continued*

```
                10,
                (SHORT) rcl.xRight - 20,        // Window size
                (SHORT) rcl.yTop - 20,
                hwndClient,                     // Owner window handle
                HWND_BOTTOM,                    // Placement window handle
                ID_BUTTON,                      // Child window ID
                NULL,                           // Control data
                NULL) ;                         // Presentation parameters


        /*---------------------------
           Create scroll bar window
        ---------------------------*/

    WinCreateWindow (
                hwndClient,                     // Parent window handle
                WC_SCROLLBAR,                   // Window class
                NULL,                           // Window text
                WS_VISIBLE                      // Window style
                    | SBS_VERT,
                (SHORT) rcl.xRight + 10,        // Window position
                10,
                (SHORT) rcl.xRight - 20,        // Window size
                (SHORT) rcl.yTop - 20,
                hwndClient,                     // Owner window handle
                HWND_BOTTOM,                    // Placement window handle
                ID_SCROLL,                      // Child window ID
                NULL,                           // Control data
                NULL) ;                         // Presentation parameters


        /*---------------------------
           Create entry field window
        ---------------------------*/

    WinCreateWindow (
                hwndClient,                     // Parent window handle
                WC_ENTRYFIELD,                  // Window class
                NULL,                           // Window text
                WS_VISIBLE                      // Window style
                    | ES_MARGIN
                    | ES_AUTOSCROLL,
                2 * (SHORT) rcl.xRight + 10,    // Window position
                10,
                (SHORT) rcl.xRight - 20,        // Window size
                (SHORT) rcl.yTop - 20,
                hwndClient,                     // Owner window handle
                HWND_BOTTOM,                    // Placement window handle
```

(continued)

Figure 3-11. The WELCOME4.C File. *continued*

```
                        ID_ENTRY,                   // Child window ID
                        NULL,                       // Control data
                        NULL) ;                     // Presentation parameters

        while (WinGetMsg (hab, &qmsg, NULL, 0, 0))
             WinDispatchMsg (hab, &qmsg) ;

        WinDestroyWindow (hwndFrame) ;
        WinDestroyMsgQueue (hmq) ;
        WinTerminate (hab) ;
        return 0 ;
        }

MRESULT EXPENTRY ClientWndProc (HWND hwnd, USHORT msg, MPARAM mp1, MPARAM mp2)
        {
        switch (msg)
             {
             case WM_COMMAND:
                  switch (COMMANDMSG(&msg)->cmd)
                       {
                       case ID_BUTTON:
                            WinAlarm (HWND_DESKTOP, WA_NOTE) ;
                            return 0 ;
                       }
                  break ;

             case WM_ERASEBACKGROUND:
                  return 1 ;
             }
        return WinDefWindowProc (hwnd, msg, mp1, mp2) ;
        }
```

The WELCOME4.DEF File

```
;----------------------------------------
; WELCOME4.DEF module definition file
;----------------------------------------

NAME            WELCOME4  WINDOWAPI

DESCRIPTION     'Creates Top-Level and 3 Children (C) Charles Petzold, 1988'
PROTMODE
HEAPSIZE        1024
STACKSIZE       8192
EXPORTS         ClientWndProc
```

Figure 3-11. *The WELCOME4 program.*

The standard window in WELCOME4 uses FCF_BORDER rather than FCF_SIZEBORDER and has no maximize icon. The window is shown in Figure 3-12.

After creating the standard window, WELCOME4 makes a call to *Win-QueryWindowRect* to obtain the rectangle structure that defines the size of the client window:

```
WinQueryWindowRect (hwndClient, &rcl) ;
```

The *xRight* field of this structure is the width of the client area in pixels. WELCOME4 divides it by 3 to be used in the three *WinCreateWindow* calls.

The first *WinCreateWindow* call creates the window based on the WC_BUTTON class:

```
WinCreateWindow (
            hwndClient,                  // Parent window handle
            WC_BUTTON,                   // Window class
            "Big Button",                // Window text
            WS_VISIBLE                   // Window style
                ¦ BS_PUSHBUTTON,
            10,                          // Window position
            10,
            (SHORT) rcl.xRight - 20,     // Initial size of window
            (SHORT) rcl.yTop - 20,
            hwndClient,                  // Owner window handle
            HWND_BOTTOM,                 // Placement window handle
            ID_BUTTON,                   // Child window ID
            NULL,                        // Control data
            NULL) ;                      // Presentation parameters
```

This call creates a large push button (such as those that appear in dialog boxes) in the left third of the client window. The text inside the button is "Big Button." Both the parent and owner are set to the *hwndClient* window handle returned from the original *WinCreateStdWindow* call. The window style uses WS_VISIBLE and BS_PUSHBUTTON. Identifiers beginning with BS ("button style") are class-specific window styles for buttons. The initial position of the window is relative to the lower-left corner of the client window. These two parameters are both set to 10 pixels to provide a small margin around the push button. The size of the window is set to one-third the width of the client window and to the height of the client window, minus 20 pixels from each dimension.

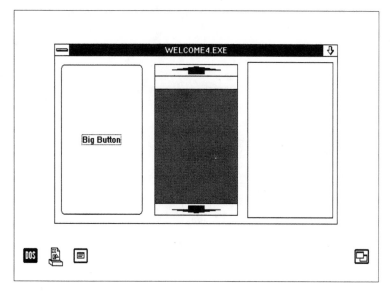

Figure 3-12. *The WELCOME4 display.*

The second *WinCreateWindow* call creates a vertical scroll bar in the middle third of the client window:

```
WinCreateWindow (
          hwndClient,                    // Parent window handle
          WC_SCROLLBAR,                  // Window class
          NULL,                          // Window text
          WS_VISIBLE                     // Window style
              ¦ SBS_VERT,
          (SHORT) rcl.xRight + 10,       // Window position
          10,
          (SHORT) rcl.xRight - 20,       // Window size
          (SHORT) rcl.yTop - 20,
          hwndClient,                    // Owner window handle
          HWND_BOTTOM,                   // Placement window handle
          ID_SCROLL,                     // Child window ID
          NULL,                          // Control data
          NULL) ;                        // Presentation parameters
```

The class is WC_SCROLLBAR, and the class-specific window style is SBS_VERT. SBS stands for ''scroll-bar style,'' and VERT indicates a vertical scroll bar.

The third *WinCreateWindow* call creates a text entry field window:

```
WinCreateWindow (
            hwndClient,                   // Parent window handle
            WC_ENTRYFIELD,                // Window class
            NULL,                         // Window text
            WS_VISIBLE,                   // Window style
                | ES_MARGIN
                | ES_AUTOSCROLL
            2 * (SHORT) rcl.xRight + 10,  // Window position
            10,
            (SHORT) rcl.xRight - 20,      // Window size
            (SHORT) rcl.yTop - 20,
            hwndClient,                   // Owner window handle
            HWND_BOTTOM,                  // Placement window handle
            ID_ENTRY,                     // Child window ID
            NULL,                         // Control data
            NULL) ;                       // Presentation parameters
```

The class is WC_ENTRYFIELD and the style bits are ES_MARGIN (to draw a border around the window) and ES_AUTOSCROLL (to scroll text horizontally within the window).

All three *WinCreateWindow* calls return the handle to the window they create, but WELCOME4 doesn't save these handles.

Although WELCOME4's button and scroll bar may appear to be somewhat grotesque, they are still functional. When you click on the button with the mouse, it flashes. When you click on various parts of the scroll bar, they, too, flash. (You can't move the scroll bar slider—that's a program's responsibility, as you'll see in the next chapter.) You can even click on the text entry field and type in some text.

These three control windows created in WELCOME4 send "notification messages" to their owner (which is the client window) when they receive user input. For example, the push button sends its owner a WM_COMMAND message when the button is clicked with the mouse. *ClientWndProc* receives this message and beeps by calling *WinAlarm*. Likewise, the control windows that make up the standard window notify their owner (the frame window) of user input. The WELCOME4 family tree is shown in Figure 3-13. This family tree shows the parent-child relationship; the owner-owned relationship is identical to this, except that the desktop window doesn't own the frame window.

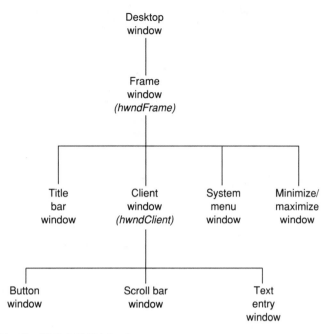

Figure 3-13. *The WELCOME4 family tree.*

Child window IDs

When the Presentation Manager (or your program) creates child windows using the *WinCreateWindow* function, each child is assigned a "child window ID" that is specified as the eleventh parameter to *WinCreateWindow*. In WELCOME4, these ID numbers are set to ID_BUTTON, ID_SCROLL, and ID_ENTRY, which are defined at the top of the program as 1, 2, and 3. The control window uses this ID to identify itself to its owner when it sends a notification message. For example, in the WM_COMMAND notification message that push buttons send, the *mp1* parameter contains this ID. Thus a window can contain many push buttons or other control windows, each with a different ID. (We'll examine this in greater detail in Chapters 11, 13, and 14.)

When the frame window creates its children, each of them is assigned an ID number. As shown in the following table, these are fixed values defined in PMWIN.H, and have identifiers beginning with the letters FID (which stands for "frame ID").

FID	*Type of Child Window*
FID_SYSMENU	System menu
FID_TITLEBAR	Title bar
FID_MINMAX	Minimize/maximize box
FID_MENU	Program's menu
FID_VERTSCROLL	Vertical scroll bar
FID_HORZSCROLL	Horizontal scroll bar
FID_CLIENT	Client window

A program can determine the window handle of a child window based on the parent window handle and the child ID:

```
hwndChild = WinWindowFromID (hwndParent, idChild) ;
```

If you need to know the window handle of the system menu window (for example), you can easily obtain it:

```
hwndSysMenu = WinWindowFromID (hwndFrame, FID_SYSMENU) ;
```

Why would you need this information? Well, you might want to send the system menu window a message. Improbable? Not at all—we'll do it in Chapter 13.

You can also determine a window's ID from its window handle:

```
idChild = WinQueryWindowUShort (hwnd, QWS_ID) ;
```

The *WinQueryWindowUShort*, *WinQueryWindowULong*, and *WinQuery-WindowPtr* functions also let you obtain a window's message queue handle, its style, and the address of the window procedure, as well as the reserved areas specified in the window class.

Styles, Classes, and IDs

By now you've seen similar identifiers connected with various parts of the standard window used in various ways. For the title bar, for example, you've seen identifiers named FCF_TITLEBAR, WC_TITLEBAR, and FID_TITLEBAR. This may all be a little confusing. Here's a table that can help you keep the identifiers straight.

The Frame Creation Flag:	Causes the Frame Window to Create a Child of Class:	With a Child Window ID Of:
FCF_TITLEBAR	WC_TITLEBAR	FID_TITLEBAR
FCF_SYSMENU	WC_MENU	FID_SYSMENU
FCF_MENU	WC_MENU	FID_MENU
FCF_MINMAX	WC_MENU	FID_MINMAX
FCF_VERTSCROLL	WC_SCROLLBAR	FID_VERTSCROLL
FCF_HORZSCROLL	WC_SCROLLBAR	FID_HORZSCROLL

The FCF identifiers are used in the *WinCreateStdWindow* call to specify the window style of the frame window. Within the Presentation Manager, a call to the *WinCreateWindow* function creates each of the control windows. The window class is one of the WC identifiers, and the child window ID is an FID identifier.

PAINTING THE CLIENT WINDOW

## CHAPTER FOUR

AN EXERCISE IN TEXT OUTPUT

The Presentation Manager is a graphical environment, and yet for many applications the display of text and numbers is more important than pictures. Although it might be nice to write a database program that can include bit-mapped images of employees' faces, the fact remains that the employees' names, addresses, and social security numbers are still the most important data. This chapter covers the basic concepts involved with displaying plain-vanilla text in the client window. Although the chapter touches on keyboard and mouse input, these subjects are discussed in more depth in Chapters 8 and 9.

When programming for the Presentation Manager, you don't use OS/2 kernel functions such as *DosWrite* and *VioWrtTTY* or C functions such as *printf* and *puts* to write text to the screen. Instead, you use functions provided by the Graphics Programming Interface (GPI) component of the Presentation Manager. (Exceptions do exist: Several high-level drawing functions such as *WinDrawText* aren't really part of GPI. Also, we'll see in Chapter 7 how you *can* use the *VioWrtTTY* function in Presentation Manager programs.) GPI functions begin with the prefix *Gpi*. Although this chapter covers only text output, many of the concepts examined here are applicable to graphics also.

Displaying Text on the Client Window

As a case study, let's write a Presentation Manager program that displays all of the information obtainable from the *WinQuerySysValue* function.

You can use *WinQuerySysValue* in a program to obtain the height and width of the screen as well as 46 other interesting pieces of information, mostly concerning the sizes of various windows created by the Presentation Manager. The first parameter to the function is the identifier HWND_DESKTOP, and the second parameter is one of the identifiers defined in PMWIN.H with the letters SV ("system value"). For example, the following call returns the height of the title bar in pixels:

```
WinQuerySysValue (HWND_DESKTOP, SV_CYTITLEBAR)
```

Like many of the values that *WinQuerySysValue* returns, this value depends on the resolution of the video display on which the Presentation Manager is running. In later chapters we'll use *WinQuerySysValue* for various purposes. Here we merely want to look at all the values. We'll display this information in the client window. The 48 items will be displayed, one per line, in three columns: the SV identifier passed to *WinQuerySysValue*, a description of the item, and the value returned from the function. The first version of the program to display these values is called SYSVALS1 and is shown in Figure 4-1.

The SYSVALS1 File

```
#--------------------
# SYSVALS1 make file
#--------------------

sysvals1.obj : sysvals1.c sysvals.h
    cl -c -G2sw -W3 sysvals1.c

sysvals1.exe : sysvals1.obj sysvals1.def
    link sysvals1, /align:16, NUL, os2, sysvals1
```

The SYSVALS.H File

```
/*--------------------------------------------------
    SYSVALS.H -- System values display structure
  ------------------------------------------------*/

#define NUMLINES (sizeof sysvals / sizeof sysvals [0])

struct
    {
    SHORT  sIndex ;
    CHAR   *szIdentifier ;
    CHAR   *szDescription ;
    }
```

(continued)

Figure 4-1. The SYSVALS.H File. *continued*

```
sysvals [] =
{
SV_SWAPBUTTON,        "SV_SWAPBUTTON",        "Mouse buttons swapped flag",
SV_DBLCLKTIME,        "SV_DBLCLKTIME",        "Mouse double click time in msec",
SV_CXDBLCLK,          "SV_CXDBLCLK",          "Mouse double click area width",
SV_CYDBLCLK,          "SV_CYDBLCLK",          "Mouse double click area height",
SV_CXSIZEBORDER,      "SV_CXSIZEBORDER",      "Sizing border width",
SV_CYSIZEBORDER,      "SV_CYSIZEBORDER",      "Sizing border height",
SV_ALARM,             "SV_ALARM",             "Alarm enabled flag",
SV_CURSORRATE,        "SV_CURSORRATE",        "Cursor blink rate",
SV_FIRSTSCROLLRATE,   "SV_FIRSTSCROLLRATE",   "Scroll bar time until repeats",
SV_SCROLLRATE,        "SV_SCROLLRATE",        "Scroll bar scroll rate",
SV_NUMBEREDLISTS,     "SV_NUMBEREDLISTS",     "Flag for numbering of lists",
SV_WARNINGFREQ,       "SV_WARNINGFREQ",       "Alarm frequency for WA_WARNING",
SV_NOTEFREQ,          "SV_NOTEFREQ",          "Alarm frequency for WA_NOTE",
SV_ERRORFREQ,         "SV_ERRORFREQ",         "Alarm frequency for WA_ERROR",
SV_WARNINGDURATION,   "SV_WARNINGDURATION",   "Alarm duration for WA_WARNING",
SV_NOTEDURATION,      "SV_NOTEDURATION",      "Alarm duration for WA_NOTE",
SV_ERRORDURATION,     "SV_ERRORDURATION",     "Alarm duration for WA_ERROR",
SV_CXSCREEN,          "SV_CXSCREEN",          "Screen width in pixels",
SV_CYSCREEN,          "SV_CYSCREEN",          "Screen height in pixels",
SV_CXVSCROLL,         "SV_CXVSCROLL",         "Vertical scroll bar width",
SV_CYHSCROLL,         "SV_CYHSCROLL",         "Horizontal scroll bar height",
SV_CYVSCROLLARROW,    "SV_CYVSCROLLARROW",    "Vertical scroll arrow height",
SV_CXHSCROLLARROW,    "SV_CXHSCROLLARROW",    "Horizontal scroll arrow width",
SV_CXBORDER,          "SV_CXBORDER",          "Border width",
SV_CYBORDER,          "SV_CYBORDER",          "Border height",
SV_CXDLGFRAME,        "SV_CXDLGFRAME",        "Dialog window frame width",
SV_CYDLGFRAME,        "SV_CYDLGFRAME",        "Dialog window frame height",
SV_CYTITLEBAR,        "SV_CYTITLEBAR",        "Title bar height",
SV_CYVSLIDER,         "SV_CYVSLIDER",         "Vertical scroll slider height",
SV_CXHSLIDER,         "SV_CXHSLIDER",         "Horizontal scroll slider width",
SV_CXMINMAXBUTTON,    "SV_CXMINMAXBUTTON",    "Minimize/Maximize button width",
SV_CYMINMAXBUTTON,    "SV_CYMINMAXBUTTON",    "Minimize/Maximize button height",
SV_CYMENU,            "SV_CYMENU",            "Menu bar height",
SV_CXFULLSCREEN,      "SV_CXFULLSCREEN",      "Full screen client window width",
SV_CYFULLSCREEN,      "SV_CYFULLSCREEN",      "Full screen client window height",
SV_CXICON,            "SV_CXICON",            "Icon width",
SV_CYICON,            "SV_CYICON",            "Icon height",
SV_CXPOINTER,         "SV_CXPOINTER",         "Pointer width",
SV_CYPOINTER,         "SV_CYPOINTER",         "Pointer height",
SV_DEBUG,             "SV_DEBUG",             "Debug version flag",
SV_CMOUSEBUTTONS,     "SV_CMOUSEBUTTONS",     "Number of mouse buttons",
SV_POINTERLEVEL,      "SV_POINTERLEVEL",      "Pointer display count",
SV_CURSORLEVEL,       "SV_CURSORLEVEL",       "Cursor display count",
```

(continued)

Figure 4-1. The SYSVALS.H File. *continued*

```
    SV_TRACKRECTLEVEL,  "SV_TRACKRECTLEVEL", "Tracking rectangle display count",
    SV_CTIMERS,         "SV_CTIMERS",        "Number of available timers",
    SV_MOUSEPRESENT,    "SV_MOUSEPRESENT",   "Mouse present flag",
    SV_CXBYTEALIGN,     "SV_CXBYTEALIGN",    "Horizontal pixel alignment value",
    SV_CYBYTEALIGN,     "SV_CYBYTEALIGN",    "Vertical pixel alignment value"
    } ;
```

The SYSVALS1.C File

```
/*-------------------------------------------------------
    SYSVALS1.C -- System Values Display Program No. 1
  -------------------------------------------------------*/

#define INCL_WIN
#define INCL_GPI
#include <os2.h>
#include <stdlib.h>
#include <string.h>
#include "sysvals.h"

MRESULT EXPENTRY ClientWndProc (HWND, USHORT, MPARAM, MPARAM) ;

int main (void)
    {
    static CHAR  szClientClass [] = "SysVals1" ;
    static ULONG flFrameFlags = FCF_TITLEBAR    | FCF_SYSMENU |
                                FCF_SIZEBORDER   | FCF_MINMAX  |
                                FCF_SHELLPOSITION | FCF_TASKLIST ;
    HAB         hab ;
    HMQ         hmq ;
    HWND        hwndFrame, hwndClient ;
    QMSG        qmsg ;

    hab = WinInitialize (0) ;
    hmq = WinCreateMsgQueue (hab, 0) ;

    WinRegisterClass (hab, szClientClass, ClientWndProc, CS_SIZEREDRAW, 0) ;

    hwndFrame = WinCreateStdWindow (HWND_DESKTOP, WS_VISIBLE,
                              &flFrameFlags, szClientClass, NULL,
                              OL, NULL, 0, &hwndClient) ;

    WinSendMsg (hwndFrame, WM_SETICON,
                    WinQuerySysPointer (HWND_DESKTOP, SPTR_APPICON, FALSE),
                    NULL) ;
```

(continued)

Figure 4-1. The SYSVALS1.C File. *continued*

```
    while (WinGetMsg (hab, &qmsg, NULL, 0, 0))
        WinDispatchMsg (hab, &qmsg) ;

    WinDestroyWindow (hwndFrame) ;
    WinDestroyMsgQueue (hmq) ;
    WinTerminate (hab) ;
    return 0 ;
    }

MRESULT EXPENTRY ClientWndProc (HWND hwnd, USHORT msg, MPARAM mp1, MPARAM mp2)
    {
    static SHORT cxChar, cxCaps, cyChar, cyDesc, cxClient, cyClient ;
    CHAR         szBuffer [10] ;
    FONTMETRICS  fm ;
    HPS          hps ;
    POINTL       ptl ;
    SHORT        sLine ;

    switch (msg)
        {
        case WM_CREATE:
            hps = WinGetPS (hwnd) ;
            GpiQueryFontMetrics (hps, (LONG) sizeof fm, &fm) ;

            cxChar = (SHORT) fm.lAveCharWidth ;
            cxCaps = (SHORT) fm.lEmInc ;
            cyChar = (SHORT) fm.lMaxBaselineExt ;
            cyDesc = (SHORT) fm.lMaxDescender ;

            WinReleasePS (hps) ;
            return 0 ;

        case WM_SIZE:
            cxClient = SHORT1FROMMP (mp2) ;
            cyClient = SHORT2FROMMP (mp2) ;
            return 0 ;

        case WM_PAINT:
            hps = WinBeginPaint (hwnd, NULL, NULL) ;
            GpiErase (hps) ;

            for (sLine = 0 ; sLine < NUMLINES ; sLine++)
                {
                ptl.x = cxCaps ;
                ptl.y = cyClient - cyChar * (sLine + 1) + cyDesc ;
```

(continued)

Figure 4-1. The SYSVALS1.C File. *continued*

```
                GpiCharStringAt (hps, &ptl,
                         (LONG) strlen (sysvals[sLine].szIdentifier),
                         sysvals[sLine].szIdentifier) ;

                ptl.x += 20 * cxCaps ;
                GpiCharStringAt (hps, &ptl,
                         (LONG) strlen (sysvals[sLine].szDescription),
                         sysvals[sLine].szDescription) ;

                ltoa (WinQuerySysValue (HWND_DESKTOP,
                         sysvals[sLine].sIndex), szBuffer, 10) ;

                ptl.x += 38 * cxChar ;
                GpiCharStringAt (hps, &ptl, (LONG) strlen (szBuffer),
                                  szBuffer) ;
                }
           WinEndPaint (hps) ;
           return 0 ;
      }
 return WinDefWindowProc (hwnd, msg, mp1, mp2) ;
 }
```

The SYSVALS1.DEF File

```
;----------------------------------------
; SYSVALS1.DEF module definition file
;----------------------------------------


NAME           SYSVALS1   WINDOWAPI

DESCRIPTION    'System Values Display No. 1 (C) Charles Petzold, 1988'
PROTMODE
HEAPSIZE       1024
STACKSIZE      8192
EXPORTS        ClientWndProc
```

Figure 4-1. *The SYSVALS1 program.*

The SYSVALS.H header file defines a structure named *sysvals* that contains all the system value identifiers and text descriptions that SYSVALS1 needs to obtain and display the information from *WinQuerySysValue*. The same SYSVALS.H file will be used in the subsequent versions of the program in this chapter. Notice that the SYSVALS1 make file recompiles the program whenever the SYSVALS1.C or SYSVALS.H file is altered.

The definition of the INCL_WIN and INCL_GPI identifiers near the top of SYSVALS1.C is required in order to include sections of the OS/2 header files that are omitted by default.

The SYSVALS1 window is shown in Figure 4-2. You might have already noticed that SYSVALS1 is seriously flawed. Never fear; we'll hammer away at it until we get it right. Despite its flaws, SYSVALS1 illustrates many of the basic concepts involved in displaying text on your client window.

	SYSVALS1.EXE	
SV_SWAPBUTTON	Mouse buttons swapped flag	0
SV_DBLCLKTIME	Mouse double click time in msec	500
SV_CXDBLCLK	Mouse double click area width	6
SV_CYDBLCLK	Mouse double click area height	6
SV_CXSIZEBORDER	Sizing border width	4
SV_CYSIZEBORDER	Sizing border height	4
SV_ALARM	Alarm enabled flag	1
SV_CURSORRATE	Cursor blink rate	500
SV_FIRSTSCROLLRATE	Scroll bar time until repeats	200
SV_SCROLLRATE	Scroll bar scroll rate	50
SV_NUMBEREDLISTS	Flag for numbering of lists	0
SV_WARNINGFREQ	Alarm frequency for warning	880
SV_NOTEFREQ	Alarm frequency for note	1760
SV_ERRORFREQ	Alarm frequency for error	440
SV_WARNINGDURATION	Alarm duration for warning	50
SV_NOTEDURATION	Alarm duration for note	100
SV_ERRORDURATION	Alarm duration for error	100
SV_CXSCREEN	Screen width in pixels	640
SV_CYSCREEN	Screen height in pixels	350
SV_CXVSCROLL	Vertical scroll bar width	17
SV_CYHSCROLL	Horizontal scroll bar height	15
SV_CYVSCROLLARROW	Vertical scroll arrow height	16
SV_CXHSCROLLARROW	Horizontal scroll arrow width	20
SV_CXBORDER	Border width	1
SV_CYBORDER	Border height	1
SV_CXDLGFRAME	Dialog window frame width	5

Figure 4-2. *The SYSVALS1 display.*

Device-independent Programming

One primary purpose of the Presentation Manager is to provide a "device-independent" environment for your applications. This means that your programs should run without change or special drivers on any machine — and in particular, with any video display adapter — on which the Presentation Manager itself runs. Some programmers who have experience with Microsoft Windows are already aware of the deep and satisfying pleasure that results from seeing their programs run without change on everything from the IBM Color/Graphics Adapter (with 640 pixels horizontally by 200 scan lines vertically) to high-resolution video adapters of 1664 by 1200. In the years to come, programmers who write applications for the Presentation Manager can experience the same pleasure in seeing their programs run on video displays of even higher resolution.

Because a display driver is one of the dynamic link libraries in the Presentation Manager, Presentation Manager applications don't require their own video display drivers. The application makes various GPI calls, the Presentation Manager calls the display driver dynamic link library, and the display driver handles the hardware screen output. Of course, you do your part by writing Presentation Manager programs that can easily adapt themselves to different environments. This involves one basic rule: Don't assume anything.

But with the Presentation Manager, there's really no need for assumptions: All the information you need concerning the video display can be obtained through various Presentation Manager functions. For example, *WinQuerySysValue* can tell you the width and height of the video display in pixels. Just about the only guarantee you have is that the video display can accommodate at least 80 text characters across and 24 text lines down when you use the standard default "system font" (which I'll discuss shortly). Of course, this doesn't mean you necessarily have access to the entire screen. Normally, your application must share the display with other programs (which explains why the results of your program should be designed to be functional in both maximized and nonmaximized windows).

Most Presentation Manager programs have a sizing border that lets the user change the size of your program's window. This has a profound consequence: Not only can you not make any assumptions about the size of your program's client window, but you can't even assume that the size will remain constant while your program is running. So the first job we'll tackle is how a program can determine the size of its client window.

The Size of the Client Window

The programs presented in Chapters 2 and 3 obtained the size of the client window by calling

```
WinQueryWindowRect (hwnd, &rcl) ;
```

The *rcl* variable is a structure of type RECTL with four fields — *xLeft*, *yBottom*, *xRight*, and *yTop*. The *WinQueryWindowRect* function fills in these fields by setting the *xLeft* and *yBottom* fields to 0 and the *xRight* and *yTop* fields to the pixel width and height of the client window. This function was convenient in the earlier programs because they used *WinDrawText* to display centered text in the client window and could simply pass the RECTL pointer directly to *DrawText*.

But SYSVALS1 doesn't use the *WinDrawText* function. *WinDrawText* works well for displaying text within a rectangle, but it's less suitable for displaying multiple lines of text, as SYSVALS1 does. Instead, SYSVALS1 uses the GPI function *GpiCharStringAt* to display the text, and *GpiCharStringAt* doesn't use the RECTL structure.

Moreover, the approach used in the previous programs required that the *WinQueryWindowRect* function be called when processing every WM_PAINT message. It's more efficient to obtain the size of the client window only when the size changes. How do you know when the size of the client window changes? Simple — the Presentation Manager sends a message to the client window procedure. That message is WM_SIZE.

The window procedure receives the first WM_SIZE message during the *WinCreateStdWindow* call. Thereafter, the window procedure receives a WM_SIZE message whenever the user changes the window's size, either by using the sizing border or by maximizing or minimizing the window. The *mp1* and *mp2* parameters that accompany a WM_SIZE message indicate the previous size of the client window and the new size of the window. The width and height of the window are given in pixels. These values are encoded in *mp1* and *mp2* as shown in Figure 4-3.

WM_SIZE is a good example of a message that encodes two unsigned short integers (the USHORT type) in a 32-bit far pointer (the MPARAM type). To help you extract the two USHORTs from the MPARAM, the PMWIN.H header file contains two macros: SHORT1FROMMP and SHORT2FROMMP. These are defined as follows:

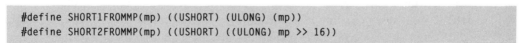

```
#define SHORT1FROMMP(mp) ((USHORT) (ULONG) (mp))
#define SHORT2FROMMP(mp) ((USHORT) ((ULONG) mp >> 16))
```

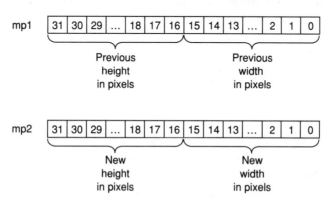

Figure 4-3. *The WM_SIZE* mp1 *and* mp2 *parameters.*

For example, you can obtain the new height of the client window with

```
SHORT2FROMMP (mp2)
```

You should use these macros rather than your own code to extract the USHORT values. On some future implementations of the Presentation Manager, the two USHORT values might be encoded in the MPARAM in a different way. The macros insulate you from the implementation.

Processing the WM_SIZE message is simple. In the client window procedure, you define two static variables named *cxClient* and *cyClient* (for example) to store the width and height of the client window:

```
static SHORT cxClient, cyClient ;
```

An *x* prefix to a variable name usually indicates a horizontal position; a *y* prefix indicates a vertical position. The *c* prefix stands for "count," and when combined with *x* indicates a width and with *y* a height. Here's how the SYSVALS1 program processes the WM_SIZE message:

```
case WM_SIZE:
    cxClient = SHORT1FROMMP (mp2) ;
    cyClient = SHORT2FROMMP (mp2) ;
    return 0 ;
```

The *cxClient* and *cyClient* variables must be defined as *static* because they are used later when processing other messages. After the first WM_SIZE message, the window procedure always has access to a valid client window size. In most cases you won't need to store or use the previous window size. You'll find similar WM_SIZE processing in most of the programs in this book. (Although the SHORT1FROMMP and SHORT2FROMMP macros extract unsigned short integer values from *mp1* and *mp2*, the values are stored in *cxClient* and *cyClient*, which are defined as signed short integers. As you'll see, the *cxClient* and *cyClient* are often used in arithmetic manipulations for which the SHORT definition is safer.)

The Presentation Space

To write to the client window, you need a handle to a "presentation space." (A presentation space is a data structure that describes an abstract display surface.) The presentation space handle is the first parameter to virtually all GPI functions and is your permission slip to use the various GPI drawing functions. The presentation space contains certain "attributes" that determine how the GPI functions work. These attributes all have default values when the presentation space is first created. You can change these attributes with GPI functions, but often the defaults are the most convenient attributes.

For example, in SYSVALS1 we probably want to display black text on a white background. These colors are attributes defined in the presentation space, and the defaults are black text on a white background. (Actually, the default colors are a little more complex than simply black and white, but I'll discuss that in Chapter 5.) We want the text to run from left to right rather than right to left or top to bottom or bottom to top; this also is defined by the default presentation space. We want the letters of the text string to be positioned top side up and not tilted in some way; the default presentation space attributes define the characters to be displayed like this. The presentation space also defines the font used to display text. In the default presentation space, this is a font known as the "system font," which is the same font that the Presentation Manager uses for text in title bars, menus, message boxes, and dialog boxes. The system font is a "proportionally spaced" Helvetica font. This means that characters have different widths. For example, a *W* is about three and one-half times wider than an *I*. Working with a proportionally spaced font certainly adds a layer of complexity to text output, but nothing insurmountable.

In this book, I'll most often use the type of presentation space called the "cached micro-PS." The cached micro-PS gives a program access to only a subset of the GPI functions, but it is often easier to use in small programs.

Because a presentation space defines an abstract drawing surface, it isn't very useful by itself (unless, of course, you own an abstract display or an abstract printer). This is why a presentation space is usually "associated with" a particular "device context." The device context refers to a device driver and the physical output device, such as the video display, a printer, or a plotter. (A device context can also describe an output device that isn't quite real, such as a "memory device context," in which a block of memory mimics a real display surface, or a "metafile device context," in which the graphics drawing functions are collected in a file.) Here's a simplified description of the relationship between a presentation space and a device context:

- The presentation space describes an abstract drawing surface.

- The device context describes a physical output device.

- When the presentation space is associated with the device context, what you draw on the presentation space by calling GPI functions will appear on the device.

The cached micro-PS, however, is always associated with the device context for the video display. More specifically, the cached micro-PS applies only to a particular window on the video display, typically your client window. When you obtain a handle to a cached micro-PS, you can't draw outside this window. It's not an error if you try to do so—the Presentation Manager simply ignores the attempt.

Getting a Handle to a Presentation Space

In using a cached micro-PS, you obtain the handle to the presentation space when you need to draw, and you ''release'' the handle when you finish drawing. After you release the handle, it's no longer valid. You have to obtain a new handle when you want to draw again. You should obtain and release the presentation space handle while processing a single message. You should *not* obtain the handle while processing one message and release it while processing another. Each time you obtain the handle, all attributes of the presentation space are set to default values. Changes you make to these attributes are lost when you release the handle.

In your window procedure, you define a variable (usually called *hps*) that is of type HPS, a handle to a presentation space:

```
HPS  hps ;
```

There are two methods for obtaining a cached micro-PS handle for your client window. The SYSVALS1 program uses both methods.

Method one: during processing of the WM_PAINT message

The first way to obtain a cached micro-PS handle is while processing the WM_PAINT message:

```
case WM_PAINT:
     hps = WinBeginPaint (hwnd, NULL, NULL) ;
         [call GPI functions]
     WinEndPaint (hps) ;
     return 0 ;
```

You should always call *WinBeginPaint* and *WinEndPaint* as a pair. Don't call *WinBeginPaint* and *WinEndPaint* while processing messages other than WM_PAINT. By setting the second parameter of *WinBeginPaint* to NULL, you request a cached micro-PS handle. Otherwise, you would set this parameter to the noncached presentation space handle you obtain from *GpiCreatePS* (a function I'll touch on in Chapters 6 and 7).

The window procedure receives a WM_PAINT message only when part of the window is invalid and must be repainted. For example, if part of your program's client window is partly off the screen and the user then moves the window so it is entirely within the screen, the area previously off the screen is marked as invalid. The Presentation Manager posts a WM_PAINT message in the window procedure's message queue.

The third parameter to *WinBeginPaint* is an optional pointer to a RECTL structure to obtain the coordinates of the rectangle encompassing the invalid area. (We'll use this in the SYSVALS3 version of the program.) The presentation space handle you obtain from *WinBeginPaint* allows you to draw only within this rectangle. When you call *WinEndPaint*, the Presentation Manager validates the entire area of the window.

Method two: during processing of other messages

You can also obtain a cached micro-PS handle while processing messages other than WM_PAINT:

```
hps = WinGetPS (hwnd) ;
    [call GPI functions]
WinReleasePS (hps) ;
```

You should always call *WinGetPS* and *WinReleasePS* as a pair. With the handle from *WinGetPS*, you can draw on any part of the client window. However, unlike *WinEndPaint*, *WinReleasePS* doesn't validate any part of the window. SYSVALS1 calls *WinGetPS* and *WinReleasePS* while processing the WM_CREATE message. I'll describe shortly what the program does during that message.

The Coordinate System

Parameters to GPI functions often specify coordinate positions and sizes. Several attributes of the presentation space define the coordinate system in effect when you draw; that is, they determine how the coordinate positions and sizes you specify in GPI functions are translated and mapped to the pixels of the output device. By default, coordinates and sizes for a cached micro-PS are specified in units of pixels, and coordinates are relative to the lower-left corner of the window, regardless of where the window is positioned on the screen. Values on the horizontal (or x) axis increase to the right; values on the vertical (or y) axis increase going up.

The notation (x, y) is often used to indicate a particular point in x and y coordinates. The point $(0, 0)$ is the lower-left corner of the client window. If you set variables *cxClient* and *cyClient* while processing the WM_SIZE message, the upper-right of the client window is (*cxClient* − *1, cyClient* − *1*). The coordinate system for a cached micro-PS is shown in Figure 4-4.

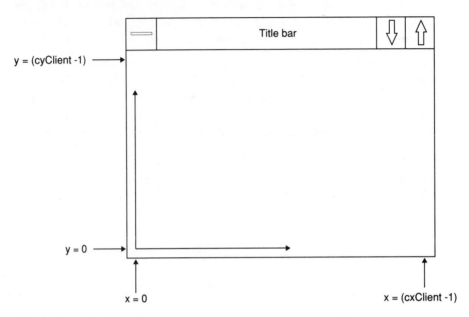

Figure 4-4. *The cached micro-PS default coordinate system.*

The Size of a Character

Because this coordinate system has an origin at the lower-left corner of the client area, it is somewhat inconvenient for displaying text, which most of us read from the top down. But that's a relatively simple adjustment you can make when it comes time to display the text. The GPI function used in SYSVALS1 to display text is *GpiCharStringAt*. This function requires the *x* and *y* coordinates of the starting position of the text. SYSVALS1 calls *GpiCharStringAt* three times—once for each of the three columns to be displayed. Thus, to properly space successive lines and columns of text, SYSVALS1 needs to know the height and width of the characters in pixels.

When you obtain a handle to a cached micro-PS, the default presentation space includes a font. Unless you change that font, the Presentation Manager uses that font for all text you write to the presentation space. The default font is called the "system font." This is the proportionally spaced font used for normal text in the Presentation Manager. You can obtain character dimensions of the current font in the presentation space by calling *GpiQueryFontMetrics*. You first define a structure of type FONTMETRICS:

```
FONTMETRICS fm ;
```

Then you call the function:

```
GpiQueryFontMetrics (hps, (LONG) sizeof fm, &fm);
```

The second parameter is the size of the structure in bytes, and the last parameter is a pointer to the structure.

On the function's return, the fields of the *fm* structure describe many of the basic characteristics of the font. Figure 4-5 shows the fields that describe the dimensions of characters. Obviously, these fields represent much more information than you need right now, but they give you a sense of just how much information is available.

All these values are LONG (32-bit) integers, as indicated by the "l" prefix.

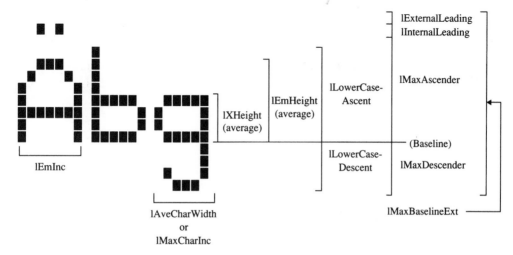

Figure 4-5. *The character dimension fields from* GpiQueryFontMetrics.

Character width

For a proportionally spaced font like the system font, the FONTMETRICS structure provides two fields that are valuable. The *lAveCharWidth* field is the weighted average width of lowercase letters based on the frequency of these letters in English. The *lEmInc* field is a weighted average width of uppercase letters. (The FONTMETRICS structure also includes a field called *lMaxCharInc*, which is the width of the widest character.) In all cases the width includes intercharacter spacing.

Character height

When it comes to character heights, the FONTMETRICS structure provides more detailed information. The *lXHeight* value is the average height above the baseline of a lowercase letter without ascenders, and *lEmHeight* is the average height of an uppercase letter. Depending on the typeface, the *lLowerCaseAscent* value could be less than *lEmHeight*, greater than *lEmHeight*, or the same. The *lInternalLeading* field is the space reserved for diacritics. For some fonts, it could be zero. The *lExternalLeading* field is the amount of white space recommended by the designer of the font to be added between lines of text. For some fonts, this also can be zero.

Interline spacing

For spacing successive lines of text, use the value returned in the *lMaxBaselineExt* field. You can also use *lMaxBaselineExt* less *lExternalLeading* if you want to get more lines of text into a smaller space. Earlier I noted that the Presentation Manager requires the screen to display at least 24 lines of 80 characters. For some low-resolution displays that holds true only if you space lines of text using the *lMaxBaselineExt* values minus *lExternalLeading*.

The size of the system font won't change during the time your program is running, so you need to obtain the character sizes only once. An excellent time to do this is while processing the WM_CREATE message, which is the approach that SYSVALS1 uses. SYSVALS1 defines four static variables to hold the average lowercase width, average uppercase width, total height, and descender height of a character:

```
static SHORT cxChar, cxCaps, cyChar, cyDesc, cxClient, cyClient ;
```

While processing WM_CREATE, SYSVALS1 obtains a handle to the presentation space, calls *WinQueryFontMetrics*, and saves the values of the *lAveCharWidth*, *lMaxBaselineExt*, and *lMaxDescender* fields:

```
case WM_CREATE:
    hps = WinGetPS (hwnd) ;

    GpiQueryFontMetrics (hps, (LONG) sizeof fm, &fm) ;

    cxChar = (SHORT) fm.lAveCharWidth ;
    cxCaps = (SHORT) fm.lEmInc ;
    cyChar = (SHORT) fm.lMaxBaselineExt ;
    cyDesc = (SHORT) fm.lMaxDescender ;

    WinReleasePS (hps) ;
    return 0 ;
```

Like the processing of the WM_SIZE message, this is fairly standard code; you'll see it frequently in Presentation Manager programs that work with simple text.

During the WM_CREATE message, SYSVALS1 obtains a handle to the presentation space only to obtain information. Attempting to draw during the WM_CREATE message is unwise, because the window isn't yet displayed on the screen. (And be forewarned that the FONTMETRICS structure is over 200 bytes long. For purposes of clarity, I've defined *fm* as a local variable in *ClientWndProc*. In most programs, the definition of *fm* and the *GpiQueryFontMetrics* call should probably be moved to a subroutine so the structure doesn't take up stack space whenever the window procedure is called.)

The WM_PAINT Message

WM_PAINT is an extremely important message. The window procedure receives a WM_PAINT message when an area of the window becomes invalid. This can happen frequently as the user moves and resizes various windows on the screen. Your Presentation Manager programs should be structured so that they can entirely update the client window on receipt of a WM_PAINT message. In many cases, this means the program can be most efficient if it draws on the client window only during the WM_PAINT message.

This certainly isn't a hard-and-fast rule. Obviously, the program can access a presentation space by calling *WinGetPS* and paint on the client window at almost any time. But the program must be able to entirely repaint the client window when it receives the WM_PAINT message anyway, so any drawing it does during other messages has to be duplicated during WM_PAINT processing. Often, however, a window procedure will determine during a message other than WM_PAINT that part of the client window should be changed. We'll see examples of how programs can themselves generate WM_PAINT messages in the SYSVALS2 and SYSVALS3 programs presented in this chapter.

The *GpiCharStringAt* Function

SYSVALS1 uses the *GpiCharStringAt* function to write text to the client area. The *At* part of the function name indicates that the function requires specific coordinates for where the text is to begin. The general syntax of *GpiCharStringAt* is

```
GpiCharStringAt (hps, &ptl, lCount, pchString) ;
```

The first parameter is a handle to the presentation space. That's the case for virtually all GPI functions. The last parameter is a pointer to a character string (as indicated by the ''pch'' prefix). The third parameter is a LONG value of the number of characters in the string. Unlike *WinDrawText*, *GpiCharStringAt* doesn't recognize zero-terminated character strings.

The second parameter to *GpiCharStringAt* is a pointer to a structure of type POINTL (which stands for "a point with LONG coordinates"). The definition of the POINTL structure in OS2DEF.H looks like this:

```
typedef struct _POINTL
    {
    LONG x ;
    LONG y ;
    }
    POINTL ;
```

It's simply a structure that specifies a point in terms of *x* and *y* coordinates. You can define a variable (the name *ptl* is standard) of type POINTL in your window procedure:

```
POINTL ptl ;
```

You then set the *x* and *y* fields of this structure before you call *GpiCharStringAt*. These *x* and *y* values indicate the starting position of the string, specifically the point corresponding to the baseline of the left side of the first character. If you use *GpiCharStringAt* with the string "go", for example, it's displayed relative to the lower-left corner of the client window, as shown in Figure 4-6.

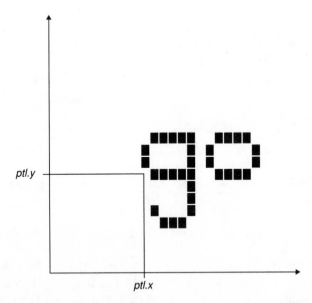

Figure 4-6. *A character string with starting coordinates set by the* GpiCharStringAt *function.*

The use of the baseline for the *y* coordinate can be a little tricky. For example, to display the string "go" in the lower-left corner of the client window, you might want to use code like this:

```
ptl.x = 0 ;
ptl.y = 0 ;

GpiCharStringAt (hps, &ptl, (LONG) 2, "go") ;
```

But the descender on the *g* won't be visible. Instead, you need to adjust the *y* coordinates for the length of the descender:

```
gpt.y = cyDesc ;
```

Numeric Formatting

If you felt disheartened when I announced at the beginning of this chapter that *printf* can't be used in Presentation Manager programs, cheer up and take a look at *sprintf*. Like *printf*, *sprintf* formats numbers and text based on a formatting string. However, rather than writing the resultant formatted text to standard output, *sprintf* stores it in a character buffer that you provide. The general syntax is

```
iLength = sprintf (szBuffer, szFormat, ...) ;
```

where *iLength* is the integer length of the zero-terminated output string that *sprintf* stores in *szBuffer*.

When you use *sprintf* in a Presentation Manager program, include the STDIO.H header file at the top of the C source code file:

```
#include <stdio.h>
```

You must also define a buffer large enough for the formatted text. For example:

```
CHAR szBuffer [80] ;
```

You can then use *sprintf* with *GpiCharStringAt* like this:

```
iLength = sprintf (szBuffer, "The sum of %d and &d is %d",
                   iNum1, iNum2, iNum1 + iNum2) ;

GpiCharStringAt (hps, &ptl, (LONG) iLength, szBuffer) ;
```

Or you can dispense with the *iLength* variable and combine both statements into one:

```
GpiCharStringAt (hps, &ptl,
        (LONG) sprintf (szBuffer, "The sum of %d and %d is %d",
                                iNum1, iNum2, iNum1 + iNum2),
        szBuffer) ;
```

This may look ugly, but it's a common construction in Presentation Manager programs.

But *sprintf* is overkill for SYSVALS1. Instead, the program can display text strings by passing them directly as the last parameter to *GpiCharStringAt* and using *strlen* to find the length of each string (required for the third parameter to *GpiCharStringAt*). For formatting the value returned from *WinQuerySysValue*, SYSVALS1 can use the C *ltoa* function.

At this point, the processing of the WM_PAINT message in SYSVALS1 should be almost comprehensible:

```
case WM_PAINT:
    hps = WinBeginPaint (hwnd, NULL, NULL) ;
    GpiErase (hps) ;

    for (sLine = 0 ; sLine < NUMLINES ; sLine++)
        {
        ptl.x = cxCaps ;
        ptl.y = cyClient - cyChar * (sLine + 1) + cyDesc ;

        GpiCharStringAt (hps, &ptl,
                    (LONG) strlen (sysvals[sLine].szIdentifier),
                    sysvals[sLine].szIdentifier) ;

        ptl.x += 20 * cxCaps ;
        GpiCharStringAt (hps, &ptl,
                    (LONG) strlen (sysvals[sLine].szDescription),
                    sysvals[sLine].szDescription) ;

        ltoa (WinQuerySysValue (HWND_DESKTOP,
                    sysvals[sLine].sIndex), szBuffer, 10) ;

        ptl.x += 38 * cxChar ;
        GpiCharStringAt (hps, &ptl, (LONG) strlen (szBuffer),
                        szBuffer) ;
        }
    WinEndPaint (hps) ;
    return 0 ;
```

Between the *WinBeginPaint* and *WinEndPaint* calls is a call to *GpiErase* (which erases the invalid rectangle) and a simple *for* loop. The NUMLINES identifier is defined in SYSVALS.H.

The *x* field of the POINTL structure is initially set to *cxCaps*. Thus every line is indented one character width from the left side of the client window. For the first line (*sLine* equals 0), the *y* field is set to (*cyClient* − *cyChar* + *cyDesc*), the top line of the client window. Each successive line begins *yChar* pixels below the previous line. The first *GpiCharStringAt* call displays the *szIdentifier* field of the sysvals structure (for example, SV_SWAPBUTTON). For the second *GpiCharStringAt* call, the *x* field of the POINTL structure is increased by 20 times the average width of an uppercase letter:

```
ptl.x += 20 * cxCaps ;
```

The *szDescription* field is then displayed. SYSVALS1 converts the value obtained from *WinQuerySysValue* by calling *ltoa*. It moves the *x* field of the POINTL structure to the right of the description column:

```
ptl.x += 38 * cxChar ;
```

It then displays the value.

The Problem with SYSVALS1

So that's it — SYSVALS1 obtains the width and height of a system font character while processing the WM_CREATE message, obtains the width and height of the client window from the WM_SIZE message, and paints the client window using this information during WM_PAINT. It's simple, and it's wrong — on most standard video displays, there's not enough room to display all 48 values obtained from *WinQuerySysValue*. SYSVALS1 always displays the values starting at the top of its client window and has no way to bring the hidden lines into view. That's a problem. But it's nothing a scroll bar can't fix.

Adding Scroll Bars

Scroll bars are an important part of the consistent user interface in the Presentation Manager. For users, scroll bars are easy to learn and to use, and they provide good visual feedback. Scroll bars are usually thought of as controlling the view of a document, as in a word-processing program, but they can be used in any program that has more to display than can fit in the client window. A vertical scroll bar, like the one shown in Figure 4-7 on the following page, is normally positioned to the right of the client window.

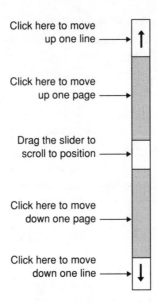

Click here to move up one line

Click here to move up one page

Drag the slider to scroll to position

Click here to move down one page

Click here to move down one line

Figure 4-7. *A vertical scroll bar and the actions it performs.*

A click on the arrow at the top of the scroll bar moves the view one line toward the beginning of the document. (This is called "scrolling up" in keeping with the user's perspective, even though the document actually scrolls down relative to the window.) Similarly, a click on the bottom arrow moves the view one line toward the end of the document.

Between the two arrows is a long area containing the moveable scroll-bar slider. Clicking above the slider moves the view one page toward the beginning of the document; clicking below the slider moves the view one page toward the end. The slider indicates the approximate position within the entire document of the portion displayed on the screen. You can move to a position in the document by dragging the slider to the relative spot in the slider area. For example, you can move to the beginning of the document by dragging the slider to the top of the slider area.

Horizontal scroll bars (normally positioned at the bottom of a client window) are used in a similar fashion to scroll documents left and right.

Creating the Scroll Bar

The first step in adding a scroll-bar interface involves changing a parameter to the *WinCreateStdWindow* call. You simply include the necessary frame creation flag identifier (FCF_HORZSCROLL, FCF_VERTSCROLL, or both) in the *flFrameFlags* variable. The Presentation Manager creates the scroll-bar windows as children of the frame window. With only this change, the scroll bars don't seem to do very much. The scroll bar colors itself with a reverse-video flash when you click on it, but that's about it.

Looks are deceiving. When you click on a scroll bar, the scroll-bar window procedure (located in the Presentation Manager) receives a mouse message. The scroll bar then posts a notification message to its owner, which is the frame window. This notification message contains information about the action of the mouse on the scroll bar. The frame window graciously sends this message to the client window procedure, which is in your program. The notification messages are WM_HSCROLL for a horizontal scroll bar and WM_VSCROLL for a vertical scroll bar.

Your client window procedure can also send messages to the scroll-bar window. These messages set the "range" and current "position" of the scroll-bar slider. To send these messages, you need to know the window handle of the scroll bar. When the Presentation Manager creates the scroll bars as part of the standard window, they are assigned predefined child ID numbers of FID_HORZSCROLL and FID_VERTSCROLL. Thus you can obtain the window handle of horizontal and vertical scroll bars by calling

```
hwndHscroll = WinWindowFromID (hwndFrame, FID_HORZSCROLL) ;
hwndVscroll = WinWindowFromID (hwndFrame, FID_VERTSCROLL) ;
```

The scroll bars' parent is *hwndFrame*. The frame window is also the parent of the client window, so you can also obtain these handles within your client window procedure by using only the *hwnd* parameter passed to the procedure. You'll probably do this while processing the WM_CREATE message:

```
hwndHscroll = WinWindowFromID (
                 WinQueryWindow (hwnd, QW_PARENT, FALSE),
                 FID_HORZSCROLL) ;

hWndVscroll = WinWindowFromID (
                 WinQueryWindow (hwnd, QW_PARENT, FALSE),
                 FID_VERTSCROLL) ;
```

Within a client window procedure, these window handles should be stored in static variables of type HWND.

The Range and Position

After obtaining the window handle of a scroll bar, the program can initialize the scroll bar to a range and slider position. When first created, a scroll bar has a default range of 0 to 100. The position of the scroll-bar slider is always a discrete integral value within this range:

- If the slider is at the top (or left) of the scroll bar, the position is 0.

- If the slider is at the bottom (or right) of the scroll bar, the position is 100.

If that 0 to 100 range isn't appropriate for your program, you can set a different range by sending the scroll bar an SBM_SETSCROLLBAR message. SBM_SETSCROLLBAR, like other messages that begin with SBM (''scrollbar message''), is a message understood only by scroll bars. Set the *mp1* parameter of this message to the initial position of the scroll-bar slider. Set *mp2* to contain the range of the scroll bar, with the minimum value in the low half of *mp2* and the maximum value in the high half. You can convert these values to an MPARAM data type using the MPFROM2SHORT macro. For example, suppose you want to set the vertical scroll-bar range to 10 through 40 and the initial position to 15. Here's the code:

```
sMinPos = 10 ;
sMaxPos = 40 ;
sPosition = 15 ;

WinSendMsg (hwndVscroll, SBM_SETSCROLLBAR,
                 MPFROM2SHORT (sPosition, 0),
                 MPFROM2SHORT (sMinPos, sMaxPos)) ;
```

If you ever need to obtain the range from the scroll bar, you can do so by sending the scroll bar an SBM_QUERYRANGE message:

```
mr = WinSendMsg (hwndVscroll, SBM_QUERYRANGE, NULL, NULL) ;
```

The minimum and maximum range positions are encoded in *mr* (a variable of type MRESULT) and can be extracted using the SHORT1FROMMR and SHORT2FROMMR macros:

```
sMinPos = SHORT1FROMMR (mr) ;
sMaxPos = SHORT2FROMMR (mr) ;
```

Receiving Notification Messages from the Scroll Bar

Scroll bars post notification messages to their owner (the frame window) when the various parts of the scroll bar are clicked on or dragged. The frame window sends these messages to the client window. For vertical scroll bars, the notification message is WM_VSCROLL; for horizontal scroll bars, it's WM_HSCROLL.

Messages from Vertical Scroll Bars

The low half of *mp1* (which you can obtain using the SHORT1FROMMP macro) contains the child window ID. For a vertical scroll bar created as part of the standard window, this is FID_VERTSCROLL. You need to examine this value only if you create multiple vertical scroll bars as children of your client window. The high half of *mp2* indicates the action of the mouse on the scroll bar. The value corresponds to an identifier defined in PMWIN.H that begins with the letter SB. Figure 4-8 shows how these values identify the mouse actions on the vertical scroll bar. The low half of *mp2* is the current position of the slider for SB_SLIDERTRACK and SB_SLIDER-POSITION actions.

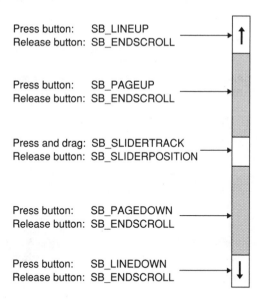

Figure 4-8. *Vertical scroll-bar action identifiers.*

Within your client window procedure, you process the WM_VSCROLL message with code that looks like this:

```
case WM_VSCROLL:
        switch (SHORT2FROMMP (mp2)
            {
            case SB_LINEUP:
                        [process line up action]
                    break ;

            case SB_PAGEUP:
                        [process page up action]
                    break ;
                        [and so forth]
```

Messages from Horizontal Scroll Bars

Horizontal scroll bars generate messages in the same way vertical scroll bars do: The notification message is WM_HSCROLL, the child window ID is FID_HORZSCROLL, and the identifiers indicating the mouse actions are those shown in Figure 4-9.

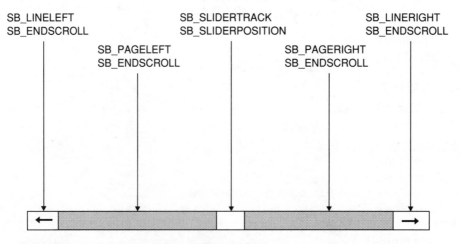

Figure 4-9. *Horizontal scroll-bar action identifiers.*

Processing Scroll-Bar Messages

You have some options in how you handle scroll-bar messages. When the user clicks on the arrows or the slider area, you receive at least two WM_VSCROLL or WM_HSCROLL messages. You get the first message when the mouse button is pressed. The action identifier is SB_LINEUP,

SB_PAGEUP, SB_LINEDOWN, or SB_PAGEDOWN for vertical scroll bars or one of the similar identifiers for horizontal scroll bars. When the button is released, you receive a WM_VSCROLL or WM_HSCROLL message with the SB_ENDSCROLL action identifier. As a general rule, you process the various "button down" messages and ignore SB_ENDSCROLL.

However, if your program requires a lot of time to process these actions, you might want to delay the processing until the mouse button is released. You can simply track how many messages you receive and do something that affects the client window *only* when you get SB_ENDSCROLL. This approach requires more complex logic and provides less feedback to the user, but it is an alternative.

The SB_SLIDERTRACK and SB_SLIDERPOSITION actions can be somewhat troublesome. As the user drags the slider up and down the scroll bar, your window procedure receives many SB_SLIDERTRACK actions.

- If your program is fast enough, you should process SB_SLIDERTRACK actions and ignore SB_SLIDERPOSITION.

- If your program has a hard time keeping up, you should process SB_SLIDERPOSITION and ignore SB_SLIDERTRACK.

(These two approaches are illustrated later in the chapter: SYSVALS2 is a slow, simple program that processes SB_SLIDERPOSITION; SYSVALS3 is optimized sufficiently to process SB_SLIDERTRACK actions on the vertical scroll bar.)

Setting the New Slider Position

The scroll-bar window itself never changes the position of the scroll-bar slider unless you tell it to. To change the position of the slider, you send the scroll bar a message. Assume the variable *sPosition* contains the new position of the vertical scroll bar. You send the scroll bar an SBM_SETPOS message in which *mp1* is the new position:

```
WinSendMsg (hwndVscroll, SBM_SETPOS, MPFROMSHORT (sPosition), NULL) ;
```

You typically send the scroll bar the SBM_SETPOS message while processing the WM_VSCROLL or WM_HSCROLL notification message *from* the scroll bar.

If you need to obtain the current position of the scroll-bar slider, you can send the scroll bar an SBM_QUERYPOS message:

```
sPosition = SHORT1FROMMR (WinSendMsg (hwndVScroll,
                                 SBM_QUERYPOS, NULL, NULL)) ;
```

The Implementation

Now we're ready to look at the SYSVALS2 program, shown in Figure 4-10. You'll need the SYSVALS.H header file from Figure 4-1 to compile the program.

The SYSVALS2 File

```
#-------------------
# SYSVALS2 make file
#-------------------

sysvals2.obj : sysvals2.c sysvals.h
    cl -c -G2sw -W3 sysvals2.c

sysvals2.exe : sysvals2.obj sysvals2.def
    link sysvals2, /align:16, NUL, os2, sysvals2
```

The SYSVALS2.C File

```
/*-----------------------------------------------------
   SYSVALS2.C -- System Values Display Program No. 2
   -----------------------------------------------------*/

#define INCL_WIN
#define INCL_GPI
#include <os2.h>
#include <stdlib.h>
#include <string.h>
#include "sysvals.h"

MRESULT EXPENTRY ClientWndProc (HWND, USHORT, MPARAM, MPARAM) ;

int main (void)
    {
    static CHAR  szClientClass [] = "SysVals2" ;
    static ULONG flFrameFlags = FCF_TITLEBAR      | FCF_SYSMENU   |
                                FCF_SIZEBORDER     | FCF_MINMAX    |
                                FCF_SHELLPOSITION  | FCF_TASKLIST  |
                                FCF_VERTSCROLL ;
    HAB          hab ;
    HMQ          hmq ;
    HWND         hwndFrame, hwndClient ;
    QMSG         qmsg ;

    hab = WinInitialize (0) ;
    hmq = WinCreateMsgQueue (hab, 0) ;
```

(continued)

Figure 4-10. The SYSVALS2.C File. *continued*

```
    WinRegisterClass (hab, szClientClass, ClientWndProc, CS_SIZEREDRAW, 0) ;

    hwndFrame = WinCreateStdWindow (HWND_DESKTOP, WS_VISIBLE,
                                    &flFrameFlags, szClientClass, NULL,
                                    OL, NULL, 0, &hwndClient) ;

    WinSendMsg (hwndFrame, WM_SETICON,
                WinQuerySysPointer (HWND_DESKTOP, SPTR_APPICON, FALSE),
                NULL) ;

    while (WinGetMsg (hab, &qmsg, NULL, 0, 0))
        WinDispatchMsg (hab, &qmsg) ;

    WinDestroyWindow (hwndFrame) ;
    WinDestroyMsgQueue (hmq) ;
    WinTerminate (hab) ;
    return 0 ;
    }

MRESULT EXPENTRY ClientWndProc (HWND hwnd, USHORT msg, MPARAM mp1, MPARAM mp2)
    {
    static HWND  hwndVscroll ;
    static SHORT cxChar, cxCaps, cyChar, cyDesc,
                 sVscrollPos, cxClient, cyClient ;
    CHAR         szBuffer [10] ;
    FONTMETRICS  fm ;
    HPS          hps ;
    POINTL       ptl ;
    SHORT        sLine ;

    switch (msg)
        {
        case WM_CREATE:
            hps = WinGetPS (hwnd) ;
            GpiQueryFontMetrics (hps, (LONG) sizeof fm, &fm) ;

            cxChar = (SHORT) fm.lAveCharWidth ;
            cxCaps = (SHORT) fm.lEmInc ;
            cyChar = (SHORT) fm.lMaxBaselineExt ;
            cyDesc = (SHORT) fm.lMaxDescender ;

            WinReleasePS (hps) ;

            hwndVscroll = WinWindowFromID (
                            WinQueryWindow (hwnd, QW_PARENT, FALSE),
                            FID_VERTSCROLL) ;
```

(continued)

Figure 4-10. The SYSVALS2.C File. *continued*

```
                    WinSendMsg (hwndVscroll, SBM_SETSCROLLBAR,
                                  MPFROM2SHORT (sVscrollPos, 0),
                                  MPFROM2SHORT (0, NUMLINES - 1)) ;
              return 0 ;

         case WM_SIZE:
              cxClient = SHORT1FROMMP (mp2) ;
              cyClient = SHORT2FROMMP (mp2) ;
              return 0 ;

         case WM_VSCROLL:
              switch (SHORT2FROMMP (mp2))
                  {
                  case SB_LINEUP:
                        sVscrollPos -= 1 ;
                        break ;

                  case SB_LINEDOWN:
                        sVscrollPos += 1 ;
                        break ;

                  case SB_PAGEUP:
                        sVscrollPos -= cyClient / cyChar ;
                        break ;

                  case SB_PAGEDOWN:
                        sVscrollPos += cyClient / cyChar ;
                        break ;

                  case SB_SLIDERPOSITION:
                        sVscrollPos = SHORT1FROMMP (mp2) ;
                        break ;
                  }
              sVscrollPos = max (0, min (sVscrollPos, NUMLINES - 1)) ;

              if (sVscrollPos != SHORT1FROMMR (WinSendMsg (hwndVscroll,
                               SBM_QUERYPOS, NULL, NULL)))
                  {
                  WinSendMsg (hwndVscroll, SBM_SETPOS,
                              MPFROMSHORT (sVscrollPos), NULL) ;
                  WinInvalidateRect (hwnd, NULL, FALSE) ;
                  }
              return 0 ;
```

(continued)

Figure 4-10. The SYSVALS2.C File. *continued*

```
          case WM_PAINT:
               hps = WinBeginPaint (hwnd, NULL, NULL) ;
               GpiErase (hps) ;

               for (sLine = 0 ; sLine < NUMLINES ; sLine++)
                   {
                   ptl.x = cxCaps ;
                   ptl.y = cyClient - cyChar * (sLine + 1 - sVscrollPos)
                                     + cyDesc ;

                   GpiCharStringAt (hps, &ptl,
                           (LONG) strlen (sysvals[sLine].szIdentifier),
                                  sysvals[sLine].szIdentifier) ;

                   ptl.x += 20 * cxCaps ;
                   GpiCharStringAt (hps, &ptl,
                           (LONG) strlen (sysvals[sLine].szDescription),
                                  sysvals[sLine].szDescription) ;

                   ltoa (WinQuerySysValue (HWND_DESKTOP,
                             sysvals[sLine].sIndex), szBuffer, 10) ;

                   ptl.x += 38 * cxChar ;
                   GpiCharStringAt (hps, &ptl, (LONG) strlen (szBuffer),
                                   szBuffer) ;
                   }
               WinEndPaint (hps) ;
               return 0 ;
          }
     return WinDefWindowProc (hwnd, msg, mp1, mp2) ;
     }
```

The SYSVALS2.DEF File

```
;--------------------------------------
; SYSVALS2.DEF module definition file
;--------------------------------------

NAME          SYSVALS2  WINDOWAPI

DESCRIPTION   'System Values Display No. 2 (C) Charles Petzold, 1988'
PROTMODE
HEAPSIZE      1024
STACKSIZE     8192
EXPORTS       ClientWndProc
```

Figure 4-10. *The SYSVALS2 program.*

The SYSVALS2 window with the vertical scroll bar is shown in Figure 4-11.

SYSVALS2.EXE		
SV_CXSIZEBORDER	Sizing border width	4
SV_CYSIZEBORDER	Sizing border height	4
SV_ALARM	Alarm enabled flag	1
SV_CURSORRATE	Cursor blink rate	500
SV_FIRSTSCROLLRATE	Scroll bar time until repeats	200
SV_SCROLLRATE	Scroll bar scroll rate	50
SV_NUMBEREDLISTS	Flag for numbering of lists	0
SV_WARNINGFREQ	Alarm frequency for warning	880
SV_NOTEFREQ	Alarm frequency for note	1760
SV_ERRORFREQ	Alarm frequency for error	440
SV_WARNINGDURATION	Alarm duration for warning	50
SV_NOTEDURATION	Alarm duration for note	100
SV_ERRORDURATION	Alarm duration for error	100
SV_CXSCREEN	Screen width in pixels	640
SV_CYSCREEN	Screen height in pixels	350
SV_CXVSCROLL	Vertical scroll bar width	17
SV_CYHSCROLL	Horizontal scroll bar height	15
SV_CYVSCROLLARROW	Vertical scroll arrow height	16
SV_CXHSCROLLARROW	Horizontal scroll arrow width	20
SV_CXBORDER	Border width	1
SV_CYBORDER	Border height	1
SV_CXDLGFRAME	Dialog window frame width	5
SV_CYDLGFRAME	Dialog window frame height	5
SV_CYTITLEBAR	Title bar height	15
SV_CYVSLIDER	Vertical scroll slider height	18
SV_CXHSLIDER	Horizontal scroll slider width	20
SV_CXMINMAXBUTTON	Minimize/Maximize button width	52

Figure 4-11. *The SYSVALS2 display.*

The only change in *main* is that the *flFrameFlags* variable now includes the identifier FCF_VERTSCROLL. This causes the Presentation Manager to create a vertical scroll bar as part of the standard window. *ClientWndProc* contains two new variables: *hwndVscroll*, which stores the handle of the scroll-bar window, and *sVscrollPos*, which stores the current position of the scroll-bar slider.

While processing the WM_CREATE message, the program obtains the window handle of the scroll bar:

```
hwndVscroll = WinWindowFromID (
              WinQueryWindow (hwnd, QW_PARENT, FALSE),
              FID_VERTSCROLL) ;
```

The program then initializes the range and slider position by sending the scroll bar a message:

```
WinSendMsg (hwndVscroll, SBM_SETSCROLLBAR,
              MPFROM2SHORT (sVscrollPos, 0),
              MPFROM2SHORT (0, NUMLINES - 1)) ;
```

The range (in *mp2*) is set to a minimum position of 0 and a maximum position of NUMLINES − 1. Thus the scroll bar has as many positions as there are lines of text. The initial value of *sVscrollPos* is 0 (because it is defined as a static variable but not explicitly initialized), so the slider is set to the topmost position.

SYSVALS2 uses the position of the vertical scroll-bar slider to determine how it displays the lines of text in the client window. The value of the slider position corresponds to the line that appears at the top of the client window, as shown in the following table:

Slider Position	*Line at Top of Client Window*
0 (top)	First
1	Second
2	Third
…	…
NUMLINES − 1 (bottom)	Last

The processing of the WM_VSCROLL message begins with the *sVscrollPos* variable being incremented or decremented, depending on the particular action of the mouse on the scroll bar:

```
case WM_VSCROLL:
     switch (SHORT2FROMMP (mp2))
          {
          case SB_LINEUP:
               sVscrollPos -= 1 ;
               break ;

          case SB_LINEDOWN:
               sVscrollPos += 1 ;
               break ;

          case SB_PAGEUP:
               sVscrollPos -= cyClient / cyChar ;
               break ;

          case SB_PAGEDOWN:
               sVscrollPos += cyClient / cyChar ;
               break ;

          case SB_SLIDERPOSITION:
               sVscrollPos = SHORT1FROMMP (mp2) ;
               break ;
          }
```

- For SB_LINEUP and SB_LINEDOWN, *sVscrollPos* is simply decremented or incremented by 1 for a change of one line.

- For SB_PAGEUP and SB_PAGEDOWN, the variable is decreased or increased by *cyClient / cyChar*, which is the number of lines that can fit in the client window.

- For the SB_SLIDERPOSITION action, the low USHORT encoded in *mp2* is the new slider position after the slider has been dragged and released.

SYSVALS2 ignores the SB_ENDSCROLL and SB_SLIDERTRACK actions.

It's possible that the new value of *sVscrollPos* is outside the range of the scroll bar. For example, the scroll-bar slider could have been at the top of the scroll bar when the user clicked the up arrow. This statement uses the *min* and *max* macros defined in STDLIB.H to bring *sVscrollPos* within the scroll bar range:

```
sVscrollPos = max (0, min (sVscrollPos, NUMLINES - 1)) ;
```

After this adjustment, it's possible that *sVscrollPos* hasn't changed at all. To determine this, the value of *sVscrollPos* is checked against the real position of the slider, which is determined by sending an SBM_QUERYPOS message to the scroll-bar window:

```
if (sVscrollPos != SHORT1FROMMR (WinSendMsg (hwndVscroll,
                                 SBM_QUERYPOS, NULL, NULL)))
    {
```

If *sVscrollPos* has changed, then the slider is set to the new position by sending it the SBM_SETPOS message:

```
WinSendMsg (hwndVscroll, SBM_SETPOS,
        MPFROMSHORT (sVscrollPos), NULL) ;
```

Finally, SYSVALS2 must update its client window to reflect the change. It must get a presentation space handle, erase the entire client window, rewrite all the lines of text, and then release the presentation space handle. It does this by calling

```
WinInvalidateRect (hwnd, NULL, FALSE) ;
```

What's this? This one *WinInvalidateRect* statement does all that? It sure does, because this statement invalidates the entire client window and causes the Presentation Manager to post a WM_PAINT message in SYSVALS2's message queue. The repainting actually occurs during the WM_PAINT message.

Earlier I discussed the idea of structuring your programs so that all drawing on the client window occurs during the WM_PAINT message. The *WinInvalidateRect* function is one of the tools that help you achieve this goal. The second parameter to *WinInvalidateRect* can be a pointer to a RECTL structure to specify that only a small rectangular area of the window is to be invalidated. Specifying NULL invalidates the whole window.

WM_PAINT Processing in SYSVALS2

Now let's look at the WM_PAINT processing. If you compare it with the WM_PAINT logic in SYSVALS1, you'll find only one changed statement. SYSVALS1 used the following statement to set the *y* field of the POINTL structure passed to *GpiCharStringAt*:

```
ptl.y = cyClient - cyChar * (sLine + 1) + cyDesc ;
```

SYSVALS2, on the other hand, uses this statement:

```
ptl.y = cyClient - cyChar * (sLine + 1 - sVscrollPos) + cyDesc ;
```

When the scroll-bar slider is at the top of the bar, *sVscrollPos* is 0, and *ptl.y* is set to the same value as in SYSVALS1. The first line of text is displayed at the top of the client window. When *sVscrollPos* is 1, then *ptl.y* is set to (*cyClient* + *cyDesc*), which means that the first line of text is displayed right above the client window, which means that it isn't displayed at all. The second line of text (when *sLine* equals 1) occupies the top line of the client window. Thus SYSVALS2 calls *GpiCharStringAt* for all 48 lines of text, but the program begins writing these lines either at the top of the client window (when *sVscrollPos* is 0) or somewhere above the client window. The Presentation Manager obligingly clips everything that falls outside the window.

This isn't very efficient WM_PAINT processing. It may not be too bad for 48 lines of text, but what if there were several hundred lines? The painting should really be restricted only to what's needed. So let's not be satisfied that we got the program working. Anybody can do that. Let's take a crack at making it better.

Optimizing the Code

The new and improved SYSVALS3 program is displayed in Figure 4-12. In addition to faster vertical scroll-bar processing and repainting, this version also includes a horizontal scroll bar for left and right scrolling. The *flFrameFlags* variable in *main* includes the frame creation flag identifiers FCF_HORZSCROLL and FCF_VERTSCROLL.

The SYSVALS3 File

```
#-------------------
# SYSVALS3 make file
#-------------------

sysvals3.obj : sysvals3.c sysvals.h
    cl -c -G2sw -W3 sysvals3.c

sysvals3.exe : sysvals3.obj sysvals3.def
    link sysvals3, /align:16, NUL, os2, sysvals3
```

The SYSVALS3.C File

```
/*-------------------------------------------------

    SYSVALS3.C -- System Values Display Program No. 3
  -----------------------------------------------*/

#define INCL_WIN
#define INCL_GPI
#include <os2.h>
#include <stdlib.h>
#include <string.h>
#include "sysvals.h"

MRESULT EXPENTRY ClientWndProc (HWND, USHORT, MPARAM, MPARAM) ;

int main (void)
    {
    static CHAR   szClientClass [] = "SysVals3" ;
    static ULONG  flFrameFlags = FCF_TITLEBAR       | FCF_SYSMENU   |
                                 FCF_SIZEBORDER     | FCF_MINMAX    |
                                 FCF_SHELLPOSITION  | FCF_TASKLIST  |
                                 FCF_VERTSCROLL     | FCF_HORZSCROLL ;
    HAB           hab ;
    HMQ           hmq ;
    HWND          hwndFrame, hwndClient ;
    QMSG          qmsg ;
```

(continued)

Figure 4-12. The SYSVALS3.C File. *continued*

```
    hab = WinInitialize (0) ;
    hmq = WinCreateMsgQueue (hab, 0) ;

    WinRegisterClass (hab, szClientClass, ClientWndProc, CS_SIZEREDRAW, 0) ;

    hwndFrame = WinCreateStdWindow (HWND_DESKTOP, WS_VISIBLE,
                                    &flFrameFlags, szClientClass, NULL,
                                    0L, NULL, 0, &hwndClient) ;

    WinSendMsg (hwndFrame, WM_SETICON,
                WinQuerySysPointer (HWND_DESKTOP, SPTR_APPICON, FALSE),
                NULL) ;

    while (WinGetMsg (hab, &qmsg, NULL, 0, 0))
        WinDispatchMsg (hab, &qmsg) ;

    WinDestroyWindow (hwndFrame) ;
    WinDestroyMsgQueue (hmq) ;
    WinTerminate (hab) ;
    return 0 ;
    }

LONG RtJustCharStringAt (HPS hps, POINTL *pptl, LONG lLength, CHAR *pchText)
    {
    POINTL aptlTextBox[TXTBOX_COUNT] ;

    GpiQueryTextBox (hps, lLength, pchText, TXTBOX_COUNT, aptlTextBox) ;

    pptl->x -= aptlTextBox[TXTBOX_CONCAT].x ;

    return GpiCharStringAt (hps, pptl, lLength, pchText) ;
    }

MRESULT EXPENTRY ClientWndProc (HWND hwnd, USHORT msg, MPARAM mp1, MPARAM mp2)
    {
    static HWND  hwndHscroll, hwndVscroll ;
    static SHORT sHscrollMax, sVscrollMax, sHscrollPos, sVscrollPos,
                 cxChar, cxCaps, cyChar, cyDesc, cxClient, cyClient,
                 cxTextTotal ;
    CHAR         szBuffer [10] ;
    FONTMETRICS  fm ;
    HPS          hps ;
    POINTL       ptl ;
    SHORT        sLine, sPaintBeg, sPaintEnd, sHscrollInc, sVscrollInc ;
    RECTL        rclInvalid ;
```

(continued)

Figure 4-12. The SYSVALS3.C File. *continued*

```
switch (msg)
    {
    case WM_CREATE:
         hps = WinGetPS (hwnd) ;
         GpiQueryFontMetrics (hps, (LONG) sizeof fm, &fm) ;

         cxChar = (SHORT) fm.lAveCharWidth ;
         cxCaps = (SHORT) fm.lEmInc ;
         cyChar = (SHORT) fm.lMaxBaselineExt ;
         cyDesc = (SHORT) fm.lMaxDescender ;

         WinReleasePS (hps) ;

         cxTextTotal = 28 * cxCaps + 38 * cxChar ;

         hwndHscroll = WinWindowFromID (
                           WinQueryWindow (hwnd, QW_PARENT, FALSE),
                           FID_HORZSCROLL) ;

         hwndVscroll = WinWindowFromID (
                           WinQueryWindow (hwnd, QW_PARENT, FALSE),
                           FID_VERTSCROLL) ;
         return 0 ;

    case WM_SIZE:
         cxClient = SHORT1FROMMP (mp2) ;
         cyClient = SHORT2FROMMP (mp2) ;

         sHscrollMax = max (0, cxTextTotal - cxClient) ;
         sHscrollPos = min (sHscrollPos, sHscrollMax) ;

         WinSendMsg (hwndHscroll, SBM_SETSCROLLBAR,
                           MPFROM2SHORT (sHscrollPos, 0),
                           MPFROM2SHORT (0, sHscrollMax)) ;

         WinEnableWindow (hwndHscroll, sHscrollMax ? TRUE : FALSE) ;

         sVscrollMax = max (0, NUMLINES - cyClient / cyChar) ;
         sVscrollPos = min (sVscrollPos, sVscrollMax) ;

         WinSendMsg (hwndVscroll, SBM_SETSCROLLBAR,
                           MPFROM2SHORT (sVscrollPos, 0),
                           MPFROM2SHORT (0, sVscrollMax)) ;

         WinEnableWindow (hwndVscroll, sVscrollMax ? TRUE : FALSE) ;
         return 0 ;
```

(continued)

Figure 4-12. The SYSVALS3.C File. *continued*

```
case WM_HSCROLL:
    switch (SHORT2FROMMP (mp2))
        {
        case SB_LINELEFT:
            sHscrollInc = -cxCaps ;
            break ;

        case SB_LINERIGHT:
            sHscrollInc = cxCaps ;
            break ;

        case SB_PAGELEFT:
            sHscrollInc = -8 * cxCaps ;
            break ;

        case SB_PAGERIGHT:
            sHscrollInc = 8 * cxCaps ;
            break ;

        case SB_SLIDERPOSITION:
            sHscrollInc = SHORT1FROMMP (mp2) - sHscrollPos;
            break ;

        default:
            sHscrollInc = 0 ;
            break ;
        }
    sHscrollInc = max (-sHscrollPos,
            min (sHscrollInc, sHscrollMax - sHscrollPos)) ;

    if (sHscrollInc != 0)
        {
        sHscrollPos += sHscrollInc ;
        WinScrollWindow (hwnd, -sHscrollInc, 0,
                    NULL, NULL, NULL, NULL, SW_INVALIDATERGN) ;

        WinSendMsg (hwndHscroll, SBM_SETPOS,
                MPFROMSHORT (sHscrollPos), NULL) ;
        }
    return 0 ;

case WM_VSCROLL:
    switch (SHORT2FROMMP (mp2))
        {
        case SB_LINEUP:
            sVscrollInc = -1 ;
            break ;
```

(continued)

Figure 4-12. The SYSVALS3.C File. *continued*

```
                case SB_LINEDOWN:
                     sVscrollInc = 1 ;
                     break ;

                case SB_PAGEUP:
                     sVscrollInc = min (-1, -cyClient / cyChar) ;
                     break ;

                case SB_PAGEDOWN:
                     sVscrollInc = max (1, cyClient / cyChar) ;
                     break ;

                case SB_SLIDERTRACK:
                     sVscrollInc = SHORT1FROMMP (mp2) - sVscrollPos;
                     break ;

                default:
                     sVscrollInc = 0 ;
                     break ;
                }
          sVscrollInc = max (-sVscrollPos,
                     min (sVscrollInc, sVscrollMax - sVscrollPos)) ;

          if (sVscrollInc != 0)
                {
                sVscrollPos += sVscrollInc ;
                WinScrollWindow (hwnd, 0, cyChar * sVscrollInc,
                           NULL, NULL, NULL, NULL, SW_INVALIDATERGN) ;

                WinSendMsg (hwndVscroll, SBM_SETPOS,
                           MPFROMSHORT (sVscrollPos), NULL) ;

                WinUpdateWindow (hwnd) ;
                }
          return 0 ;

     case WM_PAINT:
          hps = WinBeginPaint (hwnd, NULL, &rclInvalid) ;
          GpiErase (hps) ;

          sPaintBeg = max (0, sVscrollPos +
                      (cyClient - (SHORT) rclInvalid.yTop) / cyChar) ;
          sPaintEnd = min (NUMLINES, sVscrollPos +
                      (cyClient - (SHORT) rclInvalid.yBottom)
                           / cyChar + 1) ;
```

(continued)

Figure 4-12. The SYSVALS3.C File. *continued*

```
                   for (sLine = sPaintBeg ; sLine < sPaintEnd ; sLine++)
                       {
                       ptl.x = cxCaps - sHscrollPos ;
                       ptl.y = cyClient - cyChar * (sLine + 1 - sVscrollPos)
                                          + cyDesc ;

                       GpiCharStringAt (hps, &ptl,
                               (LONG) strlen (sysvals[sLine].szIdentifier),
                               sysvals[sLine].szIdentifier) ;

                       ptl.x += 20 * cxCaps ;
                       GpiCharStringAt (hps, &ptl,
                               (LONG) strlen (sysvals[sLine].szDescription),
                               sysvals[sLine].szDescription) ;

                       ltoa (WinQuerySysValue (HWND_DESKTOP,
                               sysvals[sLine].sIndex), szBuffer, 10) ;

                       ptl.x += 38 * cxChar + 6 * cxCaps ;
                       RtJustCharStringAt (hps, &ptl, (LONG) strlen (szBuffer),
                                           szBuffer) ;
                       }
              WinEndPaint (hps) ;
              return 0 ;
         }
    return WinDefWindowProc (hwnd, msg, mp1, mp2) ;
    }
```

The SYSVALS3.DEF File

```
;----------------------------------------
; SYSVALS3.DEF module definition file
;----------------------------------------

NAME          SYSVALS3   WINDOWAPI

DESCRIPTION   'System Values Display No. 3 (C) Charles Petzold, 1988'
PROTMODE
HEAPSIZE      1024
STACKSIZE     8192
EXPORTS       ClientWndProc
```

Figure 4-12. *The SYSVALS3 program.*

The SYSVALS3 window is shown in Figure 4-13.

SYSVALS3.EXE		
SV_CXBORDER	Border width	1
SV_CYBORDER	Border height	1
SV_CXDLGFRAME	Dialog window frame width	5
SV_CYDLGFRAME	Dialog window frame height	5
SV_CYTITLEBAR	Title bar height	15
SV_CYVSLIDER	Vertical scroll slider height	18
SV_CXHSLIDER	Horizontal scroll slider width	20
SV_CXMINMAXBUTTON	Minimize/Maximize button width	52
SV_CYMINMAXBUTTON	Minimize/Maximize button height	14
SV_CYMENU	Menu bar height	14
SV_CXFULLSCREEN	Full screen client window width	640
SV_CYFULLSCREEN	Full screen client window height	335
SV_CXICON	Icon width	32
SV_CYICON	Icon height	32
SV_CXPOINTER	Pointer width	32
SV_CYPOINTER	Pointer height	32
SV_DEBUG	Debug version flag	262206
SV_CMOUSEBUTTONS	Number of mouse buttons	2
SV_POINTERLEVEL	Pointer display count	0
SV_CURSORLEVEL	Cursor display count	1
SV_TRACKRECTLEVEL	Tracking rectangle display count	1
SV_CTIMERS	Number of available timers	36
SV_MOUSEPRESENT	Mouse present flag	1
SV_CXBYTEALIGN	Horizontal pixel alignment value	8
SV_CYBYTEALIGN	Vertical pixel alignment value	1

Figure 4-13. *The SYSVALS3 display.*

Right-justified Text

You'll notice I've also prettied up the display a little. In SYSVALS1 and SYSVALS2, the values returned from *WinQuerySysValue* were displayed beginning at the same horizontal pixel position. Columns of numbers are commonly displayed right justified. In SYSVALS3, the *RtJustCharStringAt* function results in right-justified text.

```
LONG RtJustCharStringAt (HPS hps, POINTL *pptl, LONG lLength, CHAR *pchText)
     {
     POINTL aptlTextBox[TXTBOX_COUNT] ;
     GpiQueryTextBox (hps, lLength, pchText, TXTBOX_COUNT, aptlTextBox) ;
     pptl->x -= aptlTextBox[TXTBOX_CONCAT].x ;
     return GpiCharStringAt (hps, pptl, lLength, pchText) ;
     }
```

This function is defined with the same parameters as *GpiCharStringAt*, but when the function is called, the *x* field of the POINTL structure should be set to the pixel position where the text should *end* rather than begin. This function uses the identifiers TXTBOX_COUNT and TXTBOX_CONCAT, defined in PMGPI.H. They are used when working with the *GpiQueryTextBox* function, which obtains an array of POINTL structures that give the coordinates of the four corners of a text string, assuming that the text begins at the point (0,0). The TXTBOX_CONCAT element of the *aptl* structure contains the coordinates of the end of the string (where more text would follow). So when the *x* coordinate of TXTBOX_CONCAT is subtracted from the *x* field of the POINTL structure passed to *RtJustCharStringAt*, the resulting value is the *x* coordinate that will result in right-justified text.

Changing the Range Based on Window Size

Another change incorporated in SYSVALS3 is that the scroll-bar range and slider position are no longer set during processing of the WM_CREATE message. Instead, a new range and position are set during each WM_SIZE message.

The primary goal is to have the last line of text be visible at the bottom of the client window. So during the WM_SIZE message, the maximum position of the vertical scroll-bar slider is calculated based on the total number of text lines and the number of lines that can fit in the client window:

```
sVscrollMax = max (0, NUMLINES - cyClient / cyChar) ;
```

The existing value of *sVscrollPos* could be outside this new range, so *sVscrollPos* is adjusted using the *min* macro:

```
sVscrollPos = min (sVscrollPos, sVscrollMax) ;
```

Then the new range and position are set by sending the scroll bar a message:

```
WinSendMsg (hwndVscroll, SBM_SETSCROLLBAR,
                         MPFROM2SHORT (sVscrollPos, 0),
                         MPFROM2SHORT (0, sVscrollMax)) ;
```

If all the text fits in the client window, then *sVscrollMax* equals 0, and there is no need for a working scroll bar. To enable or disable the scroll bar, call *WinEnableWindow* based on the value of *sVscrollMax*:

```
WinEnableWindow (hwndVscroll, sVscrollMax ? TRUE : FALSE) ;
```

A disabled scroll bar is made partly invisible and beeps if you click on it.

Scrolling the Window

Rather than immediately altering the value of *sVscrollPos*, the new WM_VSCROLL processing sets a variable named *sVscrollInc* to the incremental change in the slider position indicated by the mouse action:

```
case WM_VSCROLL:
    switch (SHORT2FROMMP (mp2))
        {
        case SB_LINEUP:
            sVscrollInc = -1 ;
            break ;

        case SB_LINEDOWN:
            sVscrollInc = 1 ;
            break ;

        case SB_PAGEUP:
            sVscrollInc = min (-1, -cyClient / cyChar) ;
            break ;

        case SB_PAGEDOWN:
            sVscrollInc = max (1, cyClient / cyChar) ;
            break ;

        case SB_SLIDERTRACK:
            sVscrollInc = SHORT1FROMMP (mp2) - sVscrollPos;
            break ;

        default:
            sVscrollInc = 0 ;
            break ;
        }
```

SYSVALS3 processes the SB_SLIDERTRACK action rather than SB_SLIDERPOSITION. This allows the program to change the client window while the user is dragging the slider with the mouse rather than after the dragging action is completed.

Next, *sVscrollInc* is adjusted based on the position of the slider and the range maximum:

```
iVscrollInc = max (-sVscrollPos,
            min (sVscrollInc, sVscrollMax - sVscrollPos));
```

If *sVscrollInc* is still nonzero, processing continues with the calculation of a new slider position:

```
sVscrollPos += sVscrollInc ;
```

In SYSVALS2, the entire window was redrawn whenever the scroll-bar position was changed. SYSVALS3 attempts to preserve part of the window by scrolling the contents of the window:

```
WinScrollWindow (hwnd, 0, cyChar * sVscrollInc,
          NULL, NULL, NULL, NULL, SW_INVALIDATERGN) ;
```

This function can scroll a rectangular area of a window up, down, left, or right. Here we're specifying that the contents of the entire window move up by *cyChar* ∗ *sVscrollInc* pixels. Thus, if the action is SB_LINEDOWN, then *sVscrollInc* is 1, and the contents of the window move up *cyChar* pixels. This means that only the last line at the bottom of the window has to be redrawn. Including SW_INVALIDATERGN as the last parameter of *WinScrollWindow* tells the Presentation Manager to invalidate the area uncovered by the scroll — the bottom line of the client window. A WM_PAINT message is placed in SYSVALS3's message queue.

Normally, SYSVALS3 would retrieve the WM_PAINT message from its message queue and repaint the window. If the scroll bar is busy receiving and processing mouse messages, however, this won't happen immediately. We can force the client window to be repainted right away with this function:

```
WinUpdateWindow (hwnd) ;
```

This causes the Presentation Manager to call *ClientWndProc* with the WM_PAINT message.

Painting Only the Invalid Rectangle

When the window procedure receives a WM_PAINT message, it's likely that only a small rectangular part of the client window is invalid and needs to be repainted. When a program obtains a presentation space handle from *WinBeginPaint*, it can paint only within that rectangular invalid area. The Presentation Manager must clip all screen output that falls outside the invalid area. But for optimum efficiency, the program itself shouldn't make any GPI calls that will eventually be ignored by the Presentation Manager.

To speed up the painting, SYSVALS3 obtains the coordinates of the rectangular invalid area. It does this in the *WinBeginPaint* function:

```
hps = WinBeginPaint (hwnd, NULL, &rclInvalid) ;
```

The Presentation Manager fills in the fields of the RECTL structure named *rclInvalid* with the coordinates of this rectangle.

SYSVALS3 then uses the *yTop* and *yBottom* fields of the RECTL structure to determine the range of lines that must be repainted:

```
sPaintBeg = max (0, sVscrollPos +
            (cyClient - (SHORT) rclInvalid.yTop) / cyChar) ;
sPaintEnd = min (NUMLINES, sVscrollPos +
            (cyClient - (SHORT) rclInvalid.yBottom) / cyChar + 1) ;
```

The *for* loop encompasses only this range:

```
for (sLine = sPaintBeg ; sLine < sPaintEnd ; sLine++)
```

The improved efficiency in processing the WM_VSCROLL and WM_PAINT messages allows SYSVALS3 to move the contents of the window during SB_SLIDERTRACK actions from the vertical scroll bar.

Adding a Keyboard Interface

Of course, if you don't have a mouse, you haven't been able to scroll SYSVALS2 or SYSVALS3 at all. So let's make one final change to the program to allow the mouseless among us to scroll the window using the cursor movement keys.

Scroll bars understand keyboard messages. However, the Presentation Manager posts keyboard messages to only one window — the window with the "input focus" (as you'll see in Chapter 8, when we examine the keyboard in more depth). If your program is active, then the window with the input focus is generally the client window rather than the scroll-bar window.

Earlier I mentioned that the frame window is the initial recipient of notification messages from the scroll bar and that the frame window sends these messages to the client window. This raises an interesting question: If the frame window passes scroll bar messages to the client window, why can't the client window pass keyboard messages to the scroll-bar window? Let's do it.

The keyboard message is called WM_CHAR. For the cursor movement keys, the high USHORT of *mp2* is a "virtual key code" (more on this in Chapter 5) that identifies the key. The PMWIN.H header file has a macro called CHARMSG that lets you extract this code. You probably want the Up Arrow, Down Arrow, Page Up, and Page Down keys to control the vertical scroll bar and the Left Arrow and Right Arrow keys to control the horizontal scroll bar. Here's the code to be added to the window procedure:

```
case WM_CHAR:
    switch (CHARMSG (&msg) ->vkey
        {
        case VK_LEFT:
        case VK_RIGHT:
            return WinSendMsg (hwndHscroll, msg, mp1, mp2) ;
        case VK_UP:
        case VK_DOWN:
        case VK_PAGEUP:
        case VK_PAGEDOWN:
            return WinSendMsg (hwndVscroll, msg, mp1, mp2) ;
        }
    break ;
```

Simple enough, wouldn't you say? With this addition, I declare the program finished. The name of the final version is simply SYSVALS without any degrading numeric suffix; the program is shown in Figure 4-14.

The SYSVALS File

```
#--------------------
# SYSVALS make file
#--------------------

sysvals.obj : sysvals.c sysvals.h
    cl -c -G2sw -W3 sysvals.c

sysvals.exe : sysvals.obj sysvals.def
    link sysvals, /align:16, NUL, os2, sysvals
```

The SYSVALS.C File

```
/*-------------------------------------------
   SYSVALS.C -- System Values Display Program
   ----------------------------------------------*/

#define INCL_WIN
#define INCL_GPI
#include <os2.h>
#include <stdlib.h>
#include <string.h>
#include "sysvals.h"

MRESULT EXPENTRY ClientWndProc (HWND, USHORT, MPARAM, MPARAM) ;

int main (void)
    {
    static CHAR  szClientClass [] = "SysVals" ;
    static ULONG flFrameFlags = FCF_TITLEBAR      | FCF_SYSMENU  |
                                FCF_SIZEBORDER     | FCF_MINMAX   |
                                FCF_SHELLPOSITION  | FCF_TASKLIST |
                                FCF_VERTSCROLL     | FCF_HORZSCROLL ;
    HAB            hab ;
    HMQ            hmq ;
    HWND           hwndFrame, hwndClient ;
    QMSG           qmsg ;

    hab = WinInitialize (0) ;
    hmq = WinCreateMsgQueue (hab, 0) ;

    WinRegisterClass (hab, szClientClass, ClientWndProc, CS_SIZEREDRAW, 0) ;

    hwndFrame = WinCreateStdWindow (HWND_DESKTOP, WS_VISIBLE,
                                    &flFrameFlags, szClientClass, NULL,
                                    OL, NULL, 0, &hwndClient) ;

    WinSendMsg (hwndFrame, WM_SETICON,
                WinQuerySysPointer (HWND_DESKTOP, SPTR_APPICON, FALSE),
                NULL) ;

    while (WinGetMsg (hab, &qmsg, NULL, 0, 0))
        WinDispatchMsg (hab, &qmsg) ;

    WinDestroyWindow (hwndFrame) ;
    WinDestroyMsgQueue (hmq) ;
    WinTerminate (hab) ;
    return 0 ;
    }
```

(continued)

Figure 4-14. The SYSVALS.C File. *continued*

```
LONG RtJustCharStringAt (HPS hps, POINTL *pptl, LONG lLength, CHAR *pchText)
    {
    POINTL aptlTextBox[TXTBOX_COUNT] ;

    GpiQueryTextBox (hps, lLength, pchText, TXTBOX_COUNT, aptlTextBox) ;

    pptl->x -= aptlTextBox[TXTBOX_CONCAT].x ;

    return GpiCharStringAt (hps, pptl, lLength, pchText) ;
    }

MRESULT EXPENTRY ClientWndProc (HWND hwnd, USHORT msg, MPARAM mp1, MPARAM mp2)
    {
    static HWND   hwndHscroll, hwndVscroll ;
    static SHORT  sHscrollMax, sVscrollMax, sHscrollPos, sVscrollPos,
                  cxChar, cxCaps, cyChar, cyDesc, cxClient, cyClient,
                  cxTextTotal ;
    CHAR          szBuffer [10] ;
    FONTMETRICS   fm ;
    HPS           hps ;
    POINTL        ptl ;
    SHORT         sLine, sPaintBeg, sPaintEnd, sHscrollInc, sVscrollInc ;
    RECTL         rclInvalid ;

    switch (msg)
        {
        case WM_CREATE:
            hps = WinGetPS (hwnd) ;

            GpiQueryFontMetrics (hps, (LONG) sizeof fm, &fm) ;

            cxChar = (SHORT) fm.lAveCharWidth ;
            cxCaps = (SHORT) fm.lEmInc ;
            cyChar = (SHORT) fm.lMaxBaselineExt ;
            cyDesc = (SHORT) fm.lMaxDescender ;

            WinReleasePS (hps) ;

            cxTextTotal = 28 * cxCaps + 38 * cxChar ;

            hwndHscroll = WinWindowFromID (
                              WinQueryWindow (hwnd, QW_PARENT, FALSE),
                              FID_HORZSCROLL) ;
```

(continued)

Figure 4-14. The SYSVALS.C File. *continued*

```
            hwndVscroll = WinWindowFromID (
                            WinQueryWindow (hwnd, QW_PARENT, FALSE),
                            FID_VERTSCROLL) ;
            return 0 ;

     case WM_SIZE:
          cxClient = SHORT1FROMMP (mp2) ;
          cyClient = SHORT2FROMMP (mp2) ;

          sHscrollMax = max (0, cxTextTotal - cxClient) ;
          sHscrollPos = min (sHscrollPos, sHscrollMax) ;

          WinSendMsg (hwndHscroll, SBM_SETSCROLLBAR,
                            MPFROM2SHORT (sHscrollPos, 0),
                            MPFROM2SHORT (0, sHscrollMax)) ;

          WinEnableWindow (hwndHscroll, sHscrollMax ? TRUE : FALSE) ;

          sVscrollMax = max (0, NUMLINES - cyClient / cyChar) ;
          sVscrollPos = min (sVscrollPos, sVscrollMax) ;

          WinSendMsg (hwndVscroll, SBM_SETSCROLLBAR,
                            MPFROM2SHORT (sVscrollPos, 0),
                            MPFROM2SHORT (0, sVscrollMax)) ;

          WinEnableWindow (hwndVscroll, sVscrollMax ? TRUE : FALSE) ;
          return 0 ;

     case WM_HSCROLL:
          switch (SHORT2FROMMP (mp2))
               {
               case SB_LINELEFT:
                    sHscrollInc = -cxCaps ;
                    break ;

               case SB_LINERIGHT:
                    sHscrollInc = cxCaps ;
                    break ;

               case SB_PAGELEFT:
                    sHscrollInc = -8 * cxCaps ;
                    break ;

               case SB_PAGERIGHT:
                    sHscrollInc = 8 * cxCaps ;
                    break ;
```

(continued)

Figure 4-14. The SYSVALS.C File. *continued*

```
                        case SB_SLIDERPOSITION:
                             sHscrollInc = SHORT1FROMMP (mp2) - sHscrollPos;
                             break ;

                        default:
                             sHscrollInc = 0 ;
                             break ;
                        }

                   sHscrollInc = max (-sHscrollPos,
                                  min (sHscrollInc, sHscrollMax - sHscrollPos)) ;

                   if (sHscrollInc != 0)
                        {
                        sHscrollPos += sHscrollInc ;
                        WinScrollWindow (hwnd, -sHscrollInc, 0,
                                       NULL, NULL, NULL, NULL, SW_INVALIDATERGN) ;

                        WinSendMsg (hwndHscroll, SBM_SETPOS,
                                  MPFROMSHORT (sHscrollPos), NULL) ;
                        }
                   return 0 ;

          case WM_VSCROLL:
               switch (SHORT2FROMMP (mp2))
                        {
                        case SB_LINEUP:
                             sVscrollInc = -1 ;
                             break ;

                        case SB_LINEDOWN:
                             sVscrollInc = 1 ;
                             break ;

                        case SB_PAGEUP:
                             sVscrollInc = min (-1, -cyClient / cyChar) ;
                             break ;

                        case SB_PAGEDOWN:
                             sVscrollInc = max (1, cyClient / cyChar) ;
                             break ;

                        case SB_SLIDERTRACK:
                             sVscrollInc = SHORT1FROMMP (mp2) - sVscrollPos;
                             break ;
```

(continued)

Figure 4-14. The SYSVALS.C File. *continued*

```
            default:
                sVscrollInc = 0 ;
                break ;
            }

        sVscrollInc = max (-sVscrollPos,
                    min (sVscrollInc, sVscrollMax - sVscrollPos)) ;

        if (sVscrollInc != 0) ;
            {
            sVscrollPos += sVscrollInc ;
            WinScrollWindow (hwnd, 0, cyChar * sVscrollInc,
                        NULL, NULL, NULL, NULL, SW_INVALIDATERGN) ;

            WinSendMsg (hwndVscroll, SBM_SETPOS,
                        MPFROMSHORT (sVscrollPos), NULL) ;
            WinUpdateWindow (hwnd) ;
            }
        return 0 ;

    case WM_CHAR:
        switch (CHARMSG(&msg)->vkey)
            {
            case VK_LEFT:
            case VK_RIGHT:
                return WinSendMsg (hwndHscroll, msg, mp1, mp2) ;
            case VK_UP:
            case VK_DOWN:
            case VK_PAGEUP:
            case VK_PAGEDOWN:
                return WinSendMsg (hwndVscroll, msg, mp1, mp2) ;
            }
        break ;

    case WM_PAINT:
        hps = WinBeginPaint (hwnd, NULL, &rclInvalid) ;
        GpiErase (hps) ;

        sPaintBeg = max (0, sVscrollPos +
                    (cyClient - (SHORT) rclInvalid.yTop) / cyChar) ;
        sPaintEnd = min (NUMLINES, sVscrollPos +
                    (cyClient - (SHORT) rclInvalid.yBottom)
                        / cyChar + 1) ;
```

(continued)

Figure 4-14. The SYSVALS.C File. *continued*

```
                    for (sLine = sPaintBeg ; sLine < sPaintEnd ; sLine++)
                        {
                        ptl.x = cxCaps - sHscrollPos ;
                        ptl.y = cyClient - cyChar * (sLine + 1 - sVscrollPos)
                                        + cyDesc ;

                        GpiCharStringAt (hps, &ptl,
                                    (LONG) strlen (sysvals[sLine].szIdentifier),
                                    sysvals[sLine].szIdentifier) ;

                        ptl.x += 20 * cxCaps ;
                        GpiCharStringAt (hps, &ptl,
                                    (LONG) strlen (sysvals[sLine].szDescription),
                                    sysvals[sLine].szDescription) ;

                        ltoa (WinQuerySysValue (HWND_DESKTOP,
                                    sysvals[sLine].sIndex), szBuffer, 10) ;

                        ptl.x += 38 * cxChar + 6 * cxCaps ;
                        RtJustCharStringAt (hps, &ptl, (LONG) strlen (szBuffer),
                                            szBuffer) ;
                        }

                WinEndPaint (hps) ;
                return 0 ;
            }
        return WinDefWindowProc (hwnd, msg, mp1, mp2) ;
        }
```

The SYSVALS.DEF File

```
;-----------------------------------
; SYSVALS.DEF module definition file
;-----------------------------------


NAME            SYSVALS    WINDOWAPI

DESCRIPTION     'System Values Display (C) Charles Petzold, 1988'
PROTMODE
HEAPSIZE        1024
STACKSIZE       8192
EXPORTS         ClientWndProc
```

Figure 4-14. *The final SYSVALS program.*

## CHAPTER FIVE

THE FIVE GPI PRIMITIVES

The world of computer graphics is often separated into two large categories: "raster" graphics and "vector" graphics. These terms refer both to graphics output devices and to the way that an application program draws graphics objects on these devices. Raster output devices display images that are made up of dots called pixels or "pels" (picture elements). Video displays, dot-matrix printers, and laser printers are all raster devices. Vector output devices — such as plotters — display images made up of lines and filled areas.

> **NOTE:** *The distinction between raster and vector devices gets a little fuzzy with devices such as the IBM 8514/A video display adapter and PostScript laser printers: Although these devices are technically raster devices, they contain a high-level graphics interface that understands and interprets vector drawing commands.*

The OS/2 Graphics Programming Interface (one of the two major components of the Presentation Manager, the other being the windowing and user interface) is fundamentally, but not exclusively, a vector graphics system: Presentation Manager programs draw graphics in terms of lines and filled areas. This approach works for every type of graphics output device — the drawing commands need only be translated by a device driver into a format the device can understand: vector drawing commands for vector output devices and pixels for raster devices.

GPI also has several functions for working with raster graphics. These functions allow a program to draw individual pixels (or, more commonly, collections of pixels called "bitmaps") on an output device. However, these functions are useful only with raster devices: Vector devices cannot adequately draw individual dots.

Vectors and rasters each have their place in the world of graphics. An architectural drawing is obviously a job for vector graphics, whereas the reproduction of a digitized photograph requires raster graphics. Accordingly, vector and raster graphics each have their place in this book: I cover vector graphics in this chapter and raster graphics in the next chapter.

The following sections describe the five GPI primitives that form the basis of the GPI vector graphics system: lines, patterned areas, text, marker symbols, and images.

GPI Primitive 1: Lines

When drawing text in Chapter 4 we specified the starting point of a text string using a POINTL structure. You also use the POINTL structure for drawing lines. POINTL is defined in OS2DEF.H like this:

```
typedef struct _POINTL
    {
    LONG x ;
    LONG y ;
    }
    POINTL ;
```

The two fields x and y define a point in terms of GPI coordinates. For a cached micro-PS, these coordinates are in units of pixels relative to the lower-left corner of the presentation space, which corresponds to the lower-left corner of the window. For convenience, I'll sometimes use the notation (x,y) to refer to a point in the presentation space. The point (0,0) is the lower-left corner of the window. The x (horizontal) coordinates increase to the right and the y (vertical) coordinates increase going up.

A structure variable of type POINTL is usually given a prefix of *ptl*. If you need only one POINTL structure variable, you can name it *ptl* and define it like this:

```
POINTL ptl ;
```

You can define an array of POINTL structures like this:

```
POINTL aptl[5] ;
```

and define a pointer to a POINTL structure like this:

```
POINTL *pptl ;
```

Simple Straight Lines

To draw a straight line, you must specify the two points that indicate the beginning and end of the line. Let's assume that *cxClient* and *cyClient* have been set to the width and height of the client window. Suppose you want to draw a diagonal line from the upper-left corner of the client window to the lower-right corner.

After obtaining a handle to a cached micro-PS from the *WinGetPS* or *WinBeginPaint* function, you set the two fields of a POINTL structure to the beginning of the line: the point (0,cyClient). You then call *GpiMove*:

```
ptl.x = 0 ;
ptl.y = cyClient ;
GpiMove (hps, &ptl) ;
```

GpiMove does not draw anything. Instead, it sets the "current position" (defined shortly) to the specified point.

You then set the two fields of the structure to the second point and call *GpiLine*:

```
ptl.x = cxClient ;
ptl.y = 0 ;
GpiLine (hps, &ptl) ;
```

GpiLine draws the line from (0,cyClient) to (cxClient,0).

Initially, it may seem annoying that drawing a single line requires four assignment statements and two function calls. The syntax of the *GpiMove* and *GpiLine* functions is defined in this way to be consistent with the *GpiPolyLine* and *GpiQueryCurrentPosition* functions discussed later in this chapter. In actual practice, it's usually not as inconvenient as it first appears to be.

The Current Position

We've just seen how the *GpiMove* function does not draw anything itself. Instead, it affects the operation of a subsequent call to *GpiLine*. The *GpiMove* function is said to set an "attribute" of the presentation space. In one sense, the presentation space is simply a data structure internal to GPI.

This data structure identifies the output device associated with the presentation space and also retains all the attributes of the presentation space.

The *GpiMove* function sets the current position to the point specified in the function. The current position is used by most GPI drawing functions as a starting position when drawing a graphics object such as a line.

When you first obtain a handle to a cached micro-PS by calling *WinGetPS* or *WinBeginPaint*, all the attributes are set to default values. The default current position is the point (0,0). When you release a presentation space handle by calling *WinReleasePS* or *WinEndPaint*, any changes you've made to the attributes are lost.

The *GpiLine* function uses the current position as a starting point for the line it draws and then sets the current position to the end of the line — the point specified in the *GpiLine* function. Thus, you can draw another line connected to the first by calling *GpiLine* again with a new point.

For example, suppose you want to draw a big ''V'' in your client window. This job requires just one call to *GpiMove* and two calls to *GpiLine*:

```
ptl.x = 0 ;
ptl.y = cyClient ;
GpiMove (hps, &ptl) ;

ptl.x = cxClient / 2 ;
ptl.y = 0 ;
GpiLine (hps, &ptl) ;

ptl.x = cxClient ;
ptl.y = cyClient ;
GpiLine (hps, &ptl) ;
```

If you enjoy typing long function names, you can use the *GpiSetCurrentPosition* function rather than *GpiMove*:

```
GpiSetCurrentPosition (hps, &ptl) ;
```

When using a cached micro-PS there is no difference between *GpiMove* and *GpiSetCurrentPosition*. You can also obtain the current position by using this function:

```
GpiQueryCurrentPosition (hps, &ptl) ;
```

Note that all four functions covered have had the same parameter syntax.

Some graphics programming languages have a function that draws a line from the current position to a point relative to the current position. GPI does not include such a function, but it's easy enough to write one:

```
LONG LineRelative (HPS hps, POINTL *pptlRelative)
    {
    POINTL ptl ;

    GpiQueryCurrentPosition (hps, &ptl) ;
    ptl.x += pptlRelative->x ;
    ptl.y += pptlRelative->y ;
    return GpiLine (hps, &ptl) ;
    }
```

The *pptl* prefix of *pptlRelative* stands for "pointer to a POINTL structure."

Throughout this chapter, we will work mostly with three types of GPI functions: functions that draw (like *GpiLine*), functions that set an attribute of the presentation space (like *GpiMove* and *GpiSetCurrentPosition*), and functions that query a presentation space attribute (like *GpiQueryCurrentPosition*). Most basic GPI functions fall into one of these three categories.

Drawing Multiple Lines

The current position stored in the presentation space allows you to draw a series of connected lines by making one call to *GpiMove* and multiple calls to *GpiLine*. However, for jobs of that type it is more efficient to use the *GpiPolyLine* function:

```
GpiPolyLine (hps, lCount, aptl) ;
```

The *aptl* parameter is an array of POINTL structures. The function draws *lCount* lines — the first from the current position to *aptl[0]*, the second from *aptl[0]* to *aptl[1]*, and so forth. The *lCount* parameter also indicates the number of points in the *aptl* array. When the function returns, the current point is set to the end of the last line it draws, the point *aptl[lCount - 1]*.

GpiPolyLine is functionally equivalent to the following:

```
for (lIndex = 0 ; lIndex < lCount ; lIndex++)
    GpiLine (hps, aptl + lIndex) ;
```

(Newcomers to C who are not yet entirely comfortable with the equivalence between array names and pointers might prefer the notation *&aptl[lIndex]* rather than *aptl+lIndex*.) However, any looping that *GpiPolyLine* performs occurs deep within a device driver. When drawing many connected lines, *GpiPolyLine* is much faster than multiple *GpiLine* calls.

The STAR5 program in Figure 5-1 shows how to draw a five-pointed star using *GpiMove* and *GpiPolyLine*.

The STAR5 File

```
#-----------------
# STAR5 make file
#-----------------

star5.obj : star5.c
    cl -c -G2sw -W3 star5.c

star5.exe : star5.obj star5.def
    link star5, /align:16, NUL, os2, star5
```

The STAR5.C File

```
/*---------------------------------
   STAR5.C -- Draws 5-Pointed Star
---------------------------------*/

#include <os2.h>

MRESULT EXPENTRY ClientWndProc (HWND, USHORT, MPARAM, MPARAM) ;

int main (void)
    {
    static CHAR  szClientClass [] = "Star5" ;
    static ULONG flFrameFlags = FCF_TITLEBAR     | FCF_SYSMENU |
                                FCF_SIZEBORDER    | FCF_MINMAX  |
                                FCF_SHELLPOSITION | FCF_TASKLIST ;
    HAB           hab ;
    HMQ           hmq ;
    HWND          hwndFrame, hwndClient ;
    QMSG          qmsg ;

    hab = WinInitialize (0) ;
    hmq = WinCreateMsgQueue (hab, 0) ;

    WinRegisterClass (hab, szClientClass, ClientWndProc, CS_SIZEREDRAW, 0) ;

    hwndFrame = WinCreateStdWindow (HWND_DESKTOP, WS_VISIBLE,
                                    &flFrameFlags, szClientClass, NULL,
                                    0L, NULL, 0, &hwndClient) ;
```

(continued)

Figure 5-1. The STAR5.C File. *continued*

```
        while (WinGetMsg (hab, &qmsg, NULL, 0, 0))
             WinDispatchMsg (hab, &qmsg) ;

        WinDestroyWindow (hwndFrame) ;
        WinDestroyMsgQueue (hmq) ;
        WinTerminate (hab) ;
        return 0 ;
        }

MRESULT EXPENTRY ClientWndProc (HWND hwnd, USHORT msg, MPARAM mp1, MPARAM mp2)
        {
        static POINTL aptlStar[5] = {-59,-81, 0,100, 59,-81, -95,31, 95,31 } ;
        static SHORT   cxClient, cyClient ;
        HPS            hps ;
        POINTL         aptl[5] ;
        SHORT          sIndex ;

        switch (msg)
             {
             case WM_SIZE:
                  cxClient = SHORT1FROMMP (mp2) ;
                  cyClient = SHORT2FROMMP (mp2) ;
                  return 0 ;

             case WM_PAINT:
                  hps = WinBeginPaint (hwnd, NULL, NULL) ;
                  GpiErase (hps) ;

                  for (sIndex = 0 ; sIndex < 5 ; sIndex++)
                       {
                       aptl[sIndex].x = cxClient / 2 + cxClient *
                                                  aptlStar[sIndex].x / 200 ;
                       aptl[sIndex].y = cyClient / 2 + cyClient *
                                                  aptlStar[sIndex].y / 200 ;
                       }
                  GpiMove (hps, aptl + 4) ;
                  GpiPolyLine (hps, 5L, aptl) ;

                  WinEndPaint (hps) ;
                  return 0 ;
             }
        return WinDefWindowProc (hwnd, msg, mp1, mp2) ;
        }
```

The STAR5.DEF File

```
;-----------------------------------
; STAR5.DEF module definition file
;-----------------------------------

NAME            STAR5     WINDOWAPI

DESCRIPTION     'Draws 5-Pointed Star (C) Charles Petzold, 1988'
PROTMODE
HEAPSIZE        1024
STACKSIZE       8192
EXPORTS         ClientWndProc
```

Figure 5-1. *The STAR5 program.*

The *aptlStar* array contains the five POINTL structures that define the star. These are specified in "virtual" coordinates, that is, a coordinate system that I fabricated. The point (0,0) is the center of the star, and the star extends 100 units in all four directions. STAR5 must convert these points so that the star fills the client window, as shown in Figure 5-2.

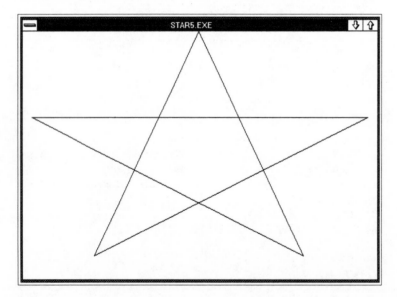

Figure 5-2. *The STAR5 display.*

STAR5 converts the virtual coordinates to client window coordinates during the *WM_PAINT* message. The *x* fields of the POINTL structures are multiplied by *cxClient* and divided by 200. This adjusts for the window width. Then half of *cxClient* is added to move the center of the star to the center of the client window. The *y* fields are adjusted similarly, and the resultant points are stored in the *aptl* array.

Notice how STAR5 calls *GpiMove* and *GpiPolyLine* to draw the star. First, it sets the current position to the *last* point in the array:

```
GpiMove (hps, aptl + 4) ;
```

(The expression *aptl + 4* is equivalent to *&aptl[4]*.) The *GpiPolyLine* function then draws five lines starting with a line to the *first* point in the array:

```
GpiPolyLine (hps, 5L, aptl) ;
```

The five lines that *GpiPolyLine* draws are as follows:

Line	Begin Point	End Point
1	aptl[4]	aptl[0]
2	aptl[0]	aptl[1]
3	aptl[1]	aptl[2]
4	aptl[2]	aptl[3]
5	aptl[3]	aptl[4]

It's necessary to initially set the current position to the last point in the array when the array defines a closed figure (like a star) and does not duplicate the first point. An alternative is to define an array of six POINTL structures, where the last point is the same as the first. In this case, you can draw the star by calling

```
GpiMove (hps, aptl) ;
GpiPolyLine (hps, 5L, aptl + 1) ;
```

STAR5 is the first program in this book that looks good when minimized and displayed as an icon at the bottom of the screen. For that reason, I've removed the logic that tells the frame window to use the SPTR_APPICON for the minimized state. To STAR5, the minimized state is simply a very small client window. When the window is minimized, *ClientWndProc* receives a WM_SIZE message with the size of this tiny window and then receives a WM_PAINT message.

Drawing Curves with *GpiPolyLine*

The *GpiPolyLine* function is deceptive. The function seems to draw a series of straight lines, and it can certainly be used for that purpose. But *GpiPolyLine* has a more important role, which is to draw curves. To do this, simply call *GpiPolyLine* with a POINTL array that defines many tiny lines.

Don't hesitate to call *GpiPolyLine* with an array of hundreds — or even thousands — of points. That's the purpose of the function. Because *GpiPolyLine* is interpreted by the device driver, it is very fast. The maximum number of points currently allowed for a *GpiPolyLine* call is 8000. This limit is based on the size of a POINTL structure (8 bytes) and the maximum size of the memory segment under the 80286 microprocessor (64 KB).

Any curve that you can define mathematically you can draw as a series of straight lines using *GpiPolyLine*. For example, suppose you want to draw one cycle of a sine curve in your client window. You can define an array of 100 POINTL structures and set the points to define the sine curve:

```
#include <math.h>              // for sin declaration
    :
POINTL aptl[100] ;
SHORT  sIndex ;
    :
for (sIndex = 0 ; sIndex < 100 ; sIndex++)
    {
    aptl[sIndex].x = (LONG) sIndex * cxClient / 100 ;
    aptl[sIndex].y = (LONG) (cyClient / 2 * (1 + sin (sIndex * 6.28 / 100))) ;
    }
```

The *x* fields of the POINTL structures range from 0 to *cxClient*. The *y* field is the value of the *sin* function over one period, scaled to the height of the client window.

To draw the sine curve, begin by setting the current position to the first point as follows:

```
GpiMove (hps, aptl) ;
```

You then use the *GpiPolyLine* function to draw 99 lines beginning at the second point:

```
GpiPolyLine (hps, 99L, aptl + 1) ;
```

Curves and Parametric Equations

The sine curve is relatively easy because the *y* coordinate is a simple function of the *x* coordinate. In general, however, this is not the case. There might be multiple *y* values for each value of *x*. A more generalized approach to drawing curves uses "parametric" equations.

In parametric equations, both the *x* and *y* coordinates of every point are calculated from functions based on a third variable, often called *t*. Intuitively, you can think of *t* as time or as some other abstract index necessary to define the entire curve. When you draw a curve using GPI functions, the values of *t* will range from 0 to the number of points that are in the POINTL array.

For example, suppose you want to draw an ellipse that fills your client window. You can start with parametric equations that define a unit circle:

$$x(t) = \cos(t)$$
$$y(t) = \sin(t)$$

For *t* ranging from 0 degrees to $2 \times \pi$ radians, these equations define a circle around the point (0,0) with a radius of 1. The ellipse is defined similarly:

$$x(t) = RX \cos(t)$$
$$y(t) = RY \sin(t)$$

The two axes of the ellipse are parallel to the horizontal and vertical axes. The horizontal ellipse axis is $2 \times RX$ in length; the vertical ellipse axis is $2 \times RY$. The ellipse is still centered around (0,0). To center it around the point (CX,CY), the formulas are

$$x(t) = CX + RX \cos(t)$$
$$y(t) = CY + RY \sin(t)$$

Here's the code to draw an ellipse centered in the client window:

```
#include <math.h>            // for sin and cos declaration
    ⋮

double dAngle ;
POINTL aptl[100] ;
SHORT  sIndex ;
    ⋮

for (sIndex = 0 ; sIndex <= 100 ; sIndex ++)
    {
    dAngle = sIndex * 6.28 / 100 ;
```

(continued)

continued

```
      aptl[sIndex].x = (LONG) (cxClient / 2 * (1 + cos (dAngle))) ;
      aptl[sIndex].y = (LONG) (cyClient / 2 * (1 + sin (dAngle))) ;
      }
GpiMove (hps, aptl) ;
GpiPolyLine (hps, 99L, aptl + 1) ;
```

In this case, both RX and CX are equal to *cxClient/2*, and RY and CY are equal to *cyClient/2*.

The SPIRAL program shown in Figure 5-3 uses a variation of these formulas to draw a spiral in its client window.

The SPIRAL File

```
#------------------
# SPIRAL make file
#------------------

spiral.obj : spiral.c
     cl -c -G2sw -W3 spiral.c

spiral.exe : spiral.obj spiral.def
     link spiral, /align:16, NUL, os2, spiral
```

The SPIRAL.C File

```
/*--------------------------------
    SPIRAL.C -- GPI Spiral Drawing
--------------------------------*/

#include <os2.h>
#include <math.h>

#define NUMPOINTS 1000
#define NUMREV    20
#define PI        3.14159

MRESULT EXPENTRY ClientWndProc (HWND, USHORT, MPARAM, MPARAM) ;
```

(continued)

Figure 5-3. The SPIRAL.C File. *continued*

```
int main (void)
    {
    static CHAR   szClientClass [] = "Spiral" ;
    static ULONG  flFrameFlags = FCF_TITLEBAR      | FCF_SYSMENU |
                                 FCF_SIZEBORDER    | FCF_MINMAX |
                                 FCF_SHELLPOSITION | FCF_TASKLIST ;

    HAB           hab ;
    HMQ           hmq ;
    HWND          hwndFrame, hwndClient ;
    QMSG          qmsg ;

    hab = WinInitialize (0) ;
    hmq = WinCreateMsgQueue (hab, 0) ;

    WinRegisterClass (hab, szClientClass, ClientWndProc, CS_SIZEREDRAW, 0) ;

    hwndFrame = WinCreateStdWindow (HWND_DESKTOP, WS_VISIBLE,
                                    &flFrameFlags, szClientClass, NULL,
                                    OL, NULL, 0, &hwndClient) ;

    while (WinGetMsg (hab, &qmsg, NULL, 0, 0))
        WinDispatchMsg (hab, &qmsg) ;

    WinDestroyWindow (hwndFrame) ;
    WinDestroyMsgQueue (hmq) ;
    WinTerminate (hab) ;
    return 0 ;
    }

MRESULT EXPENTRY ClientWndProc (HWND hwnd, USHORT msg, MPARAM mp1, MPARAM mp2)
    {
    static SHORT  cxClient, cyClient ;
    double        dAngle, dScale ;
    HPS           hps ;
    PPOINTL       pptl ;
    SEL           sel ;
    SHORT         sIndex ;

    switch (msg)
        {
        case WM_SIZE:
            cxClient = SHORT1FROMMP (mp2) ;
            cyClient = SHORT2FROMMP (mp2) ;
            return 0 ;
```

(continued)

Figure 5-3. The SPIRAL.C File. *continued*

```
        case WM_PAINT:
             hps = WinBeginPaint (hwnd, NULL, NULL) ;
             GpiErase (hps) ;

             if (!DosAllocSeg (NUMPOINTS * sizeof (POINTL), &sel, 0))
                {
                pptl = MAKEP (sel, 0) ;

                for (sIndex = 0 ; sIndex < NUMPOINTS ; sIndex ++)
                   {
                   dAngle = sIndex * 2 * PI / (NUMPOINTS / NUMREV) ;
                   dScale = 1 - (double) sIndex / NUMPOINTS ;

                   pptl[sIndex].x = (LONG) (cxClient / 2 *
                                            (1 + dScale * cos (dAngle))) ;

                   pptl[sIndex].y = (LONG) (cyClient / 2 *
                                            (1 + dScale * sin (dAngle))) ;
                   }
                GpiMove (hps, pptl) ;
                GpiPolyLine (hps, NUMPOINTS - 1L, pptl + 1) ;

                DosFreeSeg (sel) ;
                }
             WinEndPaint (hps) ;
             return 0 ;
        }
    return WinDefWindowProc (hwnd, msg, mp1, mp2) ;
    }
```

The SPIRAL.DEF File

```
;------------------------------------
; SPIRAL.DEF module definition file
;------------------------------------

NAME          SPIRAL    WINDOWAPI

DESCRIPTION   'GPI Spiral Using a Polyline (C) Charles Petzold, 1988'
PROTMODE
HEAPSIZE      1024
STACKSIZE     8192
EXPORTS       ClientWndProc
```

Figure 5-3. *The SPIRAL program.*

In effect, SPIRAL draws 20 ellipses but uniformly decreases the length of the axes to create a spiral as shown in Figure 5-4.

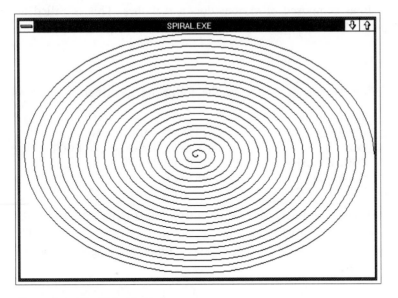

Figure 5-4. *The SPIRAL display.*

SPIRAL uses 1000 points to describe this figure. The program allocates a block of memory for this array by calling the OS/2 *DosAllocSeg* function. This function returns a selector (segment address) to the memory block, which is stored in the variable *sel*. The MAKEP macro makes a far (32-bit) pointer from *sel* and stores it in *pptl*. Note that *pptl* is not defined as a POINTL variable, but as a PPOINTL. PPOINTL is defined in OS2DEF.H as a far pointer to a POINTL structure:

```
typedef POINTL FAR *PPOINTL ;
```

The segment is freed after the drawing is finished.

You can also use the C *malloc* and *free* functions for allocating memory to store arrays of POINTL structures, in which case you would want to define the *pptl* pointer like this:

```
POINTL *pptl ;
```

Whether *pptl* is a far pointer or near pointer now depends on what memory model you specify when compiling the program. This will be compatible with the pointer returned from *malloc* and passed to *free*.

The Line Type

Up until now all the lines we have drawn have been solid lines. You can also draw lines composed of various dots and dashes. This is called the "line type attribute" and you set it with the *GpiSetLineType* function:

```
GpiSetLineType (hps, lLineType) ;
```

The *lLineType* parameter is one of the following identifiers defined in PMGPI.H:

LINETYPE_DEFAULT   LINETYPE_LONGDASH
LINETYPE_DOT   LINETYPE_DASHDOUBLEDOT
LINETYPE_SHORTDASH   LINETYPE_SOLID
LINETYPE_DASHDOT   LINETYPE_INVISIBLE
LINETYPE_DOUBLEDOT   LINETYPE_ALTERNATE

These identifiers are fairly self-explanatory. The LINETYPE_DEFAULT identifier (defined as 0L) has the same effect as LINETYPE_SOLID. The LINETYPE_ALTERNATE style draws every other pixel, giving the appearance of a gray line.

The line type is an attribute of the presentation space. When you set the line type, it affects all subsequent lines you draw until you change the line type again or release the presentation space.

You can determine the current line type by calling

```
lLineType = GpiQueryLineType (hps) ;
```

However, if you call *GpiQueryLineType* for a new presentation space without first calling *GpiSetLineType*, the function returns an identifier of LINETYPE_DEFAULT rather than LINETYPE_SOLID.

The LINETYPE program (Figure 5-5) displays lines drawn with each of these line types so that you can see what they look like.

The LINETYPE File

```
#-------------------
# LINETYPE make file
#-------------------

linetype.obj : linetype.c
    cl -c -G2sw -W3 linetype.c
```

(continued)

Figure 5-5. The LINETYPE File. *continued*

```
linetype.exe : linetype.obj linetype.def
     link linetype, /align:16, NUL, os2, linetype
```

The LINETYPE.C File

```
/*-------------------------------
   LINETYPE.C -- GPI Line Types
   -----------------------------*/

#define INCL_WIN
#define INCL_GPI
#include <os2.h>
#include <string.h>

MRESULT EXPENTRY ClientWndProc (HWND, USHORT, MPARAM, MPARAM) ;

int main (void)
    {
    static CHAR  szClientClass [] = "LineType" ;
    static ULONG flFrameFlags = FCF_TITLEBAR       | FCF_SYSMENU  |
                                FCF_SIZEBORDER     | FCF_MINMAX   |
                                FCF_SHELLPOSITION  | FCF_TASKLIST ;

    HAB          hab ;
    HMQ          hmq ;
    HWND         hwndFrame, hwndClient ;
    QMSG         qmsg ;

    hab = WinInitialize (0) ;
    hmq = WinCreateMsgQueue (hab, 0) ;

    WinRegisterClass (hab, szClientClass, ClientWndProc, CS_SIZEREDRAW, 0) ;

    hwndFrame = WinCreateStdWindow (HWND_DESKTOP, WS_VISIBLE,
                                    &flFrameFlags, szClientClass, NULL,
                                    0L, NULL, 0, &hwndClient) ;

    WinSendMsg (hwndFrame, WM_SETICON,
                WinQuerySysPointer (HWND_DESKTOP, SPTR_APPICON, FALSE),
                NULL) ;

    while (WinGetMsg (hab, &qmsg, NULL, 0, 0))
        WinDispatchMsg (hab, &qmsg) ;
```

(continued)

Figure 5-5. The LINETYPE.C File. *continued*

```
        WinDestroyWindow (hwndFrame) ;
        WinDestroyMsgQueue (hmq) ;
        WinTerminate (hab) ;
        return 0 ;
        }


MRESULT EXPENTRY ClientWndProc (HWND hwnd, USHORT msg, MPARAM mp1, MPARAM mp2)
        {
        static struct {
                    LONG lLineType ;
                    CHAR *szLineType ;
                    }
                    show [] =
                    {
                    LINETYPE_DEFAULT       , "LINETYPE_DEFAULT"       ,
                    LINETYPE_DOT           , "LINETYPE_DOT"           ,
                    LINETYPE_SHORTDASH     , "LINETYPE_SHORTDASH"     ,
                    LINETYPE_DASHDOT       , "LINETYPE_DASHDOT"       ,
                    LINETYPE_DOUBLEDOT     , "LINETYPE_DOUBLEDOT"     ,
                    LINETYPE_LONGDASH      , "LINETYPE_LONGDASH"      ,
                    LINETYPE_DASHDOUBLEDOT , "LINETYPE_DASHDOUBLEDOT" ,
                    LINETYPE_SOLID         , "LINETYPE_SOLID"         ,
                    LINETYPE_INVISIBLE     , "LINETYPE_INVISIBLE"     ,
                    LINETYPE_ALTERNATE     , "LINETYPE_ALTERNATE"
                    } ;
        static SHORT   cxClient, cyClient, cxCaps, cyChar, cyDesc,
                       sNumTypes = sizeof show / sizeof show[0] ;
        FONTMETRICS    fm ;
        HPS            hps ;
        POINTL         ptl ;
        SHORT          sIndex ;

        switch (msg)
            {
            case WM_CREATE:
                hps = WinGetPS (hwnd) ;
                GpiQueryFontMetrics (hps, (LONG) sizeof fm, &fm) ;
                cxCaps = (SHORT) fm.lEmInc ;
                cyChar = (SHORT) fm.lMaxBaselineExt ;
                cyDesc = (SHORT) fm.lMaxDescender ;
                WinReleasePS (hps) ;
                return 0 ;
```

(continued)

Figure 5-5. The LINETYPE.C File. *continued*

```
        case WM_SIZE:
             cxClient = SHORT1FROMMP (mp2) ;
             cyClient = SHORT2FROMMP (mp2) ;
             return 0 ;

        case WM_PAINT:
             hps = WinBeginPaint (hwnd, NULL, NULL) ;
             GpiErase (hps) ;

             for (sIndex = 0 ; sIndex < sNumTypes ; sIndex ++)
                 {
                 GpiSetLineType (hps, show [sIndex].lLineType) ;

                 ptl.x = cxCaps ;
                 ptl.y = cyClient - 2 * (sIndex + 1) * cyChar + cyDesc ;

                 GpiCharStringAt (hps, &ptl,
                                  (LONG) strlen (show [sIndex].szLineType),
                                  show [sIndex].szLineType) ;

                 if (cxClient > 25 * cxCaps)
                     {
                     ptl.x = 24 * cxCaps ;
                     ptl.y += cyChar / 2 - cyDesc ;
                     GpiMove (hps, &ptl) ;

                     ptl.x = cxClient - cxCaps ;
                     GpiLine (hps, &ptl) ;
                     }
                 }
             WinEndPaint (hps) ;
             return 0 ;
        }
   return WinDefWindowProc (hwnd, msg, mp1, mp2) ;
   }
```

The LINETYPE.DEF File

```
;-----------------------------------------
; LINETYPE.DEF module definition file
;-----------------------------------------

NAME            LINETYPE  WINDOWAPI

DESCRIPTION     'GPI Line Types (C) Charles Petzold, 1988'
PROTMODE
HEAPSIZE        1024
STACKSIZE       8192
EXPORTS         ClientWndProc
```

Figure 5-5. *The LINETYPE program.*

The results are shown in Figure 5-6.

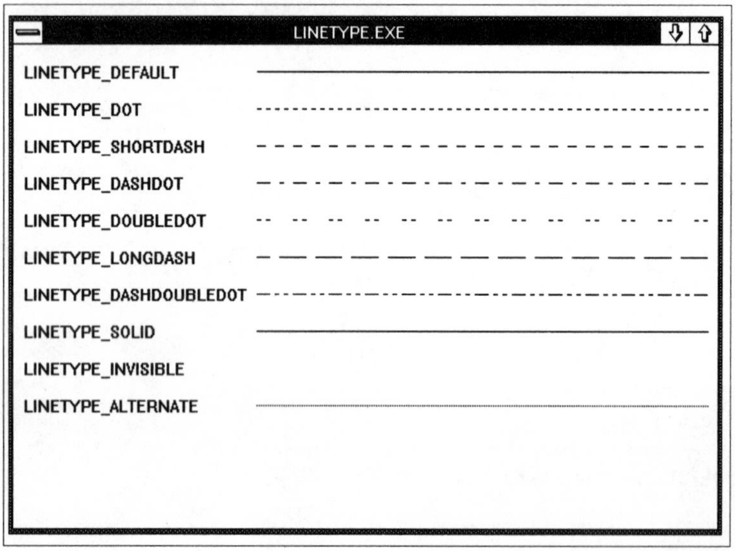

Figure 5-6. *The LINETYPE display.*

Each line type is a short sequence of dots or dashes that is repeated over the length of the line. You can use these line types when drawing multiple lines (even very short ones) with *GpiPolyLine*. When drawing each line, the device driver keeps track of which part of the short sequence it drew in the last line. The next line picks up where the last line ended. You can also use the line types with successive *GpiLine* calls. However, the device driver resets its position to the beginning of the sequence when you call *GpiMove*, *GpiSetCurrentPosition*, or *GpiSetLineType*.

Boxes and a Simple Ellipse

Probably the most common closed figure is a rectangle. You can draw a rectangle with one *GpiMove* and four *GpiLine* calls, or you can use the function that GPI provides:

```
GpiBox (hps, lOption, &ptl, 0L, 0L) ;
```

The *GpiBox* function draws a rectangle with sides parallel to the *x* and *y* axes. The position and size of the rectangle are defined by any two opposite corners of the rectangle. *GpiBox* uses the current position for one corner and the POINTL structure passed to the function for the opposite corner. *GpiBox* does not change the current position.

The *lOption* parameter can be one of the following identifiers defined in PMGPI.H:

DRO_FILL
DRO_OUTLINE
DRO_OUTLINEFILL

DRO_FILL causes the rectangle to be filled. The DRO_OUTLINE option directs GPI to draw only the outline of the rectangle. DRO_OUTLINEFILL draws the outline and fills the rectangle. GPI uses the current line type for drawing the outline. How GPI fills the interior of the rectangle is discussed in the following section on patterned areas.

Suppose *cxClient* and *cyClient* are the width and height of your client window. You want to draw an unfilled rectangle that is one half that width and height and centered in the client window. Here's the code:

```
ptl.x = xClient / 4 ;
ptl.y = yClient / 4 ;
GpiMove (hps, &ptl) ;

ptl.x *= 3 ;
ptl.y *= 3 ;
GpiBox (hps, DRO_OUTLINE, &ptl, 0L, 0L) ;
```

You can set the last two parameters of *GpiBox* to values greater than 0 to draw a rectangle with rounded corners. The general syntax of *GpiBox* is

```
GpiBox (hps, lOption, &ptl, cxEllipseAxis, cyEllipseAxis) ;
```

The last two parameters define the width and height of an ellipse. (These dimensions must be less than or equal to the width and height of the rectangle being drawn.) You can visualize GPI cutting this ellipse into four quadrants and using each quadrant of the ellipse as a corner of the box.

If *cxEllipseAxis* and *cyEllipseAxis* are set equal to the width and height of the rectangle being drawn, then *GpiBox* draws an ellipse. Here's a simple ellipse function that calculates the last two parameters of *GpiBox*:

```
#include <stdlib.h>          // For labs declaration
    ⋮

LONG Ellipse (HPS hps, LONG lOption, POINTL *pptl)
    {
    POINTL ptlCurrent ;

    GpiQueryCurrentPosition (hps, &ptlCurrent) ;

    return GpiBox (hps, lOption, pptl, labs (pptl->x - ptlCurrent.x),
                                       labs (pptl->y - ptlCurrent.y)) ;
    }
```

Like *GpiBox*, this *Ellipse* function draws a figure with axes parallel to the sides of the window. GPI provides even more versatile ellipse drawing facilities with the *GpiSetArcParams*, *GpiFullArc*, *GpiPointArc*, and *GpiPartialArc* functions. Other GPI functions that draw curves are *GpiPolySpline*, *GpiPolyFillet*, and *GpiPolyFilletSharp*.

Pixels and Device Independence

Until now, we've been working in a coordinate system based on units of pixels. To some people familiar with other graphics programming languages, the idea of working in units of pixels may seem a contradiction to the goal of writing device-independent programs. After all, what can be more device-dependent than pixels?

Pixels certainly have problems. The first is resolution. Almost every graphics output device has a different pixel resolution. A 100-pixel-high image on an IBM Color Graphics Adapter will encompass half the height of the screen. On a 300-dots-per-inch laser printer, it will be 1/3 inch high. Second, many video display adapters and dot-matrix printers use different horizontal and vertical resolutions.

Let's examine some ways to deal with these problems.

Simple Techniques

If you draw in units of pixels, you can use pixels in a device-independent manner. One simple technique (used in the SYSVALS programs in Chapter 4 and the LINETYPE program earlier in this chapter) involves basing all coordinates and dimensions on the size of the standard system font characters.

This technique is particularly useful when a program combines text with some rudimentary graphics. For example, suppose you want to write a simple database program using an index card metaphor. Each record is displayed in a simulated 3×5-inch index card on the screen. How large are the index cards in pixels? Think of a typewriter. A typewriter with a pica typeface types 10 characters per inch horizontally with 6 lines to the inch vertically. Thus a 3×5 card can fit 18 rows of 50 characters each. If *cxChar* and *cyChar* are the average width and height of a system font character, then each card is ($50 \times cxChar$) pixels wide and ($18 \times cyChar$) pixels high.

Sometimes you need to display only graphics in your window and you want the size of the objects to be based on the size of the window. In this case, you can use the technique shown earlier in the STAR5 program. The five-pointed star in that program is defined in a virtual coordinate system centered around the point (0,0) with a width of 200 units and a height of 200 units. Before drawing the object, the program scales these units to the size of the client window and translates the points so that (0,0) corresponds to the center of the window.

Of course, for some applications these approaches are not satisfactory at all. For example, how do you draw a square with sides of equal length? If the output device has different horizontal and vertical resolutions, then the horizontal and vertical dimensions of the object must be scaled differently.

The Device Context and Its Capabilities

You'll recall from Chapter 4 that a "device context" refers to a graphics output device (such as a video display or a printer) and its device driver. A presentation space is associated with a particular device context. A cached micro-PS is always associated with the device context for the video display.

A program can obtain lots of interesting information about an output device — including everything it needs to accurately scale graphics objects — by calling the *DevQueryCaps* ("query capabilities") function. To use *DevQueryCaps* for the video display, you first need a handle to the video display device context. You can obtain this easily during WM_CREATE processing by calling *WinOpenWindowDC* as shown on the next page.

```
static HDC hdc ;
    :

hdc = WinOpenWindowDC (hwnd) ;
```

Or, you can obtain a handle to the device context associated with a presentation space by calling

```
hdc = GpiQueryDevice (hps) ;
```

The PMDEV.H header file defines 39 identifiers, each beginning with the word CAPS, that you use with *DevQueryCaps*. Each identifer obtains a particular item that describes the device. Although you can obtain information about multiple items, it's easier to use *DevQueryCaps* for only one item at a time:

```
LONG lCapsValue ;
    :

DevQueryCaps (hdc, CAPS... , 1L, &lCapsValue) ;
```

The DEVCAPS program shown in Figure 5-7 obtains all the information available from *DevQueryCaps* and displays it in a simple two-column format.

The DEVCAPS File

```
#-------------------
# DEVCAPS make file
#-------------------

devcaps.obj : devcaps.c devcaps.h
    cl -c -G2sw -W3 devcaps.c

devcaps.exe : devcaps.obj devcaps.def
    link devcaps, /align:16, NUL, os2, devcaps
```

The DEVCAPS.C File

```
/*-------------------------------------------------------
   DEVCAPS.C -- Device Capabilities Display Program
   -----------------------------------------------------*/

#define INCL_WIN
#define INCL_GPI
#include <os2.h>
#include <stdlib.h>
#include <string.h>
#include "devcaps.h"

MRESULT EXPENTRY ClientWndProc (HWND, USHORT, MPARAM, MPARAM) ;

int main (void)
    {
    static CHAR   szClientClass [] = "DevCaps" ;
    static ULONG  flFrameFlags = FCF_TITLEBAR     | FCF_SYSMENU |
                                 FCF_SIZEBORDER    | FCF_MINMAX  |
                                 FCF_SHELLPOSITION | FCF_TASKLIST ;
    HAB           hab ;
    HMQ           hmq ;
    HWND          hwndFrame, hwndClient ;
    QMSG          qmsg ;

    hab = WinInitialize (0) ;
    hmq = WinCreateMsgQueue (hab, 0) ;

    WinRegisterClass (hab, szClientClass, ClientWndProc, OL, 0) ;

    hwndFrame = WinCreateStdWindow (HWND_DESKTOP, WS_VISIBLE,
                             &flFrameFlags, szClientClass, NULL,
                             OL, NULL, 0, &hwndClient) ;

    WinSendMsg (hwndFrame, WM_SETICON,
                WinQuerySysPointer (HWND_DESKTOP, SPTR_APPICON, FALSE),
                NULL) ;

    while (WinGetMsg (hab, &qmsg, NULL, 0, 0))
        WinDispatchMsg (hab, &qmsg) ;
```

(continued)

Figure 5-7. The DEVCAPS.C File. *continued*

```
        WinDestroyWindow (hwndFrame) ;
        WinDestroyMsgQueue (hmq) ;
        WinTerminate (hab) ;
        return 0 ;
        }


LONG RtJustCharStringAt (HPS hps, POINTL *pptl, LONG lLength, CHAR *pchText)
        {
        POINTL aptlTextBox[TXTBOX_COUNT] ;

        GpiQueryTextBox (hps, lLength, pchText, TXTBOX_COUNT, aptlTextBox) ;

        pptl->x -= aptlTextBox[TXTBOX_CONCAT].x ;

        return GpiCharStringAt (hps, pptl, lLength, pchText) ;
        }


MRESULT EXPENTRY ClientWndProc (HWND hwnd, USHORT msg, MPARAM mp1, MPARAM mp2)
        {
        static HDC    hdc ;
        static SHORT  cxClient, cyClient, cxCaps, cyChar, cyDesc ;
        CHAR          szBuffer [12] ;
        FONTMETRICS   fm ;
        LONG          lValue ;
        POINTL        ptl ;
        HPS           hps ;
        SHORT         sLine ;

        switch (msg)
            {
            case WM_CREATE:
                 hps = WinGetPS (hwnd) ;
                 GpiQueryFontMetrics (hps, (LONG) sizeof fm, &fm) ;
                 cxCaps = (SHORT) fm.lEmInc ;
                 cyChar = (SHORT) fm.lMaxBaselineExt ;
                 cyDesc = (SHORT) fm.lMaxDescender ;
                 WinReleasePS (hps) ;

                 hdc = WinOpenWindowDC (hwnd) ;
                 return 0 ;

            case WM_SIZE:
                 cxClient = SHORT1FROMMP (mp2) ;
                 cyClient = SHORT2FROMMP (mp2) ;
                 return 0 ;
```

(continued)

Figure 5-7. The DEVCAPS.C File. *continued*

```
        case WM_PAINT:
            hps = WinBeginPaint (hwnd, NULL, NULL) ;
            GpiErase (hps) ;

            for (sLine = 0 ; sLine < NUMLINES ; sLine++)
                {
                ptl.x = cxCaps ;
                ptl.y = cyClient - cyChar * (sLine + 2) + cyDesc ;

                if (sLine >= (NUMLINES + 1) / 2)
                    {
                    ptl.x += cxCaps * 35 ;
                    ptl.y += cyChar * (NUMLINES + 1) / 2 ;
                    }

                DevQueryCaps (hdc, devcaps[sLine].lIndex, 1L, &lValue) ;

                GpiCharStringAt (hps, &ptl,
                        (LONG) strlen (devcaps[sLine].szIdentifier),
                        devcaps[sLine].szIdentifier) ;

                ptl.x += 33 * cxCaps ;
                RtJustCharStringAt (hps, &ptl,
                        (LONG) strlen (ltoa (lValue, szBuffer, 10)),
                        szBuffer) ;
                }
            WinEndPaint (hps) ;
            return 0 ;
        }
    return WinDefWindowProc (hwnd, msg, mp1, mp2) ;
    }
```

The DEVCAPS.H File

```
/*-----------------------
   DEVCAPS.H header file
   --------------------*/

#define NUMLINES (sizeof devcaps / sizeof devcaps [0])

struct
    {
    LONG lIndex ;
```

(continued)

Figure 5-7. The DEVCAPS.H File. *continued*

```
CHAR *szIdentifier ;
}
devcaps [] =
{
CAPS_FAMILY                      , "CAPS_FAMILY"                      ,
CAPS_IO_CAPS                     , "CAPS_IO_CAPS"                     ,
CAPS_TECHNOLOGY                  , "CAPS_TECHNOLOGY"                  ,
CAPS_DRIVER_VERSION              , "CAPS_DRIVER_VERSION"              ,
CAPS_HEIGHT                      , "CAPS_HEIGHT"                      ,
CAPS_WIDTH                       , "CAPS_WIDTH"                       ,
CAPS_HEIGHT_IN_CHARS             , "CAPS_HEIGHT_IN_CHARS"             ,
CAPS_WIDTH_IN_CHARS              , "CAPS_WIDTH_IN_CHARS"              ,
CAPS_VERTICAL_RESOLUTION         , "CAPS_VERTICAL_RESOLUTION"         ,
CAPS_HORIZONTAL_RESOLUTION       , "CAPS_HORIZONTAL_RESOLUTION"       ,
CAPS_CHAR_HEIGHT                 , "CAPS_CHAR_HEIGHT"                 ,
CAPS_CHAR_WIDTH                  , "CAPS_CHAR_WIDTH"                  ,
CAPS_SMALL_CHAR_HEIGHT           , "CAPS_SMALL_CHAR_HEIGHT"           ,
CAPS_SMALL_CHAR_WIDTH            , "CAPS_SMALL_CHAR_WIDTH"            ,
CAPS_COLORS                      , "CAPS_COLORS"                      ,
CAPS_COLOR_PLANES                , "CAPS_COLOR_PLANES"                ,
CAPS_COLOR_BITCOUNT              , "CAPS_COLOR_BITCOUNT"              ,
CAPS_COLOR_TABLE_SUPPORT         , "CAPS_COLOR_TABLE_SUPPORT"         ,
CAPS_MOUSE_BUTTONS               , "CAPS_MOUSE_BUTTONS"               ,
CAPS_FOREGROUND_MIX_SUPPORT      , "CAPS_FOREGROUND_MIX_SUPPORT"      ,
CAPS_BACKGROUND_MIX_SUPPORT      , "CAPS_BACKGROUND_MIX_SUPPORT"      ,
CAPS_VIO_LOADABLE_FONTS          , "CAPS_VIO_LOADABLE_FONTS"          ,
CAPS_WINDOW_BYTE_ALIGNMENT       , "CAPS_WINDOW_BYTE_ALIGNMENT"       ,
CAPS_BITMAP_FORMATS              , "CAPS_BITMAP_FORMATS"              ,
CAPS_RASTER_CAPS                 , "CAPS_RASTER_CAPS"                 ,
CAPS_MARKER_HEIGHT               , "CAPS_MARKER_HEIGHT"               ,
CAPS_MARKER_WIDTH                , "CAPS_MARKER_WIDTH"                ,
CAPS_DEVICE_FONTS                , "CAPS_DEVICE_FONTS"                ,
CAPS_GRAPHICS_SUBSET             , "CAPS_GRAPHICS_SUBSET"             ,
CAPS_GRAPHICS_VERSION            , "CAPS_GRAPHICS_VERSION"            ,
CAPS_GRAPHICS_VECTOR_SUBSET      , "CAPS_GRAPHICS_VECTOR_SUBSET"      ,
CAPS_DEVICE_WINDOWING            , "CAPS_DEVICE_WINDOWING"            ,
CAPS_ADDITIONAL_GRAPHICS         , "CAPS_ADDITIONAL_GRAPHICS"         ,
CAPS_PHYS_COLORS                 , "CAPS_PHYS_COLORS"                 ,
CAPS_COLOR_INDEX                 , "CAPS_COLOR_INDEX"                 ,
CAPS_GRAPHICS_CHAR_WIDTH         , "CAPS_GRAPHICS_CHAR_WIDTH"         ,
CAPS_GRAPHICS_CHAR_HEIGHT        , "CAPS_GRAPHICS_CHAR_HEIGHT"        ,
CAPS_HORIZONTAL_FONT_RES         , "CAPS_HORIZONTAL_FONT_RES"         ,
CAPS_VERTICAL_FONT_RES           , "CAPS_VERTICAL_FONT_RES"
} ;
```

The DEVCAPS.DEF File

```
;-----------------------------------
; DEVCAPS.DEF module definition file
;-----------------------------------

NAME            DEVCAPS    WINDOWAPI

DESCRIPTION     'Device Capabilities (C) Charles Petzold, 1988'
PROTMODE
HEAPSIZE        1024
STACKSIZE       8192
EXPORTS         ClientWndProc
```

Figure 5-7. *The DEVCAPS program.*

When the Presentation Manager is running on an IBM Enhanced Graphics Adapter, DEVCAPS returns the information shown in Figure 5-8.

DEVCAPS.EXE			
CAPS_FAMILY	5	CAPS_BACKGROUND_MIX_SUPPORT	18
CAPS_IO_CAPS	2	CAPS_VIO_LOADABLE_FONTS	0
CAPS_TECHNOLOGY	2	CAPS_WINDOW_BYTE_ALIGNMENT	0
CAPS_DRIVER_VERSION	256	CAPS_BITMAP_FORMATS	2
CAPS_HEIGHT	350	CAPS_RASTER_CAPS	49
CAPS_WIDTH	640	CAPS_MARKER_HEIGHT	9
CAPS_HEIGHT_IN_CHARS	24	CAPS_MARKER_WIDTH	9
CAPS_WIDTH_IN_CHARS	80	CAPS_DEVICE_FONTS	0
CAPS_VERTICAL_RESOLUTION	2000	CAPS_GRAPHICS_SUBSET	0
CAPS_HORIZONTAL_RESOLUTION	2667	CAPS_GRAPHICS_VERSION	0
CAPS_CHAR_HEIGHT	12	CAPS_GRAPHICS_VECTOR_SUBSET	0
CAPS_CHAR_WIDTH	8	CAPS_DEVICE_WINDOWING	0
CAPS_SMALL_CHAR_HEIGHT	8	CAPS_ADDITIONAL_GRAPHICS	40
CAPS_SMALL_CHAR_WIDTH	8	CAPS_PHYS_COLORS	64
CAPS_COLORS	16	CAPS_COLOR_INDEX	63
CAPS_COLOR_PLANES	1	CAPS_GRAPHICS_CHAR_WIDTH	9
CAPS_COLOR_BITCOUNT	4	CAPS_GRAPHICS_CHAR_HEIGHT	12
CAPS_COLOR_TABLE_SUPPORT	0	CAPS_HORIZONTAL_FONT_RES	96
CAPS_MOUSE_BUTTONS	0	CAPS_VERTICAL_FONT_RES	72
CAPS_FOREGROUND_MIX_SUPPORT	123		

Figure 5-8. *The DEVCAPS display.*

Some information is encoded in bits in the return values. You'll need the Presentation Manager documentation and the PMDEV.H header file in order to decode it. For now, we'll look at four items: CAPS_HEIGHT and CAPS_WIDTH give the pixel dimensions of the output device (in this case the video display). CAPS_VERTICAL_RESOLUTION and CAPS-_HORIZONTAL_RESOLUTION give the resolution of the output device in the rather ungainly units of pixels per meter.

Thus, you can determine the physical dimensions of the output device (in meters) by dividing CAPS_HEIGHT by CAPS_VERTICAL_RESOLUTION and CAPS_WIDTH by CAPS_HORIZONTAL_RESOLUTION. (In most cases, these quotients will be less than 1, so you'll probably want to calculate physical dimensions in something other than meters.) You now have enough information to adjust horizontal and vertical sizes in order to draw square squares and round circles.

The CLOCK program in Chapter 10 shows how to use the CAPS_VERTICAL_RESOLUTION and CAPS_HORIZONTAL_RESOLUTION values to draw round graphics objects regardless of the different resolutions of the video display. The clock displayed by this program adjusts its size to fit the window but remains round.

Using Metric Units

You may also want to draw graphic objects in specific sizes, such as units of a fraction of an inch or millimeters. These are called "metric units."

There are a couple of ways to do this. The easy approach (described in the next section) lets GPI do most of the work. But you may prefer to retain control over metric scaling entirely within your program. For example, suppose you want to work in units of $1/10$ inch. (These units are called "Low English" because they use English measurements. "High English" units are $1/1000$ inch.)

You first need to obtain the horizontal and vertical resolution of the device:

```
static LONG cxPixelsPerMeter, cyPixelsPerMeter ;
      ⋮

DevQueryCaps (hdc, CAPS_HORIZONTAL_RESOLUTION, 1L, &cxPixelsPerMeter) ;
DevQueryCaps (hdc, CAPS_VERTICAL_RESOLUTION, 1L,&cyPixelsPerMeter) ;
```

There are 2.54 centimeters to the inch and 100 centimeters to the meter. Thus you can calculate pixels per inch by using the following method:

```
static LONG cxPixelsPerInch, cyPixelsPerInch ;
      ⋮

cxPixelsPerInch = (cxPixelsPerMeter * 254 + 5000) / 10000 ;
cyPixelsPerInch = (cyPixelsPerMeter * 254 + 5000) / 10000 ;
```

The addition of 5000 before the division gives a rounded result.

If you want to set the current position 3 inches from the left and 1½ inches from the bottom of your client window, you start by setting *ptl.x* and *ptl.y* to these values in units of ¹/₁₀₀ inch:

```
ptl.x = 300 ;
ptl.y = 150 ;
```

Now convert these coordinates to pixels:

```
ptl.x = ptl.x * cxPixelsPerInch / 100 ;
ptl.y = ptl.y * cyPixelsPerInch / 100 ;
```

Then call the *GpiMove* function.

You can also translate a pixel size or position to Low English units. For example, suppose you want to save *cxClient* and *cyClient* in these units. Here's the new WM_SIZE code:

```
case WM_SIZE:
    cxClient = SHORT1FROMMP (mp2) * 100 / cxPixelsPerInch ;
    cyClient = SHORT2FROMMP (mp2) * 100 / cyPixelsPerInch ;
    return 0 ;
```

Page Units

Rather than do your own translation between metric units and pixels, you can have GPI translate points for you. This requires that you use a function called *GpiSetPS* to set "presentation page units," which are the units you specify in GPI functions. GPI converts these page units into "device units," the normal coordinate system in units of pixels relative to the lower-left corner of the window.

To use *GpiSetPS*, you first define a structure of type SIZEL:

```
SIZEL sizl ;
```

The SIZEL structure has two fields named *cx* and *cy*. For our purposes, you can set both of these fields to zero:

```
sizl.cx = 0 ;
sizl.cy = 0 ;
```

You then call *GpiSetPS*:

```
GpiSetPS (hps, &sizl, lPageUnits);
```

The last parameter specifies the page units. It can be any of the following seven identifiers:

Page Units Identifier	Units
PU_PELS	Pixels
PU_ARBITRARY	"Square" Pixels
PU_LOMETRIC	0.1 millimeter
PU_HIMETRIC	0.01 millimeter
PU_LOENGLISH	0.01 inch
PU_HIENGLISH	0.001 inch
PU_TWIPS	$^1/_{1440}$ inch

By default, page units are set to PU_PELS. Page units of PU_ARBITRARY result in an adjustment so that horizontal units you specify in GPI functions are the same as vertical units. This is a compromise between PU_PELS and the five metric page units. The word "twips" stands for "twentieths of a point," and refers to a printer's point size, approximately $^1/_{72}$ inch. Thus $^1/_{20}$ point is $^1/_{1440}$ inch.

Be careful with *GpiSetPS*: The function resets all attributes of the presentation space to default values. Thus, if you use *GpiSetPS*, it's best to call it immediately after you obtain a presentation space handle using *WinBeginPaint* or *WinGetPS*.

The RULER program in Figure 5-9 shows how to use *GpiSetPS* to draw using Low English units.

The RULER File

```
#------------------
# RULER make file
#------------------

ruler.obj : ruler.c
     cl -c -G2sw -W3 ruler.c

ruler.exe : ruler.obj ruler.def
     link ruler, /align:16, NUL, os2, ruler
```

The RULER.C File

```
/*---------------------------
   RULER.C -- Draw a Ruler
   ------------------------*/

#define INCL_WIN
#define INCL_GPI
#include <os2.h>
#include <stdio.h>

MRESULT EXPENTRY ClientWndProc (HWND, USHORT, MPARAM, MPARAM) ;

int main (void)
    {
    static CHAR   szClientClass [] = "Ruler" ;
    static ULONG  flFrameFlags = FCF_TITLEBAR      | FCF_SYSMENU |
                                 FCF_SIZEBORDER    | FCF_MINMAX  |
                                 FCF_SHELLPOSITION | FCF_TASKLIST ;

    HAB          hab ;
    HMQ          hmq ;
    HWND         hwndFrame, hwndClient ;
    QMSG         qmsg ;

    hab = WinInitialize (0) ;
    hmq = WinCreateMsgQueue (hab, 0) ;

    WinRegisterClass (hab, szClientClass, ClientWndProc, CS_SIZEREDRAW, 0) ;

    hwndFrame = WinCreateStdWindow (HWND_DESKTOP, WS_VISIBLE,
                                    &flFrameFlags, szClientClass, NULL,
                                    0L, NULL, 0, &hwndClient) ;

    WinSendMsg (hwndFrame, WM_SETICON,
                WinQuerySysPointer (HWND_DESKTOP, SPTR_APPICON, FALSE),
                NULL) ;

    while (WinGetMsg (hab, &qmsg, NULL, 0, 0))
        WinDispatchMsg (hab, &qmsg) ;

    WinDestroyWindow (hwndFrame) ;
    WinDestroyMsgQueue (hmq) ;
    WinTerminate (hab) ;
    return 0 ;
    }
```

(continued)

Figure 5-9. The RULER.C File. *continued*

```
MRESULT EXPENTRY ClientWndProc (HWND hwnd, USHORT msg, MPARAM mp1, MPARAM mp2)
     {
     static SHORT sTick[16] = { 100, 25, 35, 25, 50, 25, 35, 25,
                                70, 25, 35, 25, 50, 25, 35, 25 } ;
     static SHORT cxClient, cyClient, cxChar, cyChar, cyDesc ;
     static SIZEL sizl ;
     CHAR          szBuffer [4] ;
     FONTMETRICS  fm ;
     HPS           hps ;
     POINTL        ptl ;
     SHORT         sIndex ;

     switch (msg)
          {
          case WM_CREATE:
               hps = WinGetPS (hwnd) ;
               GpiSetPS (hps, &sizl, PU_LOENGLISH) ;

               GpiQueryFontMetrics (hps, (LONG) sizeof fm, &fm) ;
               cxChar = (SHORT) fm.lAveCharWidth ;
               cyChar = (SHORT) fm.lMaxBaselineExt ;
               cyDesc = (SHORT) fm.lMaxDescender ;

               WinReleasePS (hps) ;
               return 0 ;

          case WM_SIZE:
               ptl.x = SHORT1FROMMP (mp2) ;
               ptl.y = SHORT2FROMMP (mp2) ;

               hps = WinGetPS (hwnd) ;
               GpiSetPS (hps, &sizl, PU_LOENGLISH) ;
               GpiConvert (hps, CVTC_DEVICE, CVTC_PAGE, 1L, &ptl) ;
               WinReleasePS (hps) ;

               cxClient = (SHORT) ptl.x ;
               cyClient = (SHORT) ptl.y ;
               return 0 ;

          case WM_PAINT:
               hps = WinBeginPaint (hwnd, NULL, NULL) ;
               GpiSetPS (hps, &sizl, PU_LOENGLISH) ;
               GpiErase (hps) ;
```

(continued)

Figure 5-9. The RULER.C File. *continued*

```
            for (sIndex = 0 ; sIndex < 16 * (SHORT) cxClient / 100 ;
                        sIndex ++)
                {
            ptl.x = 100 * sIndex / 16 ;
            ptl.y = 0 ;
            GpiMove (hps, &ptl) ;

            ptl.y = sTick [sIndex % 16] ;
            GpiLine (hps, &ptl) ;

            if (sIndex % 16 == 0)
                {
                ptl.x -= cxChar / (sIndex > 160 ? 1 : 2) ;
                ptl.y += cyDesc ;
                GpiCharStringAt (hps, &ptl,
                    (LONG) sprintf (szBuffer, "%d", sIndex / 16),
                    szBuffer) ;
                }
            }
        WinEndPaint (hps) ;
        return 0 ;
        }
    return WinDefWindowProc (hwnd, msg, mp1, mp2) ;
    }
```

The RULER.DEF File

```
;---------------------------------
; RULER.DEF module definition file
;---------------------------------

NAME            RULER       WINDOWAPI

DESCRIPTION     'Draw a Ruler (C) Charles Petzold, 1988'
PROTMODE
HEAPSIZE        1024
STACKSIZE       8192
EXPORTS         ClientWndProc
```

Figure 5-9. *The RULER program.*

RULER draws a ruler with tick marks every $1/16$ inch along the bottom of its client window, as shown in Figure 5-10 on the following page.

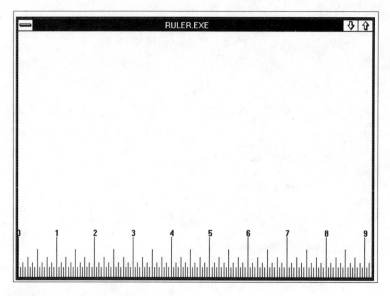

Figure 5-10. *The RULER display.*

In RULER, the *sizl* structure is defined as a static variable and implicitly initialized to zero. *ClientWndProc* calls *GpiSetPS* with the PU_LOENGLISH parameter whenever it obtains a presentation space handle, which it does three times: during the WM_CREATE, WM_SIZE, and WM_PAINT messages.

During the WM_CREATE message, the program obtains font metrics from the *GpiQueryFontMetrics* function. Because page units have been set to Low English, these font metrics are in units of $1/100$ inch.

The Low English page units don't affect nongraphics functions. For example, the WM_SIZE message will continue to report the window size in device units (pixels). For this reason, RULER must convert the window size to Low English units before saving the values in *cxClient* and *cyClient*. First, the new window size is saved in a POINTL structure:

```
ptl.x = SHORT1FROMMP (mp2) ;
ptl.y = SHORT2FROMMP (mp2) ;
```

Next, RULER gets a presention space handle and sets the page units:

```
hps = WinGetPS (hwnd) ;
GpiSetPS (hps, &sizl, PU_LOENGLISH) ;
```

The coordinates of the POINTL structure are converted to page units using *GpiConvert*, and the presentation space is released:

```
GpiConvert (hps, CVTC_DEVICE, CVTC_PAGE, 1L, &ptl) ;
WinReleasePS (hps) ;
```

The second parameter to *GpiConvert* indicates that the POINTL structure (the last parameter) is in device units. The third parameter is the units to which the POINTL structure should be converted. (You can switch these two parameters to convert from page units to device units.) The fourth parameter is the number of POINTL structures to be converted, passed as the last parameter. Finally, *cxClient* and *cyClient* are saved from the converted points as follows:

```
cxClient = (SHORT) ptl.x ;
cyClient = (SHORT) ptl.y ;
```

Thus, by the time the WM_PAINT message is processed, everything the program needs to draw the RULER (the size of the client window and the font metrics) is in units of $1/100$ inch. The *sTick* array (which has the lengths of the ruler tick marks) has also been initialized in Low English units.

This discussion of page units only scratches the surface of GPI's various transformation functions. The points you specify in GPI functions are actually in a coordinate system called "world space" and are translated to "model space," then to page units, and then to device coordinates. The *GpiSetModelTransformMatrix* and *GpiSetDefaultViewMatrix* functions allow you to perform translation, scaling, and rotation on world coordinates for more complex drawing.

GPI Primitive 2: Patterned Areas

The second GPI primitive is a pattern that fills an enclosed area. You define the area with a series of lines, and GPI fills it. The *GpiBox* function also uses a pattern to fill the box interior.

Area filling under GPI is *not* implemented as a "flood fill," such as that available with the PAINT statement in Microsoft's QuickBASIC. In a flood fill, you specify a point that is bounded by one or more existing lines. The graphics system fills the area with a pattern by searching for the boundary lines. Flood fills are possible only on raster output devices that allow the graphics system to read (as well as write) individual pixels. Instead, GPI accumulates the lines that you specify as boundaries to the area and then algorithmically fills the enclosed areas defined by these lines.

If you have already experimented with the DRO_FILL and DRO_OUTLINEFILL options of *GpiBox*, you will have noticed that GPI simply fills the box with a solid color. But that's only because the default area pattern is a solid pattern. Let's look at the other available patterns and the various ways of defining and filling an area under GPI.

Selecting the Pattern

To select the pattern that GPI uses to fill an area, you call

```
GpiSetPattern (hps, lPattern) ;
```

The *lPattern* parameter can be any one of the following 19 identifiers beginning with the prefix PATSYM ("pattern symbol"):

PATSYM_DEFAULT	PATSYM_VERT
PATSYM_DENSE1	PATSYM_HORIZ
PATSYM_DENSE2	PATSYM_DIAG1
PATSYM_DENSE3	PATSYM_DIAG2
PATSYM_DENSE4	PATSYM_DIAG3
PATSYM_DENSE5	PATSYM_DIAG4
PATSYM_DENSE6	PATSYM_NOSHADE
PATSYM_DENSE7	PATSYM_SOLID
PATSYM_DENSE8	PATSYM_HALFTONE
	PATSYM_BLANK

The PATSYM_DEFAULT and PATSYM_SOLID identifiers have the same effect; so do PATSYM_NOSHADE and PATSYM_BLANK. PATSYM_DIAG1 and PATSYM_DIAG2 are patterns composed of diagonal lines from lower left to upper right. For PATSYM_DIAG3 and PATSYM_DIAG4, the diagonal lines go from upper left to lower right.

The various PATSYM_DENSE identifiers result in shaded patterns: PATSYM_DENSE1 has the highest color density, and PATSYM_DENSE8 has the lowest color density. You can get a 50 percent shading using PATSYM_HALFTONE, which (depending on the output device) may or may not be the same as PATSYM_DENSE4 or PATSYM_DENSE5.

The PATTERNS program shown in Figure 5-11 uses the *GpiBox* function to draw all 19 patterns in its client window.

The PATTERNS File

```
#--------------------
# PATTERNS make file
#--------------------

patterns.obj : patterns.c
    cl -c -G2sw -W3 patterns.c

patterns.exe : patterns.obj patterns.def
    link patterns, /align:16, NUL, os2, patterns
```

The PATTERNS.C File

```
/*----------------------------------
   PATTERNS.C -- GPI Area Patterns
   --------------------------------*/

#define INCL_WIN
#define INCL_GPI
#include <os2.h>
#include <string.h>

MRESULT EXPENTRY ClientWndProc (HWND, USHORT, MPARAM, MPARAM) ;

int main (void)
    {
    static CHAR  szClientClass [] = "Patterns" ;
    static ULONG flFrameFlags = FCF_TITLEBAR      | FCF_SYSMENU |
                                FCF_SIZEBORDER     | FCF_MINMAX  |
                                FCF_SHELLPOSITION  | FCF_TASKLIST ;

    HAB          hab ;
    HMQ          hmq ;
    HWND         hwndFrame, hwndClient ;
    QMSG         qmsg ;

    hab = WinInitialize (0) ;
    hmq = WinCreateMsgQueue (hab, 0) ;

    WinRegisterClass (hab, szClientClass, ClientWndProc, CS_SIZEREDRAW, 0) ;

    hwndFrame = WinCreateStdWindow (HWND_DESKTOP, WS_VISIBLE,
                                    &flFrameFlags, szClientClass, NULL,
                                    0L, NULL, 0, &hwndClient) ;
```

(continued)

Figure 5-11. The PATTERNS.C File. *continued*

```
     WinSendMsg (hwndFrame, WM_SETICON,
                 WinQuerySysPointer (HWND_DESKTOP, SPTR_APPICON, FALSE),
                 NULL) ;

     while (WinGetMsg (hab, &qmsg, NULL, 0, 0))
          WinDispatchMsg (hab, &qmsg) ;

     WinDestroyWindow (hwndFrame) ;
     WinDestroyMsgQueue (hmq) ;
     WinTerminate (hab) ;
     return 0 ;
     }

MRESULT EXPENTRY ClientWndProc (HWND hwnd, USHORT msg, MPARAM mp1, MPARAM mp2)
     {
     static struct {
                    LONG lPatternSymbol ;
                    CHAR *szPatternSymbol ;
                    }
                    show [] =
                    {
                    PATSYM_DEFAULT  , "PATSYM_DEFAULT"  ,
                    PATSYM_DENSE1   , "PATSYM_DENSE1"   ,
                    PATSYM_DENSE2   , "PATSYM_DENSE2"   ,
                    PATSYM_DENSE3   , "PATSYM_DENSE3"   ,
                    PATSYM_DENSE4   , "PATSYM_DENSE4"   ,
                    PATSYM_DENSE5   , "PATSYM_DENSE5"   ,
                    PATSYM_DENSE6   , "PATSYM_DENSE6"   ,
                    PATSYM_DENSE7   , "PATSYM_DENSE7"   ,
                    PATSYM_DENSE8   , "PATSYM_DENSE8"   ,
                    PATSYM_VERT     , "PATSYM_VERT"     ,
                    PATSYM_HORIZ    , "PATSYM_HORIZ"    ,
                    PATSYM_DIAG1    , "PATSYM_DIAG1"    ,
                    PATSYM_DIAG2    , "PATSYM_DIAG2"    ,
                    PATSYM_DIAG3    , "PATSYM_DIAG3"    ,
                    PATSYM_DIAG4    , "PATSYM_DIAG4"    ,
                    PATSYM_NOSHADE  , "PATSYM_NOSHADE"  ,
                    PATSYM_SOLID    , "PATSYM_SOLID"    ,
                    PATSYM_HALFTONE , "PATSYM_HALFTONE" ,
                    PATSYM_BLANK    , "PATSYM_BLANK"    ,
                    } ;
     static SHORT  cxClient, cyClient, cxCaps, cyChar, cyDesc,
                   sNumTypes = sizeof show / sizeof show[0] ;
     FONTMETRICS   fm ;
```

(continued)

Figure 5-11. The PATTERNS.C File. *continued*

```
HPS          hps ;
POINTL       ptl ;
SHORT        sIndex ;

switch (msg)
    {
    case WM_CREATE:
        hps = WinGetPS (hwnd) ;
        GpiQueryFontMetrics (hps, (LONG) sizeof fm, &fm) ;
        cxCaps = (SHORT) fm.lEmInc ;
        cyChar = (SHORT) fm.lMaxBaselineExt ;
        cyDesc = (SHORT) fm.lMaxDescender ;
        WinReleasePS (hps) ;
        return 0 ;

    case WM_SIZE:
        cxClient = SHORT1FROMMP (mp2) ;
        cyClient = SHORT2FROMMP (mp2) ;
        return 0 ;

    case WM_PAINT:
        hps = WinBeginPaint (hwnd, NULL, NULL) ;
        GpiErase (hps) ;

        for (sIndex = 0 ; sIndex < sNumTypes ; sIndex ++)
            {
            GpiSetPattern (hps, show [sIndex].lPatternSymbol) ;

            ptl.x = (sIndex < 10 ? 1 : 33) * cxCaps ;
            ptl.y = cyClient - (sIndex % 10 * 5 + 4) * cyChar / 2
                                                + cyDesc ;

            GpiCharStringAt (hps, &ptl,
                    (LONG) strlen (show [sIndex].szPatternSymbol),
                        show [sIndex].szPatternSymbol) ;

            ptl.x = (sIndex < 10 ? 20 : 52) * cxCaps ;
            ptl.y -= cyDesc + cyChar / 2 ;
            GpiMove (hps, &ptl) ;

            ptl.x += 10 * cxCaps ;
            ptl.y += 2 * cyChar ;
            GpiBox (hps, DRO_FILL, &ptl, 0L, 0L) ;
            }
```

(continued)

Figure 5-11. The PATTERNS.C File. *continued*

```
            WinEndPaint (hps) ;
            return 0 ;
        }
    return WinDefWindowProc (hwnd, msg, mp1, mp2) ;
    }
```

The PATTERNS.DEF File

```
;------------------------------------
; PATTERNS.DEF module definition file
;------------------------------------

NAME            PATTERNS   WINDOWAPI

DESCRIPTION     'GPI Area Patterns (C) Charles Petzold, 1988'
PROTMODE
HEAPSIZE        1024
STACKSIZE       8192
EXPORTS         ClientWndProc
```

Figure 5-11. *The PATTERNS program.*

The various patterns drawn by this program are shown in Figure 5-12.

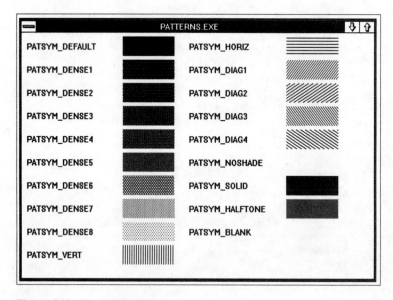

Figure 5-12. *The PATTERNS display.*

A pattern is really only a small rectangular bitmap that is repeated horizontally and vertically to fill an area. In the next chapter I'll show you how to create your own patterns for area filling.

Defining an Area

Area filling is not limited to the *GpiBox* function. You can define any area to be filled by simply drawing a series of lines between the *GpiBeginArea* and *GpiEndArea* functions:

```
GpiBeginArea (hps, lAreaFlags) ;
    [draw lines to define the area]
GpiEndArea (hps) ;
```

This is known as an "area bracket." GPI does not fill the area until you call the *GpiEndArea* function.

For example, suppose you want to draw a large filled triangle in your client window. If *cxClient* and *cyClient* are the dimensions of the client window, here's the code:

```
GpiBeginArea (hps, OL) ;

ptl.x = 0 ;
ptl.y = 0 ;
GpiMove (hps, &ptl) ;

ptl.x = cxClient / 2 ;
ptl.y = cyClient ;
GpiLine (hps, &ptl) ;

ptl.x = cxClient ;
ptl.y = 0 ;
GpiLine (hps, &ptl) ;

ptl.x = 0 ;
ptl.y = 0 ;
GpiLine (hps, &ptl) ;

GpiEndArea (hps) ;
```

The last *GpiLine* call, which closes the triangle, is not required. If you do not close the figure, GPI will close it for you by drawing a straight line to the starting point.

Only a subset of GPI functions are allowed within an area bracket. All line drawing and line attribute functions are allowed, but little else. If you call *GpiBox* within an area bracket, it should be with the DRO_OUTLINE option. If you want to use a nonsolid pattern, call *GpiSetPattern* before calling *GpiBeginArea*.

You can define more than one filled area within a single area bracket. When you call *GpiMove* in an area bracket, GPI closes the previous figure (if necessary) and starts a second figure. For example, the following code draws two filled triangles side by side in the window:

```
GpiBeginArea (hps, 0L) ;

ptl.x = 0 ;
ptl.y = 0 ;
GpiMove (hps, &ptl) ;

ptl.x = cxClient / 4 ;
ptl.y = cyClient ;
GpiLine (hps, &ptl) ;

ptl.x = cxClient / 2 ;
ptl.y = 0 ;
GpiLine (hps, &ptl) ;

GpiMove (hps, &ptl) ;

ptl.x = 3 * cxClient / 4 ;
ptl.y = cyClient ;
GpiLine (hps, &ptl) ;

ptl.x = cxClient ;
ptl.y = 0 ;
GpiLine (hps, &ptl) ;

GpiEndArea (hps) ;
```

In this case I'm letting GPI close the two triangles. The *GpiMove* call in the middle of this area bracket marks the beginning of the second triangle, which is the same as the third point of the first triangle. As part of area bracket processing, GPI closes the first triangle with a line from (cxClient/2,0) to (0,0). Similarly, the *GpiEndArea* call causes GPI to construct a boundary line from (cxClient,0) to (cxClient/2,0).

In the preceding examples, the boundary lines are not actually drawn by GPI. GPI uses the lines you specify solely for defining the enclosed area.

Whether GPI draws the boundary lines or not is governed by the second parameter to *GpiBeginArea*. It can be one of the following identifiers:

BA_NOBOUNDARY
BA_BOUNDARY

The BA_NOBOUNDARY identifier is equal to zero, so no boundary line is drawn in the preceding examples. You can also combine these identifiers by using the C bitwise OR operator with one of the following identifiers:

BA_ALTERNATE
BA_WINDING

The BA_ALTERNATE identifier is equal to zero, so that is the default if you use neither identifier. These identifiers govern whether GPI uses ''alternate'' or ''winding'' mode to fill areas.

Alternate and Winding Modes

When you draw a series of lines to define a filled area, the lines can cross each other, and the enclosed area can actually comprise several smaller sub-areas. You may not want all of these areas to be filled. The classic example is a five-pointed star that you draw with five lines. The points of the star and the interior pentagon are all sub-areas. You can have GPI fill that interior pentagon by specifying winding mode or leave it unfilled by specifying alternate mode. This is illustrated in the STARFILL program in Figure 5-13.

The STARFILL File

```
#--------------------
# STARFILL make file
#--------------------

starfill.obj : starfill.c
    cl -c -G2sw -W3 starfill.c

starfill.exe : starfill.obj starfill.def
    link starfill, /align:16, NUL, os2, starfill
```

The STARFILL.C File

```
/*----------------------------------------------
   STARFILL.C -- Alternate and Winding Modes
   ----------------------------------------------*/

#define INCL_GPI
#include <os2.h>

MRESULT EXPENTRY ClientWndProc (HWND, USHORT, MPARAM, MPARAM) ;

int main (void)
    {
    static CHAR   szClientClass [] = "StarFill" ;
    static ULONG  flFrameFlags = FCF_TITLEBAR      | FCF_SYSMENU |
                                 FCF_SIZEBORDER    | FCF_MINMAX  |
                                 FCF_SHELLPOSITION | FCF_TASKLIST ;
    HAB           hab ;
    HMQ           hmq ;
    HWND          hwndFrame, hwndClient ;
    QMSG          qmsg ;

    hab = WinInitialize (0) ;
    hmq = WinCreateMsgQueue (hab, 0) ;

    WinRegisterClass (hab, szClientClass, ClientWndProc, CS_SIZEREDRAW, 0) ;

    hwndFrame = WinCreateStdWindow (HWND_DESKTOP, WS_VISIBLE,
                                    &flFrameFlags, szClientClass,
                                    " - Alternate and Winding",
                                    0L, NULL, 0, &hwndClient) ;

    while (WinGetMsg (hab, &qmsg, NULL, 0, 0))
        WinDispatchMsg (hab, &qmsg) ;

    WinDestroyWindow (hwndFrame) ;
    WinDestroyMsgQueue (hmq) ;
    WinTerminate (hab) ;
    return 0 ;
    }

MRESULT EXPENTRY ClientWndProc (HWND hwnd, USHORT msg, MPARAM mp1, MPARAM mp2)
    {
    static POINTL aptlStar[5] = {-59,-81, 0,100, 59,-81, -95,31, 95,31 } ;
    static SHORT  cxClient, cyClient ;
    HPS           hps ;
```

(continued)

Figure 5-13. The STARFILL.C File. *continued*

```
POINTL          aptl[5] ;
SHORT           sIndex ;

switch (msg)
     {
     case WM_SIZE:
          cxClient = SHORT1FROMMP (mp2) ;
          cyClient = SHORT2FROMMP (mp2) ;
          return 0 ;

     case WM_PAINT:
          hps = WinBeginPaint (hwnd, NULL, NULL) ;
          GpiErase (hps) ;
          GpiSetPattern (hps, PATSYM_HALFTONE) ;

                         /*---------------------
                            Alternate Fill Mode
                         ---------------------*/

          for (sIndex = 0 ; sIndex < 5 ; sIndex++)
               {
               aptl[sIndex].x = cxClient / 4 + cxClient *
                                       aptlStar[sIndex].x / 400 ;
               aptl[sIndex].y = cyClient / 2 + cyClient *
                                       aptlStar[sIndex].y / 200 ;
               }

          GpiBeginArea (hps, BA_NOBOUNDARY | BA_ALTERNATE) ;
          GpiMove (hps, aptl) ;
          GpiPolyLine (hps, 4L, aptl + 1) ;
          GpiEndArea (hps) ;

                         /*--------------------
                            Winding Fill Mode
                         --------------------*/

          for (sIndex = 0 ; sIndex < 5 ; sIndex++)
               aptl[sIndex].x += cxClient / 2 ;

          GpiBeginArea (hps, BA_NOBOUNDARY | BA_WINDING) ;
          GpiMove (hps, aptl) ;
          GpiPolyLine (hps, 4L, aptl + 1) ;
          GpiEndArea (hps) ;
```

(continued)

Figure 5-13. The STARFILL.C File. *continued*

```
                    WinEndPaint (hps) ;
                    return 0 ;
            }
    return WinDefWindowProc (hwnd, msg, mp1, mp2) ;
    }
```

The STARFILL.DEF File

```
;----------------------------------------
; STARFILL.DEF module definition file
;----------------------------------------

NAME            STARFILL  WINDOWAPI

DESCRIPTION     'Alternate and Winding Modes (C) Charles Petzold, 1988'
PROTMODE
HEAPSIZE        1024
STACKSIZE       8192
EXPORTS         ClientWndProc
```

Figure 5-13. *The STARFILL program.*

As you can see in Figure 5-14, the center of the five-pointed star is filled in winding mode but not in alternate mode.

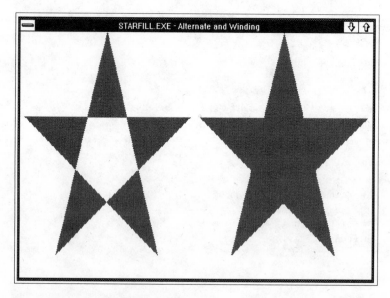

Figure 5-14. *The STARFILL display.*

At first, the difference between alternate and winding modes seems rather simple. For alternate mode, you can imagine a line drawn from a point in an enclosed area to infinity. The enclosed area is filled only if that imaginary line crosses an odd number of boundary lines. This is why the points of the star are filled but the center is not.

The example of the five-pointed star makes winding mode seem simpler than it actually is. When you're drawing a single object in an area bracket, *in most cases* winding mode will cause all enclosed areas to be filled. But there are exceptions.

To determine whether an enclosed area is filled in winding mode, you again imagine a line drawn from a point in that area to infinity:

■ If the imaginary line crosses an odd number of boundary lines, the area is filled, just as in alternate mode.

■ If the imaginary line crosses an even number of boundary lines, the area can be either filled or not filled. The area is filled if the number of boundary lines going in one direction (relative to the imaginary line) is not equal to the number of boundary lines going in the other direction.

For example, consider the object shown in Figure 5-15.

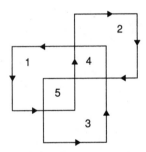

Figure 15-15. *A figure in which winding mode does not fill all interior areas.*

The arrows on the lines indicate the direction in which the lines are drawn. Both winding mode and alternate mode will fill the three enclosed L-shaped areas numbered 1 through 3. The two smaller interior areas, numbered 4 and 5, will not be filled in alternate mode. But in winding mode, area number 5 is filled because you must cross two lines going in the *same* direction to get from the inside of that area to the outside of the figure. Area number 4 is not filled. You must again cross two lines, but the two lines go in opposite directions.

Is GPI really smart enough to figure this out? Sure it is, and the ALTWIND program shown in Figure 5-16 demonstrates it.

The ALTWIND File

```
#-------------------
# ALTWIND make file
#-------------------

altwind.obj : altwind.c
    cl -c -G2sw -W3 altwind.c

altwind.exe : altwind.obj altwind.def
    link altwind, /align:16, NUL, os2, altwind
```

The ALTWIND.C File

```
/*-------------------------------------------
   ALTWIND.C -- Alternate and Winding Modes
-------------------------------------------*/

#define INCL_GPI
#include <os2.h>

MRESULT EXPENTRY ClientWndProc (HWND, USHORT, MPARAM, MPARAM) ;

int main (void)
    {
    static CHAR  szClientClass [] = "AltWind" ;
    static ULONG flFrameFlags = FCF_TITLEBAR      | FCF_SYSMENU |
                                FCF_SIZEBORDER    | FCF_MINMAX  |
                                FCF_SHELLPOSITION | FCF_TASKLIST ;
    HAB          hab ;
    HMQ          hmq ;
    HWND         hwndFrame, hwndClient ;
    QMSG         qmsg ;

    hab = WinInitialize (0) ;
    hmq = WinCreateMsgQueue (hab, 0) ;

    WinRegisterClass (hab, szClientClass, ClientWndProc, CS_SIZEREDRAW, 0) ;

    hwndFrame = WinCreateStdWindow (HWND_DESKTOP, WS_VISIBLE,
                                    &flFrameFlags, szClientClass, NULL,
                                    0L, NULL, 0, &hwndClient) ;
```

(continued)

Figure 5-16. The ALTWIND.C File. *continued*

```
      while (WinGetMsg (hab, &qmsg, NULL, 0, 0))
           WinDispatchMsg (hab, &qmsg) ;

      WinDestroyWindow (hwndFrame) ;
      WinDestroyMsgQueue (hmq) ;
      WinTerminate (hab) ;
      return 0 ;
      }

MRESULT EXPENTRY ClientWndProc (HWND hwnd, USHORT msg, MPARAM mp1, MPARAM mp2)
      {
      static POINTL aptlFigure[10] = { 10,30, 50,30, 50,90, 90,90, 90,50,
                                       30,50, 30,10, 70,10, 70,70, 10,70 } ;
      static SHORT  cxClient, cyClient ;
      HPS           hps ;
      POINTL        aptl[10] ;
      SHORT         sIndex ;

      switch (msg)
           {
           case WM_SIZE:
                cxClient = SHORT1FROMMP (mp2) ;
                cyClient = SHORT2FROMMP (mp2) ;
                return 0 ;

           case WM_PAINT:
                hps = WinBeginPaint (hwnd, NULL, NULL) ;
                GpiErase (hps) ;
                GpiSetPattern (hps, PATSYM_HALFTONE) ;

                        /*---------------------
                         Alternate Fill Mode
                        ---------------------*/

                for (sIndex = 0 ; sIndex < 10 ; sIndex++)
                     {
                     aptl[sIndex].x = cxClient * aptlFigure[sIndex].x / 200 ;
                     aptl[sIndex].y = cyClient * aptlFigure[sIndex].y / 100 ;
                     }

                GpiBeginArea (hps, BA_BOUNDARY | BA_ALTERNATE) ;
                GpiMove (hps, aptl) ;
                GpiPolyLine (hps, 9L, aptl + 1) ;
                GpiEndArea (hps) ;
```

(continued)

Figure 5-16. The ALTWIND.C File. *continued*

```
                         /*--------------------
                           Winding Fill Mode
                         --------------------*/

            for (sIndex = 0 ; sIndex < 10 ; sIndex++)
                aptl[sIndex].x += cxClient / 2 ;

            GpiBeginArea (hps, BA_BOUNDARY | BA_WINDING) ;
            GpiMove (hps, aptl) ;
            GpiPolyLine (hps, 9L, aptl + 1) ;
            GpiEndArea (hps) ;

            WinEndPaint (hps) ;
            return 0 ;
        }
    return WinDefWindowProc (hwnd, msg, mp1, mp2) ;
    }
```

The ALTWIND.DEF File

```
;-----------------------------------
; ALTWIND.DEF module definition file
;-----------------------------------

NAME            ALTWIND    WINDOWAPI

DESCRIPTION     'Alternate and Winding Modes (C) Charles Petzold, 1988'
PROTMODE
HEAPSIZE        1024
STACKSIZE       8192
EXPORTS         ClientWndProc
```

Figure 5-16. *The ALTWIND program.*

Figure 5-17 shows the ALTWIND display.

If you use *GpiBox* with the DRO_OUTLINE option within an area bracket, you need to know how GPI draws the box in order to anticipate how the intersection of the box and other closed objects will be filled in winding mode. GPI begins drawing the box at the current position. The first line it draws is horizontal, and then the box is continued from there. Thus, if the current position is the lower-left or upper-right corner of the box, the box is drawn counterclockwise.

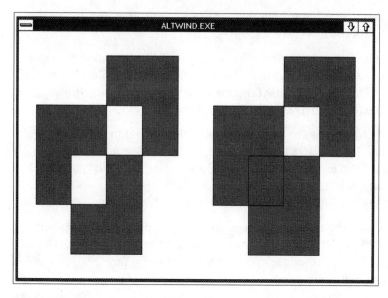

Figure 5-17. *The ALTWIND display.*

Color and Mix

All text, lines, and areas we've drawn have appeared on the window in black on a white background. Or maybe not: If you have set different "window background" and "window text" colors using the Presentation Manager Control Panel program, GPI uses these colors for the background of the window and the color of text, lines, areas, and other primitives.

The Color Index

You specify a color by calling the *GpiSetColor* function:

```
GpiSetColor (hps, lColorIndex) ;
```

The color is an attribute of the presentation space. The color you set with *GpiSetColor* affects all subsequent GPI primitives until you change the color again or release the presentation space.

Generally, the *lColorIndex* value will be one of the following identifiers:

CLR_BACKGROUND	CLR_DARKGRAY
CLR_BLUE	CLR_DARKBLUE
CLR_RED	CLR_DARKRED
CLR_PINK	CLR_DARKPINK
CLR_GREEN	CLR_DARKGREEN
CLR_CYAN	CLR_DARKCYAN
CLR_YELLOW	CLR_BROWN
CLR_NEUTRAL	CLR_PALEGRAY

Each of these color index identifiers is self-explanatory, with the exception of CLR_BACKGROUND and CLR_NEUTRAL:

- CLR_BACKGROUND is the color you set in the Presentation Manager Control Panel program as the "window background" color. By default, this is white. The *GpiErase* function erases a window using this CLR_BACKGROUND color.

- CLR_NEUTRAL is the "window text" color you set in the Control Panel Program; by default, CLR_NEUTRAL is black. For a new presentation space, all GPI primitives you draw will use the CLR_NEUTRAL color. GPI also recognizes the CLR_DEFAULT identifier, which has the same effect as CLR_NEUTRAL when used with *GpiSetColor*.

In one sense, these interpretations of the CLR_BACKGROUND and the CLR_NEUTRAL identifiers are convenient for the programmer. The user has selected these colors as his or her personal preferences for window background and foreground colors. A Presentation Manager program uses these colors by default. A user's preference, however, can sometimes defeat a feature of a program. For example, if your program uses CLR_RED text for emphasis, the text won't stand out if the user has selected red as the normal window text color.

Therefore, GPI lets you override the user's preferences and explicitly set all colors used by the program. GPI provides two additional color indexes for specifying black and white:

CLR_BLACK   CLR_WHITE

Another pair of color indexes is more appropriate for use with bitmaps:

CLR_FALSE   CLR_TRUE

On a video display, CLR_FALSE has the same effect as CLR_BLACK, and CLR_TRUE has the same effect as CLR_WHITE; on a printer, this relationship is reversed because video displays are black background devices and printers are white background devices.

You may be familiar with the IRGB (Intensity-Red-Green-Blue) color encoding of the IBM CGA, EGA, and VGA video adapters. The table on the next page shows how it corresponds to the GPI color indexes.

I	R	G	B	IRGB Color Name	Equivalent Color Index
0	0	0	0	Black	CLR_BLACK
0	0	0	1	Blue	CLR_DARKBLUE
0	0	1	0	Green	CLR_DARKGREEN
0	0	1	1	Cyan	CLR_DARKCYAN
0	1	0	0	Red	CLR_DARKRED
0	1	0	1	Magenta	CLR_DARKPINK
0	1	1	0	Brown	CLR_BROWN
0	1	1	1	Light Gray	CLR_PALEGRAY
1	0	0	0	Dark Gray	CLR_DARKGRAY
1	0	0	1	Light Blue	CLR_BLUE
1	0	1	0	Light Green	CLR_GREEN
1	0	1	1	Light Cyan	CLR_CYAN
1	1	0	0	Light Red	CLR_RED
1	1	0	1	Light Magenta	CLR_PINK
1	1	1	0	Yellow	CLR_YELLOW
1	1	1	1	White	CLR_WHITE

In literature about the IBM video adapters, "magenta" is often used to describe the color known as "pink" in GPI. In technical literature on the CGA, EGA, and VGA boards, colors with the I (intensity) bit set are traditionally referred to as "light" colors; by contrast, in GPI, most colors without the I bit set are "dark" or "pale" colors.

The COLORS program shown in Figure 5-18 displays the colors available with all 21 CLR identifiers:

The COLORS File

```
#-------------------
# COLORS make file
#-------------------

colors.obj : colors.c
    cl -c -G2sw -W3 colors.c

colors.exe : colors.obj colors.def
    link colors, /align:16, NUL, os2, colors
```

The COLORS.C File

```
/*-----------------------------------
   COLORS.C -- GPI Foreground Colors
   -----------------------------------*/

#define INCL_WIN
#define INCL_GPI
#include <os2.h>
#include <string.h>

MRESULT EXPENTRY ClientWndProc (HWND, USHORT, MPARAM, MPARAM) ;

int main (void)
    {
    static CHAR  szClientClass [] = "Colors" ;
    static ULONG flFrameFlags = FCF_TITLEBAR     | FCF_SYSMENU |
                                FCF_SIZEBORDER    | FCF_MINMAX  |
                                FCF_SHELLPOSITION | FCF_TASKLIST ;

    HAB         hab ;
    HMQ         hmq ;
    HWND        hwndFrame, hwndClient ;
    QMSG        qmsg ;

    hab = WinInitialize (0) ;
    hmq = WinCreateMsgQueue (hab, 0) ;

    WinRegisterClass (hab, szClientClass, ClientWndProc, OL, 0) ;

    hwndFrame = WinCreateStdWindow (HWND_DESKTOP, WS_VISIBLE,
                                    &flFrameFlags, szClientClass, NULL,
                                    OL, NULL, 0, &hwndClient) ;

    WinSendMsg (hwndFrame, WM_SETICON,
                WinQuerySysPointer (HWND_DESKTOP, SPTR_APPICON, FALSE),
                NULL) ;

    while (WinGetMsg (hab, &qmsg, NULL, 0, 0))
        WinDispatchMsg (hab, &qmsg) ;

    WinDestroyWindow (hwndFrame) ;
    WinDestroyMsgQueue (hmq) ;
    WinTerminate (hab) ;
    return 0 ;
    }
```

(continued)

Figure 5-18. The COLORS.C File. *continued*

```
MRESULT EXPENTRY ClientWndProc (HWND hwnd, USHORT msg, MPARAM mp1, MPARAM mp2)
    {
    static struct {
                LONG lColorIndex ;
                CHAR *szColorIndex ;
                }
                show [] =
                {
                CLR_FALSE      , "CLR_FALSE"      ,
                CLR_TRUE       , "CLR_TRUE"       ,
                CLR_DEFAULT    , "CLR_DEFAULT"    ,
                CLR_WHITE      , "CLR_WHITE"      ,
                CLR_BLACK      , "CLR_BLACK"      ,
                CLR_BACKGROUND , "CLR_BACKGROUND" ,
                CLR_BLUE       , "CLR_BLUE"       ,
                CLR_RED        , "CLR_RED"        ,
                CLR_PINK       , "CLR_PINK"       ,
                CLR_GREEN      , "CLR_GREEN"      ,
                CLR_CYAN       , "CLR_CYAN"       ,
                CLR_YELLOW     , "CLR_YELLOW"     ,
                CLR_NEUTRAL    , "CLR_NEUTRAL"    ,
                CLR_DARKGRAY   , "CLR_DARKGRAY"   ,
                CLR_DARKBLUE   , "CLR_DARKBLUE"   ,
                CLR_DARKRED    , "CLR_DARKRED"    ,
                CLR_DARKPINK   , "CLR_DARKPINK"   ,
                CLR_DARKGREEN  , "CLR_DARKGREEN"  ,
                CLR_DARKCYAN   , "CLR_DARKCYAN"   ,
                CLR_BROWN      , "CLR_BROWN"      ,
                CLR_PALEGRAY   , "CLR_PALEGRAY"
                } ;
    static SHORT  cxClient, cyClient, cxCaps, cyChar, cyDesc,
                sNumColors = sizeof show / sizeof show[0] ;
    FONTMETRICS  fm ;
    HPS          hps ;
    POINTL       ptl ;
    SHORT        sIndex ;

    switch (msg)
        {
        case WM_CREATE:
            hps = WinGetPS (hwnd) ;
            GpiQueryFontMetrics (hps, (LONG) sizeof fm, &fm) ;
            cxCaps = (SHORT) fm.lEmInc ;
            cyChar = (SHORT) fm.lMaxBaselineExt ;
```

(continued)

Figure 5-18. The COLORS.C File. *continued*

```
                cyDesc = (SHORT) fm.lMaxDescender ;
                WinReleasePS (hps) ;
                return 0 ;

        case WM_SIZE:
                cxClient = SHORT1FROMMP (mp2) ;
                cyClient = SHORT2FROMMP (mp2) ;
                return 0 ;

        case WM_PAINT:
                hps = WinBeginPaint (hwnd, NULL, NULL) ;
                GpiErase (hps) ;

                for (sIndex = 0 ; sIndex < sNumColors ; sIndex ++)
                    {
                    ptl.x = (sIndex < 11 ? 1 : 33) * cxCaps ;
                    ptl.y = cyClient - (sIndex % 11 * 5 + 4) * cyChar / 2
                                                        + cyDesc ;

                    GpiCharStringAt (hps, &ptl,
                            (LONG) strlen (show [sIndex].szColorIndex),
                                    show [sIndex].szColorIndex) ;

                    ptl.x = (sIndex < 11 ? 20 : 52) * cxCaps ;
                    ptl.y -= cyDesc + cyChar / 2 ;
                    GpiMove (hps, &ptl) ;

                    GpiSavePS (hps) ;
                    GpiSetColor (hps, show [sIndex].lColorIndex) ;

                    ptl.x += 10 * cxCaps ;
                    ptl.y += 2 * cyChar ;
                    GpiBox (hps, DRO_FILL, &ptl, 0L, 0L) ;

                    GpiRestorePS (hps, -1L) ;
                    }
                WinEndPaint (hps) ;
                return 0 ;
        }
    return WinDefWindowProc (hwnd, msg, mp1, mp2) ;
    }
```

The COLORS.DEF File

```
;------------------------------------
; COLORS.DEF module definition file
;------------------------------------

NAME            COLORS    WINDOWAPI

DESCRIPTION     'GPI Foreground Colors (C) Charles Petzold, 1988'
PROTMODE
HEAPSIZE        1024
STACKSIZE       8192
EXPORTS         ClientWndProc
```

Figure 5-18. *The COLORS program.*

This program sets the color by calling *GpiSetColor* and then calls the *GpiBox* function to draw a solid rectangle using that color.

The *GpiSetColor* function sets the color for all GPI primitives, including text. How does COLORS prevent the text from appearing in color? Very simple: COLORS calls the *GpiSavePS* function before calling *GpiSetColor* and calls *GpiRestorePS* after calling *GpiBox*. The *GpiSavePS* function saves all the attributes of the presentation space and *GpiRestorePS* restores them. If you remove these two functions from COLORS, you'll find that the text displayed by *GpiCharStringAt* will also appear in various colors.

I could have simplified COLORS a little by using the *WinFillRect* function:

```
WinFillRect (hps, &rcl, lColorIndex) ;
```

The second parameter is a pointer to a RECTL structure. The function fills that rectangle with the specified color. The *WinFillRect* function is useful for coloring the background of a client window without calling *GpiErase*:

```
WinQueryWindowRect (hps, &rcl) ;
WinFillRect (hps, &rcl, CLR_CYAN) ;
```

WinFillRect is one of the few drawing functions that begins with a *Win* prefix rather than *Gpi*. (You encountered another of these functions — *WinDrawText* — in Chapter 2.) These are high-level drawing functions that do the work of several GPI functions. They are often convenient but can be used only on a video display. Another useful high-level drawing function is *WinDrawBorder*.

Foreground Mix Mode

The use of color may seem fairly straightforward, but it's not. In general, GPI does not simply draw a color on the display. Instead, GPI performs a bitwise operation between the foreground color of the image you're drawing (the source color) and the color already on the surface of the display (the destination color). This operation is called the "mix mode" or simply the "mix."

Let's approach this by thinking about a monochrome video display that is capable of two colors: black and white. Each pixel on the display can be represented by either 0 (black) or 1 (white).

You want to draw a pixel on this display. This source pixel can be 0 or 1. The surface of the display where you want to draw this pixel (the destination) can also be either 0 or 1. The resultant color of the drawn pixel is defined by the mix mode.

There are 16 possible mix modes. These are represented by identifiers defined in PMGPI.H that begin with FM ("foreground mix"). The following table uses C notation to show the bitwise combinations of pixels:

Source (SRC): 0	0	1	1		
Destination (DEST): 0	1	0	1	Operation	Mix Mode
Result: 0	0	0	0	0	FM_ZERO
0	0	0	1	SRC & DEST	FM_AND
0	0	1	0	SRC & ~DEST	FM_MASKSRCNOT
0	0	1	1	SRC	FM_OVERPAINT
0	1	0	0	~SRC & DEST	FM_SUBTRACT
0	1	0	1	DEST	FM_LEAVEALONE
0	1	1	0	SRC ^ DEST	FM_XOR
0	1	1	1	SRC ¦ DEST	FM_OR
1	0	0	0	~(SRC ¦ DEST)	FM_NOTMERGESRC
1	0	0	1	~(SRC ^ DEST)	FM_NOTXORSRC
1	0	1	0	~DEST	FM_INVERT
1	0	1	1	SRC ¦ ~DEST	FM_MERGESRCNOT
1	1	0	0	~SRC	FM_NOTCOPYSRC
1	1	0	1	~SRC ¦ DEST	FM_MERGENOTSRC
1	1	1	0	~(SRC & DEST)	FM_NOTMASKSRC
1	1	1	1	1	FM_ONE

You can change the mix mode by calling the following function:

```
GpiSetMix (hps, lMixMode)
```

where *lMixMode* is one of the FM identifiers shown in the table. The default mix mode is FM_OVERPAINT, which transfers the color specified by the *GpiSetColor* to the destination regardless of the color of the destination. This is what we intuitively expect to happen. The PMGPI.H header file also includes the identifier FM_DEFAULT, which has the same effect as FM_OVERPAINT.

If the mix mode is set to FM_XOR, the resulting pixel will be white (1) only if either the source and destination pixels (but not both) were also white. That is, the FM_XOR mix mode causes source pixels of 1 to invert the destination and source pixels of 0 to leave it unchanged:

- If you set color to CLR_BLACK and the mix mode to FM_XOR, any lines you draw on a black background will be black, and any lines you draw on a white background will be white.

- If you set color to CLR_WHITE and the mix mode to FM_XOR, any lines you draw on a black background will be white; any lines you draw on a white background will be black.

With color, the situation gets just a little more complex. Consider the EGA and VGA display adapters in high-resolution graphics mode. These adapters use 4 bits (intensity, red, green, and blue) for each pixel. The mix mode works on each of these bits individually. For example, if a window is colored with CLR_RED, the surface of the window has its intensity and red bits set to 1 and its blue and green bits set to 0. If you set color to CLR_BLUE, the intensity and blue bits are set to 1, and the green and red bits are set to 0. You use the FM_XOR mix mode and display a line. The text is displayed in CLR_DARKPINK. The resultant red and blue bits are set to 1, and the intensity and green bits are set to 0.

The FM_ZERO mix mode causes the GPI primitive you draw to be displayed in black regardless of the destination color and the color you set with *GpiSetColor*. Similarly, FM_ONE causes a GPI primitive to be displayed in white. The FM_LEAVEALONE mix causes the GPI primitive to be invisible.

The FM_INVERT mix mode causes a GPI primitive to invert the color of the destination regardless of the color you set. For example, text drawn on a CLR_RED destination is displayed as CLR_DARKCYAN. FM_INVERT is useful for drawing and erasing an object. When you draw the same object a second time, the destination reverts to its original color. This technique is used in the WEB program in Chapter 9.

The Background Color and Mix

GPI also has two functions for setting the background color and mix:

```
GpiSetBackColor (hps, lColorIndex) ;
```

and

```
GpiSetBackMix (hps, lMixMode) ;
```

Use of the CLR_DEFAULT as a parameter to *GpiSetBackColor* has the same effect as CLR_BACKGROUND. For the *lMixMode* parameter to *GpiSetBackMix*, you use identifiers beginning with BM ("background mix") rather than FM. Not all mix modes are supported for background mixing. The supported background mixes are shown in the following table:

Source (SRC): 0	0	1	1		
Destination (DEST): 0	1	0	1	*Operation*	*Mix Mode*
Result: 0	0	1	1	SRC	BM_OVERPAINT
0	1	0	1	DEST	BM_LEAVEALONE
0	1	1	0	SRC ∧ DEST	BM_XOR
0	1	1	1	SRC ¦ DEST	BM_OR

The default background mix is BM_LEAVEALONE. (BM_DEFAULT provides the same result.) If you want to use a background color, you'll have to change the background mix to something other than BM_LEAVEALONE. Otherwise, GPI will ignore the background color.

The background color and mix don't affect lines, but do affect patterns. You'll note that many of the patterns are composed of lines or dots. These lines and dots are drawn on the display using the foreground color and foreground mix mode. The area between the lines and dots is drawn on the display using the background color and background mix mode.

For example, suppose you make the following series of function calls:

```
GpiSetColor (hps, CLR_BLUE) ;
GpiSetMix (hps, FM_OVERPAINT) ;
GpiSetBackColor (hps, CLR_RED) ;
GpiSetBackMix (hps, BM_OVERPAINT) ;
GpiSetPattern (hps, PATSYM_VERT) ;
```

When you call *GpiBox* with an option of DRO_FILL or DRO_OUTLINEFILL, the pattern will have blue vertical lines on a red background, regardless of the original color of the display.

GPI Primitive 3: Text

Text is the most common GPI primitive yet potentially the most complex because of the use of various fonts. GPI allows you to enumerate all the fonts available on the system and choose different fonts for the display of text. Many of these fonts (such as the default system font) contain characters of varying widths. In addition, you can alter the default spacing of characters to achieve such effects as justified text.

The Text Output Functions

GPI has four text output functions:

- *GpiCharStringAt*

- *GpiCharString*

- *GpiCharStringPos*

- *GpiCharStringPosAt*

The *GpiCharStringAt* and *GpiCharString* Functions

Perhaps the most common text output function is the function introduced in Chapter 4:

```
GpiCharStringAt (hps, &ptl, lLength, &cString) ;
```

The last parameter is a character array or a pointer to a character string. The *lLength* parameter is the length of this string. The POINTL structure indicates the starting position of the text. This is usually the baseline of the left side of the first character. (We'll look at an exception to this rule shortly.)

You can also use the *GpiCharString* function to display text:

```
GpiCharString (hps, lLength, &cString) ;
```

It is the same as *GpiCharStringAt*, except that the text begins at the current position. The *GpiCharStringAt* function is equivalent to

```
GpiMove (hps, &ptl) ;
GpiCharString (hps, lLength, &cString) ;
```

Following the *GpiCharString* and *GpiCharStringAt* calls, the current position is usually set to the baseline of the right side of the last character. (Again, there are exceptions.) Therefore, you can call *GpiCharString* again to continue a line of text.

The *GpiCharStringPos* and *GpiCharStringPosAt* Functions

Two other text output functions have some additional parameters:

```
GpiCharStringPos (hps, &rcl, lOptions, lLength, &cString, alIncrement) ;
GpiCharStringPosAt (hps, &ptl, &rcl, lOptions, lLength, &cString, alIncrement) ;
```

The *GpiCharStringPos* function begins the text at the current position; the *GpiCharStringPosAt* function begins the string at the POINTL structure passed as the second parameter. Information in the following discussion of *GpiCharStringPos* also applies to *GpiCharStringPosAt*.

The simplest form of *GpiCharStringPos* results from setting the *&rcl* and *alIncrement* parameters to NULL and the *lOptions* parameter to 0:

```
GpiCharStringPos (hps, NULL, OL, lLength, &cString, NULL) ;
```

In this form, the function is equivalent to *GpiCharString*. Nonzero *lOption* values cause some different results.

You can set the *lOption* parameter to CHS_LEAVEPOS:

```
GpiCharStringPos (hps, NULL, CHS_LEAVEPOS, lLength, &cString, NULL) ;
```

On return from the function, the current position will be set at the beginning of the string rather than the end. That is, the *GpiCharStringPos* function leaves the current position unchanged, but *GpiCharStringPosAt* sets the current position to the POINTL structure passed to the function.

If you include the *&rcl* parameter (a pointer to a RECTL structure), you can use the CHS_CLIP option:

```
GpiCharStringPos (hps, &rcl, CHS_CLIP, lLength, &cString, NULL) ;
```

In this case the character string will be clipped to the interior of the rectangle. Any part of the text string falling outside the rectangle will not be displayed. The *&rcl* parameter is also required for the CHS_OPAQUE option, as follows:

```
GpiCharStringPos (hps, &rcl, CHS_OPAQUE, lLength, &cString, NULL) ;
```

In this case the rectangle is colored with the current background color before the text is displayed. GPI temporarily sets the background mix to BM_OVERPAINT before coloring the rectangle.

The fourth and final option is CHS_VECTOR. This function requires that the last parameter be an array of LONG integers:

```
GpiCharStringPos (hps, NULL, CHS_VECTOR, lLength, &cString, alIncrement) ;
```

The *alIncrement* array contains *lLength* LONG values. GPI uses this array to position the successive characters in the string, thereby overriding the default spacing. The CHS_VECTOR option is the reason for the *Pos* (''position'') part of the *GpiCharStringPos* and *GpiCharStringPosAt* function names.

You can use any combination of the CHS_OPAQUE, CHS_VECTOR, CHS_LEAVEPOS, and CHS_CLIP identifiers by combining them with the C bitwise OR operator. The RECTL structure passed as the second parameter is required only for CHS_OPAQUE or CHS_CLIP. The array of LONG increment values passed as the last parameter is required only when you use CHS_VECTOR.

Text Color

The color and mix mode affect the display of characters in the text string. We've already seen how the CHS_OPAQUE option in *GpiCharStringPos* and *GpiCharStringPosAt* functions can cause GPI to use the background color to color a rectangle before displaying the text.

You can also use the background color and background mix with other forms of the text output functions. If you set the background mix to something other than BM_LEAVEALONE, the background color is used to color the small rectangular character cells that surround each character. You might want to do this if you are displaying text over some existing graphics and want the text to be more distinct. (Some GPI fonts are ''outline'' fonts and will not be affected by the background color and mix.)

Font Files

The subject of fonts is quite complex, yet we must attack it. As you discovered in Chapter 4, the default system font is proportionally spaced. Although we have been successful in working with this font, it is not appropriate for all applications. For example, a programmer's text editor or a communications program should probably use a fixed-pitch font, in which every character has the same width. We at least want to be able to switch to a fixed-pitch font. The ability to use boldface and italic versions of fonts would be nice also.

GPI supports fonts in two very different formats: "Image" fonts are stored as small bitmaps with 0 bits for the background of the character and 1 bits for the character itself. "Vector" fonts are stored as a series of straight lines and curves. This discussion is limited to image fonts.

The OS/2 Presentation Manager includes three files that contain collections of image fonts in various point sizes for various output devices. These files, and the image fonts they contain, are shown in the following table:

Font File	Font Face Name	Point Sizes
COURIER.FON	"Courier"	8, 10, 12
HELV.FON	"Helv"	8, 10, 12, 14, 18, 24
TIMES.FON	"Tms Rmn"	8, 10, 12, 14, 18, 24

> **NOTE:** *These three font files are stored in the C:\OS2\DLL directory on your hard disk. To use the fonts in these files, you must install the fonts from the Presentation Manager Control Panel. It is only necessary to install one font from each file. The Control Panel writes information to the OS2.INI file to load the fonts for use whenever you use the Presentation Manager.*

The default system font is stored in DISPLAY.DLL, the dynamic link library for the video display. It has a font face name of "System Proportional" and a point size of 12.

Each font is identified by a face name and a point size. The "Courier" font is a fixed-pitch font similar to that produced by a typewriter. The "Helv" (Helvetica) and "Tms Rmn" (Times Roman) fonts are both proportional fonts. "Helv" is a sans serif font, which means that it does not have small lines finishing off the strokes of the characters. "Tms Rmn" has serifs and is commonly used for text in magazines and books.

The point size refers to the maximum height of the characters. One point is approximately $1/72$ inch. However, if you set page units to Low English, High English, or Twips, the size of the fonts will not necessarily agree with the GPI page units. For example, a 24-point font will not be 480 twips high. The size of the fonts is based on an ideal "font resolution" for the device. You can obtain this font resolution from *DevQueryCaps* using the CAPS_HORIZONTAL_FONT_RES and CAPS_VERTICAL_FONT_RES. As you can see from Figure 5-8, these values for the EGA are set to 96 pixels and 72 pixels. This is greater than the actual resolution of the device, to allow fonts as small as 8 points to be legible on the screen.

The EASYFONT System

Working with fonts can be difficult, but I've attempted to make it a little easier for you. Figure 5-19 shows two files named EASYFONT.H and EASY-FONT.C that can greatly assist you in working with fonts in your Presentation Manager programs.

The EASYFONT.H File

```
/*---------------------------------------
   EASYFONT.H header file for EASYFONT.C
   -------------------------------------*/

BOOL EzfQueryFonts     (HPS hps) ;
LONG EzfCreateLogFont (HPS hps, LONG lcid, USHORT idFace, USHORT idSize,
                                           USHORT fsSelection) ;


#define FONTFACE_SYSTEM   0
#define FONTFACE_COUR     1
#define FONTFACE_HELV     2
#define FONTFACE_TIMES    3


#define FONTSIZE_8        0
#define FONTSIZE_10       1
#define FONTSIZE_12       2
#define FONTSIZE_14       3
#define FONTSIZE_18       4
#define FONTSIZE_24       5
```

The EASYFONT.C File

```
/*---------------------------------------------
   EASYFONT.C -- Routines for Using Image Fonts
   -------------------------------------------*/

#define INCL_GPI
#include <os2.h>
#include <stdlib.h>
#include <string.h>
#include "easyfont.h"

static SHORT sFontSize[6]   = { 80, 100, 120, 140, 180, 240 } ;
static CHAR  *szFacename[4] = { "System Proportional",
                                "Courier", "Helv", "Tms Rmn" } ;
static LONG  alMatch[4][6] ;
```

(continued)

Figure 5-19. The EASYFONT.C File. *continued*

```
BOOL EzfQueryFonts (HPS hps)
    {
    FONTMETRICS *pfm ;
    HDC         hdc ;
    LONG        lHorzRes, lVertRes, lRequestFonts, lNumberFonts ;
    SHORT       sIndex, sFace, sSize ;

    hdc = GpiQueryDevice (hps) ;
    DevQueryCaps (hdc, CAPS_HORIZONTAL_FONT_RES, 1L, &lHorzRes) ;
    DevQueryCaps (hdc, CAPS_VERTICAL_FONT_RES,   1L, &lVertRes) ;

    for (sFace = 0 ; sFace < 4 ; sFace++)
        {
        lRequestFonts = 0 ;
        lNumberFonts = GpiQueryFonts (hps, QF_PUBLIC, szFacename[sFace],
                                      &lRequestFonts, 0L, NULL) ;

        if (lNumberFonts == 0)
            continue ;

        if (lNumberFonts * sizeof (FONTMETRICS) >= 65536L)
            return FALSE ;

        pfm = malloc ((SHORT) lNumberFonts * sizeof (FONTMETRICS)) ;

        if (pfm == NULL)
            return FALSE ;

        GpiQueryFonts (hps, QF_PUBLIC, szFacename[sFace],
                       &lNumberFonts, (LONG) sizeof (FONTMETRICS), pfm) ;

        for (sIndex = 0 ; sIndex < (SHORT) lNumberFonts ; sIndex++)
            if (pfm[sIndex].sXDeviceRes == (SHORT) lHorzRes &&
                pfm[sIndex].sYDeviceRes == (SHORT) lVertRes &&
               (pfm[sIndex].fsDefn & 1) == 0)
                {
                for (sSize = 0 ; sSize < 6 ; sSize++)
                    if (pfm[sIndex].sNominalPointSize == sFontSize[sSize])
                        break ;

                if (sSize != 6)
                    alMatch[sFace][sSize] = pfm[sIndex].lMatch ;
                }

        free (pfm) ;
        }
```

(continued)

Figure 5-19. The EASYFONT.C File. *continued*

```
        return TRUE ;
        }

LONG EzfCreateLogFont (HPS hps, LONG lcid, USHORT idFace, USHORT idSize,
                                           USHORT fsSelection)
        {
        static FATTRS fat ;

        if (idFace > 3 || idSize > 5 || alMatch[idFace][idSize] == 0)
            return FALSE ;

        fat.usRecordLength = sizeof fat ;
        fat.fsSelection    = fsSelection ;
        fat.lMatch         = alMatch[idFace][idSize] ;

        strcpy (fat.szFacename, szFacename[idFace]) ;

        return GpiCreateLogFont (hps, NULL, lcid, &fat) ;
        }
```

Figure 5-19. *The EASYFONT program.*

EASYFONT.H contains declarations of the two functions in EASYFONT.C. These are *EzfQueryFonts* and *EzfCreateLogFont* ("create logical font"). In addition, EASYFONT.H contains a collection of identifiers you use as parameters to *EzfCreateLogFont*.

To use EASYFONT, include the EASYFONT.H header file in your .C source code file:

```
#include "easyfont.h"
```

Then compile and link EASYFONT.C with your program.

In a window procedure that uses fonts, obtain a handle to a presentation space during the WM_CREATE message and call *EzfQueryFonts*:

```
hps = WinGetPS (hwnd) ;
EzfQueryFonts (hps) ;
WinReleasePS (hps) ;
```

This performs all necessary initialization. Later on, whenever you need to use a non-default font, obtain a handle to a presentation space and call *EzfCreateLogFont*:

```
EzfCreateLogFont (hps, lcid, idFace, idSize, fsSelection) ;
```

The *lcid* parameter is a "local ID." It can be any number between 1 and 254. The *idFace* parameter can be any of the FONTFACE identifiers defined in EASYFONT.H. The *idSize* parameter is one of the FONTSIZE identifiers also defined in EASYFONT.H.

Not all sizes are available for all font face names. In particular, the FONTFACE_SYSTEM identifier can only be used with FONTSIZE_12. The FONTFACE_COUR identifier can only be used with FONTSIZE_8, FONT-SIZE_10, and FONTSIZE_12. *EzfCreateLogFont* returns TRUE if the font exists and FALSE otherwise. You should check the return value before attempting to use the logical font you asked for.

The *fsSelection* parameter can be any one of the following identifiers defined in OS2DEF.H:

Identifier	Meaning
FATTR_SEL_ITALIC	Italic font
FATTR_SEL_UNDERSCORE	Underlined font
FATTR_SEL_STRIKEOUT	Line drawn through characters
FATTR_SEL_BOLD	Boldface font

Use 0 if you want a normal font without any attributes.

EzfCreateLogFont creates a logical font associated with a local ID. To use this font, you pass the local ID to *GpiSetCharSet*:

```
GpiSetCharSet (hps, lcid) ;
```

After this call, you can use *GpiQueryFontMetrics* to get the dimensions of the new font. Any text you draw will be displayed with the new font. Before releasing the presentation space, go back to the default font:

```
GpiSetCharSet (hps, LCID_DEFAULT) ;
```

Then delete the local ID you used:

```
GpiDeleteSetId (hps, lcid) ;
```

You can call *EzfCreateLogFont* multiple times to create different logical fonts, each associated with a unique local ID. You then use *GpiSetCharSet* to use any one of these fonts for text output. Be sure to set the default font and delete all local IDs before releasing the presentation space.

The *EzfQueryFonts* function in EASYFONT.C first obtains the horizontal and vertical font resolution of the output device from *DevQueryCaps*. This is necessary because the font files contain image fonts for various output devices. For each of the four font faces, the function calls *GpiQueryFonts* to determine how many fonts are present and then allocates memory to store that number of FONTMETRICS structures. *GpiQueryFonts* is called again to obtain the FONTMETRICS structures for all the available fonts. Each font is checked against the device resolution and the desired point sizes. The function saves a field of the FONTMETRICS structure named *lMatch* in a static array. This value is used in the *GpiCreateLogFont* call in *EzfCreateLogFont*.

Figure 5-20 shows a program called FONTS, which uses EASYFONT to display all of the fonts available for use.

The FONTS File

```
#-----------------
# FONTS make file
#-----------------

fonts.obj : fonts.c easyfont.h
    cl -c -G2sw -W3 fonts.c

easyfont.obj : easyfont.c
    cl -c -G2sw -W3 easyfont.c

fonts.exe : fonts.obj easyfont.obj fonts.def
    link fonts easyfont, /align:16, NUL, os2, fonts
```

The FONTS.C File

```
/*---------------------------
   FONTS.C -- GPI Image Fonts
   ---------------------------*/

#define INCL_WIN
#define INCL_GPI
#include <os2.h>
#include <stdio.h>
#include <stdlib.h>
#include "easyfont.h"

#define LCID_MYFONT 1L

MRESULT EXPENTRY ClientWndProc (HWND, USHORT, MPARAM, MPARAM) ;
```

(continued)

Figure 5-20. The FONTS.C File. *continued*

```
int main (void)
    {
    static CHAR  szClientClass [] = "Fonts" ;
    static ULONG flFrameFlags = FCF_TITLEBAR       | FCF_SYSMENU   |
                                FCF_SIZEBORDER     | FCF_MINMAX    |
                                FCF_SHELLPOSITION  | FCF_TASKLIST  |
                                FCF_VERTSCROLL     | FCF_HORZSCROLL ;

    HAB          hab ;
    HMQ          hmq ;
    HWND         hwndFrame, hwndClient ;
    QMSG         qmsg ;


    hab = WinInitialize (0) ;
    hmq = WinCreateMsgQueue (hab, 0) ;

    WinRegisterClass (hab, szClientClass, ClientWndProc, CS_SIZEREDRAW, 0) ;

    hwndFrame = WinCreateStdWindow (HWND_DESKTOP, WS_VISIBLE,
                                    &flFrameFlags, szClientClass, NULL,
                                    OL, NULL, 0, &hwndClient) ;

    WinSendMsg (hwndFrame, WM_SETICON,
                WinQuerySysPointer (HWND_DESKTOP, SPTR_APPICON, FALSE),
                NULL) ;

    while (WinGetMsg (hab, &qmsg, NULL, 0, 0))
        WinDispatchMsg (hab, &qmsg) ;

    WinDestroyWindow (hwndFrame) ;
    WinDestroyMsgQueue (hmq) ;
    WinTerminate (hab) ;
    return 0 ;
    }

MRESULT EXPENTRY ClientWndProc (HWND hwnd, USHORT msg, MPARAM mp1, MPARAM mp2)
    {
    static CHAR   *szFace[] = { "System", "Courier",
                               "Helv",   "Tms Rmn" } ;
    static CHAR   *szSize[] = { "8", "10", "12", "14", "18", "24" } ;
    static CHAR   *szSel[]  = { "Normal",     "Italic", "Underscore",
                               "Strike-out", "Bold" } ;
    static CHAR   szBuffer[80] ;
    static HWND   hwndVscroll, hwndHscroll ;
    static USHORT idFace[] = { FONTFACE_SYSTEM, FONTFACE_COUR,
                               FONTFACE_HELV,   FONTFACE_TIMES } ;
```

(continued)

Figure 5-20. The FONTS.C File. *continued*

```
        static USHORT  idSize[] = { FONTSIZE_8,  FONTSIZE_10, FONTSIZE_12,
                                    FONTSIZE_14, FONTSIZE_18, FONTSIZE_24 } ;
        static USHORT  afsSel[] = { 0, FATTR_SEL_ITALIC,    FATTR_SEL_UNDERSCORE,
                                    FATTR_SEL_STRIKEOUT, FATTR_SEL_BOLD } ;
        static SHORT   sVscrollMax = sizeof idFace / sizeof idFace[0] - 1,
                       sHscrollMax = sizeof afsSel / sizeof afsSel[0] - 1,
                       cxClient, cyClient, sHscrollPos, sVscrollPos ;
        FONTMETRICS    fm ;
        HPS            hps;
        HWND           hwndFrame ;
        POINTL         ptl ;
        SHORT          sIndex ;

        switch (msg)
            {
            case WM_CREATE:
                hps = WinGetPS (hwnd) ;
                EzfQueryFonts (hps) ;
                WinReleasePS (hps) ;

                hwndFrame   = WinQueryWindow (hwnd, QW_PARENT, FALSE),
                hwndVscroll = WinWindowFromID (hwndFrame, FID_VERTSCROLL) ;
                hwndHscroll = WinWindowFromID (hwndFrame, FID_HORZSCROLL) ;

                WinSendMsg (hwndVscroll, SBM_SETSCROLLBAR,
                            MPFROM2SHORT (sVscrollPos, 0),
                            MPFROM2SHORT (0, sVscrollMax)) ;

                WinSendMsg (hwndHscroll, SBM_SETSCROLLBAR,
                            MPFROM2SHORT (sHscrollPos, 0),
                            MPFROM2SHORT (0, sHscrollMax)) ;
                return 0 ;

            case WM_SIZE:
                cxClient = SHORT1FROMMP (mp2) ;
                cyClient = SHORT2FROMMP (mp2) ;
                return 0 ;

            case WM_VSCROLL:
                switch (SHORT2FROMMP (mp2))
                    {
                    case SB_LINEUP:
                    case SB_PAGEUP:
                        sVscrollPos = max (0, sVscrollPos - 1) ;
                        break ;
```

(continued)

Figure 5-20. The FONTS.C File. *continued*

```
                         case SB_LINEDOWN:
                         case SB_PAGEDOWN:
                              sVscrollPos = min (sVscrollMax, sVscrollPos + 1) ;
                              break ;

                         case SB_SLIDERPOSITION:
                              sVscrollPos = SHORT1FROMMP (mp2) ;
                              break ;

                         default:
                              return 0 ;
                         }
                    WinSendMsg (hwndVscroll, SBM_SETPOS,
                              MPFROM2SHORT (sVscrollPos, 0), NULL) ;

                    WinInvalidateRect (hwnd, NULL, FALSE) ;
                    return 0 ;

          case WM_HSCROLL:
               switch (SHORT2FROMMP (mp2))
                    {
                    case SB_LINELEFT:
                    case SB_PAGELEFT:
                         sHscrollPos = max (0, sHscrollPos - 1) ;
                         break ;

                    case SB_LINERIGHT:
                    case SB_PAGERIGHT:
                         sHscrollPos = min (sHscrollMax, sHscrollPos + 1) ;
                         break ;

                    case SB_SLIDERPOSITION:
                         sHscrollPos = SHORT1FROMMP (mp2) ;
                         break ;

                    default:
                         return 0 ;
                    }
               WinSendMsg (hwndHscroll, SBM_SETPOS,
                         MPFROM2SHORT (sHscrollPos, 0), NULL) ;

               WinInvalidateRect (hwnd, NULL, FALSE) ;
               return 0 ;

          case WM_CHAR:
               switch (CHARMSG(&msg)->vkey)
```

(continued)

Figure 5-20. The FONTS.C File. *continued*

```
                        {
                   case VK_LEFT:
                   case VK_RIGHT:
                        return WinSendMsg (hwndHscroll, msg, mp1, mp2) ;
                   case VK_UP:
                   case VK_DOWN:
                   case VK_PAGEUP:
                   case VK_PAGEDOWN:
                        return WinSendMsg (hwndVscroll, msg, mp1, mp2) ;
                        }
               break ;

          case WM_PAINT:
               hps = WinBeginPaint (hwnd, NULL, NULL) ;
               GpiErase (hps) ;

               ptl.x = 0 ;
               ptl.y = cyClient ;

               for (sIndex = 0 ; sIndex < 6 ; sIndex++)
                    if (EzfCreateLogFont (hps, LCID_MYFONT,
                                          idFace[sVscrollPos],
                                          idSize[sIndex],
                                          afsSel[sHscrollPos]))
                         {
                         GpiSetCharSet (hps, LCID_MYFONT) ;
                         GpiQueryFontMetrics (hps, (LONG) sizeof fm, &fm) ;

                         ptl.y -= fm.lMaxBaselineExt ;

                         GpiCharStringAt (hps, &ptl,
                              (LONG) sprintf (szBuffer, "%s, %s point, %s",
                                             szFace[sVscrollPos],
                                             szSize[sIndex],
                                             szSel[sHscrollPos]),
                              szBuffer) ;

                         GpiSetCharSet (hps, LCID_DEFAULT) ;
                         GpiDeleteSetId (hps, LCID_MYFONT) ;
                         }

               WinEndPaint (hps) ;
               return 0 ;
          }
     return WinDefWindowProc (hwnd, msg, mp1, mp2) ;
     }
```

The FONTS.DEF File

```
;----------------------------------------
; FONTS.DEF module definition file
;----------------------------------------

NAME            FONTS       WINDOWAPI

DESCRIPTION     'Displays GPI Image Fonts (C) Charles Petzold, 1988'
PROTMODE
HEAPSIZE        1024
STACKSIZE       8192
EXPORTS         ClientWndProc
```

Figure 5-20. *The FONTS program.*

Several programs in upcoming chapters (KEYLOOK and TYPEAWAY in Chapter 8 and HEAD in Chapter 14) use EASYFONT to obtain a fixed-pitch Courier font for text output.

You'll notice that the FONTS make file also compiles EASYFONT.C and links EASYFONT.OBJ with the program. FONTS.C includes EASYFONT.H for the function declarations and definitions of the FONTFACE and FONT-SIZE identifiers.

Each screen in FONTS shows all the available font sizes for a particular face name and *fsSelection* attribute (such as italics). You change the *fsSelection* attribute using the horizontal scroll bar and the face name using the vertical scroll bar. The "Tms Rmn" italic fonts are shown in Figure 5-21.

GPI Primitive 4: Marker Symbols

"Markers" are small symbols about the same size as a system font character. (To determine the size of a marker, call *DevQueryCaps* with the CAPS_MARKER_WIDTH and CAPS_MARKER_HEIGHT identifiers.) You can use markers as bullets or data points on a line graph.

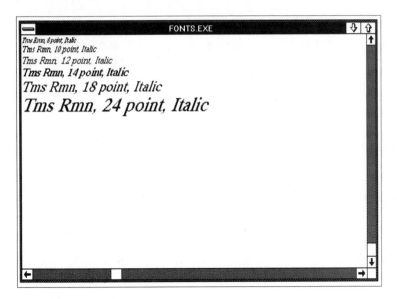

Figure 5-21. *The FONTS display.*

Drawing a Marker

You can draw a marker by calling the following function:

```
GpiMarker (hps, &ptl) ;
```

GPI draws the marker with its center at the point specified in the POINTL structure. The current position is also set to that point.

You can also draw a series of markers:

```
GpiPolyMarker (hps, l Number, aptl) ;
```

The *aptl* parameter is an array of *lNumber* POINTL structures. Like *GpiPolyLine*, *GpiPolyMarker* is more efficient than multiple *GpiMarker* calls because the repetition occurs within the device driver. The current position is set to the last point.

If you use markers to indicate data points on a line graph, you can use the same array of POINTL structures for drawing the line and drawing the markers. For example, suppose *aptl* contains *sNum* data points for the graph. This code will draw the line and the markers:

```
GpiMove (hps, aptl) ;
GpiPolyLine (hps, sNum - 1L, aptl + 1) ;
GpiPolyMarker (hps, (LONG) sNum, aptl) ;
```

Selecting a Different Marker Symbol

The default marker has the appearance of a small x and has the name MARKSYM_CROSS. You can use the *GpiSetMarker* function to select a different marker:

```
GpiSetMarker (hps, lSymbol) ;
```

The *lSymbol* parameter can be any of the following identifiers:

MARKSYM_DEFAULT	MARKSYM_EIGHTPOINTSTAR
MARKSYM_CROSS	MARKSYM_SOLIDDIAMOND
MARKSYM_PLUS	MARKSYM_SOLIDSQUARE
MARKSYM_DIAMOND	MARKSYM_DOT
MARKSYM_SQUARE	MARKSYM_SMALLCIRCLE
MARKSYM_SIXPOINTSTAR	MARKSYM_BLANK

The MARKSYM_DEFAULT identifier has the same effect as MARKSYM_CROSS.

The marker is drawn using the current color and mix. The background of the rectangle that encompasses the marker is drawn using the current background color and background mix.

GPI Primitive 5: Images

I began this chapter by noting that GPI is fundamentally a vector graphics system. But this final GPI primitive looks like it belongs more to the realm of raster graphics. An "image" is a collection of bytes whose bits define a little picture. Each bit corresponds to a display pixel.

You display an image by calling

```
GpiImage (hps, 0L, &sizl, lLength, abData) ;
```

The last parameter is an array of bytes that is *lLength* bytes long. This is the image data. The third parameter is a pointer to a SIZEL structure. The SIZEL structure is similar to the POINTL structure except that the fields are named *cx* and *cy*. This structure defines the width and height of the image in pixels.

The data in *abData* is organized with the top row of bits first. The first byte contains the 8 leftmost bits of this row. The most significant bit of the first byte is the leftmost pixel. Each row of bits must begin with a new byte; if the width of the image is not a multiple of 8, the last few bits of the last byte

of each row are not used. Thus you can calculate *lLength* using the following formula:

```
lLength = (sizl.cx + 7) / 8 * sizl.cy ;
```

The leftmost pixel of the top row is displayed at the current position.
GpiImage does not change the current position. The 1 bits are displayed
with the current foreground color and mix, and the 0 bits are displayed with
the current background color and mix.

The IMAGECAT program shown in Figure 5-22 uses the *GpiImage* function
to draw a little cat in the center of the client window.

The IMAGECAT File

```
#-------------------
# IMAGECAT make file
#-------------------

imagecat.obj : imagecat.c
    cl -c -G2sw -W3 imagecat.c

imagecat.exe : imagecat.obj imagecat.def
    link imagecat, /align:16, NUL, os2, imagecat
```

The IMAGECAT.C File

```
/*----------------------------------------
   IMAGECAT.C -- Cat drawn using GpiImage
   ----------------------------------------*/

#define INCL_WIN
#define INCL_GPI
#include <os2.h>
#include <stdlib.h>

MRESULT EXPENTRY ClientWndProc (HWND, USHORT, MPARAM, MPARAM) ;

int main (void)
    {
    static CHAR  szClientClass [] = "ImageCat" ;
    static ULONG flFrameFlags = FCF_TITLEBAR      | FCF_SYSMENU  |
                                FCF_SIZEBORDER     | FCF_MINMAX   |
                                FCF_SHELLPOSITION  | FCF_TASKLIST ;
```

(continued)

Figure 5-22. The IMAGECAT.C File. *continued*

```
    HAB         hab ;
    HMQ         hmq ;
    HWND        hwndFrame, hwndClient ;
    QMSG        qmsg ;

    hab = WinInitialize (0) ;
    hmq = WinCreateMsgQueue (hab, 0) ;

    WinRegisterClass (hab, szClientClass, ClientWndProc, CS_SIZEREDRAW, 0) ;

    hwndFrame = WinCreateStdWindow (HWND_DESKTOP, WS_VISIBLE,
                                    &flFrameFlags, szClientClass, NULL,
                                    0L, NULL, 0, &hwndClient) ;

    while (WinGetMsg (hab, &qmsg, NULL, 0, 0))
        WinDispatchMsg (hab, &qmsg) ;

    WinDestroyWindow (hwndFrame) ;
    WinDestroyMsgQueue (hmq) ;
    WinTerminate (hab) ;
    return 0 ;
    }

MRESULT EXPENTRY ClientWndProc (HWND hwnd, USHORT msg, MPARAM mp1, MPARAM mp2)
    {
    static BYTE  abCat [] = {
                        0x01, 0xF8, 0x1F, 0x80, 0x01, 0x04, 0x20, 0x80,
                        0x00, 0x8F, 0xF1, 0x00, 0x00, 0x48, 0x12, 0x00,
                        0x00, 0x28, 0x14, 0x00, 0x00, 0x1A, 0x58, 0x00,
                        0x00, 0x08, 0x10, 0x00, 0x00, 0xFC, 0x3F, 0x00,
                        0x00, 0x09, 0x90, 0x00, 0x00, 0xFC, 0x3F, 0x00,
                        0x00, 0x08, 0x10, 0x00, 0x00, 0x07, 0xE0, 0x00,
                        0x00, 0x08, 0x10, 0x00, 0x00, 0x08, 0x10, 0xC0,
                        0x00, 0x08, 0x10, 0x20, 0x00, 0x10, 0x08, 0x10,
                        0x00, 0x10, 0x08, 0x08, 0x00, 0x10, 0x08, 0x04,
                        0x00, 0x20, 0x04, 0x04, 0x00, 0x20, 0x04, 0x04,
                        0x00, 0x20, 0x04, 0x04, 0x00, 0x40, 0x02, 0x04,
                        0x00, 0x40, 0x02, 0x04, 0x00, 0x40, 0x02, 0x04,
                        0x00, 0xC0, 0x03, 0x04, 0x00, 0x9C, 0x39, 0x08,
                        0x00, 0xA2, 0x45, 0x08, 0x00, 0xA2, 0x45, 0x10,
                        0x00, 0xA2, 0x45, 0xE0, 0x00, 0xA2, 0x45, 0x00,
                        0x00, 0xA2, 0x45, 0x00, 0x00, 0xFF, 0xFF, 0x00 } ;
    static SHORT cxClient, cyClient ;
    HPS         hps ;
    POINTL      ptl ;
    SIZEL       sizl ;
```

(continued)

Figure 5-22. The IMAGECAT.C File. *continued*

```
    switch (msg)
        {
        case WM_SIZE:
             cxClient = SHORT1FROMMP (mp2) ;
             cyClient = SHORT2FROMMP (mp2) ;
             return 0 ;

        case WM_PAINT:
             hps = WinBeginPaint (hwnd, NULL, NULL) ;
             GpiErase (hps) ;

             ptl.x = cxClient / 2 - 16 ;
             ptl.y = cyClient / 2 + 16 ;
             GpiMove (hps, &ptl) ;

             sizl.cx = 32 ;
             sizl.cy = 32 ;
             GpiImage (hps, 0L, &sizl, (LONG) sizeof abCat, abCat) ;

             WinEndPaint (hps) ;
             return 0 ;
        }
    return WinDefWindowProc (hwnd, msg, mp1, mp2) ;
    }
```

The IMAGECAT.DEF File

```
;----------------------------------------
; IMAGECAT.DEF module definition file
;----------------------------------------

NAME            IMAGECAT   WINDOWAPI

DESCRIPTION     'Cat Drawn Using GpiImage (C) Charles Petzold, 1988'
PROTMODE
HEAPSIZE        1024
STACKSIZE       8192
EXPORTS         ClientWndProc
```

Figure 5-22. *The IMAGECAT program.*

The cat is 32 pixels high and 32 pixels wide. It will look a little different on various output devices. Figure 5-23 on the following page shows what it looks like on an EGA.

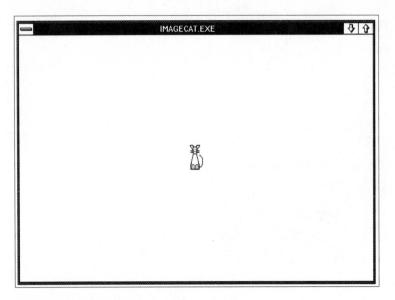

Figure 5-23. *The IMAGECAT display.*

The *GpiImage* function is easy to use but extremely limited. For example, the function cannot alter the size of the displayed image to accommodate various output devices. If *GpiImage* were the only way to display bitmapped data in GPI, it would be important despite its limitations.

Fortunately, *GpiImage* pales in comparison to the *WinDrawBitMap* and *GpiBitBlt* functions, which are the subject of the next chapter. Among other things, we'll use these functions to stretch that little cat to fill the entire client window.

BITMAPS AND BITBLTS

GPI is fundamentally a vector graphics drawing system and can display graphics on both vector and raster output devices. For output to a vector device, the GPI drawing commands are translated into commands the output device understands. For output to a raster device, which displays an image composed of color dots called pixels or pels, the device driver must translate the GPI drawing commands into displayable pixels. If GPI were based on a raster model, then output to a vector device would be nearly impossible.

But GPI is not limited to vector graphics. A Presentation Manager program can also draw pixels on a raster output device. Of course, drawing pixels one at a time can be very slow: The IBM Video Graphics Array (VGA) adapter running in its 640-by-480 graphics mode displays 307,200 pixels on the screen. A laser printer with 300-dots-per-inch resolution requires about 8 million pixels to define an 8½-by-11-inch page.

Instead, a Presentation Manager program that draws pixels usually works with "bitmaps." A bitmap is an array of data organized into rows and columns in which the bits correspond to pixels on the raster output device.

A bitmap can represent either a monochrome or a color image:

- In a monochrome bitmap, each bit corresponds to one pixel. When a monochrome bitmap is displayed, a 0 bit usually corresponds to the background color and a 1 bit is the foreground color.

- In a color bitmap, each pixel requires multiple bits to represent color.

This chapter is generally restricted to monochrome bitmaps but will touch on color when necessary.

Bitmaps are most suitable for small objects that must be frequently redrawn. For example, the mouse pointer you see on the Presentation Manager screen is stored as two bitmaps. Each time you move the mouse, the Presentation Manager must redraw the two bitmaps on the display.

Bitmaps are highly device dependent. Because a bitmap represents an object as a series of pixels, it is usually designed for a particular device. A bitmap designed for the 640-by-350 resolution of the IBM Enhanced Graphics Adapter (EGA) will be distorted when displayed on a VGA. (You can compensate for this by stretching the bitmap, but this introduces other distortions.)

Moreover, not all output devices are raster devices. Although every graphics output device attached to the Presentation Manager can handle vector graphics, only a raster output device can handle bitmaps. In short, don't expect to display a bitmap on a plotter. Even if the device driver could translate the bitmap into approximate plotter commands, the plotter would take a very long time to draw it.

The Bit-Block Transfer

You can think of the entire video display as one big bitmap. The pixels you see on the screen are represented by bits stored in memory on the video display adapter board. Any rectangular area of the video display is also a bitmap. Each bitmap has a size—the number of rows and columns of pixels it contains.

Let's begin our journey into the world of bitmaps by copying a bitmap from one area of the video display to another. This is a job for the powerful *GpiBitBlt* function.

Bitblt (pronounced "bit blit") stands for "bit-block transfer." The term was first used in graphics in connection with the SmallTalk system designed at Xerox Palo Alto Research Center (PARC). In SmallTalk, all graphics output operations are based around the bitblt. Among programmers, "blt" is often used as a verb, as in: "Blt the bitmap on the screen."

The *GpiBitBlt* function is a pixel-mover, or (more vividly) a raster-blaster. As you'll see, the term "transfer" doesn't entirely do justice to the *GpiBitBlt* function. The function actually performs a bitwise operation on pixels and can result in some interesting effects.

Simple Use of *GpiBitBlt*

The MINMAX1 program shown in Figure 6-1 uses the *GpiBitBlt* function to copy the program's minimize-maximize menu (located in the upper-right corner of the frame window) to its client window.

The MINMAX1 File

```
#-------------------
# MINMAX1 make file
#-------------------

minmax1.obj : minmax1.c
    cl -c -G2sw -W3 minmax1.c

minmax1.exe : minmax1.obj minmax1.def
    link minmax1, /align:16, NUL, os2, minmax1
```

The MINMAX1.C File

```
/*----------------------------------------------
   MINMAX1.C -- Bitblt of Minimize-Maximize Menu
  --------------------------------------------*/

#define INCL_WIN
#include <os2.h>

MRESULT EXPENTRY ClientWndProc (HWND, USHORT, MPARAM, MPARAM) ;

int main (void)
    {
    static CHAR  szClientClass [] = "MinMax1" ;
    static ULONG flFrameFlags = FCF_TITLEBAR       | FCF_SYSMENU |
                                FCF_SIZEBORDER      | FCF_MINMAX  |
                                FCF_SHELLPOSITION   | FCF_TASKLIST ;

    HAB          hab ;
    HMQ          hmq ;
    HWND         hwndFrame, hwndClient ;
    QMSG         qmsg ;

    hab = WinInitialize (0) ;
    hmq = WinCreateMsgQueue (hab, 0) ;

    WinRegisterClass (hab, szClientClass, ClientWndProc, CS_SIZEREDRAW, 0) ;
```

(continued)

Figure 6-1. The MINMAX1.C File. *continued*

```
        hwndFrame = WinCreateStdWindow (HWND_DESKTOP, WS_VISIBLE,
                                    &flFrameFlags, szClientClass, NULL,
                                    OL, NULL, O, &hwndClient) ;


        WinSendMsg (hwndFrame, WM_SETICON,
                    WinQuerySysPointer (HWND_DESKTOP, SPTR_APPICON, FALSE),
                    NULL) ;


        while (WinGetMsg (hab, &qmsg, NULL, 0, 0))
            WinDispatchMsg (hab, &qmsg) ;


        WinDestroyWindow (hwndFrame) ;
        WinDestroyMsgQueue (hmq) ;
        WinTerminate (hab) ;
        return 0 ;
        }

MRESULT EXPENTRY ClientWndProc (HWND hwnd, USHORT msg, MPARAM mp1, MPARAM mp2)
        {
        static LONG  cxMinMax, cyMinMax ;
        static SHORT cxClient, cyClient ;
        HPS          hps ;
        POINTL       aptl[3] ;
        LONG         lRow, lCol ;


        switch (msg)
            {
            case WM_CREATE:
                cxMinMax = WinQuerySysValue (HWND_DESKTOP, SV_CXMINMAXBUTTON) ;
                cyMinMax = WinQuerySysValue (HWND_DESKTOP, SV_CYMINMAXBUTTON) ;
                return 0 ;

            case WM_SIZE:
                cxClient = SHORT1FROMMP (mp2) ;
                cyClient = SHORT2FROMMP (mp2) ;
                return 0 ;

            case WM_PAINT:
                hps = WinBeginPaint (hwnd, NULL, NULL) ;

                GpiErase (hps) ;
```

(continued)

Figure 6-1. The MINMAX1.C File. *continued*

```
            for (lRow = 0 ; lRow <= cyClient / cyMinMax ; lRow++)
                for (lCol = 0 ; lCol <= cxClient / cxMinMax ; lCol++)
                    {
                    aptl[0].x = lCol * cxMinMax ;        // target
                    aptl[0].y = lRow * cyMinMax ;        //   lower left

                    aptl[1].x = aptl[0].x + cxMinMax ; // target
                    aptl[1].y = aptl[0].y + cyMinMax ; //   upper right

                    aptl[2].x = cxClient - cxMinMax ;  // source
                    aptl[2].y = cyClient ;             //   lower left

                    GpiBitBlt (hps, hps, 3L, aptl, ROP_SRCCOPY, BBO_AND) ;
                    }
            WinEndPaint (hps) ;
            return 0 ;
        }
    return WinDefWindowProc (hwnd, msg, mp1, mp2) ;
    }
```

The MINMAX1.DEF File

```
;-------------------------------------
; MINMAX1.DEF module definition file
;-------------------------------------


NAME            MINMAX1    WINDOWAPI

DESCRIPTION     'Bitblt of Min-Max Menu (C) Charles Petzold, 1988'
PROTMODE
HEAPSIZE        1024
STACKSIZE       8192
EXPORTS         ClientWndProc
```

Figure 6-1. *The MINMAX1 program.*

But why stop at one bitblt? In fact, MINMAX1 fills its client window with multiple copies of the minimize-maximize window, as shown in Figure 6-2 on the following page. *GpiBitBlt* transfers pixels from a rectangular area on one presentation space (called the "source") to a rectangular area on another presentation space (the "target," or "destination"). In MINMAX1, the two presentation spaces are the same: the cached micro-PS associated with the program's client window. The source rectangle is the minimize-maximize menu; the destination is various rectangles on the client window.

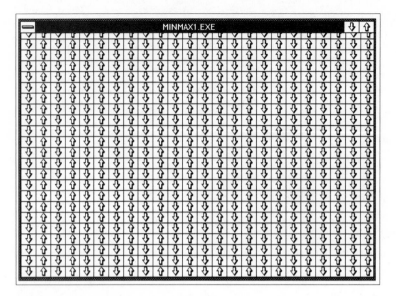

Figure 6-2. *The MINMAX1 display.*

MINMAX1's minimize-maximize menu is outside the program's client window, so you may be surprised that *GpiBitBlt* can access that area of the display. When you're using a cached micro-PS, GPI only prohibits *writing* outside the window. GPI does indeed allow *GpiBitBlt* to access an area outside the window's limits. However, if MINMAX1 tries to repaint its client window when part of the minimize-maximize menu is off the screen or partially obscured, the image within the client window will reflect that by displaying random data. *GpiBitBlt* is reading from the screen — if the image isn't on the screen, the function can't read it.

MINMAX1 calls the *GpiBitBlt* function during the WM_PAINT message based on information obtained during WM_CREATE and WM_SIZE. During the WM_CREATE message, MINMAX1 calls *WinQuerySysValue* to get the size of the minimize-maximize menu. It saves the dimensions in *cxMinMax* and *cyMinMax*. During the WM_SIZE message, MINMAX1 saves the size of the client window in *cxClient* and *cyClient*, as usual. MINMAX1 uses these variables to determine the number of times it calls *GpiBitBlt* during the WM_PAINT message.

As used in MINMAX1, the *GpiBitBlt* function requires an array of three POINTL structures. This array is defined in *ClientWndProc* like this:

```
POINTL aptl[3] ;
```

During the WM_PAINT message, MINMAX1 sets the three POINTL structures with the coordinates (relative to the lower-left corner of the client window) of both the source and destination rectangles, as shown in the following table:

POINTL Structure	Meaning
aptl[0]	Target (or destination) of lower-left corner of bitmap
aptl[1]	Target (or destination) of upper-right corner of bitmap
aptl[2]	Lower-left corner of source bitmap

For each copy of the minimize-maximize menu that MINMAX1 draws, *aptl[2]* is set to the lower-left corner of the source rectangle (that is, the lower-left corner of the minimize-maximize menu) relative to the lower-left corner of the client window:

```
aptl[2].x = cxClient - cxMinMax ;
aptl[2].y = cyClient ;
```

For the first *GpiBitBlt* call during the WM_PAINT message, MINMAX1 sets *aptl[0]* to the point (0,0), which is the lower-left corner of the client window. The *aptl[1]* structure indicates the width and height of the destination rectangle relative to *aptl[0]*. This is shown in Figure 6-3.

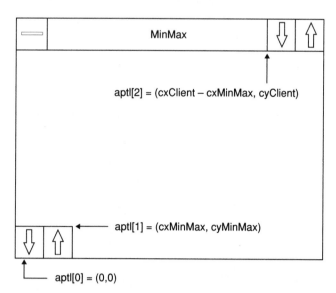

Figure 6-3. *The* aptl *array coordinates for the first* GpiBitBlt *call in MINMAX1.*

For the subsequent *GpiBitBlt* calls in MINMAX1, *aptl[0]* and *aptl[1]* are the lower-left corner and upper-right corner of the target rectangle. This may be a little confusing: *aptl[1]* is documented as the upper-right corner of the destination rectangle, but in MINMAX1 it really indicates the size of the source bitmap. (We'll see why it's specified this way in this next section.)

MINMAX1 passes the *aptl* array to *GpiBitBlt*:

```
GpiBitBlt (hps, hps, 3L, aptl, ROP_SRCCOPY, BBO_AND) ;
```

The general syntax of *GpiBitBlt* is as follows:

```
GpiBitBlt (hpsDest, hpsSource, lNumPoints, aptl, lRasterOp,
           lCompressionType) ;
```

In the case of MINMAX1, the source presentation space (*hpsSource*) and the destination presentation space (*hpsDest*) are the same. The *lNumPoints* parameter indicates the number of POINTL structures passed as the fourth parameter, in this case three. I'll discuss the last two parameters later in this chapter.

Stretching the Bitmap

The third parameter to *GpiBitBlt*, *lNumPoints*, indicates the number of POINTL structures in the array passed as the fourth parameter.

- If you want the copy of the bitmap to be the same size and orientation as the source bitmap (as is the case in MINMAX1), set the *lNumPoints* parameter to 3L.

- If you want to change the size of the bitmap as it is copied, you can use a fourth POINTL structure in the array and specify *lNumPoint* as 4L. This is illustrated in the MINMAX2 program shown in Figure 6-4.

The MINMAX2 File

```
#-------------------
# MINMAX2 make file
#-------------------

minmax2.obj : minmax2.c
    cl -c -G2sw -W3 minmax2.c

minmax2.exe : minmax2.obj minmax2.def
    link minmax2, /align:16, NUL, os2, minmax2
```

The MINMAX2.C File

```
/*-----------------------------------------------
   MINMAX2.C -- Bitblt of Minimize-Maximize Menu
   -----------------------------------------------*/

#define INCL_WIN
#include <os2.h>

MRESULT EXPENTRY ClientWndProc (HWND, USHORT, MPARAM, MPARAM) ;

int main (void)
    {
    static CHAR  szClientClass [] = "MinMax2" ;
    static ULONG flFrameFlags = FCF_TITLEBAR       | FCF_SYSMENU |
                                FCF_SIZEBORDER     | FCF_MINMAX  |
                                FCF_SHELLPOSITION  | FCF_TASKLIST ;
    HAB          hab ;
    HMQ          hmq ;
    HWND         hwndFrame, hwndClient ;
    QMSG         qmsg ;

    hab = WinInitialize (0) ;
    hmq = WinCreateMsgQueue (hab, 0) ;

    WinRegisterClass (hab, szClientClass, ClientWndProc, CS_SIZEREDRAW, 0) ;

    hwndFrame = WinCreateStdWindow (HWND_DESKTOP, WS_VISIBLE,
                                    &flFrameFlags, szClientClass, NULL,
                                    0L, NULL, 0, &hwndClient) ;

    WinSendMsg (hwndFrame, WM_SETICON,
                WinQuerySysPointer (HWND_DESKTOP, SPTR_APPICON, FALSE),
                NULL) ;

    while (WinGetMsg (hab, &qmsg, NULL, 0, 0))
        WinDispatchMsg (hab, &qmsg) ;

    WinDestroyWindow (hwndFrame) ;
    WinDestroyMsgQueue (hmq) ;
    WinTerminate (hab) ;
    return 0 ;
    }

MRESULT EXPENTRY ClientWndProc (HWND hwnd, USHORT msg, MPARAM mp1, MPARAM mp2)
    {
    static LONG  cxMinMax, cyMinMax ;
    static SHORT cxClient, cyClient ;
```

(continued)

Figure 6-4. The MINMAX2.C File. *continued*

```
HPS         hps ;
POINTL      aptl[4] ;

switch (msg)
    {
    case WM_CREATE:
         cxMinMax = WinQuerySysValue (HWND_DESKTOP, SV_CXMINMAXBUTTON) ;
         cyMinMax = WinQuerySysValue (HWND_DESKTOP, SV_CYMINMAXBUTTON) ;
         return 0 ;

    case WM_SIZE:
         cxClient = SHORT1FROMMP (mp2) ;
         cyClient = SHORT2FROMMP (mp2) ;
         return 0 ;

    case WM_PAINT:
         hps = WinBeginPaint (hwnd, NULL, NULL) ;
         GpiErase (hps) ;

         aptl[0].x = 0 ;                      // target lower left
         aptl[0].y = 0 ;

         aptl[1].x = cxClient ;               // target upper right
         aptl[1].y = cyClient ;

         aptl[2].x = cxClient - cxMinMax ;    // source lower left
         aptl[2].y = cyClient ;

         aptl[3].x = cxClient ;               // source upper right
         aptl[3].y = cyClient + cyMinMax ;

         GpiBitBlt (hps, hps, 4L, aptl, ROP_SRCCOPY, BBO_AND) ;

         WinEndPaint (hps) ;
         return 0 ;
    }
return WinDefWindowProc (hwnd, msg, mp1, mp2) ;
}
```

The MINMAX2.DEF File

```
;------------------------------------
; MINMAX2.DEF module definition file
;------------------------------------

NAME          MINMAX2    WINDOWAPI

DESCRIPTION   'Bitblt of Min-Max Menu (C) Charles Petzold, 1988'
PROTMODE
HEAPSIZE      1024
STACKSIZE     8192
EXPORTS       ClientWndProc
```

Figure 6-4. *The MINMAX2 program.*

MINMAX2 calls *GpiBitBlt* only once during the WM_PAINT message, but it does so in style: The minimize-maximize menu is stretched to fill the entire client window, as shown in Figure 6-5.

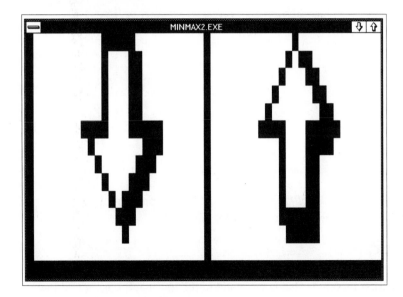

Figure 6-5. *The MINMAX2 display.*

When you use an array of four POINTL structures in the *GpiBitBlt* function, they are interpreted as shown on the next page.

POINTL Structure	Meaning
aptl[0]	Target (or destination) of lower-left corner of bitmap
aptl[1]	Target (or destination) of upper-right corner of bitmap
aptl[2]	Lower-left corner of source bitmap
aptl[3]	Upper-right corner of source bitmap

In MINMAX2, the destination points are the lower-left and upper-right corners of the client window. The two source points are the lower-left and the upper-right corners of the minimize-maximize window. This is shown in Figure 6-6.

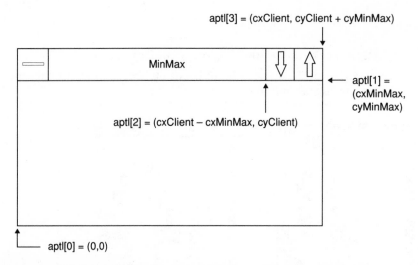

Figure 6-6. *The* aptl *array coordinates for the* GpiBitBlt *call in MINMAX2.*

Now you can see that *aptl[1]* really indicates the upper-right corner of the target rectangle rather than the size of the bitmap.

Flipping the Bitmap

The *aptl[0]* and *aptl[1]* elements of the POINTL array specify the points of the destination rectangle that correspond to the lower-left corner and lower-right corner of the source bitmap. The MINMAX2 program in Figure 6-4 sets *aptl[0]* and *aptl[1]* as shown on the next page.

```
aptl[0].x = 0 ;
aptl[0].y = 0 ;

aptl[1].x = cxClient ;
aptl[1].y = cyClient ;
```

But these two points do not have to be the lower-left corner and lower-right corner of the destination rectangle. You can use any two opposite points for a variety of effects. For example, if you'd like to turn the image upside down, use

```
aptl[0].x = 0 ;
aptl[0].y = cyClient ;

aptl[1].x = cxClient ;
aptl[1].y = 0 ;
```

The lower-left corner of the source bitmap is copied to *aptl[0]*, which is now the upper-left corner of the client window. The upper-right corner of the source bitmap is copied to *aptl[1]*, the lower-right corner of the client window.

To display the minimize-maximize menu flipped around the vertical axis, use

```
aptl[0].x = xClient ;
aptl[0].y = 0 ;

aptl[1].x = 0 ;
aptl[1].y = yClient ;
```

To display the minimize-maximize menu flipped on both axes, use

```
aptl[0].x = cxClient ;
aptl[0].y = cyClient ;

aptl[1].x = 0 ;
aptl[1].y = 0 ;
```

When you flip a bitmap around the horizontal or vertical axis, you must specify four points in the *aptl* array, even if the bitmap is not being altered in size. The rule is simple: Use three points in the *aptl* array when you do not wish to change the size or orientation of the source bitmap. Use four points otherwise.

Different Presentation Spaces

The preceding examples use the same presentation space for both the source and the target. You can modify the MINMAX2.C source code file to use different presentation spaces. The destination presentation space is still the cached micro-PS for the client window, but the source presentation space can be the cached micro-PS for the minimize-maximize menu.

To use this approach, you need another variable of type HPS to store the source presentation space handle:

```
HPS   hpsMinMax ;
```

During the WM_PAINT message, you can obtain *hpsMinMax* like this:

```
hpsMinMax = WinGetPS (
              WinWindowFromID (
                WinQueryWindow (hwnd, QW_PARENT, FALSE),
                  FID_MINMAX) ;
```

The *WinQueryWindow* function obtains the handle of the frame window (which is the parent of the client window), *WinWindowFromID* returns the handle to the minimize-maximize menu window, and *WinGetPS* obtains a cached micro-PS for this window.

> **NOTE:** *At first, it seems rude to get a presentation space handle for a window that does not belong to your program. But the window really is part of your program. You created the minimize-maximize window by calling* WinCreateStdWindow. *Although the window procedure for this window is within the Presentation Manager, the window belongs to your program. You can do what you want with it.*

The *aptl[0]* and *aptl[1]* structures are set to the same values shown in MINMAX2.C. But the coordinates of the source bitmap are now relative to the lower-left corner of the source presentation space:

```
aptl[2].x = 0 ;
aptl[2].y = 0 ;

aptl[3].x = cxMinMax ;
aptl[3].y = cyMinMax ;
```

The *GpiBitBlt* call specifies *hpsMinMax* as the source presentation space:

```
GpiBitBlt (hps, hpsMinMax, 4L, aptl, ROP_SRCCOPY, BBO_AND) ;
```

Remember to release the presentation space handle of the minimize-maximize menu when you're finished with it:

```
WinReleasePS (hpsMinMax) ;
```

The Raster Operations

In MINMAX1 and MINMAX2, the source bitmap is simply copied from one area of the screen to another. This is the result of specifying ROP_SRCCOPY as the fifth parameter—the raster operation—to *GpiBitBlt*. ROP_SRCCOPY is only 1 of 256 raster operations you can use in *GpiBitBlt*. Let's experiment with a few others in MINMAX2 and then investigate the raster operations more methodically.

Try replacing ROP_SRCCOPY with ROP_NOTSRCCOPY. As the name suggests, this raster operation inverts the colors of the bitmap as it is copied: On the client window, the black area of the minimize-maximize menu becomes white, and white becomes black. Try ROP_ZERO: The entire client window is painted black. ROP_ONE causes the entire client window to be painted white.

Now try replacing the *GpiBitBlt* call in MINMAX2 with the following two statements:

```
GpiSetPattern (hps, PATSYM_HALFTONE) ;
GpiBitBlt (hps, hps, 4L, aptl, ROP_MERGECOPY, BBO_AND) ;
```

In this case, the black area of the minimize-maximize menu remains black when copied to the client window, but the white area is displayed as the PATSYM_HALFTONE pattern. Here's another one:

```
GpiSetPattern (hps, PATSYM_HORIZ) ;
GpiBitBlt (hps, hps, 4L, aptl, ROP_PATCOPY, BBO_AND) ;
```

This simply fills the entire client window with the PATSYM_HORIZ pattern. Now try adding two more statements so that you call *GpiSetPattern* and *GpiBitBlt* twice:

```
GpiSetPattern (hps, PATSYM_HORIZ) ;
GpiBitBlt (hps, hps, 4L, aptl, ROP_PATCOPY, BBO_AND) ;
GpiSetPattern (hps, PATSYM_VERT) ;
GpiBitBlt (hps, hps, 4L, aptl, ROP_PATPAINT, BBO_AND) ;
```

This one (shown in Figure 6-7) is strange: The black area of the minimize-maximize menu is now copied as white, and the white area is a pattern of black dots which (if you think about it) appears to be an "intersection" of the horizontal and vertical line patterns.

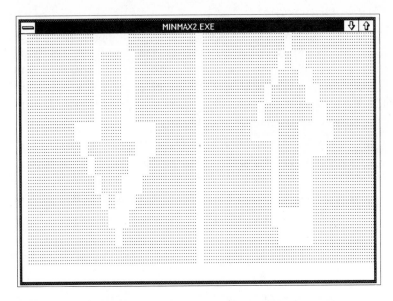

Figure 6-7. *The MINMAX2 display with a different raster operation.*

Just what on earth is going on here?

As I mentioned earlier, the *GpiBitBlt* function is not simply a bit-transfer function. It actually performs a bitwise operation between the following three bitmaps:

- Source: The source bitmap, expanded or compressed (if necessary) to be the same size as the destination rectangle.

- Destination: The destination rectangle before the *GpiBitBlt* call.

- Pattern: The current pattern of the destination presentation space, repeated horizontally and vertically to be the same size as the destination rectangle.

The result of this bitwise operation is copied to the destination rectangle.

The raster operations are conceptually similar to the mix modes we encountered in Chapter 5. The mix modes govern the way in which a graphics object (such as a line) is combined with a destination. You'll recall that there were 16 foreground mix modes—all the unique results obtained when 0s and 1s in the object are combined with 0s and 1s in the destination.

The raster operations used in *GpiBitBlt* involve a combination of three objects, and this results in 256 raster operations. There are 256 ways to combine a source bitmap, a destination bitmap, and a pattern. Fifteen of these raster operations are common enough to be given names (some of them rather obscure) in PMGPI.H. The raster operation identifiers all begin with the prefix ROP. If you examine how they're defined in PMGPI.H, you'll see that each is defined as a number (which also seems rather obscure):

```
#define ROP_NOTSRCCOPY  0x0033L
#define ROP_SRCCOPY     0x00CCL
#define ROP_PATCOPY     0x00F0L
```

Those numbers have real meaning. They define how the source, destination, and pattern bitmaps are combined.

Figure 6-8 shows the 15 raster operations that have names.

Pattern:	1	1	1	1	0	0	0	0			
Source:	1	1	0	0	1	1	0	0			
Destination:	1	0	1	0	1	0	1	0	*Operation*	*Value*	*Identifier*
Result:	0	0	0	0	0	0	0	0	0	0x00	ROP_ZERO
	0	0	0	1	0	0	0	1	~(S ¦ D)	0x11	ROP_NOTSRCERASE
	0	0	1	1	0	0	1	1	~S	0x33	ROP_NOTSRCCOPY
	0	1	0	0	0	1	0	0	S & ~D	0x44	ROP_SRCERASE
	0	1	0	1	0	1	0	1	~D	0x55	ROP_DSTINVERT
	0	1	0	1	1	0	1	0	P ^ D	0x5A	ROP_PATINVERT
	0	1	1	0	0	1	1	0	S ^ D	0x66	ROP_SRCINVERT
	1	0	0	0	1	0	0	0	S & D	0x88	ROP_SRCAND
	1	0	1	1	1	0	1	1	~S ¦ D	0xBB	ROP_MERGEPAINT
	1	1	0	0	0	0	0	0	P & S	0xC0	ROP_MERGECOPY
	1	1	0	0	1	1	0	0	S	0xCC	ROP_SRCCOPY
	1	1	1	0	1	1	1	0	S ¦ D	0xEE	ROP_SRCPAINT
	1	1	1	1	0	0	0	0	P	0xF0	ROP_PATCOPY
	1	1	1	1	1	0	1	1	P ¦ ~S ¦ D	0xFB	ROP_PATPAINT
	1	1	1	1	1	1	1	1	1	0xFF	ROP_ONE

Figure 6-8. *The 15 raster operations that have names defined in PMGPI.H.*

This is an extremely important table, so let's spend a little time examining it.

The numeric values of the ROP identifiers are listed in the second-to-last column. These numbers are the hexadecimal representations of the "result" bits shown in the first eight columns. These bits are the result of a bitwise operation between the pattern, source, and destination bits shown at the top. The Operation column uses C syntax to show how the pattern, source, and destination are combined.

To begin understanding this table, it's easiest to assume that you're dealing with a monochrome system in which 0 is black and 1 is white. The result of the ROP_ZERO operation is all zeros regardless of the source, destination, and pattern, so the destination will be colored black. Similarly, ROP_ONE always causes the destination to be colored white.

Let's take another look at these four lines of code shown earlier:

```
GpiSetPattern (hps, PATSYM_HORIZ) ;
GpiBitBlt (hps, hps, 4L, aptl, ROP_PATCOPY, BBO_AND) ;
GpiSetPattern (hps, PATSYM_VERT) ;
GpiBitBlt (hps, hps, 4L, aptl, ROP_PATPAINT, BBO_AND) ;
```

This code was responsible for the display in Figure 6-7. As you can see from the table in Figure 6-8, ROP_PATCOPY causes the result bits to be the same as the pattern bits. The source and destination bitmaps are essentially ignored. In other words, ROP_PATCOPY simply copies the current pattern to the destination rectangle.

The ROP_PATPAINT raster operation involves a more complex operation. The result is equal to

P | ~S | D

When the source bitmap is black (a 0 bit), the result is always white (a 1 bit). Figure 6-7 verifies this. When the source is white (1), the result is also white if either the pattern or the destination is white. In other words, the result will be black only if the source is white and both the pattern and the destination are black. Again, Figure 6-7 verifies this. Black dots appeared in the white area of the source bitmap where the lines of the pattern that were already on the destination intersected the lines of the current pattern.

When a raster operation does not require a source bitmap, you can set the second parameter of *GpiBitBlt* (the handle to the source presentation space) to NULL and the third parameter (the number of POINTL structures in the array) to 2L. This will speed up the drawing. The preceding example can also be written as

```
GpiSetPattern (hps, PATSYM_HORIZ) ;
GpiBitBlt (hps, NULL, 2L, aptl, ROP_PATCOPY, BBO_AND) ;
GpiSetPattern (hps, PATSYM_VERT) ;
GpiBitBlt (hps, hps, 4L, aptl, ROP_PATPAINT, BBO_AND) ;
```

You don't need to use one of the predefined identifiers for the raster operation parameter to *GpiBitBlt*. You can use any number between 0 and 255. The hard part is determining what number to use for a particular effect. Here are some examples:

Suppose you want to copy the white area of a source bitmap as white, but you want to display the PATSYM_HALFTONE pattern where the bitmap is black. You set up a little table similar to the one shown at the top of Figure 6-8 and work out the bits:

Pattern:	1	1	1	1	0	0	0	0	
Source:	1	1	0	0	1	1	0	0	
Destination:	1	0	1	0	1	0	1	0	Value
Result:	1	1	1	1	1	1	0	0	0xFC

When the source is 1 (white), the result is also 1. When the source is 0 (black), the result is the pattern. Thus the raster operation is 0xFC. Here's the code:

```
GpiSetPattern (hps, PATSYM_HALFTONE) ;
GpiBitBlt (hps, hps, 4L, aptl, 0xFC, BBO_AND) ;
```

Simple, right?

Let's try another. Where the source is white, you want the result to be colored with horizontal lines, and where the source is black, you want vertical lines. First, color the destination area using PATSYM_HORIZ and then set the pattern to PATSYM_VERT:

```
GpiSetPattern (hps, PATSYM_HORIZ) ;
GpiBitBlt (hps, NULL, 2L, aptl, ROP_PATCOPY, BBO_AND) ;
GpiSetPattern (hps, PATSYM_VERT) ;
```

Now all you need is a raster operation that does the following: When the source is 1 (white), the result is the destination; when the source is 0 (black), the result is the pattern. Here's the table:

Pattern:	1	1	1	1	0	0	0	0	
Source:	1	1	0	0	1	1	0	0	
Destination:	1	0	1	0	1	0	1	0	Value
Result:	1	0	1	1	1	0	0	0	0xB8

And here's the *GpiBitBlt* function that uses this raster operation:

```
GpiBitBlt (hps, hps, 4L, aptl, 0xB8L, BBO_AND) ;
```

Raster Operations and Color

As I discussed in Chapter 5, a color display uses multiple bits for each pixel. For example, the EGA and VGA in high-resolution modes use 4 bits per pixel and can display 16 colors simultaneously. Although both the EGA and VGA can map these 4 bits to any one of 64 possible colors on the EGA (or 262,144 possible colors on the VGA), the mapping is usually defined so that the 4 bits represent an IRGB (Intensity-Red-Green-Blue) color scheme.

Like the mix mode in Chapter 5, the *GpiBitBlt* function performs the bitwise operation between each of these color bits separately. For example, if the destination is CLR_RED (intensity and red bits set to 1) and the source is CLR_PALEBLUE (blue bit set to 1), then an ROP_SRCPAINT raster operation will color the destination as CLR_PINK (intensity, red, and blue bits set to 1).

If you are using a color display, and you have used the Presentation Manager Control Panel to set your window background and window text colors to something other than white and black, the preceding descriptions of some raster operations probably did not agree with your observations. Instead, you saw results that included the CLR_BACKGROUND and CLR_NEUTRAL colors.

Here's why: When the *GpiBitBlt* function performs a bitwise operation on a source, destination, and pattern, all three bitmaps must have the same color format. *GpiBitBlt* performs the operation on the color bits separately.

Patterns are stored as monochrome bitmaps. They have 1 bit per pixel. During *GpiBitBlt* the pattern must be converted to a color bitmap. That is, on the EGA and VGA, each bit of the pattern must be converted to 4 bits so that they can be combined with the source and destination. GPI does this by converting the 1 bits to the 4 IRGB bits that describe the current presentation space foreground color (the CLR_NEUTRAL color by default) and the 0 bits to the 4 IRGB bits for the current presentation space background color (CLR_BACKGROUND by default).

I guarantee this will be confusing at first. By default, CLR_NEUTRAL is black and CLR_BACKGROUND is white. This means that 1 bits in the pattern become black and 0 bits become white, which is exactly the opposite of the interpretation of bits in a monochrome system.

For example, the PATSYM_VERT pattern is mostly 0 bits except for the vertical lines, which are 1 bits. In a monochrome system, for example, PATSYM_VERT would have white lines on a black background. But when the pattern is converted to a color bitmap (as it must be for GPI to display it on a color screen), the pattern appears as CLR_NEUTRAL lines on a CLR_BACKGROUND background, or black on white by default.

Bitblt Compression

I haven't yet discussed the last parameter to *GpiBitBlt*. This parameter governs how a source bitmap is altered when it is compressed to a smaller destination. Three options are available: BBO_OR, BBO_AND, and BBO_IGNORE.

If you considered the problem of stretching or compressing a bitmap, you probably assumed that GPI simply duplicates rows and columns of pixels to stretch a bitmap. This is correct. You may also have assumed that GPI simply eliminates rows and columns of pixels to compress a bitmap. But that's only one of the three options—the one you get when you use BBO_IGNORE, which is often not satisfactory.

For example, suppose you have a source bitmap that has a white background and a 1-pixel-wide outline of a square in black. When GPI compresses the bitmap, the rows and columns of the bitmap containing the black lines could be the rows and columns that GPI eliminates. The result will be entirely white.

When you have a bitmap with a black image on a white background, use BBO_AND. GPI will not eliminate whole rows and columns but instead will combine adjacent rows and columns of the bitmap with a bitwise AND operation. A result pixel will be white only if both adjacent pixels are also white. With a white image on a black background, use BBO_OR. Adjacent rows and columns are combined with a bitwise OR operation so that a result will be black only if adjacent pixels are black.

BBO_IGNORE is for use with color bitmaps. For color bitmaps, BBO_OR and BBO_AND can result in the creation of colors not in the original bitmap, even when you're using ROP_SRCCOPY.

Bitmap Handles and Bitmap Drawing

We've been blting bitmaps around the video display but we haven't really gotten our hands on a bitmap, and it's not quite clear what we could do with one anyway.

Let's temporarily abandon the *GpiBitBlt* function and approach bitmaps from another direction. We'll first try getting a handle to a bitmap and drawing the bitmap on the video display. After we nail down a couple of additional concepts, we can again bring *GpiBitBlt* into our collection of tools.

The System Bitmaps

If you've been exploring the Presentation Manager programming utilities, you may have discovered that ICONEDIT can create a file containing a monochrome bitmap. In ICONEDIT you color in the black and white pixels with a mouse and then save the bitmap as a file with the extension .BMP. In Chapter 12, you'll see how you can use that bitmap as a ''resource'' in a program, load it into memory, and display it on the screen.

But you needn't jump ahead that far yet. The Presentation Manager and the File System program themselves use bitmaps occasionally. These are called ''system bitmaps.'' These bitmaps are stored as resources in DISPLAY.DLL, the device driver for the video display. As I mentioned earlier, bitmaps are very device dependent and must often be different sizes for different video display drivers. Accordingly, the bitmaps are stored in the video display device driver.

In preparation for getting your hands on a bitmap, you must define a variable to store a bitmap handle. A bitmap handle is of type HBITMAP:

```
HBITMAP hbm ;
```

An HBITMAP variable begins with *hbm* by convention. Now you can call *WinGetSysBitmap*:

```
hbm = WinGetSysBitmap (HWND_DESKTOP, idSysBitmap) ;
```

This function returns a handle to a copy of a system bitmap. The *idSysBitmap* parameter is one of the identifiers defined in PMWIN.H that begins with SBMP.

When you've finished using the bitmap, you should delete it:

```
GpiDeleteBitmap (hbm) ;
```

It's okay to delete a bitmap you obtain from *WinGetSysBitmap*. You're not deleting the system bitmap itself, only the copy that was made for you.

Drawing a Bitmap

If you look over the identifiers beginning with SBMP, you'll find SBMP_MINBUTTON and SBMP_MAXBUTTON. Of course! The Presentation Manager has to draw the minimize-maximize menu somehow. What it uses are these system bitmaps.

This can only mean that you're not yet done with the MINMAX series of programs. It's time for MINMAX3, which is shown in Figure 6-9.

The MINMAX3 File

```
#-------------------
# MINMAX3 make file
#-------------------

minmax3.obj : minmax3.c
    cl -c -G2sw -W3 minmax3.c

minmax3.exe : minmax3.obj minmax3.def
    link minmax3, /align:16, NUL, os2, minmax3
```

The MINMAX3.C File

```
/*-----------------------------------------
   MINMAX3.C -- Minimize-Maximize Bitmap
   -------------------------------------*/

#define INCL_WIN
#include <os2.h>

MRESULT EXPENTRY ClientWndProc (HWND, USHORT, MPARAM, MPARAM) ;

int main (void)
    {
    static CHAR  szClientClass [] = "MinMax3" ;
    static ULONG flFrameFlags = FCF_TITLEBAR       | FCF_SYSMENU |
                                FCF_SIZEBORDER      | FCF_MINMAX  |
                                FCF_SHELLPOSITION   | FCF_TASKLIST ;
    HAB          hab ;
    HMQ          hmq ;
    HWND         hwndFrame, hwndClient ;
    QMSG         qmsg ;

    hab = WinInitialize (0) ;
    hmq = WinCreateMsgQueue (hab, 0) ;
```

(continued)

Figure 6-9. The MINMAX3.C File. *continued*

```
         WinRegisterClass (hab, szClientClass, ClientWndProc, CS_SIZEREDRAW, 0) ;

         hwndFrame = WinCreateStdWindow (HWND_DESKTOP, WS_VISIBLE,
                                         &flFrameFlags, szClientClass, NULL,
                                         OL, NULL, 0, &hwndClient) ;

         while (WinGetMsg (hab, &qmsg, NULL, 0, 0))
              WinDispatchMsg (hab, &qmsg) ;

         WinDestroyWindow (hwndFrame) ;
         WinDestroyMsgQueue (hmq) ;
         WinTerminate (hab) ;
         return 0 ;
         }

MRESULT EXPENTRY ClientWndProc (HWND hwnd, USHORT msg, MPARAM mp1, MPARAM mp2)
         {
         static SHORT   cxClient, cyClient ;
         HBITMAP        hbmMin, hbmMax ;
         HPS            hps ;
         POINTL         aptl [2] ;

         switch (msg)
              {
              case WM_SIZE:
                   cxClient = SHORT1FROMMP (mp2) ;
                   cyClient = SHORT2FROMMP (mp2) ;
                   return 0 ;

              case WM_PAINT:
                   hps = WinBeginPaint (hwnd, NULL, NULL) ;

                   hbmMin = WinGetSysBitmap (HWND_DESKTOP, SBMP_MINBUTTON) ;
                   hbmMax = WinGetSysBitmap (HWND_DESKTOP, SBMP_MAXBUTTON) ;

                   aptl[0].x = 0 ;                // Target lower left
                   aptl[0].y = 0 ;
                   aptl[1].x = cxClient / 2 ;      // Target upper right
                   aptl[1].y = cyClient ;

                   WinDrawBitmap (hps, hbmMin, NULL, aptl,
                              CLR_NEUTRAL, CLR_BACKGROUND, DBM_STRETCH) ;

                   aptl[0].x = cxClient / 2 ;      // Target left
                   aptl[1].x = cxClient ;          // Target right
```

(continued)

Figure 6-9. The MINMAX3.C File. *continued*

```
                WinDrawBitmap (hps, hbmMax, NULL, aptl,
                              CLR_NEUTRAL, CLR_BACKGROUND, DBM_STRETCH) ;

                GpiDeleteBitmap (hbmMin) ;
                GpiDeleteBitmap (hbmMax) ;

                WinEndPaint (hps) ;
                return 0 ;
            }
        return WinDefWindowProc (hwnd, msg, mp1, mp2) ;
        }
```

The MINMAX3.DEF File

```
;----------------------------------------
; MINMAX3.DEF module definition file
;----------------------------------------


NAME          MINMAX3    WINDOWAPI

DESCRIPTION   'Min-Max Bitmap (C) Charles Petzold, 1988'
PROTMODE
HEAPSIZE      1024
STACKSIZE     8192
EXPORTS       ClientWndProc
```

Figure 6-9. *The MINMAX3 program.*

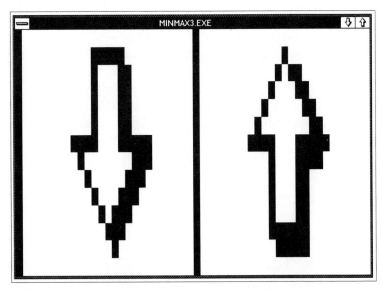

Figure 6-10. *The MINMAX3 display.*

While processing the WM_PAINT message, MINMAX3 obtains handles to the minimize and maximize bitmaps by calling *WinGetSysBitmap* twice. It stores the handles in *hbmMin* and *hbmMax*. The program then draws the two bitmaps on its client window by calling *WinDrawBitmap* and deletes the bitmaps using *GpiDeleteBitmap*. The MINMAX3 display is shown in Figure 6-10.

The *WinDrawBitmap* Function

As you can tell by the *Win* prefix, *WinDrawBitmap* is a high-level drawing function. It is certainly convenient and will be welcomed by Microsoft Windows programmers. (Windows had no comparable function.) But you'll soon see that GPI offers a better approach to drawing bitmaps.

The general syntax of *WinDrawBitmap* is

```
WinDrawBitmap (hps, hbm, &rclSource, &ptlDest, clrForeground,
               clrBackground, fsOptions) ;
```

The third parameter, *&rclSource*, is a pointer to a RECTL structure defining a rectangular area of the bitmap you want to draw. If you set this parameter to NULL (as MINMAX3 does), *WinDrawBitmap* draws the entire bitmap.

The fourth parameter specifies the destination coordinates. If you do not include DBM_STRETCH in the options, this parameter points to a POINTL structure specifying the lower-left corner of the destination. If you use DBM_STRETCH, the parameter is an array of two POINTL structures specifying the lower-left corner and upper-right corner. Alternatively, you can use a pointer to a RECTL structure for this parameter and cast it to a PPOINTL (a pointer to a POINTL structure).

You specify two colors for the bitmap, *clrForeground* and *clrBackground*. The *clrForeground* is used for the 1 bits of the bitmap and *clrBackground* is used for the 0 bits. (MINMAX3 uses both CLR_NEUTRAL and CLR_BACKGROUND.) If you have not changed the window background and window text colors in the Presentation Manager Control Panel, the minimize and maximize bitmaps are drawn as black arrows on a white background. Alternatively, you can use the DBM_IMAGEATTRS option in the final parameter to use the colors currently selected for drawing images.

The *fsOptions* parameter can be a combination (using the C bitwise OR operator) of the following identifiers:

Identifier	Meaning
DBM_NORMAL	Draw the bitmap normally
DBM_INVERT	Invert the colors of the bitmap
DBM_HALFTONE	Draw only every other bit of the bitmap
DBM_STRETCH	Stretch the bitmap to fit the target area
DBM_IMAGEATTRS	Use the image attributes for color

The DBM_NORMAL identifier is defined as 0, so that is the default whenever you use a 0 as the last parameter. Both the DBM_INVERT and DBM_HALFTONE flags allow you to use a small subset of the 256 raster operations to draw the bitmap. *WinDrawBitmap* uses the bitmap as the source and temporarily sets the current pattern to PATSYM_HALFTONE (which consists of alternating 0 and 1 bits). The last parameter to *WinDrawBitmap* is equivalent to the following raster operations:

WinDrawBitmap Parameter	Raster Operation
DBM_NORMAL	ROP_SRCCOPY
DBM_INVERT	ROP_NOTSRCCOPY
DBM_HALFTONE	0xFC (P ¦ S)
DBM_INVERT ¦ DBM_HALFTONE	0x30 (P & ~S)

Remember that GPI converts both the source and pattern to a color bitmap before performing the logical operation on each set of color bits. Thus, when you use ROP_NOTSRCCOPY, the 1 bits in the bitmap are colored with the inverse of the ROP_NEUTRAL color and the 0 bits are colored with the inverse of ROP_BACKGROUND.

Getting Bitmap Information

We managed to obtain handles to system bitmaps and draw them on the MINMAX3 client window without knowing the size of the bitmaps. If you need this information, you can obtain it. First you define a variable of type BITMAPINFOHEADER:

```
BITMAPINFOHEADER bmp ;
```

The recommended prefix for structures of this type is *bmp*, which actually stands for "bitmap parameters." The BITMAPINFOHEADER structure is defined in PMGPI.H:

```
typedef struct _BITMAPINFOHEADER
    {
    ULONG  cbFix ;
    USHORT cx ;
    USHORT cy ;
    USHORT cPlanes ;
    USHORT cBitCount ;
    }
    BITMAPINFOHEADER ;
```

You first set the *cbFix* field as the size of the structure, which is 12 bytes. Then you pass a pointer to this structure to *GpiQueryBitmapParameters*:

```
GpiQueryBitmapParameters (hbm, &bmp) ;
```

On return from the function, the *cx* and *cy* fields will contain the width and height of the bitmap in pixels. For a monochrome bitmap (such as all the system bitmaps), the *cPlanes* and *cBitCount* fields are 1. For color bitmaps, these two fields describe how the bitmap is organized to represent color.

You also use the BITMAPINFOHEADER structure when creating a bitmap. Let's get to it.

Working with Bitmaps

I mentioned earlier that you can create a bitmap using the ICONEDIT program and store that bitmap as a resource in your program. This is certainly an easy approach to creating a bitmap and using it. But we'll wait for Chapter 12 to see how that is done. Meanwhile, it is instructive to create bitmaps and work with them directly in a program.

The Bitmap Bits

What do you need to create a bitmap that represents an image? One major requirement is obviously the bits themselves. In a program, these bits are usually stored as an array of BYTE (unsigned character) values. For a monochrome bitmap, this array is organized as follows:

- The array begins with the bottom row of bits.

- The first byte in each row is the leftmost eight pixels.

- The most significant bit in each byte is the leftmost pixel.

- The number of bits in each row must be a multiple of the size of a ULONG (32 bits). If the bitmap width is not a multiple of 32, the row must be padded at the right.

- A 1 bit represents the foreground color (by default, black), and a 0 bit represents the background color (by default, white).

For example, suppose you want to create a small bitmap that contains the word "HELLO." You want the letters to be colored with the foreground color (black, by default). The background will be white (by default). You can picture such a bitmap like this:

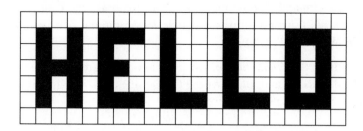

This is a "21-by-7" bitmap, with 7 rows of 21 bits each. You can represent the bitmap as a string of bits where the background bits are 0 and the foreground bits are 1:

```
0 0 0 0 0 0 0 0 0 0 0 0 0 0 0 0 0 0 0 0 0
0 1 0 1 0 1 1 1 0 1 0 0 0 1 0 0 0 1 1 1 0
0 1 0 1 0 1 0 0 0 1 0 0 0 1 0 0 0 1 0 1 0
0 1 1 1 0 1 1 0 0 1 0 0 0 1 0 0 0 1 0 1 0
0 1 0 1 0 1 0 0 0 1 0 0 0 1 0 0 0 1 0 1 0
0 1 0 1 0 1 1 1 0 1 1 1 0 1 1 1 0 1 1 1 0
0 0 0 0 0 0 0 0 0 0 0 0 0 0 0 0 0 0 0 0 0
```

Group each set of 8 bits into a byte. The leftmost bits are most significant. Each row must be padded at the right for a multiple of 4 bytes per row. It doesn't matter whether you pad the rows with 0s or 1s:

```
0x00 0x00 0x00 0x00
0x57 0x44 0x70 0x00
0x54 0x44 0x50 0x00
0x76 0x44 0x50 0x00
0x54 0x44 0x50 0x00
0x57 0x77 0x70 0x00
0x00 0x00 0x00 0x00
```

Now reverse the order of the rows so that the array begins with the bottom row. You can define the resultant array in a program like this:

```
static BYTE abHello [] = { 0x00, 0x00, 0x00, 0x00,
                           0x57, 0x77, 0x70, 0x00,
                           0x54, 0x44, 0x50, 0x00,
                           0x76, 0x44, 0x50, 0x00,
                           0x54, 0x44, 0x50, 0x00,
                           0x57, 0x44, 0x70, 0x00,
                           0x00, 0x00, 0x00, 0x00 } ;
```

Bitmap Creation and Initialization

To create a bitmap based on an array of bits, you use the *GpiCreateBitmap* function. This function returns a handle to the bitmap that you store in a variable of type HBITMAP.

Before calling *GpiCreateBitmap*, you need two structures that are very similar: BITMAPINFO and BITMAPINFOHEADER. You've already seen the BITMAPINFOHEADER structure:

```
typedef struct _BITMAPINFOHEADER
    {
    ULONG  cbFix ;
    USHORT cx ;
    USHORT cy ;
    USHORT cPlanes ;
    USHORT cBitCount ;
    }
    BITMAPINFOHEADER ;
```

The prefix for a BITMAPINFOHEADER structure is *bmp*.

The first five BITMAPINFO fields are the same as BITMAPINFOHEADER, but a sixth field, an array of one RGB structure, is added:

```
typedef struct _BITMAPINFO
    {
    ULONG  cbFix ;
    USHORT cx ;
    USHORT cy ;
    USHORT cPlanes ;
    USHORT cBitCount ;
    RGB    argbColor[1] ;
    }
    BITMAPINFO ;
```

By convention, a BITMAPINFO structure variable begins with *bmi*. The RGB structure defines a color as a combination of red, green, and blue bytes:

```
typedef struct _RGB
     {
     BYTE bBlue ;
     BYTE bGreen ;
     BYTE bRed ;
     }
     RGB ;
```

Each byte can range from 0 through 0xFF (255). When all 3 bytes are set to 0, the color is black. When all 3 bytes are set to 255, the color is white. You need one RGB structure for each color in the bitmap. For example, if the bitmap has 4 color bits per pixel, you need an array of 16 RGB structures, one for each of the 16 possible colors. These structures indicate to GPI what real color corresponds to each combination of 4 bits. For a monochrome bitmap (which we'll be creating), you need an array of two RGB structures.

In both structures, the *cbFix* field is set to the *fixed* size of the structure, which in both cases is 12 bytes. The *cx* and *cy* fields specify the size of the bitmap in bits. The *cPlanes* and *cBitCount* fields indicate how bits in the bitmap are organized to represent color. For a monochrome bitmap, these two fields are set to 1.

So, to create a bitmap to contain the *abHello* array of bits, first define a BITMAPINFOHEADER structure variable and set the fields like this:

```
BITMAPINFOHEADER bmp ;
     ....

bmp.cbFix = sizeof bmp ;
bmp.cx = 21 ;
bmp.cy = 7 ;
bmp.cPlanes = 1 ;
bmp.cBitCount = 1 ;
```

The BITMAPINFO structure is set up similarly, but it needs two RGB values that define how the 0 and 1 bits are interpreted. For a monochrome bitmap, the three fields of the first RGB structure should be set to 0, and the three fields of the second structure should be set to 255.

And now we have a little problem. We need to define values of *argbColor[0]* and *argbColor[1]*, but the definition of the BITMAPINFO structure is large enough to accommodate only one RGB structure. We need a BITMAPINFO structure large enough for two RGB structures. Here's one way to do it. Don't define a structure of type BITMAPINFO like this:

```
BITMAPINFO bmi ;
```

Instead, define a pointer to a BITMAPINFO structure:

```
BITMAPINFO *pbmi ;
```

Then use *malloc* to allocate enough local memory for the structure:

```
pbmi = malloc (sizeof (BITMAPINFO) + sizeof (RGB)) ;
```

The *cbFix* field is set equal to the size of the BITMAPINFO structure excluding the *argbColor* field, so you can set the fields of the structure like this:

```
pbmi->cbFix = sizeof bmp ;
pbmi->cx = 21 ;
pbmi->cy = 7
pbmi->cPlanes = 1 ;
pbmi->cBitCount = 1 ;
pbmi->argbColor[0].bBlue  = 0 ;
pbmi->argbColor[0].bGreen = 0 ;
pbmi->argbColor[0].bRed   = 0 ;
pbmi->argbColor[1].bBlue  = 255 ;
pbmi->argbColor[1].bGreen = 255 ;
pbmi->argbColor[1].bRed   = 255 ;
```

Now we're ready to call *GpiCreateBitmap* using the *abHello* array and these two structures:

```
hbm = GpiCreateBitmap (hps, &bmp, CBM_INIT, abHello, pbmi) ;
```

The first parameter to *GpiCreateBitmap* is a handle to a presentation space. For bitmaps to be displayed on the screen, you can use the handle returned from *WinGetPS*. If possible, GPI will use part of the video memory to store the bitmap. Even if the bitmap is stored in system memory, it is always associated with a particular device. The CBM_INIT identifier indicates that we want the bitmap to be initialized with the *abHello* data after the bitmap is created.

After you call *GpiCreateBitmap*, you want to free the memory used for the BITMAPINFO structure:

```
free (pbmi) ;
```

When your program is finished using a bitmap, the bitmap should be deleted:

```
GpiDeleteBitmap (hbm) ;
```

You can also create a bitmap without initializing it. In this case, the bitmap initially contains random data. If we simply wanted to create an un-initialized 21-by-7 bitmap, the *GpiCreateBitmap* function would be

```
hbm = GpiCreateBitmap (hps, &bmp, OL, NULL, NULL) ;
```

Notice that only the BITMAPINFOHEADER structure is required for this variation of the *GpiCreateBitmap* call. You don't need to tell GPI how to interpret color information when creating the uninitialized bitmap.

The Bit Cat

Now that we have some of the concepts down, let's look at a program that creates and displays a bitmap. Rather than the simple "HELLO" bitmap described previously, this program uses a more interesting bitmap. Remember the cat we displayed in Chapter 5 using *GpiImage*? We'll now display that cat as a bitmap. BITCAT1 is shown in Figure 6-11.

The BITCAT1 File

```
#-------------------
# BITCAT1 make file
#-------------------

bitcat1.obj : bitcat1.c bitcat.h
    cl -c -G2sw -W3 bitcat1.c

bitcat1.exe : bitcat1.obj bitcat1.def
    link bitcat1, /align:16, NUL, os2, bitcat1
```

The BITCAT1.C File

```
/*-------------------------------------------
   BITCAT1.C -- Bitmap Creation and Display
   -----------------------------------------*/

#define INCL_WIN
#define INCL_GPI
#include <os2.h>
#include <stdlib.h>
#include "bitcat.h"
```

(continued)

Figure 6-11. The BITCAT1.C File. *continued*

```
MRESULT EXPENTRY ClientWndProc (HWND, USHORT, MPARAM, MPARAM) ;

int main (void)
    {
    static CHAR   szClientClass [] = "BitCat1" ;
    static ULONG  flFrameFlags = FCF_TITLEBAR      | FCF_SYSMENU |
                                 FCF_SIZEBORDER    | FCF_MINMAX  |
                                 FCF_SHELLPOSITION | FCF_TASKLIST ;

    HAB         hab ;
    HMQ         hmq ;
    HWND        hwndFrame, hwndClient ;
    QMSG        qmsg ;

    hab = WinInitialize (0) ;
    hmq = WinCreateMsgQueue (hab, 0) ;

    WinRegisterClass (hab, szClientClass, ClientWndProc, CS_SIZEREDRAW, 0) ;

    hwndFrame = WinCreateStdWindow (HWND_DESKTOP, WS_VISIBLE,
                                    &flFrameFlags, szClientClass, NULL,
                                    OL, NULL, 0, &hwndClient) ;

    while (WinGetMsg (hab, &qmsg, NULL, 0, 0))
        WinDispatchMsg (hab, &qmsg) ;

    WinDestroyWindow (hwndFrame) ;
    WinDestroyMsgQueue (hmq) ;
    WinTerminate (hab) ;
    return 0 ;
    }

MRESULT EXPENTRY ClientWndProc (HWND hwnd, USHORT msg, MPARAM mp1, MPARAM mp2)
    {
    static HBITMAP    hbm ;
    BITMAPINFO        *pbmi ;
    BITMAPINFOHEADER  bmp ;
    HPS               hps ;
    RECTL             rcl ;

    switch (msg)
        {
        case WM_CREATE:

                        /*-------------------------------------
                           Create 32-by-32 monochrome bitmap
                        -----------------------------------*/
```

(continued)

Figure 6-11. The BITCAT1.C File. *continued*

```
                bmp.cbFix      = sizeof bmp ;
                bmp.cx         = 32 ;
                bmp.cy         = 32 ;
                bmp.cPlanes    = 1 ;
                bmp.cBitCount  = 1 ;

                pbmi = malloc (sizeof (BITMAPINFO) + sizeof (RGB)) ;

                pbmi->cbFix      = sizeof bmp ;
                pbmi->cx         = 32 ;
                pbmi->cy         = 32 ;
                pbmi->cPlanes    = 1 ;
                pbmi->cBitCount  = 1;

                pbmi->argbColor[0].bBlue  = 0 ;
                pbmi->argbColor[0].bGreen = 0 ;
                pbmi->argbColor[0].bRed   = 0 ;
                pbmi->argbColor[1].bBlue  = 0xFF ;
                pbmi->argbColor[1].bGreen = 0xFF ;
                pbmi->argbColor[1].bRed   = 0xFF ;

                hps = WinGetPS (hwnd) ;
                hbm = GpiCreateBitmap (hps, &bmp, CBM_INIT, abBitCat, pbmi) ;

                WinReleasePS (hps) ;
                free (pbmi) ;
                return 0 ;

        case WM_PAINT:
                hps = WinBeginPaint (hwnd, NULL, NULL) ;

                WinQueryWindowRect (hwnd, &rcl) ;

                WinDrawBitmap (hps, hbm, NULL, (PPOINTL) &rcl,
                            CLR_NEUTRAL, CLR_BACKGROUND, DBM_STRETCH) ;

                WinDrawBitmap (hps, hbm, NULL, (PPOINTL) &rcl,
                            CLR_NEUTRAL, CLR_BACKGROUND, DBM_NORMAL) ;

                WinEndPaint (hps) ;
                return 0 ;

        case WM_DESTROY:
                GpiDeleteBitmap (hbm) ;
                return 0 ;
        }
    return WinDefWindowProc (hwnd, msg, mp1, mp2) ;
    }
```

The BITCAT.H File

```
/*----------------------
   BITCAT.H header file
----------------------*/

static BYTE abBitCat[] = {0x00, 0xFF, 0xFF, 0x00, 0x00, 0xA2, 0x45, 0x00,
                          0x00, 0xA2, 0x45, 0x00, 0x00, 0xA2, 0x45, 0xE0,
                          0x00, 0xA2, 0x45, 0x10, 0x00, 0xA2, 0x45, 0x08,
                          0x00, 0x9C, 0x39, 0x08, 0x00, 0xC0, 0x03, 0x04,

                          0x00, 0x40, 0x02, 0x04, 0x00, 0x40, 0x02, 0x04,
                          0x00, 0x40, 0x02, 0x04, 0x00, 0x20, 0x04, 0x04,
                          0x00, 0x20, 0x04, 0x04, 0x00, 0x20, 0x04, 0x04,
                          0x00, 0x10, 0x08, 0x04, 0x00, 0x10, 0x08, 0x08,

                          0x00, 0x10, 0x08, 0x10, 0x00, 0x08, 0x10, 0x20,
                          0x00, 0x08, 0x10, 0xC0, 0x00, 0x08, 0x10, 0x00,
                          0x00, 0x07, 0xE0, 0x00, 0x00, 0x08, 0x10, 0x00,
                          0x00, 0xFC, 0x3F, 0x00, 0x00, 0x09, 0x90, 0x00,

                          0x00, 0xFC, 0x3F, 0x00, 0x00, 0x08, 0x10, 0x00,
                          0x00, 0x1A, 0x58, 0x00, 0x00, 0x28, 0x14, 0x00,
                          0x00, 0x48, 0x12, 0x00, 0x00, 0x8F, 0xF1, 0x00,
                          0x01, 0x04, 0x20, 0x80, 0x01, 0xF8, 0x1F, 0x80 } ;
```

The BITCAT1.DEF File

```
;---------------------------------------
; BITCAT1.DEF module definition file
;---------------------------------------

NAME          BITCAT1   WINDOWAPI

DESCRIPTION   'Bitmap Creation and Display (C) Charles Petzold, 1988'
PROTMODE
HEAPSIZE      1024
STACKSIZE     8192
EXPORTS       ClientWndProc
```

Figure 6-11. *The BITCAT1 program.*

The *abBitCat* array in BITCAT.H contains the bytes that define the picture of the cat. Note that the rows are in reverse order from the rows used in *GpiImage*. (*GpiImage* requires the top row first.) The BITCAT1 program creates the 32-by-32 bitmap during the WM_CREATE message and deletes it during the WM_DESTROY message.

During the WM_PAINT message, BITCAT1 draws the bitmap twice using the *WinDrawBitmap* function. The first call draws the bitmap to fill the entire client window. The second call draws the bitmap in the lower-left corner of the client window in its actual pixel size. This is shown in Figure 6-12.

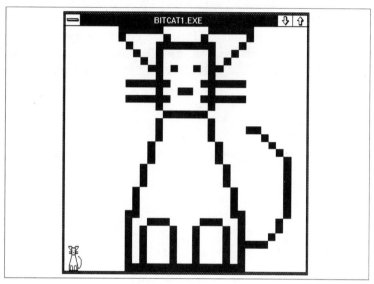

Figure 6-12. *The BITCAT1 display.*

Bitmaps and Bitblts

I mentioned earlier that the *WinDrawBitmap* function is convenient but that GPI has a better way to draw a bitmap using our old friend, the *GpiBitBlt* function. This will be demonstrated shortly in the BITCAT2 program.

You may resist this new method at first because BITCAT2.C is longer than BITCAT1.C and somewhat more complex. However, this method unleashes all the power available in the *GpiBitBlt* function when drawing a bitmap. This is where bitmaps and bitblts come together as two related tools.

You'll recall that *GpiBitBlt* transfers a bitmap from one presentation space to another, possibly combining it with the current pattern set in the destination presentation space. There doesn't seem to be any place in the function for a handle to a bitmap. To use the *GpiBitBlt* function to draw a bitmap, we must first make the bitmap part of a presentation space. This requires a concept that is very important for working with bitmaps: the memory device context.

The Memory Device Context

In Chapter 5 we worked briefly with the device context for the video display. "Device context" is a term used to describe the combination of an output device and its device driver. A presentation space is associated with a device context. When you call GPI drawing functions for a particular presentation space, GPI draws the objects on the device context associated with the presentation space.

We're going to create a device context that exists only in memory. This device context is not a real output device. It is called the memory device context. To create this device context, you call *DevOpenDC* with a second parameter set to the identifier OD_MEMORY and the other parameters as shown here:

```
hdcMemory = DevOpenDC (hab, OD_MEMORY, "*", OL, NULL, NULL) ;
```

You then create a presentation space associated with this memory device context by calling *GpiCreatePS*:

```
hpsMemory = GpiCreatePS (hab, hdcMemory, &sizl,
                   PU_PELS  | GPIF_DEFAULT |
                   GPIT_MICRO | GPIA_ASSOC) ;
```

This presentation space is associated with the memory device context. The third parameter is a pointer to a structure of type SIZEL with two fields named *cx* and *cy*. Before calling *GpiCreatePS*, you set these two fields to 0.

Here comes the crucial step: You call *GpiSetBitmap* to set a bitmap in this presentation space:

```
GpiSetBitmap (hpsMemory, hbm) ;
```

This function seems a little strange at first. Near the beginning of this chapter I said that you could imagine the entire video display as one big bitmap. The video adapter board contains a large block of memory that contains (in one form or another) the digital representation of the image on the screen.

When you call *GpiSetBitmap*, the bitmap becomes the display surface of the memory device context associated with the presentation space. You can then use this presentation space as a source (or destination) with functions such as *GpiBitBlt*. Moreover, anything you draw on this presentation space is actually drawn on the bitmap.

When you are finished using the presentation space, the memory device context, and the bitmap, you destroy them in this order:

```
GpiDestroyPS (hpsMemory) ;
DevCloseDC (hdcMemory) ;
GpiDeleteBitmap (hbm) ;
```

Now let's look at BITCAT2, which uses this approach. The program is shown in Figure 6-13.

The BITCAT2 File

```
#-------------------
# BITCAT2 make file
#-------------------

bitcat2.obj : bitcat2.c bitcat.h
    cl -c -G2sw -W3 bitcat2.c

bitcat2.exe : bitcat2.obj bitcat2.def
    link bitcat2, /align:16, NUL, os2, bitcat2
```

The BITCAT2.C File

```
/*--------------------------------------------
   BITCAT2.C -- Bitmap Creation and Display
  ------------------------------------------*/

#define INCL_WIN
#define INCL_GPI
#include <os2.h>
#include <stdlib.h>
#include "bitcat.h"

MRESULT EXPENTRY ClientWndProc (HWND, USHORT, MPARAM, MPARAM) ;

HAB   hab ;

int main (void)
    {
    static CHAR  szClientClass [] = "BitCat2" ;
    static ULONG flFrameFlags = FCF_TITLEBAR        | FCF_SYSMENU  |
                                FCF_SIZEBORDER      | FCF_MINMAX   |
                                FCF_SHELLPOSITION | FCF_TASKLIST ;
    HMQ           hmq ;
    HWND          hwndFrame, hwndClient ;
```

(continued)

Figure 6-13. The BITCAT2.C File. *continued*

```
    QMSG          qmsg ;

    hab = WinInitialize (0) ;
    hmq = WinCreateMsgQueue (hab, 0) ;

    WinRegisterClass (hab, szClientClass, ClientWndProc, CS_SIZEREDRAW, 0) ;

    hwndFrame = WinCreateStdWindow (HWND_DESKTOP, WS_VISIBLE,
                                    &flFrameFlags, szClientClass, NULL,
                                    OL, NULL, 0, &hwndClient) ;

    while (WinGetMsg (hab, &qmsg, NULL, 0, 0))
        WinDispatchMsg (hab, &qmsg) ;

    WinDestroyWindow (hwndFrame) ;
    WinDestroyMsgQueue (hmq) ;
    WinTerminate (hab) ;
    return 0 ;
    }

MRESULT EXPENTRY ClientWndProc (HWND hwnd, USHORT msg, MPARAM mp1, MPARAM mp2)
    {
    static HBITMAP    hbm ;
    static HDC        hdcMemory ;
    static HPS        hpsMemory ;
    static SHORT      cxClient, cyClient ;
    BITMAPINFO        *pbmi ;
    BITMAPINFOHEADER  bmp ;
    HPS               hps ;
    POINTL            aptl [4] ;
    SIZEL             sizl ;

    switch (msg)
        {
        case WM_CREATE:

                        /*----------------------------------------------------
                           Open memory DC and create PS associated with it
                        --------------------------------------------------*/

                hdcMemory = DevOpenDC (hab, OD_MEMORY, "*", OL, NULL, NULL) ;

                sizl.cx = 0 ;
                sizl.cy = 0 ;
```

(continued)

Figure 6-13. The BITCAT2.C File. *continued*

```
hpsMemory = GpiCreatePS (hab, hdcMemory, &sizl,
                          PU_PELS  | GPIF_DEFAULT |
                          GPIT_MICRO | GPIA_ASSOC) ;

                /*---------------------------
                   Create 32 by 32 bitmap
                 ------------------------*/

bmp.cbFix    = sizeof bmp ;
bmp.cx       = 32 ;
bmp.cy       = 32 ;
bmp.cPlanes  = 1 ;
bmp.cBitCount = 1 ;

hbm = GpiCreateBitmap (hpsMemory, &bmp, OL, NULL, NULL) ;

                /*--------------------------------
                   Select bitmap into memory PS
                 -----------------------------*/

GpiSetBitmap (hpsMemory, hbm) ;

                /*----------------------------------------
                   Set bitmap bits from abBitCat array
                 -------------------------------------*/

pbmi = malloc (sizeof (BITMAPINFO) + sizeof (RGB)) ;

pbmi->cbFix    = sizeof bmp ;
pbmi->cx       = 32 ;
pbmi->cy       = 32 ;
pbmi->cPlanes  = 1 ;
pbmi->cBitCount = 1 ;

pbmi->argbColor[0].bBlue  = 0 ;
pbmi->argbColor[0].bGreen = 0 ;
pbmi->argbColor[0].bRed   = 0 ;
pbmi->argbColor[1].bBlue  = 0xFF ;
pbmi->argbColor[1].bGreen = 0xFF ;
pbmi->argbColor[1].bRed   = 0xFF ;

GpiSetBitmapBits (hpsMemory, OL, 32L, abBitCat, pbmi) ;

free (pbmi) ;
return 0 ;
```

(continued)

Figure 6-13. The BITCAT2.C File. *continued*

```
        case WM_SIZE:
             cxClient = SHORT1FROMMP (mp2) ;
             cyClient = SHORT2FROMMP (mp2) ;
             return 0 ;

        case WM_PAINT:
             hps = WinBeginPaint (hwnd, NULL, NULL) ;

             aptl[0].x = 0 ;                        // target lower left
             aptl[0].y = 0 ;

             aptl[1].x = cxClient ;                 // target upper right
             aptl[1].y = cyClient ;

             aptl[2].x = 0 ;                        // source lower left
             aptl[2].y = 0 ;

             aptl[3].x = 32 ;                       // source upper right
             aptl[3].y = 32 ;

             GpiBitBlt (hps, hpsMemory, 4L, aptl, ROP_SRCCOPY, BBO_AND) ;

             aptl[1] = aptl[3] ;                    // target upper right

             GpiBitBlt (hps, hpsMemory, 3L, aptl, ROP_SRCCOPY, BBO_AND) ;

             WinEndPaint (hps) ;
             return 0 ;

        case WM_DESTROY:
             GpiDestroyPS (hpsMemory) ;
             DevCloseDC (hdcMemory) ;
             GpiDeleteBitmap (hbm) ;
             return 0 ;
        }
   return WinDefWindowProc (hwnd, msg, mp1, mp2) ;
   }
```

The BITCAT2.DEF File

```
;------------------------------------
; BITCAT2.DEF module definition file
;------------------------------------

NAME          BITCAT2   WINDOWAPI

DESCRIPTION   'Bitmap Creation and Display (C) Charles Petzold, 1988'
PROTMODE
HEAPSIZE      1024
STACKSIZE     8192
EXPORTS       ClientWndProc
```

Figure 6-13. *The BITCAT2 program.*

The BITCAT2 program also requires the BITCAT.H header file from Figure 6-11. As you can see from Figure 6-14, the program shows the same output as BITCAT1:

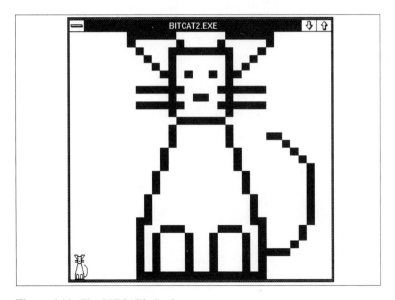

Figure 6-14. *The BITCAT2 display.*

During the WM_CREATE message, BITCAT2 opens a memory device context and creates a presentation space associated with that device context. BITCAT2 creates an initialized 32-by-32 bitmap exactly like BITCAT1. But then it calls *GpiSetBitmap* to set the bitmap in the presentation space.

During the WM_PAINT message, BITCAT2 uses the *GpiBitBlt* function to draw the bitmap on the display. The source presentation space is simply the presentation space associated with the memory device context. Although BITCAT2 uses ROP_SRCCOPY, it could also select a nondefault pattern in the destination presentation space and use *GpiBitBlt* with all 256 raster operations.

For drawing bitmaps, GPI also provides a function similar to *GpiBitBlt* — called *GpiWCBitBlt*. (The WC stands for "word coordinates.") The second parameter is a handle to a bitmap rather than a handle to a source presentation space.

Drawing on the Memory Device Context

I said earlier that the bitmap is the display surface of the memory device context. Thus, when you use normal GPI functions to draw on the presentation space associated with this memory device context, you're actually drawing on the bitmap. This is one reason why you can create a bitmap without initializing it. You can create an image on the bitmap by simply drawing on the presentation space.

This is shown in the HELLOBIT program in Figure 6-15.

The HELLOBIT File

```
#--------------------
# HELLOBIT make file
#--------------------

hellobit.obj : hellobit.c
      cl -c -G2sw -W3 hellobit.c

hellobit.exe : hellobit.obj hellobit.def
      link hellobit, /align:16, NUL, os2, hellobit
```

The HELLOBIT.C File

```
/*-----------------------------------
   HELLOBIT.C -- "Hello, world" Bitmap
   ------------------------------------*/

#define INCL_WIN
#define INCL_GPI
#include <os2.h>
```

(continued)

Figure 6-15. The HELLOBIT.C File. *continued*

```
MRESULT EXPENTRY ClientWndProc (HWND, USHORT, MPARAM, MPARAM) ;


HAB  hab ;


int main (void)
    {
    static CHAR  szClientClass [] = "HelloBit" ;
    static ULONG flFrameFlags = FCF_TITLEBAR      | FCF_SYSMENU |
                                FCF_SIZEBORDER    | FCF_MINMAX  |
                                FCF_SHELLPOSITION | FCF_TASKLIST ;
    HMQ          hmq ;
    HWND         hwndFrame, hwndClient ;
    QMSG         qmsg ;


    hab = WinInitialize (0) ;
    hmq = WinCreateMsgQueue (hab, 0) ;


    WinRegisterClass (hab, szClientClass, ClientWndProc, CS_SIZEREDRAW, 0) ;


    hwndFrame = WinCreateStdWindow (HWND_DESKTOP, WS_VISIBLE,
                                    &flFrameFlags, szClientClass, NULL,
                                    0L, NULL, 0, &hwndClient) ;


    WinSendMsg (hwndFrame, WM_SETICON,
                WinQuerySysPointer (HWND_DESKTOP, SPTR_APPICON, FALSE),
                NULL) ;


    while (WinGetMsg (hab, &qmsg, NULL, 0, 0))
        WinDispatchMsg (hab, &qmsg) ;


    WinDestroyWindow (hwndFrame) ;
    WinDestroyMsgQueue (hmq) ;
    WinTerminate (hab) ;
    return 0 ;
    }


MRESULT EXPENTRY ClientWndProc (HWND hwnd, USHORT msg, MPARAM mp1, MPARAM mp2)
    {
    static CHAR        szHello [] = " Hello, world " ;
    static HBITMAP     hbm ;
    static HDC         hdcMemory ;
    static HPS         hpsMemory ;
    static SHORT       cxClient, cyClient, cxString, cyString ;
    BITMAPINFOHEADER   bmp ;
    HPS                hps ;
    POINTL             aptl [4], ptl ;
```

(continued)

Figure 6-15. The HELLOBIT.C File. *continued*

```
SHORT            x, y ;
SIZEL            sizl ;

switch (msg)
     {
     case WM_CREATE:


                    /*---------------------------------------------------
                              Open memory DC and create PS associated with it
                    --------------------------------------------------*/


               hdcMemory = DevOpenDC (hab, OD_MEMORY, "*", OL, NULL, NULL) ;

               sizl.cx = 0 ;
               sizl.cy = 0 ;
               hpsMemory = GpiCreatePS (hab, hdcMemory, &sizl,
                                   PU_PELS   ¦ GPIF_DEFAULT ¦
                                   GPIT_MICRO ¦ GPIA_ASSOC) ;


                    /*-------------------------------------
                              Determine dimensions of text string
                    -----------------------------------*/


               GpiQueryTextBox (hpsMemory, sizeof szHello - 1L,
                          szHello, 4L, aptl) ;

               cxString = (SHORT) (aptl [TXTBOX_TOPRIGHT].x -
                                   aptl [TXTBOX_TOPLEFT].x) ;

               cyString = (SHORT) (aptl [TXTBOX_TOPLEFT].y -
                                   aptl [TXTBOX_BOTTOMLEFT].y) ;


                    /*---------------------------------------------
                              Create bitmap and set it in the memory PS
                    -------------------------------------------*/


               bmp.cbFix     = sizeof bmp ;
               bmp.cx        = cxString ;
               bmp.cy        = cyString ;
               bmp.cPlanes   = 1 ;
               bmp.cBitCount = 1 ;

               hbm = GpiCreateBitmap (hpsMemory, &bmp, OL, OL, NULL) ;

               GpiSetBitmap (hpsMemory, hbm) ;
```

(continued)

Figure 6-15. The HELLOBIT.C File. *continued*

```
                        /*-----------------------------------------
                         Write the text string to the memory PS
                        -----------------------------------------*/

        ptl.x = 0 ;
        ptl.y = - aptl [TXTBOX_BOTTOMLEFT].y ;

        GpiSetColor (hpsMemory, CLR_TRUE) ;
        GpiSetBackColor (hpsMemory, CLR_FALSE) ;
        GpiSetBackMix (hpsMemory, BM_OVERPAINT) ;
        GpiCharStringAt (hpsMemory, &ptl, sizeof szHello - 1L,
                         szHello) ;
        return 0 ;

    case WM_SIZE:
        cxClient = SHORT1FROMMP (mp2) ;
        cyClient = SHORT2FROMMP (mp2) ;
        return 0 ;

    case WM_PAINT:
        hps = WinBeginPaint (hwnd, NULL, NULL) ;

        for (y = 0 ; y <= cyClient / cyString ; y++)
            for (x = 0 ; x <= cxClient / cxString ; x++)
                {
                aptl[0].x = x * cxString ;        // target lower left
                aptl[0].y = y * cyString ;

                aptl[1].x = aptl[0].x + cxString ; // upper right
                aptl[1].y = aptl[0].y + cyString ;

                aptl[2].x = 0 ;                    // source lower left
                aptl[2].y = 0 ;

                GpiBitBlt (hps, hpsMemory, 3L, aptl, ROP_SRCCOPY,
                           BBO_AND) ;
                }
        WinEndPaint (hps) ;
        return 0 ;

    case WM_DESTROY:
        GpiDestroyPS (hpsMemory) ;
        DevCloseDC (hdcMemory) ;
        GpiDeleteBitmap (hbm) ;
        return 0 ;
    }
return WinDefWindowProc (hwnd, msg, mp1, mp2) ;
}
```

The HELLOBIT.DEF File

```
;-------------------------------------
; HELLOBIT.DEF module definition file
;-------------------------------------

NAME          HELLOBIT  WINDOWAPI

DESCRIPTION   '"Hello, world" Bitmap (C) Charles Petzold, 1988'
PROTMODE
HEAPSIZE      1024
STACKSIZE     8192
EXPORTS       ClientWndProc
```

Figure 6-15. *The HELLOBIT program.*

HELLOBIT creates a memory device context and a presentation space associated with this memory device context during the WM_CREATE message. Then it determines the dimension of the text "Hello, world" by calling *GpiQueryTextBox*. The program creates a bitmap of these dimensions and sets the bitmap in the memory device context.

HELLOBIT then writes the text string on the presentation space by calling *GpiCharStringAt*. The bitmap is monochrome, so the foreground color is set

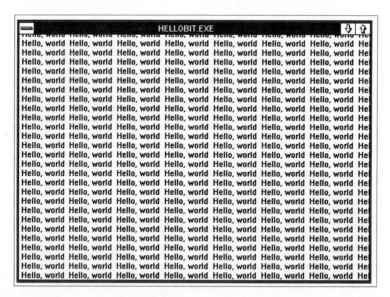

Figure 6-16. *The HELLOBIT display.*

to CLR_TRUE (1 bits), and the background color to CLR_FALSE (0 bits). These are the best color values to use with monochrome bitmaps. HELLOBIT also sets the background mix to BM_OVERPAINT so that the background is filled in with 0 bits.

During the WM_PAINT message, HELLOBIT covers the window with copies of this bitmap by calling *GpiBitBlt*. This is shown in Figure 6-16.

As in BITCAT2, the presentation space, device context, and bitmap are destroyed during the WM_DESTROY message.

You might want to try a variation of HELLOBIT that uses *WinDrawBitmap* during the WM_PAINT message. In this case, you don't need the memory device context or presentation space after you initialize the bitmap by calling *GpiCharStringAt*. You can destroy them after that call:

```
GpiDestroyPS (hpsMemory) ;
DevCloseDC (hdcMemory) ;
```

During the WM_DESTROY message you need only destroy the bitmap. Thus the memory device context and presentation space serve simply as a mold to draw on the bitmap. You can then destroy the mold (calling *GpiDestroyPS* and *DevCloseDC*), leaving the bitmap behind.

One common use of a memory device context is for a "shadow bitmap." You create a bitmap large enough to encompass the client window and select that into a presentation space associated with a memory device context. Whenever you draw on the window, you also draw on the presentation space. During the WM_PAINT message, you can update the client window with a simple *GpiBitBlt* call. This approach is shown in the SKETCH program in Chapter 9.

When a bitmap is set in a presentation space associated with a memory device context, you can set the bitmap bits with an array of data using *GpiSetBitmapBits*. This is yet another way to initialize a bitmap. You can also obtain the bitmap bits and store them in an array by calling *GpiQueryBitmapBits*.

Customized Patterns

Another use for bitmaps is to create your own customized patterns for area filling. A pattern is based on an 8-by-8 bitmap. When a pattern is used to fill an area, the bitmap is simply repeated horizontally and vertically.

For example, suppose you want to use a pattern that looks like a brick wall. Assuming you want the brick itself to be the foreground color (1 bits) and the cement between the bricks to be the background color (0 bits), the bit-map that you begin with might look like this:

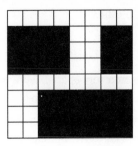

These bits (padded at the right so each row is 32 bits) are stored in the *abBrick* array in the BRICKS program in Figure 6-17.

The BRICKS File

```
#------------------
# BRICKS make file
#------------------

bricks.obj : bricks.c
    cl -c -G2sw -W3 bricks.c

bricks.exe : bricks.obj bricks.def
    link bricks, /align:16, NUL, os2, bricks
```

The BRICKS.C File

```
/*--------------------------------------------
    BRICKS.C -- Customized Pattern from Bitmap
  --------------------------------------------*/

#define INCL_WIN
#define INCL_GPI
#include <os2.h>
#include <stdlib.h>

#define LCID_BRICKS_BITMAP    1L

MRESULT EXPENTRY ClientWndProc (HWND, USHORT, MPARAM, MPARAM) ;

int main (void)
    {
```

(continued)

Figure 6-17. The BRICKS.C File. *continued*

```c
       static CHAR   szClientClass [] = "Bricks" ;
       static ULONG  flFrameFlags = FCF_TITLEBAR     | FCF_SYSMENU  |
                                    FCF_SIZEBORDER   | FCF_MINMAX   |
                                    FCF_SHELLPOSITION | FCF_TASKLIST ;

       HAB           hab ;
       HMQ           hmq ;
       HWND          hwndFrame, hwndClient ;
       QMSG          qmsg ;

       hab = WinInitialize (0) ;
       hmq = WinCreateMsgQueue (hab, 0) ;

       WinRegisterClass (hab, szClientClass, ClientWndProc, CS_SIZEREDRAW, 0) ;

       hwndFrame = WinCreateStdWindow (HWND_DESKTOP, WS_VISIBLE,
                                       &flFrameFlags, szClientClass, NULL,
                                       0L, NULL, 0, &hwndClient) ;

       while (WinGetMsg (hab, &qmsg, NULL, 0, 0))
            WinDispatchMsg (hab, &qmsg) ;

       WinDestroyWindow (hwndFrame) ;
       WinDestroyMsgQueue (hmq) ;
       WinTerminate (hab) ;
       return 0 ;
       }

MRESULT EXPENTRY ClientWndProc (HWND hwnd, USHORT msg, MPARAM mp1, MPARAM mp2)
       {
       static BYTE       abBrick [] = {
                                       0x00, 0x00, 0x00, 0x00,
                                       0xF3, 0x00, 0x00, 0x00,
                                       0xF3, 0x00, 0x00, 0x00,
                                       0xF3, 0x00, 0x00, 0x00,
                                       0x00, 0x00, 0x00, 0x00,
                                       0x3F, 0x00, 0x00, 0x00,
                                       0x3F, 0x00, 0x00, 0x00,
                                       0x3F, 0x00, 0x00, 0x00
                                       } ;
       static HBITMAP    hbm ;
       static POINTL     aptl [2] ;
       BITMAPINFO        *pbmi ;
       BITMAPINFOHEADER  bmp ;
       HPS               hps ;
```

(continued)

Figure 6-17. The BRICKS.C File. *continued*

```
switch (msg)
    {
    case WM_CREATE:
                    /*-----------------------
                        Create 8-by-8 bitmap
                    ----------------------*/

        bmp.cbFix     = sizeof bmp ;
        bmp.cx       = 8 ;
        bmp.cy       = 8 ;
        bmp.cPlanes  = 1 ;
        bmp.cBitCount = 1 ;

        pbmi = malloc (sizeof (BITMAPINFO) + sizeof (RGB)) ;

        pbmi->cbFix     = sizeof bmp ;
        pbmi->cx       = 8 ;
        pbmi->cy       = 8 ;
        pbmi->cPlanes  = 1 ;
        pbmi->cBitCount = 1 ;

        pbmi->argbColor[0].bBlue  = 0 ;
        pbmi->argbColor[0].bGreen = 0 ;
        pbmi->argbColor[0].bRed   = 0 ;
        pbmi->argbColor[1].bBlue  = 0xFF ;
        pbmi->argbColor[1].bGreen = 0xFF ;
        pbmi->argbColor[1].bRed   = 0xFF ;

        hps = WinGetPS (hwnd) ;
        hbm = GpiCreateBitmap (hps, &bmp, CBM_INIT, abBrick, pbmi) ;

        WinReleasePS (hps) ;
        free (pbmi) ;
        return 0 ;

    case WM_SIZE:
        aptl[1].x = SHORT1FROMMP (mp2) ;
        aptl[1].y = SHORT2FROMMP (mp2) ;
        return 0 ;

    case WM_PAINT:
        hps = WinBeginPaint (hwnd, NULL, NULL) ;

        GpiSetBitmapId (hps, hbm, LCID_BRICKS_BITMAP) ;
        GpiSetPatternSet (hps, LCID_BRICKS_BITMAP) ;
```

(continued)

Figure 6-17. The BRICKS.C File. *continued*

```
            GpiBitBlt (hps, NULL, 2L, aptl, ROP_PATCOPY, BBO_AND) ;

            GpiSetPatternSet (hps, LCID_DEFAULT) ;
            GpiDeleteSetId (hps, LCID_BRICKS_BITMAP) ;

            WinEndPaint (hps) ;
            return 0 ;

        case WM_DESTROY:
            GpiDeleteBitmap (hbm) ;
            return 0 ;
        }
    return WinDefWindowProc (hwnd, msg, mp1, mp2) ;
    }
```

The BRICKS.DEF File

```
;-----------------------------------
; BRICKS.DEF module definition file
;-----------------------------------


NAME            BRICKS      WINDOWAPI

DESCRIPTION     'Customized Pattern from Bitmap (c) Charles Petzold, 1988'
PROTMODE
HEAPSIZE        1024
STACKSIZE       8192
EXPORTS         ClientWndProc
```

Figure 6-17. *The BRICKS program.*

During the WM_CREATE message, BRICKS creates an 8-by-8 bitmap initialized with these bits. During the WM_PAINT message, the bitmap is first tagged with an ID number:

```
GpiSetBitmapId (hps, hbm, LCID_BRICKS_BITMAP) ;
```

The LCID_BRICKS_BITMAP is defined in BRICKS.C as 1. (LCID stands for "local id.") The bitmap is now an available pattern. You can use the *GpiSetPatternSet* function to make this pattern the current pattern:

```
GpiSetPatternSet (hps, LCID_BRICKS_BITMAP) ;
```

Notice that this is the *GpiSetPatternSet* function rather than the *GpiSet-Pattern* function normally used for selecting a pattern.

BRICKS uses the *GpiBitBlt* function with the ROP_PATCOPY raster operation to fill the window with the bitmap, as shown in Figure 6-18.

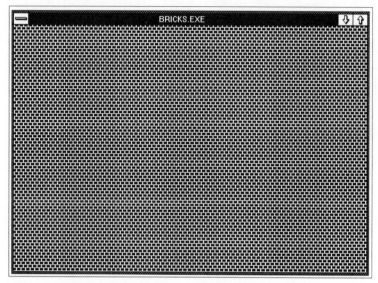

Figure 6-18. *The BRICKS display.*

The program could also have used *GpiBox* with the DRO_FILL or DRO_OUTLINEFILL option to display the bricks pattern. After BRICKS uses the pattern, the current pattern set is established as the default pattern set (containing all predefined patterns):

```
GpiSetPatternSet (hps, LCID_DEFAULT) ;
```

The LCID_DEFAULT identifier is defined in PMGPI.H. BRICKS then deletes the local ID:

```
GpiDeleteSetId (hps, LCID_BRICKS_BITMAP) ;
```

You can define up to 254 customized patterns using local IDs ranging from 1 through 254. When you want to use a customized pattern, you call *GpiSet-PatternSet* with the local ID. When you want to use a predefined pattern, you first call *GpiSetPatternSet* with LCID_DEFAULT and then use *GpiSet-Pattern* with a PATSYM identifier.

The local IDs for these customized patterns become part of the presentation space. Before releasing a cached micro-PS by calling *WinReleasePS* or *WinEndPaint*, you should set the pattern to the default and delete all the IDs. A bitmap cannot be deleted while it has a local ID. You can obtain the bitmap handle tagged with a local ID by calling *GpiQueryBitmapHandle*:

```
hbm = GpiQueryBitmapHandle (hps, lcid) ;
```

You'll recall from the last chapter that you use local IDs when creating fonts. You cannot use the same local ID for both a bitmap and a pattern at the same time. Also keep in mind that the *GpiSetPS* function deletes all local IDs.

Drawing Pixels

Finally, GPI has two functions that might seem important when you first begin programming for the OS/2 Presentation Manager. The *GpiSetPel* function sets an individual pixel to the current foreground color:

```
GpiSetPel (hps, &ptl) ;
```

The *GpiQueryPel* function obtains the color of an individual pixel:

```
lColor = GpiQueryPel (hps, &ptl) ;
```

These two functions are used so infrequently in Presentation Manager programming that you can just about ignore them.

ADVANCED VIO: THE EASY WAY OUT

When OS/2 1.0 was first released, many programmers were favorably impressed by the collection of VIO ("video input/output") functions included in the operating system. These VIO functions gave character-mode OS/2 applications a fast, high-level interface to the video display. Unlike DOS applications, OS/2 1.0 applications can achieve good video performance without directly accessing the video display hardware.

The Presentation Manager is not a character-mode environment. It uses other functions (such as *GpiCharStringAt*) to display text on a window. But the OS/2 VIO functions are too good to abandon entirely. After all, some applications don't need graphics. It seems reasonable that the Presentation Manager allow such applications to write to their client window as if the window were a character-mode device. The AVIO ("Advanced VIO") — an enhancement to the OS/2 1.0 VIO interface, designed specifically for Presentation Manager programs — allows them to do just that.

The Presentation Manager intercepts all VIO calls from all applications running in the Presentation Manager session. This serves two purposes. First, it allows many character-mode programs originally written for OS/2 1.0 to run in a window. The Presentation Manager intercepts the VIO calls and routes the output to the program's window. Although they cannot take advantage of Presentation Manager features (such as graphics, menus, and dialog boxes), these OS/2 1.0 programs are accessible to users because they run in a window in the Presentation Manager session. (Character-mode programs running in other sessions continue to use the normal, unintercepted VIO interface.)

Second, the Presentation Manager also intercepts VIO calls from Presentation Manager programs that use Advanced VIO for displaying text. The text output is converted to graphics and displayed on the window that the program creates.

In general, using AVIO is easier than using GPI. Rather than specifying a coordinate position where a text string is to begin, the program specifies a character row and column position relative to the upper-left corner of the client window. The big disadvantage of AVIO is that precise placement of text is not possible. Each character you display is placed in a character cell. All character cells are the same width and height. Proportional spacing and techniques such as subscripting are not possible. However, a Presentation Manager program using AVIO can also display graphics (including text) on the same window by using the normal GPI interface.

AVIO Mechanics

Let's begin by examining a simple program called AVIO1 (Figure 7-1) that uses several AVIO functions to display the first paragraph of Lewis Carroll's *Alice in Wonderland* in its client window.

The AVIO1 File

```
#-----------------
# AVIO1 make file
#-----------------

aviol.obj : aviol.c
    cl -c -G2sw -W3 aviol.c

aviol.exe : aviol.obj aviol.def
    link aviol, /align:16, NUL, os2, aviol
```

The AVIO1.C File

```
/*------------------------------------------
    AVIO1.C -- Advanced VIO Display of Text
  ---------------------------------------*/

#define INCL_WIN
#define INCL_VIO
#define INCL_AVIO
#include <os2.h>
#include <string.h>
```

(continued)

Figure 7-1. The AVIO1.C File. *continued*

```
#define VIDEOWIDTH 40

MRESULT EXPENTRY ClientWndProc (HWND, USHORT, MPARAM, MPARAM) ;

HAB   hab ;

int main (void)
    {
    static CHAR  szClientClass [] = "Avio1" ;
    static ULONG flFrameFlags = FCF_TITLEBAR      | FCF_SYSMENU |
                                FCF_SIZEBORDER    | FCF_MINMAX  |
                                FCF_SHELLPOSITION | FCF_TASKLIST ;
    HMQ          hmq ;
    HWND         hwndFrame, hwndClient ;
    QMSG         qmsg ;

    hab = WinInitialize (0) ;
    hmq = WinCreateMsgQueue (hab, 0) ;

    WinRegisterClass (hab, szClientClass, ClientWndProc, CS_SIZEREDRAW, 0) ;

    hwndFrame = WinCreateStdWindow (HWND_DESKTOP, WS_VISIBLE,
                                    &flFrameFlags, szClientClass, NULL,
                                    OL, NULL, 0, &hwndClient) ;

    WinSendMsg (hwndFrame, WM_SETICON,
                WinQuerySysPointer (HWND_DESKTOP, SPTR_APPICON, FALSE),
                NULL) ;

    while (WinGetMsg (hab, &qmsg, NULL, 0, 0))
        WinDispatchMsg (hab, &qmsg) ;

    WinDestroyWindow (hwndFrame) ;
    WinDestroyMsgQueue (hmq) ;
    WinTerminate (hab) ;
    return 0 ;
    }

MRESULT EXPENTRY ClientWndProc (HWND hwnd, USHORT msg, MPARAM mp1, MPARAM mp2)
    {
    static CHAR  *aszAlice [] = {
                                "Alice was beginning to get very tired of",
                                "sitting by her sister on the bank and of",
                                "having nothing to do: once or twice she",
                                "had peeped into the book her sister was",
```

(continued)

Figure 7-1. The AVIO1.C File. *continued*

```
                                       "reading, but it had no pictures or ",
                                       "conversations in it, \"and what is the",
                                       "use of a book,\" thought Alice, \"without",
                                       "pictures or conversations?\""
                                       } ;
     static HPS    hps ;
     static HVPS   hvps ;
     static SHORT  sNumLines = sizeof aszAlice / sizeof aszAlice[0] ;
     HDC           hdc ;
     SHORT         sRow ;
     SIZEL         sizl ;

     switch (msg)
          {
          case WM_CREATE:
               hdc = WinOpenWindowDC (hwnd) ;

               sizl.cx = sizl.cy = 0 ;
               hps = GpiCreatePS (hab, hdc, &sizl, PU_PELS    | GPIF_DEFAULT |
                                                  GPIT_MICRO | GPIA_ASSOC) ;

               VioCreatePS (&hvps, sNumLines, VIDEOWIDTH, 0, 1, NULL) ;
               VioAssociate (hdc, hvps) ;

               for (sRow = 0 ; sRow < sNumLines ; sRow++)
                    VioWrtCharStr (aszAlice[sRow],
                                   strlen (aszAlice[sRow]),
                                   sRow, 0, hvps) ;
               return 0 ;

          case WM_SIZE:
               WinDefAVioWindowProc (hwnd, msg, mp1, mp2) ;
               return 0 ;

          case WM_PAINT:
               WinBeginPaint (hwnd, hps, NULL) ;
               GpiErase (hps) ;

               VioShowBuf (0, 2 * sNumLines * VIDEOWIDTH, hvps) ;

               WinEndPaint (hps) ;
               return 0 ;

          case WM_DESTROY:
               VioAssociate (NULL, hvps) ;
```

(continued)

Figure 7-1. The AVIO1.C File. *continued*

```
            VioDestroyPS (hvps) ;
            GpiDestroyPS (hps) ;
            return 0 ;
        }
    return WinDefWindowProc (hwnd, msg, mp1, mp2) ;
    }
```

The AVIO1.DEF File

```
;-----------------------------------
; AVIO1.DEF module definition file
;-----------------------------------


NAME           AVIO1      WINDOWAPI

DESCRIPTION    'Advanced VIO Display of Text (C) Charles Petzold, 1988'
HEAPSIZE       1024
STACKSIZE      8192
EXPORTS        ClientWndProc
```

Figure 7-1. *The AVIO1 program.*

The AVIO1 window is shown in Figure 7-2.

Figure 7-2. *The AVIO1 display.*

You'll notice a little problem with AVIO1: The text displayed by the program appears as light gray letters on a black background. This is, of course, the default for text in a character-mode session. However, the rest of the window has a white background (or whatever color you set for the window background in the Presentation Manager Control Program). We'll take care of this problem later.

You'll notice that the AVIO1.C file begins with the definition of two identifiers:

```
#define INCL_VIO
#define INCL_AVIO
```

The first identifier enables the declaration of OS/2 1.0 VIO functions and structures in the BSESUB.H header file. The second identifier causes the PMAVIO.H header file to be included; this file declares the additional functions supported by the Presentation Manager AVIO interface.

Creating and Destroying

To use AVIO, a program first creates an AVIO presentation space by calling *VioCreatePS*. A program that uses AVIO for most of its window output will probably create the presentation space while processing the WM_CREATE message in the window procedure. The general syntax of *VioCreatePS* is

```
VioCreatePS (&hvps, cyDisplay, cxDisplay, 0, cbAttrs, 0) ;
```

> **NOTE:** *In the initial release of the Presentation Manager, the fourth and last parameters must be set to 0.*

The first parameter is a pointer to a variable of type HVPS ("handle to a VIO presentation space"), which you can define like this:

```
HVPS hvps ;
```

The *VioCreatePS* function stores the handle to the AVIO presentation space in this variable. You use the *hvps* handle with the VIO functions in the same way that you use the *hps* handle with the GPI functions, except that *hvps* is the last parameter to the VIO functions rather than the first parameter.

When you create an AVIO presentation space, the Presentation Manager creates a "virtual display buffer" for you. This is simply a block of memory organized into rows and columns of characters. You specify the dimensions of this virtual display buffer by using the parameters *cxDisplay* (number of characters per row) and *cyDisplay* (number of rows).

The *cbAttrs* parameter must be either 1 or 3. This specifies the number of "attribute" bytes associated with each character. When *cbAttrs* is set to 1, each character has 1 attribute byte. Within the virtual display buffer, the character and attribute bytes alternate (character first and then attribute). The attribute is compatible with the attribute byte used in character modes of the IBM Color Graphics Adapter (CGA), Enhanced Graphics Adapter (EGA), and Video Graphics Array (VGA). The attribute byte indicates the foreground and background colors of the character. (I'll discuss the alternative use of 3 attribute bytes later in this chapter.)

The total number of bytes required for the AVIO virtual display buffer is the product of *cxDisplay*, *cyDisplay*, and the number of bytes associated with each character (2 if *cbAttrs* is set to 1, or 4 if *cbAttrs* is set to 3). The total size of the AVIO virtual display buffer cannot exceed 65,536 bytes. Once you create an AVIO presentation space, you cannot change the dimensions or number of attribute bytes.

When first created, the virtual display buffer is cleared to simulate a blank screen. The character bytes are set to spaces, and the attribute bytes are set to 7, which is light gray text on a black background.

The AVIO1 program in Figure 7-1 needs to display only *sNumLines* rows of text with a maximum width of VIDEOWIDTH (defined in the beginning of the AVIO1.C file). Thus the program creates a presentation space just large enough for this output:

```
VioCreatePS (&hvps, sNumLines, VIDEOWIDTH, 0, 1, NULL) ;
```

You'll notice that the *VioCreatePS* function has no parameter to specify the window for which the AVIO presentation space is to be used. After a program creates an AVIO presentation space, it must "associate" the presentation space with a screen device context for a particular window. As you saw in Chapter 5, you can obtain a device context for a window by calling

```
hdc = WinOpenWindowDC (hwnd) ;
```

You then associate the AVIO presentation space with this device context:

```
VioAssociate (hdc, hvps) ;
```

Before your program terminates, it should disassociate the AVIO presentation space from the device context:

```
VioAssociate (NULL, hvps) ;
```

and destroy the presentation space:

```
VioDestroyPS (hvps) ;
```

You'll probably do this during the WM_DESTROY message.

AVIO1 also creates a micro-PS during the WM_CREATE message. This presentation space is associated with the same device context as the AVIO presentation space:

```
hps = GpiCreatePS (hab, hdc, &sizl, PU_PELS | GPIF_DEFAULT |
                                    GPIT_MICRO | GPIA_ASSOC) ;
```

This micro-PS is also destroyed during the WM_DESTROY message:

```
GpiDestroyPS (hps) ;
```

Creating this micro-PS is not strictly required, but it helps out during WM_PAINT processing.

Writing to the Presentation Space

OS/2 1.0 has seven VIO functions that let you display text on the screen. A Presentation Manager program can use these same seven functions to display text on the AVIO virtual display buffer. The function used in AVIO1.C is *VioWrtCharStr*. (The other functions are discussed later in this chapter.)

The general syntax of *VioWrtCharStr* is

```
VioWrtCharStr (&chString, cbString, usRow, usCol, hvps) ;
```

The first parameter is a pointer to a character string; the second parameter is to the length of this string. The *usRow* and *usCol* parameters indicate the character row and column in which the first character of the string will be displayed. The top row is row 0; the leftmost column is column 0.

You can write to the AVIO virtual display buffer any time after you create it. (Because the text in AVIO1's window does not change, AVIO1 does this during the WM_CREATE message.) However, when you write to the AVIO virtual display buffer during the WM_CREATE message, the text is *not* displayed on the program's window because the window is not yet visible. You must still update the window during the WM_PAINT message.

Updating the Window

To display text on the window, you must update the window from the AVIO virtual display buffer. Two functions do this: *VioShowBuf*, which was included in OS/2 1.0, and *VioShowPS*, which is new with the Presentation Manager.

The AVIO1 program uses *VioShowBuf*, which has a general syntax as follows:

```
VioShowBuf (usByteOffset, usLength, hvps) ;
```

The function updates *usLength* bytes beginning at the *usByteOffset* from the start of the virtual display buffer.

When the window is visible, you can call *VioShowPS* or *VioShowBuf* at any time to update the window. However, as you saw in previous chapters, it's often best to organize your programs so they write to the window only during the WM_PAINT message. Here's how AVIO1 does it:

```
case WM_PAINT:
    WinBeginPaint (hwnd, hps, NULL) ;
    GpiErase (hps) ;
    VioShowBuf (0, 2 * sNumLines*VIDEOWIDTH, hvps) ;
    WinEndPaint (hps) ;

    return 0 ;
```

Note that the second parameter to *WinEndPaint* is the micro-PS handle obtained during WM_CREATE. The presentation space handle is associated with the device context for the window. The AVIO presentation space is also associated with the same device context. This ensures that any updating of the window affects only the invalid area. Note that you can also display graphics to the window by using the *hps* handle in GPI calls.

If you want to restrict the *VioShowBuf* call to the invalid rectangle of the window (which is often more efficient), you can pass a pointer to a RECTL structure as the last parameter of *WinBeginPaint*. You must then convert the pixel coordinates of this rectangle into character rows and columns before calling *VioShowBuf*. (As I'll discuss later in this chapter, you can obtain the dimensions of the AVIO character cell by calling *VioGetDeviceCellSize*.)

Processing WM_SIZE Messages

Every window procedure that uses an AVIO presentation space must pass the WM_SIZE message to *WinDefAVioWindowProc*. You can do your own WM_SIZE processing before or after this call:

```
case WM_SIZE:

     . . . .

     WinDefAVioWindowProc (hwnd, msg, mp1, mp2) ;

     . . . .

     return 0 ;
```

The AVIO Presentation Space

When you first encountered the GPI presentation space, the concept may have been somewhat difficult to grasp. You eventually saw how the presentation space is associated with a device context and how it stores various attributes that affect how the GPI functions work on the device.

The AVIO presentation space is conceptually much simpler. The most important part of the AVIO presentation space is the virtual display buffer that you write on when you call VIO functions. The presentation space also includes a current cursor position, cursor shape, and origin, as well as other information.

The Virtual Display Buffer

When you create an AVIO presentation space, you define the row and column dimensions of a display surface and the number of attribute bytes associated with each character. The Presentation Manager allocates a block of memory to use for the virtual display buffer.

You can think of this virtual display buffer as comprising a series of cells. Each cell is either 2 or 4 bytes long and comprises a character and 1 or 3 attribute bytes, depending on the *cbAttrs* parameter in the *VioCreatePS* function.

For example, an AVIO presentation space of 5 rows and 10 columns has a virtual display buffer either 100 or 200 bytes long. The buffer begins with the cell in the upper-left corner (row 0 and column 0) and continues with the cells in the first row. The other rows follow. This organization is shown in Figure 7-3.

	0	1	2	3	4	5	6	7	8	9
0	0	1	2	3	4	5	6	7	8	9
1	10	11	12	13	14	15	16	17	18	19
2	20	21	22	23	24	25	26	27	28	29
3	30	31	32	33	34	35	36	37	38	39
4	40	41	42	43	44	45	46	47	48	49

Column (header); Row (side header)

Figure 7-3. *Organization of cells in the AVIO virtual display buffer that has 5 rows and 10 cells per row.*

Character and Attributes

When creating the presentation space, you have a choice of using 1 or 3 attribute bytes per cell.

The option of 1 attribute byte provides compatibility with character modes of the IBM CGA, EGA, and VGA. Hence, the organization of the virtual display buffer is familiar to any programmer who has worked with character-mode video output on PC compatibles under MS-DOS or OS/2. Each cell is 2 bytes long. The first byte is the character, and the second is the attribute. This is shown in Figure 7-4. The byte offset is measured from the beginning of the virtual display buffer.

Byte offset: 0   1   2   3   4   5   . . .

| Char 0 | Attr 0 | Char 1 | Attr 1 | Char 2 | Attr 2 | . . . |

Figure 7-4. *The organization of characters and attributes when using 1 attribute byte.*

The attribute byte comprises two 4-bit color codes, as shown in Figure 7-5. The lower 4 bits indicate the character color, and the upper 4 bits indicate the background color.

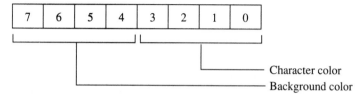

| 7 | 6 | 5 | 4 | 3 | 2 | 1 | 0 |

Character color
Background color

Figure 7-5. *The AVIO attribute byte.*

These 4-bit color values describe a color based on an IRGB (Intensity-Red-Green-Blue) encoding as shown in Figure 7-6.

		AVIO Colors			Traditional	
I	R	G	B	Value	Color Names	Equivalent GPI Color
0	0	0	0	0	Black	CLR_BLACK
0	0	0	1	1	Blue	CLR_BLUE
0	0	1	0	2	Green	CLR_DARKGREEN
0	0	1	1	3	Cyan	CLR_DARKCYAN
0	1	0	0	4	Red	CLR_DARKRED
0	1	0	1	5	Magenta	CLR_DARKPINK
0	1	1	0	6	Brown	CLR_BROWN
0	1	1	1	7	Light gray	CLR_PALEGRAY
1	0	0	0	8	Dark gray	CLR_DARKGRAY
1	0	0	1	9	Light blue	CLR_BLUE
1	0	1	0	10	Light green	CLR_GREEN
1	0	1	1	11	Light cyan	CLR_CYAN
1	1	0	0	12	Light red	CLR_RED
1	1	0	1	13	Light magenta	CLR_PINK
1	1	1	0	14	Light yellow	CLR_YELLOW
1	1	1	1	15	White	CLR_WHITE

Figure 7-6. *The color values used in the AVIO attribute byte.*

For example, an attribute byte of 0x1E is yellow text (14 or 0xE) on a blue background (1). These color values do *not* correspond to the values of the GPI color identifiers, so don't use GPI color indices (like CLR_BLUE) for attribute bytes.

> **NOTE:** *Programmers familiar with character-mode programming will note that the interpretation of the attribute is not* exactly *the same as in the default operation of the CGA, EGA, and VGA. By default, these video boards interpret the high bit of the attribute as a "blinking" bit rather than as an intensity of the background color. Advanced VIO does not support blinking characters.*

When you set the *cbAttrs* parameter in *VioCreatePS* to 3, each cell has 4 bytes. The first byte is the character, the second is the normal attribute described above, and the third is an extended attribute byte. This is shown in Figure 7-7. The fourth byte of each cell is used internally by the Presentation Manager for double-byte character set support.

Byte offset: 0 1 2 3 4 5 6 7 . . .

| Char 0 | Attr 0 | Ext. Attr 0 | | Char 1 | Attr 1 | Ext. Attr 1 | | . . . |

Figure 7-7. *The organization of characters and attributes with the use of 3 attribute bytes.*

The extended attribute byte is shown in Figure 7-8.

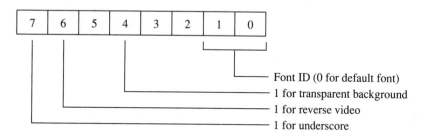

Figure 7-8. *The AVIO extended attribute byte.*

When you set bit 4 to 1, the background of the character cell is not colored by the background color. Whatever was there remains there. (This is useful when you mix AVIO text and graphics.) When bit 6 is set to 1, foreground and background colors are switched for the character. Bit 7 underlines the character.

Writing Directly to the Buffer

When you call functions such as *VioWrtCharStr* to display text on an AVIO presentation space, the text is stored in the virtual display buffer and, if possible, displayed on the window.

You can also write directly on the virtual display buffer. To do this, you must first obtain a far pointer to the beginning of the buffer by calling *VioGetBuf*. Your program can then write on the buffer using normal C pointer manipulation. But this text will not automatically be displayed on the window. You must update the window from the buffer with *VioShowPS* or *VioShowBuf*.

You need to define a few variables in preparation for calling *VioGetBuf*:

```
PCHAR pVideoBuffer ;
ULONG ulVideoBuffer ;
ULONG usVideoLength ;
```

You call *VioGetBuf* like this:

```
VioGetBuf (&ulVideoBuffer, &usVideoLength, hvps) ;
```

On return from the function, *ulVideoBuffer* is a far pointer to the beginning of the logical video buffer stored as a ULONG integer. The returned value of *usVideoLength* is the length of the buffer in bytes. You already know this length: It's the number of rows times the number of columns times the number of bytes per cell (2 or 4).

The first parameter to *VioGetBuf* is declared in the BSESUB.H header file as a pointer to a ULONG value, but it's really a pointer to a PCHAR (which itself is a far pointer to CHAR), so you can cast it into PCHAR like this:

```
pVideoBuffer = (PCHAR) ulVideoBuffer ;
```

Let's assume that *cxDisplay* is the width of the AVIO presentation space and *cbAttrs* is the number of attribute bytes. If you wanted to write the letter A in the *sRow* and *sCol* position of the virtual display buffer, you would use the following syntax:

$$*(pVideoBuffer + sRow * cxDisplay * (cbAttrs + 1) + sCol) = \text{'A'} ;$$

Of course, this syntax is somewhat clumsy for general use. You will probably want to define a macro that makes the code a little clearer.

Or, you could use the approach shown in the AVIO2 program in Figure 7-9.

The AVIO2 File

```
#------------------
# AVIO2 make file
#------------------

avio2.obj : avio2.c
    cl -c -G2sw -W3 avio2.c

avio2.exe : avio2.obj avio2.def
    link avio2, /align:16, NUL, os2, avio2
```

The AVIO2.C File

```
/*-----------------------------------------
   AVIO2.C -- Advanced VIO Display of Text
   -----------------------------------------*/

#define INCL_WIN
#define INCL_VIO
#define INCL_AVIO
#include <os2.h>

#define VIDEOWIDTH 40

typedef struct
    {
    CHAR ch ;
    CHAR attr ;
    }
    VIDEO [][VIDEOWIDTH] ;

typedef VIDEO FAR *PVIDEO ;

MRESULT EXPENTRY ClientWndProc (HWND, USHORT, MPARAM, MPARAM) ;

HAB   hab ;

int main (void)
    {
    static CHAR    szClientClass [] = "Avio2" ;
    static ULONG   flFrameFlags = FCF_TITLEBAR      | FCF_SYSMENU  |
                                  FCF_SIZEBORDER    | FCF_MINMAX   |
                                  FCF_SHELLPOSITION | FCF_TASKLIST ;
    HMQ            hmq ;
    HWND           hwndFrame, hwndClient ;
    QMSG           qmsg ;

    hab = WinInitialize (0) ;
    hmq = WinCreateMsgQueue (hab, 0) ;

    WinRegisterClass (hab, szClientClass, ClientWndProc, CS_SIZEREDRAW, 0) ;

    hwndFrame = WinCreateStdWindow (HWND_DESKTOP, WS_VISIBLE,
                                    &flFrameFlags, szClientClass, NULL,
                                    0L, NULL, 0, &hwndClient) ;
```

(continued)

Figure 7-9. The AVIO2.C File. *continued*

```
        WinSendMsg (hwndFrame, WM_SETICON,
                    WinQuerySysPointer (HWND_DESKTOP, SPTR_APPICON, FALSE),
                    NULL) ;

        while (WinGetMsg (hab, &qmsg, NULL, 0, 0))
             WinDispatchMsg (hab, &qmsg) ;

        WinDestroyWindow (hwndFrame) ;
        WinDestroyMsgQueue (hmq) ;
        WinTerminate (hab) ;
        return 0 ;
        }

MRESULT EXPENTRY ClientWndProc (HWND hwnd, USHORT msg, MPARAM mp1, MPARAM mp2)
        {
        static CHAR  *aszAlice [] = {
                                "Alice was beginning to get very tired of",
                                "sitting by her sister on the bank and of",
                                "having nothing to do: once or twice she",
                                "had peeped into the book her sister was",
                                "reading, but it had no pictures or",
                                "conversations in it, \"and what is the",
                                "use of a book,\" thought Alice, \"without",
                                "pictures or conversations?\""
                                } ;
        static HPS    hps ;
        static HVPS   hvps ;
        static PVIDEO pvideo ;
        static SHORT  sNumLines = sizeof aszAlice / sizeof aszAlice[0] ;
        static USHORT usVideoLength ;
        HDC           hdc ;
        RECTL         rcl ;
        SHORT         sRow, sCol ;
        SIZEL         sizl ;
        ULONG         ulVideoBuffer ;

        switch (msg)
            {
            case WM_CREATE:
                hdc = WinOpenWindowDC (hwnd) ;

                sizl.cx = sizl.cy = 0 ;
                hps = GpiCreatePS (hab, hdc, &sizl, PU_PELS  | GPIF_DEFAULT |
                                                   GPIT_MICRO | GPIA_ASSOC) ;
```

(continued)

Figure 7-9. The AVIO2.C File. *continued*

```
              VioCreatePS (&hvps, sNumLines, VIDEOWIDTH, 0, 1, NULL) ;
              VioAssociate (hdc, hvps) ;

              VioGetBuf (&ulVideoBuffer, &usVideoLength, hvps) ;
              pvideo = (PVIDEO) ulVideoBuffer ;

              for (sRow = 0 ; sRow < sNumLines ; sRow++)
                   for (sCol = 0 ; sCol < VIDEOWIDTH ; sCol++)
                        (*pvideo) [sRow][sCol].attr = '\x1E' ;

              for (sRow = 0 ; sRow < sNumLines ; sRow++)
                   for (sCol = 0 ; aszAlice [sRow][sCol] ; sCol++)
                        (*pvideo) [sRow][sCol].ch = aszAlice [sRow][sCol] ;

              return 0 ;

         case WM_SIZE:
              WinDefAVioWindowProc (hwnd, msg, mp1, mp2) ;
              return 0 ;

         case WM_PAINT:
              WinBeginPaint (hwnd, hps, NULL) ;

              WinQueryWindowRect (hwnd, &rcl) ;
              WinFillRect (hps, &rcl, CLR_DARKBLUE) ;

              VioShowBuf (0, usVideoLength, hvps) ;

              WinEndPaint (hps) ;
              return 0 ;

         case WM_DESTROY:
              VioAssociate (NULL, hvps) ;
              VioDestroyPS (hvps) ;
              GpiDestroyPS (hps) ;
              return 0 ;
         }
    return WinDefWindowProc (hwnd, msg, mp1, mp2) ;
    }
```

The AVIO2.DEF File

```
;-------------------------------------
; AVIO2.DEF module definition file
;-------------------------------------

NAME            AVIO2       WINDOWAPI

DESCRIPTION     'Advanced VIO Display of Text (C) Charles Petzold, 1988'
HEAPSIZE        1024
STACKSIZE       8192
EXPORTS         ClientWndProc
```

Figure 7-9. *The AVIO2 program.*

The method shown here works only when the width of the AVIO presentation space is a constant and is known during compilation of the program.

If you're using 1 attribute byte and VIDEOWIDTH is the width of the AVIO presentation space, you can define a new data type called VIDEO like this:

```
typedef struct
    {
    CHAR ch ;
    CHAR attr ;
    }
    VIDEO [][VIDEOWIDTH] ;
```

The data type VIDEO is a two-dimensional array of structures. The first dimension is the row, and the second is the column. Define another new data type called PVIDEO that is a far pointer to VIDEO:

```
typedef VIDEO FAR *PVIDEO ;
```

Within the window procedure, you define the variable *pvideo* as a PVIDEO (a pointer to a VIDEO array of structures):

```
static PVIDEO pvideo ;
```

The *VioGetBuf* call is the same as shown above, but now cast *ulVideoBuffer* into *pvideo*:

```
pvideo = (PVIDEO) ulVideoBuffer ;
```

To store an 'A' in the *sRow* row and *sCol* column, you use

```
(*pvideo)[sRow][sCol].ch = 'A' ;
```

To set the attribute to 0x1E (yellow text on a blue background), use

```
(*pvideo)[sRow][sCol].attr = '\x1E' ;
```

AVIO2 initializes the virtual display buffer using two sets of *for* loops. The first sets all the attributes of the virtual display buffer to \x1E. The second transfers the text into the character positions of the buffer.

Before updating the window during the WM_PAINT message, AVIO2 erases the background of its window using *WinFillRect* rather than *GpiErase*:

```
WinQueryWindowRect (hwnd, &rcl) ;
WinFillRect (hps, &rcl, CLR_DARKBLUE) ;
```

Thus the background of the window is the same as the background of the character cells. This is one way to take care of the color difference between AVIO and GPI.

The Size of the Display Buffer

Before calling *VioCreatePS*, you must determine the row and column dimensions of the virtual display buffer. The entire size of this buffer (rows times columns times number of bytes per cell) cannot exceed 65,536 bytes.

You'll probably find that an application using AVIO fits into one of the following four categories:

1. Programs that require a virtual display buffer smaller than the size of the screen and that probably use a fixed-size window to display the entire buffer at all times. AVIO1 and AVIO2 are examples of this type of program, although the window is not a fixed size. (Fixed-size windows are demonstrated in the FREEMEM and DIGCLOCK programs shown in Chapter 10.)

2. Programs that require a buffer of a constant size that may be larger than the size of the screen. The SYSVALS4 program, shown later in this chapter, is of this type. The program provides a facility to scroll the presentation space within the window.

3. Programs that use a virtual display buffer to display part of a document. The buffer should be large enough to encompass the entire client window when the window is maximized. The output is adjusted to the window size. A character-mode word-processing or spreadsheet program fits this category.

4. Programs that use a teletype output mode to display character data. This category might include modem communications programs.

For categories 1 and 2, the size of the presentation space can be easily determined by the program before it calls the *VioCreatePS* function. Category 3 programs must determine the number of character rows and columns that can be displayed when the window is maximized. You can do this by calling *WinQuerySysValue* with both the CV_CXFULLSCREEN and SV_CYFULLSCREEN parameters to get the pixel dimensions of the maximized client window, and dividing by the AVIO character cell width and height that you obtain by calling *VioGetDeviceCellSize* (described later in this chapter).

With a category 4 program (such as a modem communications program), you probably want a width of 80 columns and a maximum number of lines. (With the 1-byte attributes, the AVIO presentation space can be 409 lines long.) This lets you retain and scroll back information that has scrolled past the top of the window.

Other Presentation Space Data

Besides the virtual display buffer, the AVIO presentation space retains other data, including

- The origin (the character row and column displayed in the upper left corner of the window)

- The row and column cursor position

- The cursor size and whether it's displayed or hidden

- The dimension in pixels of the character cell

- The code page (or character set)

- Font information

You can query or change these attributes using various VIO and AVIO functions that I'll describe in the next section.

The VIO and AVIO Functions

Advanced VIO supports only a subset of the OS/2 1.0 VIO functions. These are listed in Figure 7-10 along with additional AVIO functions available under the Presentation Manager.

OS/2 1.0 VIO Functions Usable in a Presentation Manager Program		Additional Presentation Manager AVIO Functions
VioGetAnsi	VioSetAnsi	VioAssociate
VioGetBuf	VioSetCp	VioCreateLogFont
VioGetConfig	VioSetCurPos	VioCreatePS
VioGetCp	VioSetCurType	VioDeleteSetId
VioGetCurPos	VioShowBuf	VioDestroyPS
VioGetCurType	VioWrtCellStr	VioGetDeviceCellSize
VioReadCellStr	VioWrtCharStr	VioGetOrg
VioReadCharStr	VioWrtCharStrAtt	VioQueryFonts
VioScrollDn	VioWrtNAttr	VioQuerySetIds
VioScrollLf	VioWrtNCell	VioSetDeviceCellSize
VioScrollRt	VioWrtNChar	VioSetOrg
VioScrollUp	VioWrtTTY	VioShowPS

Figure 7-10. *VIO functions available to a Presentation Manager program.*

The following sections describe how the VIO functions work in the AVIO presentation space. The functions are grouped according to purpose:

- Cursor Position and Size Functions

- Output Functions

- ANSI Control Sequences

- Input Functions

- Scrolling Functions

- Origin Functions

- Cell Size Functions

- Virtual Display Buffer Functions

- Miscellaneous VIO Functions

Except for the *VioCreatePS* function, all VIO functions require the *hvps* handle as the last parameter.

Cursor Position and Size Functions

AVIO displays a cursor only if the program calls *VioWrtTTY* (described shortly). When you first create an AVIO presentation space, the cursor is positioned at the upper-left corner (row 0, column 0). You can change the cursor position by calling

```
VioSetCurPos (usRow, usCol, hvps) ;
```

You do not need to call *VioShowBuf* or *VioShowPS* to display the new cursor position.

To obtain the current position of the cursor, call

```
VioGetCurPos (&usRow, &usCol, hvps) ;
```

Note that this function requires two pointers to variables that receive the row and column position. For example, to move the cursor back one position (but not to the left of column 0), you can use the following code:

```
USHORT usRow, usCol ;

    ....

VioGetCurPos (&usRow, &usCol, hvps) ;

if (usCol > 0)
    VioSetCurPos (usRow, --usCol, hvps) ;
```

The only other VIO function that changes the position of the cursor is *VioWrtTTY*.

By default, the cursor is an underline similar to the hardware cursor supported by most video boards in character modes. Unlike the hardware cursor, the AVIO cursor does not blink. You can change the size of the cursor or make it invisible using *VioSetCurType*. This function requires a structure of type VIOCURSORINFO defined in BSESUB.H:

```
typedef struct _VIOCURSORINFO
    {
    USHORT yStart ;
    USHORT cEnd ;
    USHORT cx ;
    USHORT attr ;
    }
    VIOCURSORINFO ;
```

By convention, a structure of type VIOCURSORINFO begins with the prefix *vioci*. You define such a variable like this:

```
VIOCURSORINFO vioci ;
```

To obtain the current VIOCURSORINFO settings, use

```
VioGetCurType (&vioci, hvps) ;
```

To set new values, use

```
VioSetCurType (&vioci, hvps) ;
```

You don't need to make a call to *VioShowBuf* or *VioShowPS* after you change the cursor size.

The height of the cursor is specified by the *yStart* and *cEnd* fields, which are in units of pixels measured from the top of a character, starting with 0. (To determine the height of a character in pixels, you use the *VioGetDevice-CellSize* function described under "Cell Size Functions.") The *cEnd* field must be greater than or equal to the *yStart* field. If the two fields are equal, the cursor is 1 pixel high.

For example, suppose that characters are 10 pixels high. To create a box cursor the full height of the character, you can use the following code:

```
VioGetCurType (&vioci, hvps) ;

vioci.yStart = 0 ;
vioci.cEnd = 9 ;

VioSetCurType (&vioci, hvps) ;
```

The Presentation Manager displays the cursor in reverse video, so the character is still visible.

The width of the cursor is specified by *cx*. Because the cursor can be only 1 character wide, you can only set this field equal to 1 (which indicates the cursor is 1 character wide) or 0 (which indicates a default width, again 1 character wide).

You can set the *attr* field to −1 to hide the cursor, or to any other value to display the cursor. The function on the next page hides the cursor.

```
VOID HideCursor (HVPS hvps)
     {
     VIOCURSORINFO vioci ;

     VioGetCurType (&vioci, hvps) ;
     vioci.attr = -1 ;
     VioSetCurType (&vioci, hvps) ;
     }
```

If a program does not use *VioWrtTTY* for displaying output (as in AVIO1), the cursor will be hidden anyway. This function shows the cursor again:

```
VOID ShowCursor (HVPS hvps)
     {
     VIOCURSORINFO vioci ;

     VioGetCurType (&vioci, hvps) ;
     vioci.attr = 0 ;
     VioSetCurType (&vioci, hvps) ;
     }
```

As you'll learn in Chapter 8, it's a good practice to hide a cursor when a program loses the input focus and to display the cursor when the program gains the input focus. The presence of the cursor indicates to the user when the program can accept keyboard input.

Output Functions

Seven VIO functions let you display text or attributes on the virtual display buffer. The first six of these functions require parameters to specify the row and column position where the text or attributes begin.

You've already seen how the *VioWrtCharStr* function works in AVIO1.C:

```
VioWrtCharStr (&chCharString, cbCharString, usRow, usCol, hvps)
```

This function requires a pointer to a character string and the length of the string. The function does not affect the attributes already set for the cells.

You can also write a string of cells. Each cell is a character followed by 1 attribute byte or 3 attribute bytes:

```
VioWrtCellStr (&chCellString, cbCellString, usRow, usCol, hvps)
```

The *cbCellString* parameter is the number of bytes in the string: an even number for single attribute bytes and a multiple of 4 for extended attributes.

In practice, this function is rather awkward to use. It makes most sense when used in conjunction with *VioReadCellStr* (described under "Input Functions").

You can also write a character string that uses the same attribute for all characters in the string:

```
VioWrtCharStrAtt (&chCharString, cbCharString, usRow, usCol, &bAttr, hvps)
```

The *&bAttr* parameter is a pointer to 1 byte or 3 bytes. For example, suppose you want to display the text "Hello" at row 0 and column 1. You're using 3 attribute bytes and you want underlined yellow letters on a blue background. The statement is

```
VioWrtCharStrAtt ("Hello", 5, 0, 1, "\x1E\x80\0", hvps) ;
```

The following three functions display the same character, the same attribute, or the same cell repeated a specified number of times:

```
VioWrtNChar (&chChar, cbRepetition, usRow, usCol, hvps)
VioWrtNAttr (&bAttr, cbRepetition, usRow, usCol, hvps)
VioWrtNCell (&bCell, cbRepetition, usRow, usCol, hvps)
```

The *&chChar* parameter in *VioWrtNChar* points to a 1-byte string. The *&bAttr* parameter in *VioWrtNAttr* points to a 1-byte or 3-byte string. The *&bCell* parameter in *VioWrtNCell* points to a 2-byte or 4-byte string.

For example, suppose *cxDisplay* is the width of the AVIO presentation space in characters, *cyDisplay* is the height in rows, and you're using the 1 attribute byte option. You can set the entire AVIO virtual display buffer to yellow asterisks on a blue background by calling

```
VioWrtNCell ("*\x1E", cxDisplay * cyDisplay, 0, 0, hvps) ;
```

The *VioWrtNAttr* function is useful for highlighting (or un-highlighting) a text string already in the virtual display buffer.

None of these six functions changes the cursor position: Output that continues past the end of a line wraps to the next line; output that exceeds the length of the virtual display buffer is ignored. Control codes, such as tabs and carriage returns, are displayed as characters—they are not interpreted.

The seventh, and highest-level, text-output function is *VioWrtTTY*:

```
VioWrtTTY (&chCharString, cbCharString, hvps) ;
```

The first parameter is a pointer to a text string, and the second parameter is the number of characters in the string. *VioWrtTTY* displays the text string starting at the current cursor position and leaves the cursor at the next position following the end of the text.

As with the first six output functions, text displayed by *VioWrtTTY* wraps at the end of a line. However, *VioWrtTTY* doesn't ignore text that exceeds the length of the virtual display buffer. Instead, it scrolls the contents of the virtual display buffer up one line to continue displaying the text on the last line. The first line in the virtual display buffer is lost.

VioWrtTTY also recognizes and interprets five control codes. These characters are not displayed:

Control Character	Action
Bell ('\a')	Beeps the speaker.
Backspace ('\b')	Moves the cursor back one position without deleting, but not beyond column 0.
Tab ('\t')	Inserts spaces to the next column position that is a multiple of 8.
Linefeed ('\n')	Moves the cursor down one line (and possibly scrolls the contents of the virtual display buffer).
Carriage return ('\r')	Moves the cursor to the beginning of the current line.

VioWrtTTY also recognizes ANSI control sequences if ANSI processing is enabled.

ANSI Control Sequences

The AVIO version of *VioWrtTTY* supports a small subset (Figure 7-11) of control sequences defined by American National Standards document X3.64-1979, ''Additional Controls for Use with American National Standard Code for Information Interchange [ASCII].'' These are commonly referred to as ''ANSI control sequences.'' You can mix ANSI control sequences with text strings that you pass to *VioWrtTTY*. These control sequences let you set the cursor position and foreground and background colors.

> **NOTE:** *Some ANSI control sequences recognized by the character-mode VIO interface are not recognized by AVIO.*

ANSI Sequence	Action
"\33[2J"	Erases screen with current attribute and sets the cursor to the upper-left corner.
"\33[K"	Erases line starting from current cursor position using current attribute.
"\33[*row;col*H"	Sets cursor to *row* and *col*.
"\33[*row;col*f"	Sets cursor to *row* and *col*.
"\33[*n*A"	Moves cursor up *n* rows.
"\33[*n*B"	Moves cursor down *n* rows.
"\33[*n*C"	Moves cursor forward *n* columns.
"\33[*n*D"	Moves cursor backward *n* columns.
"\33[s"	Saves current cursor position.
"\33[u"	Restores cursor position from saved value.
"\33[*x;...;x*m"	Sets attributes.

Figure 7-11. *ANSI control sequences recognized by the AVIO version of* VioWrtTTY.

Keep the following points in mind as you work with the control sequences:

- The first character of the control sequence is always an ASCII escape character (\33 in octal or \x1B in hexadecimal). The second character is always a left bracket.

- The two control sequences that set a cursor position use row and column values starting at 1 rather than 0. (Thus the upper-left corner of the virtual display buffer is row 1 and column 1.)

- The four functions that move the cursor *n* positions do not move the cursor past the boundaries of the virtual display buffer.

- The functions that save and restore the cursor position cannot be nested.

The last control sequence shown in Figure 7-11 sets colors that are used for text displayed after the control sequence and for erasing the virtual display buffer. *x* can be one or more of the numbers shown in Figure 7-12.

Color	Foreground	Background
Black	30	40
Red	31	41
Green	32	42
Yellow	33	43
Blue	34	44
Magenta	35	45
Cyan	36	46
White	37	47

Figure 7-12. *Values used in setting attributes using ANSI.*   *(continued)*

Figure 7-12. *continued*

Other Attributes	Value
Reset attributes to default:	0
Bold (light) foreground:	1
Reverse video:	7
Hide characters:	8

For example, if you want to use yellow (light brown) characters on a blue background, you can set that attribute and clear the virtual display buffer using the following statement:

```
VioWrtTTY ("\33[33;44;1m\33[2J", 14, hvps) ;
```

By default, ANSI processing is enabled. You can disable ANSI processing by calling the following function:

```
VioSetAnsi (ANSI_OFF, hvps) ;
```

You can enable it again by calling

```
VioSetAnsi (ANSI_ON, hvps) ;
```

The only reasons for disabling ANSI processing are to display the character associated with the ASCII escape code or to implement another terminal emulation protocol that uses the escape code. You can determine whether ANSI processing is enabled or disabled by calling

```
VioGetAnsi (&usAnsiState, hvps) ;
```

On return from the function, the variable *usAnsiState* is set to either ANSI_ON or ANSI_OFF.

Using C Output Functions

You may be aware that three "console" output functions included in the Microsoft C libraries use *VioWrtTTY* to write to the screen. These functions are *putch* (display a character), *cputs* (display a zero-terminated string), and *cprintf* (display a formatted string similar to *printf*). The *cputs* and *cprintf* functions call *putch* for each character they display. The functions are declared in the CONIO.H header file.

At first it may seem possible to use these functions to write on an AVIO presentation space. But that's not so. The simple reason: The *putch* function included in the C libraries calls *VioWrtTTY* with the last parameter set to 0 rather than to *hvps*. The zero parameter is the value that OS/2 character-mode applications use.

However, in your program you can define a new version of *putch* that uses *hvps* as the last parameter to *VioWrtTTY*. To do this you need to define *hvps* as a global variable:

```
#include <conio.h>  // declaration of putch

    ....

HVPS hvps ;          // handle to AVIO PS must be global!

    ....

int putch (char ch)
    {
    return VioWrtTTY (&ch, 1, hvps) ;
    }
```

If you do this, then *cputs* and *cprintf* both write output to the AVIO virtual display buffer. Unlike *puts*, *cputs* does not append a newline character to the string, so you'll want to use "\r\n" to move the cursor to the next line. Unlike *printf*, *cprintf* does not translate the C newline character (\n) into a carriage return and linefeed sequence, so you'll probably want to use \r\n to go to the beginning of the next line rather than just \n.

But keep in mind that *cputs* and *cprintf* will be somewhat slow because they call *VioWrtTTY* for each character individually. It is much more efficient to call *VioWrtTTY* for a whole string of characters. If you want to use *cputs*, you'll get better performance by defining a new version of the function:

```
#include <conio.h>  // declaration of cputs
#include <string.h> // declaration of strlen

    ....

HVPS hvps ;          // handle to AVIO PS must be global!

    ....

int cputs (char *psz)
    {
    return VioWrtTTY (psz, strlen (psz), hvps) ;
    }
```

A more efficient version of *cprintf* is slightly more difficult but certainly not impossible. It uses the *vsprintf* function, which is similar to *sprintf* but with an important difference: The *vsprintf* function accepts a pointer to the items to be formatted rather than accepting the items themselves. This allows arguments passed on a stack to be used by the *vsprintf* function. The *va_start*, *va_arg*, and *va_end* macros defined in STDARG.H help in creating this new *cprintf* function:

```
#include <conio.h>        // declaration of cprintf
#include <stdio.h>        // declaration of vsprintf
#include <stdarg.h>       // declaration of va_start, etc.

    ....

#define MAXLENGTH 80      // maximum length of formatted string

    ....

HVPS hvps ;               // handle to AVIO PS must be global!

    ....

int cprintf (char *szFormat, ...)
    {
    CHAR    chBuffer [MAXLENGTH] ;
    SHORT   sLength ;
    va_list pArguments ;

    va_start (pArguments, szFormat) ;
    sLength = vsprintf (chBuffer, szFormat, pArguments) ;

    VioWrtTTY (chBuffer, sLength, hvps) ;

    va_end (pArguments) ;
    return sLength ;
    }
```

Input Functions

Two VIO functions can read from the virtual display buffer:

```
VioReadCellStr (&chCellString, &cb, usRow, usCol, hvps) ;
VioReadCharStr (&chCharString, &cb, usRow, usCol, hvps) ;
```

In both cases, the first parameter is a pointer to a buffer that receives the cell string or character string. The second parameter is a pointer to a USHORT variable that you set to the number of bytes you want to read. On return from the function, the *cb* parameter indicates the number of bytes actually read. This could be fewer than the number you specified if the count exceeds the size of the virtual display buffer.

The *VioReadCellStr* function can be used to save an area of the virtual display. You restore the area with *VioWrtCellStr*. (You can use *VioReadCharStr* and *VioWrtCharStr* instead if you don't need to save and restore the attributes.) You can also use *VioReadCellStr* in conjunction with *VioWrtCellStr* to alter part of the virtual display. For example, suppose you use the 3-attribute option and you want to alter a 20-character string by setting reverse video. Here's the code:

```
BYTE    bCellBuffer [20][4] ;
USHORT  i, cb ;


    . . . .


cb = 20 * 4 ;

VioReadCellStr (bCellBuffer, &cb, usRow, usCol, hvps) ;

for (i = 0 ; i < 20 ; i++)
        bCellBuffer [i][2] |= '\x40' ;

VioWrtCellStr (bCellBuffer, cb, usRow, usCol, hvps) ;
```

Scrolling Functions

Four VIO functions scroll a rectangular area of the virtual display buffer up, down, left, and right. You specify upper-left and lower-right character positions, the number of lines to scroll, and the cell that is used to fill the area left uncovered by the scroll.

The most common scrolling function is the one that scrolls a rectangular area up:

```
VioScrollUp (usTopRow, usLeftCol, usBottomRow, usRightCol,
             cbLines, &bCell, hvps) ;
```

The scrolled area is a rectangle that includes the *usTopRow* and *usBottomRow* rows and the *usLeftCol* and *usRightCol* columns.

- *usTopRow* must be less than or equal to *usBottomRow*.

- *usLeftCol* must be less than or equal to *usRightCol*.

The *cbLines* parameter indicates the number of lines to scroll. (The function doesn't do anything if *cbLines* is 0.) The area at the bottom of the rectangle left uncovered by the scroll is filled with the cell specified as the pointer to *bCell*.

If your values for *usBottomRow*, *usRightCol*, or *cbLines* exceed the maximum, they are set to the maximum. Thus, it is customary to use −1 (equivalent to 65,535 when interpreted as an unsigned value) when you want to use the maximums. For example, to scroll the entire contents of the virtual buffer up one line, use

```
VioScrollUp (0, 0, -1, -1, 1, " \7", hvps) ;
```

The top line of the virtual buffer is lost. The last line is filled with blanks with the attribute 7 (the default light gray on black color). If you were using 3 attributes, the cell string would be \7\0\0.

To blank the entire virtual buffer, set the *cbLines* parameter to a maximum value:

```
VioScrollUp (0, 0, -1, -1, -1, " \x1E", hvps) ;
```

The function to scroll a rectangular area down has the same syntax:

```
VioScrollDn (usTopRow, usLeftCol, usBottomRow, usRightCol, cbLines,
            &bCell, hvps) ;
```

The lines on the bottom are lost. The lines on top are filled with *bCell*.

The following two functions scroll an area left or right:

```
VioScrollLf (usTopRow, usLeftCol, usBottomRow, usRightCol, cbColumns, &bCell, hvps) ;
VioScrollRt (usTopRow, usLeftCol, usBottomRow, usRightCol, cbColumns, &bCell, hvps) ;
```

The syntax is the same as that used in the other two scrolling functions except that the fifth parameter is the number of columns rather than the number of lines. These functions will have no effect if the *cbColumns* parameter is set to 0.

Keep in mind that these scrolling functions move the contents of the virtual display buffer and result in one or more lines or columns being lost from the buffer. You may prefer to use *VioSetOrg* to move the virtual display buffer relative to the window rather than to move cells within the buffer.

Origin Functions

Normally the upper-left corner of the virtual display buffer (row 0 and column 0) is displayed in the upper-left corner of the window. You can change that through use of the *VioSetOrg* function:

```
VioSetOrg (sRow, sCol, hvps) ;
```

After this call, the *sRow* and *sCol* position in the virtual display buffer is displayed in the upper-left corner of the window. The SYSVALS4 program shown later in this chapter uses this function to shift data within the window. You can obtain the current origin by calling

```
VioGetOrg (&sRow, &sCol, hvps) ;
```

Cell Size Functions

When using GPI functions for character output, you obtain the dimensions of a character by calling *GpiQueryFontMetrics*. With AVIO, you use *VioGetDeviceCellSize*:

```
VioGetDeviceCellSize (&cyChar, &cxChar, hvps) ;
```

On return from the function, *cyChar* and *cxChar* will be set to the height and width, in pixels, of the character cell.

You can also set a new cell size by calling

```
VioSetDeviceCellSize (cyChar, cxChar, hvps) ;
```

However, this function is more limited than you may initially assume. The AVIO interface supports (at most) two cell sizes: a large cell size and a small cell size. Initially, the cell size is large, roughly approximating the size of characters in a character-mode session. When a program's window is maximized, the client window can display at least 25 rows of 80 characters using this cell size.

You can switch to the smaller cell size by calling *VioSetDeviceCellSize* with very low values:

```
VioSetDeviceCellSize (1, 1, hvps) ;
```

You then use *VioGetDeviceCellSize* to determine what size the character cells *really* are.

You can also obtain this information by using *DevQueryCaps*. The CAPS_CHAR_HEIGHT and CAPS_CHAR_WIDTH parameters report the large cell size, and the CAPS_SMALL_CHAR_HEIGHT and CAPS-_SMALL_CHAR_WIDTH parameters report the small cell size. (You may want to run the DEVCAPS program from Chapter 5 to see what these sizes are for your particular display adapter.) If *DevQueryCaps* returns 0 for the CAPS_SMALL_CHAR_HEIGHT and CAPS_SMALL_CHAR_WIDTH parameters, then a small cell size is not available.

When the Presentation Manager runs an OS/2 1.0 program in a window, it includes the "Small Font" option on the program's system menu. This lets the user select a small cell size if one is available. After switching to the small cell size, the system menu allows switching back with the "Large Font" option. You may want to provide a similar facility for your Presentation Manager programs that use AVIO.

Virtual Display Buffer Functions

As you saw in AVIO2, a program can obtain a pointer to the virtual display buffer and write to it directly. The *VioGetBuf* function returns a pointer to the buffer as a ULONG value. The size of the buffer in bytes is returned in *usVideoLength*:

```
VioGetBuf (&ulVideoBuffer, &usVideoLength, hvps) ;
```

When writing directly to the buffer, you need to update the window from the buffer by calling *VioShowBuf* or *VioShowPS*. The various *VioWrt* functions write text and attributes to the buffer and (if possible) to the window.

Two functions update the window from the virtual display buffer. The first is a VIO function included in OS/2 1.0:

```
VioShowBuf (usByteOffset, usLength, hvps) ;
```

The *usByteOffset* parameter is an offset in bytes from the beginning of the virtual display buffer. The *usLength* parameter indicates the number of bytes to update.

The second function is an AVIO function:

```
VioShowPS (sHeight, sWidth, sCellOffset, hvps) ;
```

This updates a rectangle of cells that is *sHeight* characters high and *sWidth* characters wide with the upper-left corner at the *sCellOffset* character. Note that this function always updates complete cells. The *sCellOffset* is the number of character cells from the beginning of the buffer; the *usByteOffset* parameter in *VioShowBuf* specifies a starting position in bytes.

For example, suppose your virtual display buffer is 10 characters wide and has 1 attribute byte. Each row has 10 cells (20 bytes). You want to update the second and third rows. The *VioShowBuf* call is

```
VioShowBuf (20, 40, hvps) ;
```

The *VioShowPS* call is

```
VioShowPS (2, 10, 10, hvps) ;
```

You should call one of these two functions during the WM_PAINT message to update the invalid area of the window.

Miscellaneous VIO Functions

Three other OS/2 1.0 VIO functions are supported under the Presentation Manager AVIO interface.

The *VioGetConfig* uses a structure of type VIOCONFIGINFO:

```
struct _VIOCONFIGINFO
    {
    USHORT cb ;
    USHORT adapter ;
    USHORT display ;
    ULONG cbMemory ;
    }
    VIOCONFIGINFO ;
```

You define a structure of type VIOCONFIGINFO, set the *cb* field to the size of the structure, and pass a pointer to the structure to *VioGetConfig*:

```
VIOCONFIGINFO vioin ;

    . . . .

vioin.cb = sizeof VIOCONFIGINFO ;

VioGetConfig (0, &vioin, hvps) ;
```

The first parameter of *VioGetConfig* must be set to 0. On return from the function, the *adapter* and *display* fields contain codes that identify the video adapter and display. The *cbMemory* field is not available under the AVIO interface. It's unlikely that this function provides meaningful information to a Presentation Manager program.

The Return of SYSVALS

After enduring several versions of the SYSVALS program in Chapter 4, you may have thought we were done with it. No such luck. SYSVALS is back! The AVIO version is called SYSVALS4 and is shown in Figure 7-13.

The SYSVALS4 File

```
#--------------------
# SYSVALS4 make file
#--------------------

sysvals4.obj : sysvals4.c sysvals.h
    cl -c -G2sw -W3 sysvals4.c

sysvals4.exe : sysvals4.obj sysvals4.def
    link sysvals4, /align:16, NUL, os2, sysvals4
```

The SYSVALS4.C File

```
/*-------------------------------------------------------------
    SYSVALS4.C -- System Values Display Program using AVIO
   -------------------------------------------------------*/

#define INCL_WIN
#define INCL_GPI
#define INCL_VIO
#define INCL_AVIO
#include <os2.h>
#include <stdio.h>
#include <stdlib.h>
#include "sysvals.h"

#define MAXWIDTH 60

MRESULT EXPENTRY ClientWndProc (HWND, USHORT, MPARAM, MPARAM) ;

HAB  hab ;
```

(continued)

Figure 7-13. The SYSVALS4.C File. *continued*

```
int main (void)
    {
    static CHAR  szClientClass [] = "SysVals4" ;
    static ULONG flFrameFlags = FCF_TITLEBAR      | FCF_SYSMENU   |
                                FCF_SIZEBORDER    | FCF_MINMAX    |
                                FCF_SHELLPOSITION | FCF_TASKLIST  |
                                FCF_VERTSCROLL    | FCF_HORZSCROLL ;

    HMQ          hmq ;
    HWND         hwndFrame, hwndClient ;
    QMSG         qmsg ;

    hab = WinInitialize (0) ;
    hmq = WinCreateMsgQueue (hab, 0) ;

    WinRegisterClass (hab, szClientClass, ClientWndProc, 0L, 0) ;

    hwndFrame = WinCreateStdWindow (HWND_DESKTOP, WS_VISIBLE,
                                    &flFrameFlags, szClientClass, NULL,
                                    0L, NULL, 0, &hwndClient) ;

    WinSendMsg (hwndFrame, WM_SETICON,
                WinQuerySysPointer (HWND_DESKTOP, SPTR_APPICON, FALSE),
                NULL) ;

    while (WinGetMsg (hab, &qmsg, NULL, 0, 0))
        WinDispatchMsg (hab, &qmsg) ;

    WinDestroyWindow (hwndFrame) ;
    WinDestroyMsgQueue (hmq) ;
    WinTerminate (hab) ;
    return 0 ;
    }

BYTE RgbToVioColor (COLOR clrRgb)
    {
    BYTE bIrgb ;
    RGB  rgb ;

    rgb = MAKETYPE (clrRgb, RGB) ;

    if (rgb.bBlue  >= 0x80) bIrgb |= '\x01' ;
    if (rgb.bGreen >= 0x80) bIrgb |= '\x02' ;
    if (rgb.bRed   >= 0x80) bIrgb |= '\x04' ;
```

(continued)

Figure 7-13. The SYSVALS4.C File. *continued*

```
        if (rgb.bBlue >= 0xC0 || rgb.bGreen >= 0xC0 || rgb.bRed >= 0xC0)
            bIrgb |= 8 ;

        if (bIrgb == 0 && rgb.bBlue >= 0x40 && rgb.bGreen >= 0x40 &&
                          rgb.bRed   >= 0x40)
            bIrgb = 8 ;

        return bIrgb ;
        }

BYTE ConstructDefaultAttribute (VOID)
        {
        return RgbToVioColor (
                    WinQuerySysColor (HWND_DESKTOP, SYSCLR_WINDOW, 0L)) << 4 |
                RgbToVioColor (
                    WinQuerySysColor (HWND_DESKTOP, SYSCLR_WINDOWTEXT, 0L)) ;
        }

MRESULT EXPENTRY ClientWndProc (HWND hwnd, USHORT msg, MPARAM mp1, MPARAM mp2)
        {
        static BYTE     bBlankCell [2] = " " ;
        static HVPS     hvps ;
        static HWND     hwndHscroll, hwndVscroll ;
        static HPS      hps ;
        static SHORT    sHscrollPos, sVscrollPos,
                        cxChar, cyChar, cxClient, cyClient ;
        CHAR            szBuffer [80] ;
        HDC             hdc ;
        SIZEL           sizl ;
        USHORT          usRow ;

        switch (msg)
            {
            case WM_CREATE:
                hdc = WinOpenWindowDC (hwnd) ;

                sizl.cx = sizl.cy = 0 ;
                hps = GpiCreatePS (hab, hdc, &sizl, PU_PELS    | GPIF_DEFAULT |
                                                    GPIT_MICRO | GPIA_ASSOC) ;

                VioCreatePS (&hvps, NUMLINES, MAXWIDTH, 0, 1, NULL) ;
                VioAssociate (hdc, hvps) ;
                VioGetDeviceCellSize (&cyChar, &cxChar, hvps) ;
```

(continued)

Figure 7-13. The SYSVALS4.C File. *continued*

```
           bBlankCell[1] = ConstructDefaultAttribute () ;
           VioScrollUp (0, 0, -1, -1, -1, bBlankCell, hvps) ;

           for (usRow = 0 ; usRow < NUMLINES ; usRow++)
               VioWrtCharStr (szBuffer,
                               sprintf (szBuffer, "%-20s%-35s%5ld",
                                        sysvals[usRow].szIdentifier,
                                        sysvals[usRow].szDescription,
                                        WinQuerySysValue (HWND_DESKTOP,
                                        sysvals[usRow].sIndex)),
                               usRow, 0, hvps) ;

           hwndHscroll = WinWindowFromID (
                           WinQueryWindow (hwnd, QW_PARENT, FALSE),
                           FID_HORZSCROLL) ;

           WinSendMsg (hwndHscroll, SBM_SETSCROLLBAR,
                           MPFROM2SHORT (sHscrollPos, 0),
                           MPFROM2SHORT (0, MAXWIDTH - 1)) ;

           hwndVscroll = WinWindowFromID (
                           WinQueryWindow (hwnd, QW_PARENT, FALSE),
                           FID_VERTSCROLL) ;

           WinSendMsg (hwndVscroll, SBM_SETSCROLLBAR,
                           MPFROM2SHORT (sVscrollPos, 0),
                           MPFROM2SHORT (0, NUMLINES - 1)) ;
           return 0 ;

      case WM_SIZE:
           cxClient = SHORT1FROMMP (mp2) ;
           cyClient = SHORT2FROMMP (mp2) ;

           WinDefAVioWindowProc (hwnd, msg, mp1, mp2) ;
           return 0 ;

      case WM_HSCROLL:
           switch (SHORT2FROMMP (mp2))
               {
               case SB_LINELEFT:
                   sHscrollPos -= 1 ;
                   break ;

               case SB_LINERIGHT:
                   sHscrollPos += 1 ;
                   break ;
```

(continued)

Figure 7-13. The SYSVALS4.C File. *continued*

```
                    case SB_PAGELEFT:
                         sHscrollPos -= 8 ;
                         break ;

                    case SB_PAGERIGHT:
                         sHscrollPos += 8 ;
                         break ;

                    case SB_SLIDERPOSITION:
                         sHscrollPos = SHORT1FROMMP (mp2) ;
                         break ;
                    }
               sHscrollPos = max (0, min (sHscrollPos, MAXWIDTH - 1)) ;

               if (sHscrollPos != SHORT1FROMMR (WinSendMsg (hwndHscroll,
                                    SBM_QUERYPOS, NULL, NULL)))
                    {
                    VioSetOrg (sVscrollPos, sHscrollPos, hvps) ;

                    WinSendMsg (hwndHscroll, SBM_SETPOS,
                              MPFROM2SHORT (sHscrollPos, 0), NULL) ;
                    }
               return 0 ;

          case WM_VSCROLL:
               switch (SHORT2FROMMP (mp2))
                    {
                    case SB_LINEUP:
                         sVscrollPos -= 1 ;
                         break ;

                    case SB_LINEDOWN:
                         sVscrollPos += 1 ;
                         break ;

                    case SB_PAGEUP:
                         sVscrollPos -= cyClient / cyChar ;
                         break ;

                    case SB_PAGEDOWN:
                         sVscrollPos += cyClient / cyChar ;
                         break ;
```

(continued)

Figure 7-13. The SYSVALS4.C File. *continued*

```
                        case SB_SLIDERPOSITION:
                             sVscrollPos = SHORT1FROMMP (mp2) ;
                             break ;
                     }
             sVscrollPos = max (0, min (sVscrollPos, NUMLINES - 1)) ;

             if (sVscrollPos != SHORT1FROMMR (WinSendMsg (hwndVscroll,
                                 SBM_QUERYPOS, NULL, NULL)))
                     {
                     VioSetOrg (sVscrollPos, sHscrollPos, hvps) ;

                     WinSendMsg (hwndVscroll, SBM_SETPOS,
                                 MPFROM2SHORT (sVscrollPos, 0), NULL) ;
                     }
             return 0 ;

        case WM_CHAR:
             switch (CHARMSG(&msg)->vkey)
                     {
                     case VK_LEFT:
                     case VK_RIGHT:
                          return WinSendMsg (hwndHscroll, msg, mp1, mp2) ;
                     case VK_UP:
                     case VK_DOWN:
                     case VK_PAGEUP:
                     case VK_PAGEDOWN:
                          return WinSendMsg (hwndVscroll, msg, mp1, mp2) ;
                     }
             break ;

        case WM_PAINT:
             WinBeginPaint (hwnd, hps, NULL) ;
             GpiErase (hps) ;

             VioShowBuf (0, MAXWIDTH * NUMLINES * 2, hvps) ;

             WinEndPaint (hps) ;
             return 0 ;

        case WM_DESTROY:
             VioAssociate (NULL, hvps) ;
             VioDestroyPS (hvps) ;
             GpiDestroyPS (hps) ;
             return 0 ;
        }
    return WinDefWindowProc (hwnd, msg, mp1, mp2) ;
    }
```

The SYSVALS4.DEF File

```
;------------------------------------
; SYSVALS4.DEF module definition file
;------------------------------------

NAME            SYSVALS4  WINDOWAPI

DESCRIPTION     'System Values Display using AVIO (C) Charles Petzold, 1988'
PROTMODE
HEAPSIZE        1024
STACKSIZE       8192
EXPORTS         ClientWndProc
```

Figure 7-13. *The SYSVALS4 program.*

To compile this program you'll also need the SYSVALS.H header file from Chapter 4.

SYSVALS4 calculates an attribute that provides the same window background and window text colors that the user selected in the Presentation Manager Control Panel program. This requires a little work. The *Construct-DefaultAttribute* function first calls *WinQuerySysColor* to obtain the window background and text colors. These are returned in ULONG values in which red, green, and blue bytes (each ranging from 0 to 255) are encoded. The *RgbToVioColor* function converts these RGB values into the 4-bit IRGB encoding. These two 4-bit values are combined into 1 byte in the *Construct-DefaultAttribute* routine. *ClientWndProc* then uses this attribute with the *VioScrollUp* function to clear the AVIO virtual display buffer. The text is written to the AVIO buffer using *VioWrtCharStr*.

Processing the WM_HSCROLL and WM_VSCROLL messages is fairly straightforward. SYSVALS4 simply uses the current scroll-bar positions to set the new origin. The Presentation Manager then updates the window from this new origin without any additional code.

WM_PAINT processing is similarly straightforward. SYSVALS4 simply calls *VioShowBuf* to update the entire window.

GETTING INPUT

## CHAPTER EIGHT

TAPPING INTO THE KEYBOARD

Despite the sophisticated user interface of the Presentation Manager (including the mouse, menus, and dialog boxes), the keyboard is still the primary means of user input in most applications. Even if you write a Presentation Manager program that makes extensive use of the mouse, you should also include a keyboard interface that duplicates the mouse functions. As you probably know, many users still simply refuse to allow a mouse anywhere near their desk. The Presentation Manager doesn't require a mouse, so your programs shouldn't either.

A Presentation Manager program receives keyboard input in the form of messages. You process these keyboard messages in the same way you process other messages. In fact, because user input is closer to one's intuitive concept of a message, working with these keyboard messages should be easier in some ways than handling other types of messages.

As you've seen in previous programs, the Presentation Manager itself handles a large part of keyboard processing. The keystrokes involved in choosing an item from the system menu are handled outside the client window procedure, as are the keyboard accelerators that duplicate system menu options. Many child window controls (discussed in Chapter 11) have their own keyboard interface. The Presentation Manager also takes care of keyboard processing in a program's menu (Chapter 13) and dialog boxes (Chapter 14). But this isn't to say that keyboard handling is easy. The Presentation Manager delivers a lot of information to your program with the keyboard message. You need to recognize what is important and what you can safely ignore.

Keyboard processing becomes more complex if you want to ensure that your programs can survive the transition to a system with a foreign keyboard. By "foreign keyboard" I mean any type of keyboard that is different from the one you have on your desk. This includes a variety of European keyboards, keyboards used in Far Eastern countries that generate double-byte character codes, and even keyboards for non-PC computers that might someday run versions of the Presentation Manager. The Presentation Manager has a device-independent keyboard interface, but—as is the case with other device-independent interfaces—you have to help. You can even design your Presentation Manager programs so that they can be recompiled for a system with a keyboard that generates codes in the EBCDIC (Extended Binary Coded Decimal Interchange Code) character set used on IBM mainframes and minicomputers.

The Keyboard and Codes

A keyboard always generates numeric codes of various sorts. Within a program, you make an implicit assumption about how these codes relate to the keys that generate them.

You can think of the keyboard in one of two ways—as a collection of distinct physical keys or as a means of generating character codes. When you treat the keyboard as a collection of keys, any code generated by the keyboard must identify the key and indicate whether the key is being pressed or released. When you treat the keyboard as a character input device, a code generated by a particular keystroke identifies a unique character in a character set. For a U.S. keyboard on the PC, this character set is ASCII. For a European keyboard, however, it is an extended ASCII character set that includes accented letters and other symbols not in the standard ASCII character set. For a keyboard on an IBM mainframe, it is the EBCDIC character set. If you obtain a character code from the keyboard and echo it to the display, it should look the same as the character printed on the top of the key. That is, the visual appearance of the character on the screen shouldn't surprise the user. This requires that the keyboard driver and display driver are working with the same character set or "codepage."

Because many of the keys on the keyboard aren't associated with character codes, you must usually treat the keyboard as both a collection of keys and a character generator. You can divide the keyboard into four general groups of keys:

- Toggle keys—The Caps Lock, Num Lock, and Scroll Lock keys and possibly the Insert key. Pressing the key turns the state of the key on; pressing it again turns the state off.

- Shift keys—The Shift, Ctrl, and Alt keys. The shift keys affect the interpretation of other keys.

- Noncharacter keys—The function keys, the cursor movement keys, Pause, Escape, Delete, and possibly the Insert key. These keys aren't associated with characters but instead often direct a program to carry out a particular action.

- Character keys—The letter, number, and symbol keys, the Spacebar, the Tab key, Backspace, and Enter. (The Tab, Backspace, and Enter keys can also be treated as noncharacter keys.)

Often a single physical key can generate different character codes depending on the shift keys. For example, the A key generates a lowercase *a* or an uppercase *A* depending on the Shift key. Sometimes two different physical keys (such as the two Enter keys on an IBM enhanced keyboard) can generate the same character code.

The Presentation Manager handles the keyboard somewhat differently from other PC keyboard interfaces with which you may be more familiar. To put this into perspective, let's examine these other keyboard interfaces.

Pre-OS/2 Keyboard Processing

The hardware of the keyboard on a PC generates a "hardware scan code." This is an 8-bit code that identifies the physical key and indicates whether the key is being pressed or released. Hardware scan codes are usually numbered sequentially across the rows of keys.

In the world of real mode and MS-DOS, the PC BIOS processes each keystroke through its Interrupt 09H handler. For hardware scan codes corresponding to shift keys and toggle keys, the Interrupt 09H handler stores the current state of the key. For character keys, the hardware scan code is converted into an ASCII character code based on the state of the shift and toggle keys and is stored in a small buffer. For noncharacter keys, the hardware scan code is converted into an "extended keyboard code" and also stored in the buffer.

A program running under MS-DOS can obtain keystrokes from the buffer through various MS-DOS function calls or the BIOS Interrupt 16H. For character keys, Interrupt 16H returns the ASCII character code and the hardware scan code. For noncharacter keys, the extended keyboard code is returned, and the ASCII code is set to 0.

In summary, the PC BIOS works with three types of codes:

- Hardware scan code—Generated from keyboard hardware.

- Extended keyboard code—Identifies noncharacter keys in combination with the Shift, Ctrl, or Alt key.

- ASCII character code — Identifies character keys based on the Shift, Ctrl, or Caps Lock key.

The OS/2 Kernel and the Keyboard

When OS/2 is running, the keyboard is handled by the OS/2 kernel rather than the PC BIOS. However, the OS/2 keyboard interface closely mimics the operation of the BIOS. A program running under the OS/2 kernel obtains keyboard input by calling the *DosRead*, *KbdCharIn*, or *KbdStringIn* function. The *KbdCharIn* function is the most general and is similar to Interrupt 16H. The keyboard information from *KbdCharIn* is stored in a structure of type KBDKEYINFO.

Two fields of KBDKEYINFO identify the key. The *chChar* field contains an ASCII character code. If this field is 0, the *chScan* field contains an extended keyboard code. (Despite the name of this field, and the OS/2 kernel documentation, this field does *not* contain a hardware scan code.) The *fsState* field is a 16-bit integer with flags that identify the current state of the shift and toggle keys.

Enter the Presentation Manager

Rather than use *DosRead* or the *Kbd* functions to obtain keyboard input, a Presentation Manager program receives keyboard information in the form of messages. These messages contain more information about keyboard activity than is available from the OS/2 *KbdCharIn* function. When a key is pressed or released, the Presentation Manager decodes the key and stores the information about the keystroke in a system message queue. This keyboard message is later routed to the message queue of the window with the input focus (a concept discussed later in this chapter) and then retrieved by the program.

Where the Presentation Manager differs from other PC keyboard interfaces is mostly in the treatment of the noncharacter keys. The Presentation Manager doesn't use the extended keyboard codes because they are too dependent on the specific hardware of the PC and would make little sense for versions of the Presentation Manager adapted for different hardware. Instead, an attempt has been made to virtualize the codes for noncharacter keys. A fourth type of keyboard code has been introduced — the "virtual key code." Like the hardware scan code, the virtual key code generally identifies a physical key and isn't dependent on a particular shift state. (There are a couple of exceptions.)

Armed with this historical perspective, let's examine the Presentation Manager keyboard message.

The WM_CHAR Message

In most cases a Presentation Manager program can obtain all the information it needs about keyboard input by processing the WM_CHAR message in the client window procedure. The information encoded in the *mp1* and *mp2* parameters is shown in Figure 8-1.

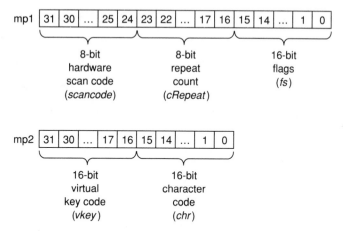

Figure 8-1. *The WM_CHAR* mp1 *and* mp2 *parameters.*

You can use a variety of macros defined in PMWIN.H — such as SHORT1-FROMMP and CHAR3FROMMP — to extract each of these fields. Or you can use a macro called CHARMSG designed specifically for processing WM_CHAR messages. You use CHARMSG like this:

```
CHARMSG (&msg) -> identifier
```

where *identifier* is one of the identifiers in parentheses shown in Figure 8-1. This macro references the *mp1* and *mp2* parameters to the window procedure from the stack.

> **NOTE:** *If you want to use CHARMSG in a subroutine called from the window procedure, you must pass* msg, mp1, *and* mp2 *to the subroutine (in that order), and the subroutine must be defined as PASCAL.*

The lower 16 bits of *mp1* contain a series of flags that further describe the keyboard message. The individual flags can be extracted using identifiers beginning with the letters KC defined in the PMWIN.H header file. These flags are shown in Figure 8-2 on the following page.

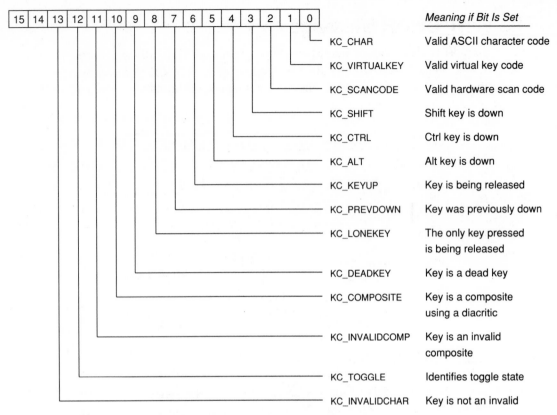

	Meaning if Bit Is Set
KC_CHAR	Valid ASCII character code
KC_VIRTUALKEY	Valid virtual key code
KC_SCANCODE	Valid hardware scan code
KC_SHIFT	Shift key is down
KC_CTRL	Ctrl key is down
KC_ALT	Alt key is down
KC_KEYUP	Key is being released
KC_PREVDOWN	Key was previously down
KC_LONEKEY	The only key pressed is being released
KC_DEADKEY	Key is a dead key
KC_COMPOSITE	Key is a composite using a diacritic
KC_INVALIDCOMP	Key is an invalid composite
KC_TOGGLE	Identifies toggle state
KC_INVALIDCHAR	Key is not an invalid

Figure 8-2. *Flags defined in the WM_CHAR* mp1 *parameter.*

You can test these flags with one of two expressions:

```
SHORT1FROMMP (mp1) & KC_SHIFT
```

or

```
CHARMSG (&msg) -> fs & KC_SHIFT
```

Both expressions return a nonzero value if the KC_SHIFT flag is set (meaning the Shift key is down) or 0 if the flag is 0 (meaning the Shift key is up).

Looking at the Keys

As I discuss the various codes and flags in the *mp1* and *mp2* parameters, you may find it helpful to observe what the Presentation Manager actually gives your program in the WM_CHAR message when you press a particular key. To do this, you can use the KEYLOOK program, shown in Figure 8-3.

The KEYLOOK File

```
#-------------------
# KEYLOOK make file
#-------------------

keylook.obj : keylook.c
    cl -c -G2sw -W3 keylook.c

easyfont.obj : easyfont.c
    cl -c -G2sw -W3 easyfont.c

keylook.exe : keylook.obj easyfont.obj keylook.def
    link keylook easyfont, /align:16, NUL, os2, keylook
```

The KEYLOOK.C File

```c
/*-----------------------------------------
   KEYLOOK.C -- Displays WM_CHAR Messages
   -----------------------------------------*/

#define INCL_WIN
#define INCL_GPI
#include <os2.h>
#include <stdio.h>
#include "easyfont.h"

#define LCID_FIXEDFONT 1L
#define MAX_KEYS       100

MRESULT EXPENTRY ClientWndProc (HWND, USHORT, MPARAM, MPARAM) ;

CHAR szClientClass [] = "KeyLook" ;
HAB  hab ;

int main (void)
    {
    static ULONG flFrameFlags = FCF_TITLEBAR      | FCF_SYSMENU |
                                FCF_SIZEBORDER     | FCF_MINMAX  |
                                FCF_SHELLPOSITION | FCF_TASKLIST ;
    HMQ           hmq ;
    HWND          hwndFrame, hwndClient ;
    QMSG          qmsg ;

    hab = WinInitialize (0) ;
    hmq = WinCreateMsgQueue (hab, 0) ;
```

(continued)

Figure 8-3. The KEYLOOK.C File. *continued*

```
    WinRegisterClass (hab, szClientClass, ClientWndProc, CS_SIZEREDRAW, 0) ;

    hwndFrame = WinCreateStdWindow (HWND_DESKTOP, WS_VISIBLE,
                                    &flFrameFlags, szClientClass, NULL,
                                    OL, NULL, 0, &hwndClient) ;
    if (hwndFrame != NULL)
        {
        WinSendMsg (hwndFrame, WM_SETICON,
                    WinQuerySysPointer (HWND_DESKTOP, SPTR_APPICON, FALSE),
                    NULL) ;

        while (WinGetMsg (hab, &qmsg, NULL, 0, 0))
            WinDispatchMsg (hab, &qmsg) ;

        WinDestroyWindow (hwndFrame) ;
        }
    WinDestroyMsgQueue (hmq) ;
    WinTerminate (hab) ;
    return 0 ;
    }

MRESULT EXPENTRY ClientWndProc (HWND hwnd, USHORT msg, MPARAM mp1, MPARAM mp2)
    {
    static CHAR    szHeader [] = "Scan  Rept  IN TG IC CM DK LK PD KU"
                                 " AL CT SH SC VK CH  Virt  Char" ;
    static CHAR    szUndrLn [] = "----  ----  -- -- -- -- -- -- -- --"
                                 " -- -- -- -- -- --  ----  ----" ;
    static CHAR    szFormat [] = "%4X %4dx  %2d %2d %2d %2d %2d %2d %2d %2d"
                                 " %2d %2d %2d %2d %2d %2d  %4X  %4X  %c" ;

    static SHORT   cxChar, cyChar, cyDesc, cxClient, cyClient, sNextKey ;
    static struct {
                  MPARAM mp1 ;
                  MPARAM mp2 ;
                  BOOL   fValid ;
                  }
                  key [MAX_KEYS] ;
    CHAR           szBuffer [80] ;
    FONTMETRICS    fm ;
    HPS            hps ;
    POINTL         ptl ;
    RECTL          rcl, rclInvalid ;
    SHORT          sKey, sIndex, sFlag ;
```

(continued)

Figure 8-3. The KEYLOOK.C File. *continued*

```
switch (msg)
    {
    case WM_CREATE:
        hps = WinGetPS (hwnd) ;
        EzfQueryFonts (hps) ;

        if (!EzfCreateLogFont (hps, LCID_FIXEDFONT, FONTFACE_COUR,
                                                    FONTSIZE_10, 0))
            {
            WinReleasePS (hps) ;

            WinMessageBox (HWND_DESKTOP, HWND_DESKTOP,
                "Cannot find a fixed-pitch font.  Load the Courier "
                "fonts from the Control Panel and try again.",
                szClientClass, 0, MB_OK | MB_ICONEXCLAMATION) ;

            return 1 ;
            }

        GpiSetCharSet (hps, LCID_FIXEDFONT) ;

        GpiQueryFontMetrics (hps, (LONG) sizeof fm, &fm) ;
        cxChar = (SHORT) fm.lAveCharWidth ;
        cyChar = (SHORT) fm.lMaxBaselineExt ;
        cyDesc = (SHORT) fm.lMaxDescender ;

        GpiSetCharSet (hps, LCID_DEFAULT) ;
        GpiDeleteSetId (hps, LCID_FIXEDFONT) ;
        WinReleasePS (hps) ;
        return 0 ;

    case WM_SIZE:
        cxClient = SHORT1FROMMP (mp2) ;
        cyClient = SHORT2FROMMP (mp2) ;
        return 0 ;

    case WM_CHAR:
        key [sNextKey].mp1 = mp1 ;
        key [sNextKey].mp2 = mp2 ;
        key [sNextKey].fValid = TRUE ;

        sNextKey = (sNextKey + 1) % MAX_KEYS ;
```

(continued)

Figure 8-3. The KEYLOOK.C File. *continued*

```
              WinSetRect (hwnd, &rcl,
                         0, 2 * cyChar, cxClient, cyClient - 2 * cyChar) ;

              WinScrollWindow (hwnd, 0, cyChar, &rcl, &rcl, NULL, NULL,
                                            SW_INVALIDATERGN) ;
              WinUpdateWindow (hwnd) ;
              return 0 ;

     case WM_PAINT:
              hps = WinBeginPaint (hwnd, NULL, &rclInvalid) ;
              GpiErase (hps) ;
              EzfCreateLogFont (hps, LCID_FIXEDFONT, FONTFACE_COUR,
                                                FONTSIZE_10, 0) ;
              GpiSetCharSet (hps, LCID_FIXEDFONT) ;

              ptl.x = cxChar ;
              ptl.y = cyDesc ;
              GpiCharStringAt (hps, &ptl, sizeof szHeader - 1L, szHeader) ;

              ptl.y += cyChar ;
              GpiCharStringAt (hps, &ptl, sizeof szUndrLn - 1L, szUndrLn) ;

              for (sKey = 0 ; sKey < MAX_KEYS ; sKey++)
                  {
                  ptl.y += cyChar ;

                  sIndex = (sNextKey - sKey - 1 + MAX_KEYS) % MAX_KEYS ;

                  if (ptl.y > rclInvalid.yTop ||
                          ptl.y > cyClient - 2 * cyChar ||
                              !key [sIndex].fValid)
                      break ;

                  mp1 = key [sIndex].mp1 ;
                  mp2 = key [sIndex].mp2 ;

                  sFlag = CHARMSG(&msg)->fs ;

                  GpiCharStringAt (hps, &ptl,
                      (LONG) sprintf (szBuffer, szFormat,
                              CHARMSG(&msg)->scancode,
                              CHARMSG(&msg)->cRepeat,
                              sFlag & KC_INVALIDCHAR ? 1 : 0,
                              sFlag & KC_TOGGLE      ? 1 : 0,
```

(continued)

Figure 8-3. **The KEYLOOK.C File.** *continued*

```
                                    sFlag & KC_INVALIDCOMP ? 1 : 0,
                                    sFlag & KC_COMPOSITE   ? 1 : 0,
                                    sFlag & KC_DEADKEY     ? 1 : 0,
                                    sFlag & KC_LONEKEY     ? 1 : 0,
                                    sFlag & KC_PREVDOWN    ? 1 : 0,
                                    sFlag & KC_KEYUP       ? 1 : 0,
                                    sFlag & KC_ALT         ? 1 : 0,
                                    sFlag & KC_CTRL        ? 1 : 0,
                                    sFlag & KC_SHIFT       ? 1 : 0,
                                    sFlag & KC_SCANCODE    ? 1 : 0,
                                    sFlag & KC_VIRTUALKEY  ? 1 : 0,
                                    sFlag & KC_CHAR        ? 1 : 0,
                                    CHARMSG(&msg)->vkey,
                                    CHARMSG(&msg)->chr,
                                    sFlag & KC_CHAR ? CHARMSG(&msg)->chr : ' '),
                              szBuffer) ;
                 }
          ptl.y = cyClient - cyChar + cyDesc ;
          GpiCharStringAt (hps, &ptl, sizeof szHeader - 1L, szHeader) ;

          ptl.y -= cyChar ;
          GpiCharStringAt (hps, &ptl, sizeof szUndrLn - 1L, szUndrLn) ;

          GpiSetCharSet (hps, LCID_DEFAULT) ;
          GpiDeleteSetId (hps, LCID_FIXEDFONT) ;
          WinEndPaint (hps) ;
          return 0 ;
       }
    return WinDefWindowProc (hwnd, msg, mp1, mp2) ;
    }
```

The KEYLOOK.DEF File

```
;-------------------------------------
; KEYLOOK.DEF module definition file
;-------------------------------------


NAME           KEYLOOK   WINDOWAPI

DESCRIPTION    'Key Look Program (C) Charles Petzold, 1988'
PROTMODE
HEAPSIZE       1024
STACKSIZE      8192
EXPORTS        ClientWndProc
```

Figure 8-3. *The KEYLOOK program.*

Compiling KEYLOOK also requires the EASYFONT.C and EASYFONT.H files from Chapter 5. KEYLOOK uses a fixed-pitch Courier font to ease the display of WM_CHAR information in the window. If a Courier font is not available, KEYLOOK displays a message box and returns 1 from the WM_CREATE message. This aborts creation of the program's window and causes the *WinCreateStdWindow* cell in *main* to return NULL. Figure 8-4 shows KEYLOOK running under the Presentation Manager after the word *Keyboard* has been typed.

```
┌─────────────────────────────────────────────────────────────────────┐
│ ▬                            KEYLOOK.EXE                        ⇩│⇧  │
│ Scan  Rept  IN TG IC CM DK LK PD KU AL CT SH SC VK CH  Virt   Char   │
│ ────  ────  ── ── ── ── ── ── ── ── ── ── ── ── ── ──  ────   ────   │
│                                                                      │
│                                                                      │
│                                                                      │
│                                                                      │
│   2A   1x    0  1  0  0  0  0  0  0  0  0  1  1  1  0     9      0    │
│   25   1x    0  0  0  0  0  0  0  0  0  0  1  1  0  1     0     4B  K │
│   25   1x    0  0  0  0  0  1  0  1  0  0  1  1  0  0     0   254B    │
│   2A   1x    0  1  0  0  0  0  0  0  1  0  0  1  1  0     9      0    │
│   12   1x    0  0  0  0  0  0  0  0  0  0  0  1  0  1     0     65  e │
│   12   1x    0  0  0  0  0  1  0  1  0  0  0  1  0  0     0   1265    │
│   15   1x    0  0  0  0  0  0  0  0  0  0  0  1  0  1     0     79  y │
│   15   1x    0  0  0  0  0  1  0  1  0  0  0  1  0  0     0   1579    │
│   30   1x    0  0  0  0  0  0  0  0  0  0  0  1  0  1     0     62  b │
│   30   1x    0  0  0  0  0  1  0  1  0  0  0  1  0  0     0   3062    │
│   18   1x    0  0  0  0  0  0  0  0  0  0  0  1  0  1     0     6F  o │
│   18   1x    0  0  0  0  0  1  0  1  0  0  0  1  0  0     0   186F    │
│   1E   1x    0  0  0  0  0  0  0  0  0  0  0  1  0  1     0     61  a │
│   1E   1x    0  0  0  0  0  1  0  1  0  0  0  1  0  0     0   1E61    │
│   13   1x    0  0  0  0  0  0  0  0  0  0  0  1  0  1     0     72  r │
│   13   1x    0  0  0  0  0  1  0  1  0  0  0  1  0  0     0   1372    │
│   20   1x    0  0  0  0  0  0  0  0  0  0  0  1  0  1     0     64  d │
│   20   1x    0  0  0  0  0  1  0  1  0  0  0  1  0  0     0   2064    │
│ ────  ────  ── ── ── ── ── ── ── ── ── ── ── ── ── ──  ────   ────   │
│ Scan  Rept  IN TG IC CM DK LK PD KU AL CT SH SC VK CH  Virt   Char   │
└─────────────────────────────────────────────────────────────────────┘
```

Figure 8-4. *The KEYLOOK display.*

KEYLOOK displays the contents of each WM_CHAR message it receives, starting with the high fields of *mp1* and working down. The heading in KEYLOOK uses abbreviations to identify this information:

Heading	Description
Scan	Hardware scan code in hexadecimal
Rept	Repeat count in decimal
IN	KC_INVALIDCHAR flag (0 or 1)
TG	KC_TOGGLE flag
IC	KC_INVALIDCOMP flag
CM	KC_COMPOSITE flag
DK	KC_DEADKEY flag
LK	KC_LONEKEY flag
PD	KC_PREVDOWN flag

(continued)

Heading	Description
KU	KC_KEYUP flag
AL	KC_ALT flag
CT	KC_CTRL flag
SH	KC_SHIFT flag
SC	KC_SCANCODE flag
VK	KC_VIRTUALKEY flag
CH	KC_CHAR flag
Virt	Virtual key code in hexadecimal
Char	ASCII character code in hexadecimal

Following the hexadecimal representation of the character code, KEYLOOK also displays the character itself.

The Three Keyboard Codes

The *mp1* and *mp2* parameters accompanying the WM_CHAR message contain three codes that identify the key or character. These are the hardware scan code, the virtual key code, and the character code.

Hardware Scan Code

If the KC_SCANCODE bit is set, the upper 8 bits of *mp1* contain a valid hardware scan code. The KC_SCANCODE bit is set for all WM_CHAR messages you receive in a window procedure. The hardware scan code can be extracted with the expression

```
CHAR4FROMMP (mp1)
```

or

```
CHARMSG (& msg) -> scancode
```

Presentation Manager programs usually ignore this code. The hardware scan codes will be quite different for non-PCs running a future version of the Presentation Manager. Using this code will guarantee that you'll have to modify your programs to run on these machines. You're on your own here. There is no support in the header files for using these codes; you'll have to do some research on scan code values in the PC technical reference manuals. (But that won't prevent me from using the scan code in the ORGAN program shown at the end of this chapter.)

Virtual Key Code

If the KC_VIRTUALKEY bit is set, the upper 16 bits of *mp2* contain a valid virtual key code. The virtual key code can be extracted with the expression

```
SHORT2FROMMP (mp2)
```

or

```
CHARMSG (&msg) -> vkey
```

If the KC_VIRTUALKEY flag is 0, the upper 16 bits of *mp2* are also set to 0. The virtual key code is used for keys that don't generate characters. The code generally identifies the key being pressed or released independent of the shift states. (The major exception is for the keyboard number pad.) I'll discuss the virtual key codes in detail later in this chapter.

Character Code

If the KC_CHAR flag is set, the lower 16 bits of *mp2* contain a valid character code. A character code is present in the WM_CHAR message only when the key is being pressed (that is, the KC_KEYUP flag is 0) and the key generates a character. While processing the WM_CHAR message, you can obtain the character code with the expression

```
SHORT1FROMMP (mp2)
```

or

```
CHARMSG (&msg) -> chr
```

The character code reflects the state of the Shift key at the time the key is pressed. On IBM PCs and compatibles, this character code is usually from the ASCII character set. For European keyboards, however, the character code could have a value of 128 or above for letters and symbols not present in the ASCII character set. You can better code your programs for easy adaptation to other implementations of the Presentation Manager by making no assumptions about the character set.

If you run KEYLOOK and type a letter key in combination with the Ctrl key, you'll notice that the Presentation Manager sets neither KC_VIR-TUALKEY nor KC_CHAR flag to 1 for the letter key.

This presents a problem for programs that need to recognize Ctrl-letter key combinations, such as modem communications programs that need to recognize Ctrl-letter combinations typed at the keyboard in order to send the ASCII control code to the communications port. For example, when the user types Ctrl-S to suspend incoming data, the program needs to convert that key combination to an ASCII code of 0x13 (known as XOFF).

These Ctrl-letter keys have to be handled as a special case: If the KC_VIRTUALKEY, KC_CHAR, and KC_KEYUP flags are set to 0, the KC_CTRL flag is set to 1, and if the character code is not 0, the character code is the ASCII code of the letter being typed. You can convert that character code to an ASCII control code with this expression:

```
(CHARMSG(&msg)->chr) & 0x1F
```

Processing Virtual Keys and Characters

The processing of a WM_CHAR message in a window procedure is often divided into two parts: processing character keys and processing noncharacter keys. For a few keys (Enter, Backspace, Space, and Tab) both the KC_VIRTUALKEY and KC_CHAR flags are set. You can process these keys as virtual keys or character keys. The number pad generates both virtual codes and character codes if Num Lock is on. I'll discuss the number pad shortly.

The easiest approach is to examine the KC_CHAR flag first and process the character keys if the flag is set. You can then check the KC_VIRTUALKEY and process noncharacter keys. The code looks something like this:

```
case WM_CHAR:
        [other program lines]
    if (CHARMSG (&msg) -> fs & KC_CHAR)
        {
        switch (CHARMSG (&msg) -> chr)
            {
                    [process character keys]
            }
        }

    else if (CHARMSG (&msg) -> fs & KC_VIRTUALKEY)
        {
        switch (CHARMSG (&msg) -> vkey)
            {
                    [process noncharacter keys]
            }
        }
        [other program lines]
    return 1;
```

The two sections marked "process character keys" and "process non-character keys" each have a series of *case* statements for processing particular keys or characters.

A Closer Look at Virtual Key Codes

When processing a virtual key, you use a *switch* and *case* construction to compare the virtual key code to identifiers beginning with VK defined in the PMWIN.H header file. The virtual key codes defined in PMWIN.H fall into several categories. Here is the group of identifiers for the function keys:

VK_F1	VK_F7	VK_F13	VK_F19
VK_F2	VK_F8	VK_F14	VK_F20
VK_F3	VK_F9	VK_F15	VK_F21
VK_F4	VK_F10	VK_F16	VK_F22
VK_F5	VK_F11	VK_F17	VK_F23
VK_F6	VK_F12	VK_F18	VK_F24

A machine that runs the Presentation Manager is required to have only the first ten function keys on the keyboard. The others are optional. The function keys don't generate character codes. The F10 key invokes the menu in Presentation Manager programs, so VK_MENU is defined to be the same as VK_F10.

The cursor movement keys generate the following virtual key codes:

VK_LEFT	VK_UP	VK_PAGEUP	VK_HOME
VK_RIGHT	VK_DOWN	VK_PAGEDOWN	VK_END

The Insert and Delete keys generate the following virtual key codes:

VK_DELETE
VK_INSERT

The IBM enhanced keyboard has a set of dedicated cursor movement keys and Insert and Delete. These keys always generate the virtual key codes just shown. The KC_CHAR flag is 0.

The number pad on IBM keyboards can be used for either typing numbers or for cursor movement, or for Insert or Delete. If Num Lock is toggled off, the number pad generates virtual key codes and not character codes. If Num Lock is toggled on, the number pad generates the virtual key codes as well as character codes for numbers and the decimal point. For this reason, it's best to process character keys before virtual keys.

The Shift key reverses the meaning of Num Lock for the number pad keys. The virtual key codes for the number pad are important only if your program needs to differentiate between characters from the number pad and the same characters generated otherwise.

The Spacebar, Tab, Enter, and Backspace keys generate both virtual codes and character codes. Their virtual key codes are as follows:

VK_SPACE   VK_NEWLINE
VK_TAB   VK_ENTER
VK_BACKSPACE

The VK_NEWLINE code is generated from the Enter key on the main keyboard, and VK_ENTER is generated from the Enter key on the number pad of the IBM enhanced keyboard. You can process any of these five keys as virtual keys or character keys.

One slightly problematic key combination is Shift-Tab. This combination generates a virtual key code of VK_BACKTAB. But the character code is the same as for an unshifted Tab key. If you differentiate between a Tab and a Shift-Tab, you'll want to process the VK_BACKTAB virtual key *before* processing character keys. Or you can check the state of the KC_SHIFT flag while processing Tab as a character key.

Although an ASCII character code is defined for Escape, the Escape key generates only a virtual key code: VK_ESC.

The following virtual key code identifiers are for the shift and toggle keys:

VK_SHIFT   VK_NUMLOCK
VK_CTRL   VK_SCRLLOCK
VK_ALT   VK_ALTGRAF
VK_CAPSLOCK

The VK_ALTGRAF key is the right Alt key on some European versions of the IBM enhanced keyboard.

Certain key combinations generate these virtual key codes:

VK_BREAK   VK_PRINTSCRN
VK_PAUSE   VK_SYSRQ

Although the Presentation Manager does nothing with these key combinations, you may want to process them.

Finally, there are three virtual key codes that you *never* receive with a WM_CHAR message:

VK_BUTTON1   VK_BUTTON2   VK_BUTTON3

These refer to mouse buttons. I discuss how to use these identifiers in the next chapter.

Going Down, Going Up

If the user simply presses and releases a key, the window procedure usually receives two WM_CHAR messages. The KC_KEYUP flag in the WM_CHAR *mpl* parameter indicates whether the message signals a key press or release.

	KC_KEYUP
Key is pressed	0
Key is released	1

For character keys, the KC_CHAR flag is set (and the character code is valid) for key presses. For the Alt key, the window procedure receives only one WM_CHAR message, for the key press. The frame window uses the release of the Alt key to activate the program's window. For the F1 and F10 keys, the window procedure receives a WM_CHAR message only for the release. The window procedure receives a WM_HELP message for the F1 key press.

Often the key-down and key-up WM_CHAR messages come in pairs with nothing in between, but that's not always the case. For example, when the user presses the Shift key and a letter and then releases the letter and the Shift key, the program receives four WM_CHAR messages in this order:

	KC_KEYUP	Virtual Key	Character
Press Shift	0	VK_SHIFT	0
Press A key	0	0	A
Release A key	1	0	A
Release Shift	1	VK_SHIFT	0

For most purposes, you can ignore these WM_CHAR messages when the KC_KEYUP bit is set to 1. Thus the processing of the WM_CHAR message can include logic like this:

```
case WM_CHAR:
    [other program lines]
    if (CHARMSG (&msg) -> fs &KC_KEYUP)
        return 0;
    [other program lines]
```

If the user presses the key and holds it down, the program receives a series of WM_CHAR messages because of the typematic action of the key. This is indicated by the KC_PREVDOWN flag:

	KC_KEYUP	*KC_PREVDOWN*
Key is pressed	0	0
Key is held down	0	1
Key is released	1	0

You receive one WM_CHAR message when the key is initially pressed, a series of messages as the key is held down, and a final WM_CHAR message when the key is released. A program can use the KC_PREVDOWN flag to distinguish between an initial key press and a typematic repeat of a key. Note that the KC_PREVDOWN flag is *not* set when the key is released, even though the key was previously down.

The *mp1* parameter also contains an 8-bit repeat count that you can extract with the expression

```
CHAR3FROMMP (mp1)
```

or

```
CHARMSG (&msg) -> cRepeat
```

Most often, this value is 1. It can be greater than 1 only for a typematic repeat, when the KC_KEYUP flag is 0 and KC_PREVDOWN is 1. A repeat count greater than 1 indicates that the keyboard hardware generated a typematic repeat of a keystroke while a WM_CHAR message for the same key was still in the message queue. What it *really* indicates is that your program can't keep up with the pace of typematic key repeats.

How you handle the repeat count requires some thought. We've all experienced the nuisance of "overscrolling" a word-processing document or spreadsheet. By ignoring the repeat count, you avoid this problem. But you probably always want to use the repeat count when processing character input. This usually involves a simple *for* loop in the WM_CHAR processing:

```
for (sRepeat = 0 ; sRepeat < CHARMSG (&msg) -> cRepeat; sRepeat++)
    {
        [process key]
    }
```

The KC_LONEKEY flag is set only for a key release. It indicates that no other key was pressed between the time the key was pressed and released. You can ignore the KC_LONEKEY flag unless you think of a particular application for it.

The Shift States

The KC_SHIFT, KC_CTRL, and KC_ALT flags in the WM_CHAR *mp1* parameter indicate the state of the Shift, Ctrl, and Alt keys at the time a key was pressed or released. When the flag is set to 1, it means that the shift key was pressed. You can also use the *WinGetKeyState* function (discussed later in this chapter) to obtain this information. When you process a character key, you don't have to look at the KC_SHIFT flag because the character code itself is based on the current state of the Shift key. The shift-state information is most useful during WM_CHAR messages for noncharacter keys, particularly the cursor movement keys.

The KC_TOGGLE flag is most useful for the Caps Lock, Num Lock, and Scroll Lock keys if your program displays the current state of these keys. The KC_TOGGLE flag is set if the keystroke is turning on the lock state. However, you can treat any key as a toggle key by examining this flag.

The KC_DEADKEY, KC_COMPOSITE, and KC_INVALIDCOMP flags are used with "dead keys" generated from some European keyboards. I'll discuss these flags in reference to the upcoming TYPEAWAY program.

Other Keyboard Messages and Functions

Although processing the WM_CHAR message is the most important part of keyboard handling, it's not the only part: Several other important concepts, messages, and functions relate to the keyboard. We'll look at these and then apply this information in a program that illustrates several aspects of keyboard handling.

Active Windows and Focus Windows

The keyboard must be shared among all applications running under the Presentation Manager. When a keyboard event occurs, the Presentation Manager stores the information about the event in its own system message queue. The Presentation Manager later converts this event to a WM_CHAR message posted to a particular program message queue for a particular window. The window that gets the WM_CHAR message is the window with the "input focus," sometimes also called the "focus window."

The concept of input focus is closely related to the concept of "active window." The active window is always a top-level window, that is, a child of the desktop window. The active window is positioned above all other top-level windows on the screen. A standard window frame indicates that it is active by highlighting its title bar. A dialog box indicates that it is active by highlighting its border. The user generally controls which window is active by using the Alt-Esc or Alt-Tab key combinations to switch from one window to another or by clicking on a particular window with the mouse.

The focus window (if any) is always the active window itself or a descendant of the active window. The Presentation Manager posts WM_CHAR messages to the focus window. When a program first creates a standard window, the frame window is the active window, and the client window is the focus window.

Thus in a standard window without any additional child windows, the client window procedure always receives WM_CHAR messages when the frame window is active. (If the program creates some children of the client window, these child windows can get the input focus. We'll examine this subject more in Chapter 11.) If a particular descendant of the active window has the input focus when the user changes the active window by pressing Alt-Esc or Alt-Tab, the same descendant regains the input focus when the frame window again becomes active.

The Presentation Manager sends a WM_SETFOCUS message to a window procedure when the window is gaining the input focus or losing the input focus. A program can determine which window has the input focus by calling the *WinQueryFocus* function. We'll use this message and function in the TYPEAWAY program coming up soon.

I mentioned at the beginning of this section that the Presentation Manager first stores keyboard messages in a system message queue. It does this because one of these messages (an Alt-Tab key combination, for instance) could change the active window and hence the window with the input focus. The messages for the keys that follow the Alt-Tab must go to a different program. This wouldn't work properly if the messages were posted in a program's message queue when the keystrokes occurred.

Getting Keyboard States

A program can obtain the state of a particular key at any time by calling

```
sKeyState = WinGetKeyState (HWND_DESKTOP, sVirtKey) ;
```

The *sVirtKey* parameter can be any of the virtual key identifiers beginning with VK. The *sKeyState* return value has the high bit set if the key is down. Because *WinGetKeyState* returns a signed short integer, you can determine if a key is down by simply testing if the return value is negative. The low bit is set if the key is toggled on. The low bit has little meaning for keys other than toggle keys, but it can allow you to treat any key as a toggle key.

WinGetKeyState is synchronized with the WM_CHAR messages. It reports that a particular key is pressed or released only if the WM_CHAR message for the press or release has already been retrieved from the message queue. This synchronization is to your advantage: If you call *WinGetKeyState* during processing of a WM_CHAR message, it reports the state of keys at the time of the keyboard action that resulted in the message. If you need to know the state of a key "right now" rather than as of the most recent WM_CHAR message, you can call the *WinGetPhysKeyState* function instead.

Using a Cursor

When you process keystrokes, you often echo characters to the client window. To indicate where the next character will appear in the client window, a program can create a cursor.

> **NOTE:** *The terminology used in Microsoft Windows is different from the Presentation Manager terminology. The small bitmap on the screen that you move with the mouse is called the "pointer." In Windows it is called the cursor. The Presentation Manager cursor is a small blinking box or line generally indicating an entry point for keyboard input. In Windows this is called the "caret." There are no carets in the Presentation Manager. You point with the mouse and curse with the keyboard.*

You create a cursor using the function

```
WinCreateCursor (hwnd, xPos, yPos, cxWidth, cyHeight, fsFlags, &rclClip) ;
```

The *xPos* and *yPos* parameters indicate where the lower-left corner of the cursor is to appear relative to the lower-left corner of *hwnd*. Generally, the lower-left corner of the cursor corresponds to the lower-left corner of a character cell.

The *cxWidth* and *cyHeight* parameters are the size of the cursor. You can use 0 for either of the two parameters to set the size equal to the width of a thin border. These are the most common combinations of *cxWidth* and *cyHeight* (based on *cxChar* and *cyChar* character dimensions):

cxWidth	cyHeight	Cursor Form
cxChar	*cyChar*	Box
cxChar	0	Underline
0	*cyChar*	Vertical line

The box and underline cursors most closely mimic cursors in nongraphics programs. The vertical line cursor is the best suited for use with a font with variable character widths because you can position the vertical line between two adjacent characters. If you use a box or underline cursor with a variable-pitch font, you have to change the width of the cursor as it's moved over the characters. This requires that you destroy and recreate the cursor — a nuisance for you, and an annoyance to the user, who would be faced with a pulsating cursor.

The *fsFlags* parameter can be CURSOR_SOLID (which equals 0, so it's the default) for a solid cursor or CURSOR_HALFTONE for a cursor with only half the bits present. You can use the C bitwise OR operator to include the CURSOR_FLASH flag and make a blinking cursor. If you create a box cursor, you can include the CURSOR_FRAME flag to draw only the frame of the cursor and not the interior.

The last parameter to *WinCreateCursor* is a pointer to a RECTL structure, which defines a clipping region relative to *hwnd*. The cursor won't be visible outside this rectangle. Specifying NULL for this parameter sets the clipping region equal to the entire area of the window at the time of the *WinCreateCursor* call.

When the cursor is first created, it is invisible. You can show it by calling

```
WinShowCursor (hwnd, TRUE) ;
```

You can hide the cursor by calling

```
WinShowCursor (hwnd, FALSE) ;
```

You need to hide the cursor when you write to the screen during a message other than WM_PAINT.

After the cursor is created, you can change the position with another call to *WinCreateCursor*:

```
WinCreateCursor (hwnd, xPos, yPos, 0, 0, CURSOR_SETPOS, NULL) ;
```

This is a special version of the *WinCreateCursor* call. The size and clipping region parameters are ignored. The only flag you can use is CURSOR-_SETPOS. (Do *not*, however, use CURSOR_SETPOS when you are creating the cursor.)

Finally, to destroy the cursor, you call

```
WinDestroyCursor (hwnd) ;
```

When using a cursor, you must remember this very important rule: Only one cursor can be present in the Presentation Manager at any time. Do *not* create a cursor during the WM_CREATE message and destroy it during WM_DESTROY. Instead, you create the cursor when the window gets the input focus and destroy the cursor when the window loses the input focus. And take note of this: If the clipping region of the cursor depends on the size of the window (as it does if you specify NULL as the last parameter to *WinCreateCursor* when you create the cursor), you should destroy and recreate the cursor when you receive a WM_SIZE message. This is the only way to change the clipping region of the cursor.

The cursor logic can be tricky, so let's look at the code involved with maintaining a cursor in the context of a program that also does other keyboard handling.

Sample Keyboard Processing

The TYPEAWAY program, shown in Figure 8-5, demonstrates several of the concepts covered in this chapter. When TYPEAWAY's window first appears, the cursor is positioned in the upper-left corner of the client window. To use the program, simply type away. What you type is what you see.

The TYPEAWAY File

```
#--------------------
# TYPEAWAY make file
#--------------------

typeaway.obj : typeaway.c
    cl -c -G2sw -W3 typeaway.c

easyfont.obj : easyfont.c
    cl -c -G2sw -W3 easyfont.c

typeaway.exe : typeaway.obj easyfont.obj typeaway.def
    link typeaway easyfont, /align:16, NUL, os2, typeaway
```

The TYPEAWAY.C File

```
/*--------------------------------
   TYPEAWAY.C -- Typing Program
   ------------------------------*/

#define INCL_WIN
#define INCL_GPI
#include <os2.h>
#include <stdio.h>
#include <stdlib.h>
#include "easyfont.h"

#define LCID_FIXEDFONT 1L
#define BUFFER(x,y) (*(pBuffer + y * xMax + x))

MRESULT EXPENTRY ClientWndProc (HWND, USHORT, MPARAM, MPARAM) ;

CHAR szClientClass [] = "TypeAway" ;
HAB  hab ;

int main (void)
    {
    static ULONG flFrameFlags = FCF_TITLEBAR       | FCF_SYSMENU |
                                FCF_SIZEBORDER     | FCF_MINMAX  |
                                FCF_SHELLPOSITION  | FCF_TASKLIST ;

    HMQ         hmq ;
    HWND        hwndFrame, hwndClient ;
    QMSG        qmsg ;

    hab = WinInitialize (0) ;
    hmq = WinCreateMsgQueue (hab, 0) ;

    WinRegisterClass (hab, szClientClass, ClientWndProc, CS_SIZEREDRAW, 0) ;

    hwndFrame = WinCreateStdWindow (HWND_DESKTOP, WS_VISIBLE,
                                &flFrameFlags, szClientClass, NULL,
                        0L, NULL, 0, &hwndClient) ;
    if (hwndFrame != NULL)
        {
        WinSendMsg (hwndFrame, WM_SETICON,
                    WinQuerySysPointer (HWND_DESKTOP, SPTR_APPICON, FALSE),
                    NULL) ;
```

(continued)

Figure 8-5. The TYPEAWAY.C File. *continued*

```
                    while (WinGetMsg (hab, &qmsg, NULL, 0, 0))
                         WinDispatchMsg (hab, &qmsg) ;

                    WinDestroyWindow (hwndFrame) ;
                    }
          WinDestroyMsgQueue (hmq) ;
          WinTerminate (hab) ;
          return 0 ;
          }


VOID GetCharXY (HPS hps, SHORT *pcxChar, SHORT *pcyChar, SHORT *pcyDesc)
          {
          FONTMETRICS fm ;

          GpiQueryFontMetrics (hps, (LONG) sizeof fm, &fm) ;
          *pcxChar = (SHORT) fm.lAveCharWidth ;
          *pcyChar = (SHORT) fm.lMaxBaselineExt ;
          *pcyDesc = (SHORT) fm.lMaxDescender ;
          }


MRESULT EXPENTRY ClientWndProc (HWND hwnd, USHORT msg, MPARAM mp1, MPARAM mp2)
          {
          static BOOL  fInsertMode = FALSE ;
          static CHAR  *pBuffer ;
          static SHORT cxClient, cyClient, cxChar, cyChar, cyDesc,
                         xCursor, yCursor, xMax,  yMax ;
          BOOL          fProcessed ;
          CHAR          szBuffer [20] ;
          HPS           hps ;
          POINTL        ptl ;
          RECTL         rcl ;
          SHORT         sRep, s ;

          switch (msg)
               {
               case WM_CREATE:
                    hps = WinGetPS (hwnd) ;
                    EzfQueryFonts (hps) ;

                    if (!EzfCreateLogFont (hps, LCID_FIXEDFONT, FONTFACE_COUR,
                                                        FONTSIZE_10, 0))

                         {
                         WinReleasePS (hps) ;
```

(continued)

Figure 8-5. The TYPEAWAY.C File. *continued*

```
                        WinMessageBox (HWND_DESKTOP, HWND_DESKTOP,
                             "Cannot find a fixed-pitch font.  Load the Courier "
                             "fonts from the Control Panel and try again.",
                             szClientClass, 0, MB_OK | MB_ICONEXCLAMATION) ;

                        return 1 ;
                        }

               GpiSetCharSet (hps, LCID_FIXEDFONT) ;

               GetCharXY (hps, &cxChar, &cyChar, &cyDesc) ;

               GpiSetCharSet (hps, LCID_DEFAULT) ;
               GpiDeleteSetId (hps, LCID_FIXEDFONT) ;
               WinReleasePS (hps) ;
               return 0 ;

          case WM_SIZE:
               cxClient = SHORT1FROMMP (mp2) ;
               cyClient = SHORT2FROMMP (mp2) ;

               xMax = min (255, cxClient / cxChar) ;
               yMax = min (255, cyClient / cyChar - 2) ;

               if (pBuffer != NULL)
                    free (pBuffer) ;

               if (NULL == (pBuffer = malloc (xMax * yMax + 1)))
                    {
                    WinMessageBox (HWND_DESKTOP, hwnd,
                         "Cannot allocate memory for text buffer.\n"
                         "Try a smaller window.", szClientClass, 0,
                         MB_OK | MB_ICONEXCLAMATION) ;

                    xMax = yMax = 0 ;
                    }
               else
                    {
                    for (s = 0 ; s < xMax * yMax ; BUFFER (s++, 0) = ' ') ;

                    xCursor = 0 ;
                    yCursor = 0 ;
                    }
```

(continued)

Figure 8-5. The TYPEAWAY.C File. *continued*

```
            if (hwnd == WinQueryFocus (HWND_DESKTOP, FALSE))
                {
                WinDestroyCursor (hwnd) ;

                WinCreateCursor (hwnd, 0, cyClient - cyChar,
                                 cxChar, cyChar,
                                 CURSOR_SOLID | CURSOR_FLASH, NULL) ;

                WinShowCursor (hwnd, xMax > 0 && yMax > 0) ;
                }
            return 0 ;

      case WM_SETFOCUS:
            if (SHORT1FROMMP (mp2))
                {
                WinCreateCursor (hwnd, cxChar * xCursor,
                                 cyClient - cyChar * (1 + yCursor),
                                 cxChar, cyChar,
                                 CURSOR_SOLID | CURSOR_FLASH, NULL) ;

                WinShowCursor (hwnd, xMax > 0 && yMax > 0) ;
                }
            else
                WinDestroyCursor (hwnd) ;
            return 0 ;

      case WM_CHAR:
            if (xMax == 0 || yMax == 0)
                return 0 ;

            if (CHARMSG(&msg)->fs & KC_KEYUP)
                return 0 ;

            if (CHARMSG(&msg)->fs & KC_INVALIDCHAR)
                return 0 ;

            if (CHARMSG(&msg)->fs & KC_INVALIDCOMP)
                {
                xCursor = (xCursor + 1) % xMax ;         // Advance cursor
                if (xCursor == 0)
                    yCursor = (yCursor + 1) % yMax ;

                WinAlarm (HWND_DESKTOP, WA_ERROR) ;       // And beep
                }
```

(continued)

Figure 8-5. The TYPEAWAY.C File. *continued*

```
for (sRep = 0 ; sRep < CHARMSG(&msg)->cRepeat ; sRep++)
    {
    fProcessed = FALSE ;

    ptl.x = xCursor * cxChar ;
    ptl.y = cyClient - cyChar * (yCursor + 1) + cyDesc ;

                   /*---------------------------
                        Process some virtual keys
                     ----------------------------*/

    if (CHARMSG(&msg)->fs & KC_VIRTUALKEY)
        {
        fProcessed = TRUE ;

        switch (CHARMSG(&msg)->vkey)
            {
                      /*---------------
                           Backspace key
                         ---------------*/

            case VK_BACKSPACE:
                if (xCursor > 0)
                    {
                    WinSendMsg (hwnd, WM_CHAR,
                        MPFROM2SHORT (KC_VIRTUALKEY, 1),
                        MPFROM2SHORT (0, VK_LEFT)) ;

                    WinSendMsg (hwnd, WM_CHAR,
                        MPFROM2SHORT (KC_VIRTUALKEY, 1),
                        MPFROM2SHORT (0, VK_DELETE)) ;
                    }
                break ;

                      /*---------
                           Tab key
                         ---------*/

            case VK_TAB:
                s = min (8 - xCursor % 8, xMax - xCursor) ;

                WinSendMsg (hwnd, WM_CHAR,
                    MPFROM2SHORT (KC_CHAR, s),
                    MPFROM2SHORT ((USHORT) ' ', 0)) ;
```

(continued)

Figure 8-5. The TYPEAWAY.C File. *continued*

```
                                break ;

                                /*------------------------
                                  Backtab (Shift-Tab) key
                                -------------------------*/

                    case VK_BACKTAB:
                        if (xCursor > 0)
                            {
                            s = (xCursor - 1) % 8 + 1 ;

                            WinSendMsg (hwnd, WM_CHAR,
                                MPFROM2SHORT (KC_VIRTUALKEY, s),
                                MPFROM2SHORT (0, VK_LEFT)) ;
                            }
                        break ;

                                /*------------------------
                                  Newline and Enter keys
                                -------------------------*/

                    case VK_NEWLINE:
                    case VK_ENTER:
                        xCursor = 0 ;
                        yCursor = (yCursor + 1) % yMax ;
                        break ;

                    default:
                        fProcessed = FALSE ;
                        break ;
                    }
                }

                /*------------------------
                  Process character keys
                -------------------------*/

    if (!fProcessed && CHARMSG(&msg)->fs & KC_CHAR)
        {
                                        // Shift line if fInsertMode
        if (fInsertMode)
            for (s = xMax - 1 ; s > xCursor ; s--)
                BUFFER (s, yCursor) =
                    BUFFER (s - 1, yCursor) ;
```

(continued)

Figure 8-5. The TYPEAWAY.C File. *continued*

```
                                          // Store character in buffer

                  BUFFER (xCursor, yCursor) =
                                  (CHAR) CHARMSG(&msg)->chr ;

                                          // Display char or new line

                  WinShowCursor (hwnd, FALSE) ;
                  hps = WinGetPS (hwnd) ;

                  EzfCreateLogFont (hps, LCID_FIXEDFONT,
                                  FONTFACE_COUR, FONTSIZE_10, 0) ;
                  GpiSetCharSet (hps, LCID_FIXEDFONT) ;
                  GpiSetBackMix (hps, BM_OVERPAINT) ;

                  if (fInsertMode)
                      GpiCharStringAt (hps, &ptl,
                                  (LONG) (xMax - xCursor),
                                  & BUFFER (xCursor, yCursor)) ;
                  else
                      GpiCharStringAt (hps, &ptl, 1L,
                                  (CHAR *) & CHARMSG(&msg)->chr) ;

                  GpiSetCharSet (hps, LCID_DEFAULT) ;
                  GpiDeleteSetId (hps, LCID_FIXEDFONT) ;
                  WinReleasePS (hps) ;
                  WinShowCursor (hwnd, TRUE) ;

                                          // Increment cursor

                  if (!(CHARMSG(&msg)->fs & KC_DEADKEY))
                      if (0 == (xCursor = (xCursor + 1) % xMax))
                          yCursor = (yCursor + 1) % yMax ;

                  fProcessed = TRUE ;
                  }

                  /*---------------------------------
                  Process remaining virtual keys
                  ---------------------------------*/
```

(continued)

Figure 8-5. The TYPEAWAY.C File. *continued*

```
                if (!fProcessed && CHARMSG(&msg)->fs & KC_VIRTUALKEY)
                    {
                    fProcessed = TRUE ;

                    switch (CHARMSG(&msg)->vkey)
                        {
                                    /*-----------------------
                                      Cursor movement keys
                                      ----------------------*/

                        case VK_LEFT:
                                xCursor = (xCursor - 1 + xMax) % xMax ;

                                if (xCursor == xMax - 1)
                                        yCursor = (yCursor - 1 + yMax) % yMax ;
                                break ;

                        case VK_RIGHT:
                                xCursor = (xCursor + 1) % xMax ;

                                if (xCursor == 0)
                                        yCursor = (yCursor + 1) % yMax ;
                                break ;

                        case VK_UP:
                                yCursor = max (yCursor - 1, 0) ;
                                break ;

                        case VK_DOWN:
                                yCursor = min (yCursor + 1, yMax - 1) ;
                                break ;

                    case VK_PAGEUP:
                                yCursor = 0 ;
                                break ;

                    case VK_PAGEDOWN:
                                yCursor = yMax - 1 ;
                                break ;

                        case VK_HOME:
                                xCursor = 0 ;
                                break ;
```

(continued)

Figure 8-5. The TYPEAWAY.C File. *continued*

```
                          case VK_END:
                               xCursor = xMax - 1 ;
                               break ;


                                    /*------------
                                        Insert key
                                      ------------*/

                          case VK_INSERT:
                               fInsertMode = fInsertMode ? FALSE : TRUE ;
                               WinSetRect (hab, &rcl, 0, 0,
                                           cxClient, cyChar) ;
                               WinInvalidateRect (hwnd, &rcl, FALSE) ;
                               break ;


                                    /*------------
                                        Delete key
                                      ------------*/

                     case VK_DELETE:
                          for (s = xCursor ; s < xMax - 1 ; s++)
                               BUFFER (s, yCursor) =
                                    BUFFER (s + 1, yCursor) ;

                          BUFFER (xMax, yCursor) = ' ' ;

                          WinShowCursor (hwnd, FALSE) ;
                          hps = WinGetPS (hwnd) ;
                          EzfCreateLogFont (hps, LCID_FIXEDFONT,
                                  FONTFACE_COUR, FONTSIZE_10, 0) ;
                          GpiSetCharSet (hps, LCID_FIXEDFONT) ;
                          GpiSetBackMix (hps, BM_OVERPAINT) ;

                          GpiCharStringAt (hps, &ptl,
                                  (LONG) (xMax - xCursor),
                                  & BUFFER (xCursor, yCursor)) ;

                          GpiSetCharSet (hps, LCID_DEFAULT) ;
                          GpiDeleteSetId (hps, LCID_FIXEDFONT) ;
                          WinReleasePS (hps) ;
                          WinShowCursor (hwnd, TRUE) ;
                          break ;
```

(continued)

Figure 8-5. The TYPEAWAY.C File. *continued*

```
                                 default:
                                        fProcessed = FALSE ;
                                        break ;
                                 }
                          }
                   }
           WinCreateCursor (hwnd, cxChar * xCursor,
                                  cyClient - cyChar * (1 + yCursor),
                                  0, 0, CURSOR_SETPOS, NULL) ;

           return 0 ;

      case WM_PAINT:
           hps = WinBeginPaint (hwnd, NULL, NULL) ;
           GpiErase (hps) ;
           EzfCreateLogFont (hps, LCID_FIXEDFONT, FONTFACE_COUR,
                                                  FONTSIZE_10, 0) ;
           GpiSetCharSet (hps, LCID_FIXEDFONT) ;

           ptl.x = cxChar ;
           ptl.y = cyDesc ;
           GpiCharStringAt (hps, &ptl,
                           (LONG) sprintf (szBuffer, "Insert Mode: %s",
                                           fInsertMode ? "ON" : "OFF"),
                           szBuffer) ;

           ptl.x = 0 ;
           ptl.y = 3 * cyChar / 2 ;
           GpiMove (hps, &ptl) ;

           ptl.x = cxClient ;
           GpiLine (hps, &ptl) ;

           if (xMax > 0 && yMax > 0)
               {
               for (s = 0 ; s < yMax ; s++)
                   {
                   ptl.x = 0 ;
                   ptl.y = cyClient - cyChar * (s + 1) + cyDesc ;

                   GpiCharStringAt (hps, &ptl, (LONG) xMax,
                                              & BUFFER (0, s)) ;
```

(continued)

Figure 8-5. **The TYPEAWAY.C File.** *continued*

```
                    }
              }
         GpiSetCharSet (hps, LCID_DEFAULT) ;
         GpiDeleteSetId (hps, LCID_FIXEDFONT) ;
         WinEndPaint (hps) ;
         return 0 ;

    case WM_DESTROY:
         if (pBuffer != NULL)
              free (pBuffer) ;
         break ;
    }
return WinDefWindowProc (hwnd, msg, mp1, mp2) ;
}
```

The TYPEAWAY.DEF File

```
;----------------------------------------
; TYPEAWAY.DEF module definition file
;----------------------------------------


NAME           TYPEAWAY  WINDOWAPI

DESCRIPTION    'Typing Program (C) Charles Petzold, 1988'
PROTMODE
HEAPSIZE       1024
STACKSIZE      8192
EXPORTS        ClientWndProc
```

Figure 8-5. *The TYPEAWAY program.*

TYPEAWAY uses a fixed-pitch Courier font and requires the EASYFONT.C EASYFONT.H files shown in Chapter 5.

You can move the cursor to any position within the client window using the cursor movement keys. They work as follows:

Key	Cursor Movement
Right Arrow	One character right (wraps to next line)
Left Arrow	One character left (wraps to previous line)
Down Arrow	One line down
Up Arrow	One line up

(continued)

Key	Cursor Movement
Home	Beginning of line
End	End of line
Page Up	Top line (same column position)
Page Down	Bottom line (same column position)

TYPEAWAY also processes the following keys:

Key	Action
Insert	Turn Insert mode on and off
Delete	Delete character at cursor position, move rest of line to left
Return	Move cursor to beginning of next line
Tab	Move cursor to next tab position based on 8-column increments
Shift-Tab	Move cursor to previous tab position
Backspace	Delete character to left of cursor, move rest of line to left

The characters you type are stored in a block of memory allocated using *malloc*. This allows TYPEAWAY to re-create the client window when the window procedure receives a WM_PAINT message. TYPEAWAY frees this memory block and allocates a new one whenever the size of the window changes. This means that the contents of the buffer aren't preserved following a WM_SIZE message.

Let's first isolate the cursor logic, because that is perhaps the trickiest to deal with. Cursor creation and destruction occur during processing of the WM_SETFOCUS message:

```
case WM_SETFOCUS:
    if (SHORT1FROMMP (mp2))
        {
        WinCreateCursor (hwnd, cxChar * xCursor,
                         cyClient - cyChar * (1 + yCursor,
                         cxChar, cyChar,
                         CURSOR_SOLID | CURSOR_FLASH, NULL) ;

        WinShowCursor (hwnd, xMax > 0 && yMax > 0) ;
        }
    else
        WinDestroyCursor (hwnd) ;
    return 0 ;
```

The *mp2* parameter is nonzero if the window is getting the input focus and 0 if it's losing the input focus. These two types of WM_SETFOCUS messages are equally balanced during the lifetime of a window. This ensures that the program doesn't attempt to create a second cursor or destroy a nonexistent cursor. The window loses the input focus before it's destroyed, at which time the cursor will also be destroyed.

When the TYPEAWAY client window receives the input focus, it creates a solid blinking cursor and positions it based on the size of the client area, the size of a character, and the cursor position (in terms of a row and column) stored in the variables *xCursor* and *yCursor*. The *WinShowCursor* function normally requires TRUE as the second parameter to display the cursor. The *xMax* and *yMax* variables are the number of character columns and rows in the client window, so this code displays the cursor only if the client window can fit at least one character.

The cursor is also destroyed and re-created during processing of the WM_SIZE message. This is necessary to change the clipping region of the cursor when the window size changes. But note that TYPEAWAY does this only if the client window has the input focus. Otherwise, the cursor doesn't exist and will be re-created during the next WM_SETFOCUS message.

```
if (hwnd == WinQueryFocus (HWND_DESKTOP, FALSE))
    {
    WinDestroyCursor (hwnd) ;

    WinCreateCursor (hwnd, 0, cyClient - cyChar,
                     cxChar, cyChar,
                     CURSOR_SOLID | CURSOR_FLASH, NULL) ;

    WinShowCursor (hwnd, xMax > 0 && yMax > 0) ;
    }
```

The cursor is automatically hidden during a WM_PAINT message. This prevents a program from writing over the cursor. However, if you write on the window during messages other than WM_PAINT (as TYPEAWAY does), you must hide and show the cursor. TYPEAWAY writes on the window during WM_CHAR. Before calling *WinGetPS*, the cursor is hidden:

```
WinShowCursor (hwnd, FALSE) ;
```

After a call to *WinReleasePS*, the cursor is shown again:

```
WinShowCursor (hwnd, TRUE) ;
```

After the key has been processed and the character (if any) written to the client window, the cursor is repositioned:

```
WinCreateCursor (hwnd, cxChar * xCursor,
                 cyClient - cyChar * (1 + yCursor),
                 0, 0, CURSOR_SETPOS, NULL) ;
```

The processing of the WM_CHAR message is fairly straightfoward and easy to follow because of the *switch* and *case* structure. The program first checks to see that at least one character can fit in the client window:

```
if (xMax == 0 || yMax == 0)
    return 0 ;
```

It then checks to see that the message is for a key press:

```
if (CHARMSG (&msg) -> fs & KC_KEYUP)
    return 0 ;
```

Most of the key processing logic is repeated based on the repeat count:

```
for (sRep = 0 ; sRep < CHARMSG (&msg) -> cRepeat ; sRep++)
    {
```

TYPEAWAY also throws away WM_CHAR messages whenever the KC-_INVALIDCHAR flag is set. (This is rarely the case.)

I've chosen to process some virtual keys first. These are the Backspace, Tab, Shift-Tab, and Enter keys, which also generate character codes.

The Backspace, Tab, and Shift-Tab keys are processed by sending the window function other WM_CHAR messages. This simplifies the logic for these keys. The character keys are processed next by displaying the character at the current cursor position. Then, the remaining virtual keys (cursor movement keys, Insert, and Delete) are processed.

Dead Keys and Foreign Language Keyboards

TYPEAWAY shows the correct processing of "dead keys" and "composite keys." These keys are generated on some foreign language keyboards to create characters containing diacritics (sometimes called accent marks). These characters require two keystrokes. The first keystroke is the diacritic itself and is called a "dead key." The second keystroke is a letter and is called a "composite key." The letter is combined with the diacritic mark to form a composite character.

You can process dead keys and composite keys using the KC_DEADKEY, KC_COMPOSITE, and KC_INVALIDCOMP flags that accompany the WM_CHAR message. This will allow your program to be converted more easily to a foreign language. If foreign language conversion is not of concern to you, you can ignore these flags. A compromise approach is to throw away WM_CHAR messages when the KC_DEADKEY flag is set. Near the beginning of your WM_CHAR processing, you'd have

```
if (CHARMSG(&msg)->fs & KC_DEADKEY)
    return 0 ;
```

But this doesn't give good feedback to the user or provide error processing of incorrect combinations of dead keys and letters.

If you add dead-key logic to your program, you'll need to test the logic. You must make the Presentation Manager believe that it is running on a foreign language keyboard that uses dead keys (for example, the German keyboard). You can do this by adding (or changing) the following statements in your CONFIG.SYS file:

```
COUNTRY  = 049
CODEPAGE = 850, 437
DEVINFO  = KBD, GR, [path] KEYBOARD.DCP
DEVINFO  = SCR, EGA, [path] VIOTBL.DCP
```

[path] is the path where the KEYBOARD.DCP and VIOTBL.DCP files are located. If you have a VGA rather than an EGA, use VGA in the second DEVINFO statement.

After you reboot your system, you'll probably find that using this German keyboard is not easy. The Y and Z keys are reversed, and all the symbols are in different places. You can switch to the U.S. keyboard and codepage using the following OS/2 commands:

```
KEYB US
CHCP 437
```

When you want to switch to German for running KEYLOOK or TYPEAWAY or to test one of your own programs, run

```
KEYB GR
CHCP 850
```

Here's how dead keys work: A German user who wishes to type a letter with a diacritic first presses the dead key. The key corresponding to the + and = key on the U.S. keyboard generates dead keys on the German keyboard. When unshifted, the dead key is an acute diacritic (é). When shifted, the dead key is a grave diacritic (è). A Presentation Manager program should display this diacritic but not advance the cursor.

The user then follows this dead key with an uppercase or lowercase A, E, I, O, or U. The resultant character is the letter with the diacritic. The program displays this character and advances the cursor. If the user wants to type the acute or grave mark by itself, he or she follows the dead key by pressing the Spacebar. A dead key followed by any other key is considered an error, and the program should indicate this by beeping. In this case, your program should advance the cursor past the diacritic and display the new key anyway, just as if the dead key were followed by the Spacebar and then the new key.

The code in TYPEAWAY that is necessary to correctly handle dead-key combinations is not very large. You can consider three cases:

Case 1: If the KC_CHAR and KC_DEADKEY flags are set, the character code is the code for the diacritic. You display this character, but do not advance the cursor. In TYPEAWAY, this is handled at the end of the section that processes character keys. The character is stored in the buffer and displayed, but the cursor is advanced only if the KC_DEADKEY flag is not set.

Case 2: If the KC_CHAR and KC_COMPOSITE flags are set, the character accompanying the message will be the composite character. (If the dead key is followed by a Spacebar, the character code accompanying the WM_CHAR message for the Spacebar is the previous dead-key character.) You display the character and advance the cursor. This is exactly how you process a normal character key, so you do not need to check the KC_COMPOSITE flag. TYPEAWAY ignores it.

Case 3: If the KC_INVALIDCOMP flag is set, the dead key was followed by a character or virtual key that cannot be combined with the dead key. You advance the cursor past the dead key and beep the speaker to indicate an error. Then you process the WM_CHAR message as usual. In TYPEAWAY, this is done near the beginning of the WM_CHAR message processing.

Code Pages and Character Sets

If you've had some earlier programming experience with the PC and you're familiar with the PC's extended character set, you may be wondering where some of these composite characters come from, because not all of them are supported by the PC character set.

By default, the Presentation Manager does not use the PC character set for text written to the window using GPI functions. The "old PC" character set is codepage 437. The default codepage for GPI is called the "new PC" character set, and is codepage 850. In codepage 850 some of the line-drawing characters are replaced with composite characters.

Under AVIO, the situation is a little different: AVIO will use the system default codepage (which is 437) unless the CONFIG.SYS file has a CODEPAGE statement. In this case, AVIO uses the first codepage in the CODEPAGE statement and can be switched to the other using the *VioSetCp* function. The OS/2 CHCP (change codepage) command affects the AVIO codepage but not the GPI codepage.

If you need to convert a text string to upper case, do not use the C functions available for this purpose. These functions will work only with ASCII codes under 128. Instead, use the *WinUpper* and *WinUpperChar* functions and use *WinCompareStrings* for sorting.

Reading Character Strings

Because a program gets WM_CHAR messages one at a time, there doesn't seem to be anything in the Presentation Manager that corresponds to the *KbdStringIn* function to read an entire character string. In the Presentation Manager you do this a little differently. You create a child window control of the predefined WC_ENTRYFIELD class. This window accepts typed input, understands cursor movement keys, and can even scroll the input left and right if it's too long to fit in the window. We'll create such a child window control in Chapter 14.

Breaking the Rules

Presentation Manager programming often seems to involve so many rules that it can feel good to break a few. The final program in this chapter does just that. Earlier I warned you against using the scan code that accompanies the WM_CHAR message. For reasons I'll discuss shortly, this final program uses the scan code.

The Presentation Manager programs we've written so far have used the hardware of the PC (such as the video display) only through the software interface provided by OS/2 and the Presentation Manager. But this program directly accesses the PC hardware to control the speaker. Perhaps even more shocking is the fact that part of the program is written in assembly language rather than C.

Playing Music on the Keyboard

The ORGAN program shown in Figure 8-6 lets you play your keyboard as if it were a 7-octave organ.

The ORGAN File

```
#----------------
# ORGAN make file
#----------------

organ.obj : organ.c organ.h
    cl -c -G2sw -W3 organ.c

speaker.obj : speaker.asm
    masm speaker ;

organ.exe : organ.obj speaker.obj organ.def
    link organ speaker, /align:16, NUL, os2, organ
```

The ORGAN.C File

```
/*--------------------------------------------
    ORGAN.C --  Play Organ from Keyboard
  --------------------------------------*/

#define INCL_DOS
#define INCL_WIN
#define INCL_GPI
#include <os2.h>
#include "organ.h"

MRESULT EXPENTRY ClientWndProc (HWND, USHORT, MPARAM, MPARAM) ;
VOID    EXPENTRY Speaker (USHORT usFreq) ;

SHORT  xOffset, yOffset, cxCaps, cyChar ;
USHORT usLastScan ;
```

(continued)

Figure 8-6. The ORGAN.C File. *continued*

```
int main (void)
    {
    static CHAR  szClientClass [] = "Organ" ;
    static ULONG flFrameFlags = FCF_TITLEBAR       | FCF_SYSMENU |
                                 FCF_SIZEBORDER     | FCF_MINMAX  |
                                 FCF_SHELLPOSITION  | FCF_TASKLIST ;

    HAB          hab ;
    HMQ          hmq ;
    HWND         hwndFrame, hwndClient ;
    QMSG         qmsg ;

    if (DosPortAccess (0, 0, 0x42, 0x61))   // Don't run if port access fails
        return 1 ;

    hab = WinInitialize (0) ;
    hmq = WinCreateMsgQueue (hab, 0) ;

    WinRegisterClass (hab, szClientClass, ClientWndProc, CS_SIZEREDRAW, 0) ;

    hwndFrame = WinCreateStdWindow (HWND_DESKTOP, WS_VISIBLE,
                                    &flFrameFlags, szClientClass, NULL,
                                    0L, NULL, 0, &hwndClient) ;

    WinSendMsg (hwndFrame, WM_SETICON,
                WinQuerySysPointer (HWND_DESKTOP, SPTR_APPICON, FALSE),
                NULL) ;

    while (WinGetMsg (hab, &qmsg, NULL, 0, 0))
        WinDispatchMsg (hab, &qmsg) ;

    WinDestroyWindow (hwndFrame) ;
    WinDestroyMsgQueue (hmq) ;
    WinTerminate (hab) ;
    DosPortAccess (0, 1, 0x42, 0x61) ;
    return 0 ;
    }

VOID DrawKey (HPS hps, USHORT usScanCode, BOOL fInvert)
    {
    RECTL rcl ;

    rcl.xLeft   = 3 * cxCaps * key[usScanCode].xPos / 2 + xOffset ;
    rcl.yBottom = 3 * cyChar * key[usScanCode].yPos / 2 + yOffset ;
```

(continued)

Figure 8-6. The ORGAN.C File. *continued*

```
      rcl.xRight  = rcl.xLeft   + 3 * cxCaps ;
      rcl.yTop    = rcl.yBottom + 3 * cyChar / 2 ;

      WinDrawText (hps, -1, key[usScanCode].szKey, &rcl,
                   CLR_NEUTRAL, CLR_BACKGROUND,
                   DT_CENTER ¦ DT_VCENTER ¦ DT_ERASERECT) ;
      if (fInvert)
          WinInvertRect (hps, &rcl) ;

      WinDrawBorder (hps, &rcl, 1, 1, CLR_NEUTRAL, CLR_BACKGROUND,
                     DB_STANDARD) ;
      }

VOID ProcessKey (HPS hps, USHORT usScanCode, USHORT fsFlags)
      {
      static USHORT ausOctFreq [] = { 262, 277, 294, 311, 330, 349,
                                      370, 392, 415, 440, 466, 494 } ;
      USHORT        usOct, usFreq ;

      if (usScanCode >= NUMSCANS)                    // No scan codes over 53
          return ;
      if ((usOct = key[usScanCode].sOctave) == -1)  // Non-music key
          return ;

      if (fsFlags & KC_KEYUP)                        // For key up
          {
          if (usLastScan == usScanCode)             // If that's the note
              {
              Speaker (0) ;                         // turn off speaker
              DrawKey (hps, usScanCode, FALSE) ;    // and redraw key
              usLastScan = 0 ;
              }
          return ;
          }
      if (fsFlags & KC_PREVDOWN)                     // Ignore typematics
          return ;

      usFreq = ausOctFreq [key[usScanCode].sNote] ; // Get frequency

      if (fsFlags & KC_SHIFT)
          usOct += fsFlags & KC_ALT ? 2 : 1 ;       // Higher octave
      else if (fsFlags & KC_CTRL)
          usOct -= fsFlags & KC_ALT ? 2 : 1 ;       // Lower octave
```

(continued)

Figure 8-6. The ORGAN.C File. *continued*

```
        if (usOct > 4)                                      // Shift frequency
            usFreq <<= (usOct - 4) ;                        //   for octave
        else if (usOct < 4)
            usFreq >>= (4 - usOct) ;

        Speaker (usFreq) ;                                  // Turn on speaker
        DrawKey (hps, usScanCode, TRUE) ;                   // Draw the inverted key

        if (usLastScan != 0)
            DrawKey (hps, usLastScan, FALSE) ;              // Redraw previous key
        usLastScan = usScanCode ;                           // Save scan code
        }

MRESULT EXPENTRY ClientWndProc (HWND hwnd, USHORT msg, MPARAM mp1, MPARAM mp2)
    {
    FONTMETRICS fm ;
    HPS         hps ;
    SHORT       cxClient, cyClient ;
    USHORT      usScanCode ;

    switch (msg)
        {
        case WM_CREATE:
            hps = WinGetPS (hwnd) ;
            GpiQueryFontMetrics (hps, (LONG) sizeof fm, &fm) ;
            cxCaps = (SHORT) fm.lEmInc ;
            cyChar = (SHORT) fm.lMaxBaselineExt ;
            WinReleasePS (hps) ;
            return 0 ;

        case WM_SIZE:
            cxClient = SHORT1FROMMP (mp2) ;
            cyClient = SHORT2FROMMP (mp2) ;

            xOffset = (cxClient - 25 * 3 * cxCaps / 2) / 2 ;
            yOffset = (cyClient - 6 * cyChar) / 2 ;
            return 0 ;

        case WM_CHAR:
            if (!(CHARMSG(&msg)->fs & KC_SCANCODE))
                break ;
```

(continued)

Figure 8-6. The ORGAN.C File. *continued*

```
                    hps = WinGetPS (hwnd) ;
                    ProcessKey (hps, CHARMSG(&msg)->scancode, CHARMSG(&msg)->fs) ;
                    WinReleasePS (hps) ;
                    return 0 ;

            case WM_PAINT:
                    hps = WinBeginPaint (hwnd, NULL, NULL) ;
                    GpiErase (hps) ;

                    for (usScanCode = 0 ; usScanCode < NUMSCANS ; usScanCode++)
                        if (key[usScanCode].xPos != -1)
                            DrawKey (hps, usScanCode, usScanCode == usLastScan) ;

                    WinEndPaint (hps) ;
                    return 0 ;
            }
        return WinDefWindowProc (hwnd, msg, mp1, mp2) ;
        }
```

The ORGAN.H File

```
/*----------------------
   ORGAN.H header file
   --------------------*/

#define NUMSCANS    (sizeof key / sizeof key[0])

struct
    {
    SHORT sOctave ;
    SHORT sNote ;
    SHORT yPos ;
    SHORT xPos ;
    CHAR  *szKey ;
    }
    key [] =
    {
                                // Scan  Char  Oct  Note
                                // ----  ----  ---  ----
    -1, -1, -1, -1, NULL,       //  0    None
    -1, -1, -1, -1, NULL,       //  1    Esc
    -1, -1,  3,  0, "",         //  2     1
     4,  1,  3,  2, "C#",       //  3     2     4   C#
```

(continued)

Figure 8-6. The ORGAN.H File. *continued*

```
 4,  3,  3,  4, "D#",    //  4     3    4    D#
-1, -1,  3,  6, "",      //  5     4
 4,  6,  3,  8, "F#",    //  6     5    4    F#
 4,  8,  3, 10, "G#",    //  7     6    4    G#
 4, 10,  3, 12, "A#",    //  8     7    4    A#
-1, -1,  3, 14, "",      //  9     8
 5,  1,  3, 16, "C#",    // 10     9    5    C#
 5,  3,  3, 18, "D#",    // 11     0    5    D#
-1, -1,  3, 20, "",      // 12     -
 5,  6,  3, 22, "F#",    // 13     =    5    F#
-1, -1, -1, -1, NULL,    // 14     Back

-1, -1, -1, -1, NULL,    // 15     Tab
 4,  0,  2,  1, "C",     // 16     q    4    C
 4,  2,  2,  3, "D",     // 17     w    4    D
 4,  4,  2,  5, "E",     // 18     e    4    E
 4,  5,  2,  7, "F",     // 19     r    4    F
 4,  7,  2,  9, "G",     // 20     t    4    G
 4,  9,  2, 11, "A",     // 21     y    4    A
 4, 11,  2, 13, "B",     // 22     u    4    B
 5,  0,  2, 15, "C",     // 23     i    5    C
 5,  2,  2, 17, "D",     // 24     o    5    D
 5,  4,  2, 19, "E",     // 25     p    5    E
 5,  5,  2, 21, "F",     // 26     [    5    F
 5,  7,  2, 23, "G",     // 27     ]    5    G
-1, -1, -1, -1, NULL,    // 28     Ent

-1, -1, -1, -1, NULL,    // 29     Ctrl
 2,  8,  1,  2, "G#",    // 30     a    2    G#
 2, 10,  1,  4, "A#",    // 31     s    2    A#
-1, -1,  1,  6, "",      // 32     d
 3,  1,  1,  8, "C#",    // 33     f    3    C#
 3,  3,  1, 10, "D#",    // 34     g    3    D#
-1, -1,  1, 12, "",      // 35     h
 3,  6,  1, 14, "F#",    // 36     j    3    F#
 3,  8,  1, 16, "G#",    // 37     k    3    G#
 3, 10,  1, 18, "A#",    // 38     l    3    A#
-1, -1,  1, 20, "",      // 39     ;
 4,  1,  1, 22, "C#",    // 40     '    4    C#
-1, -1, -1, -1, NULL,    // 41     `

-1, -1, -1, -1, NULL,    // 42     Shift
-1, -1, -1, -1, NULL,    // 43     \
 2,  9,  0,  3, "A",     // 44     z    2    A
```

(continued)

Figure 8-6. The ORGAN.H File. *continued*

```
    2, 11,  0,  5, "B",      // 45    x    2    B
    3,  0,  0,  7, "C",      // 46    c    3    C
    3,  2,  0,  9, "D",      // 47    v    3    D
    3,  4,  0, 11, "E",      // 48    b    3    E
    3,  5,  0, 13, "F",      // 49    n    3    F
    3,  7,  0, 15, "G",      // 50    m    3    G
    3,  9,  0, 17, "A",      // 51    ,    3    A
    3, 11,  0, 19, "B",      // 52    .    3    B
    4,  0,  0, 21, "C"       // 53    /    4    C
} ;
```

The SPEAKER.ASM File

```
;----------------------------------------------------
; SPEAKER.ASM -- Ring 2 routine for ORGAN program
;               (Accesses Intel 8255 Timer chip)
;----------------------------------------------------


            PUBLIC    Speaker
            .286
            .MODEL    MEDIUM, PASCAL


            .DATA
ClockFreq   dd    1193180


            .CODE     SPEAKER-TEXT
Speaker     PROC FAR   Frequency:WORD
            Cli                                    ; Disable interrupts


            Mov  BX, Frequency                     ; Get parameter from stack
            Or   BX, BX                            ; Check if it's zero
            Jz   TurnOff                           ; If so, turn off sound


            Mov  AL, 10110110b                     ; Set flags for programming
            Out  43h, AL


            Mov  AX, WORD PTR [ClockFreq]          ; Calculate timer frequency
            Mov  DX, WORD PTR [ClockFreq + 2]
            Div  BX


            Out  42h, AL                           ; Output low byte
            Jmp  $ + 2                             ; Delay
```

(continued)

Figure 8-6. The SPEAKER.ASM File. *continued*

```
               Mov  AL, AH                    ; Output high byte
               Out  42h, AL
               Jmp  $ + 2                      ; Delay

               In   AL, 61h                    ; Get 8255 bits
               Jmp  $ + 2                      ; Delay

               Or   AL, 00000011b              ; Set bits for speaker
               Out  61h, AL                    ; Set 8255 bits
               Jmp  Return

TurnOff:       In   AL, 61h                    ; Get 8255 bits
               Jmp  $ + 2                      ; Delay
               And  AL, 11111101b              ; Set bits for no speaker
               Out  61h, AL                    ; Set 8255 bits

Return:        Sti                             ; Enable interrupts
               Ret
Speaker        ENDP
               END
```

The ORGAN.DEF File

```
;----------------------------------
; ORGAN.DEF module definition file
;----------------------------------

NAME           ORGAN       WINDOWAPI

DESCRIPTION    'Play Organ from Keyboard (C) Charles Petzold, 1988'
PROTMODE
HEAPSIZE       1024
STACKSIZE      8192
SEGMENTS       SPEAKER_TEXT    IOPL
EXPORTS        ClientWndProc
               Speaker       1
```

Figure 8-6. *The ORGAN program.*

To run ORGAN, you'll need the following line in your CONFIG.SYS file:

```
IOPL=YES
```

If this line is not in CONFIG.SYS, edit the file to include the line and reboot.

The program displays part of the keyboard in the window, as shown in Figure 8-7.

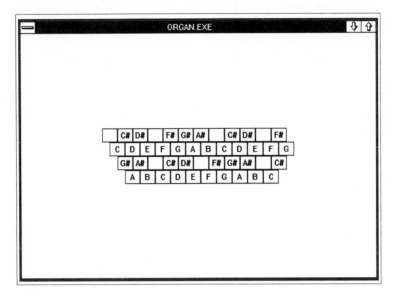

Figure 8-7. *The ORGAN display.*

The keys are labeled with the notes they generate. When you press any key, the key is displayed in reverse video as the note is played. The note stops when you release the key. You can shift up one octave by pressing the Shift key before you press the note key, and you can shift up two octaves by pressing Shift and Alt together. Pressing Ctrl shifts down one octave; Ctrl and Alt shift down two octaves. Due to the limitations of the PC's sound generation hardware, you can play only one note at a time.

When Scan Codes Are Important

The ORGAN.H header file contains a structure called *key* that maps scan codes into note and octave combinations. The *yPos* and *xPos* fields of this structure are used within ORGAN.C to draw the keyboard on the screen.

All the keys that play notes generate character codes, but I decided to use scan codes to allow ORGAN to be used with European keyboards. For example, the letter key in the lower-left corner of the keyboard is a Z on a U.S. keyboard but a Y on a German keyboard. Moreover, many of the symbol keys on foreign language keyboards are different than those on the U.S. keyboards.

The scan codes, however, are the same for U.S. keyboards and foreign language keyboards. The scan code for the lower-left-letter key is always a 44 regardless whether the key generates a Z or a Y. This allows ORGAN to be used on a wider variety of keyboards. Just don't expect to be able to simply recompile ORGAN for versions of the Presentation Manager that may someday run on non-PC hardware. ORGAN is very much dependent on the PC.

Using IOPL Segments

When you press a key in ORGAN, the note sounds and continues to sound until you release the key. The only mechanisms for generating sounds in OS/2 are the *DosBeep* function supported in the OS/2 kernel and the *WinAlarm* function. Both of these functions make a tone for a specified period of time.

But in ORGAN the length of this tone depends on how long the key is pressed. Therefore, I had to use a different approach. This required writing a function that directly accesses the hardware of the PC's speaker. This function is called *Speaker* and is in the SPEAKER.ASM file. It takes one 2-byte parameter, which is the frequency in Hertz. A zero parameter turns the speaker off.

Under OS/2, functions that access the hardware of the PC must be placed in special segments called IOPL ("I/O privilege level") segments. These segments run in priority level 2 rather than the normal priority level 3. IOPL segments must be identified as such in the module definition file. This is indicated in the SEGMENTS statement:

```
SEGMENTS  SPEAKER_TEXT  IOPL
```

The *Speaker* function is in a segment called SPEAKER_TEXT, and the IOPL keyword tells LINK to flag this segment as an IOPL segment. The entry point to the *Speaker* function must also be listed in the EXPORTS section of the module definition file along with *ClientWndProc*:

```
EXPORTS   ClientWndProc
          Speaker        1
```

The 1 that follows the *Speaker* function name indicates the number of WORD parameters to the function.

I wrote the *Speaker* function in assembly language because it is not normally possible to call functions located in a ring 3 segment from a function in a ring 2 segment. Because the rest of ORGAN runs in ring 3, the *Speaker* function can't make calls to C library functions. However, *Speaker* needs to make a 32-bit divide; if *Speaker* were written in C, that would require a C library function call.

Otherwise, the program is fairly straightforward. The *DrawKey* function is responsible for drawing the keys on the window, and *ProcessKey* is responsible for determining what frequency to use for a particular keyboard message.

Of course, you might not like the idea of directly accessing the PC hardware in a Presentation Manager program, and I tend to agree. But still, it's nice to know that if you want to, you can.

TAMING THE MOUSE

All user input to a Presentation Manager program comes from the keyboard and the mouse. The keyboard is adequate for alphanumeric input and rudimentary cursor movement. The mouse provides a more intimate connection between the user and the objects on the screen. As an extension of the user's fingers, the mouse can point, grab, and move. As you've seen in the sample programs from previous chapters, the Presentation Manager takes care of all mouse input involving menus, scroll bars, and the moving and sizing of windows. Your programs will be concerned mostly with mouse activity that occurs within the client window.

When you program for the Presentation Manager, however, the mouse must be viewed as secondary to the keyboard—the Presentation Manager doesn't require a mouse. Obviously, some programs (drawing programs and page-composition programs) become awkward when controlled solely from the keyboard, so in those cases you might feel justified in not providing a keyboard interface that duplicates all the mouse functions. That's up to you. Just be aware that if your program requires a mouse, it won't be usable by all Presentation Manager users.

The Presentation Manager supports a mouse that has one, two, or three buttons. You must decide how many mouse buttons you'll use in your program. The easiest approach is to go for the lowest common denominator and use only one mouse button.

Mouse and Pointer Basics

Let's begin with a few simple definitions, starting with the distinction between the mouse and the pointer. The mouse is the object that sits on the desk. The pointer is a small bitmapped picture on the screen. When you move the mouse with your hand, the Presentation Manager moves the pointer.

Clicking the mouse is pressing and releasing a mouse button. Double-clicking is pressing and releasing the mouse button twice in succession. To qualify as a double click, both clicks must occur within a fixed period of time (by default, half a second) and with the pointer in approximately the same area of the screen (within an area of about half a system font character). Dragging the mouse is holding down the mouse button and moving the mouse. For example, you drag the mouse when you change the position or size of a window.

More About the Pointer

The Presentation Manager moves the pointer in response to mouse movements. The Presentation Manager includes several predefined pointer shapes, with the most familiar being the arrow pointer used by default on most windows. Four other predefined pointers (double-headed arrows of various types) are used on the sizing border. You can also create your own customized pointers, as described in Chapter 12.

The displayed size of the mouse pointer is dependent on the resolution of the video display. For example, on the IBM EGA a pointer is 32 pixels wide and 32 pixels high. On an IBM CGA a pointer is only 16 pixels high because the vertical resolution is lower. (A program can obtain the dimensions of the pointer from *WinQuerySysValue* using the SV_CXPOINTER and SV_CYPOINTER parameters.) Every pointer has a "hot spot," which is a single pixel position within the pointer bitmap. For the standard arrow pointer, the hot spot is the tip of the arrow. The Presentation Manager uses the hot spot as the position of the pointer.

The Pointer Position

Programs that use the mouse for input must often determine the position of the pointer or, more precisely, the coordinates of the pointer's hot spot. Such programs can make this determination in three ways: by calling *WinQueryPointerPos*; by calling *WinQueryMsgPos*; or by processing WM-_MOUSEMOVE messages.

The *WinQueryPointerPos* Function

This function fills in the *x* and *y* fields of the POINTL structure with the current pointer position in screen coordinates, relative to the lower-left corner of the screen:

```
WinQueryPointerPos (HWND_DESKTOP, &ptl) ;
```

You can call this function at any time.

The *WinQueryMsgPos* Function

You can use the second method, the *WinQueryMsgPos* function, while processing a message in a window procedure. This function reports the screen coordinates of the pointer at the time a message was last placed in the program's message queue:

```
WinQueryMsgPos (hab, &ptl) ;
```

If the window procedure calls this function while processing a nonqueued message, this pointer position could be long out of date. The pointer position obtained from *WinQueryMsgPos* is originally part of the QMSG structure that the Presentation Manager fills in when you retrieve a message from the message queue with *WinGetMsg*. However, the pointer position isn't passed to the window procedure along with the more important QMSG fields (the window handle, message number, *mp1*, and *mp2*). You use *WinQueryMsgPos* to get this field. This function is sometimes useful when you need to determine the pointer position at the time a key on the keyboard was pressed.

Both *WinQueryPointerPos* and *WinQueryMsgPos* return the pointer coordinates relative to the lower-left corner of the screen, but the functions don't necessarily return the same value. *WinQueryPointerPos* returns the pointer position at the time the function is called, whereas *WinQueryMsgPos* returns the position at the time the message currently being processed was posted in the message queue.

Processing the WM_MOUSEMOVE Message

The third way to obtain the pointer position is by processing the WM_MOUSEMOVE message in the window procedure. The pointer coordinates are stored in *mp1*. You can extract the *x* (horizontal) coordinate with the expression

```
xPointer = SHORT1FROMMP (mp1) ;
```

and extract the *y* (vertical) coordinate using

```
yPointer = SHORT2FROMMP (mp1) ;
```

> **NOTE:** *The PMWIN.H header file also includes a MOUSEMSG macro that is similar to the CHARMSG macro discussed in Chapter 8. You can use MOUSEMSG to obtain the pointer position like this:*

```
case WM_MOUSEMOVE:
     xPointer = MOUSEMSG (&msg) -> x ;
     yPointer = MOUSEMSG (&msg) -> y ;
```

Unlike the pointer position obtained from *WinQueryPointerPos* and *Win-QueryMsgPos*, the pointer position in the WM_MOUSEMOVE message is in window coordinates relative to the lower-left corner of the window receiving the message. Under normal circumstances, a window procedure receives WM_MOUSEMOVE messages only when the pointer is positioned over the window. Thus the coordinates in *mp1* won't be negative. (The exception is when a program "captures the mouse," a technique I'll discuss later in this chapter.)

You'll recall from Chapter 8 that a window procedure receives WM_CHAR messages when the window has the input focus. The mouse is handled differently—a window procedure receives WM_MOUSEMOVE messages when the pointer is positioned over the window, regardless of the active window and the focus window. If the mouse pointer is positioned over overlapping windows, the topmost window receives the WM_MOUSEMOVE message.

Processing WM_MOUSEMOVE messages is generally the easiest way for a program to determine the pointer position, for two reasons:

- The message notifies a window procedure when the mouse has moved.

- The coordinates of the pointer position are relative to the window rather than the screen.

WM_MOUSEMOVE Message Default Processing

After processing most messages, the window procedure returns a 0. Any message that a window procedure does not process must be passed to *Win-DefWindowProc* for default processing.

But WM_MOUSEMOVE messages should be handled a little differently. The Presentation Manager documentation recommends that a window procedure return 1 if it processes a WM_MOUSEMOVE message and 0 if it does not. But this is just a convention. The value you return from the window procedure is not used for anything important—it is simply returned from the *WinDispatchMsg* call that originally dispatched the WM_MOUSEMOVE message to the window procedure.

Rather than return a 0 or 1 from the window procedure, you'll probably want to conclude your WM_MOUSEMOVE processing with a *break* statement. This will cause *WinDefWindowProc* to be called for the same message. *WinDefWindowProc* processes WM_MOUSEMOVE messages by setting the pointer shape to the default tilted arrow.

If you had the source code to *WinDefWindowProc*, you'd find that it looked something like this:

```
MRESULT APIENTRY WinDefWindowProc (HPS hps, USHORT msg, MPARAM mp1, MPARAM mp2)
    {

        ⋮

    switch (msg)
        {

            ⋮

        case WM_MOUSEMOVE:
            WinSetPointer (HWND_DESKTOP,
                WinQuerySysPointer (HWND_DESKTOP, SPTR_ARROW, FALSE)) ;
            return 0 ;

            ⋮

        }
    return 0 ;
    }
```

The *WinQuerySysPointer* function returns a handle to a system pointer. The SPTR_ARROW identifier refers to the tilted arrow pointer. The *WinSetPointer* call uses that pointer handle to set the pointer shape.

If you want a different pointer shape when the pointer is positioned on your client window, you can call *WinSetPointer* while you are processing WM_MOUSEMOVE and return from the window procedure without calling *WinDefWindowProc*. You can set the pointer to any of the system pointers (obtained from *WinQuerySysPointer* using the SPTR identifiers) or to a customized pointer (discussed in Chapter 12).

If you do not call *WinSetPointer* while processing the WM_MOUSEMOVE message, you should call *WinDefWindowProc* so the tilted arrow pointer is set. Otherwise, you may find that the pointer used by another window (for example, the double-headed arrows used by the sizing border window) continues to be used when the pointer is inside the client window.

Processing WM_MOUSEMOVE Messages

The WEB program, shown in Figure 9-1, processes WM_MOUSEMOVE messages. Whenever this program receives a WM_MOUSEMOVE message, it draws a series of lines from the pointer position encoded in *mpl* to the four corners and four sides of the client window. The pattern looks like a web (Figure 9-2). As you move the mouse around the window, the center of the web follows. When you move the mouse outside the client window, the client window stops receiving WM_MOUSEMOVE messages; thus the web stops changing shape.

The WEB File

```
#---------------
# WEB make file
#---------------

web.obj : web.c
     cl -c -G2sw -W3 web.c

web.exe : web.obj web.def
     link web, /align:16, NUL, os2, web
```

The WEB.C File

```
/*---------------------------------------
   WEB.C -- Mouse Movement Demo Program
---------------------------------------*/

#define INCL_WIN
#define INCL_GPI
#include <os2.h>

MRESULT EXPENTRY ClientWndProc (HWND, USHORT, MPARAM, MPARAM) ;

int main (void)
    {
    static CHAR   szClientClass [] = "Web" ;
    static ULONG  flFrameFlags = FCF_TITLEBAR       | FCF_SYSMENU |
                                 FCF_SIZEBORDER      | FCF_MINMAX  |
                                 FCF_SHELLPOSITION | FCF_TASKLIST ;
```

(continued)

Figure 9-1. The WEB.C File. *continued*

```
        HAB          hab ;
        HMQ          hmq ;
        HWND         hwndFrame, hwndClient ;
        QMSG         qmsg ;

        hab = WinInitialize (0) ;
        hmq = WinCreateMsgQueue (hab, 0) ;

        WinRegisterClass (hab, szClientClass, ClientWndProc,
                          CS_SIZEREDRAW ¦ CS_SYNCPAINT, 0) ;

        hwndFrame = WinCreateStdWindow (HWND_DESKTOP, WS_VISIBLE,
                                        &flFrameFlags, szClientClass, NULL,
                                        OL, NULL, 0, &hwndClient) ;

        WinSendMsg (hwndFrame, WM_SETICON,
                    WinQuerySysPointer (HWND_DESKTOP, SPTR_APPICON, FALSE),
                    NULL) ;

        while (WinGetMsg (hab, &qmsg, NULL, 0, 0))
            WinDispatchMsg (hab, &qmsg) ;

        WinDestroyWindow (hwndFrame) ;
        WinDestroyMsgQueue (hmq) ;
        WinTerminate (hab) ;
        return 0 ;
        }

VOID DrawWeb (HPS hps, POINTL *pptlPointerPos, POINTL *pptlClient)
        {
        POINTL ptl ;
                                        // Lower Left --> Pointer --> Upper Right
        ptl.x = 0 ;
        ptl.y = 0 ;
        GpiMove (hps, &ptl) ;
        GpiLine (hps, pptlPointerPos) ;
        GpiLine (hps, pptlClient) ;
                                        // Upper Left --> Pointer --> Lower Right
        ptl.x = 0 ;
        ptl.y = pptlClient->y ;
        GpiMove (hps, &ptl) ;
        GpiLine (hps, pptlPointerPos) ;

        ptl.x = pptlClient->x ;
        ptl.y = 0 ;
        GpiLine (hps, &ptl) ;
                                        // Lower Center --> Pointer --> Upper Center
```

(continued)

Figure 9-1. The WEB.C File. *continued*

```
        ptl.x = pptlClient->x / 2 ;
        ptl.y = 0 ;
        GpiMove (hps, &ptl) ;
        GpiLine (hps, pptlPointerPos) ;

        ptl.y = pptlClient->y ;
        GpiLine (hps, &ptl) ;
                                    // Left Center --> Pointer --> Right Center
        ptl.x = 0 ;
        ptl.y = pptlClient->y / 2 ;
        GpiMove (hps, &ptl) ;
        GpiLine (hps, pptlPointerPos) ;

        ptl.x = pptlClient->x ;
        GpiLine (hps, &ptl) ;
        }

MRESULT EXPENTRY ClientWndProc (HWND hwnd, USHORT msg, MPARAM mp1, MPARAM mp2)
        {
        static POINTL ptlClient, ptlPointerPos ;
        HPS          hps ;

        switch (msg)
            {
            case WM_SIZE:
                 ptlClient.x = SHORT1FROMMP (mp2) ;
                 ptlClient.y = SHORT2FROMMP (mp2) ;
                 return 0 ;

            case WM_MOUSEMOVE:
                 hps = WinGetPS (hwnd) ;
                 GpiSetMix (hps, FM_INVERT) ;

                 DrawWeb (hps, &ptlPointerPos, &ptlClient) ;

                 ptlPointerPos.x = MOUSEMSG(&msg)->x ;
                 ptlPointerPos.y = MOUSEMSG(&msg)->y ;

                 DrawWeb (hps, &ptlPointerPos, &ptlClient) ;

                 WinReleasePS (hps) ;
                 break ;                     // do default processing

            case WM_PAINT:
                 hps = WinBeginPaint (hwnd, NULL, NULL) ;
                 GpiErase (hps) ;
                 GpiSetMix (hps, FM_INVERT) ;
```

(continued)

Figure 9-1. The WEB.C File. *continued*

```
            DrawWeb (hps, &ptlPointerPos, &ptlClient) ;

            WinEndPaint (hps) ;
            return 0 ;
        }
    return WinDefWindowProc (hwnd, msg, mp1, mp2) ;
    }
```

The WEB.DEF File

```
;--------------------------------
; WEB.DEF module definition file
;--------------------------------

NAME            WEB  WINDOWAPI

DESCRIPTION     'Mouse Movement Demo Program (C) Charles Petzold, 1988'
PROTMODE
HEAPSIZE        1024
STACKSIZE       8192
EXPORTS         ClientWndProc
```

Figure 9-1. *The WEB program.*

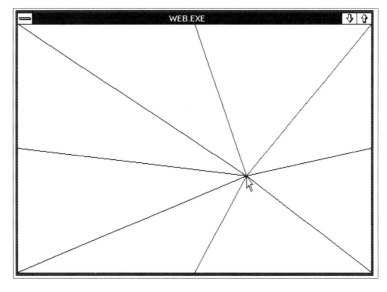

Figure 9-2. *The WEB display.*

Erasing and Redrawing

WEB draws lines using a series of *GpiMove* and *GpiLine* calls in the *DrawWeb* function. When WEB receives a WM_MOUSEMOVE message, it must erase the lines previously drawn and draw new lines based on the new mouse position. One way to erase the old lines is to write over them using a different mix mode. The default mix mode, called FM_OVERPAINT, causes any object you draw to overpaint whatever was previously in the client window. You can instead set a mix mode of FM_INVERT:

```
GpiSetMix (hps, FM_INVERT) ;
```

This causes the Presentation Manager to draw the lines by inverting the color of the client window background. Thus if you set the mix mode to FM_INVERT and draw over the old lines, the lines are effectively erased.

The WM_MOUSEMOVE code first sets the mix mode to FM_INVERT and then calls *DrawWeb* to erase the previous web:

```
case WM_MOUSEMOVE:
     hps = WinGetPS (hwnd) ;
     GpiSetMix (hps, FM_INVERT) ;

     DrawWeb (hps, &ptlPointerPos, &ptlClient) ;
```

The new position of the pointer is stored in *ptlPointerPos*, and the program calls *DrawWeb* again to draw the new web:

```
     ptlPointerPos.x = MOUSEMSG (&msg) -> x ;
     ptlPointerPos.y = MOUSEMSG (&msg) -> y ;

     DrawWeb (hps, &ptlPointerPos, &ptlClient) ;

     WinReleasePS (hps) ;
     break ;
```

But there's a bug in this web. Both WM_MOUSEMOVE and WM_PAINT are queued messages. The WM_PAINT message is a low-priority message. If both a WM_MOUSEMOVE message and a WM_PAINT message are in the message queue, WM_MOUSEMOVE is retrieved first.

If the pointer is positioned over a window when the window is first created, the Presentation Manager places an initial WM_MOUSEMOVE message in the program's message queue even if the mouse isn't moving during that time. This is often the first queued message the window procedure receives. The WM_PAINT message is usually the second queued message. But the code in WEB assumes that the window procedure receives a WM_PAINT message (and draws an initial web) before the first WM_MOUSEMOVE message (which begins by erasing the previous web). The fix for this is relatively easy. The window class is given a CS_SYNCPAINT style:

```
WinRegisterClass (hab, szClientClass, ClientWndProc,
                CS_SIZEREDRAW : CS_SYNCPAINT, 0) ;
```

This class style makes WM_PAINT messages nonqueued. The window procedure receives a WM_PAINT message immediately whenever part of the window is invalid. The first WM_PAINT message then precedes the first WM_MOUSEMOVE message.

If you move the mouse quickly within WEB's client area, you'll notice a lag between the position of the pointer and the center of the web. This results from the delay between the time the WM_MOUSEMOVE message is posted and the time it is actually processed. You can force the web to follow the movement of the mouse more closely by replacing the following two statements:

```
ptlPointerPos.x = MOUSEMSG (&msg) -> x ;
ptlPointerPos.y = MOUSEMSG (&msg) -> y ;
```

with the following code:

```
WinQueryPointerPos (HWND_DESKTOP, &ptlPointerPos) ;
WinMapWindowPoints (HWND_DESKTOP, hwnd, &ptlPointerPos, 1) ;
```

The WM_MOUSEMOVE message continues to notify the window procedure of a change in the pointer position, but the program obtains a more up-to-date pointer position from the *WinQueryPointerPos* function. The position must be converted from screen coordinates to client window coordinates with *WinMapWindowPoints*.

You'll notice with both methods that no matter how quickly you move the mouse around the client window, the program never has to "catch up" to a stream of unprocessed WM_MOUSEMOVE messages. That's because the Presentation Manager doesn't fill up your message queue with a lot of WM_MOUSEMOVE messages—it posts them only as quickly as you can process them. If the queue already contains a WM_MOUSEMOVE message when a new WM_MOUSEMOVE message is ready, the Presentation Manager replaces the message currently in the queue. Therefore, only one WM_MOUSEMOVE message exists at a time in the message queue.

Mouse Buttons and Hit-Testing

A mouse can have one, two, or three buttons. A program can obtain the number of mouse buttons from *WinQuerySysValue*:

```
lNumButtons = WinQuerySysValue (HWND_DESKTOP, SV_CMOUSEBUTTONS) ;
```

If the return value is 0, no mouse is installed. A program can check for the presence of a mouse in this manner or by calling *WinQuerySysValue* with the SV_MOUSEPRESENT parameter.

The PMWIN.H header file defines several identifiers you use in button-related functions and messages. These identifiers contain the words BUTTON1, BUTTON2, and BUTTON3 to refer to the three buttons. The following table shows how these identifiers normally correspond to the actual buttons on the mouse:

Number of Mouse Buttons	*BUTTON1*	*Identifier* *BUTTON2*	*BUTTON3*
One	Center	—	—
Two	Left	Right	—
Three	Left	Center	Right

You can write your programs for a three-button mouse and then include special logic to mimic the third button for a two-button mouse and the second and third buttons for a one-button mouse. But the easiest approach is to assume that the mouse has only one button and to work entirely with the functions and messages that pertain to BUTTON1. The Presentation Manager's own window procedures for the menu, scroll bar, sizing border, title bar, push buttons, and so forth all work this way.

Left-handed users often prefer to use their index finger for the first button. For this reason, the Presentation Manager Control Panel allows the user to switch the orientation of the buttons, like this:

Number of Mouse Buttons	BUTTON1	Identifier BUTTON2	BUTTON3
One	Center	—	—
Two	Right	Left	—
Three	Right	Center	Left

This swapping of the mouse buttons is invisible to your program; you needn't worry about it. The user knows which physical button is the first button, and that's all that's important. (But if you're writing a training program that draws a mouse on the screen and labels the buttons, you can determine if the mouse buttons have been swapped by calling *WinQuerySysValue* with the SV_SWAPBUTTON parameter.)

A program can determine whether a mouse button is currently pressed or released by calling *WinGetKeyState*, the function used in Chapter 8 to determine the state of keys on the keyboard:

```
sKeyState = WinGetKeyState (HWND_DESKTOP, VK_BUTTON1) ;
```

The high bit of *sKeyState* is set (*sKeyState* is negative) if the first mouse button is currently down. You can use the VK_BUTTON2 and VK_BUTTON3 identifiers to determine the state of the second and third buttons.

Button Messages

A window procedure is notified of button presses and releases by messages:

Button	Pressed	Released
1	WM_BUTTON1DOWN	WM_BUTTON1UP
2	WM_BUTTON2DOWN	WM_BUTTON2UP
3	WM_BUTTON3DOWN	WM_BUTTON3UP

If the user presses and releases the mouse button twice to qualify as a double click, the window procedure receives the two messages shown above for the first click and the following pair of messages for the second click:

Button	Pressed Again	Released
1	WM_BUTTON1DBLCLK	WM_BUTTON1UP
2	WM_BUTTON2DBLCLK	WM_BUTTON2UP
3	WM_BUTTON3DBLCLK	WM_BUTTON3UP

The Presentation Manager routes these messages to window procedures in the same way it routes the WM_MOUSEMOVE message: The window underneath the pointer at the time of the button action determines the window procedure that receives the message. The pointer position is stored in the *mpl* parameter, just as it is in the WM_MOUSEMOVE message.

WinDefWindowProc performs some important default processing of button down messages:

```
case WM_BUTTON1DOWN:
case WM_BUTTON2DOWN:
case WM_BUTTON3DOWN:
    WinSetActiveWindow (HWND_DESKTOP, hwnd) ;

    hwndOwner = WinQueryWindow (hwnd, QW_OWNER, FALSE) ;

    if (hwndOwner != NULL)
        return WinSendMsg (hwndOwner, msg, mp1, mp2) ;
    else
        return 0 ;
```

The *WinSetActiveWindow* call sets the active window to *hwnd*. If *hwnd* is not a top-level window, then *hwnd* is a descendant of a top-level window and that top-level window becomes active. This allows the user to bring a window to the foreground by clicking the client area with the mouse. You should either include a call to *WinSetActiveWindow* in your button down processing or call *WinDefWindowProc*.

WinDefWindowProc also sends the message to the window's owner, under the assumption that, if the window is not interested in the message, the window's owner might be.

Hit-Testing

When you draw graphic figures or text on the screen, you determine the coordinates of each object (whether figure or text) and call the appropriate GPI functions to draw it. Often a program uses a mouse interface to allow a user to point to and manipulate these graphic objects. But that means your program must work backward from the pointer coordinates to determine which of these objects the mouse is pointing to. This process is called "hit-testing." Hit-testing can be complex, particularly if your client window contains figures that overlap or contains text in a variable-pitch font. To help out, GPI includes a built-in facility to draw a series of objects and then determine which object coincides with a particular point. You'll want to use this facility for complex hit-testing, but for simple hit-testing, you can use the old-fashioned techniques, which I'll discuss in this section.

Simple Hit-Testing

The CHECKER1 program, shown in Figure 9-3, demonstrates some simple hit-testing logic. The program draws 25 rectangles in a 5-by-5 grid. When you click within one of these rectangles, CHECKER1 draws an X in the rectangle. When you click again, the X disappears.

The CHECKER1 File

```
#--------------------
# CHECKER1 make file
#--------------------

checker1.obj : checker1.c
    cl -c -G2sw -W3 checker1.c

checker1.exe : checker1.obj checker1.def
    link checker1, /align:16, NUL, os2, checker1
```

The CHECKER1.C File

```
/*---------------------------------------------
   CHECKER1.C -- Mouse Hit-Test Demo Program
  ---------------------------------------------*/

#define INCL_WIN
#include <os2.h>

#define DIVISIONS 5

MRESULT EXPENTRY ClientWndProc (HWND, USHORT, MPARAM, MPARAM) ;

int main (void)
    {
    static CHAR   szClientClass [] = "Checker1" ;
    static ULONG  flFrameFlags = FCF_TITLEBAR      | FCF_SYSMENU |
                                 FCF_SIZEBORDER    | FCF_MINMAX  |
                                 FCF_SHELLPOSITION | FCF_TASKLIST ;
    HAB           hab ;
    HMQ           hmq ;
    HWND          hwndFrame, hwndClient ;
    QMSG          qmsg ;
```

(continued)

Figure 9-3. The CHECKER1.C File. *continued*

```
      hab = WinInitialize (0) ;
      hmq = WinCreateMsgQueue (hab, 0) ;

      WinRegisterClass (hab, szClientClass, ClientWndProc, CS_SIZEREDRAW, 0) ;

      hwndFrame = WinCreateStdWindow (HWND_DESKTOP, WS_VISIBLE,
                                      &flFrameFlags, szClientClass, NULL,
                                      OL, NULL, 0, &hwndClient) ;

      while (WinGetMsg (hab, &qmsg, NULL, 0, 0))
          WinDispatchMsg (hab, &qmsg) ;

      WinDestroyWindow (hwndFrame) ;
      WinDestroyMsgQueue (hmq) ;
      WinTerminate (hab) ;
      return 0 ;
      }

VOID DrawLine (HPS hps, LONG x1, LONG y1, LONG x2, LONG y2)
      {
      POINTL ptl ;

      ptl.x = x1 ;  ptl.y = y1 ;  GpiMove (hps, &ptl) ;
      ptl.x = x2 ;  ptl.y = y2 ;  GpiLine (hps, &ptl) ;
      }

MRESULT EXPENTRY ClientWndProc (HWND hwnd, USHORT msg, MPARAM mp1, MPARAM mp2)
      {
      static BOOL  fBlockState [DIVISIONS] [DIVISIONS] ;
      static SHORT xBlock, yBlock ;
      HPS          hps ;
      RECTL        rcl ;
      SHORT        x, y ;

      switch (msg)
          {
          case WM_SIZE:
              xBlock = SHORT1FROMMP (mp2) / DIVISIONS ;
              yBlock = SHORT2FROMMP (mp2) / DIVISIONS ;
              return 0 ;

          case WM_BUTTON1DOWN:
          case WM_BUTTON1DBLCLK:
              if (xBlock > 0 && yBlock > 0)
                  {
                  x = MOUSEMSG(&msg)->x / xBlock ;
                  y = MOUSEMSG(&msg)->y / yBlock ;
```

(continued)

Figure 9-3. The CHECKER1.C File. *continued*

```
                if (x < DIVISIONS && y < DIVISIONS)
                    {
                    fBlockState [x][y] = !fBlockState [x][y] ;

                    rcl.xRight = xBlock + (rcl.xLeft   = x * xBlock) ;
                    rcl.yTop   = yBlock + (rcl.yBottom = y * yBlock) ;

                    WinInvalidateRect (hwnd, &rcl, FALSE) ;
                    }
                else
                    WinAlarm (HWND_DESKTOP, WA_WARNING) ;
                }
            else
                WinAlarm (HWND_DESKTOP, WA_WARNING) ;

            break ;                         // do default processing

        case WM_PAINT:
            hps = WinBeginPaint (hwnd, NULL, NULL) ;
            GpiErase (hps) ;

            if (xBlock > 0 && yBlock > 0)
                for (x = 0 ; x < DIVISIONS ; x++)
                    for (y = 0 ; y < DIVISIONS ; y++)
                        {
                        rcl.xRight = xBlock + (rcl.xLeft   = x * xBlock);
                        rcl.yTop   = yBlock + (rcl.yBottom = y * yBlock);

                        WinDrawBorder (hps, &rcl, 1, 1,
                                       CLR_NEUTRAL, CLR_BACKGROUND,
                                       DB_STANDARD ¦ DB_INTERIOR) ;

                        if (fBlockState [x][y])
                            {
                            DrawLine (hps, rcl.xLeft,  rcl.yBottom,
                                           rcl.xRight, rcl.yTop) ;

                            DrawLine (hps, rcl.xLeft,  rcl.yTop,
                                           rcl.xRight, rcl.yBottom) ;
                            }
                        }
            WinEndPaint (hps) ;
            return 0 ;
        }
    return WinDefWindowProc (hwnd, msg, mp1, mp2) ;
    }
```

The CHECKER1.DEF File

```
;-----------------------------------
; CHECKER1.DEF module definition file
;-----------------------------------

NAME            CHECKER1   WINDOWAPI

DESCRIPTION     'Mouse Hit-Test Program No. 1 (C) Charles Petzold, 1988'
PROTMODE
HEAPSIZE        1024
STACKSIZE       8192
EXPORTS         ClientWndProc
```

Figure 9-3. *The CHECKER1 program.*

The CHECKER1 display is shown in Figure 9-4.

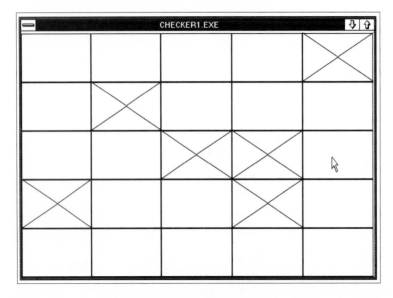

Figure 9-4. *The CHECKER1 display.*

Each rectangle in CHECKER1 has the same width and height. The program determines the dimensions of the rectangles during the WM_SIZE message by dividing the client window width and height by 5. These dimensions are stored in *xBlock* and *yBlock*. The *fBlockState* array stores the state (checked or not checked) of each block. The state is TRUE if the rectangle contains an X and FALSE if it doesn't. The WM_PAINT message code tests the values in this array to determine if it should draw the Xs in the rectangles.

The WM_BUTTON1DOWN code must work backward from the pointer coordinates to determine the particular block being clicked on. Because all the blocks are the same height and width, this task is fairly trivial, requiring only that the pointer coordinates be divided by the rectangle size:

```
x = MOUSEMSG (&msg) -> x / xBlock ;
y = MOUSEMSG (&msg) -> y / yBlock ;
```

The values of *x* and *y* can range from 0 to 4, identifying the rectangle that the user clicked on. The value of *fBlockState* for that rectangle is inverted:

```
fBlockState [x][y] = !fBlockState [x][y] ;
```

The rectangle is then invalidated to generate a WM_PAINT message. If the width or height of the client window isn't equally divisible by 5, the program leaves a strip across the right or top of the window that isn't covered by any of the rectangles. If the user clicks on that area, the *x* or *y* value (calculated as shown above) will be greater than 4, in which case CHECKER1 beeps to indicate the error.

Before we proceed to a more sophisticated hit-testing technique, let's add a keyboard interface to this program.

Emulating the Mouse with the Keyboard

I said at the outset of this chapter that you should write your Presentation Manager programs so they are usable with either a mouse or the keyboard. So far, I've been shamelessly ignoring that rule in order to concentrate on mouse logic. The CHECKER2 program, shown in Figure 9-5, adds a keyboard interface to CHECKER1. You can use the cursor movement keys to move the pointer from rectangle to rectangle. The Spacebar or Enter key draws an X or removes the X in the rectangle under the pointer.

The CHECKER2 File

```
#--------------------
# CHECKER2 make file
#--------------------

checker2.obj : checker2.c
    cl -c -G2sw -W3 checker2.c

checker2.exe : checker2.obj checker2.def
    link checker2, /align:16, NUL, os2, checker2
```

The CHECKER2.C File

```
/*-----------------------------------------------------------------
   CHECKER2.C -- Mouse Hit-Test Demo Program with Keyboard Interface
   -------------------------------------------------------------------*/

#define INCL_WIN
#include <os2.h>
#include <stdlib.h>

#define DIVISIONS 5

MRESULT EXPENTRY ClientWndProc (HWND, USHORT, MPARAM, MPARAM) ;

int main (void)
    {
    static CHAR  szClientClass [] = "Checker2" ;
    static ULONG flFrameFlags = FCF_TITLEBAR      | FCF_SYSMENU |
                                FCF_SIZEBORDER     | FCF_MINMAX  |
                                FCF_SHELLPOSITION  | FCF_TASKLIST ;

    HAB         hab ;
    HMQ         hmq ;
    HWND        hwndFrame, hwndClient ;
    QMSG        qmsg ;

    hab = WinInitialize (0) ;
    hmq = WinCreateMsgQueue (hab, 0) ;

    WinRegisterClass (hab, szClientClass, ClientWndProc, CS_SIZEREDRAW, 0) ;

    hwndFrame = WinCreateStdWindow (HWND_DESKTOP, WS_VISIBLE,
                                    &flFrameFlags, szClientClass, NULL,
                                    0L, NULL, 0, &hwndClient) ;

    while (WinGetMsg (hab, &qmsg, NULL, 0, 0))
        WinDispatchMsg (hab, &qmsg) ;

    WinDestroyWindow (hwndFrame) ;
    WinDestroyMsgQueue (hmq) ;
    WinTerminate (hab) ;
    return 0 ;
    }

VOID DrawLine (HPS hps, LONG x1, LONG y1, LONG x2, LONG y2)
    {
    POINTL ptl ;
```

(continued)

Figure 9-5. The CHECKER2.C File. *continued*

```
        ptl.x = x1 ;  ptl.y = y1 ;  GpiMove (hps, &ptl) ;
        ptl.x = x2 ;  ptl.y = y2 ;  GpiLine (hps, &ptl) ;
        }

MRESULT EXPENTRY ClientWndProc (HWND hwnd, USHORT msg, MPARAM mp1, MPARAM mp2)
     {
     static BOOL  fBlockState [DIVISIONS] [DIVISIONS] ;
     static SHORT xBlock, yBlock ;
     HPS          hps ;
     POINTL       ptl ;
     RECTL        rcl ;
     SHORT        x, y ;

     switch (msg)
          {
          case WM_SIZE:
               xBlock = SHORT1FROMMP (mp2) / DIVISIONS ;
               yBlock = SHORT2FROMMP (mp2) / DIVISIONS ;
               return 0 ;

          case WM_BUTTON1DOWN:
          case WM_BUTTON1DBLCLK:
               if (xBlock > 0 && yBlock > 0)
                    {
                    x = MOUSEMSG(&msg)->x / xBlock ;
                    y = MOUSEMSG(&msg)->y / yBlock ;

                    if (x < DIVISIONS && y < DIVISIONS)
                         {
                         fBlockState [x][y] = !fBlockState [x][y] ;

                         rcl.xRight = xBlock + (rcl.xLeft   = x * xBlock) ;
                         rcl.yTop   = yBlock + (rcl.yBottom = y * yBlock) ;

                         WinInvalidateRect (hwnd, &rcl, FALSE) ;
                         }
                    else
                         WinAlarm (HWND_DESKTOP, WA_WARNING) ;
                    }
               else
                    WinAlarm (HWND_DESKTOP, WA_WARNING) ;

               break ;                        // do default processing

          case WM_SETFOCUS:
               if (WinQuerySysValue (HWND_DESKTOP, SV_MOUSEPRESENT) == 0)
```

(continued)

Figure 9-5. The CHECKER2.C File. *continued*

```
                    WinShowPointer (HWND_DESKTOP,
                                    SHORT1FROMMP (mp2) ? TRUE : FALSE) ;
        return 0 ;

case WM_CHAR:
        if (xBlock == 0 || yBlock == 0)
            break ;

        if (CHARMSG(&msg)->fs & KC_KEYUP)
            break ;

        if (!(CHARMSG(&msg)->fs & KC_VIRTUALKEY))
            break ;

        WinQueryPointerPos (HWND_DESKTOP, &ptl) ;
        WinMapWindowPoints (HWND_DESKTOP, hwnd, &ptl, 1) ;

        x = max (0, min (DIVISIONS - 1, (SHORT) ptl.x / xBlock)) ;
        y = max (0, min (DIVISIONS - 1, (SHORT) ptl.y / yBlock)) ;

        switch (CHARMSG(&msg)->vkey)
            {
            case VK_LEFT:
                x-- ;
                break ;

            case VK_RIGHT:
                x++ ;
                break ;

            case VK_DOWN:
                y-- ;
                break ;

            case VK_UP:
                y++ ;
                break ;

            case VK_HOME:
                x = 0 ;
                y = DIVISIONS - 1 ;
                break ;
```

(continued)

Figure 9-5. The CHECKER2.C File. *continued*

```
                     case VK_END:
                         x = DIVISIONS - 1 ;
                         y = 0 ;
                         break ;

                     case VK_NEWLINE:
                     case VK_ENTER:
                     case VK_SPACE:
                         WinSendMsg (hwnd, WM_BUTTON1DOWN,
                             MPFROM2SHORT (x * xBlock, y * yBlock), NULL) ;
                         break ;

                     default:
                         return 0 ;
                     }
                x = (x + DIVISIONS) % DIVISIONS ;
                y = (y + DIVISIONS) % DIVISIONS ;

                ptl.x = x * xBlock + xBlock / 2 ;
                ptl.y = y * yBlock + yBlock / 2 ;

                WinMapWindowPoints (hwnd, HWND_DESKTOP, &ptl, 1) ;
                WinSetPointerPos (HWND_DESKTOP, (SHORT) ptl.x, (SHORT) ptl.y) ;
                return 0 ;

          case WM_PAINT:
                hps = WinBeginPaint (hwnd, NULL, NULL) ;
                GpiErase (hps) ;

                if (xBlock > 0 && yBlock > 0)
                     for (x = 0 ; x < DIVISIONS ; x++)
                         for (y = 0 ; y < DIVISIONS ; y++)
                             {
                             rcl.xRight = xBlock + (rcl.xLeft   = x * xBlock);
                             rcl.yTop   = yBlock + (rcl.yBottom = y * yBlock);

                             WinDrawBorder (hps, &rcl, 1, 1,
                                         CLR_NEUTRAL, CLR_BACKGROUND,
                                         DB_STANDARD | DB_INTERIOR) ;

                             if (fBlockState [x][y])
                                 {
                                 DrawLine (hps, rcl.xLeft, rcl.yBottom,
                                             rcl.xRight, rcl.yTop) ;
```

(continued)

Figure 9-5. The CHECKER2.C File. *continued*

```
                                    DrawLine (hps, rcl.xLeft,  rcl.yTop,
                                              rcl.xRight, rcl.yBottom) ;
                        }
                }
        WinEndPaint (hps) ;
        return 0 ;
    }
  return WinDefWindowProc (hwnd, msg, mp1, mp2) ;
}
```

The CHECKER2.DEF File

```
;------------------------------------
; CHECKER2.DEF module definition file
;------------------------------------


NAME            CHECKER2  WINDOWAPI

DESCRIPTION     'Mouse Hit-Test Program No. 2 (C) Charles Petzold, 1988'
PROTMODE
HEAPSIZE        1024
STACKSIZE       8192
EXPORTS         ClientWndProc
```

Figure 9-5. *The CHECKER2 program.*

The first problem to be solved in a program like this involves the pointer it-self. If no mouse is installed, how can the program use the pointer? Well, it's easier than you may think. Even if a mouse isn't installed, the pointer still exists and has a position on the display. You can determine that posi-tion from *WinQueryPointerPos* and set the position by calling *WinSet-PointerPos*. If there's no mouse, calling *WinSetPointerPos* is the only way to move the pointer. Obviously, a user without a mouse would be annoyed to have a pointer sitting in the center of the display, so the Presentation Man-ager hides the pointer to make it invisible.

The Presentation Manager maintains a value called the "pointer level," which determines whether the pointer is visible. Initially, the pointer level is set to 0 if a mouse is installed and to 1 if a mouse isn't installed. To decre-ment the pointer level, call

```
WinShowPointer (HWND_DESKTOP, TRUE) ;
```

The Presentation Manager will not decrement the pointer level below zero. To increment the pointer level, make the following call:

```
WinShowPointer (HWND_DESKTOP, FALSE) ;
```

The Presentation Manager displays the pointer only if the pointer level is equal to 0. (You can obtain the current pointer level from *WinQuerySysValue* with the SV_POINTERLEVEL parameter.)

CHECKER2 shows how this works in practice. The program calls *WinShow-Pointer* in only one place — while processing the WM_SETFOCUS message:

```
case WM_SETFOCUS:
    if (WinQuerySysValue (HWND_DESKTOP, SV_MOUSEPRESENT) == 0)
        WinShowPointer (HWND_DESKTOP,
                        SHORT1FROMMP (mp2) ? TRUE : FALSE) ;
    return 0 ;
```

You'll recall from the discussion of WM_SETFOCUS in Chapter 8 that *mp2* is TRUE if the window is gaining the input focus and FALSE if the window is losing the input focus.

If a mouse isn't installed (indicated by a 0 value returned from *Win-QuerySysValue* with the SV_MOUSEPRESENT parameter), the initial pointer level is 1, and the pointer is hidden. When CHECKER2 gets the input focus, it decrements the pointer level to 0. The pointer becomes visible. When CHECKER2 loses the input focus, the pointer level is incremented back to 1 to hide the pointer again.

This logic thus allows CHECKER2 to display the pointer whenever it has the input focus. Normally, input focus has nothing to do with the pointer. But CHECKER2 uses the keyboard to mimic the action of the mouse. It only makes sense to display the pointer when CHECKER2 has the input focus, because that's when CHECKER2 gets WM_CHAR messages.

The button and repainting logic in *ClientWndProc* is the same as that in CHECKER1. The bulk of the new code is the addition of WM_CHAR processing. When CHECKER2 receives a WM_CHAR message, it obtains the position of the pointer in screen coordinates and converts the position to client window coordinates:

```
WinQueryPointerPos (HWND_DESKTOP, &ptl) ;
WinMapWindowPoints (HWND_DESKTOP, hwnd, &ptl, 1) ;
```

The pointer could be outside the client window entirely. The program determines the values of x and y (ranging from 0 to 4) that identify the rectangle closest to the pointer:

```
x = max (0, min (DIVISIONS - 1, (SHORT) ptl.x / xBlock)) ;
y = max (0, min (DIVISIONS - 1, (SHORT) ptl.y / yBlock)) ;
```

(The identifier DIVISIONS is defined as 5 near the top of the program.)
These values of *x* and *y* are then incremented or decremented depending on
the particular cursor movement key being pressed. The VK_NEWLINE,
VK_ENTER, and VK_SPACE keys are processed by sending the window a
WM_BUTTON1DOWN message to simulate a mouse button action.

The new *x* and *y* values must then be converted back to a pointer position.
The following formulas calculate a point in window coordinates at the center of the rectangle identified by *x* and *y*:

```
ptl.x = x * xBlock + xBlock / 2 ;
ptl.y = y * yBlock + yBlock / 2 ;
```

CHECKER2 then converts that point to window coordinates and sets the
new pointer position:

```
WinMapWindowPoints (hwnd, HWND_DESKTOP, &ptl, 1) ;
WinSetPointerPos (HWND_DESKTOP, (SHORT) ptl.x, (SHORT) ptl.y) ;
```

Hit-Testing with Children

Now let's try a different approach to hit-testing — one that involves creating child windows that process WM_BUTTON1DOWN messages themselves.
The CHECKER3 program is shown in Figure 9-6.

The CHECKER3 File

```
#--------------------
# CHECKER3 make file
#--------------------

checker3.obj : checker3.c
    cl -c -G2sw -W3 checker3.c

checker3.exe : checker3.obj checker3.def
    link checker3, /align:16, NUL, os2, checker3
```

The CHECKER3.C File

```
/*-------------------------------------------------------------------
    CHECKER3.C -- Mouse Hit-Test Demo Program with Child Windows
   -------------------------------------------------------------------*/

#define INCL_WIN
#include <os2.h>
```

(continued)

Figure 9-6. The CHECKER3.C File. *continued*

```
#define DIVISIONS 5

MRESULT EXPENTRY ClientWndProc (HWND, USHORT, MPARAM, MPARAM) ;
MRESULT EXPENTRY ChildWndProc  (HWND, USHORT, MPARAM, MPARAM) ;

HAB  hab ;

int main (void)
    {
    static CHAR  szClientClass [] = "Checker3" ;
    static ULONG flFrameFlags = FCF_TITLEBAR      | FCF_SYSMENU |
                                FCF_SIZEBORDER    | FCF_MINMAX  |
                                FCF_SHELLPOSITION | FCF_TASKLIST ;

    HMQ          hmq ;
    HWND         hwndFrame, hwndClient ;
    QMSG         qmsg ;

    hab = WinInitialize (0) ;
    hmq = WinCreateMsgQueue (hab, 0) ;

    WinRegisterClass (hab, szClientClass, ClientWndProc, CS_SIZEREDRAW, 0) ;

    hwndFrame = WinCreateStdWindow (HWND_DESKTOP, WS_VISIBLE,
                                    &flFrameFlags, szClientClass, NULL,
                                    0L, NULL, 0, &hwndClient) ;

    while (WinGetMsg (hab, &qmsg, NULL, 0, 0))
        WinDispatchMsg (hab, &qmsg) ;

    WinDestroyWindow (hwndFrame) ;
    WinDestroyMsgQueue (hmq) ;
    WinTerminate (hab) ;
    return 0 ;
    }

VOID DrawLine (HPS hps, LONG x1, LONG y1, LONG x2, LONG y2)
    {
    POINTL ptl ;

    ptl.x = x1 ; ptl.y = y1 ; GpiMove (hps, &ptl) ;
    ptl.x = x2 ; ptl.y = y2 ; GpiLine (hps, &ptl) ;
    }
```

(continued)

Figure 9-6. The CHECKER3.C File. *continued*

```
MRESULT EXPENTRY ClientWndProc (HWND hwnd, USHORT msg, MPARAM mp1, MPARAM mp2)
    {
    static CHAR szChildClass [] = "Checker3.Child" ;
    static HWND hwndChild [DIVISIONS][DIVISIONS] ;
    SHORT      xBlock, yBlock, x, y ;

    switch (msg)
        {
        case WM_CREATE:
            WinRegisterClass (hab, szChildClass, ChildWndProc,
                              CS_SIZEREDRAW, sizeof (USHORT)) ;

            for (x = 0 ; x < DIVISIONS ; x++)
                for (y = 0 ; y < DIVISIONS ; y++)

                    hwndChild [x][y] =
                        WinCreateWindow (
                                hwnd,          // Parent window
                                szChildClass,  // Window class
                                NULL,          // Window text
                                WS_VISIBLE,    // Window style
                                0, 0, 0, 0,    // Position & size
                                hwnd,          // Owner window
                                HWND_BOTTOM,   // Placement
                                y << 8 | x,    // Child window ID
                                NULL,          // Control data
                                NULL) ;        // Pres. Params
            return 0 ;

        case WM_SIZE:
            xBlock = SHORT1FROMMP (mp2) / DIVISIONS ;
            yBlock = SHORT2FROMMP (mp2) / DIVISIONS ;

            for (x = 0 ; x < DIVISIONS ; x++)
                for (y = 0 ; y < DIVISIONS ; y++)

                    WinSetWindowPos (hwndChild [x][y], NULL,
                        x * xBlock, y * yBlock, xBlock, yBlock,
                        SWP_MOVE | SWP_SIZE) ;
            return 0 ;

        case WM_BUTTON1DOWN:
        case WM_BUTTON1DBLCLK:
            WinAlarm (HWND_DESKTOP, WA_WARNING) ;
            break ;                            // do default processing
```

(continued)

Figure 9-6. The CHECKER3.C File. *continued*

```
              case WM_ERASEBACKGROUND:
                   return 1 ;
              }
        return WinDefWindowProc (hwnd, msg, mp1, mp2) ;
        }

MRESULT EXPENTRY ChildWndProc (HWND hwnd, USHORT msg, MPARAM mp1, MPARAM mp2)
     {
     HPS   hps ;
     RECTL rcl ;

     switch (msg)
          {
          case WM_CREATE:
               WinSetWindowUShort (hwnd, 0, 0) ;
               return 0 ;

          case WM_BUTTON1DOWN:
          case WM_BUTTON1DBLCLK:
               WinSetActiveWindow (HWND_DESKTOP, hwnd) ;
               WinSetWindowUShort (hwnd, 0, !WinQueryWindowUShort (hwnd, 0)) ;
               WinInvalidateRect (hwnd, NULL, FALSE) ;
               return 0 ;

          case WM_PAINT:
               hps = WinBeginPaint (hwnd, NULL, NULL) ;

               WinQueryWindowRect (hwnd, &rcl) ;

               WinDrawBorder (hps, &rcl, 1, 1, CLR_NEUTRAL, CLR_BACKGROUND,
                                   DB_STANDARD | DB_INTERIOR) ;

               if (WinQueryWindowUShort (hwnd, 0))
                   {
                   DrawLine (hps, rcl.xLeft,  rcl.yBottom,
                                  rcl.xRight, rcl.yTop) ;
                   DrawLine (hps, rcl.xLeft,  rcl.yTop,
                                  rcl.xRight, rcl.yBottom) ;
                   }
               WinEndPaint (hps) ;
               return 0 ;
          }
     return WinDefWindowProc (hwnd, msg, mp1, mp2) ;
     }
```

The CHECKER3.DEF File

```
;------------------------------------
; CHECKER3.DEF module definition file
;------------------------------------

NAME            CHECKER3  WINDOWAPI

DESCRIPTION     'Mouse Hit-Test Program No. 3 (C) Charles Petzold, 1988'
PROTMODE
HEAPSIZE        1024
STACKSIZE       8192
EXPORTS         ClientWndProc
                ChildWndProc
```

Figure 9-6. *The CHECKER3 program.*

While processing the WM_CREATE message, *ClientWndProc* registers another window class named ''Checker3.Child.'' Windows that are created based on the ''Checker3.Child'' class use the *ChildWndProc* window procedure for message processing. CHECKER3 then creates 25 child windows based on the ''Checker3.Child'' class:

```
for (x = 0 ; x < DIVISIONS ; x++)
    for (y = 0 ; y < DIVISIONS ; y++)

        hwndChild [x] [y] =
            WinCreateWindow (
                    hwnd,                 // Parent window
                    szChildClass,         // Window class
                    NULL,                 // Window text
                    WS_VISIBLE,           // Window style
                    0, 0, 0, 0,           // Position & size
                    hwnd,                 // Owner window
                    HWND_BOTTOM,          // Placement
                    y << 8 | x,           // Child window ID
                    NULL,                 // Control data
                    NULL) ;               // Pres. Params
```

You've seen *WinCreateWindow* before. I used it in the WELCOME4 program in Chapter 3 to create three child windows based on predefined window classes. CHECKER3 uses *WinCreateWindow* to create windows based on the ''Checker3.Child'' class.

In the *WinCreateWindow* function, the size and position parameters for these 25 child windows are all set to 0. The windows must be sized and positioned based on the size of CHECKER3's client window. The sizing and positioning occur during the WM_SIZE message:

```
case WM_SIZE:
    xBlock = SHORT1FROMMP (mp2) / DIVISIONS ;
    yBlock = SHORT2FROMMP (mp2) / DIVISIONS ;

    for (x = 0 ; x < DIVISIONS ; x++)
        for (y = 0 ; y < DIVISIONS ; y++)

            WinSetWindowPos (hwndChild [x] [y], NULL,
                x * xBlock, y * yBlock, xBlock, yBlock,
                SWP_MOVE | SWP_SIZE) ;
    return 0 ;
```

Each child window is set to one-fifth the height and one-fifth the width of CHECKER3's client window. Basically, instead of drawing 25 rectangles, CHECKER3 creates 25 child windows of the same size and position as the rectangles in CHECKER1 and CHECKER2. *ClientWndProc* doesn't do much else except call *WinAlarm* when it receives a WM_BUTTON1DOWN message. *ClientWndProc* receives this message only if the mouse is clicked in an area of the client window not covered by one of the children.

Messages to the 25 child windows are processed in *ChildWndProc*. When CHECKER3 registers the "Checker3.Child" window class, it reserves 2 bytes of additional space (the size of a USHORT) for each window created based on that class:

```
WinRegisterClass (hab, szChildClass, ChildWndProc,
            CS_SIZEREDRAW, sizeof (USHORT)) ;
```

ChildWndProc can access that USHORT by calling the *WinSetWindowUShort* and *WinQueryWindowUShort* functions. It uses the space to store the current state (X or no X) of the window. *ChildWndProc* initializes the reserved USHORT to 0 (meaning no X) when it receives a WM_CREATE message:

```
case WM_CREATE:
    WinSetWindowUShort (hwnd, 0, 0) ;
    return 0 ;
```

ChildWndProc actually receives 25 WM_CREATE messages, 1 for each of the 25 child windows. For each WM_CREATE message, the value of *hwnd* is different. A different reserved USHORT is initialized to 0 with each message.

Each of the 25 child windows also receives a WM_PAINT message. Each window paints itself. The logic is somewhat simpler than in CHECKER1 and CHECKER2 because the rectangle and the lines encompass the entire area of the child window. For example, to paint the rectangle around the window, the child need only obtain its window rectangle from *WinQuery-WindowRect* and use that RECT structure directly in *WinDrawBorder*:

```
WinQueryWindowRect (hwnd, &rcl) ;

WinDrawBorder (hps, &rcl, 1, 1, CLR_NEUTRAL, CLR_BACKGROUND,
               DB_STANDARD ¦ DB_INTERIOR) ;
```

The processing of the WM_BUTTON1DOWN message is also quite simple:

```
case WM_BUTTON1DOWN:
case WM_BUTTON1DBLCLK:
    WinSetActiveWindow (HWND_DESKTOP, hwnd) ;
    WinSetWindowUShort (hwnd, 0, !WinQueryWindowUShort (hwnd, 0)) ;
    WinInvalidateRect (hwnd, NULL, FALSE) ;
    return 0 ;
```

A particular child window receives a WM_BUTTON1DOWN message when the child is underneath the pointer when the button was clicked. The code here obtains the value stored in the reserved USHORT using *WinQuery-WindowUShort*, inverts it, and then stores it again using *WinSetWin-dowUShort*. The entire area of the child window is then invalidated to generate a WM_PAINT message for that child.

CHECKER3.C is longer than CHECKER1.C. My explanation of CHECKER3 is longer than my explanation of CHECKER1. Despite that, I claim that CHECKER3 is simpler than CHECKER1. The reason? There's no real hit-testing in this program. If the child gets hit with a mouse click, it changes the state of itself without even examining the pointer position. If the rect-angles in CHECKER1 were all different sizes, the hit-testing in that pro-gram would obviously be much more complex. But if the child windows in CHECKER3 were all different sizes, the logic in *ChildWndProc* wouldn't have to be changed at all.

Just as you use subroutines to modularize your programs, you can use child windows to modularize the area of the client window and simplify mouse message processing.

Tracking and Capturing

So far we've seen a program that processes WM_MOUSEMOVE messages and a series of three programs that process WM_BUTTON1DOWN messages. However, often you'll have to use a combination of mouse movement and mouse button messages. You begin an action when a button is pressed, follow the movement of the mouse around the window, and then finish up when the button is released. This is sometimes called "tracking" the mouse, and some complexities are involved.

Simple Mouse Tracking

The BLOKOUT1 program in Figure 9-7 uses simple mouse tracking logic.

The BLOKOUT1 File

```
#--------------------
# BLOKOUT1 make file
#--------------------

blokout1.obj : blokout1.c
    cl -c -G2sw -W3 blokout1.c

blokout1.exe : blokout1.obj blokout1.def
    link blokout1, /align:16, NUL, os2, blokout1
```

The BLOKOUT1.C File

```
/*------------------------------------------
    BLOKOUT1.C -- Mouse Button Demo Program
  ------------------------------------------*/

#define INCL_WIN
#define INCL_GPI
#include <os2.h>

MRESULT EXPENTRY ClientWndProc (HWND, USHORT, MPARAM, MPARAM) ;

int main (void)
```

(continued)

Figure 9-7. The BLOKOUT1.C File. *continued*

```
    {
    static CHAR  szClientClass [] = "BlokOut1" ;
    static ULONG flFrameFlags = FCF_TITLEBAR      | FCF_SYSMENU |
                                FCF_SIZEBORDER    | FCF_MINMAX |
                                FCF_SHELLPOSITION | FCF_TASKLIST ;

    HAB         hab ;
    HMQ         hmq ;
    HWND        hwndFrame, hwndClient ;
    QMSG        qmsg ;


    hab = WinInitialize (0) ;
    hmq = WinCreateMsgQueue (hab, 0) ;


    WinRegisterClass (hab, szClientClass, ClientWndProc, CS_SIZEREDRAW, 0) ;


    hwndFrame = WinCreateStdWindow (HWND_DESKTOP, WS_VISIBLE,
                                   &flFrameFlags, szClientClass, NULL,
                                   0L, NULL, 0, &hwndClient) ;


    WinSendMsg (hwndFrame, WM_SETICON,
                WinQuerySysPointer (HWND_DESKTOP, SPTR_APPICON, FALSE),
                NULL) ;


    while (WinGetMsg (hab, &qmsg, NULL, 0, 0))
        WinDispatchMsg (hab, &qmsg) ;


    WinDestroyWindow (hwndFrame) ;
    WinDestroyMsgQueue (hmq) ;
    WinTerminate (hab) ;
    return 0 ;
    }

VOID DrawBoxOutline (HWND hwnd, POINTL *pptlStart, POINTL *pptlEnd)
    {
    HPS hps ;


    hps = WinGetPS (hwnd) ;
    GpiSetMix (hps, FM_INVERT) ;


    GpiMove (hps, pptlStart) ;
    GpiBox (hps, DRO_OUTLINE, pptlEnd, 0L, 0L) ;
```

(continued)

Figure 9-7. The BLOKOUT1.C File. *continued*

```
    WinReleasePS (hps) ;
    }

MRESULT EXPENTRY ClientWndProc (HWND hwnd, USHORT msg, MPARAM mp1, MPARAM mp2)
    {
    static BOOL    fButtonDown, fValidBox ;
    static POINTL  ptlStart, ptlEnd, ptlBoxStart, ptlBoxEnd ;
    HPS            hps ;

    switch (msg)
        {
        case WM_BUTTON1DOWN:
            ptlStart.x = ptlEnd.x = MOUSEMSG(&msg)->x ;
            ptlStart.y = ptlEnd.y = MOUSEMSG(&msg)->y ;

            DrawBoxOutline (hwnd, &ptlStart, &ptlEnd) ;

            fButtonDown = TRUE ;
            break ;                    // do default processing

        case WM_MOUSEMOVE:
            if (fButtonDown)
                {
                DrawBoxOutline (hwnd, &ptlStart, &ptlEnd) ;

                ptlEnd.x = MOUSEMSG(&msg)->x ;
                ptlEnd.y = MOUSEMSG(&msg)->y ;

                DrawBoxOutline (hwnd, &ptlStart, &ptlEnd) ;
                }
            break ;                    // do default processing

        case WM_BUTTON1UP:
            if (fButtonDown)
                {
                DrawBoxOutline (hwnd, &ptlStart, &ptlEnd) ;

                ptlBoxStart = ptlStart ;
                ptlBoxEnd.x = MOUSEMSG(&msg)->x ;
                ptlBoxEnd.y = MOUSEMSG(&msg)->y ;

                fButtonDown = FALSE ;
                fValidBox = TRUE ;
                WinInvalidateRect (hwnd, NULL, FALSE) ;
                }
            return 0 ;
```

(continued)

Figure 9-7. The BLOKOUT1.C File. *continued*

```
        case WM_PAINT:
            hps = WinBeginPaint (hwnd, NULL, NULL) ;
            GpiErase (hps) ;

            if (fValidBox)
                {
                GpiMove (hps, &ptlBoxStart) ;
                GpiBox (hps, DRO_OUTLINEFILL, &ptlBoxEnd, 0L, 0L) ;
                }
            if (fButtonDown)
                {
                GpiSetMix (hps, FM_INVERT) ;

                GpiMove (hps, &ptlStart) ;
                GpiBox (hps, DRO_OUTLINE, &ptlEnd, 0L, 0L) ;
                }
            WinEndPaint (hps) ;
            return 0 ;
        }
    return WinDefWindowProc (hwnd, msg, mp1, mp2) ;
    }
```

The BLOKOUT1.DEF File

```
;----------------------------------------
; BLOKOUT1.DEF module definition file
;----------------------------------------

NAME            BLOKOUT1   WINDOWAPI

DESCRIPTION     'Mouse Button Demo Program (C) Charles Petzold, 1988'
PROTMODE
HEAPSIZE        1024
STACKSIZE       8192
EXPORTS         ClientWndProc
```

Figure 9-7. *The BLOKOUT1 program.*

You can use this program to block out a rectangular area within the client window. When you press button 1, BLOKOUT1 saves the pointer position and uses it as one corner of a rectangle. You then move the mouse with the button pressed. The current position of the pointer is the opposite corner of the rectangle. As you move the mouse, BLOKOUT1 displays the rectangle outline. When you release the mouse button, the program draws the filled rectangle.

Figure 9-8 shows one rectangle already drawn and another rectangle in progress.

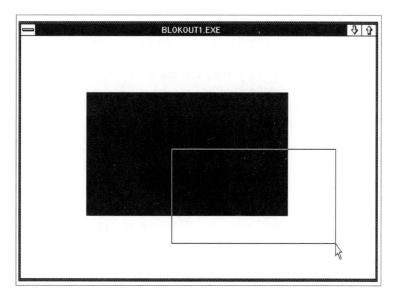

Figure 9-8. *The BLOKOUT1 display.*

When *ClientWndProc* receives a WM_BUTTON1DOWN message, it saves the position of the pointer in two static POINTL structures:

```
ptlStart.x = ptlEnd.x = MOUSEMSG(&msg) -> x ;
ptlStart.y = ptlEnd.y = MOUSEMSG(&msg) -> y ;
```

It then calls the function *DrawBoxOutline* to draw a rectangle using *GpiBox* with the FM_INVERT mix mode between these two points. (The rectangle will be only one pixel after this first call to *DrawBoxOutline*.) The *fButton-Down* variable is set to TRUE so that the program knows the button is down during subsequent messages.

The WM_MOUSEMOVE message is processed only if *fButtonDown* is TRUE. *DrawBoxOutline* is called again to erase the previous box, the new pointer position is stored in *ptlEnd*, and the new rectangle outline is drawn.

The WM_BUTTON1UP message is also processed only if *fButtonDown* is TRUE. *ClientWndProc* first erases the previous rectangle and then saves the two opposite corners in the POINTL structures *ptlBoxStart* and *ptlBoxEnd*. The *fButtonDown* variable is set to FALSE and the client window is invalidated. The WM_PAINT processing draws a filled rectangle based on these two points.

At first, nothing seems to be wrong with this program. But a problem does exist.

The Problem

Try this: What happens if you press the mouse button within BLOKOUT1's client window but then move the pointer outside the window? BLOKOUT1 will stop receiving the WM_MOUSEMOVE messages. Now you release the mouse button. BLOKOUT1 doesn't get that WM_BUTTON1UP message because the pointer is outside the client window.

Now move the mouse pointer back within BLOKOUT1's client window. *ClientWndProc* still thinks the mouse button is pressed because *fButtonDown* is set to TRUE! This is clearly not good. The program doesn't know what's going on.

An alternative is to dispense with the *fButtonDown* variable and use *WinGetKeyState* to test the state of the button during the WM_MOUSEMOVE message. But this is also a problem. What happens if you press the mouse button outside of BLOKOUT1's client window and then move the pointer inside? *WinGetKeyState* will report that the mouse button is pressed, but BLOKOUT1 will not have a valid starting point for the rectangle because the button was pressed outside the client window.

How about using a combination of the *fButtonDown* logic and the *WinGetKeyState* function? You're welcome to try, but think a bit about what you really want to do here. You want the ability to follow the mouse pointer even when it ventures outside the client window. You want to process *all* of the WM_MOUSEMOVE messages between WM_BUTTON1DOWN and WM_BUTTON1UP, regardless of whether the mouse is inside or outside the client window.

You can do this. It's called "capturing the mouse."

The Solution—Capturing the Mouse

Capturing the mouse is simpler than baiting a mousetrap. You simply call

```
WinSetCapture (HWND_DESKTOP, hwnd) ;
```

After you call *WinSetCapture*, all mouse messages will be directed to *hwnd*'s window procedure regardless of where the pointer is positioned.

(Note that the coordinates of the pointer will still be relative to the lower-left corner of the window, so they could be negative.) To release the mouse, use the following call:

```
WinSetCapture (HWND_DESKTOP, NULL) ;
```

A window that has captured the mouse is called the "capture window." Only one window can be the capture window at any time. You can obtain the window handle of the capture window by calling *WinQueryCapture*. The function returns NULL if there is no capture window, as is usually the case.

The BLOKOUT2 program, shown in Figure 9-9, demonstrates how to capture the mouse.

The BLOKOUT2 File

```
#-------------------
# BLOKOUT2 make file
#-------------------

blokout2.obj : blokout2.c
    cl -c -G2sw -W3 blokout2.c

blokout2.exe : blokout2.obj blokout2.def
    link blokout2, /align:16, NUL, os2, blokout2
```

The BLOKOUT2.C File

```
/*-----------------------------------------------------
    BLOKOUT2.C -- Mouse Button & Capture Demo Program
  -----------------------------------------------------*/

#define INCL_WIN
#define INCL_GPI
#include <os2.h>

MRESULT EXPENTRY ClientWndProc (HWND, USHORT, MPARAM, MPARAM) ;

int main (void)
    {
    static CHAR  szClientClass [] = "BlokOut2" ;
    static ULONG flFrameFlags = FCF_TITLEBAR       | FCF_SYSMENU |
                                FCF_SIZEBORDER     | FCF_MINMAX  |
                                FCF_SHELLPOSITION | FCF_TASKLIST ;
    HAB          hab ;
    HMQ          hmq ;
```

(continued)

Figure 9-9. The BLOKOUT2.C File. *continued*

```
        HWND        hwndFrame, hwndClient ;
        QMSG        qmsg ;

        hab = WinInitialize (0) ;
        hmq = WinCreateMsgQueue (hab, 0) ;

        WinRegisterClass (hab, szClientClass, ClientWndProc, CS_SIZEREDRAW, 0) ;

        hwndFrame = WinCreateStdWindow (HWND_DESKTOP, WS_VISIBLE,
                                    &flFrameFlags, szClientClass, NULL,
                                    OL, NULL, 0, &hwndClient) ;

        WinSendMsg (hwndFrame, WM_SETICON,
                    WinQuerySysPointer (HWND_DESKTOP, SPTR_APPICON, FALSE),
                    NULL) ;

        while (WinGetMsg (hab, &qmsg, NULL, 0, 0))
            WinDispatchMsg (hab, &qmsg) ;

        WinDestroyWindow (hwndFrame) ;
        WinDestroyMsgQueue (hmq) ;
        WinTerminate (hab) ;
        return 0 ;
        }

VOID DrawBoxOutline (HWND hwnd, POINTL *pptlStart, POINTL *pptlEnd)
        {
        HPS hps ;

        hps = WinGetPS (hwnd) ;
        GpiSetMix (hps, FM_INVERT) ;

        GpiMove (hps, pptlStart) ;
        GpiBox (hps, DRO_OUTLINE, pptlEnd, OL, OL) ;

        WinReleasePS (hps) ;
        }

MRESULT EXPENTRY ClientWndProc (HWND hwnd, USHORT msg, MPARAM mp1, MPARAM mp2)
        {
        static BOOL   fCapture, fValidBox ;
        static POINTL ptlStart, ptlEnd, ptlBoxStart, ptlBoxEnd ;
        HPS           hps ;

        switch (msg)
            {
```

(continued)

Figure 9-9. The BLOKOUT2.C File. *continued*

```
        case WM_BUTTON1DOWN:
             ptlStart.x = ptlEnd.x = MOUSEMSG(&msg)->x ;
             ptlStart.y = ptlEnd.y = MOUSEMSG(&msg)->y ;

             DrawBoxOutline (hwnd, &ptlStart, &ptlEnd) ;

             WinSetCapture (HWND_DESKTOP, hwnd) ;
             fCapture = TRUE ;
             break ;                        // do default processing

        case WM_MOUSEMOVE:
             if (fCapture)
                 {
                 DrawBoxOutline (hwnd, &ptlStart, &ptlEnd) ;

                 ptlEnd.x = MOUSEMSG(&msg)->x ;
                 ptlEnd.y = MOUSEMSG(&msg)->y ;

                 DrawBoxOutline (hwnd, &ptlStart, &ptlEnd) ;
                 }
             break ;                        // do default processing

        case WM_BUTTON1UP:
             if (fCapture)
                 {
                 DrawBoxOutline (hwnd, &ptlStart, &ptlEnd) ;

                 ptlBoxStart = ptlStart ;
                 ptlBoxEnd.x = MOUSEMSG(&msg)->x ;
                 ptlBoxEnd.y = MOUSEMSG(&msg)->y ;

                 WinSetCapture (HWND_DESKTOP, NULL) ;
                 fCapture = FALSE ;
                 fValidBox = TRUE ;
                 WinInvalidateRect (hwnd, NULL, FALSE) ;
                 }
             return 0 ;

        case WM_CHAR:
             if (fCapture && CHARMSG(&msg)->fs   &  KC_VIRTUALKEY &&
                         !(CHARMSG(&msg)->fs   &  KC_KEYUP)       &&
                         CHARMSG(&msg)->vkey == VK_ESC)
                 {
                 DrawBoxOutline (hwnd, &ptlStart, &ptlEnd) ;

                 WinSetCapture (HWND_DESKTOP, NULL) ;
```

(continued)

Figure 9-9. The BLOKOUT2.C File. *continued*

```
                    fCapture - FALSE ;
                }
            return 0 ;

        case WM_PAINT:
            hps = WinBeginPaint (hwnd, NULL, NULL) ;
            GpiErase (hps) ;

            if (fValidBox)
                {
                GpiMove (hps, &ptlBoxStart) ;
                GpiBox (hps, DRO_OUTLINEFILL, &ptlBoxEnd, 0L, 0L) ;
                }
            if (fCapture)
                {
                GpiSetMix (hps, FM_INVERT) ;
                GpiMove (hps, &ptlStart) ;
                GpiBox (hps, DRO_OUTLINE, &ptlEnd, 0L, 0L) ;
                }
            WinEndPaint (hps) ;
            return 0 ;
        }
    return WinDefWindowProc (hwnd, msg, mp1, mp2) ;
    }
```

The BLOKOUT2.DEF File

```
;-------------------------------------
; BLOKOUT2.DEF module definition file
;-------------------------------------

NAME            BLOKOUT2  WINDOWAPI

DESCRIPTION     'Mouse Button & Capture Demo Program (C) Charles Petzold, 1988'
PROTMODE
HEAPSIZE        1024
STACKSIZE       8192
EXPORTS         ClientWndProc
```

Figure 9-9. *The BLOKOUT2 program.*

BLOKOUT2 captures the mouse on a WM_BUTTON1DOWN message.
Rather than using the *fButtonDown* variable from BLOKOUT1, BLOKOUT2
uses an *fCapture* variable that it sets to TRUE when the mouse is captured.

If the size of the BLOKOUT2 window is less than the full screen, you'll notice that BLOKOUT2 continues to receive WM_MOUSEMOVE messages even when you move the pointer outside the client window. When you release the button (either while the pointer is inside or outside the client window), BLOKOUT2 releases the mouse.

BLOKOUT2 also processes the WM_CHAR message. If you press the Escape key while blocking out a rectangle, the program erases the rectangle you've been drawing and releases the mouse. This is how you can cancel the block-out. Otherwise, much of BLOKOUT2 is exactly the same as BLOKOUT1. Capturing the mouse adds very little overhead to mouse processing and helps out a lot in many cases.

The Presentation Manager *WinTrackRect* function is also a big help in jobs that require a rectangle to be stretched or moved using the mouse and keyboard, particularly when the rectangle must be displayed outside the program's window. The title bar window and sizing border window use *WinTrackRect* to let you move and resize the standard window. I'll show you how to use the *WinTrackRect* in the BLOWUP program in Chapter 15.

The SKETCH Program

You've heard of CAD programs? You've heard of paint programs? The program in Figure 9-10 is neither of these. It's called SKETCH and is just about the most primitive drawing program possible.

The SKETCH File

```
#-----------------
# SKETCH make file
#-----------------

sketch.obj : sketch.c
     cl -c -G2sw -W3 sketch.c

sketch.exe : sketch.obj sketch.def
     link sketch, /align:16, NUL, os2, sketch
```

The SKETCH.C File

```
/*------------------------------------------
   SKETCH.C -- Mouse Sketching Program
   ------------------------------------*/

#define INCL_WIN
```

(continued)

Figure 9-10. The SKETCH.C File. *continued*

```
#define INCL_GPI
#include <os2.h>

MRESULT EXPENTRY ClientWndProc (HWND, USHORT, MPARAM, MPARAM) ;

HAB  hab ;

int main (void)
    {
    static CHAR  szClientClass [] = "Sketch" ;
    static ULONG flFrameFlags = FCF_TITLEBAR      | FCF_SYSMENU  |
                                FCF_SIZEBORDER    | FCF_MINMAX   |
                                FCF_SHELLPOSITION | FCF_TASKLIST ;
    HMQ          hmq ;
    HWND         hwndFrame, hwndClient ;
    QMSG         qmsg ;

    hab = WinInitialize (0) ;
    hmq = WinCreateMsgQueue (hab, 0) ;

    WinRegisterClass (hab, szClientClass, ClientWndProc, CS_SIZEREDRAW, 0) ;

    hwndFrame = WinCreateStdWindow (HWND_DESKTOP, WS_VISIBLE,
                                    &flFrameFlags, szClientClass, NULL,
                                    0L, NULL, 0, &hwndClient) ;

    if (hwndFrame == NULL)
        WinMessageBox (HWND_DESKTOP, HWND_DESKTOP,
                       "Not enough memory to create the "
                       "bitmap used for storing images.",
                       szClientClass, 0, MB_OK | MB_ICONEXCLAMATION) ;
    else
        {
        WinSendMsg (hwndFrame, WM_SETICON,
                    WinQuerySysPointer (HWND_DESKTOP, SPTR_APPICON, FALSE),
                    NULL) ;

        while (WinGetMsg (hab, &qmsg, NULL, 0, 0))
            WinDispatchMsg (hab, &qmsg) ;

        WinDestroyWindow (hwndFrame) ;
        }

    WinDestroyMsgQueue (hmq) ;
    WinTerminate (hab) ;
    return 0 ;
    }
```

(continued)

Figure 9-10. The SKETCH.C File. *continued*

```
MRESULT EXPENTRY ClientWndProc (HWND hwnd, USHORT msg, MPARAM mp1, MPARAM mp2)
    {
    static BOOL       fButton1Down, fButton2Down ;
    static HBITMAP    hbm ;
    static HDC        hdcMemory ;
    static HPS        hpsMemory ;
    static POINTL     ptlPointerPos, aptl [3] ;
    BITMAPINFOHEADER  bmp ;
    HPS               hpsWindow ;
    LONG              cxFullScrn, cyFullScrn ;
    SIZEL             sizl ;

    switch (msg)
        {
        case WM_CREATE:
            cxFullScrn = WinQuerySysValue (HWND_DESKTOP, SV_CXFULLSCREEN) ;
            cyFullScrn = WinQuerySysValue (HWND_DESKTOP, SV_CYFULLSCREEN) ;


                        /*--------------------------
                          Create Memory DC and PS
                          --------------------------*/


            hdcMemory = DevOpenDC (hab, OD_MEMORY, "*", 0L, NULL, NULL) ;

            sizl.cx = 0 ;
            sizl.cy = 0 ;
            hpsMemory = GpiCreatePS (hab, hdcMemory, &sizl,
                                   PU_PELS    | GPIF_DEFAULT |
                                   GPIT_MICRO | GPIA_ASSOC) ;


                        /*------------------------------------------------
                          Create monochrome bitmap, return 1 if cannot
                          ----------------------------------------------*/


            bmp.cbFix     = sizeof bmp ;
            bmp.cx        = (SHORT) cxFullScrn ;
            bmp.cy        = (SHORT) cyFullScrn ;
            bmp.cPlanes   = 1 ;
            bmp.cBitCount = 1 ;
            hbm = GpiCreateBitmap (hpsMemory, &bmp, 0L, 0L, NULL) ;

            if (hbm == NULL)
                {
                GpiDestroyPS (hpsMemory) ;
                DevCloseDC (hdcMemory) ;
                return 1 ;
                }
```

(continued)

Figure 9-10. The SKETCH.C File. *continued*

```
                            /*---------------------------------------
                            Set bitmap in memory PS and clear it
                            ---------------------------------------*/

          GpiSetBitmap (hpsMemory, hbm) ;

          aptl[1].x = cxFullScrn ;
          aptl[1].y = cyFullScrn ;
          GpiBitBlt (hpsMemory, NULL, 2L, aptl, ROP_ZERO, BBO_OR) ;
          return 0 ;

     case WM_BUTTON1DOWN:
          if (!fButton2Down)
              WinSetCapture (HWND_DESKTOP, hwnd) ;

          ptlPointerPos.x = MOUSEMSG(&msg)->x ;
          ptlPointerPos.y = MOUSEMSG(&msg)->y ;

          fButton1Down = TRUE ;
          break ;                       // do default processing

     case WM_BUTTON1UP:
          if (!fButton2Down)
              WinSetCapture (HWND_DESKTOP, NULL) ;

          fButton1Down = FALSE ;
          return 0 ;

     case WM_BUTTON2DOWN:
          if (!fButton1Down)
              WinSetCapture (HWND_DESKTOP, hwnd) ;

          ptlPointerPos.x = MOUSEMSG(&msg)->x ;
          ptlPointerPos.y = MOUSEMSG(&msg)->y ;

          fButton2Down = TRUE ;
          break ;                       // do default processing

     case WM_BUTTON2UP:
          if (!fButton1Down)
              WinSetCapture (HWND_DESKTOP, NULL) ;
```

(continued)

Figure 9-10. The SKETCH.C File. *continued*

```
            fButton2Down = FALSE ;
            return 0 ;

    case WM_MOUSEMOVE:
            if (!fButton1Down && !fButton2Down)
                break ;

            hpsWindow = WinGetPS (hwnd) ;

            GpiSetColor (hpsMemory, fButton1Down ? CLR_TRUE : CLR_FALSE) ;
            GpiSetColor (hpsWindow,
                        fButton1Down ? CLR_NEUTRAL : CLR_BACKGROUND) ;

            GpiMove (hpsMemory, &ptlPointerPos) ;
            GpiMove (hpsWindow, &ptlPointerPos) ;

            ptlPointerPos.x = MOUSEMSG(&msg)->x ;
            ptlPointerPos.y = MOUSEMSG(&msg)->y ;

            GpiLine (hpsMemory, &ptlPointerPos) ;
            GpiLine (hpsWindow, &ptlPointerPos) ;

            WinReleasePS (hpsWindow) ;
            break ;                         // do default processing

    case WM_PAINT:
            hpsWindow = WinBeginPaint (hwnd, NULL, (PRECTL) aptl) ;

            aptl[2] = aptl[0] ;

            GpiBitBlt (hpsWindow, hpsMemory, 3L, aptl, ROP_SRCCOPY,
                        BBO_OR) ;

            WinEndPaint (hpsWindow) ;
            return 0 ;

    case WM_DESTROY:
            GpiDestroyPS (hpsMemory) ;
            DevCloseDC (hdcMemory) ;
            GpiDeleteBitmap (hbm) ;
            return 0 ;
    }
return WinDefWindowProc (hwnd, msg, mp1, mp2) ;
}
```

The SKETCH.DEF File

```
;-----------------------------------
; SKETCH.DEF module definition file
;-----------------------------------

NAME            SKETCH    WINDOWAPI

DESCRIPTION     'Mouse Sketching Program (C) Charles Petzold, 1988'
PROTMODE
HEAPSIZE        1024
STACKSIZE       8192
EXPORTS         ClientWndProc
```

Figure 9-10. *The SKETCH program.*

To draw in SKETCH, you press button 1 and move the mouse. To erase (or, more precisely, to draw in the background color) you press button 2 and move the mouse. To clear the entire window, you.... Well, you have to end the program, load it again, and start all over. (I said that this is a primitive program.) Figure 9-11 shows the SKETCH program with the word ''Hello'' drawn on the window, an homage to those early advertisements for the Apple Macintosh.

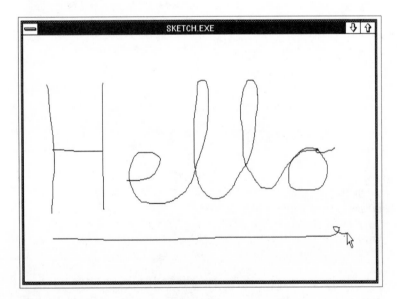

Figure 9-11. *The SKETCH display.*

During the WM_CREATE message, SKETCH creates a monochrome bitmap the size of the maximized window. If this is not possible, SKETCH returns 1 from the WM_CREATE message. Returning 1 from WM_CREATE causes the creation of the standard window to be aborted. In *main*, SKETCH checks the value of *hwndFrame* to see if *WinCreateStdWindow* was successful. If not, SKETCH displays a message box informing the user of the problem.

This bitmap is used in a memory device context for saving any drawing you do and updating the window during the WM_PAINT message. A bitmap used in this way is sometimes called a "shadow bitmap." Whenever SKETCH draws something on the window, it also draws the same thing on the bitmap. Consequently, WM_PAINT processing is very simple. All that's required is a *GpiBitBlt* call to update the window from the bitmap.

## CHAPTER TEN

SETTING THE TIMER

The Presentation Manager timer is a form of input that periodically notifies a window procedure when a specified amount of time has elapsed. Your program specifies this time in the *WinStartTimer* function. The Presentation Manager then periodically posts WM_TIMER messages to the program's window procedure.

A clock is the most obvious application for a timer. The WM_TIMER messages signal the program to update the clock display. (Later in this chapter we'll write two clock programs that use the timer.) You can also use the timer to periodically update a status report (as is done in the FREEMEM program also shown in this chapter) or to pace screen activity for animation or computer-aided instruction.

Why the Timer Is Necessary

In previous chapters you've seen how the Presentation Manager provides alternatives to several categories of OS/2 kernel functions. For example, a Presentation Manager program doesn't use the OS/2 kernel VIO functions to write to the display (unless, of course, the application uses the Advanced VIO facility). Instead, the program writes to the screen using the Presentation Manager GPI functions. Similarly, a Presentation Manager program doesn't use the OS/2 kernel KBD or MOU functions for keyboard or mouse input. Instead, the program processes keyboard and mouse input in the form of messages.

The Presentation Manager timer is also a substitute for OS/2 kernel functions — specifically those functions that involve suspending a thread of execution. For example, if you were to write a clock program for the OS/2 kernel, you would probably use the *DosSleep* function to suspend the thread for a set period of time. On return from *DosSleep*, the program updates the clock and calls *DosSleep* again. But in a single-thread Presentation Manager program, *DosSleep* would suspend the normal processing of messages in that thread—even messages for such basic tasks as moving and resizing the window or selecting an item from the program's system menu. It's clear that for the Presentation Manager, which requires threads to process messages as quickly as possible (window procedures should take no longer than one-tenth of a second to process a message), you shouldn't call functions such as *DosSleep* or *DosSemSetWait* in a message queue thread if you want optimum performance. That's why the Presentation Manager includes the timer. Message queue threads use the timer to regain periodic control in the absence of user input and other messages to the thread's windows. Chapter 17 discusses some alternatives to this use of the timer, including the use of multiple threads of execution.

Timer Basics

The timer is a fairly simple facility involving two functions and one message. The Presentation Manager defines two ways to set a timer. Both use the same *WinStartTimer* function but in a somewhat different format. The first method is by far the most common.

The Common Method of Using a Timer

The BEEPER1 program, shown in Figure 10-1, shows how to start a timer, process WM_TIMER messages, and stop the timer. BEEPER1 sets the timer to go off once every second. The window procedure responds to a WM_TIMER message by beeping and changing the color of its client window, alternating between red and blue.

The BEEPER1 File

```
#-------------------
# BEEPER1 make file
#-------------------

beeper1.obj : beeper1.c
    cl -c -G2sw -W3 beeper1.c

beeper1.exe : beeper1.obj beeper1.def
    link beeper1, /align:16, NUL, os2, beeper1
```

The BEEPER1.C File

```
/*--------------------------------------------
   BEEPER1.C -- Timer Demo Program No. 1
--------------------------------------------*/

#define INCL_WIN
#include <os2.h>

#define ID_TIMER 1

MRESULT EXPENTRY ClientWndProc (HWND, USHORT, MPARAM, MPARAM) ;

int main (void)
    {
    static char  szClientClass [] = "Beeper1" ;
    static ULONG flFrameFlags = FCF_TITLEBAR      | FCF_SYSMENU |
                                FCF_SIZEBORDER    | FCF_MINMAX  |
                                FCF_SHELLPOSITION | FCF_TASKLIST ;
    HAB          hab ;
    HMQ          hmq ;
    HWND         hwndFrame, hwndClient ;
    QMSG         qmsg ;

    hab = WinInitialize (0) ;
    hmq = WinCreateMsgQueue (hab, 0) ;

    WinRegisterClass (hab, szClientClass, ClientWndProc, OL, 0) ;

    hwndFrame = WinCreateStdWindow (HWND_DESKTOP, WS_VISIBLE,
                                    &flFrameFlags, szClientClass, NULL,
                                    OL, NULL, 0, &hwndClient) ;

    WinStartTimer (hab, hwndClient, ID_TIMER, 1000) ;

    while (WinGetMsg (hab, &qmsg, NULL, 0, 0))
        WinDispatchMsg (hab, &qmsg) ;

    WinStopTimer (hab, hwndClient, ID_TIMER) ;

    WinDestroyWindow (hwndFrame) ;
    WinDestroyMsgQueue (hmq) ;
    WinTerminate (hab) ;
    return 0 ;
    }
```

(continued)

Figure 10-1. The BEEPER1.C File. *continued*

```
MRESULT EXPENTRY ClientWndProc (HWND hwnd, USHORT msg, MPARAM mp1, MPARAM mp2)
    {
    static BOOL fFlipFlop ;
    HPS         hps ;
    RECTL       rcl ;

    switch (msg)
        {
        case WM_TIMER:
            WinAlarm (HWND_DESKTOP, WA_NOTE) ;
            fFlipFlop = !fFlipFlop ;
            WinInvalidateRect (hwnd, NULL, FALSE) ;
            return 0 ;

        case WM_PAINT:
            hps = WinBeginPaint (hwnd, NULL, NULL) ;

            WinQueryWindowRect (hwnd, &rcl) ;
            WinFillRect (hps, &rcl, fFlipFlop ? CLR_BLUE : CLR_RED) ;

            WinEndPaint (hps) ;
            return 0 ;
        }
    return WinDefWindowProc (hwnd, msg, mp1, mp2) ;
    }
```

The BEEPER1.DEF File

```
;-------------------------------------
; BEEPER1.DEF module definition file
;-------------------------------------

NAME            BEEPER1     WINDOWAPI

DESCRIPTION     'Timer Demo Program No. 1 (C) Charles Petzold, 1988'
PROTMODE
HEAPSIZE        1024
STACKSIZE       8192
EXPORTS         ClientWndProc
```

Figure 10-1. *The BEEPER1 program.*

The general syntax of the *WinStartTimer* function is

```
WinStartTimer (hab, hwnd, idTimer, usMsecInterval) ;
```

The *hwnd* parameter is the window handle that designates which window function receives the WM_TIMER messages. The *idTimer* parameter is a number you select to identify this particular timer. The *usMsecInterval* parameter specifies a time interval in milliseconds (msec). This is the rate at which the Presentation Manager posts the WM_TIMER messages in the message queue. The value can range from 0 (which delivers WM_TIMER messages as fast as the computer's hardware clock) to 65,535 msec, or a little more than a minute.

BEEPER1 starts a timer in *main* immediately following the *WinCreateStdWindow* call:

```
WinStartTimer (hab, hwndClient, ID_TIMER, 1000) ;
```

This tells the Presentation Manager to post a WM_TIMER message to *hwndClient* once every 1000 msec. The ID_TIMER identifier is defined near the top of the program:

```
#define ID_TIMER 1
```

The low USHORT of the *mp1* parameter that accompanies the WM_TIMER message is this ID number.

BEEPER1 processes the WM_TIMER messages in *ClientWndProc*:

```
case WM_TIMER:
    WinAlarm (HWND_DESKTOP, WA_NOTE) ;
    fFlipFlop = !fFlipFlop ;
    WinInvalidateRect (hwnd, NULL, FALSE) ;
    return 0 ;
```

The code simply beeps the speaker, inverts the value of the static BOOL variable *fFlipFlop*, and calls *WinInvalidateRect* to invalidate the entire client window and generate a WM_PAINT message. During the WM_PAINT message, BEEPER1 uses the *fFlipFlop* variable to determine the color (blue or red) used to paint the client window:

```
WinQueryWindowRect (hwnd, &rcl) ;
WinFillRect (hps, &rcl, fFlipFlop ? CLR_BLUE: CLR_RED) ;
```

The window procedure receives WM_TIMER messages during the entire time the window exists. Only when BEEPER1 exits the message queue in *main* on receipt of a WM_QUIT message does the program stop the timer:

```
WinStopTimer (hab, hwndClient, ID_TIMER) ;
```

BEEPER1 then terminates normally.

A program doesn't need to start and stop the timer in *main.* If the program doesn't need a timer for the entire duration of the program, it can start or stop the timer from the window procedure. Although BEEPER1 causes its client window to be repainted once a second by calling *WinInvalidateRect*, a program can also call *WinGetPS* to do some painting while processing the WM_TIMER message. The CLOCK program shown later in this chapter paints during the WM_TIMER message.

Timer Imprecision

If you can tolerate the program's incessant beeping, you can learn a lot about the timer by experimenting with BEEPER1 while running other Presentation Manager programs. The first discovery is that the timer is not a precise and regular clock tick. There are several reasons for this.

The resolution of the timer depends on the resolution of the hardware clock in the computer. Under 0S/2, the hardware clock generates an interrupt every 31.25 msec, or 32 times per second. The rate of the WM_TIMER messages on a PC is always an integral multiple of 32 msec. You can't receive WM_TIMER messages more frequently than 32 msec.

The WM_TIMER message isn't sent directly to the window procedure but is instead placed in the program's message queue. (Actually, the Presentation Manager handles WM_TIMER messages a little differently than it does other queued messages: WM_TIMER messages are not actually placed in the queue. Programs needn't worry about this, however.) WM_TIMER messages are low priority—*WinGetMsg* retrieves other queued messages (except WM_PAINT) before WM_TIMER messages. There can be a delay between the time the message is placed in the queue and the time the window procedure gets it. However, the Presentation Manager doesn't load a message queue with multiple WM_TIMER messages if the program can't process them. The message queue never contains more than one timer message of a particular timer ID.

Limited Availability of Timers

The Presentation Manager allows only a limited number of timers to be set throughout the system. (The initial release of the Presentation Manager is limited to 40 timers.) A program can determine how many timers are still available in the Presentation Manager by calling

```
lAvailTimers = WinQuerySysValue (HWND_DESKTOP, SV_CTIMERS) ;
```

However, it's often easier to simply call *WinStartTimer*. If *WinStartTimer* returns 0, then no timer was available.

If your program can't work properly without a timer (as is obviously the case for a clock application), then the program has no choice but to terminate if no timer is available. You should display a message box informing the user of this problem. If you set the timer in *main* after the *WinCreateStd-Window* call, here is one way of dealing with the lack of an available timer:

```
hwndFrame = WinCreateStdWindow (...) ;

if (WinStartTimer (hab, hwndClient, ID_TIMER, 1000))
    {
    while (WinGetMsg (hab, &qmsg, NULL, 0, 0))
        WinDispatchMsg (hab, &qmsg) ;

    WinStopTimer (hab, hwndClient, ID_TIMER) ;
    }
else
    WinMessageBox (HWND_DESKTOP, hwndClient,
                "Too many clocks or timers",
                "Program Name", 0, MB_OK | MB_ICONEXCLAMATION) ;

WinDestroyWindow (hwndFrame) ;
```

If *WinStartTimer* returns a nonzero value, the program enters the message loop and later calls *WinStopTimer* when it exits the message loop. Otherwise, the program displays a message box, destroys the frame window, and terminates normally. You should perform this check in every program you write that uses a timer.

A One-Shot Timer

In some applications you may not need a timer that repeatedly sends WM_TIMER messages. Instead, you may want to send only one WM_TIMER message after a specified period of time. In this case you can set the timer normally and call *WinStopTimer* during processing of the WM_TIMER message:

```
case WM_TIMER:
        [other program lines]
    WinStopTimer (hab, hwnd, ID_TIMER) ;
    return 0 ;
```

Calling *WinStopTimer* not only stops future WM_TIMER messages but also clears the message queue of any pending WM_TIMER messages. You'll never receive a stray WM_TIMER message after you call *WinStopTimer*.

A Timer Over 65$^1/_2$ Seconds

The maximum timer interval is 65,535 msec, or 65½ seconds. If you need a timer interval greater than this (for example, 30 minutes), you can first set a static variable that contains the duration in minutes:

```
usMinuteWait = 30 ;
```

You then set a timer for 1 minute:

```
WinStartTimer (hab, hwnd, ID_TIMER, 60000) ;
```

During WM_TIMER processing you decrement and test *usMinuteWait*:

```
case WM_TIMER:
    if (--usMinuteWait == 0)
        {
            [other program lines]
        }
    return 0 ;
```

An alternative method is to call *DosGetDateTime* to get the current time when you first start the timer. During the WM_TIMER message you can call *DosGetDateTime* again to determine if 30 minutes have elapsed.

The *WinGetCurrentTime* function can also be helpful here. This function returns the elapsed time in milliseconds since OS/2 was first booted. This is a ULONG value that rolls over to 0 every 49 days. Let's assume again that you want to set a 30-minute timer interval. First, define a static ULONG variable:

```
static ULONG ulStartTime ;
```

Then call *WinGetCurrentTime* and *WinStartTimer*:

```
ulStartTime = WinGetCurrentTime (hab) ;
WinStartTimer (hab, hwnd, ID_TIMER, 60000) ;
```

During the WM_TIMER message, check to see if 30 minutes have elapsed:

```
case WM_TIMER:
     if (WinGetCurrentTime (hab) - ulStartTime > 30 * 60 * 1000)
         {
              [other program lines]
         }
     return 0 ;
```

Resetting the Timer Time

You may need to change the interval of the WM_TIMER messages. For example, you may have originally set the timer for one-second intervals:

```
WinStartTimer (hab, hwnd, ID_TIMER, 1000) ;
```

If you later need to change that to five-second intervals, you can simply call *WinStartTimer* again with the same timer ID and a different elapsed time:

```
WinStartTimer (hab, hwnd, ID_TIMER, 5000) ;
```

Using Multiple Timers

If you want, you can set multiple timers in your program. Suppose you want one timer for one-second intervals and another timer for one-minute intervals. You first define two IDs:

```
#define ID_SECTIMER 1
#define ID_MINTIMER 2
```

To start the timers, make two *WinStartTimer* calls:

```
WinStartTimer (hab, hwnd, ID_SECTIMER, 1000) ;
WinStartTimer (hab, hwnd, ID_MINTIMER, 60000) ;
```

The processing of the WM_TIMER message can use a *switch* and *case* construction to do different processing based on the timer ID stored in *mp1*:

```
case WM_TIMER:
    switch (SHORT1FROMMP (mp1))
        {
        case ID_SECTIMER:
                    [once-per-second processing]
            return 0 ;

        case ID_MINTIMER:
                    [once-per-minute processing]
            return 0 ;
        }
    break ;
```

Before your program terminates, it stops both timers:

```
WinStopTimer (hab, hwnd, ID_SECTIMER) ;
WinStopTimer (hab, hwnd, ID_MINTIMER) ;
```

But considering that the Presentation Manager makes available only a limited number of timers, you should feel a little guilty about hogging system resources like this. A better approach is to set only one timer (the one with the shortest interval) and then derive longer intervals from that.

The Timers You Don't Set

Even if you never call *WinStartTimer* in your program, WM_TIMER messages may still be posted through your message queue and even dispatched to your client window procedure. Sometimes you need to make special provisions for these messages.

You'll recall that the TYPEAWAY program in Chapter 8 creates a blinking cursor. The blink is controlled by a timer. Because the client window procedure in TYPEAWAY doesn't explicitly process WM_TIMER messages, the messages are passed on to *WinDefWindowProc*. That's where the cursor-blinking logic is. If you add the following lines to TYPEAWAY's client window procedure, the cursor won't blink:

```
case WM_TIMER:
    return 0 ;
```

Child window scroll bars and edit fields (discussed in Chapters 11 and 14) also use the timer to blink their cursors. If you create a scroll bar or edit window, the WM_TIMER messages come through the program's message queue but are dispatched to the window procedure associated with the child window.

If you set a timer in a program that also creates a blinking cursor, you should process only those WM_TIMER messages with the ID number you use (for example, ID_TIMER). All other WM_TIMER messages should be passed on to *WinDefWindowProc*. The logic looks like this:

```
case WM_TIMER:
    if (SHORT1FROMMP (mp1) == ID_TIMER)
        {
            [process timer message]
        return 0 ;
        }
    break ;
```

If you set multiple timers, you can use *switch* and *case* statements and *break* for the *default* case.

The IDs for the cursor, scroll bar, and flashing window timers are defined in PMWIN.H using the identifiers TID_CURSOR, TID_SCROLL, and TID_FLASHWINDOW. These are set equal to 0xFFFF, 0xFFFE, and 0xFFFD, so you should avoid using those IDs for any other timers.

The Uncommon Method of Using a Timer

The examples in all of the preceding sections of this chapter use the following form of the *WinStartTimer* call:

```
WinStartTimer (hab, hwnd, idTimer, usMsecInterval) ;
```

where *idTimer* is a predefined constant.

The second form of the *WinStartTimer* function requires that you first define a variable to store the timer ID:

```
USHORT idTimer ;
```

You then call the *WinStartTimer* function like this:

```
idTimer = WinStartTimer (hab, NULL, 0, usMsecInterval) ;
```

The second parameter (normally set to the window handle) is set to NULL in this form of *WinStartTimer*. The Presentation Manager ignores the third parameter and instead returns a timer ID (or 0 if no timer was available) from the function. You use this ID when stopping the timer:

```
WinStopTimer (hab, NULL, idTimer) ;
```

This form of *WinStartMessage* requires that the WM_TIMER message be handled in a special way. Although the message is posted to the message queue associated with the thread, the window handle of the message is set to NULL. This means that the message won't be dispatched to a window procedure. Instead, it must be processed immediately after it is retrieved from the message queue. The BEEPER2 program, shown in Figure 10-2, shows how this is done.

The BEEPER2 File

```
#-------------------
# BEEPER2 make file
#-------------------

beeper2.obj : beeper2.c
    cl -c -G2sw -W3 beeper2.c

beeper2.exe : beeper2.obj beeper2.def
    link beeper2, /align:16, NUL, os2, beeper2
```

The BEEPER2.C File

```
/*-----------------------------------------
   BEEPER2.C -- Timer Demo Program No. 2
------------------------------------------*/

#define INCL_WIN
#include <os2.h>

MRESULT EXPENTRY ClientWndProc (HWND, USHORT, MPARAM, MPARAM) ;

BOOL fFlipFlop ;
```

(continued)

Figure 10-2. The BEEPER2.C File. *continued*

```
int main (void)
    {
    static char  szClientClass [] = "Beeper2" ;
    static ULONG flFrameFlags = FCF_TITLEBAR      | FCF_SYSMENU |
                                FCF_SIZEBORDER    | FCF_MINMAX  |
                                FCF_SHELLPOSITION | FCF_TASKLIST ;
    HAB          hab ;
    HMQ          hmq ;
    HWND         hwndFrame, hwndClient ;
    QMSG         qmsg ;
    USHORT       idTimer ;

    hab = WinInitialize (0) ;
    hmq = WinCreateMsgQueue (hab, 0) ;

    WinRegisterClass (hab, szClientClass, ClientWndProc, CS_SIZEREDRAW, 0) ;

    hwndFrame = WinCreateStdWindow (HWND_DESKTOP, WS_VISIBLE,
                                    &flFrameFlags, szClientClass, NULL,
                                    OL, NULL, 0, &hwndClient) ;

    idTimer = WinStartTimer (hab, NULL, 0, 1000) ;

    while (WinGetMsg (hab, &qmsg, NULL, 0, 0))
        {
        if (qmsg.msg == WM_TIMER && SHORT1FROMMP (qmsg.mp1) == idTimer)
            {
            WinAlarm (HWND_DESKTOP, WA_NOTE) ;
            fFlipFlop = !fFlipFlop ;
            WinInvalidateRect (hwndClient, NULL, FALSE) ;
            }
        else
            WinDispatchMsg (hab, &qmsg) ;
        }

    WinStopTimer (hab, NULL, idTimer) ;

    WinDestroyWindow (hwndFrame) ;
    WinDestroyMsgQueue (hmq) ;
    WinTerminate (hab) ;
    return 0 ;
    }
```

(continued)

Figure 10-2. The BEEPER2.C File. *continued*

```
MRESULT EXPENTRY ClientWndProc (HWND hwnd, USHORT msg, MPARAM mp1, MPARAM mp2)
    {
    HPS   hps ;
    RECTL rcl ;

    switch (msg)
        {
        case WM_PAINT:
             hps = WinBeginPaint (hwnd, NULL, NULL) ;

             WinQueryWindowRect (hwnd, &rcl) ;
             WinFillRect (hps, &rcl, fFlipFlop ? CLR_BLUE : CLR_RED) ;

             WinEndPaint (hps) ;
             return 0 ;
        }
    return WinDefWindowProc (hwnd, msg, mp1, mp2) ;
    }
```

The BEEPER2.DEF File

```
;------------------------------------
; BEEPER2.DEF module definition file
;------------------------------------


NAME            BEEPER2    WINDOWAPI

DESCRIPTION     'Timer Demo Program No. 2 (C) Charles Petzold, 1988'
PROTMODE
HEAPSIZE        1024
STACKSIZE       8192
EXPORTS         ClientWndProc
```

Figure 10-2. *The BEEPER2 program.*

BEEPER2 doesn't process the WM_TIMER message in its client window
procedure but instead has the timer logic within the message loop, as shown
on the next page.

```
while (WinGetMsg (hab, &qmsg, NULL, 0, 0))
    {
    if (qmsg.msg == WM_TIMER && SHORT1FROMMP (qmsg.mp1) == idTimer)
        {
        WinAlarm (HWND_DESKTOP, WA_NOTE) ;
        fFlipFlop = !fFlipFlop ;
        WinInvalidateRect (hwndClient, NULL, FALSE) ;
        }
    else
        WinDispatchMsg (hab, &qmsg) ;
    }
```

BEEPER2 checks to see if the *msg* field of the QMSG structure is equal to WM_TIMER and if the low USHORT of the *mp1* parameter is equal to the timer ID returned from *WinStartTimer*. If the check is successful, BEEPER2 proceeds like BEEPER1 when it received a WM_TIMER message. If not, BEEPER2 dispatches the message to the window procedure. This form of the *WinStartTimer* function might be appropriate for a program that creates several threads of execution and needs a timer in a thread that doesn't create any windows.

If you move or resize BEEPER2's window, or invoke the system menu, you'll notice that the WM_TIMER messages seemingly stop. These operations involve the use of a different message loop than the one in your program, so any WM_TIMER message in the queue is ignored.

Three Timer Programs

Now let's put what we've learned into practice by writing three useful programs—a free memory display and two clocks (one digital, one analog).

A Free Memory Display

The FREEMEM program, shown in Figure 10-3 on the following pages, is the Presentation Manager version of a program that I originally wrote for Microsoft Windows (*Programming Windows,* Microsoft Press, 1988). Some Windows programmers have found FREEMEM useful as a simple debugging aid. The program creates a tiny window and positions it at the lower-left corner of the display. The window displays, in bytes, the amount of free memory in OS/2. The display is updated every second—that's where the timer helps out.

The FREEMEM File

```
#-------------------
# FREEMEM make file
#-------------------

freemem.obj : freemem.c
    cl -c -G2sw -W3 freemem.c

freemem.exe : freemem.obj freemem.def
    link freemem, /align:16, NUL, os2, freemem
```

The FREEMEM.C File

```c
/*-----------------------------------
   FREEMEM.C -- Free Memory Display
   ---------------------------------*/

#define INCL_WIN
#define INCL_GPI
#define INCL_DOS
#include <os2.h>
#include <string.h>

#define ID_TIMER 1

MRESULT EXPENTRY ClientWndProc (HWND, USHORT, MPARAM, MPARAM) ;
VOID    SizeTheWindow (HWND) ;

int main (void)
    {
    static CHAR  szClientClass[] = "FreeMem" ;
    static ULONG flFrameFlags = FCF_TITLEBAR | FCF_SYSMENU |
                                FCF_BORDER   | FCF_TASKLIST ;

    HAB          hab ;
    HMQ          hmq ;
    HWND         hwndFrame, hwndClient ;
    QMSG         qmsg ;

    hab = WinInitialize (0) ;
    hmq = WinCreateMsgQueue (hab, 0) ;

    WinRegisterClass (hab, szClientClass, ClientWndProc, OL, 0) ;
```

(continued)

Figure 10-3. The FREEMEM.C File. *continued*

```
    hwndFrame = WinCreateStdWindow (HWND_DESKTOP, WS_VISIBLE,
                                    &flFrameFlags, szClientClass, NULL,
                                    OL, NULL, 0, &hwndClient) ;

    SizeTheWindow (hwndFrame) ;

    if (WinStartTimer (hab, hwndClient, ID_TIMER, 1000))
        {
        while (WinGetMsg (hab, &qmsg, NULL, 0, 0))
            WinDispatchMsg (hab, &qmsg) ;

        WinStopTimer (hab, hwndClient, ID_TIMER) ;
        }
    else
        WinMessageBox (HWND_DESKTOP, hwndClient,
                       "Too many clocks or timers",
                       szClientClass, 0, MB_OK | MB_ICONEXCLAMATION) ;

    WinDestroyWindow (hwndFrame) ;
    WinDestroyMsgQueue (hmq) ;
    WinTerminate (hab) ;
    return 0 ;
    }

VOID SizeTheWindow (HWND hwndFrame)
    {
    static CHAR szText [] = "1,234,567,890 bytes" ;
    HPS         hps ;
    POINTL      aptl[TXTBOX_COUNT] ;
    RECTL       rcl ;

    hps = WinGetPS (hwndFrame) ;
    GpiQueryTextBox (hps, sizeof szText - 1L, szText, TXTBOX_COUNT, aptl) ;
    WinReleasePS (hps) ;

    rcl.yBottom = 0 ;
    rcl.yTop    = 3 * (aptl[TXTBOX_TOPLEFT].y -
                       aptl[TXTBOX_BOTTOMLEFT].y) / 2 ;
    rcl.xLeft   = 0 ;
    rcl.xRight  = (sizeof szText + 1L) * (aptl[TXTBOX_BOTTOMRIGHT].x -
                   aptl[TXTBOX_BOTTOMLEFT].x) / (sizeof szText - 1L) ;

    WinCalcFrameRect (hwndFrame, &rcl, FALSE) ;
```

(continued)

Figure 10-3. The FREEMEM.C File. *continued*

```
        WinSetWindowPos (hwndFrame, NULL, (SHORT) rcl.xLeft, (SHORT) rcl.yBottom,
                         (SHORT) (rcl.xRight - rcl.xLeft),
                         (SHORT) (rcl.yTop - rcl.yBottom), SWP_SIZE | SWP_MOVE) ;
        }

VOID FormatNumber (CHAR *pchResult, ULONG ulValue)
        {
        BOOL  fDisplay = FALSE ;
        SHORT sDigit ;
        ULONG ulQuotient, ulDivisor = 1000000000L ;

        for (sDigit = 0 ; sDigit < 10 ; sDigit++)
            {
            ulQuotient = ulValue / ulDivisor ;

            if (fDisplay || ulQuotient > 0 || sDigit == 9)
                {
                fDisplay = TRUE ;

                *pchResult++ = (CHAR) ('0' + ulQuotient) ;

                if ((sDigit % 3 == 0) && sDigit != 9)
                    *pchResult++ = ',' ;
                }
            ulValue -= ulQuotient * ulDivisor ;
            ulDivisor /= 10 ;
            }
        *pchResult = '\0' ;
        }

MRESULT EXPENTRY ClientWndProc (HWND hwnd, USHORT msg, MPARAM mp1, MPARAM mp2)
        {
        static RECTL rcl ;
        static ULONG ulFreeMem, ulPrevMem ;
        CHAR         szBuffer [24] ;
        HPS          hps;

        switch (msg)
            {
            case WM_SIZE:
                WinQueryWindowRect (hwnd, &rcl) ;
                return 0 ;

            case WM_TIMER:
                DosMemAvail (&ulFreeMem) ;
```

(continued)

Figure 10-3. The FREEMEM.C File. *continued*

```
                    if (ulFreeMem != ulPrevMem)
                        {
                        WinInvalidateRect (hwnd, NULL, FALSE) ;
                        ulPrevMem = ulFreeMem ;
                        }
                    return 0 ;

            case WM_PAINT:
                    hps = WinBeginPaint (hwnd, NULL, NULL) ;

                    FormatNumber (szBuffer, ulFreeMem) ;
                    strcat (szBuffer, " bytes") ;

                    WinDrawText (hps, -1, szBuffer, &rcl,
                                CLR_NEUTRAL, CLR_BACKGROUND,
                                DT_CENTER | DT_VCENTER | DT_ERASERECT) ;

                    WinEndPaint (hps) ;
                    return 0 ;
            }
        return WinDefWindowProc (hwnd, msg, mp1, mp2) ;
    }
```

The FREEMEM.DEF File

```
;-------------------------------------
; FREEMEM.DEF module definition file
;-------------------------------------

NAME            FREEMEM   WINDOWAPI

DESCRIPTION     'Free Memory Display (C) Charles Petzold, 1988'
PROTMODE
HEAPSIZE        1024
STACKSIZE       8192
EXPORTS         ClientWndProc
```

Figure 10-3. *The FREEMEM program.*

FREEMEM starts the timer in *main* and displays a message box if *WinStart-Timer* returns 0. The processing of the WM_TIMER message in *Client-WndProc* is simple, as shown on the next page.

```
case WM_TIMER:
    DosMemAvail (&ulFreeMem) ;

    if (ulFreeMem != ulPrevMem)
        {
        WinInvalidateRect (hwnd, NULL, FALSE) ;
        ulPrevMem = ulFreeMem ;
        }
    return 0 ;
```

DosMemAvail is an OS/2 kernel function that returns the size of the largest contiguous block of free memory, which isn't necessarily the same as total free memory. For example, if you specify that the DOS compatibility box is less than 640 KB (or if you run a protected mode–only session), the lower 640 KB of memory won't be included in the value reported by *DosMem-Avail*, because that memory isn't contiguous with memory above 1 MB. Nor will *DosMemAvail* show memory that could become available by swapping or discarding memory segments or by compacting free memory.

FREEMEM saves the previous free memory size in *ulPrevMem*. Only if that size differs from the current value returned from *DosMemAvail* will FREEMEM invalidate the window to generate a WM_PAINT message. The WM_PAINT processing calls the function *FormatNumber* to convert the memory size into a text string with comma separators.

FREEMEM creates a window of a fixed size positioned in a set area of the display, so it is worthwhile to take a closer look at how this is done. The *WinCreateStdWindow* function in FREEMEM uses frame creation flags of FCF_TITLEBAR, FCF_SYSMENU, FCF_BORDER, and FCF_TASKLIST. The FCF_SIZEBORDER, FCF_MINMAX, and FCF_SHELLPOSITION flags are not used.

Because the window doesn't contain the minimize/maximize menu, the Minimize and Maximize options on the system menu are grayed and disabled.

A program that does not use the the FCF_SHELLPOSITION flag when creating the standard window must call *WinSetWindowPos* to give the frame window a size and position. This is done in FREEMEM's *SizeTheWindow* function. Because the size of the client window must be based on the size of the text string it displays, the function first calls *GpiQueryTextBox* for a maximum possible string length. *SizeTheWindow* then defines the screen coordinates of a RECTL structure that contains the position and size of this client window.

The positioning of the client window at the lower-left corner of the screen is indicated by the *yBottom* and *xLeft* fields. To allow a little margin around the text, the client window rectangle is set to 1½ times the height of the text box with a width sufficient for the string plus a slight margin.

That RECTL structure is the position and size of the client window. The *WinCalcFrameRect* function converts this rectangle to a frame window position and size:

```
WinCalcFrameRect (hwndFrame, &rcl, FALSE) ;
```

SizeTheWindow can then set the position and size of the frame window:

```
WinSetWindowPos (hwndFrame, NULL, (SHORT) rcl.xLeft, (SHORT) rcl.yBottom,
                 (SHORT) (rcl.xRight - rcl.xLeft),
                 (SHORT) (rcl.yTop - rcl.yBottom), SWP_SIZE | SWP_MOVE) ;
```

This window won't be the active window. Because the program's purpose is to display some information, FREEMEM needn't be the active window when it is first displayed. If we wanted FREEMEM to be the active window when it is first displayed, we could include SWP_ACTIVATE among the last parameters to *WinSetWindowPos*.

Figure 10-4 shows FREEMEM running in the lower-left corner of the Presentation Manager.

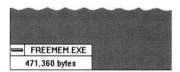

Figure 10-4. *The FREEMEM display.*

A Digital Clock

Figure 10-5, on the following pages, shows the DIGCLOCK program, a digital clock that occupies a small window positioned at the lower-right corner of the display. The clock displays the day of the week, the date (month/day/year), and the time. It is updated (with help from the Presentation Manager timer) every second.

The DIGCLOCK File

```
#--------------------
# DIGCLOCK make file
#--------------------

digclock.obj : digclock.c
     cl -c -G2sw -W3 digclock.c

digclock.exe : digclock.obj digclock.def
     link digclock, /align:16, NUL, os2, digclock
```

The DIGCLOCK.C File

```
/*-----------------------------
   DIGCLOCK.C -- Digital Clock
   ----------------------------*/

#define INCL_WIN
#define INCL_GPI
#define INCL_DOS
#include <os2.h>
#include <stdio.h>

#define ID_TIMER 1

MRESULT EXPENTRY ClientWndProc (HWND, USHORT, MPARAM, MPARAM) ;
VOID    SizeTheWindow (HWND) ;

int main (void)
    {
    static CHAR   szClientClass[] = "DigClock" ;
    static ULONG  flFrameFlags = FCF_TITLEBAR | FCF_SYSMENU |
                                 FCF_BORDER   | FCF_TASKLIST ;
    HAB           hab ;
    HMQ           hmq ;
    HWND          hwndFrame, hwndClient ;
    QMSG          qmsg ;

    hab = WinInitialize (0) ;
    hmq = WinCreateMsgQueue (hab, 0) ;

    WinRegisterClass (hab, szClientClass, ClientWndProc, 0L, 0) ;
```

(continued)

Figure 10-5. The DIGCLOCK.C File. *continued*

```
        hwndFrame = WinCreateStdWindow (HWND_DESKTOP, WS_VISIBLE,
                                        &flFrameFlags, szClientClass, NULL,
                                        OL, NULL, 0, &hwndClient) ;
        SizeTheWindow (hwndFrame) ;

        if (WinStartTimer (hab, hwndClient, ID_TIMER, 1000))
            {
            while (WinGetMsg (hab, &qmsg, NULL, 0, 0))
                WinDispatchMsg (hab, &qmsg) ;

            WinStopTimer (hab, hwndClient, ID_TIMER) ;
            }
        else
            WinMessageBox (HWND_DESKTOP, hwndClient,
                           "Too many clocks or timers",
                           szClientClass, 0, MB_OK | MB_ICONEXCLAMATION) ;

        WinDestroyWindow (hwndFrame) ;
        WinDestroyMsgQueue (hmq) ;
        WinTerminate (hab) ;
        return 0 ;
        }

VOID SizeTheWindow (HWND hwndFrame)
    {
    FONTMETRICS fm ;
    HPS         hps ;
    RECTL       rcl ;

    hps = WinGetPS (hwndFrame) ;
    GpiQueryFontMetrics (hps, (LONG) sizeof fm, &fm) ;
    WinReleasePS (hps) ;

    rcl.yBottom = 0 ;
    rcl.yTop    = 11 * fm.lMaxBaselineExt / 4 ;
    rcl.xRight  = WinQuerySysValue (HWND_DESKTOP, SV_CXSCREEN) ;
    rcl.xLeft   = rcl.xRight - 16 * fm.lEmInc ;

    WinCalcFrameRect (hwndFrame, &rcl, FALSE) ;

    WinSetWindowPos (hwndFrame, NULL, (SHORT) rcl.xLeft, (SHORT) rcl.yBottom,
                     (SHORT) (rcl.xRight - rcl.xLeft),
                     (SHORT) (rcl.yTop - rcl.yBottom), SWP_SIZE | SWP_MOVE) ;
    }
```

(continued)

Figure 10-5. The DIGCLOCK.C File. *continued*

```
VOID UpdateTime (HWND hwnd, HPS hps)
    {
    static BOOL        fHaveCtryInfo = FALSE ;
    static CHAR        *szDayName [] = { "Sun", "Mon", "Tue", "Wed",
                                         "Thu", "Fri", "Sat" } ;
    static CHAR        szDateFormat [] = " %s   %d%s%02d%s%02d " ;
    static COUNTRYCODE ctryc = { 0, 0 } ;
    static COUNTRYINFO ctryi ;
    CHAR               szBuffer [20] ;
    DATETIME           dt ;
    RECTL              rcl ;
    USHORT             usDataLength ;

                /*-------------------------------------------
                    Get Country Information, Date, and Time
                -------------------------------------------*/

    if (!fHaveCtryInfo)
        {
        DosGetCtryInfo (sizeof ctryi, &ctryc, &ctryi, &usDataLength) ;
        fHaveCtryInfo = TRUE ;
        }
    DosGetDateTime (&dt) ;
    dt.year %= 100 ;

                /*-------------
                    Format Date
                -------------*/
                                    /*-----------------
                                        mm/dd/yy format
                                    -----------------*/
    if (ctryi.fsDateFmt == 0)

        sprintf (szBuffer, szDateFormat, szDayName [dt.weekday],
                        dt.month, ctryi.szDateSeparator,
                        dt.day,   ctryi.szDateSeparator, dt.year) ;

                                    /*-----------------
                                        dd/mm/yy format
                                    -----------------*/
    else if (ctryi.fsDateFmt == 1)
```

(continued)

Figure 10-5. The DIGCLOCK.C File. *continued*

```
        sprintf (szBuffer, szDateFormat, szDayName [dt.weekday],
                            dt.day,   ctryi.szDateSeparator,
                            dt.month, ctryi.szDateSeparator, dt.year) ;

                                    /*-----------------
                                       yy/mm/dd format
                                    -----------------*/
    else
        sprintf (szBuffer, szDateFormat, szDayName [dt.weekday],
                            dt.year,  ctryi.szDateSeparator,
                            dt.month, ctryi.szDateSeparator, dt.day) ;

            /*--------------
               Display Date
            --------------*/

WinQueryWindowRect (hwnd, &rcl) ;
rcl.yBottom += 5 * rcl.yTop / 11 ;
WinDrawText (hps, -1, szBuffer, &rcl, CLR_NEUTRAL, CLR_BACKGROUND,
            DT_CENTER | DT_VCENTER) ;

            /*-------------
               Format Time
            -------------*/
                                    /*-----------------
                                       12-hour format
                                    -----------------*/
if ((ctryi.fsTimeFmt & 1) == 0)

        sprintf (szBuffer, " %d%s%02d%s%02d %cm ",
                            (dt.hours + 11) % 12 + 1, ctryi.szTimeSeparator,
                            dt.minutes, ctryi.szTimeSeparator,
                            dt.seconds, dt.hours / 12 ? 'p' : 'a') ;

                                    /*-----------------
                                       24-hour format
                                    -----------------*/
    else
        sprintf (szBuffer, " %02d%s%02d%s%02d ",
                            dt.hours,   ctryi.szTimeSeparator,
                            dt.minutes, ctryi.szTimeSeparator, dt.seconds) ;
```

(continued)

Figure 10-5. The DIGCLOCK.C File. *continued*

```
               /*---------------
                 Display Time
                 --------------*/


     WinQueryWindowRect (hwnd, &rcl) ;
     rcl.yTop -= 5 * rcl.yTop / 11 ;
     WinDrawText (hps, -1, szBuffer, &rcl, CLR_NEUTRAL, CLR_BACKGROUND,
                  DT_CENTER | DT_VCENTER) ;

     }


MRESULT EXPENTRY ClientWndProc (HWND hwnd, USHORT msg, MPARAM mp1, MPARAM mp2)
     {
     HPS   hps;

     switch (msg)
         {
         case WM_TIMER:
             hps = WinGetPS (hwnd) ;
             GpiSetBackMix (hps, BM_OVERPAINT) ;

             UpdateTime (hwnd, hps) ;

             WinReleasePS (hps) ;
             return 0 ;

         case WM_PAINT:
             hps = WinBeginPaint (hwnd, NULL, NULL) ;
             GpiErase (hps) ;

             UpdateTime (hwnd, hps) ;

             WinEndPaint (hps) ;
             return 0 ;
         }
     return WinDefWindowProc (hwnd, msg, mp1, mp2) ;
     }
```

The DIGCLOCK.DEF File

```
;--------------------------------------
; DIGCLOCK.DEF module definition file
;--------------------------------------

NAME            DIGCLOCK  WINDOWAPI

DESCRIPTION     'Digital Clock (C) Charles Petzold, 1988'
PROTMODE
HEAPSIZE        1024
STACKSIZE       8192
EXPORTS         ClientWndProc
```

Figure 10-5. *The DIGCLOCK program.*

To position and size the window, DIGCLOCK uses a technique similar to that used in FREEMEM. To allow a little margin around the two lines of text, I made the client window 2¾ times the height and 16 times the width of an average system font uppercase letter:

```
rcl.yBottom = 0 ;
rcl.yTop    = 11 * fm.lMaxBaselineExt / 4 ;
rcl.xRight  = WinQuerySysValue (HWND_DESKTOP, SV_CXSCREEN) ;
rcl.xLeft   = rcl.xRight - 16 * fm.lEmInc ;
```

DIGCLOCK processes its WM_TIMER message by invalidating the client window. The WM_PAINT message calls the *UpdateTime* function to display the date and time. *UpdateTime* makes use of two OS/2 kernel functions — *DosGetDateTime* to obtain the date and time and *DosGetCtryInfo* to obtain information about the format of the date and time applicable for the country specified in the user's CONFIG.SYS file. Thus the format of the date and time in DIGCLOCK looks much like the format used in the OS/2 DATE, TIME, and DIR commands. The *UpdateTime* function is mostly a collection of various *sprintf* statements that format the date and time for display. The function writes the two lines of text to its client window using *WinDrawText*.

Figure 10-6 on the following page shows DIGCLOCK running in the lower-right corner of the Presentation Manager.

Figure 10-6. *The DIGCLOCK display.*

An Analog Clock

An analog clock program doesn't have to worry about different date and time formats, but the complexity of the graphics more than outweighs that convenience. The analog CLOCK program is shown in Figure 10-7. Most of the code in this program is devoted to displaying the face and hands of the clock, so that's what I'll discuss in this section.

The CLOCK File

```
#-----------------
# CLOCK make file
#-----------------

clock.obj : clock.c
     cl -c -G2sw -W3 clock.c

clock.exe : clock.obj clock.def
     link clock, /align:16, NUL, os2, clock
```

The CLOCK.C File

```
/*------------------------
   CLOCK.C -- Analog Clock
   ------------------------*/

#define INCL_WIN
#define INCL_GPI
#include <os2.h>
#include <stdlib.h>

#define ID_TIMER 1

typedef struct
    {
    SHORT cxClient ;
    SHORT cyClient ;
    SHORT cxPixelDiam ;
```

(continued)

Figure 10-7. The CLOCK.C File. *continued*

```
        SHORT cyPixelDiam ;
        }
        WINDOWINFO ;

typedef WINDOWINFO *PWINDOWINFO ;

MRESULT EXPENTRY ClientWndProc (HWND, USHORT, MPARAM, MPARAM) ;

int main (void)
        {
        static CHAR   szClientClass[] = "Clock" ;
        static ULONG  flFrameFlags = FCF_TITLEBAR      | FCF_SYSMENU |
                                     FCF_SIZEBORDER    | FCF_MINMAX  |
                                     FCF_SHELLPOSITION | FCF_TASKLIST ;

        HAB           hab ;
        HMQ           hmq ;
        HWND          hwndFrame, hwndClient ;
        QMSG          qmsg ;

        hab = WinInitialize (0) ;
        hmq = WinCreateMsgQueue (hab, 0) ;

        WinRegisterClass (hab, szClientClass, ClientWndProc, CS_SIZEREDRAW, 0) ;

        hwndFrame = WinCreateStdWindow (HWND_DESKTOP, WS_VISIBLE,
                                        &flFrameFlags, szClientClass, NULL,
                                        0L, NULL, 0, &hwndClient) ;

        if (WinStartTimer (hab, hwndClient, ID_TIMER, 1000))
            {
            while (WinGetMsg (hab, &qmsg, NULL, 0, 0))
                WinDispatchMsg (hab, &qmsg) ;

            WinStopTimer (hab, hwndClient, ID_TIMER) ;
            }
        else
            WinMessageBox (HWND_DESKTOP, hwndClient,
                           "Too many clocks or timers",
                           szClientClass, 0, MB_OK | MB_ICONEXCLAMATION) ;

        WinDestroyWindow (hwndFrame) ;
        WinDestroyMsgQueue (hmq) ;
        WinTerminate (hab) ;
        return 0 ;
        }
```

(continued)

Figure 10-7. The CLOCK.C File. *continued*

```
VOID RotatePoint (POINTL aptl[], SHORT sNum, SHORT sAngle)
    {
    static SHORT sSin [60] =
                  {
                      0,  105,  208,  309,  407,  500,  588,  669,  743,  809,
                    866,  914,  951,  978,  995, 1000,  995,  978,  951,  914,
                    866,  809,  743,  669,  588,  500,  407,  309,  208,  105,
                      0, -104, -207, -308, -406, -499, -587, -668, -742, -808,
                   -865, -913, -950, -977, -994, -999, -994, -977, -950, -913,
                   -865, -808, -742, -668, -587, -499, -406, -308, -207, -104
                  } ;
    POINTL       ptlTemp ;
    SHORT        sIndex ;
    for (sIndex = 0 ; sIndex < sNum ; sIndex++)
        {
        ptlTemp.x = (aptl[sIndex].x * sSin [(sAngle + 15) % 60] +
                     aptl[sIndex].y * sSin [sAngle]) / 1000 ;

        ptlTemp.y = (aptl[sIndex].y * sSin [(sAngle + 15) % 60] -
                     aptl[sIndex].x * sSin [sAngle]) / 1000 ;

        aptl[sIndex] = ptlTemp ;
        }
    }

VOID ScalePoint (POINTL aptl[], SHORT sNum, PWINDOWINFO pwi)
    {
    SHORT sIndex ;

    for (sIndex = 0 ; sIndex < sNum ; sIndex++)
        {
        aptl[sIndex].x = aptl[sIndex].x * pwi->cxPixelDiam / 200 ;
        aptl[sIndex].y = aptl[sIndex].y * pwi->cyPixelDiam / 200 ;
        }
    }

VOID TranslatePoint (POINTL aptl[], SHORT sNum, PWINDOWINFO pwi)
    {
    SHORT sIndex ;
```

(continued)

Figure 10-7. The CLOCK.C File. *continued*

```
            for (sIndex = 0 ; sIndex < sNum ; sIndex++)
                {
                aptl[sIndex].x += pwi->cxClient / 2 ;
                aptl[sIndex].y += pwi->cyClient / 2 ;
                }
            }


VOID DrawHand (HPS hps, POINTL aptlIn[], SHORT sNum, SHORT sAngle,
               PWINDOWINFO pwi)
        {
        POINTL aptl [5] ;
        SHORT  sIndex ;

        for (sIndex = 0 ; sIndex < sNum ; sIndex++)
             aptl [sIndex] = aptlIn [sIndex] ;

        RotatePoint    (aptl, sNum, sAngle) ;
        ScalePoint     (aptl, sNum, pwi) ;
        TranslatePoint (aptl, sNum, pwi) ;

        GpiMove (hps, aptl) ;
        GpiPolyLine (hps, sNum - 1L, aptl + 1) ;
        }

MRESULT EXPENTRY ClientWndProc (HWND hwnd, USHORT msg, MPARAM mp1, MPARAM mp2)
        {
        static DATETIME    dtPrevious ;
        static HDC         hdc ;
        static LONG        xPixelsPerMeter, yPixelsPerMeter ;
        static POINTL      aptlHour   [5] = { 0,-15, 10,0, 0,60, -10,0, 0,-15 },
                           aptlMinute [5] = { 0,-20,  5,0, 0,80,  -5,0, 0,-20 },
                           aptlSecond [2] = { 0,  0,  0,80 } ;
        static WINDOWINFO wi ;
        DATETIME          dt ;
        HPS               hps ;
        POINTL            aptl [3] ;
        SHORT             sDiamMM, sAngle ;

        switch (msg)
            {
            case WM_CREATE:
                hdc = WinOpenWindowDC (hwnd) ;

                DevQueryCaps (hdc, CAPS_VERTICAL_RESOLUTION,
                                  1L, &yPixelsPerMeter) ;
```

(continued)

Figure 10-7. The CLOCK.C File. *continued*

```
                   DevQueryCaps (hdc, CAPS_HORIZONTAL_RESOLUTION,
                                 1L, &xPixelsPerMeter) ;

                   DosGetDateTime (&dtPrevious) ;
                   dtPrevious.hours = (dtPrevious.hours * 5) % 60 +
                                      dtPrevious.minutes / 12 ;
                   return 0 ;

          case WM_SIZE:
                   wi.cxClient = SHORT1FROMMP (mp2) ;
                   wi.cyClient = SHORT2FROMMP (mp2) ;

                   sDiamMM = (SHORT) min (wi.cxClient * 1000L / xPixelsPerMeter,
                                          wi.cyClient * 1000L / yPixelsPerMeter) ;

                   wi.cxPixelDiam = (SHORT) (xPixelsPerMeter * sDiamMM / 1000) ;
                   wi.cyPixelDiam = (SHORT) (yPixelsPerMeter * sDiamMM / 1000) ;
                   return 0 ;

          case WM_TIMER:
                   DosGetDateTime (&dt) ;
                   dt.hours = (dt.hours * 5) % 60 + dt.minutes / 12 ;

                   hps = WinGetPS (hwnd) ;
                   GpiSetColor (hps, CLR_BACKGROUND) ;

                   DrawHand (hps, aptlSecond, 2, dtPrevious.seconds, &wi) ;

                   if (dt.hours   != dtPrevious.hours ||
                       dt.minutes != dtPrevious.minutes)
                       {
                       DrawHand (hps, aptlHour,   5, dtPrevious.hours,   &wi) ;
                       DrawHand (hps, aptlMinute, 5, dtPrevious.minutes, &wi) ;
                       }

                   GpiSetColor (hps, CLR_NEUTRAL) ;

                   DrawHand (hps, aptlHour,   5, dt.hours,   &wi) ;
                   DrawHand (hps, aptlMinute, 5, dt.minutes, &wi) ;
                   DrawHand (hps, aptlSecond, 2, dt.seconds, &wi) ;

                   WinReleasePS (hps) ;
                   dtPrevious = dt ;
                   return 0 ;
```

(continued)

Figure 10-7. The CLOCK.C File. *continued*

```
      case WM_PAINT:
           hps = WinBeginPaint (hwnd, NULL, NULL) ;
           GpiErase (hps) ;

           for (sAngle = 0 ; sAngle < 60 ; sAngle++)
               {
               aptl[0].x = 0 ;
               aptl[0].y = 90 ;

               RotatePoint    (aptl, 1, sAngle) ;
               ScalePoint     (aptl, 1, &wi) ;
               TranslatePoint (aptl, 1, &wi) ;

               aptl[2].x = aptl[2].y = sAngle % 5 ? 2 : 10 ;

               ScalePoint (aptl + 2, 1, &wi) ;

               aptl[0].x -= aptl[2].x / 2 ;
               aptl[0].y -= aptl[2].y / 2 ;

               aptl[1].x = aptl[0].x + aptl[2].x ;
               aptl[1].y = aptl[0].y + aptl[2].y ;

               GpiMove (hps, aptl) ;
               GpiBox (hps, DRO_OUTLINEFILL, aptl + 1,
                           aptl[2].x, aptl[2].y) ;
               }
           DrawHand (hps, aptlHour,   5, dtPrevious.hours,   &wi) ;
           DrawHand (hps, aptlMinute, 5, dtPrevious.minutes, &wi) ;
           DrawHand (hps, aptlSecond, 2, dtPrevious.seconds, &wi) ;

           WinEndPaint (hps) ;
           return 0 ;
      }
 return WinDefWindowProc (hwnd, msg, mp1, mp2) ;
 }
```

The CLOCK.DEF File

```
;-----------------------------------
; CLOCK.DEF module definition file
;-----------------------------------

NAME            CLOCK       WINDOWAPI

DESCRIPTION     'Analog Clock (C) Charles Petzold, 1988'
PROTMODE
HEAPSIZE        1024
STACKSIZE       8192
EXPORTS         ClientWndProc
```

Figure 10-7. *The CLOCK program.*

Figure 10-8 shows CLOCK dominating the full Presentation Manager session.

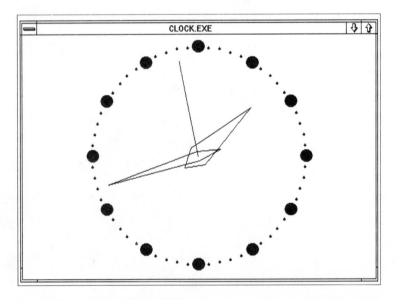

Figure 10-8. *The CLOCK display.*

To draw a round clock face, CLOCK defines its own coordinate system. The center of the clock (which is positioned in the center of the client window) is the point (0, 0) in this coordinate system. The horizontal and vertical axes both range from −100 to +100.

While processing the WM_CREATE message, CLOCK obtains two values from *DevQueryCaps* that report the horizontal and vertical resolution of the display in pixels per meter:

```
DevQueryCaps (hdc, CAPS_VERTICAL_RESOLUTION, 1L, &yPixelsPerMeter) ;
DevQueryCaps (hdc, CAPS_HORIZONTAL_RESOLUTION, 1L, &xPixelsPerMeter) ;
```

During the WM_SIZE message, the diameter of the clock face in millimeters is calculated based on the width and height of the client window:

```
sDiamMM = (SHORT) min (wi.cxClient * 1000L / xPixelsPerMeter,
                       wi.cyClient * 1000L / yPixelsPerMeter) ;
```

This value is then converted to a diameter in pixels for both the horizontal and vertical axes:

```
wi.cxPixelDiam = (SHORT) (xPixelsPerMeter * sDiamMM / 1000) ;
wi.cyPixelDiam = (SHORT) (yPixelsPerMeter * sDiamMM / 1000) ;
```

As I noted above, CLOCK defines its own coordinates to range from −100 to +100 on the horizontal and vertical axes. Thus, on the horizontal axis, the width in pixels of the clock face is *cxPixelDiam*, but this corresponds to 200 units in CLOCK's coordinate system.

CLOCK has two functions to translate one or more POINTL structures from its own coordinate system to the window coordinates used in the GPI functions: *ScalePoint* and *TranslatePoint*.

ScalePoint uses the relationship between these two coordinate systems to convert a point in CLOCK's coordinate system to pixels:

```
aptl[sIndex].x = aptl[sIndex].x * pwi->cxPixelDiam / 200 ;
aptl[sIndex].y = aptl[sIndex].y * pwi->cyPixelDiam / 200 ;
```

CLOCK's coordinate system defines (0, 0) as the center of the client window. The point (0, 0) in window coordinates is the lower-left corner of the window. *TranslatePoint* converts the point accordingly:

```
aptl[sIndex].x += pwi->cxClient / 2 ;
aptl[sIndex].y += pwi->cyClient / 2 ;
```

The more complex aspect of CLOCK involves the rotation of points around the clock face. Let's look at an example. The hour hand of the clock is defined as an array of POINTL structures that specify a starting position and four line segments:

```
static POINTL aptlHour [5] = { 0,-15, 10,0, 0,60, -10,0, 0,-15 }
```

But these are the coordinates only when the hour hand points straight up, at midnight or noon. What are the coordinates of the hour hand at 3:00? To get those coordinates, the points have to be rotated 90 degrees clockwise around a circle. Time for a trigonometry refresher: If the original point is (x, y) and the clockwise angle of rotation is α, then the new point (x', y') is calculated with the following formulas:

$$x' = x \; COS \; \alpha + y \; SIN \; \alpha$$
$$y' = y \; COS \; \alpha - x \; SIN \; \alpha$$

This is done in the *RotatePoint* function. Because a clock face is divided into 60 increments, all that's needed are 60 sine and cosine values in increments of 6 degrees. The cosines can be derived from the sines by offsetting the angle by 90 degrees.

To avoid introducing floating-point math in CLOCK (which would increase the CLOCK.EXE size considerably), the *sSin* array in *RotatePoint* contains the 60 required sine values scaled by a factor of 1000. The rotation formulas in *RotatePoint* are

```
ptlTemp.x = (aptl[sIndex].x * sSin [(sAngle + 15) % 60] +
            aptl[sIndex].y * sSin [sAngle]) / 1000 ;

ptlTemp.y = (aptl[sIndex].y * sSin [(sAngle + 15) % 60] -
            aptl[sIndex].x * sSin [sAngle]) / 1000 ;

aptl[sIndex] = ptlTemp ;
```

The *DrawHand* function in CLOCK is passed an array of points that define a clock hand at 12:00. It calls the *RotatePoint, ScalePoint,* and the *TranslatePoint* functions to rotate the points and convert them from CLOCK's coordinate system to window coordinates. *DrawHand* then calls *GpiMove* and *GpiPolyLine* to draw the hand. During processing of the WM_PAINT message, CLOCK draws the face of the clock and the three hands at the current time. Processing during the WM_TIMER message updates the position of the clock hands based on the new time obtained from *DosGetDateTime*.

CONTROL WINDOWS: PUTTING THE CHILDREN TO WORK

Control windows (sometimes called "child window controls" or simply "controls") are child windows that take the form of objects such as buttons, scroll bars, list boxes, and text entry fields. A control window processes mouse and keyboard input and notifies its owner of significant input events. Although the input originates with the keyboard and the mouse, it is filtered through the control, so you can treat control windows as additional means of input to your program.

For example, in a spreadsheet program you might want to display a small push button labeled "Recalculate" on your client window. You can do this in one of two ways. The first way requires the program itself to draw the push button on the client window. The client window procedure then has to process mouse messages and do some hit-testing to determine when the user clicks on the push button. But an easier approach is to create a push button control window that is a child of your client window. The window procedure for the push button window is inside the Presentation Manager. That window procedure draws the button, processes the mouse messages, and sends your client window a message when the button is clicked. By putting child windows to work, your program can delegate the drawing and the mouse hit-testing jobs.

We've already explored some of the concepts involved in creating and using control windows. The WELCOME4 program in Chapter 3 created a push button, scroll bar, and text-entry field based on preregistered window classes. Creating each control window required only one *WinCreateWindow* call. (The only problem was that WELCOME4 didn't know quite what to do with these control windows after it created them.)

Although the control windows in WELCOME4 were based on preregistered window classes, you can also create your own classes of control windows. For example, the CHECKER3 program in Chapter 9 created 25 child windows on the surface of its client. These child windows processed mouse clicks by drawing or erasing an X mark on the child window. The child windows added a layer of processing between the user and CHECKER3's client window that simplified mouse input processing.

CHECKER3's client window was ignorant of the state (X or no X) of each of the 25 child windows. But it's not difficult to imagine each of the child windows sending messages to the client window whenever the child window was checked or unchecked. We might also have added a facility that allowed the client window to send the child window a message requesting information about the state of a particular rectangle. Had we done this in CHECKER3, the child windows would have been sophisticated enough to qualify as control windows.

Control windows appear most often in dialog boxes. You'll discover in Chapter 14 that defining the position and size of control windows in a dialog box is simplified by using a dialog box template. The dialog box logic within the Presentation Manager also assists greatly in much of the overhead involved with using controls, including shifting the keyboard input focus between the windows. However, it's a good exercise to create a few control windows yourself to get a better understanding of dialog boxes and a greater appreciation for the work the Presentation Manager assumes when you use dialog boxes.

Control Window Basics

Using control windows involves three major jobs:

- You create a control window by calling *WinCreateWindow*. Most often, the window class has been preregistered by the Presentation Manager, which means that the window procedure for the class is in the Presentation Manager PMWIN.DLL dynamic link library. You specify the style, position, and size of the control window, and *WinCreateWindow* returns a handle to the window. The program can later adjust the position and size of the control by calling the *WinSetWindowPos* function.

- Your program can send messages to the control window using *Win-SendMsg*. These messages can either set the state of a control or query the current state. The identifiers for the messages you send to controls begin with a prefix that indicates the type of control window that responds to the message. For example, messages that begin with BM are messages you send to button controls, and messages that begin with SBM are messages you send to scroll-bar controls.

- You receive notification messages from the control window when a significant input event occurs. This usually results from the user clicking on the control window with the mouse or — if the control window has the input focus — pressing a key that affects the control. The notification messages are usually WM_COMMAND and WM_CONTROL messages for most control windows and WM_VSCROLL and WM_HSCROLL messages for scroll bars.

Creating the Window

You create a control window by calling the *WinCreateWindow* function, which generally looks like this:

```
hwnd = WinCreateWindow (
              hwndParent,       // Parent window
              szClass,          // Window class
              szText,           // Text
              WS_ ...,          // Window style
              xPosition,        // Position
              yPosition,
              cxWidth,          // Width
              cyHeight,         // Height
              hwndOwner,        // Owner window
              hwndPlacement,    // Placement
              id,               // Child ID
              pCtrlData,        // Ctrl data
              pPresParams) ;    // Pres params
```

When you create a control window based on a preregistered window class, the last two parameters (far pointers to control data and presentation parameters) are often set to NULL. The other parameters are described in the following paragraphs.

The Predefined Window Classes

In the CHECKER3 program in Chapter 9, the window class parameter in *WinCreateWindow* was a text string identifying a window class that the program registered. For control windows based on a preregistered window class, this parameter is an identifier beginning with the letters WC. These identifiers are as follows:

Preregistered Window Class	Type of Window
WC_FRAME	Standard frame window
WC_BUTTON	Push button, check box, and so forth
WC_MENU	Menu (including system menu and minimize/maximize menu)
WC_STATIC	Static text string and rectangle
WC_ENTRYFIELD	Text entry field
WC_LISTBOX	List box
WC_SCROLLBAR	Scroll bar
WC_TITLEBAR	Standard title bar

The WC_FRAME identifier isn't commonly used in the *WinCreateWindow* function because *WinCreateStdWindow* creates a frame window. The WC_MENU and WC_TITLEBAR identifiers refer to windows that are usually part of the standard window created with *WinCreateStdWindow*. Excluding those identifiers leaves us with the five most common control window classes, which are WC_BUTTON, WC_STATIC, WC_ENTRYFIELD, WC_LISTBOX, and WC_SCROLLBAR. The sample programs throughout this chapter create controls of the WC_BUTTON, WC_STATIC, and WC_SCROLLBAR classes.

The Window Style

The window style parameter of *WinCreateWindow* is one or more identifiers that define the appearance and functionality of the window. The style identifiers you use depend on the window class. For example, when creating a scroll-bar control window, you specify either SBS_VERT or SBS_HORZ, depending on whether you want a vertical or horizontal scroll bar. When you create a button control, the window style identifies the button as a push button, a radio button, or a check box. The identifier WS_VISIBLE usually is included in the window style. If you omit it, the window is created but not displayed. You must later call *WinShowWindow* to display the window.

Some control windows (such as buttons) display text, which you specify in the text parameter to *WinCreateWindow*. You can later change the text using the *WinSetWindowText* function. The position parameters give the coordinates of the lower-left corner of the control relative to the lower-left corner of its parent window. The size parameters specify the control's width and height. You can change the position and size using the *WinSetWindowPos* function.

The Owner and the Parent

When you create a child window, you assign it both a parent window and an owner window. The parent window determines where the control is positioned. The position parameters in *WinCreateWindow* specify the coordinates of the control window relative to the lower-left corner of the control's parent. If the parent window is moved, the child window is moved also. Like all child windows, a control window is clipped on the surface of its parent. It can't appear outside the area its parent occupies.

The control window sends notification messages not to its parent but to its owner. The window procedure associated with the owner window is responsible for interpreting these notification messages. Usually, the same window serves as both the parent and the owner of the control. For example, if you create a control window on the surface of your client window, the client window is usually both the parent and the owner of the control window. You can specify a different parent and owner if you want the notification messages to be processed by a window other than the one on which the control is located.

A third window handle can be passed to the *WinCreateWindow* function to specify how overlapping siblings appear on the screen. (This is identified as *hwndPlacement* in the *WinCreateWindow* call on page 475.) This parameter must be either a window handle of a sibling, HWND_TOP, or HWND_BOTTOM. The terminology often becomes confusing: An HWND_BOTTOM window obscures an HWND_TOP window if the two windows overlap. If you specify a handle of a sibling window, that sibling will be obscured by the new window if the windows overlap. If you create several sibling windows using HWND_TOP, the most recently created window will be obscured by the others. Specifying HWND_BOTTOM for several siblings causes the most recently created window to obscure the siblings that it overlaps.

If your child windows do not overlap, you can use either HWND_TOP or HWND_BOTTOM for all of them.

The Child ID

The child ID is a very important parameter of the *WinCreateWindow* function. This ID number should be unique for each child of a particular window. The control window uses the ID to identify itself when it sends the owner a notification message. You can use any number you want for a child ID, but it's safest to use numbers less than 32,768 so as not to conflict with predefined IDs used by the frame window. If you create many control windows, you should choose IDs that let you conveniently determine which control is sending you a notification message and what you do with information from the control. For example, the sample programs in this chapter often use the IDs as indexes to arrays.

Although the *WinCreateWindow* function returns a handle to the child window, it's not essential that you save it. You can always determine the child window handle from the child ID by using the following function:

```
hwndChild = WinWindowFromID (hwnd, id) ;
```

The *hwnd* parameter is the window handle of the parent of *hwndChild*. The *id* parameter is the ID you specify when creating the child window.

Knowing the handle of a child window, you can also obtain the ID:

```
id = WinQueryWindowUShort (hwndChild, QWS_ID) ;
```

The Button Class

Let's begin with buttons, which are almost the simplest type of control window. (Static control windows are actually simpler because they don't process input at all.) When you create a button control window, you specify the WC_BUTTON window class in the *WinCreateWindow* function. The window style indicates the type of button. The most common button window styles are BS_PUSHBUTTON, BS_CHECKBOX, and BS_RADIOBUTTON.

A push button is a rounded rectangle that contains text. When you click on the button with the mouse or — if the button has the input focus — press the Spacebar, the button flashes and sends a notification message to its owner. Push buttons generally signal simple actions: "Do this."

A check box is a small square (about the height of a character) followed by a text string. Clicking the button with the mouse causes an X to appear in the box; clicking it again removes the X. A program often uses check boxes for various program options.

A radio button is a small circle followed by text. Like a check box, a radio button can be either checked or unchecked. Clicking on the radio button checks it, but clicking again doesn't uncheck it. Generally, a group of radio buttons is used to indicate mutually exclusive options. When the user checks one button, the program unchecks all the other buttons in the same group, just as the buttons on a car radio do.

A Push Button Demonstration Program

The BUTTONS1 program, shown in Figure 11-1, creates two push buttons labeled "Smaller" and "Larger." These buttons appear in the center of the client window. When you click with the mouse on the button labeled "Smaller," the program's window decreases in size by 10 percent. When you click on "Larger," the window size increases by 10 percent.

The BUTTONS1 File

```
#--------------------
# BUTTONS1 make file
#--------------------

buttons1.obj : buttons1.c
    cl -c -G2sw -W3 buttons1.c

buttons1.exe : buttons1.obj buttons1.def
    link buttons1, /align:16, NUL, os2, buttons1
```

The BUTTONS1.C File

```
/*-------------------------------------------
   BUTTONS1.C -- Push Button Demonstration
   -----------------------------------------*/

#define INCL_WIN
#define INCL_GPI
#include <os2.h>

MRESULT EXPENTRY ClientWndProc (HWND, USHORT, MPARAM, MPARAM) ;

int main (void)
    {
    static CHAR  szClientClass[] = "Buttons1" ;
    static ULONG flFrameFlags = FCF_TITLEBAR      | FCF_SYSMENU  |
                                FCF_SIZEBORDER     | FCF_MINMAX   |
                                FCF_SHELLPOSITION | FCF_TASKLIST ;

    HAB          hab ;
    HMQ          hmq ;
    HWND         hwndFrame, hwndClient ;
    QMSG         qmsg ;
```

(continued)

Figure 11-1. The BUTTONS1.C File. *continued*

```
hab = WinInitialize (0) ;
    hmq = WinCreateMsgQueue (hab, 0) ;

    WinRegisterClass (hab, szClientClass, ClientWndProc, CS_SIZEREDRAW, 0) ;

    hwndFrame = WinCreateStdWindow (HWND_DESKTOP, WS_VISIBLE,
                                    &flFrameFlags, szClientClass, NULL,
                                    OL, NULL, 0, &hwndClient) ;

    WinSendMsg (hwndFrame, WM_SETICON,
                WinQuerySysPointer (HWND_DESKTOP, SPTR_APPICON, FALSE),
                NULL) ;

    while (WinGetMsg (hab, &qmsg, NULL, 0, 0))
        WinDispatchMsg (hab, &qmsg) ;

    WinDestroyWindow (hwndFrame) ;
    WinDestroyMsgQueue (hmq) ;
    WinTerminate (hab) ;
    return 0 ;
    }

MRESULT EXPENTRY ClientWndProc (HWND hwnd, USHORT msg, MPARAM mp1, MPARAM mp2)
    {
    static CHAR  *szButtonLabel[] = { "Smaller", "Larger" } ;
    static HWND  hwndFrame, hwndButton[2] ;
    static SHORT cxClient, cyClient, cxChar, cyChar ;
    FONTMETRICS  fm ;
    HPS          hps ;
    SHORT        id ;
    RECTL        rcl ;

    switch (msg)
        {
        case WM_CREATE :
            hwndFrame = WinQueryWindow (hwnd, QW_PARENT, FALSE) ;

            hps = WinGetPS (hwnd) ;
            GpiQueryFontMetrics (hps, (LONG) sizeof fm, &fm) ;
            cxChar = (SHORT) fm.lAveCharWidth ;
            cyChar = (SHORT) fm.lMaxBaselineExt ;
            WinReleasePS (hps) ;
```

(continued)

Figure 11-1. The BUTTONS1.C File. *continued*

```
                        for (id = 0 ; id < 2 ; id++)
                            hwndButton[id] = WinCreateWindow (
                                            hwnd,               // Parent
                                            WC_BUTTON,          // Class
                                            szButtonLabel[id],  // Text
                                            WS_VISIBLE |        // Style
                                                BS_PUSHBUTTON,
                                            0, 0,               // Position
                                            12 * cxChar,        // Width
                                            2 * cyChar,         // Height
                                            hwnd,               // Owner
                                            HWND_BOTTOM,        // Placement
                                            id,                 // ID
                                            NULL,               // Ctrl data
                                            NULL) ;             // Pres params
               return 0 ;

          case WM_SIZE :
               cxClient = SHORT1FROMMP (mp2) ;
               cyClient = SHORT2FROMMP (mp2) ;

               for (id = 0 ; id < 2 ; id++)
                   WinSetWindowPos (hwndButton[id], NULL,
                           cxClient / 2 + (14 * id - 13) * cxChar,
                           (cyClient - 2 * cyChar) / 2,
                           0, 0, SWP_MOVE) ;
               return 0 ;

          case WM_COMMAND:
               WinQueryWindowRect (hwnd, &rcl) ;
               WinMapWindowPoints (hwnd, HWND_DESKTOP, (PPOINTL) &rcl, 2) ;

               switch (COMMANDMSG(&msg)->cmd)              // Child ID
                   {
                   case 0:                                // "Smaller"
                        rcl.xLeft   += cxClient / 20 ;
                        rcl.xRight  -= cxClient / 20 ;
                        rcl.yBottom += cyClient / 20 ;
                        rcl.yTop    -= cyClient / 20 ;
                        break ;
```

(continued)

Figure 11-1. The BUTTONS1.C File. *continued*

```
              case 1:                                     // "Larger"
                    rcl.xLeft   -= cxClient / 20 ;
                    rcl.xRight  += cxClient / 20 ;
                    rcl.yBottom -= cyClient / 20 ;
                    rcl.yTop    += cyClient / 20 ;
                    break ;

              }
         WinCalcFrameRect (hwndFrame, &rcl, FALSE) ;

         WinSetWindowPos (hwndFrame, NULL,
                         (SHORT) rcl.xLeft, (SHORT) rcl.yBottom,
                         (SHORT) rcl.xRight - (SHORT) rcl.xLeft,
                         (SHORT) rcl.yTop   - (SHORT) rcl.yBottom,
                         SWP_MOVE | SWP_SIZE) ;

         return 0 ;

    case WM_ERASEBACKGROUND:
         return 1 ;
    }
return WinDefWindowProc (hwnd, msg, mp1, mp2) ;
}
```

The BUTTONS1.DEF File

```
;------------------------------------
; BUTTONS1.DEF module definition file
;------------------------------------

NAME           BUTTONS1  WINDOWAPI

DESCRIPTION    'Push Button Demo (C) Charles Petzold, 1988'
PROTMODE
HEAPSIZE       1024
STACKSIZE      8192
EXPORTS        ClientWndProc
```

Figure 11-1. *The BUTTONS1 program.*

Figure 11-2 shows BUTTONS1 running under the Presentation Manager. The ''Larger'' button is in the process of being triggered by the mouse.

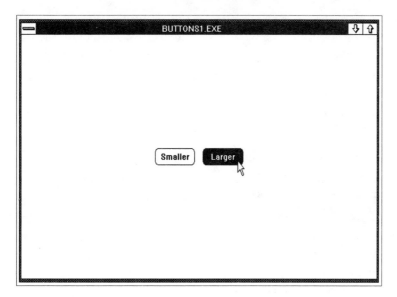

Figure 11-2. *The BUTTONS1 display.*

BUTTONS1 creates these two push buttons during processing of the WM_CREATE message in *ClientWndProc*:

```
for (id = 0 ; id < 2 ; id++)
    hwndButton [id] = WinCreateWindow (
                        hwnd,                   // Parent
                        WC_BUTTON,              // Class
                        szButtonLabel [id],     // Text
                        WS_VISIBLE |            // Style
                            BS_PUSHBUTTON,
                        0, 0,                   // Position
                        12 * cxChar,            // Width
                        2 * cyChar,             // Height
                        hwnd,                   // Owner
                        HWND_BOTTOM,            // Placement
                        id,                     // ID
                        NULL,                   // Ctrl data
                        NULL) ;                 // Pres params
```

The window handles are saved in the *hwndButton* array. The two IDs are set to 0 and 1, as are the indexes to this array. The *szButtonLabel* array contains the two text strings that appear inside the buttons.

The height of the buttons is set to 2 times the height of a character, which is a standard height for push buttons. The width of a push button should be at least the length of the text string inside the button plus two additional character widths. Twelve times the width of a character is adequate for the two buttons in this program.

The position parameters of *WinCreateWindow* are set to 0. Because the buttons will be positioned in the center of the client window, the position can be determined only when the program knows the size of the client window. This requires that *ClientWndProc* call *WinSetWindowPos* during the WM_SIZE message:

```
for (id = 0 ; id < 2 ; id++)
    WinSetWindowPos (hwndButton [id], NULL,
            cxClient / 2 + (14 * id - 13) * cxChar,
            (cyClient - 2 * cyChar) / 2,
            0, 0, SWP_MOVE) ;
```

The third and fourth parameters give the position of the control relative to the lower-left corner of the client window. These messy-looking formulas place the buttons side by side in the center of the client window. (Such formulas disappear when you work with controls in dialog boxes.)

Push buttons send WM_COMMAND messages to their owners when they are clicked on. The following *mp1* and *mp2* parameters accompany the WM_COMMAND message:

WM_COMMAND Parameter	Meaning
SHORT1FROMMP (mp1)	Child ID
SHORT1FROMMP (mp2)	CMDSRC_PUSHBUTTON
SHORT2FROMMP (mp2)	Nonzero for mouse input; 0 for keyboard input

The CMDSRC_PUSHBUTTON identifier indicates that the WM_COMMAND message is sent by a push button. (As you'll see in Chapter 13, menus and keyboard accelerators also send WM_COMMAND messages to the client window. In these cases the low USHORT of *mp2* is either CMDSRC_MENU or CMDSRC_ACCELERATOR.) The only way to identify the push button sending the message is to examine the child ID in the low USHORT of *mp1*, which is why it's so important to give each push button a unique ID.

PMWIN.H contains a COMMANDMSG macro that you can use like the CHARMSG and MOUSEMSG macros. The following expression returns the child window ID:

```
COMMANDMSG (&msg) -> cmd
```

The following expression identifies the source of the message:

```
COMMANDMSG (&msg) -> source
```

The following expression is TRUE if the mouse was used:

```
COMMANDMSG (&msg) -> fMouse
```

In the BUTTONS1 program, the push button on the left (containing the text "Smaller") has an ID of 0. The push button with the text "Larger" has an ID of 1. The processing of the WM_COMMAND message in BUTTONS1.C is structured like this:

```
case WM_COMMAND:
    [other program lines]
    switch (COMMANDMSG (&msg) -> cmd)
        {
        case 0:
            [process message from "Smaller" push button]
            break ;

        case 1:
            [process message from "Larger" push button]
            break ;
        }
    [other program lines]
    return 0 ;
```

When *ClientWndProc* receives a WM_COMMAND message, it must alter the size of the program's window. The program first obtains the client window's rectangle from *WinQueryWindowRect* and then translates the coordinates to window coordinates using *WinMapWindowPoints*. Depending on the ID of the push button that sent the message, BUTTONS1 adjusts the four fields of the rectangle to increase or decrease the size. It then determines the frame rectangle that corresponds to this client rectangle by calling *WinCalcFrameRect*. BUTTONS1 then sets the new size and position of the frame rectangle by calling *WinSetWindowPos*.

When BUTTONS1 calls *WinSetWindowPos*, the client window procedure receives a WM_SIZE message. As I've mentioned, BUTTONS1 responds to this by calling *WinSetWindowPos* to set the new position of the push button controls. Because the frame window is resized equally in all four directions and the push button controls are always positioned in the center of the window, the push buttons remain in the same position relative to the screen.

Controls and Keyboard Input Focus

When you click on one of the push buttons in BUTTONS1, the push button obtains the input focus, as indicated by a dotted line around the text of the button. Whenever a push button has the input focus, you can also press the Spacebar to trigger the button. However, this is the only keystroke that the push button responds to in a meaningful way. When a dialog box contains push buttons and other controls, you can move the input focus between controls by using the Tab key and, sometimes, the cursor movement keys. The dialog box logic in the Presentation Manager adds this additional keyboard interface — it isn't part of the keyboard logic in individual control windows. In the COLORSCR program shown later in this chapter, we'll examine a way to add a keyboard interface to move the input focus between control windows.

Radio Buttons to Indicate Choices

The BUTTONS1 program created two push button control windows. Now let's go a little further and write a program that has a few more controls. The DRAWLINE program, shown in Figure 11-3, creates 26 control windows — 24 radio buttons and two group boxes.

The DRAWLINE File

```
#--------------------
# DRAWLINE make file
#--------------------

drawline.obj : drawline.c
    cl -c -G2sw -W3 drawline.c

drawline.exe : drawline.obj drawline.def
    link drawline, /align:16, NUL, os2, drawline
```

The DRAWLINE.C File

```
/*----------------------------------------------
   DRAWLINE.C -- Draw line from radio buttons
   ------------------------------------------*/

#define INCL_WIN
#define INCL_GPI
#include <os2.h>
```

(continued)

Figure 11-3. The DRAWLINE.C File. *continued*

```
MRESULT EXPENTRY ClientWndProc (HWND, USHORT, MPARAM, MPARAM) ;

int main (void)
    {
    static CHAR  szClientClass[] = "DrawLine" ;
    static ULONG flFrameFlags = FCF_TITLEBAR      | FCF_SYSMENU |
                                FCF_SIZEBORDER    | FCF_MINMAX  |
                                FCF_SHELLPOSITION | FCF_TASKLIST ;

    HAB          hab ;
    HMQ          hmq ;
    HWND         hwndFrame, hwndClient ;
    QMSG         qmsg ;

    hab = WinInitialize (0) ;
    hmq = WinCreateMsgQueue (hab, 0) ;

    WinRegisterClass (hab, szClientClass, ClientWndProc, CS_SIZEREDRAW, 0) ;

    hwndFrame = WinCreateStdWindow (HWND_DESKTOP, WS_VISIBLE,
                                    &flFrameFlags, szClientClass, NULL,
                                    0L, NULL, 0, &hwndClient) ;

    WinSendMsg (hwndFrame, WM_SETICON,
                WinQuerySysPointer (HWND_DESKTOP, SPTR_APPICON, FALSE),
                NULL) ;

    while (WinGetMsg (hab, &qmsg, NULL, 0, 0))
        WinDispatchMsg (hab, &qmsg) ;

    WinDestroyWindow (hwndFrame) ;
    WinDestroyMsgQueue (hmq) ;
    WinTerminate (hab) ;
    return 0 ;
    }

MRESULT EXPENTRY ClientWndProc (HWND hwnd, USHORT msg, MPARAM mp1, MPARAM mp2)
    {
    static CHAR   *szGroupText[] = { "Color", "Type" } ;
    static CHAR   *szColorText[] = { "Background", "Blue",      "Red",
                                     "Pink",       "Green",     "Cyan",
                                     "Yellow",     "Neutral",   "Dark Gray",
                                     "Dark Blue",  "Dark Red",  "Dark Pink",
                                     "Dark Green", "Dark Cyan", "Brown",
                                     "Pale Gray" } ;
```

(continued)

Figure 11-3. The DRAWLINE.C File. *continued*

```
      static CHAR    *szTypeText [] = { "Dot",       "Short Dash",
                                        "Dash Dot", "Double Dot",
                                        "Long Dash", "Dash Double Dot",
                                        "Solid",    "Invisible" } ;
      static HWND    hwndGroup[2], hwndRadioColor[8], hwndRadioType[8] ;
      static POINTL aptl[5] ;
      static SHORT   sCurrentColor = 7,   // Neutral
                     sCurrentType  = 6 ;  // Solid
FONTMETRICS    fm ;
HPS            hps ;
SHORT          s, id, cxChar, cyChar ;

switch (msg)
     {
     case WM_CREATE :
          hps = WinGetPS (hwnd) ;
          GpiQueryFontMetrics (hps, (LONG) sizeof fm, &fm) ;
          cxChar = (SHORT) fm.lAveCharWidth ;
          cyChar = (SHORT) fm.lMaxBaselineExt ;
          WinReleasePS (hps) ;

          for (s = 0 ; s < 2 ; s++)

               hwndGroup[s] = WinCreateWindow (
                         hwnd,              // Parent
                         WC_STATIC,         // Class
                         szGroupText[s],    // Text
                         WS_VISIBLE |       // Style
                              SS_GROUPBOX,
                         (8 + 42 * s) * cxChar,
                         4 * cyChar,        // Position
                         (26 + 12 * (1 - s)) *
                              cxChar,       // Width
                         14 * cyChar,       // Height
                         hwnd,              // Owner
                         HWND_TOP,          // Placement
                         s + 24,            // ID
                         NULL,              // Ctrl data
                         NULL) ;            // Pres params

          for (s = 0 ; s < 16 ; s++)
```

(continued)

Figure 11-3. The DRAWLINE.C File. *continued*

```
                  hwndRadioColor[s] = WinCreateWindow (
                                    hwnd,            // Parent
                                    WC_BUTTON,       // Class
                                    szColorText[s],  // Text
                                    WS_VISIBLE |     // Style
                                        BS_RADIOBUTTON,
                                    (10 + (s > 7 ? 18 : 0))
                                        * cxChar,    // X Position
                                    (31 - 3 * (s % 8))
                                        * cyChar / 2, // Y Position
                                    16 * cxChar,     // Width
                                    3 * cyChar / 2,  // Height
                                    hwnd,            // Owner
                                    HWND_BOTTOM,     // Placement
                                    s,               // ID
                                    NULL,            // Ctrl data
                                    NULL) ;          // Pres params


         for (s = 0 ; s < 8 ; s++)

                  hwndRadioType[s]  = WinCreateWindow (
                                    hwnd,            // Parent
                                    WC_BUTTON,       // Class
                                    szTypeText[s],   // Text
                                    WS_VISIBLE |     // Style
                                        BS_RADIOBUTTON,
                                    52 * cxChar,     // Position
                                    (31 - 3 * s) * cyChar / 2,
                                    22 * cxChar,     // Width
                                    3 * cyChar / 2,  // Height
                                    hwnd,            // Owner
                                    HWND_BOTTOM,     // Placement
                                    s + 16,          // ID
                                    NULL,            // Ctrl data
                                    NULL) ;          // Pres params


    WinSendMsg (hwndRadioColor[sCurrentColor],
               BM_SETCHECK, MPFROMSHORT (1), NULL) ;

    WinSendMsg (hwndRadioType[sCurrentType],
               BM_SETCHECK, MPFROMSHORT (1), NULL) ;

    aptl[0].x = aptl[3].x = aptl[4].x = 4 * cxChar ;
    aptl[1].x = aptl[2].x = 80 * cxChar ;
```

(continued)

Figure 11-3. The DRAWLINE.C File. *continued*

```
                aptl[0].y = aptl[1].y = aptl[4].y = 2 * cyChar ;
                aptl[2].y = aptl[3].y = 20 * cyChar ;

                return 0 ;

        case WM_CONTROL:
                id = SHORT1FROMMP (mp1) ;

                if (id < 16)                // Color IDs
                    {
                    WinSendMsg (hwndRadioColor[sCurrentColor],
                            BM_SETCHECK, MPFROMSHORT (0), NULL) ;

                    sCurrentColor = id ;

                    WinSendMsg (hwndRadioColor[sCurrentColor],
                            BM_SETCHECK, MPFROMSHORT (1), NULL) ;
                    }

                else if (id < 24)          // Line Type IDs
                    {
                    WinSendMsg (hwndRadioType[sCurrentType],
                            BM_SETCHECK, MPFROMSHORT (0), NULL) ;

                    sCurrentType = id - 16 ;

                    WinSendMsg (hwndRadioType[sCurrentType],
                            BM_SETCHECK, MPFROMSHORT (1), NULL) ;
                    }
                WinInvalidateRect (hwnd, NULL, TRUE) ;
                return 0 ;

        case WM_PAINT:
                hps = WinBeginPaint (hwnd, NULL, NULL) ;
                GpiErase (hps) ;

                GpiSetColor (hps, (LONG) sCurrentColor) ;
                GpiSetLineType (hps, sCurrentType + LINETYPE_DOT) ;
                GpiMove (hps, aptl) ;
                GpiPolyLine (hps, 4L, aptl + 1) ;

                WinEndPaint (hps) ;
                return 0 ;
        }
    return WinDefWindowProc (hwnd, msg, mp1, mp2) ;
    }
```

The DRAWLINE.DEF File

```
;--------------------------------------
; DRAWLINE.DEF module definition file
;--------------------------------------

NAME            DRAWLINE  WINDOWAPI

DESCRIPTION     'Draw Line from Radio Buttons (C) Charles Petzold, 1988'
PROTMODE
HEAPSIZE        1024
STACKSIZE       8192
EXPORTS         ClientWndProc
```

Figure 11-3. *The DRAWLINE program.*

DRAWLINE displays two groups of mutually exclusive radio buttons. You specify a line color with one group and a line type (dotted, dashed, solid, and so forth) with the other group. DRAWLINE responds by drawing four-line segments (using the *GpiPolyLine* function) based on the color and line type you choose. Each group of radio buttons is enclosed in a "group box," which is a control window of the WC_STATIC class. A group box looks like a box with some text at the top. The group box doesn't process keyboard and mouse input and doesn't send messages to its owner.

As in BUTTONS1, DRAWLINE creates the control windows in *Client-WndProc* during processing of the WM_CREATE message. The IDs for the first sixteen radio buttons (those that specify the line color) are 0 through 15. The IDs for the eight line-type radio buttons are 16 through 23. The two group boxes have IDs of 24 and 25. DRAWLINE avoids processing the WM_SIZE message by positioning these control windows relative to the lower-left corner of the client window. This allows the position to be specified in the original *WinCreateWindow* function. When you first execute DRAWLINE, you may have to increase the size of the window to see all the controls. The DRAWLINE window is shown in Figure 11-4 on the following page.

After DRAWLINE creates the sixteen radio buttons, it sends BM_SET-CHECK messages to two radio buttons:

```
WinSendMsg (hwndRadioColor [sCurrentColor],
          BM_SETCHECK, MPFROMSHORT (1), NULL) ;

WinSendMsg (hwndRadioType [sCurrentType],
          BM_SETCHECK, MPFROMSHORT (1), NULL) ;
```

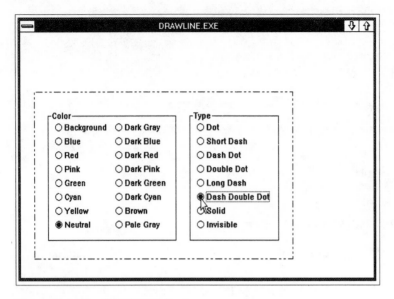

Figure 11-4. *The DRAWLINE display.*

The BM_SETCHECK message tells a radio button to check or uncheck itself, depending on the value of *mp1*. These two statements cause a check to appear in the default radio button in each group—the buttons labeled "Neutral" and "Solid." The program keeps track of which radio button is checked in each group with the two static variables *sCurrentColor* and *sCurrentType*. When the program begins, the two variables are initialized to 7 and 6, which are the values of CLR_NEUTRAL and LINETYPE_SOLID.

When a radio button control is clicked, the control window sends its owner a WM_CONTROL message (not the WM_COMMAND message a push button sends its owner). The *mp1* and *mp2* parameters for radio buttons are:

WM_CONTROL Parameter	*Meaning*
SHORT1FROMMP (mp1)	Child ID
SHORT2FROMMP (mp1)	Notification code
mp2	Control window handle

As in the WM_COMMAND message, the control window identifies itself by the child ID in the low USHORT of *mp1*. (Although the *mp2* parameter also identifies the control because it contains the control's window handle, some controls that send their owners WM_CONTROL messages use *mp2* for other purposes.)

The high USHORT of *mp1* is a notification code. Radio buttons send WM_CONTROL messages to their owners to indicate one of two occurrences, as shown on the next page.

Notification Code	Meaning
BN_CLICKED	Clicked with mouse
BN_DBLCLICKED	Double-clicked with mouse

DRAWLINE ignores the notification code and accepts either a single click or a double click.

DRAWLINE processes the WM_CONTROL message by first obtaining the ID number from *mp1*:

```
case WM_CONTROL:
    id = SHORT1FROMMP (mp1) ;
```

If the ID number is from 0 to 15, the radio button being clicked is in the first group of buttons—those that specify the line color. DRAWLINE must uncheck the currently checked radio button in the group and then check the radio button that has sent it the WM_CONTROL message:

```
if (id < 16)              // Color IDs
    {
    WinSendMsg (hwndRadioColor [sCurrentColor],
            BM_SETCHECK, MPFROMSHORT (0), NULL) ;

    sCurrentColor = id ;

    WinSendMsg (hwndRadioColor [sCurrentColor],
            BM_SETCHECK, MPFROMSHORT (1), NULL) ;
    }
```

Notice that the ID number is used as an array index and as the value stored in *sCurrentColor*. If the ID is from 16 to 23, the radio button is in the second group (line type):

```
else if (id < 24)         // Line type IDs
    {
    WinSendMsg (hwndRadioType [sCurrentType],
            BM_SETCHECK, MPFROMSHORT (0), NULL) ;

    sCurrentType = id - 16 ;

    WinSendMsg (hwndRadioType [sCurrentType],
            BM_SETCHECK, MPFROMSHORT (1), NULL) ;
    }
```

Here the ID must be adjusted by subtracting 16 before it's used as an array index and saved in *sCurrentType*. In either case, the client window is invalidated to generate a WM_PAINT message:

```
WinInvalidateRect (hwnd, NULL, TRUE) ;
```

During processing of WM_PAINT, DRAWLINE uses the *sCurrentColor* and *sCurrentType* variables to set the color and line type:

```
GpiSetColor (hps, (LONG) sCurrentColor) ;
GpiSetLineType (hps, sCurrentType + LINETYPE_DOT) ;
```

It then draws the line in the specified color and type.

The Scroll-Bar Class

A program uses scroll bars to allow a user to specify a single value from a continuous range of integer values (even though the user may not think of the scroll bar in quite this way). As you saw in the series of SYSVALS programs in Chapter 4, you can add a vertical and a horizontal scroll bar to the standard window by including the frame creation flags FCF_VERTSCROLL and FCF_HORZSCROLL in the *WinCreateStdWindow* function. The vertical scroll bar is always positioned to the right of the client window, and the horizontal scroll bar is always positioned below the client window. (They are children of the frame window rather than the client window.) The scroll bars send messages to their owner (the frame window), which then passes the messages to the client window. You can also create vertical or horizontal scroll-bar control windows anywhere on your client window. These scroll bars send messages to their owner, which most often is the client.

The COLORSCR program, shown in Figure 11-5, shows how this is done. This program creates three vertical scroll bars — labeled "Red," "Green," and "Blue" — in the left half of its client window. Each has a range from 0 to 255. As you move the slider on each scroll bar, the right half of the client window uses the *WinFillRect* function to color itself with the composite color based on the red, green, and blue values.

The COLORSCR File

```
#--------------------
# COLORSCR make file
#--------------------

colorscr.obj : colorscr.c
     cl -c -G2sw -W3 colorscr.c

colorscr.exe : colorscr.obj colorscr.def
     link colorscr, /align:16, NUL, os2, colorscr
```

The COLORSCR.C File

```
/*----------------------------------------------------------
   COLORSCR.C -- Color Scroll using child window controls
   ----------------------------------------------------------*/

#define INCL_WIN
#define INCL_GPI
#include <os2.h>
#include <stdlib.h>

MRESULT EXPENTRY ClientWndProc (HWND, USHORT, MPARAM, MPARAM) ;
MRESULT EXPENTRY ScrollProc (HWND, USHORT, MPARAM, MPARAM) ;


HWND  hwndScroll[3], hwndFocus ;
PFNWP pfnOldScroll[3] ;

int main (void)
    {
    static CHAR  szClientClass[] = "ColorScr" ;
    static ULONG flFrameFlags = FCF_TITLEBAR      | FCF_SYSMENU |
                                FCF_SIZEBORDER    | FCF_MINMAX  |
                                FCF_SHELLPOSITION | FCF_TASKLIST ;

    HAB          hab ;
    HMQ          hmq ;
    HWND         hwndFrame, hwndClient ;
    QMSG         qmsg ;

    hab = WinInitialize (0) ;
    hmq = WinCreateMsgQueue (hab, 0) ;

    WinRegisterClass (hab, szClientClass, ClientWndProc, CS_SIZEREDRAW, 0) ;
```

(continued)

Figure 11-5. The COLORSCR.C File. *continued*

```
        hwndFrame = WinCreateStdWindow (HWND_DESKTOP, WS_VISIBLE,
                                        &flFrameFlags, szClientClass, NULL,
                                        OL, NULL, O, &hwndClient) ;

        WinSetFocus (HWND_DESKTOP, hwndFocus = hwndScroll[0]) ;

        WinSendMsg (hwndFrame, WM_SETICON,
                    WinQuerySysPointer (HWND_DESKTOP, SPTR_APPICON, FALSE),
                    NULL) ;

        while (WinGetMsg (hab, &qmsg, NULL, 0, 0))
            WinDispatchMsg (hab, &qmsg) ;

        WinDestroyWindow (hwndFrame) ;
        WinDestroyMsgQueue (hmq) ;
        WinTerminate (hab) ;
        return 0 ;
        }

MRESULT EXPENTRY ClientWndProc (HWND hwnd, USHORT msg, MPARAM mp1, MPARAM mp2)
        {
        static CHAR    *szColorLabel[] = { "Red", "Green", "Blue" } ;
        static HWND    hwndLabel[3], hwndValue[3] ;
        static SHORT   cyChar, sColor[3] ;
        static RECTL   rclRightHalf ;
        CHAR           szBuffer[10] ;
        FONTMETRICS    fm ;
        HPS            hps ;
        SHORT          s, id, cxClient, cyClient ;

        switch (msg)
            {
            case WM_CREATE :
                hps = WinGetPS (hwnd) ;
                GpiQueryFontMetrics (hps, (LONG) sizeof fm, &fm) ;
                cyChar = (SHORT) fm.lMaxBaselineExt ;
                WinReleasePS (hps) ;

                for (s = 0 ; s < 3 ; s++)
                    {
                    hwndScroll[s] = WinCreateWindow (
                                        hwnd,              // Parent
                                        WC_SCROLLBAR,      // Class
```

(continued)

Figure 11-5. The COLORSCR.C File. *continued*

```
                               NULL,              // Text
                               WS_VISIBLE |       // Style
                                   SBS_VERT,
                               0, 0,              // Position
                               0, 0,              // Size
                               hwnd,              // Owner
                               HWND_BOTTOM,       // Placement
                               s,                 // ID
                               NULL,              // Ctrl data
                               NULL) ;            // Pres params

        hwndLabel[s]  = WinCreateWindow (
                               hwnd,              // Parent
                               WC_STATIC,         // Class
                               szColorLabel[s],   // Text
                               WS_VISIBLE |       // Style
                                 SS_TEXT | DT_CENTER,
                               0, 0,              // Position
                               0, 0,              // Size
                               hwnd,              // Owner
                               HWND_BOTTOM,       // Placement
                               s + 3,             // ID
                               NULL,              // Ctrl data
                               NULL) ;            // Pres params

        hwndValue[s]  = WinCreateWindow (
                               hwnd,              // Parent
                               WC_STATIC,         // Class
                               "0",               // Text
                               WS_VISIBLE |       // Style
                                 SS_TEXT | DT_CENTER,
                               0, 0,              // Position
                               0, 0,              // Size
                               hwnd,              // Owner
                               HWND_BOTTOM,       // Placement
                               s + 6,             // ID
                               NULL,              // Ctrl data
                               NULL) ;            // Pres params

        pfnOldScroll[s] =
                WinSubclassWindow (hwndScroll[s], ScrollProc) ;
```

(continued)

Figure 11-5. The COLORSCR.C File. *continued*

```
                    WinSendMsg (hwndScroll[s], SBM_SETSCROLLBAR,
                           MPFROM2SHORT (0, 0), MPFROM2SHORT (0, 255)) ;
               }
          return 0 ;

     case WM_SIZE :
          cxClient = SHORT1FROMMP (mp2) ;
          cyClient = SHORT2FROMMP (mp2) ;

          for (s = 0 ; s < 3 ; s++)
               {
               WinSetWindowPos (hwndScroll[s], NULL,
                           (2 * s + 1) * cxClient / 14, 2 * cyChar,
                           cxClient / 14, cyClient - 4 * cyChar,
                           SWP_SIZE | SWP_MOVE) ;

               WinSetWindowPos (hwndLabel[s], NULL,
                           (4 * s + 1) * cxClient / 28,
                           cyClient - 3 * cyChar / 2,
                           cxClient / 7, cyChar,
                           SWP_SIZE | SWP_MOVE) ;

               WinSetWindowPos (hwndValue[s], NULL,
                           (4 * s + 1) * cxClient / 28, cyChar / 2,
                           cxClient / 7, cyChar,
                           SWP_SIZE | SWP_MOVE) ;
               }

          WinQueryWindowRect (hwnd, &rclRightHalf) ;
          rclRightHalf.xLeft = rclRightHalf.xRight / 2 ;
          return 0 ;

     case WM_VSCROLL :
          id = SHORT1FROMMP (mp1) ;              // ID of scroll bar

          switch (SHORT2FROMMP (mp2))
               {
               case SB_LINEDOWN :
                    sColor[id] = min (255, sColor[id] + 1) ;
                    break ;

               case SB_LINEUP :
                    sColor[id] = max (0, sColor[id] - 1) ;
                    break ;
```

(continued)

Figure 11-5. The COLORSCR.C File. *continued*

```
                          case SB_PAGEDOWN :
                               sColor[id] = min (255, sColor[id] + 16) ;
                               break ;

                          case SB_PAGEUP :
                               sColor[id] = max (0, sColor[id] - 16) ;
                               break ;

                          case SB_SLIDERTRACK :
                               sColor[id] = SHORT1FROMMP (mp2) ;
                               break ;

                          default :
                               return 0 ;
                          }
                     WinSendMsg (hwndScroll[id], SBM_SETPOS,
                               MPFROM2SHORT (sColor[id], 0), NULL) ;

                     WinSetWindowText (hwndValue[id],
                                        itoa (sColor[id], szBuffer, 10)) ;
                     WinInvalidateRect (hwnd, &rclRightHalf, FALSE) ;
                     return 0 ;

                case WM_PAINT:
                     hps = WinBeginPaint (hwnd, NULL, NULL) ;

                     GpiCreateLogColorTable (hps, LCOL_RESET, LCOLF_RGB,
                                                  0L, 0L, NULL) ;

                     WinFillRect (hps, &rclRightHalf, (ULONG) sColor[0] << 16 |
                                                      (ULONG) sColor[1] <<  8 |
                                                      (ULONG) sColor[2]) ;
                     WinEndPaint (hps) ;
                     return 0 ;

                case WM_ERASEBACKGROUND:
                     return 1 ;
                }
          return WinDefWindowProc (hwnd, msg, mp1, mp2) ;
          }

MRESULT EXPENTRY ScrollProc (HWND hwnd, USHORT msg, MPARAM mp1, MPARAM mp2)
     {
```

(continued)

Figure 11-5. The COLORSCR.C File. *continued*

```
    USHORT id ;

    id = WinQueryWindowUShort (hwnd, QWS_ID) ;    // ID of scroll bar

    switch (msg)
        {
        case WM_CHAR:
            if (!(CHARMSG(&msg)->fs & KC_VIRTUALKEY))
                break ;

            switch (CHARMSG(&msg)->vkey)
                {
                case VK_TAB:
                    if (!(CHARMSG(&msg)->fs & KC_KEYUP))
                        {
                        hwndFocus = hwndScroll[(id + 1) % 3] ;
                        WinSetFocus (HWND_DESKTOP, hwndFocus) ;
                        }
                    return 1 ;

                case VK_BACKTAB:
                    if (!(CHARMSG(&msg)->fs & KC_KEYUP))
                        {
                        hwndFocus = hwndScroll[(id + 2) % 3] ;
                        WinSetFocus (HWND_DESKTOP, hwndFocus) ;
                        }
                    return 1 ;

                default:
                    break ;
                }
            break ;

        case WM_BUTTON1DOWN:
            WinSetFocus (HWND_DESKTOP, hwndFocus = hwnd) ;
            break ;
        }
    return pfnOldScroll[id] (hwnd, msg, mp1, mp2) ;
    }
```

The COLORSCR.DEF File

```
;-------------------------------------
; COLORSCR.DEF module definition file
;-------------------------------------

NAME          COLORSCR  WINDOWAPI

DESCRIPTION   'Color Scroll (C) Charles Petzold, 1988'
PROTMODE
HEAPSIZE      1024
STACKSIZE     8192
EXPORTS       ClientWndProc
              ScrollProc
```

Figure 11-5. *The COLORSCR program.*

COLORSCR creates nine control windows—three scroll-bar windows and six static text windows. Three static text windows are positioned on top of the scroll bars and display the labels "Red," "Green," and "Blue." The text windows on the bottom of each scroll bar display the current position (0 through 255) of the scroll bar. These values correspond directly to the red, green, and blue values used to create the composite color. The COLORSCR window is shown in Figure 11-6.

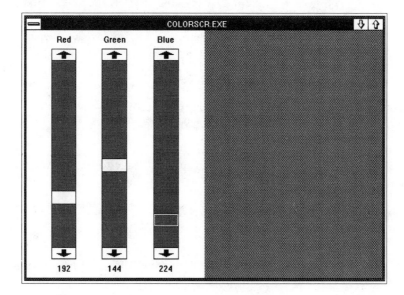

Figure 11-6. *The COLORSCR display.*

The nine windows are created during processing of the WM_CREATE message in *ClientWndProc*. The child IDs and the arrays the program uses for storing the window handles are as follows:

Window Type	Child ID	Window Handle Array
Scroll bar	0 to 2	*hwndScroll*
Static text	3 to 5	*hwndLabel*
Static text	6 to 8	*hwndValue*

The three scroll bars have the window class WC_SCROLLBAR and the window style WS_VISIBLE ¦ SBS_VERT. The SBS_VERT style indicates that the scroll bars are vertical. COLORSCR gives the six static text windows the window style WS_VISIBLE ¦ SS_TEXT ¦ DT_CENTER. The SS_TEXT identifier is one of several window styles available for windows of the WC_STATIC class. The DT_CENTER identifier is normally used with the *WinDrawText* function, but you can also use it as a window style with SS_TEXT to center the text within the width of the window. The position and size parameters are set to 0 in the *WinCreateWindow* call. *ClientWndProc* positions and sizes the windows during the WM_SIZE message.

When you include scroll bars as part of the standard window, vertical scroll bars always have a standard width, and horizontal scroll bars always have a standard height. You can obtain these standard widths and heights from the *WinQuerySysValue* function using the SV_CXVSCROLL and SV_CYHSCROLL parameters. However, when you create scroll bars using the *WinCreateWindow* function, the scroll bars can be any size you want. You can make long, thin scroll bars or short, pudgy scroll bars. COLORSCR always sets the width of the three vertical scroll bars at $1/14$ the width of the client window. This is done while processing the WM_SIZE message. If you want to use standard widths and heights for the scroll bars you create in your programs, get the values from *WinQuerySysValue*.

After creating the scroll bars during the WM_CREATE message, COLORSCR sends them a SBM_SETSCROLLBAR message to set the range and current position:

```
WinSendMsg (hwndScroll [s], SBM_SETSCROLLBAR,
            MPFROM2SHORT (0, 0), MPFROM2SHORT (0, 255)) ;
```

The SYSVALS programs in Chapter 4 use this same message.

Processing the Scroll-Bar Messages

The scroll bars in COLORSCR send WM_VSCROLL messages to the client window. WM_VSCROLL and WM_HSCROLL messages are accompanied by *mp1* and *mp2* parameters as follows:

WM_xSCROLL Parameter	Meaning
SHORT1FROMMP (mp1)	Child ID
SHORT2FROMMP (mp1)	0
SHORT1FROMMP (mp2)	Slider position (for some commands)
SHORT2FROMMP (mp2)	Command

This is the same information used for scroll bars created in a standard window. The SYSVALS program didn't look at the control ID, because the program had only one vertical scroll bar and one horizontal scroll bar. If you include scroll bars as part of the standard window and then create additional scroll bars using *WinCreateWindow*, you can differentiate the scroll bars by examining the ID number. The scroll bars that are part of the standard window have the predefined IDs FID_VERTSCROLL and FID_HORZSCROLL.

COLORSCR defines a static array named *sColor* to store the current position of each of the three scroll bars. The index to this array is the same as the scroll-bar ID. The processing of the WM_VSCROLL message thus begins by obtaining the ID number from *mp1*:

```
case WM_VSCROLL :
    id = SHORT1FROMMP (mp1) ;
```

COLORSCR then alters the appropriate value stored in *sColor* based on the scroll-bar command in the high USHORT of *mp2*:

```
switch (SHORT2FROMMP (mp2))
    {
    case SB_LINEDOWN :
        sColor [id] = min (255, sColor [id] + 1) ;
        break ;

    case SB_LINEUP :
        sColor [id] = max (0, sColor [id] - 1) ;
        break ;
```

(continued)

continued

```
case SB_PAGEDOWN :
     sColor [id] = min (255, sColor [id] + 16) ;
     break ;

case SB_PAGEUP :
     sColor [id] = max (0, sColor [id] - 16) ;
     break ;

case SB_SLIDERTRACK :
     sColor [id] = SHORT1FROMMP (mp2) ;
     break ;

default :
     return 0 ;
}
```

The program sets a new position of the scroll-bar slider by sending it an SBM_SETPOS message. The window handle of the scroll bar is stored in the *hwndScroll* array that is also indexed by the ID number:

```
WinSendMsg (hwndScroll [id], SBM_SETPOS,
          MPFROM2SHORT (sColor [id], 0), NULL) ;
```

COLORSCR must also change the text in the static control window displayed at the bottom of the scroll bar. It does this by first converting the number to its ASCII value using the C function *itoa* and then calling *WinSetWindowText*. The window handles are stored in the *hwndValue* array:

```
WinSetWindowText (hwndValue [id],
               itoa (sColor [id], szBuffer, 10)) ;
```

The right half of the client window is then invalidated to generate a WM_PAINT message:

```
WinInvalidateRect (hwnd, &rclRightHalf, FALSE) ;
```

The *rclRightHalf* RECTL structure contains the coordinates of the right half of the client window. These are set during the WM_SIZE message.

The WM_PAINT processing is fairly simple. COLORSCR first calls *GpiCreateLogColorTable* to specify that color indexes are to be interpreted as 32-bit RGB values:

```
GpiCreateLogColorTable (hps, LCOL_RESET, LCOLF_RGB,
                        0L, 0L, NULL) ;
```

The program then combines the current red, green, and blue color values stored in the *sColor* array into one ULONG and calls *WinFillRect* to color the right half of the client window with that color:

```
WinFillRect (hps, &rclRightHalf, (ULONG) sColor [0] << 16 |
                                 (ULONG) sColor [1] <<  8 |
                                 (ULONG) sColor [2]) ;
```

Changing the Keyboard Input Focus

Unlike BUTTONS1 and DRAWLINE, COLORSCR has a complete keyboard interface and doesn't require a mouse. You can move the position of the scroll-bar slider using the cursor movement arrow keys, and you can move the keyboard input focus from one scroll bar to another using the Tab and Shift-Tab keys.

As you saw in the SYSVALS program in Chapter 4, the scroll bars include their own keyboard interface for the cursor movement keys. Once a scroll-bar window has the keyboard input focus, it can understand and interpret these keys. That's not the problem. The problem is that once a control window gets the input focus, it doesn't properly interpret the Tab key. We need to find a way to give a scroll bar the input focus (so that it uses the cursor movement keys) and then be able to take away the input focus when the Tab key is pressed. But how can *ClientWndProc* know that the Tab key is pressed when the scroll bar is getting all the WM_CHAR messages?

The solution involves a technique called "window subclassing." Essentially, this technique allows your program to get first dibs on all messages sent to a particular window created by your program (but not windows created by other programs). You can process some of these messages and then allow the window's normal window procedure to process the others. You can prevent the normal window procedure from receiving some messages, or you can alter messages before they get to the window procedure.

Let's look at COLORSCR to see how this works in practice. Toward the end of COLORSCR.C is a function called *ScrollProc* that is defined as if it were a normal window procedure. It is an EXPENTRY function, has a return value of MRESULT, and accepts the four parameters normally passed to window procedures. *ScrollProc* is also included in the EXPORTS section of the COLORSCR.DEF module definition file:

```
EXPORTS        ClientWndProc
               ScrollProc
```

Don't forget to do this!

After creating the three scroll-bar windows during processing of the WM_CREATE message, COLORSCR calls *WinSubclassWindow* to specify that all messages to these three scroll-bar windows should be sent to *ScrollProc* instead:

```
pfnOldScroll[s] =
        WinSubclassWindow (hwndScroll[s], ScrollProc) ;
```

The *pfnOldScroll* array is a global variable defined near the top of COLORSCR.C:

```
PFNWP pfnOldScroll[3] ;
```

This array holds the addresses of the original window procedures for the three scroll bars.

Now let's look at *ScrollProc*. When a message is sent to any of the three scroll bars, *ScrollProc* gets the message rather than the normal scroll-bar window procedure. *ScrollProc* obtains the control ID associated with the scroll-bar window receiving the message:

```
id = WinQueryWindowUShort (hwnd, QWS_ID) ;
```

ScrollProc then checks to see if the message is WM_CHAR, if the message contains a valid virtual key code, if the key is being pressed, and if the virtual key is VK_TAB or VK_BACKTAB.

For VK_TAB, *ScrollProc* determines the window handle that is to receive the input focus:

```
hwndFocus = hwndScroll[(id + 1) % 3]
```

The new focus window is the scroll bar with the next highest ID. *ScrollProc* then uses this *hwndFocus* variable to set the new focus window:

```
WinSetFocus (HWND_DESKTOP, hwndFocus) ;
```

ScrollProc also sets the focus to one of the scroll bars when it receives a WM_BUTTON1DOWN message.

ScrollProc sends all messages (except the VK_TAB and VK_BACKTAB keystrokes) to the old scroll-bar window procedure stored in *pfnOldScroll*:

```
return pfnOldScroll [id] (hwnd, msg, mp1, mp2) ;
```

This allows the normal processing in the scroll-bar window procedure to occur.

Of course, we must make sure that the first scroll bar gets the input focus when the program starts up. Following the *WinCreateStdWindow* call in *main*, COLORSCR sets the input focus to the first window:

```
WinSetFocus (HWND_DESKTOP, hwndFocus = hwndScroll [0]) ;
```

Without this statement, the first scroll bar wouldn't get the input focus until it was clicked.

Creating Your Own Controls

In Chapter 9's CHECKER3 program you created child windows that helped simplify mouse processing. These child windows were not really control windows because they had two deficiencies: They had no keyboard interface and they did not notify their owner when they were toggled. Now let's try something similar, but this time let's make the children full-fledged control windows.

In this exercise, we're going to reinvent the push button. While we're at it, we're going to make our push buttons look a little prettier than the ones built into the Presentation Manager. This new push button will be square and (through use of color) will have a 3-D appearance.

Mouse Capture and Input Focus

You may want to experiment with BUTTONS1 (and other programs that create control windows based on the predefined window classes) to help you understand what is going on in the window procedure for the control.

For example, you'll find in BUTTONS1 that triggering the button with the mouse requires that you both press and release the mouse button while the pointer is positioned within the control. If you press the mouse button when the pointer is within the control, the control is inverted. If you move the mouse pointer outside the control with the mouse button pressed, the control returns to normal. Moving the pointer back within the button causes the button colors to be inverted again.

Obviously the window procedure is capturing the mouse (a concept discussed in Chapter 9). This is the only way the window procedure can detect that the mouse pointer has moved outside the control window.

Clicking the push button with the mouse causes a dotted outline to appear around the text. This indicates that the control has the input focus and requires that the window procedure give itself the input focus when the button is clicked. When the push button has the input focus, you can also trigger the button by pressing the Spacebar. This requires that the window procedure for the control also process some keystrokes.

The Square Button Window Procedure

Let's look first at the SQBTN.C file shown in Figure 11-7.

```
/*-------------------------------------------------------------------
      SQBTN.C -- Contains window procedure for square 3D push button
   -------------------------------------------------------------------*/

#define INCL_WIN
#define INCL_GPI
#include <os2.h>
#include <malloc.h>
#include <string.h>


#define LCID_ITALIC 1L

            /*-------------------------------------------------------
                  Structure for storing data unique to each window
               ----------------------------------------------------*/
typedef struct
    {
    PSZ  pszText ;
    BOOL fHaveCapture ;
    BOOL fHaveFocus ;
    BOOL fInsideRect ;
    BOOL fSpaceDown ;
    }
```

(continued)

Figure 11-7. *continued*

```
    SQBTN ;

typedef SQBTN FAR *PSQBTN ;
MRESULT EXPENTRY SqBtnWndProc (HWND, USHORT, MPARAM, MPARAM) ;
VOID             DrawButton   (HWND, HPS, PSQBTN) ;

HAB  hab ;

        /*-------------------------------------------------------------
                RegisterSqBtnClass function available to other modules
        ------------------------------------------------------------*/

BOOL RegisterSqBtnClass (HAB habIn)
    {
    hab = habIn ;

    return WinRegisterClass (hab, "SqBtn", SqBtnWndProc,
                    CS_SIZEREDRAW, sizeof (PSQBTN)) ;
    }

        /*--------------------------------------------
                String functions that accept far pointers
        -------------------------------------------*/

USHORT fstrlen (PCHAR pch)
    {
    USHORT usLen ;
    for (usLen = 0 ; pch[usLen] ; usLen++) ;
    return usLen ;
    }

PCHAR fstrcpy (PCHAR pchDst, PCHAR pchSrc)
    {
    USHORT usIndex ;
    for (usIndex = 0 ; pchDst[usIndex] = pchSrc[usIndex] ; usIndex++) ;
    return pchDst ;
    }

        /*-------------------------------
                SqBtnWndProc window procedure
        ------------------------------*/
```

(continued)

Figure 11-7. *continued*

```
MRESULT EXPENTRY SqBtnWndProc (HWND hwnd, USHORT msg, MPARAM mp1, MPARAM mp2)
    {
    BOOL          fTestInsideRect ;
    HPS           hps ;
    PCREATESTRUCT pcrst ;
    POINTL        ptl ;
    PSQBTN        pSqBtn ;
    PWNDPARAMS    pwprm ;
    RECTL         rcl ;

    pSqBtn = WinQueryWindowPtr (hwnd, 0) ;

    switch (msg)
        {
        case WM_CREATE:
            pSqBtn = _fmalloc (sizeof (SQBTN)) ;

                    // Initialize structure

            pSqBtn->fHaveCapture = FALSE ;
            pSqBtn->fHaveFocus   = FALSE ;
            pSqBtn->fInsideRect  = FALSE ;
            pSqBtn->fSpaceDown   = FALSE ;

                    // Get window text from creation structure

            pcrst = (PCREATESTRUCT) PVOIDFROMMP (mp2) ;

            pSqBtn->pszText = _fmalloc (1 + fstrlen (pcrst->pszText)) ;
            fstrcpy (pSqBtn->pszText, pcrst->pszText) ;

            WinSetWindowPtr (hwnd, 0, pSqBtn) ;
            return 0 ;

        case WM_SETWINDOWPARAMS:
            pwprm = (PWNDPARAMS) PVOIDFROMMP (mp1) ;

                    // Get window text from window parameter structure

            if (pwprm->fsStatus & WPM_TEXT)
                {
                _ffree (pSqBtn->pszText) ;
                pSqBtn->pszText = _fmalloc (1 + pwprm->cchText) ;
```

(continued)

Figure 11-7. *continued*

```
                       fstrcpy (pSqBtn->pszText, pwprm->pszText) ;
                       }
               return 1 ;

     case WM_QUERYWINDOWPARAMS:
          pwprm == (PWNDPARAMS) PVOIDFROMMP (mp1) ;

                       // Set window parameter structure fields

          if (pwprm->fsStatus & WPM_CCHTEXT)
              pwprm->cchText = fstrlen (pSqBtn->pszText) ;

          if (pwprm->fsStatus & WPM_TEXT)
              fstrcpy (pwprm->pszText, pSqBtn->pszText) ;

          if (pwprm->fsStatus & WPM_CBPRESPARAMS)
              pwprm->cbPresParams = 0 ;

          if (pwprm->fsStatus & WPM_PRESPARAMS)
              pwprm->pPresParams = NULL ;

          if (pwprm->fsStatus & WPM_CBCTLDATA)
              pwprm->cbCtlData = 0 ;

          if (pwprm->fsStatus & WPM_CTLDATA)
              pwprm->pCtlData = NULL ;

          return 1 ;

     case WM_BUTTON1DOWN:
          WinSetFocus (HWND_DESKTOP, hwnd) ;
          WinSetCapture (HWND_DESKTOP, hwnd) ;
          pSqBtn->fHaveCapture = TRUE ;
          pSqBtn->fInsideRect  = TRUE ;
          WinInvalidateRect (hwnd, NULL, FALSE) ;
          return 0 ;

     case WM_MOUSEMOVE:
          if (!pSqBtn->fHaveCapture)
              break ;

          WinQueryWindowRect (hwnd, &rcl) ;
          ptl.x = MOUSEMSG(&msg)->x ;
          ptl.y = MOUSEMSG(&msg)->y ;
```

(continued)

Figure 11-7. *continued*

```
                    // Test if mouse pointer is still in window

        fTestInsideRect = WinPtInRect (hab, &rcl, &ptl) ;

        if (pSqBtn->fInsideRect != fTestInsideRect)
            {
            pSqBtn->fInsideRect = fTestInsideRect ;
            WinInvalidateRect (hwnd, NULL, FALSE) ;
            }
        break ;

case WM_BUTTON1UP:
        if (!pSqBtn->fHaveCapture)
            break ;

        WinSetCapture (HWND_DESKTOP, NULL) ;
        pSqBtn->fHaveCapture = FALSE ;
        pSqBtn->fInsideRect  = FALSE ;

        WinQueryWindowRect (hwnd, &rcl) ;
        ptl.x = MOUSEMSG(&msg)->x ;
        ptl.y = MOUSEMSG(&msg)->y ;

                    // Post WM_COMMAND if mouse pointer is in window

        if (WinPtInRect (hab, &rcl, &ptl))
            WinPostMsg (WinQueryWindow (hwnd, QW_OWNER, FALSE),
                WM_COMMAND,
                MPFROMSHORT (WinQueryWindowUShort (hwnd, QWS_ID)),
                MPFROM2SHORT (CMDSRC_OTHER, TRUE)) ;

        WinInvalidateRect (hwnd, NULL, FALSE) ;
        return 0 ;

case WM_ENABLE:
        WinInvalidateRect (hwnd, NULL, FALSE) ;
        return 0 ;

case WM_SETFOCUS:
        pSqBtn->fHaveFocus = SHORT1FROMMP (mp2) ;
        WinInvalidateRect (hwnd, NULL, FALSE) ;
        return 0 ;
```

(continued)

Figure 11-7. *continued*

```
          case WM_CHAR:
              if (!(CHARMSG(&msg)->fs & KC_VIRTUALKEY) ||
                    CHARMSG(&msg)->vkey != VK_SPACE      ||
                    CHARMSG(&msg)->fs & KC_PREVDOWN)
                  break ;

                       // Post WM_COMMAND when space bar is released

              if (!(CHARMSG(&msg)->fs & KC_KEYUP))
                  pSqBtn->fSpaceDown = TRUE ;
              else
                  {
                  pSqBtn->fSpaceDown = FALSE ;
                  WinPostMsg (WinQueryWindow (hwnd, QW_OWNER, FALSE),
                      WM_COMMAND,
                      MPFROMSHORT (WinQueryWindowUShort (hwnd, QWS_ID)),
                      MPFROM2SHORT (CMDSRC_OTHER, FALSE)) ;
                  }
              WinInvalidateRect (hwnd, NULL, FALSE) ;
              return 0 ;

          case WM_PAINT:
              hps = WinBeginPaint (hwnd, NULL, NULL) ;
              DrawButton (hwnd, hps, pSqBtn) ;
              WinEndPaint (hps) ;
              return 0 ;

          case WM_DESTROY:
              _ffree (pSqBtn->pszText) ;
              _ffree (pSqBtn) ;
              return 0 ;
          }
      return WinDefWindowProc (hwnd, msg, mp1, mp2) ;
      }


      /*----------------------------------------------------------
          Draws filled and outlined polygon (used by DrawButton)
      ----------------------------------------------------------*/

VOID Polygon (HPS hps, LONG lPoints, POINTL aptl[], LONG lColor)
      {
          // Draw interior in specified color
```

(continued)

Figure 11-7. *continued*

```
     GpiSavePS (hps) ;
     GpiSetColor (hps, lColor) ;

     GpiBeginArea (hps, BA_NOBOUNDARY | BA_ALTERNATE) ;
     GpiMove (hps, aptl) ;
     GpiPolyLine (hps, lPoints - 1, aptl + 1) ;
     GpiEndArea (hps) ;

     GpiRestorePS (hps, -1L) ;

               // Draw boundary in default color

     GpiMove (hps, aptl + lPoints - 1) ;
     GpiPolyLine (hps, lPoints, aptl) ;
     }


       /*-----------------------
          Draws square button
          ---------------------*/

VOID DrawButton (HWND hwnd, HPS hps, PSQBTN pSqBtn)
     {
     FATTRS       fat ;
     FONTMETRICS  fm ;
     HDC          hdc ;
     LONG         lColor, lHorzRes, lVertRes, cxEdge, cyEdge ;
     POINTL       aptl[10], aptlTextBox[TXTBOX_COUNT], ptlShadow, ptlText ;
     RECTL        rcl ;

               // Find 2 millimeter edge width in pixels

     hdc = GpiQueryDevice (hps) ;
     DevQueryCaps (hdc, CAPS_HORIZONTAL_RESOLUTION, 1L, &lHorzRes) ;
     DevQueryCaps (hdc, CAPS_VERTICAL_RESOLUTION,   1L, &lVertRes) ;

     cxEdge = lHorzRes / 500 ;
     cyEdge = lVertRes / 500 ;

               // Set up coordinates for drawing the button

     WinQueryWindowRect (hwnd, &rcl) ;

     aptl[0].x = 0 ;                      aptl[0].y = 0 ;
     aptl[1].x = cxEdge ;                 aptl[1].y = cyEdge ;
     aptl[2].x = rcl.xRight - cxEdge ;    aptl[2].y = cyEdge ;
```

(continued)

Figure 11-7. *continued*

```
aptl[3].x = rcl.xRight - 1 ;        aptl[3].y = 0 ;
aptl[4].x = rcl.xRight - 1 ;        aptl[4].y = rcl.yTop - 1 ;
aptl[5].x = rcl.xRight - cxEdge ;   aptl[5].y = rcl.yTop - cyEdge ;
aptl[6].x = cxEdge ;                aptl[6].y = rcl.yTop - cyEdge ;
aptl[7].x = 0 ;                     aptl[7].y = rcl.yTop - 1 ;
aptl[8].x = 0 ;                     aptl[8].y = 0 ;
aptl[9].x = cxEdge ;                aptl[9].y = cyEdge ;

        // Paint edges at bottom and right side

GpiSetColor (hps, CLR_BLACK) ;
lColor = (pSqBtn->fInsideRect || pSqBtn->fSpaceDown) ?
                    CLR_PALEGRAY : CLR_DARKGRAY ;
Polygon (hps, 4L, aptl + 0, lColor) ;
Polygon (hps, 4L, aptl + 2, lColor) ;

        // Paint edges at top and left side

lColor = (pSqBtn->fInsideRect || pSqBtn->fSpaceDown) ?
                    CLR_DARKGRAY : CLR_WHITE ;
Polygon (hps, 4L, aptl + 4, lColor) ;
Polygon (hps, 4L, aptl + 6, lColor) ;

        // Paint interior area

GpiSavePS (hps) ;
GpiSetColor (hps, (pSqBtn->fInsideRect || pSqBtn->fSpaceDown) ?
                    CLR_DARKGRAY : CLR_PALEGRAY) ;
GpiMove (hps, aptl + 1) ;
GpiBox (hps, DRO_FILL, aptl + 5, 0L, 0L) ;
GpiRestorePS (hps, -1L) ;
GpiBox (hps, DRO_OUTLINE, aptl + 5, 0L, 0L) ;

        // If button has focus, use italic font

GpiQueryFontMetrics (hps, (LONG) sizeof fm, &fm) ;

if (pSqBtn->fHaveFocus)
    {
    fat.usRecordLength  = sizeof fat ;
    fat.fsSelection     = FATTR_SEL_ITALIC ;
    fat.lMatch          = 0 ;
    fat.idRegistry      = fm.idRegistry ;
    fat.usCodePage      = fm.usCodePage ;
```

(continued)

Figure 11-7. *continued*

```
            fat.lMaxBaselineExt = fm.lMaxBaselineExt ;
            fat.lAveCharWidth   = fm.lAveCharWidth ;
            fat.fsType          = 0 ;
            fat.fsFontUse       = 0 ;
            strcpy (fat.szFacename, fm.szFacename) ;

            GpiCreateLogFont (hps, NULL, LCID_ITALIC, &fat) ;
            GpiSetCharSet (hps, LCID_ITALIC) ;
            }
                // Calculate text position

    GpiQueryTextBox (hps, (LONG) fstrlen (pSqBtn->pszText), pSqBtn->pszText,
                        TXTBOX_COUNT, aptlTextBox) ;

    ptlText.x = (rcl.xRight - aptlTextBox[TXTBOX_CONCAT].x) / 2 ;
    ptlText.y = (rcl.yTop   - aptlTextBox[TXTBOX_TOPLEFT].y -
                        aptlTextBox[TXTBOX_BOTTOMLEFT].y) / 2 ;

    ptlShadow.x = ptlText.x + fm.lAveCharWidth    / 3 ;
    ptlShadow.y = ptlText.y - fm.lMaxBaselineExt / 8 ;

                // Display text shadow in black, and text in white

    GpiSetColor (hps, CLR_BLACK) ;
    GpiCharStringAt (hps, &ptlShadow, (LONG) fstrlen (pSqBtn->pszText),
                                    pSqBtn->pszText) ;
    GpiSetColor (hps, CLR_WHITE) ;
    GpiCharStringAt (hps, &ptlText, (LONG) fstrlen (pSqBtn->pszText),
                                    pSqBtn->pszText) ;

                // X out button if the window is not enabled

    if (!WinIsWindowEnabled (hwnd))
        {
        GpiMove (hps, aptl + 1) ;
        GpiLine (hps, aptl + 5) ;
        GpiMove (hps, aptl + 2) ;
        GpiLine (hps, aptl + 6) ;
        }
            // Clean up

    if (pSqBtn->fHaveFocus)
        {
        GpiSetCharSet (hps, LCID_DEFAULT) ;
        GpiDeleteSetId (hps, LCID_ITALIC) ;
        }
    }
```

Figure 11-7. *The SQBTN.C file.*

This file contains several functions. Two functions are called from outside the module: *RegisterSqBtnClass* registers a window class called "SqBtn" that uses the window procedure *SqBtnWndProc*, another function in SQBTN.C. *RegisterSqBtnClass* also saves the process's anchor block handle in a global variable for later use in the window procedure.

Often a program creates more than one child window based on the same window class. This means that you cannot use static variables to store information unique to each child window: These static variables would be shared by all windows based on that class that are created within the same process. For this reason, only automatic variables (used during the course of processing a single message) are defined within *SqBtnWndProc*.

Information unique to each window is stored in a structure of type SQBTN, defined in the SQBTN.C file. When *RegisterSqBtnClass* registers the window class, the last parameter of *WinRegisterClass* is set to the size of a far pointer to the SQBTN structure. This reserves some memory space that is unique to each window. During the WM_CREATE message, *SqBtnWndProc* calls _*fmalloc* (a version of *malloc* that returns a far pointer) to allocate a block of memory the size of the SQBTN structure. The pointer returned by _*fmalloc* is stored in the variable *pSqBtn*. After the fields of this structure are initialized, the pointer is saved in the memory reserved by the *WinRegisterClass* function:

```
WinSetWindowPtr (hwnd, 0, pSqBtn) ;
```

The WM_CREATE message is the first message the window procedure processes when creating a new window. For all other messages, the pointer stored in the reserved area will be valid. *SqBtnWndProc* obtains that pointer before processing any specific message:

```
pSqBtn = WinQueryWindowPtr (hwnd, 0) ;
```

This allows the window procedure to use the window-specific information stored in the structure.

Some windows have a "window text" that the window displays. For example, push buttons display their window text in the center of the button. Windows that have a window text must save the text themselves. This requires some additional processing in the WM_CREATE message. During WM_CREATE, a pointer to the initial window text of the window (which is the string passed as the window text parameter to *WinCreateWindow*) is stored in the *pszText* field of a CREATESTRUCT structure for the window.

The *mp2* message parameter contains a pointer to this structure. *SqBtn-WndProc* must determine the length of this text, allocate memory for storing the text by calling *_fmalloc*, copy the text into this memory, and save the pointer returned from *_fmalloc* in the SQBTN structure.

Now we have a little problem because we're compiling for small model but the pointer to this text in the CREATESTRUCT structure is a far pointer. This means that we cannot use the normal C *strlen* and *strcpy* functions for working with this string. For this reason, the SQBTN.C file has two functions named *fstrlen* and *fstrcpy*, which are equivalent to *strlen* and *strcpy* but which use far pointers. (Another way around this problem is to compile for medium or large model.)

The window text can be changed by a call to *WinSetWindowText* and queried by a call to *WinQueryWindowText*. These functions send WM_SETWIN-DOWPARAMS and WM_QUERYWINDOWPARAMS messages, respectively, to the window procedure. This requires that *SqBtnWndProc* also process these two messages. Again the *fstrlen* and *fstrcpy* functions are used in working with the text string.

During the WM_BUTTON1DOWN message, *SqBtnWndProc* captures the mouse and sets the *fHaveCapture* field in the SQBTN structure to TRUE. The window procedure tests this field during the WM_MOUSEMOVE and WM_BUTTON1UP message to determine if it can ignore the message. For both of these messages, *SqBtnWndProc* uses the *WinPtInRect* to determine if the mouse pointer is still within the area occupied by the control window. If the mouse pointer is within the window during a WM_BUTTON1UP message, *SqBtnWndProc* posts a WM_COMMAND message to its owner.

The WM_COMMAND message can also be posted during the WM_CHAR message. The window procedure posts this message when the Spacebar is released. Because *SqBtnWndProc* will receive WM_CHAR messages only when the control has the input focus, it need not check that it has the input focus when processing the keystrokes.

During the WM_PAINT message, *SqBtnWndProc* calls *DrawButton* to draw the button. The processing is lengthy but does nothing we didn't see in Chapter 5 when exploring the GPI functions. Rather than outlining text to indicate the button's input focus, I decided to display italic text instead.

Creating the Square Buttons

To test this new window class, we need a program that creates a couple of square 3-D buttons. This is BUTTONS2, shown in Figure 11-8.

The BUTTONS2 File

```
#--------------------
# BUTTONS2 make file
#--------------------

buttons2.obj : buttons2.c
    cl -c -G2sw -W3 buttons2.c

sqbtn.obj : sqbtn.c
    cl -c -G2sw -W3 sqbtn.c

buttons2.exe : buttons2.obj sqbtn.obj buttons2.def
    link buttons2 sqbtn, /align:16, NUL, os2, buttons2
```

The BUTTONS2.C File

```
/*---------------------------------------------
   BUTTONS2.C -- Square Button Demonstration
   ---------------------------------------------*/

#define INCL_WIN
#define INCL_GPI
#include <os2.h>

BOOL RegisterSqBtnClass (HAB) ;               // In SQBTN.C

MRESULT EXPENTRY ClientWndProc (HWND, USHORT, MPARAM, MPARAM) ;

HAB  hab ;

int main (void)
    {
    static CHAR   szClientClass[] = "Buttons2" ;
    static ULONG  flFrameFlags = FCF_TITLEBAR      | FCF_SYSMENU  |
                                 FCF_SIZEBORDER    | FCF_MINMAX   |
                                 FCF_SHELLPOSITION | FCF_TASKLIST ;
    HMQ           hmq ;
    HWND          hwndFrame, hwndClient ;
    QMSG          qmsg ;

    hab = WinInitialize (0) ;
    hmq = WinCreateMsgQueue (hab, 0) ;

    WinRegisterClass (hab, szClientClass, ClientWndProc, CS_SIZEREDRAW, 0) ;
```

(continued)

Figure 11-8. The BUTTONS2.C File. *continued*

```
        hwndFrame = WinCreateStdWindow (HWND_DESKTOP, WS_VISIBLE,
                                   &flFrameFlags, szClientClass, NULL,
                                   OL, NULL, O, &hwndClient) ;


    WinSendMsg (hwndFrame, WM_SETICON,
                WinQuerySysPointer (HWND_DESKTOP, SPTR_APPICON, FALSE),
                NULL) ;


    while (WinGetMsg (hab, &qmsg, NULL, O, O))
         WinDispatchMsg (hab, &qmsg) ;


    WinDestroyWindow (hwndFrame) ;
    WinDestroyMsgQueue (hmq) ;
    WinTerminate (hab) ;
    return 0 ;
    }

MRESULT EXPENTRY ClientWndProc (HWND hwnd, USHORT msg, MPARAM mp1, MPARAM mp2)
    {
    static CHAR  szSqBtnClass[] = "SqBtn",
                 *szButtonLabel[] = { "Smaller", "Larger" } ;
    static HWND  hwndFrame, hwndButton[2] ;
    static SHORT cxClient, cyClient, cxChar, cyChar ;
    FONTMETRICS  fm ;
    HPS          hps ;
    SHORT        id ;
    RECTL        rcl ;

    switch (msg)
        {
        case WM_CREATE :
            hwndFrame = WinQueryWindow (hwnd, QW_PARENT, FALSE) ;

            hps = WinGetPS (hwnd) ;
            GpiQueryFontMetrics (hps, (LONG) sizeof fm, &fm) ;
            cxChar = (SHORT) fm.lAveCharWidth ;
            cyChar = (SHORT) fm.lMaxBaselineExt ;
            WinReleasePS (hps) ;

            RegisterSqBtnClass (hab) ;

            for (id = 0 ; id < 2 ; id++)
                    hwndButton[id] = WinCreateWindow (
```

(continued)

Figure 11-8. The BUTTONS2.C File. *continued*

```
                                hwnd,               // Parent
                                "SqBtn",            // Class
                                szButtonLabel[id],  // Text
                                WS_VISIBLE,         // Style
                                0, 0,               // Position
                                12 * cxChar,        // Width
                                2 * cyChar,         // Height
                                hwnd,               // Owner
                                HWND_BOTTOM,        // Placement
                                id,                 // ID
                                NULL,               // Ctrl data
                                NULL) ;             // Pres params

          return 0 ;

     case WM_SIZE :
          cxClient = SHORT1FROMMP (mp2) ;
          cyClient = SHORT2FROMMP (mp2) ;

          for (id = 0 ; id < 2 ; id++)
               WinSetWindowPos (hwndButton[id], NULL,
                       cxClient / 2 + (14 * id - 13) * cxChar,
                       (cyClient - 2 * cyChar) / 2,
                       0, 0, SWP_MOVE) ;
          return 0 ;

     case WM_COMMAND:
          WinQueryWindowRect (hwnd, &rcl) ;
          WinMapWindowPoints (hwnd, HWND_DESKTOP, (PPOINTL) &rcl, 2) ;

          switch (COMMANDMSG(&msg)->cmd)           // Child ID
               {
               case 0:                             // "Smaller"
                    rcl.xLeft   += cxClient / 20 ;
                    rcl.xRight  -= cxClient / 20 ;
                    rcl.yBottom += cyClient / 20 ;
                    rcl.yTop    -= cyClient / 20 ;
                    break ;

               case 1:                             // "Larger"
                    rcl.xLeft   -= cxClient / 20 ;
                    rcl.xRight  += cxClient / 20 ;
                    rcl.yBottom -= cyClient / 20 ;
                    rcl.yTop    += cyClient / 20 ;
                    break ;
               }
```

(continued)

Figure 11-8. The BUTTONS2.C File. *continued*

```
                WinCalcFrameRect (hwndFrame, &rcl, FALSE) ;

                WinSetWindowPos (hwndFrame, NULL,
                                  (SHORT) rcl.xLeft, (SHORT) rcl.yBottom,
                                  (SHORT) rcl.xRight - (SHORT) rcl.xLeft,
                                  (SHORT) rcl.yTop   - (SHORT) rcl.yBottom,
                                  SWP_MOVE : SWP_SIZE) ;

                return 0 ;
          case WM_ERASEBACKGROUND:
                return 1 ;
          }
     return WinDefWindowProc (hwnd, msg, mp1, mp2) ;
     }
```

The BUTTONS2.DEF File

```
;----------------------------------------
; BUTTONS2.DEF module definition file
;----------------------------------------


NAME          BUTTONS2  WINDOWAPI

DESCRIPTION   'Square Button Demo (C) Charles Petzold, 1988'
PROTMODE
HEAPSIZE      1024
STACKSIZE     8192
EXPORTS       ClientWndProc
              SqBtnWndProc
```

Figure 11-8. *The BUTTONS2 program.*

You'll notice that the BUTTONS2 make file compiles both SQBTN.C and BUTTONS2.C and links them. The BUTTONS2.DEF file lists both *Client-WndProc* and *SqBtnWndProc* in the EXPORTS section.

BUTTONS2 is almost identical to BUTTONS1. The only real difference is that *ClientWndProc* calls *RegisterSqBtnClass* during the WM_CREATE message. This is the routine in SQBTN.C. The two push buttons are created based on the "SqBtn" class.

Figure 11-9 shows BUTTONS2 running under the Presentation Manager.

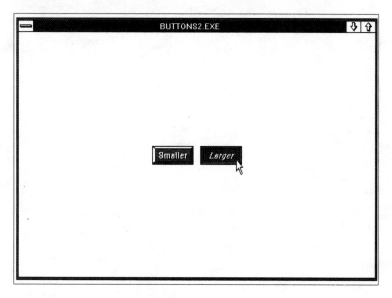

Figure 11-9. *The BUTTONS2 display.*

You might like the look of square 3-D push buttons and wonder if you could somehow use them in dialog boxes. We'll do exactly that in Chapter 14.

USING RESOURCES

BITMAPS, ICONS, POINTERS, AND STRINGS

Until now, our Presentation Manager programs have been missing a few features. The programs haven't included a menu bar across the top of the window, or dialog boxes invoked from menu items, or even a customized icon displayed when the program's window is minimized.

Icons, menus, and dialog boxes are all examples of program "resources." Resources are read-only data segments that are stored in a program's .EXE file but that are not part of the program's normal code and data segments. In most cases, resources aren't loaded into memory when OS/2 runs the program—the resources reside on disk in the .EXE file until specifically needed. When resources are loaded into memory, the memory blocks they occupy are read-only segments. Thus OS/2 can allow the resources in memory to be shared by multiple instances of the same program. OS/2 can also discard resources if memory space is needed and then later reload them from the .EXE file.

The Presentation Manager BSEDOS.H header file defines 15 resource types, but only the first 10 are commonly used by programs. The identifiers for these resource types begin with the letters RT (as listed in the table on the following page). You can also define your own resource types. This chapter covers bitmaps, icons and pointers, text strings, and programmer-defined resources. Menus and keyboard accelerator tables are covered in Chapter 13 and dialog boxes in Chapter 14.

Using resources in your Presentation Manager programs is an option rather than a requirement. If you want, you can instead define menus, dialog boxes, icons, and so forth in the program's normal data segment. However, you'll find that using resources is easier, because the OS/2 Software Development Kit includes several tools to help you create and edit resources. We'll examine one of these tools (the ICONEDIT program) in this chapter.

Resource Type	Description
RT_POINTER	Icon or mouse pointer
RT_BITMAP	Bitmap
RT_MENU	Menu template
RT_DIALOG	Dialog box template
RT_STRING	Text string
RT_FONTDIR	Font directory
RT_FONT	Font
RT_ACCELTABLE	Keyboard accelerator table
RT_RCDATA	Programmer-defined data
RT_MESSAGE	Message string

Basic Concepts

A program's .EXE file (or a dynamic link library's .DLL file) is divided into several sections, as shown in Figure 12-1. Following the new .EXE header, each of the program's code and data segments occupies a separate block in the .EXE file. Tables in the header allow OS/2 to identify the beginning of each segment in the .EXE file, the size of the segment, and characteristics of the segment. Resources are organized similarly. They follow the normal code and data segments in the .EXE file and likewise are identified by tables in the header section. You can thus think of an OS/2 program as comprising code segments, data segments, and resource segments.

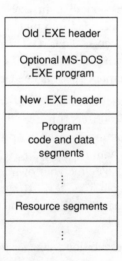

Figure 12-1. *The OS/2 .EXE and .DLL file format.*

Each resource (with the exception of the RT_STRING and RT_MESSAGE types) occupies a separate segment in the .EXE file. Text and message strings are stored with multiple strings in each segment. Most of the resources are stored in a special format that is unique for that resource type. Your program doesn't need to know the format of the resource in the .EXE file, because the Presentation Manager usually loads the resource and takes care of any translation necessary to put it into a format suitable for use with other Presentation Manager functions.

OS/2 Kernel Support of Resources

Each resource in the program's .EXE file is identified by a "type ID" and a "name ID," both of which are 16-bit numbers. The identifiers beginning with RT ("resource type") correspond to type IDs of 1 through 15. The Presentation Manager reserves type ID numbers up through 255 for its own use. You are free to use resource type IDs of 256 and above for programmer-defined resource types. The name ID uniquely identifies a particular resource of a particular type. For example, a .EXE file can have several bit-map resources, each of which occupies a different segment in the .EXE file. They all have a type ID of RT_BITMAP, but each bitmap has a different name ID.

The OS/2 kernel includes a function called *DosGetResource* that allows a program to load resources from the .EXE file into memory. (For the moment, let's ignore the problem of how the resources get into the .EXE file in the first place.) Generally, a Presentation Manager program needs to use *DosGetResource* only for the programmer-defined resources. For the predefined resource types, the Presentation Manager includes other functions to load resources. But given that these Presentation Manager functions ultimately use the *DosGetResource* function to load the resource into memory, it's worthwhile to understand this function.

Before calling *DosGetResource*, you need several variables:

```
USHORT idType, idName ;
SEL    selResource ;
PVOID  pResource ;
```

Based on the values of *idType* and *idName*, *DosGetResource* loads a resource from the program's .EXE file into memory and returns the segment selector of the memory block containing the resource:

```
DosGetResource (NULL, idType, idName, &selResource) ;
```

You then convert the segment selector to a long (or far) address with the MAKEP macro:

```
pResource = MAKEP (selResource, 0) ;
```

The memory segment belongs to your process. You can use *pResource* as a normal far pointer to access the resource. But because the memory segment is read-only, you can't write to it. Otherwise, it's a normal memory segment. You can use *DosSizeSeg* to find the size of the segment and *DosFreeSeg* to free the segment from memory.

When the first parameter of *DosGetResource* is NULL, OS/2 loads the resource from the program's .EXE file. You can also load a resource from a dynamic link library. Let's assume the dynamic link library containing the resource is named MYLIB.DLL. You first need to define a variable of type HMODULE to hold the module handle:

```
HMODULE hmod ;
```

You then call *DosLoadModule* to obtain the module handle:

```
DosLoadModule (NULL, 0, "MYLIB", &hmod) ;
```

The first parameter of *DosLoadModule* can optionally be set to the address of a buffer area that OS/2 uses if it can't obtain the module handle. Generally, OS/2 will fill this buffer by using the name of the module that contributed to the failure of the function. The second parameter is the length of this buffer.

After you obtain the module handle, you can use it as the first parameter to *DosGetResource* to load a resource from the dynamic link library:

```
DosGetResource (hmod, usTypeID, usNameID, &selResource) ;
```

After you free the resource segment and no longer need it, you can free the module handle:

```
DosFreeModule (hmod) ;
```

I'll discuss the use of dynamic link libraries in more depth in Chapter 16.

The OS/2 Kernel Message Facility

Although the *DosGetResource* function allows you to load resources of any type into memory, the only use of resources within the OS/2 kernel is for "message strings." These are text strings that contain replaceable parameters to display messages from OS/2 and the various OS/2 commands. The MKMSGF.EXE program creates a binary file with the extension .MSG based on an ASCII file containing message texts and codes. The MSGBIND.EXE program then adds these messages as resources to a program's .EXE file. An OS/2 program can either access a message from the .MSG file or load the message from its own .EXE file using the *DosGetMessage* function. If the message text has replaceable parameters (indicated by *%1*, *%2*, and so forth), the *DosGetMessage* function can insert other text (such as filenames) into the message text. Because the messages aren't in the program's normal data segments, OS/2 programs that use this messaging facility can be customized more easily for foreign-language markets.

The Resource Script

Although Presentation Manager programs can use the OS/2 message facility, they also need resources of other types. To add these resources to a program's .EXE file, the programmer first prepares an ASCII file called a "resource script." By convention, this file has the extension .RC. The resource script file includes some resources in an ASCII format and can also reference other files that contain binary resources, such as icons, mouse pointers, and bitmaps. Figure 12-2 on the following page shows a sample resource script named SAMPLE.RC that contains a reference to an icon file, a menu template, a keyboard accelerator table, and a string table. It's not important right now that you understand the format of the statements in this file. We'll cover the details as we study each resource in depth.

The keywords POINTER, MENU, ACCELTABLE, and STRINGTABLE all correspond to predefined resource types. The SAMPLE.ICO file referenced by the POINTER statement is a separate binary file containing a bitmap of the program's icon. You'll also note that the file contains several identifiers beginning with the letters ID, IDM, IDS, and IDD. Some of these are resource name IDs. They are all constants defined in a separate header file, SAMPLE.H, shown in Figure 12-3 on page 533. This header file must also be included in the program's C source code file so that the program can refer to these resources using the identifiers.

```
/*---------------------------------------------
   SAMPLE.RC -- Sample Resource Script File
---------------------------------------------*/


#include <os2.h>
#include "sample.h"

POINTER ID_RESOURCE sample.ico

MENU ID_RESOURCE
    {
    SUBMENU "~File",              IDM_FILE
        {
        MENUITEM "~New",              IDM_NEW
        MENUITEM "~Open...",          IDM_OPEN
        MENUITEM "~Save",             IDM_SAVE
        MENUITEM "Save ~As...",       IDM_SAVEAS
        MENUITEM SEPARATOR
        MENUITEM "E~xit",             IDM_EXIT
        MENUITEM "A~bout Sample...",  IDM_ABOUT
        }
    SUBMENU "~Edit",              IDM_EDIT
        {
        MENUITEM "~Undo\tAlt+BkSp",   IDM_UNDO
        MENUITEM SEPARATOR
        MENUITEM "Cu~t\tDel",         IDM_CUT
        MENUITEM "~Copy\tCtrl+Ins",   IDM_COPY
        MENUITEM "~Paste\tShift+Ins", IDM_PASTE
        MENUITEM "C~lear\tShift+Del", IDM_CLEAR
        }
    MENUITEM "F1=Help",      IDM_HELP, MIS_HELP ¦ MIS_BUTTONSEPARATOR
    }

ACCELTABLE ID_RESOURCE
    {
    VK_BACKSPACE,  IDM_UNDO,   VIRTUALKEY, ALT
    VK_DELETE,     IDM_CUT,    VIRTUALKEY
    VK_INSERT,     IDM_COPY,   VIRTUALKEY, CONTROL
    VK_INSERT,     IDM_PASTE,  VIRTUALKEY, SHIFT
    VK_DELETE,     IDM_CLEAR,  VIRTUALKEY, SHIFT
    }

STRINGTABLE
    {
    IDS_APPNAME,     "Sample"
    IDS_TITLEBAR,    "Sample Titlebar Text"
    }
```

Figure 12-2. *The SAMPLE.RC file.*

```
/*--------------------------------------------------------
    SAMPLE.H -- Sample Header File for Resource IDs
  ------------------------------------------------------*/

#define ID_RESOURCE 1

    /*------------------
        IDM -- Menu IDs
      ----------------*/

#define IDM_FILE     10
#define IDM_NEW      11
#define IDM_OPEN     12
#define IDM_SAVE     13
#define IDM_SAVEAS   14
#define IDM_EXIT     15
#define IDM_ABOUT    16

#define IDM_EDIT     20
#define IDM_UNDO     21
#define IDM_CUT      22
#define IDM_COPY     23
#define IDM_PASTE    24
#define IDM_CLEAR    25

#define IDM_HELP     30

    /*------------------
        IDS -- String IDs
      ----------------*/

#define IDS_APPNAME     1
#define IDS_TITLEBAR    2
```

Figure 12-3. *The SAMPLE.H file.*

The Resource Compiler

The ASCII resource script must be compiled to a binary form. By convention, the extension of the compiled resource file is .RES. The compiled resources must then be added to the program's .EXE file or to the dynamic link library's .DLL file. Both of these jobs—compiling the resources and adding them to the .EXE file—are handled by the RC.EXE resource compiler. You can do them separately or in a single step.

Compiling the Resources

To compile the ASCII .RC file into a binary .RES file without adding the resources to a .EXE file, use the command

```
RC -r SAMPLE
```

The .RC extension on SAMPLE is assumed. This command creates a SAMPLE.RES file.

Adding the Resources to .EXE

To add the compiled resources to the .EXE file, use the command

```
RC SAMPLE.RES
```

This adds the compiled resources in SAMPLE.RES to the SAMPLE.EXE file. (If the .EXE file contains any resources already, they are replaced with the new resources.) Optionally, you can include the name of the .EXE file if it's different from the .RES file:

```
RC SAMPLE.RES MYEXE.EXE
```

The .RES extension is required in this form of the command to differentiate it from the next form of the command.

Compiling and Adding as a Single Step

You can do both jobs in one step with the command

```
RC SAMPLE
```

The .RC extension on SAMPLE is assumed. This command compiles the resources to create a SAMPLE.RES file and then adds the resources to the SAMPLE.EXE file. If the name of the .EXE file is different from the .RC file, you can use

```
RC SAMPLE MYEXE.EXE
```

Presentation Manager programmers usually set up their make files to compile the resources and add them to the .EXE file in two separate steps. This results in a faster edit-make-run cycle because compiling the resources often takes much longer than adding them to the .EXE file. During development of a program, you'll generally make more changes to the C source code file than to the resource script file. You don't need to recompile the resources. Instead, you want to compile the C source code file, link it, and add the compiled resources. Typically, a make file for a program containing resources looks like SAMPLE, shown in Figure 12-4.

```
#-------------------
# SAMPLE make file
#-------------------

sample.obj : sample.c sample.h
    cl -c -G2sw -W2 sample.c

sample.res : sample.rc sample.h sample.ico
    rc -r sample

sample.exe : sample.obj sample.def sample.res
    link sample, /align:16, NUL, os2, sample
    rc sample.res
```

Figure 12-4. *The SAMPLE make file.*

The first compile step indicates that SAMPLE.C and SAMPLE.H are dependent files for the creation of SAMPLE.OBJ. The header file defines constants used by the program to reference the resources. The second step in the make file runs RC.EXE with the *-r* parameter to compile the ASCII SAMPLE.RC file into a binary SAMPLE.RES file. This step also requires both SAMPLE.H and SAMPLE.ICO. The third step is executed if SAMPLE.OBJ, SAMPLE.DEF, or SAMPLE.RES is updated. This links the program and then adds the resources to the .EXE file using RC.EXE again.

If you make a lot of changes to the resource script file, you'll probably want to avoid re-linking each time. Adding a couple of extra lines to the make file (shown in Figure 12-5) will speed things up.

```
#-------------------
# SAMPLE make file
#-------------------

sample.obj : sample.c sample.h
    cl -c -G2sw -W2 sample.c

sample.res : sample.rc sample.h sample.ico
    rc -r sample

sample.exe : sample.obj sample.def
    link sample, /align:16, NUL, os2, sample
    rc sample.res

sample.exe : sample.res
    rc sample.res
```

Figure 12-5. *A better SAMPLE make file for a program with resources.*

Note that the LINK step is not run if only SAMPLE.RES has changed. Instead, the resources in the .EXE file are replaced in the last RC step.

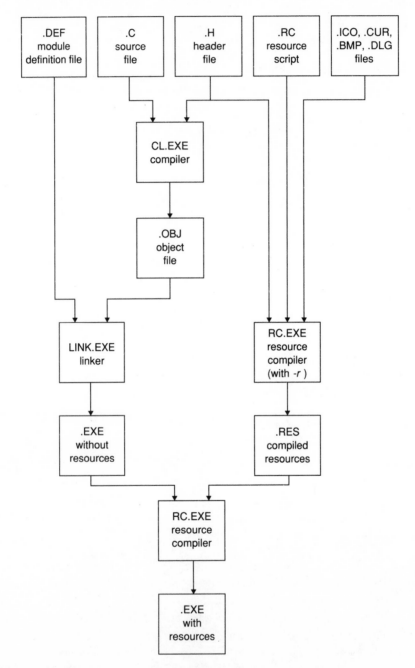

Figure 12-6. *The process of creating a Presentation Manager program that uses resources.*

Figure 12-6 shows the general procedure for creating a Presentation Manager program that uses resources. You create the source code files listed in the five boxes across the top of the diagram. The rest of the process is handled by the make file.

Bitmap Resources

We learned about bitmaps in Chapter 6. A bitmap is a block of memory organized by rows and columns where the bits represent a graphical image. In a monochrome bitmap, each bit in the bitmap corresponds to a display pixel. A color bitmap requires two or more bits per pixel to contain color information. The Presentation Manager and Graphics Programming Interface include several functions for creating, manipulating, and displaying bitmaps. Although we were able to define a bitmap in a program by a series of bytes in Chapter 6, it's usually much easier to create the bitmap in the Presentation Manager ICONEDIT program.

Creating a Bitmap in ICONEDIT

ICONEDIT is a Presentation Manager program that lets you create icons, mouse pointers, and monochrome bitmaps. You draw the image using the mouse. To create a new bitmap in ICONEDIT, choose New from the File menu, choose Bitmap from the dialog box, and enter a width and height in pixels.

The bitmap is initially all white, which means that every bit is set to 1. You use the mouse buttons to color the pixels. From the menu you can display a grid and select different pen sizes. When you're finished, choose Save As from the File menu and enter a filename. ICONEDIT adds a .BMP extension, which is standard for a bitmap. A header section in the .BMP file contains the height and width of the bitmap, the number of color planes (which equals 1 for a monochrome bitmap), the number of color bits per pixel (also 1), and the color table. More complete documentation on using ICONEDIT is included in the OS/2 Programmer's Toolkit.

Using the Bitmap Resource in a Program

After you create a bitmap file, you need to reference the bitmap filename in a resource script and assign the bitmap a name ID. In the program you use that name ID to load the bitmap into memory. Assuming the program's name is SAMPLE and the bitmap file is SAMPLE.BMP, the SAMPLE.RC resource script file contains the following statement to reference the bitmap file:

```
BITMAP idName sample.bmp
```

The *idName* value is simply an unsigned 16-bit number or an identifier defined in a header file *#define* statement. BITMAP is a resource compiler keyword. When you compile the resource script and add the resources to the program's .EXE file, the .EXE file contains a resource with a type ID of RT_BITMAP and a name ID of *idName*.

A program loads a bitmap resource into memory using the *GpiLoadBitmap* function. First, the program must define a variable of type HBITMAP:

```
HBITMAP hbm ;
```

The *GpiLoadBitmap* function returns a handle to the bitmap:

```
hbm = GpiLoadBitmap (hps, hmod, idName, lWidth, lHeight) ;
```

The *GpiLoadBitmap* function works only with resources of the RT_BITMAP type. The name ID identifies the particular RT_BITMAP resource.

The *hps* parameter to *GpiLoadBitmap* is a handle to a presentation space. The Presentation Manager uses this handle for two purposes. The first is to convert the colors of the bitmap into a form suitable for the device context. (Because we're working with a monochrome bitmap in this example, the bitmap can be loaded without any color conversion.) The second purpose of the presentation space handle is to allow GPI to store the bitmap in part of the device's memory. For example, the Enhanced Graphics Adapter has a maximum of 256 KB of memory, but only 112 KB are used for display purposes. The Presentation Manager can store the bitmap in free display memory. Graphics coprocessors on some video boards can more efficiently display bitmaps if they are stored in an unused region of display memory. For a monochrome bitmap, you can set the *hps* parameter to NULL, and the Presentation Manager will store the bitmap in normal memory.

The *hmod* parameter is set to NULL if you're loading the bitmap from the program's .EXE file. Otherwise, this is the module handle of a dynamic link library file. The *idName* is the ID number of the bitmap you want to load. The *lWidth* and *lHeight* parameters indicate the resultant size of the bitmap when the Presentation Manager loads it into memory. The bitmap can be compressed or stretched. If you set both parameters to 0L, the bitmap will retain the size you specified when you created the bitmap file in ICONEDIT.

Before the program terminates, you delete the bitmap from memory:

```
GpiDeleteBitmap (hbm) ;
```

A Sample Program

The LOADBMP1 program, shown in Figure 12-7, demonstrates how to include a bitmap as a resource in a program, load the bitmap into memory, and display it on the client window. The LOADBMP.BMP file is a 64-by-32-pixel bitmap file that was created in ICONEDIT in about 10 seconds (and looks it).

The LOADBMP1 File

```
#-------------------
# LOADBMP1 make file
#-------------------

loadbmp1.obj : loadbmp1.c loadbmp.h
     cl -c -G2sw -W3 loadbmp1.c

loadbmp.res : loadbmp.rc loadbmp.h loadbmp.bmp
     rc -r loadbmp

loadbmp1.exe : loadbmp1.obj loadbmp1.def
     link loadbmp1, /align:16, NUL, os2, loadbmp1
     rc loadbmp.res loadbmp1.exe

loadbmp1.exe : loadbmp.res
     rc loadbmp.res loadbmp1.exe
```

The LOADBMP1.C File

```
/*-------------------------------------------------------
    LOADBMP1.C -- Loads a Bitmap Resource and Draws it
  -------------------------------------------------------*/

#define INCL_WIN
#include <os2.h>
#include "loadbmp.h"

MRESULT EXPENTRY ClientWndProc (HWND, USHORT, MPARAM, MPARAM) ;

int main (void)
    {
    static CHAR  szClientClass [] = "LoadBmp1" ;
    static ULONG flFrameFlags = FCF_TITLEBAR     | FCF_SYSMENU |
                                FCF_SIZEBORDER   | FCF_MINMAX  |
                                FCF_SHELLPOSITION | FCF_TASKLIST ;
```

(continued)

Figure 12-7. The LOADBMP1.C File. *continued*

```
        HAB         hab ;
        HMQ         hmq ;
        HWND        hwndFrame, hwndClient ;
        QMSG        qmsg ;

        hab = WinInitialize (0) ;
        hmq = WinCreateMsgQueue (hab, 0) ;

        WinRegisterClass (hab, szClientClass, ClientWndProc, CS_SIZEREDRAW, 0) ;

        hwndFrame = WinCreateStdWindow (HWND_DESKTOP, WS_VISIBLE,
                                        &flFrameFlags, szClientClass, NULL,
                                        OL, NULL, 0, &hwndClient) ;

        while (WinGetMsg (hab, &qmsg, NULL, 0, 0))
            WinDispatchMsg (hab, &qmsg) ;

        WinDestroyWindow (hwndFrame) ;
        WinDestroyMsgQueue (hmq) ;
        WinTerminate (hab) ;
        return 0 ;
        }

MRESULT EXPENTRY ClientWndProc (HWND hwnd, USHORT msg, MPARAM mp1, MPARAM mp2)
        {
        static SHORT cxClient, cyClient ;
        HBITMAP     hbm ;
        HPS         hps ;
        POINTL      ptl ;

        switch (msg)
            {
            case WM_SIZE:
                cxClient = SHORT1FROMMP (mp2) ;
                cyClient = SHORT2FROMMP (mp2) ;
                return 0 ;

            case WM_PAINT:
                hps = WinBeginPaint (hwnd, NULL, NULL) ;
                GpiErase (hps) ;

                hbm = GpiLoadBitmap (hps, NULL, IDB_HELLO,
                                    (LONG) cxClient, (LONG) cyClient) ;
                if (hbm)
```

(continued)

Figure 12-7. The LOADBMP1.C File. *continued*

```
                        {
                        ptl.x = 0 ;
                        ptl.y = 0 ;

                        WinDrawBitmap (hps, hbm, NULL, &ptl,
                                        CLR_NEUTRAL, CLR_BACKGROUND, DBM_NORMAL) ;

                        GpiDeleteBitmap (hbm) ;
                        }
                WinEndPaint (hps) ;
                return 0 ;
        }
    return WinDefWindowProc (hwnd, msg, mp1, mp2) ;
    }
```

The LOADBMP.H File

```
/*------------------------
   LOADBMP.H header file
   ----------------------*/

#define IDB_HELLO 55
```

The LOADBMP.RC File

```
/*----------------------------------
   LOADBMP.RC resource script file
   -------------------------------*/

#include "loadbmp.h"

BITMAP IDB_HELLO loadbmp.bmp
```

The LOADBMP.BMP File

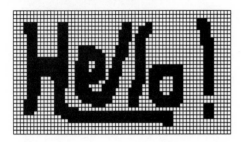

The LOADBMP1.DEF File

```
;----------------------------------------
; LOADBMP1.DEF module definition file
;----------------------------------------

NAME            LOADBMP1   WINDOWAPI

DESCRIPTION     'Loads Bitmap Resource and Draws it (C) Charles Petzold, 1988'
PROTMODE
HEAPSIZE        1024
STACKSIZE       8192
EXPORTS         ClientWndProc
```

Figure 12-7. *The LOADBMP1 program.*

I decided to give the bitmap a name ID of 55. The identifier IDB_HELLO is defined in LOADBMP.H for this purpose:

```
#define IDB_HELLO 55
```

The IDB prefix stands for ''ID for a bitmap.''

This statement in the LOADBMP.RC resource script file references the file containing the bitmap:

```
BITMAP IDB_HELLO loadbmp.bmp
```

The LOADBMP.RC resource script is compiled by the following command in the make file:

```
rc -r loadbmp
```

The resource compiler creates a binary LOADBMP.RES file that contains the entire LOADBMP.BMP file. When RC.EXE is run the second time in the make file, the bitmap resource in LOADBMP.RES is added to the LOADBMP1.EXE file:

```
rc loadbmp.res loadbmp1.exe
```

Following this step, the LOADBMP1.EXE file includes a resource segment containing the entire bitmap. The header section of the .EXE file identifies the resource type ID (RT_BITMAP) and name ID (55). The program can then get access to that resource.

During the WM_PAINT message in LOADBMP1.C, the bitmap resource is loaded into memory and stretched to fill the size of the client window:

```
hbm = GpiLoadBitmap (hps, NULL, IDB_HELLO,
                    (LONG) cxClient, (LONG) cyClient) ;
```

Note that the second parameter is set to NULL to indicate that the resource is part of the program's .EXE file. The IDB_HELLO identifier is the name ID of the resource defined in LOADBMP.H. (Obviously, I could have dispensed with the LOADBMP.H file in this example and used 55 in place of IDB_HELLO in both the resource script and the program. But for more complex resources such as menus and dialog boxes, the header file becomes very important, so we might as well get accustomed to using it.)

GpiLoadBitmap returns NULL if the bitmap can't be loaded into memory. The rest of the WM_PAINT logic continues only if *hbm* isn't NULL:

```
if (hbm)
    {
    ptl.x = 0 ;
    ptl.y = 0 ;

    WinDrawBitmap (hps, hbm, NULL, &ptl,
                CLR_NEUTRAL, CLR_BACKGROUND, DBM_NORMAL) ;

    GpiDeleteBitmap (hbm) ;
    }
```

This draws the bitmap on the client window and then deletes it from memory. The LOADBMP1 window is shown in Figure 12-8 on the following page.

Figure 12-8. *The LOADBMP1 display.*

An Alternative Approach to Loading Bitmaps

LOADBMP1 loads the bitmap and then deletes it whenever it needs to re-paint the client window. Another approach is to load the bitmap during the WM_CREATE message, keep it in memory for the duration of the program, and then delete it during the WM_DESTROY message.

The LOADBMP2 program, shown in Figure 12-9, illustrates this approach. The LOADBMP.H, LOADBMP.RC, and LOADBMP.BMP files from Figure 12-7 are also required to compile the program.

The LOADBMP2 File

```
#--------------------
# LOADBMP2 make file
#--------------------

loadbmp2.obj : loadbmp2.c loadbmp.h
    cl -c -G2sw -W3 loadbmp2.c

loadbmp.res : loadbmp.rc loadbmp.h loadbmp.bmp
    rc -r loadbmp
```

(continued)

Figure 12-9. The LOADBMP2 File. *continued*

```
loadbmp2.exe : loadbmp2.obj loadbmp2.def
     link loadbmp2, /align:16, NUL, os2, loadbmp2
     rc loadbmp.res loadbmp2.exe

loadbmp2.exe : loadbmp.res
     rc loadbmp.res loadbmp2.exe
```

The LOADBMP2.C File

```
/*------------------------------------------------------
   LOADBMP2.C -- Loads a Bitmap Resource and Draws it
   ------------------------------------------------------*/

#define INCL_WIN
#include <os2.h>
#include "loadbmp.h"

MRESULT EXPENTRY ClientWndProc (HWND, USHORT, MPARAM, MPARAM) ;

int main (void)
    {
    static CHAR  szClientClass [] = "LoadBmp2" ;
    static ULONG flFrameFlags = FCF_TITLEBAR      | FCF_SYSMENU |
                                FCF_SIZEBORDER     | FCF_MINMAX  |
                                FCF_SHELLPOSITION | FCF_TASKLIST ;

    HAB         hab ;
    HMQ         hmq ;
    HWND        hwndFrame, hwndClient ;
    QMSG        qmsg ;

    hab = WinInitialize (0) ;
    hmq = WinCreateMsgQueue (hab, 0) ;

    WinRegisterClass (hab, szClientClass, ClientWndProc, CS_SIZEREDRAW, 0) ;

    hwndFrame = WinCreateStdWindow (HWND_DESKTOP, WS_VISIBLE,
                                    &flFrameFlags, szClientClass, NULL,
                                    0L, NULL, 0, &hwndClient) ;

    while (WinGetMsg (hab, &qmsg, NULL, 0, 0))
        WinDispatchMsg (hab, &qmsg) ;
```

(continued)

Figure 12-9. The LOADBMP2.C File. *continued*

```
      WinDestroyWindow (hwndFrame) ;
      WinDestroyMsgQueue (hmq) ;
      WinTerminate (hab) ;
      return 0 ;
      }

MRESULT EXPENTRY ClientWndProc (HWND hwnd, USHORT msg, MPARAM mp1, MPARAM mp2)
      {
      static HBITMAP hbm ;
      HPS            hps ;
      RECTL          rcl ;

      switch (msg)
          {
          case WM_CREATE:
              hps = WinGetPS (hwnd) ;
              hbm = GpiLoadBitmap (hps, NULL, IDB_HELLO, OL, OL) ;
              WinReleasePS (hps) ;
              return 0 ;

          case WM_PAINT:
              hps = WinBeginPaint (hwnd, NULL, NULL) ;
              GpiErase (hps) ;

              WinQueryWindowRect (hwnd, &rcl) ;

              if (hbm)
                  WinDrawBitmap (hps, hbm, NULL, (PPOINTL) &rcl,
                                 CLR_NEUTRAL, CLR_BACKGROUND, DBM_STRETCH) ;

              WinEndPaint (hps) ;
              return 0 ;

          case WM_DESTROY:
              if (hbm)
                  GpiDeleteBitmap (hbm) ;
              return 0 ;
          }
      return WinDefWindowProc (hwnd, msg, mp1, mp2) ;
      }
```

The LOADBMP2.DEF File

```
;------------------------------------
; LOADBMP2.DEF module definition file
;------------------------------------

NAME            LOADBMP2  WINDOWAPI

DESCRIPTION     'Loads Bitmap Resource and Draws it (C) Charles Petzold, 1988'
PROTMODE
HEAPSIZE        1024
STACKSIZE       8192
EXPORTS         ClientWndProc
```

Figure 12-9. *The LOADBMP2 program.*

In LOADBMP2.C, the last two parameters of *GpiLoadBitmap* are set to 0, so the bitmap isn't stretched when loaded into memory:

```
case WM_CREATE:
    hps = WinGetPS (hwnd) ;
    hbm = GpiLoadBitmap (hps, NULL, IDB_HELLO, 0L, 0L) ;
    WinReleasePS (hps) ;
    return 0 ;
```

The WM_PAINT logic stretches the bitmap in the *WinDrawBitmap* function:

```
WinQueryWindowRect (hwnd, &rcl) ;

if (hbm)
    WinDrawBitmap (hps, hbm, NULL, (PPOINTL) &rcl,
                   CLR_NEUTRAL, CLR_BACKGROUND, DBM_STRETCH) ;
```

LOADBMP2 deletes the bitmap while processing the WM_DESTROY message:

```
case WM_DESTROY:
    if (hbm)
        GpiDeleteBitmap (hbm) ;
    return 0 ;
```

It's OK to handle small bitmaps in this way, but you should be leery of keeping large bitmaps in memory for long periods. Although the Presentation Manager can discard bitmaps from memory and reload them from the program's .EXE file, common courtesy requires that you not be piggy with memory space.

Icons and Mouse Pointers

Icons and customized mouse pointers are identical in structure and are often interchangeable. In fact, both icon and pointer resources are stored in the program's .EXE file with a resource type of RT_POINTER. Some Presentation Manager functions that seemingly apply to pointers (*WinLoadPointer* and *WinDestroyPointer*, for example) can also be used with icons.

You can use icons in your program in two ways: as a symbolic representation of the program when the program's top-level window is minimized, and as little pictures you can draw on the program's client window. You can create and use a customized mouse pointer in your program to substitute for the default mouse pointer. For example, the ICONEDIT program itself has a customized mouse pointer that looks like a paintbrush.

Designing Icons and Pointers

You use ICONEDIT to create icons and pointers. ICONEDIT saves icon files with a .ICO extension and pointer files with a .PTR extension. When you create an icon or pointer in ICONEDIT, it's important that you understand how these images are used by the Presentation Manager.

The first issue is resolution. The Presentation Manager always displays an icon or pointer in a pixel dimension that is appropriate for the video display adapter on which the Presentation Manager is running. A program can obtain this dimension by calling the *WinQuerySysValue* function with parameters of SV_CXICON, SV_CYICON, SV_CXPOINTER, and SV_CYPOINTER. For most video display adapters, the Presentation Manager uses the same dimensions for both icons and pointers. The following table shows these dimensions for the most common display adapters:

Width	*Height*	*Display Adapter*
32	16	Color Graphics Adapter (640 x 200)
		Enhanced Graphics Adapter (640 x 200)
32	32	Enhanced Graphics Adapter (640 x 350)
		Video Graphics Array (640 x 480)
64	64	Future high-resolution adapters

When you create a new icon or pointer, you can pick one of these three resolutions in which to edit the image. ICONEDIT saves the image in the .ICO or .PTR file in the editing dimension you choose. A 64-by-64 .ICO file is about eight times as large as a 32-by-16 .ICO file. When your program loads an icon or pointer into memory, the Presentation Manager adjusts the size of the image to match the video display adapter. For example, if the icon resource in your program's .EXE file is 32 by 32, the Presentation Manager eliminates every other row when displaying the icon on a Color Graphics Adapter and duplicates every row and column for a future high-resolution adapter.

If you want to create icons and pointers that look satisfactory on every type of adapter and that take up the least amount of space in the .EXE file, use the 32-by-16 resolution. But be aware that they may appear grainy on an EGA or a high-resolution adapter. The other extreme is to create 64-by-64 icons and pointers. These will look great on a future high-resolution adapter, but they may not do so well on the video adapters most commonly used today. Editing icons and pointers in a 32-by-32 resolution is a good compromise between these extremes, particularly considering that the Color Graphics Adapter is quickly becoming obsolete.

The second major consideration when designing icons and pointers is color. Icons and pointers are made up of a pair of monochrome bitmaps. When you design an icon or pointer in ICONEDIT, you can color pixels in either black, white, "screen," or "inverse screen." The "screen" color is transparent. When the Presentation Manager displays the icon or pointer, whatever was originally behind it shows through. The "inverse screen" color inverts the background behind the image. A black background becomes white, white becomes black, and green becomes magenta.

These four colors correspond to the bits in the two bitmaps that make up an icon or pointer, as shown in the following table:

Bitmap 1	Bitmap 2	Resultant Color
0	0	Black
1	0	White
0	1	Screen
1	1	Inverse screen

When the Presentation Manager displays the icon or pointer, it first draws Bitmap 2 on the screen using a bitwise AND operation (the raster operation ROP_SRCAND). The 1 bits in Bitmap 2 preserve the color bits on the screen;

the 0 bits in Bitmap 2 set the screen bits to 0 (black). The Presentation Manager then draws Bitmap 1 on the screen using an exclusive OR operation (the raster operation ROP_SRCINVERT). The 0 bits in Bitmap 1 preserve the screen image, and the 1 bits invert the screen image. Using C notation for the logical operations, the display is altered by the following formula:

Display = (Display & Bitmap2) ^ Bitmap1

Because an icon or pointer can be displayed against a background of almost any color, a few simple rules apply in designing the images:

- If the icon or pointer is mostly black, give it a white outline.

- If the icon or pointer is mostly white, give it a black outline.

- Use the "screen" color to make the icon or pointer nonrectangular (such as the common arrow pointer).

- Use "inverse screen" to add a dash of inverted color when the icon or pointer is displayed against a color background.

Referencing the File in the Resource Script

The statements in your resource script that reference the icon and pointer files are very similar to the statement used for bitmaps. You reference an icon file as a resource with the following statement:

```
POINTER idName sample.ico
```

You reference a pointer file with the following statement:

```
POINTER idName sample.ptr
```

POINTER is a keyword recognized by RC.EXE.

The use of the POINTER keyword for both icons and pointers may seem a little strange. As I mentioned earlier, icons and pointers are identical in structure and are in many ways interchangeable. Both icons and pointers are stored in a program's .EXE file with a resource type of RT_POINTER. If a different keyword (for example, ICON) were used to identify icons in a resource script, you might be tempted to use the same name ID for an icon resource and a pointer resource. The name IDs for any icons and pointers in a resource script must be unique.

Six Steps to Adding an Icon to a Program

By far the most common use of an icon is for a symbolic representation of a program when the window is minimized. You can add such an icon to a program through these six steps:

1. Create an icon in ICONEDIT. Give the file the same name as your program but with a .ICO extension; for example, SAMPLE.ICO.

2. Create a SAMPLE.RC resource script file containing a POINTER statement. For example:

```
POINTER 555 sample.ico
```

This statement defines a pointer resource (which is actually an icon) with a name ID of 555.

3. Change your program's make file so that it looks like this:

```
sample.obj : sample.c
    cl -c -G2sw -W2 sample.c

sample.res : sample.rc sample.ico
    rc -r sample

sample.exe : sample.obj sample.def
    link sample, /align:16, NUL, os2, sample
    rc sample.res

sample.exe : sample.res
    rc sample.res
```

4. Change the definition of *flFrameFlags* to include the FCF_ICON style:

```
static ULONG flFrameFlags = FCF_TITLEBAR        | FCF_SYSMENU   |
                            FCF_SIZEBORDER      | FCF_MINMAX    |
                            FCF_SHELLPOSITION   | FCF_TASKLIST  |
                            FCF_ICON ;
```

5. Change the call to *WinCreateStdWindow* so the second-to-last parameter is the name ID of the bitmap:

```
hwndFrame = WinCreateStdWindow (HWND_DESKTOP, WS_VISIBLE,
                        &flFrameFlags, szClientClass, NULL,
                        0L, NULL, 555, &hwndClient) ;
```

6. If you have a *WinSendMsg* call to send the frame window a
WM_SETICON message, remove it.

You're done. Remake the program.

As you'll see in the next chapter, the second-to-last parameter to
WinCreateStdWindow is actually the name ID of three different resources.
If you include the frame creation flag FCF_MENU, the Presentation Man-
ager uses that same name ID to load the program's menu. If you include
FCF_ACCELTABLE, the same name ID references the program's keyboard
accelerator table.

You might want to use an identifier defined in a header file for the name ID
of these three resources. In the programs in this chapter and the next two
chapters, I use the identifier ID_RESOURCE for this purpose and define it
to be equal to 1. In this case, a SAMPLE.H header file has the following
statement:

```
#define ID_RESOURCE 1
```

The SAMPLE.RC resource script looks like this:

```
#include "sample.h"

POINTER ID_RESOURCE sample.ico
```

The SAMPLE make file is changed so that it recompiles the source code file
and resource script file if the header file changes:

```
sample.obj : sample.c sample.h
    cl -c -G2sw -W2 sample.c

sample.res : sample.rc sample.ico sample.h
    rc -r sample

sample.exe : sample.obj sample.def
    link sample, /align:16, NUL, os2, sample
    rc sample.res

sample.exe : sample.res
    rc sample.res
```

The SAMPLE.C file includes the header file near the top of the program:

```
#include "sample.h"
```

and the second to last parameter of the *WinCreateStdWindow* function uses the defined name rather than a number:

```
hwndFrame = WinCreateStdWindow (HWND_DESKTOP, WS_VISIBLE
                                &flFrameFlags, szClientClass, NULL,
                                OL, NULL, ID_RESOURCE, &hwndClient ;
```

Drawing Icons and Setting Pointers

Besides using an icon as a symbolic representation of a program, you can also draw an icon on your client window. Because of the similarity between icons and pointers, the functions for loading and destroying icons are the same as those used for pointers.

You first define a handle of type HPOINTER to store a handle to the icon:

```
HPOINTER hIcon ;
```

You then load the icon into memory using the *WinLoadPointer* function:

```
hIcon = WinLoadPointer (HWND_DESKTOP, hmod, idName) ;
```

The *hmod* parameter is NULL if the icon is stored in the program's .EXE file. You can then display the icon on a presentation space using the following function:

```
WinDrawPointer (hps, x, y, hIcon, sFlags) ;
```

where *x* and *y* are the coordinates of the presentation space corresponding to the lower-left corner of the icon. The *sFlags* parameter can be DP_NORMAL to draw the icon normally, DP_INVERTED to invert the icon, and DP_HALFTONED to draw only every other bit of the icon. You might want to use icons in this way in a menu that you create and manage. You use the inverted icon when the user selects an option and the "halftoned" icon when a menu option is disabled.

Before your program terminates, you destroy the icon:

```
WinDestroyPointer (hIcon) ;
```

You can also use the *WinLoadPointer* and *WinDestroyPointer* functions with mouse pointers. If you create a customized mouse pointer and include it in your resource script, you can get a handle to the pointer in your program like this:

```
hptr = WinLoadPointer (HWND_DESKTOP, hmod, idName) ;
```

You'll probably do this during the WM_CREATE message. The *hptr* variable is defined as type HPOINTER.

The easiest way for your program to use this new pointer is to set the pointer during the WM_MOUSEMOVE message:

```
case WM_MOUSEMOVE:
    WinSetPointer (HWND_DESKTOP, hptr) ;
        [other program lines]
```

You can also test the coordinates of the mouse pointer during the WM_MOUSEMOVE message and set a different pointer depending on where the pointer is located in the client area. If you divide your client area into several areas with the use of child windows, each child window might set its own pointer.

During processing of the WM_DESTROY message, you destroy the pointer:

```
WinDestroyPointer (hptr) ;
```

The RESOURCE program, shown in Figure 12-10, contains an icon and a pointer resource. The icon is a square pattern that shows the four colors (black, white, "screen," and "inverse screen"). The program references the icon name ID in the *WinCreateStdWindow* call and while processing the WM_CREATE message. RESOURCE draws the icon on the four corners of its client window and shows what the "halftoned" and inverted icons look like. The customized pointer is displayed whenever the mouse is within RESOURCE's client window.

The RESOURCE File

```
#--------------------
# RESOURCE make file
#--------------------

resource.obj : resource.c resource.h
    cl -c -G2sw -W3 resource.c

resource.res : resource.rc resource.h resource.ico resource.ptr
    rc -r resource

resource.exe : resource.obj resource.def
    link resource, /align:16, NUL, os2, resource
    rc resource.res

resource.exe : resource.res
    rc resource.res
```

The RESOURCE.C File

```
/*-------------------------------------------------
   RESOURCE.C -- Uses an Icon and Pointer Resource
   -----------------------------------------------*/

#define INCL_WIN
#define INCL_GPI
#include <os2.h>
#include "resource.h"

MRESULT EXPENTRY ClientWndProc (HWND, USHORT, MPARAM, MPARAM) ;

int main (void)
    {
    static CHAR   szClientClass [] = "Resource" ;
    static ULONG  flFrameFlags = FCF_TITLEBAR       | FCF_SYSMENU   |
                                 FCF_SIZEBORDER     | FCF_MINMAX    |
                                 FCF_SHELLPOSITION  | FCF_TASKLIST  |
                                 FCF_ICON ;
    HAB           hab ;
    HMQ           hmq ;
    HWND          hwndFrame, hwndClient ;
    QMSG          qmsg ;

    hab = WinInitialize (0) ;
    hmq = WinCreateMsgQueue (hab, 0) ;
```

(continued)

Figure 12-10. The RESOURCE.C File. *continued*

```
     WinRegisterClass (hab, szClientClass, ClientWndProc, CS_SIZEREDRAW, 0) ;

     hwndFrame = WinCreateStdWindow (HWND_DESKTOP, WS_VISIBLE,
                                     &flFrameFlags, szClientClass, NULL,
                                     OL, NULL, ID_RESOURCE, &hwndClient) ;

     while (WinGetMsg (hab, &qmsg, NULL, 0, 0))
          WinDispatchMsg (hab, &qmsg) ;

     WinDestroyWindow (hwndFrame) ;
     WinDestroyMsgQueue (hmq) ;
     WinTerminate (hab) ;
     return 0 ;
     }

MRESULT EXPENTRY ClientWndProc (HWND hwnd, USHORT msg, MPARAM mp1, MPARAM mp2)
     {
     static HPOINTER hIcon, hptr ;
     static SHORT    cxClient, cyClient, cxIcon, cyIcon ;
     HPS             hps ;
     RECTL           rcl ;

     switch (msg)
          {
          case WM_CREATE:
               hIcon = WinLoadPointer (HWND_DESKTOP, NULL, ID_RESOURCE) ;
               hptr  = WinLoadPointer (HWND_DESKTOP, NULL, IDP_CIRCLE) ;

               cxIcon = (SHORT) WinQuerySysValue (HWND_DESKTOP, SV_CXICON) ;
               cyIcon = (SHORT) WinQuerySysValue (HWND_DESKTOP, SV_CYICON) ;
               return 0 ;

          case WM_SIZE:
               cxClient = SHORT1FROMMP (mp2) ;
               cyClient = SHORT2FROMMP (mp2) ;
               return 0 ;

          case WM_MOUSEMOVE:
               WinSetPointer (HWND_DESKTOP, hptr) ;
               return 1 ;

          case WM_PAINT:
               hps = WinBeginPaint (hwnd, NULL, NULL) ;
```

(continued)

Figure 12-10. The RESOURCE.C File. *continued*

```
              WinQueryWindowRect (hwnd, &rcl) ;
              WinFillRect (hps, &rcl, CLR_CYAN) ;

              WinDrawPointer (hps, 0, 0, hIcon, DP_NORMAL) ;
              WinDrawPointer (hps, 0, cyClient - cyIcon, hIcon, DP_NORMAL) ;
              WinDrawPointer (hps, cxClient - cyIcon, 0, hIcon, DP_NORMAL) ;
              WinDrawPointer (hps, cxClient - cxIcon, cyClient - cyIcon,
                                   hIcon, DP_NORMAL) ;

              WinDrawPointer (hps, cxClient / 3, cyClient / 2, hIcon,
                                                 DP_HALFTONED) ;
              WinDrawPointer (hps, 2 * cxClient / 3, cyClient / 2, hIcon,
                                                 DP_INVERTED) ;
              WinEndPaint (hps) ;
              return 0 ;

         case WM_DESTROY:
              WinDestroyPointer (hIcon) ;
              WinDestroyPointer (hptr) ;
              return 0 ;
         }
    return WinDefWindowProc (hwnd, msg, mp1, mp2) ;
    }
```

The RESOURCE.H File

```
/*-----------------------
   RESOURCE.H header file
   -----------------------*/


#define ID_RESOURCE 1
#define IDP_CIRCLE  2
```

The RESOURCE.RC File

```
/*-----------------------------------
   RESOURCE.RC resource script file
   ----------------------------------*/


#include "resource.h"

POINTER ID_RESOURCE resource.ico
POINTER IDP_CIRCLE  resource.ptr
```

The RESOURCE.ICO File

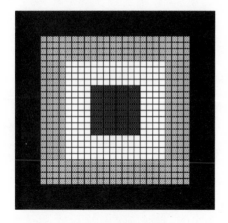

The RESOURCE.PTR File

The RESOURCE.DEF File

```
;-------------------------------------
; RESOURCE.DEF module definition file
;-------------------------------------

NAME            RESOURCE   WINDOWAPI

DESCRIPTION     'Icon and Pointer Resources (C) Charles Petzold, 1988'
PROTMODE
HEAPSIZE        1024
STACKSIZE       8192
EXPORTS         ClientWndProc
```

Figure 12-10. *The RESOURCE program.*

The String Resource

For bitmaps, icons, and pointers, there are some clear advantages to using resources rather than defining the images in your program's source code file. The ICONEDIT utility lets you draw the image and save it as a binary file — you don't have to worry about the format of the bits and bytes. So the next type of resource — the text string — may initially seem a little strange. Rather than put text strings in your C source code file, you can instead include them in the program's resource script. But why on earth would you want to do this?

As you'll see in the next two chapters, a program's resource script also contains the program's menu and dialog box templates. If the resource script also contains all the text strings used by the program, converting the program to a foreign language requires that only the resource script (or files referenced by the resource script) be changed. The .C source code file doesn't even have to be recompiled. Of course, if your programs are intended only for yourself, a few friends, your corporation, or a domestic market, then using string resources provides no benefit, except perhaps — if the strings are handled properly — a slight saving in memory space when the program is running under the Presentation Manager.

Defining and Loading String Resources

You include strings in a resource script using the STRINGTABLE block:

```
STRINGTABLE
    {
    idString1, "This little string went to market"
    idString2, "This little string stayed home"
        [other string definitions]
    }
```

A resource script can have only one string table that contains all the program's strings. Each string is one line long, with a maximum of 255 characters. You can use the keywords BEGIN and END rather than the curly brackets if you're nostalgic for Pascal syntax.

In your program you load a particular string into a character array with the following function:

```
WinLoadString (hab, hmod, idString, sBufferLen, achBuffer) ;
```

As in the previous resource-loading functions, *hmod* is NULL if the strings are resources in the program's .EXE file. The function copies up to *(sBufferLen − 1)* characters into the character array addressed by *achBuffer* and appends a 0 character.

To use the *WinLoadString* function, you need a character array in your program large enough to hold the string:

```
CHAR achString [256] ;
     [other program lines]
WinLoadString (hab, NULL, idString, sizeof achString, achString) ;
```

Following this statement, *achString* contains the NULL-terminated string that was identified by *idString* in the resource script.

You probably want to load strings only when you need them for display purposes. In that case, make the string arrays local variables in functions so that the space is freed up when the function ends.

Using Strings for Error Messages

Here's an example of how a program can use strings to display error messages in a message box. Suppose your program works with files and has three error messages: "File is not found," "File is too large to edit," and "File is read-only." You first define three identifiers in the program's header file:

```
#define IDS_FILENOTFOUND 1
#define IDS_FILETOOBIG   2
#define IDS_FILEREADONLY 3
```

The string table in the resource script looks like this:

```
STRINGTABLE
    {
    IDS_FILENOTFOUND, "File %s not found."
    IDS_FILETOOBIG,   "File %s too large to edit."
    IDS_FILEREADONLY, "File %s is read-only."
    }
```

In your program you define a function that displays one of these messages with a particular filename:

```
VOID ErrorMessage (HWND hwnd, USHORT usErrorNum, CHAR * szFileName)
    {
    CHAR    achString [40] ;
    CHAR    achFormattedString [60] ;

    WinLoadString (hab, NULL, usErrorNum, sizeof achString, achString) ;

    sprintf (achFormattedString, achString, szFileName) ;

    WinMessageBox (HWND_DESKTOP, hwnd, achFormattedString,
                   NULL, 0, MB_OK | MB_ICONEXCLAMATION) ;
    }
```

When the program needs to display the "File is not found" message, it calls the *ErrorMessage* function with the IDS_FILENOTFOUND identifier and the filename:

```
ErrorMessage (hwnd, IDS_FILENOTFOUND, szFileName) ;
```

String Resource Storage

The string IDs in the STRINGTABLE block aren't treated the same way as the name IDs for bitmaps, icons, and cursors. Up to 16 strings are consolidated in the same resource segment in the program's .EXE file. All the strings with string IDs of 0 through 15 are in the same segment. The name ID for that segment is 1. The string IDs of 16 through 31 are in another segment with a name ID of 2.

When you call *WinLoadString*, the Presentation Manager loads an entire resource segment into memory (containing up to 16 strings) and then copies the particular string you want into the array in your program's data segment. For this reason, you can conserve memory space if you assign string IDs in logical groups. For example, if one section of your program uses five strings and another section uses four strings, make the IDs of the first five strings 0 through 4 and the IDs of the other four strings 16 through 19.

Programmer-defined Resources

The programmer-defined resource provides a way for you to attach arbitrary data to your program's .EXE file and load it into memory during program execution. Perhaps this data is in a binary form, and it's inconvenient to make it part of the program's source code file. Or perhaps you have a large text file (for example, a file that contains reams of "help" text) that your program must access. Make it a programmer-defined resource.

The POEPOEM program, shown in Figure 12-11, shows how this is done. This program displays the text of Edgar Allan Poe's "Annabel Lee" in its client window. The text of the poem is a programmer-defined resource. The program's resource script also defines the text strings used in the program in a string table, as well as the program's icon.

The POEPOEM File

```
#-------------------
# POEPOEM make file
#-------------------

poepoem.obj : poepoem.c poepoem.h
    cl -c -G2sw -W3 poepoem.c

poepoem.res : poepoem.rc poepoem.ico poepoem.asc poepoem.h
    rc -r poepoem

poepoem.exe : poepoem.obj poepoem.def
    link poepoem, /align:16, NUL, os2, poepoem
    rc poepoem.res

poepoem.exe : poepoem.res
    rc poepoem.res
```

The POEPOEM.C File

```
/*-----------------------------------------------------------
   POEPOEM.C -- Demonstrates Programmer-defined Resources
   -------------------------------------------------------*/

#define INCL_WIN
#define INCL_GPI
#define INCL_DOS
#include <os2.h>
```

(continued)

Figure 12-11. The POEPOEM.C File. *continued*

```
#include <stdlib.h>
#include "poepoem.h"

MRESULT EXPENTRY ClientWndProc (HWND, USHORT, MPARAM, MPARAM) ;

int main (void)
    {
    static CHAR  szClientClass [10] ;
    static CHAR  szTitleBar [40] ;
    static ULONG flFrameFlags = FCF_TITLEBAR       | FCF_SYSMENU   |
                                FCF_SIZEBORDER     | FCF_MINMAX    |
                                FCF_SHELLPOSITION  | FCF_TASKLIST  |
                                FCF_VERTSCROLL     | FCF_ICON ;

    HAB          hab ;
    HMQ          hmq ;
    HWND         hwndFrame, hwndClient ;
    QMSG         qmsg ;

    hab = WinInitialize (0) ;
    hmq = WinCreateMsgQueue (hab, 0) ;

    WinLoadString (hab, NULL, IDS_CLASS, sizeof szClientClass, szClientClass);
    WinLoadString (hab, NULL, IDS_TITLE, sizeof szTitleBar,    szTitleBar) ;

    WinRegisterClass (hab, szClientClass, ClientWndProc, CS_SIZEREDRAW, 0) ;

    hwndFrame = WinCreateStdWindow (HWND_DESKTOP, WS_VISIBLE,
                                    &flFrameFlags, szClientClass, szTitleBar,
                                    0L, NULL, ID_RESOURCE, &hwndClient) ;

    while (WinGetMsg (hab, &qmsg, NULL, 0, 0))
         WinDispatchMsg (hab, &qmsg) ;

    WinDestroyWindow (hwndFrame) ;
    WinDestroyMsgQueue (hmq) ;
    WinTerminate (hab) ;
    return 0 ;
    }

MRESULT EXPENTRY ClientWndProc (HWND hwnd, USHORT msg, MPARAM mp1, MPARAM mp2)
    {
    static HWND   hwndScroll ;
    static PCHAR  pResource ;
```

(continued)

Figure 12-11. The POEPOEM.C File. *continued*

```
static SEL      selResource ;
static SHORT    cxClient, cyClient, cxChar, cyChar, cyDesc,
                sScrollPos, sNumLines ;
FONTMETRICS     fm ;
HPS             hps ;
PCHAR           pText ;
POINTL          ptl ;
SHORT           sLineLength, sLine ;
ULONG           ulSegSize ;

switch (msg)
    {
    case WM_CREATE:

                /*----------------------------------------------
                    Load the resource, get size and address
                -------------------------------------------*/

            DosGetResource (NULL, IDT_TEXT, IDT_POEM, &selResource) ;
            DosSizeSeg (selResource, &ulSegSize) ;
            pResource = MAKEP (selResource, 0) ;

                /*----------------------------------------------------
                    Determine how many text lines are in resource
                -----------------------------------------------*/

            pText = pResource ;

            while (pText - pResource < (USHORT) ulSegSize)
                {
                if (*pText == '\0' ¦¦ *pText == '\x1A')
                    break ;

                if (*pText == '\r')
                    sNumLines ++ ;

                pText++ ;
                }

                /*---------------------------------------------
                    Initialize scroll bar range and position
                -------------------------------------------*/

            hwndScroll = WinWindowFromID (
                            WinQueryWindow (hwnd, QW_PARENT, FALSE),
                            FID_VERTSCROLL) ;
```

(continued)

Figure 12-11. The POEPOEM.C File. *continued*

```
                  WinSendMsg (hwndScroll, SBM_SETSCROLLBAR,
                                  MPFROM2SHORT (sScrollPos, 0),
                                  MPFROM2SHORT (0, sNumLines - 1)) ;


                  /*----------------------
                      Query character size
                      ---------------------*/


             hps = WinGetPS (hwnd) ;

             GpiQueryFontMetrics (hps, (LONG) sizeof fm, &fm) ;
             cxChar = (SHORT) fm.lAveCharWidth ;
             cyChar = (SHORT) fm.lMaxBaselineExt ;
             cyDesc = (SHORT) fm.lMaxDescender ;

             WinReleasePS (hps) ;
             return 0 ;

        case WM_SIZE:
             cxClient = SHORT1FROMMP (mp2) ;
             cyClient = SHORT2FROMMP (mp2) ;
             return 0 ;

        case WM_CHAR:
             return WinSendMsg (hwndScroll, msg, mp1, mp2) ;

        case WM_VSCROLL:
             switch (SHORT2FROMMP (mp2))
                 {
                 case SB_LINEUP:
                      sScrollPos -= 1 ;
                      break ;

                 case SB_LINEDOWN:
                      sScrollPos += 1 ;
                      break ;

                 case SB_PAGEUP:
                      sScrollPos -= cyClient / cyChar ;
                      break ;

                 case SB_PAGEDOWN:
                      sScrollPos += cyClient / cyChar ;
                      break ;
```

(continued)

Figure 12-11. The POEPOEM.C File. *continued*

```
                          case SB_SLIDERPOSITION:
                               sScrollPos = SHORT1FROMMP (mp2) ;
                               break ;
                          }
                     sScrollPos = max (0, min (sScrollPos, sNumLines - 1)) ;

                     if (sScrollPos != (SHORT) WinSendMsg (hwndScroll,
                                                         SBM_QUERYPOS, 0L, 0L))
                          {
                          WinSendMsg (hwndScroll, SBM_SETPOS,
                                      MPFROM2SHORT (sScrollPos, 0), NULL) ;
                          WinInvalidateRect (hwnd, NULL, FALSE) ;
                          }
                     return 0 ;

           case WM_PAINT:
                hps = WinBeginPaint (hwnd, NULL, NULL) ;
                GpiErase (hps) ;

                pText = pResource ;

                for (sLine = 0 ; sLine < sNumLines ; sLine++)
                     {
                     sLineLength = 0 ;

                     while (pText [sLineLength] != '\r')
                          sLineLength ++ ;

                     ptl.x = cxChar ;
                     ptl.y = cyClient - cyChar * (sLine + 1 - sScrollPos)
                                   + cyDesc ;

                     GpiCharStringAt (hps, &ptl, (LONG) sLineLength, pText) ;

                     pText += sLineLength + 2 ;
                     }
                WinEndPaint (hps) ;
                return 0 ;

           case WM_DESTROY:
                DosFreeSeg (selResource) ;
                return 0 ;
           }
     return WinDefWindowProc (hwnd, msg, mp1, mp2) ;
     }
```

The POEPOEM.H File

```
/*-------------------------
    POEPOEM.H header file
    ---------------------*/

#define ID_RESOURCE      1

#define IDT_TEXT      1024
#define IDT_POEM         1

#define IDS_CLASS        0
#define IDS_TITLE        1
```

The POEPOEM.RC File

```
/*---------------------------------
    POEPOEM.RC resource script file
    -------------------------------*/

#include "poepoem.h"

POINTER ID_RESOURCE poepoem.ico

RESOURCE IDT_TEXT IDT_POEM poepoem.asc

STRINGTABLE
    {
    IDS_CLASS, "PoePoem"
    IDS_TITLE, " - ""Annabel Lee"" by Edgar Allan Poe"
    }
```

The POEPOEM.ICO File

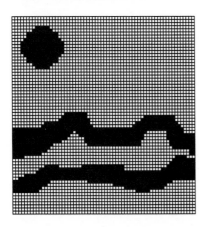

The POEPOEM.ASC File

```
It was many and many a year ago,
     In a kingdom by the sea,
That a maiden there lived whom you may know
     By the name of Annabel Lee;
And this maiden she lived with no other thought
     Than to love and be loved by me.


I was a child and she was a child
     In this kingdom by the sea,
But we loved with a love that was more than love --
     I and my Annabel Lee --
With a love that the winged seraphs of Heaven
     Coveted her and me.


And this was the reason that, long ago,
     In this kingdom by the sea,
A wind blew out of a cloud, chilling
     My beautiful Annabel Lee;
So that her highborn kinsmen came
     And bore her away from me,
To shut her up in a sepulchre
     In this kingdom by the sea.


The angels, not half so happy in Heaven,
     Went envying her and me --
Yes! that was the reason (as all men know,
     In this kingdom by the sea)
That the wind came out of the cloud by night,
     Chilling and killing my Annabel Lee.


But our love it was stronger by far than the love
     Of those who were older than we --
     Of many far wiser than we --
And neither the angels in Heaven above
     Nor the demons down under the sea
Can ever dissever my soul from the soul
     Of the beautiful Annabel Lee:


For the moon never beams, without bringing me dreams
     Of the beautiful Annabel Lee;
And the stars never rise, but I feel the bright eyes
     Of the beautiful Annabel Lee:
And so, all the night-tide, I lie down by the side
```

(continued)

Figure 12-11. **The POEPOEM.ASC File.** *continued*

```
Of my darling -- my darling -- my life and my bride,
    In her sepulchre there by the sea --
    In her tomb by the sounding sea.


                                        [May, 1849]
```

The POEPOEM.DEF File

```
;-------------------------------------
; POEPOEM.DEF module definition file
;-------------------------------------

NAME            POEPOEM    WINDOWAPI

DESCRIPTION     'Programmer-defined Resource (C) Charles Petzold, 1988'
PROTMODE
HEAPSIZE        1024
STACKSIZE       8192
EXPORTS         ClientWndProc
```

Figure 12-11. *The POEPOEM program.*

The POEPOEM.ASC file contains the text of the poem. This text is made a programmer-defined resource by referencing it in the resource script with this statement:

```
RESOURCE IDT_TEXT IDT_POEM poepoem.asc
```

The IDT_TEXT and IDT_POEM identifiers are defined in POEPOEM.H:

```
#define IDT_TEXT        1024
#define IDT_POEM           1
```

IDT_TEXT is the resource type ID. Programmer-defined resources must have type IDs of 256 or greater. IDT_POEM is the name ID.

During processing of the WM_CREATE message, POEPOEM obtains a segment selector to the resource by calling the OS/2 *DosGetResource* function:

```
DosGetResource (NULL, IDT_TEXT, IDT_POEM, &selResource) ;
```

When OS/2 loads the resource into memory, it allocates a memory block and returns the selector to the memory block in the *selResource* variable, which is defined as type SEL. POEPOEM converts this selector to a far pointer using the MAKEP macro:

```
pResource = MAKEP (selResource, 0) ;
```

A program can also use other OS/2 functions with this memory block, such as *DosSizeSeg* to find the size of the segment:

```
DosSizeSeg (selResource, &ulSegSize) ;
```

The only action that a program can't take is to write on this memory block. Resources loaded into memory using *DosGetResource* are always read-only. However, a program can allocate another memory block using *DosAllocSeg* and copy the data for later modification.

During the WM_CREATE message, POEPOEM determines the number of lines of text in the poem and sets the range of a scroll bar accordingly. All WM_CHAR messages to the client window are sent to the scroll bar to give the program a complete keyboard interface. POEPOEM displays the text during the WM_PAINT message. The only assumption it makes is that each line of text is terminated by a carriage return and a linefeed.

During the WM_DESTROY message, POEPOEM frees the memory block:

```
DosFreeSeg (selResource) ;
```

You'll notice that POEPOEM.C itself contains no displayable text. The text used in the title bar is defined in the resource script. We've thus made it easier for translators to convert the program to a foreign-language version. Of course, they would also need to translate the text of ''Annabel Lee,'' which is a far more challenging job.

MENUS AND KEYBOARD ACCELERATORS

The menu is an important part of the consistent user interface in Presentation Manager programs. Users learn a new program more quickly if the program has a menu that works like the menus in other Presentation Manager programs.

In one sense, putting a menu in a Presentation Manager program is fairly easy. You define the menu template in a resource script file, and you process WM_COMMAND messages from the menu in your client window procedure. The Presentation Manager takes care of all the keyboard and mouse processing involved with the menu. However, menus are also one of the more complex aspects of the Presentation Manager's windowing environment because they can be extensively tailored to the program's needs.

Let's nail down some terminology first. A "menu" is a control window created by *WinCreateStdWindow* as part of the standard window. A menu contains several items, each of which can be selected using either the mouse or the keyboard. The horizontal menu that appears below the window's title bar is called the program's "main menu" or "top-level menu" or the "action bar." I've generally used the term *top-level menu* for this.

Some menu items invoke another menu called a "popup menu" or a "drop-down menu" or a "pull-down menu" or a "submenu." I'll use the term *submenu* because that's the word used in several identifiers defined in the Presentation Manager header files. From the perspective of a program, each submenu is a separate window. Thus, when you create a top-level menu that invokes three submenus, you're actually creating four menu-control windows.

A Presentation Manager program also usually contains three other menu-control windows. One is the system menu, which contains one item—a little bitmapped picture to the left of the title bar. The system menu invokes a submenu. The minimize/maximize icon to the right of the title bar is also a menu. It contains two items, both of which are bitmaps.

Menu items can be "enabled" or "disabled." A disabled menu item appears in gray text. Although the user can click on a disabled menu item or use the keyboard to move a reverse-video bar to the menu item, the menu beeps and does not send a WM_COMMAND message to the program.

Conventional Menus

The CONVMENU program, shown in Figure 13-1, contains a conventional menu and demonstrates some sample menu processing. This program and the discussion that follows cover just about everything you'll need to know to implement a menu in most of your programs. The CONVMENU program also contains a keyboard accelerator table. Keyboard accelerators are key combinations that usually duplicate some menu items.

The CONVMENU File

```
#--------------------
# CONVMENU make file
#--------------------

convmenu.obj : convmenu.c convmenu.h
    cl -c -G2sw -W3 convmenu.c

convmenu.res : convmenu.rc convmenu.h
    rc -r convmenu

convmenu.exe : convmenu.obj convmenu.def
    link convmenu, /align:16, NUL, os2, convmenu
    rc convmenu.res

convmenu.exe : convmenu.res
    rc convmenu.res
```

The CONVMENU.C File

```
/*------------------------------------
   CONVMENU.C -- Conventional Menu Use
   ------------------------------------*/

#define INCL_WIN
#define INCL_GPI
#include <os2.h>
#include "convmenu.h"

#define ID_TIMER    1

MRESULT EXPENTRY ClientWndProc (HWND, USHORT, MPARAM, MPARAM) ;

CHAR szClientClass[] = "ConvMenu" ;
HAB  hab ;

int main (void)
    {
    static ULONG flFrameFlags = FCF_TITLEBAR     | FCF_SYSMENU   |
                                FCF_SIZEBORDER   | FCF_MINMAX    |
                                FCF_SHELLPOSITION | FCF_TASKLIST |
                                FCF_MENU         | FCF_ACCELTABLE ;
    HMQ          hmq ;
    HWND         hwndFrame, hwndClient ;
    QMSG         qmsg ;

    hab = WinInitialize (0) ;
    hmq = WinCreateMsgQueue (hab, 0) ;

    WinRegisterClass (hab, szClientClass, ClientWndProc, 0L, 0) ;

    hwndFrame = WinCreateStdWindow (HWND_DESKTOP, WS_VISIBLE,
                                    &flFrameFlags, szClientClass, NULL,
                                    0L, NULL, ID_RESOURCE, &hwndClient) ;

    WinSendMsg (hwndFrame, WM_SETICON,
                WinQuerySysPointer (HWND_DESKTOP, SPTR_APPICON, FALSE),
                NULL) ;

    while (TRUE)
        {
        while (WinGetMsg (hab, &qmsg, NULL, 0, 0))
            WinDispatchMsg (hab, &qmsg) ;
```

(continued)

Figure 13-1. The CONVMENU.C File. *continued*

```
            if (MBID_OK == WinMessageBox (HWND_DESKTOP, hwndClient,
                                "Really want to end program?",
                                szClientClass, 0,
                                MB_OKCANCEL | MB_ICONQUESTION))

                break ;

            WinCancelShutdown (hmq, FALSE) ;
            }

    WinDestroyWindow (hwndFrame) ;
    WinDestroyMsgQueue (hmq) ;
    WinTerminate (hab) ;
    return 0 ;
    }

MRESULT EXPENTRY ClientWndProc (HWND hwnd, USHORT msg, MPARAM mp1, MPARAM mp2)
    {
    static BOOL  fTimerGoing = FALSE ;
    static COLOR colBackground [] = {
                                0xFFFFFFL, 0xC0C0C0L, 0x808080L,
                                0x404040L, 0x000000L
                                } ;
    static HWND  hwndMenu ;
    static SHORT sCurrentBackground = IDM_WHITE ;
    HPS         hps ;
    RECTL       rcl ;

    switch (msg)
        {
        case WM_CREATE:
            hwndMenu = WinWindowFromID (
                        WinQueryWindow (hwnd, QW_PARENT, FALSE),
                        FID_MENU) ;
            return 0 ;

        case WM_INITMENU:
            switch (SHORT1FROMMP (mp1))
                {
                case IDM_TIMER:
                    WinSendMsg (hwndMenu, MM_SETITEMATTR,
                            MPFROM2SHORT (IDM_START, TRUE),
                            MPFROM2SHORT (MIA_DISABLED,
                                    !fTimerGoing &&
```

(continued)

Figure 13-1. The CONVMENU.C File. *continued*

```
                        WinQuerySysValue (HWND_DESKTOP, SV_CTIMERS) ?
                                  0 : MIA_DISABLED)) ;

                   WinSendMsg (hwndMenu, MM_SETITEMATTR,
                             MPFROM2SHORT (IDM_STOP, TRUE),
                             MPFROM2SHORT (MIA_DISABLED,
                                    fTimerGoing ? 0 : MIA_DISABLED)) ;
                   return 0 ;
              }
         break ;

    case WM_COMMAND:
         switch (COMMANDMSG(&msg)->cmd)
              {
              case IDM_NEW:
                   WinMessageBox (HWND_DESKTOP, hwnd,
                             "Bogus \"New\" Dialog",
                             szClientClass, 0, MB_OK | MB_ICONASTERISK) ;
                   return 0 ;

              case IDM_OPEN:
                   WinMessageBox (HWND_DESKTOP, hwnd,
                             "Bogus \"Open\" Dialog",
                             szClientClass, 0, MB_OK | MB_ICONASTERISK) ;
                   return 0 ;

              case IDM_SAVE:
                   WinMessageBox (HWND_DESKTOP, hwnd,
                             "Bogus \"Save\" Dialog",
                             szClientClass, 0, MB_OK | MB_ICONASTERISK) ;
                   return 0 ;

              case IDM_SAVEAS:
                   WinMessageBox (HWND_DESKTOP, hwnd,
                             "Bogus \"Save As\" Dialog",
                             szClientClass, 0, MB_OK | MB_ICONASTERISK) ;
                   return 0 ;

              case IDM_EXIT:
                   WinSendMsg (hwnd, WM_CLOSE, 0L, 0L) ;
                   return 0 ;
```

(continued)

Figure 13-1. The CONVMENU.C File. *continued*

```
          case IDM_ABOUT:
               WinMessageBox (HWND_DESKTOP, hwnd,
                         "Bogus \"About\" Dialog",
                         szClientClass, 0, MB_OK ¦ MB_ICONASTERISK) ;
               return 0 ;

          case IDM_START:
               if (WinStartTimer (hab, hwnd, ID_TIMER, 1000))
                    fTimerGoing = TRUE ;
               else
                    WinMessageBox (HWND_DESKTOP, hwnd,
                         "Too many clocks or timers",
                         szClientClass, 0,
                         MB_OK ¦ MB_ICONEXCLAMATION) ;
               return 0 ;

          case IDM_STOP:
               WinStopTimer (hab, hwnd, ID_TIMER) ;
               fTimerGoing = FALSE ;
               return 0 ;

          case IDM_WHITE:
          case IDM_LTGRAY:
          case IDM_GRAY:
          case IDM_DKGRAY:
          case IDM_BLACK:
               WinSendMsg (hwndMenu, MM_SETITEMATTR,
                         MPFROM2SHORT (sCurrentBackground, TRUE),
                         MPFROM2SHORT (MIA_CHECKED, 0)) ;

               sCurrentBackground = COMMANDMSG(&msg)->cmd ;

               WinSendMsg (hwndMenu, MM_SETITEMATTR,
                         MPFROM2SHORT (sCurrentBackground, TRUE),
                         MPFROM2SHORT (MIA_CHECKED, MIA_CHECKED)) ;

               WinInvalidateRect (hwnd, NULL, FALSE) ;
               return 0 ;
          }
     break ;
```

(continued)

Figure 13-1. The CONVMENU.C File. *continued*

```
        case WM_HELP:
             WinMessageBox (HWND_DESKTOP, hwnd,
                            "Help not yet implemented",
                            szClientClass, 0, MB_OK | MB_ICONEXCLAMATION) ;
             return 0 ;

        case WM_TIMER:
             WinAlarm (HWND_DESKTOP, WA_NOTE) ;
             return 0 ;

        case WM_PAINT:
             hps = WinBeginPaint (hwnd, NULL, NULL) ;
             GpiSavePS (hps) ;

             GpiCreateLogColorTable (hps, OL, LCOLF_RGB, OL, OL, NULL) ;

             WinQueryWindowRect (hwnd, &rcl) ;

             WinFillRect (hps, &rcl,
                          colBackground [sCurrentBackground - IDM_WHITE]) ;

             GpiRestorePS (hps, -1L) ;
             WinEndPaint (hps) ;
             return 0 ;

        case WM_DESTROY:
             if (fTimerGoing)
                  {
                  WinStopTimer (hab, hwnd, ID_TIMER) ;
                  fTimerGoing = FALSE ;
                  }
             return 0 ;
        }
   return WinDefWindowProc (hwnd, msg, mp1, mp2) ;
   }
```

The CONVMENU.H File

```
/*------------------------
   CONVMENU.H header file
   ------------------------*/

#define ID_RESOURCE        1

#define IDM_FILE           1      // Top-level items
```

(continued)

Figure 13-1. **The CONVMENU.H File.** *continued*

```
#define IDM_TIMER          2
#define IDM_BACKGROUND     3
#define IDM_TOPEXIT        4
#define IDM_HELP           5

#define IDM_NEW            10    // "File" submenu
#define IDM_OPEN           11
#define IDM_SAVE           12
#define IDM_SAVEAS         13
#define IDM_ABOUT          14

#define IDM_START          20    // "Timer" submenu
#define IDM_STOP           21

#define IDM_WHITE          30    // "Background" submenu
#define IDM_LTGRAY         31
#define IDM_GRAY           32        // Program logic assumes these
#define IDM_DKGRAY         33        // five numbers are consecutive
#define IDM_BLACK          34

#define IDM_EXIT           40    // "Exit" submenu
#define IDM_RESUME         41
```

The CONVMENU.RC File

```
/*-----------------------------------
   CONVMENU.RC resource script file
   ----------------------------------*/


#include <os2.h>
#include "convmenu.h"

MENU ID_RESOURCE
    {
    SUBMENU "~File",                IDM_FILE
        {
        MENUITEM "~New",                    IDM_NEW
        MENUITEM "~Open...",                IDM_OPEN
        MENUITEM "~Save\tShift+F3",         IDM_SAVE
        MENUITEM "Save ~As...",             IDM_SAVEAS
        MENUITEM SEPARATOR
        MENUITEM "A~bout ConvMenu...",      IDM_ABOUT
        }
```

(continued)

Figure 13-1. The CONVMENU.RC File. *continued*

```
    SUBMENU "~Timer",                IDM_TIMER
        {
        MENUITEM "~Start",                   IDM_START
        MENUITEM "S~top",                    IDM_STOP,, MIA_DISABLED
        }
    SUBMENU "~Background",           IDM_BACKGROUND
        {
        MENUITEM "~White\tCtrl+W",           IDM_WHITE,, MIA_CHECKED
        MENUITEM "~Light Gray\tCtrl+L",      IDM_LTGRAY
        MENUITEM "~Gray\tCtrl+G",            IDM_GRAY
        MENUITEM "~Dark Gray\tCtrl+D",       IDM_DKGRAY
        MENUITEM "~Black\tCtrl+B",           IDM_BLACK
        }
    SUBMENU "E~xit",                IDM_TOPEXIT
        {
        MENUITEM "E~xit ConvMenu...\tF3",  IDM_EXIT
        MENUITEM "~Resume ConvMenu",       IDM_RESUME
        }
    MENUITEM "F1=Help",              IDM_HELP, MIS_HELP | MIS_BUTTONSEPARATOR
    }


ACCELTABLE ID_RESOURCE
    {
    VK_F3, IDM_SAVE,   VIRTUALKEY, SHIFT
    VK_F3, IDM_EXIT,   VIRTUALKEY
    "^W",  IDM_WHITE
    "^L",  IDM_LTGRAY
    "^G",  IDM_GRAY
    "^D",  IDM_DKGRAY
    "^B",  IDM_BLACK
    }
```

The CONVMENU.DEF File

```
;------------------------------------
; CONVMENU.DEF module definition file
;------------------------------------


NAME         CONVMENU   WINDOWAPI

DESCRIPTION  'Conventional Menu Demo (C) Charles Petzold, 1988'
PROTMODE
HEAPSIZE     1024
STACKSIZE    8192
EXPORTS      ClientWndProc
```

Figure 13-1. *The CONVMENU program.*

The File submenu in CONVMENU contains standard options that don't do anything in this program except display some message boxes. (In the next chapter you'll see how to invoke dialog boxes from menu items.) The Timer menu starts and stops the timer. The timer causes the program to beep once a second. When the timer is active, the Start option is disabled; when the timer is inactive, the Stop option is disabled. The Background menu changes the background color of the client window. This menu uses check marks to indicate the current color.

Defining the Menu

You define a menu template in a resource script file. The menu template begins with the MENU statement, which indicates the resource name ID of the menu. The menu in CONVMENU.RC has a resource name ID of ID_RESOURCE, which is defined in CONVMENU.H. The actual definition of the menu is enclosed within a pair of curly brackets:

```
MENU ID_RESOURCE
    {
        [menu definition]
    }
```

If you want, you can use the BEGIN and END keywords rather than the curly brackets.

Between the curly brackets, you specify the items on the top-level menu by one or more MENUITEM or SUBMENU statements. The SUBMENU statement indicates a menu item that invokes a submenu, and the MENUITEM statement indicates a menu item that doesn't:

```
MENU ID_RESOURCE
    {
    SUBMENU "~File",        IDM_FILE
        {
            [definition of submenu]
        }
    SUBMENU "~Timer",       IDM_TIMER
        {
            [definition of submenu]
        }
    SUBMENU "~Background",  IDM_BACKGROUND
        {
            [definition of submenu]
        }
```

(continued)

continued

```
SUBMENU "E~xit",          IDM_TOPEXIT
    {
            [definition of submenu]
    }
MENUITEM "F1=Help",       IDM_HELP, MIS_HELP ¦ MIS_BUTTONSEPARATOR
}
```

Thus the top-level menu in CONVMENU contains the options "File," "Timer," "Background," and "F1=Help."

The syntax of the MENUITEM and SUBMENU statements is the same. Each statement contains a text string and a menu item ID followed by optional style and attribute identifiers:

```
MENUITEM "Text", idMenuItem [,[style flags][, attribute flags]]
SUBMENU  "Text", idMenuItem [,[style flags][, attribute flags]]
```

The text string is the text that appears in the menu. A tilde (~) character causes the letter that follows the tilde to be underlined when the text is displayed. A user can type that letter in combination with the Alt key to select the menu item from the keyboard. The underlined letters within the top-level menu and each submenu should be unique. It's recommended that you use the first letter, the first consonant, or a subsequent consonant.

The menu item ID is a 16-bit number that the Presentation Manager uses to identify the menu item in messages from the menu to your client window. You also use the menu item ID to send messages to the menu. The menu definition in CONVMENU.RC uses identifiers that are defined in CONV-MENU.H and begin with the letters IDM ("ID for a menu item").

The optional styles and attributes are one or more identifiers beginning with the letters MIS ("menu item style") or MIA ("menu item attribute"). I'll describe these styles and attributes shortly.

The SUBMENU statement indicates a menu item that invokes a submenu. The submenu is defined by one or more MENUITEM statements within a pair of curly brackets that follow the SUBMENU statement, like this:

```
SUBMENU "~Timer",         IDM_TIMER
    {
    MENUITEM "~Start",    IDM_START
    MENUITEM "S~top",     IDM_STOP,,   MIA_DISABLED
    }
```

This indicates that the Timer item on the top-level menu invokes a submenu containing the items Start and Stop. Multiple levels of submenu nesting are supported but not often used.

The text in submenu items can contain a tab character indicated by "\t." The text that follows the tab character appears to the right when the submenu is displayed. You generally use this to indicate the keyboard accelerator for the menu item, as in the submenu invoked by File:

```
SUBMENU "~File",              IDM_FILE
    {
    MENUITEM "~New",                IDM_NEW
    MENUITEM "~Open...",            IDM_OPEN
    MENUITEM "~Save\tShift+F3",     IDM_SAVE
    MENUITEM "Save ~As...",         IDM_SAVEAS
    MENUITEM SEPARATOR
    MENUITEM "A~bout ConvMenu...",IDM_ABOUT
    }
```

The F3 key in combination with the Shift key is a keyboard accelerator for Save. This text only indicates to the user what the keyboard accelerators are. I'll discuss later how you make these key combinations function as keyboard accelerators.

The ellipsis (...) in some text strings indicates that the item invokes a dialog box. The File submenu also includes the following line, which draws a horizontal line between the Save As and the About menu items:

```
MENUITEM SEPARATOR
```

ID Confusion

We first worked with IDs in connection with child windows. A child window ID is assigned by the program when it creates a child window. The child window uses this ID to identify itself to its parent. In the last chapter we began working with resource type IDs and resource name IDs. These IDs identify unique resources within a program.

Now we have menu item IDs. Don't confuse these with resource name IDs or child window IDs. The menu item ID identifies a particular menu item within a top-level menu or a submenu. (However, the menu item IDs are sometimes related to child window IDs. For example, IDM_FILE is the menu item ID of the File item on CONVMENU's top-level menu. It is also the child window ID of the submenu invoked by the File item. But the submenu isn't a child window of the top-level menu. This is obvious, because the submenu is displayed outside the area occupied by the top-level menu.)

The Styles and Attributes

Every menu item has a style and an attribute, each of which is represented within the Presentation Manager by bit flags within a 16-bit integer. You can override the default style and attribute using identifiers beginning with MIS and MIA in the menu definition.

Styles

Styles fall into several groups of mutually exclusive options. The first four style bits determine the contents of the visible part of the menu item:

Style Bit	Description
MIS_TEXT	Text string
MIS_BITMAP	Bitmap
MIS_SEPARATOR	Horizontal dividing line in submenu
MIS_OWNERDRAW	Item that will be drawn by program

When you omit a style identifier for a menu item, RC.EXE uses the MIS_STRING style as a default. In CONVMENU's menu, all menu items (except the separator bar in the File menu) have the MIS_STRING style. In the GRAFMENU program shown later in this chapter, we'll use the MIS_BITMAP style. The MIS_SEPARATOR style serves as an alternative to using the MENUITEM SEPARATOR statement. The MIS_OWNERDRAW style requires that your program itself draw the item whenever the menu is displayed. The Presentation Manager sends the client window procedure WM_MEASUREITEM and WM_DRAWITEM messages when the item must be drawn.

The next group of style bits determines the organization of the menu items in rows and columns:

Style Bit	Description
MIS_BREAK	Menu item starts in a new row or column
MIS_BREAKSEPARATOR	Menu item starts in a new row or column with a line drawn between the rows or columns
MIS_BUTTONSEPARATOR	Menu item is separated by a bar — the user can't use the cursor movement keys to move to the item

The MIS_BREAK and MIS_BREAKSEPARATOR styles are used most often in submenus that contain a large number of items. These styles aren't required in top-level menus because the Presentation Manager automatically breaks the menu into multiple lines when the window is too narrow to display the menu as a single line. The menu in CONVMENU uses the MIS_BUTTONSEPARATOR style for the "F1=Help" item. This places the item at the far right of the top-level menu.

The next set of style bits determines the message that the Presentation Manager sends the program when a menu item has been chosen by the user. Normally, the message is WM_COMMAND. These two bits override that:

Style Bit	Description
MIS_SYSCOMMAND	Choosing menu item generates a WM_SYSCOMMAND message
MIS_HELP	Choosing menu item generates a WM_HELP message

The WM_SYSCOMMAND message is usually reserved for system menu items. Because these items generate WM_SYSCOMMAND messages, you can process WM_COMMAND messages from the menu without worrying about receiving system menu messages. The "F1=Help" item in CONVMENU's menu has the MIS_HELP style to generate a WM_HELP message.

Although these last two menu item styles have little to do with each other, in a practical sense they are mutually exclusive. In a resource script menu template, the MIS_SUBMENU style is assumed when you use the SUBMENU statement rather than a MENUITEM statement.

Style Bit	Description
MIS_SUBMENU	Item invokes a submenu
MIS_STATIC	Item can't be chosen

Attributes

These five identifiers determine the attribute of the menu item:

Attribute Bit	Description
MIA_NODISMISS	If item in submenu is chosen, the submenu remains down
MIA_FRAMED	Item is enclosed in a box (top-level menu only; used by Presentation Manager when item is selected)
MIA_CHECKED	Check mark appears to left of item (submenu only)
MIA_DISABLED	Item is shown in gray text and can't be chosen
MIA_HILITED	Item is shown in reverse video (used by Presentation Manager when item is selected)

The difference between a menu style and a menu attribute is fairly simple: A program can change an item's attribute but not its style (unless the entire item is replaced).

The MIA_CHECKED and MIA_DISABLED attributes are used in CONV-MENU.RC for the White and Stop menu items respectively. You'll see shortly how a program can change these attributes.

Including the Menu in the Standard Window

You make the menu part of the standard window by including the FCF_MENU frame creation flag in the definition of *flFrameFlags*, just as you include the FCF_ICON flag discussed in the last chapter.

When the frame flags include FCF_MENU, the second to last parameter of *WinCreateStdWindow* must be set to the resource name ID of the menu, which, in CONVMENU.RC, is ID_RESOURCE. The Presentation Manager uses this same resource name ID for loading the program's icon when the frame flags include FCF_ICON and for loading the program's keyboard accelerator table when the frame flags include FCF_ACCELTABLE.

After the *WinCreateStdWindow* function returns, you can obtain the handle of the top-level menu by using the following function:

```
hwndMenu = WinWindowFromID (hwndFrame, FID_MENU) ;
```

Or, within the client window procedure, you can use

```
hwndMenu = WinWindowFromID (
          WinQueryWindow (hwnd, QW_PARENT, FALSE),
          FID_MENU) ;
```

Often the client window procedure obtains the window handle of the menu during the WM_CREATE message and stores it in a static variable for later use.

Receiving Menu Messages

The Presentation Manager sends the frame window procedure WM_COM-MAND messages when the user chooses an enabled menu item from the menu. (This message will be WM_SYSCOMMAND or WM_HELP if the menu item style includes the MIS_SYSCOMMAND or MIS_HELP style bit.) The frame window passes the messages to the client window procedure. If a disabled menu item is chosen, no WM_COMMAND message is generated.

The *mpl* and *mp2* parameters that accompany a WM_COMMAND message are shown below:

WM_COMMAND Parameters	Description
SHORT1FROMMP (*mpl*)	Menu item ID
SHORT1FROMMP (*mp2*)	CMDSRC_MENU
SHORT2FROMMP (*mp2*)	Nonzero if selected by mouse, 0 if selected by keyboard

WM_COMMAND is the same message that a push button window sends its owner. For a push button, the low USHORT of *mpl* is the child window ID, and the low USHORT of *mp2* is CMDSRC_PUSHBUTTON. Keyboard accelerators send WM_COMMAND messages with the low USHORT of *mpl* equal to CMDSRC_ACCELERATOR. If you're receiving WM_COMMAND messages from menus, accelerators, and push buttons, it's easiest to ignore *mp2* and test only the low USHORT of *mpl*. You should thus make all ID numbers unique unless you deliberately want the program to process WM_COMMAND messages from two or more different sources in the same way. (This is often the case with keyboard accelerators, because you use them to duplicate menu items.) As you learned in Chapter 11, you can also use the COMMANDMSG macro for decoding the message parameters of a WM_COMMAND message. For example, the expression

```
COMMANDMSG (&msg) -> cmd
```

is the menu item ID.

In *ClientWndProc*, the processing of the WM_COMMAND message looks like this:

```
case WM_COMMAND:
    switch (COMMANDMSG (&msg) -> cmd)
        {
            [case statements for menu item IDs]
        }
    break ;
```

You'll note that the *switch* and *case* construction includes *case* statements only for IDs associated with menu items in the menu's MENUITEM statements. The window procedure never receives WM_COMMAND messages for the menu item IDs in SUBMENU statements because these items invoke submenus and aren't commands in themselves. The WM_COMMAND processing in CONVMENU.C also lacks a *case* statement for IDM_HELP because that menu item generates a WM_HELP message. In the WM_COMMAND message processing, the IDM_NEW, IDM_OPEN, IDM_SAVE, IDM_SAVEAS, and IDM_ABOUT items cause the program to display message boxes. Normally, these items would cause the program to create and display a dialog box.

Working with Checked Menu Items

The submenu invoked by the Background item on CONVMENU's top-level menu allows the user to choose one of five colors that the program uses to color the background of the client window:

```
SUBMENU "~Background",   IDM_BACKGROUND
    {
    MENUITEM "~White\tCtrl+W",        IDM_WHITE,, MIA_CHECKED
    MENUITEM "~Light Gray\tCtrl+L",   IDM_LTGRAY
    MENUITEM "~Gray\tCtrl+G",         IDM_GRAY
    MENUITEM "~Dark Gray\tCtrl+D",    IDM_DKGRAY
    MENUITEM "~Black\tCtrl+B",        IDM_BLACK
    }
```

When the Presentation Manager first creates the window, the White item appears with a check mark to the left of the text. Check marks are used most often for mutually exclusive menu options, as is the case here.

Within *ClientWndProc*, the *sCurrentBackground* variable is initialized with the menu item ID of the checked item:

```
static SHORT sCurrentBackground = IDM_WHITE ;
```

When *ClientWndProc* receives a WM_COMMAND message for one of the five items in this submenu, it must remove the check mark from the item currently checked, add a check mark to the item that the user has chosen, and change the color of the client window.

Processing of the WM_COMMAND message is the same for all five items in this submenu:

```
case WM_COMMAND:
    switch (COMMANDMSG (&msg) -> cmd)
        {
            [other program lines]
        case IDM_WHITE:
```

(continued)

continued

```
        case IDM_LTGRAY:
        case IDM_GRAY:
        case IDM_DKGRAY:
        case IDM_BLACK:
```

To process these commands, CONVMENU first removes the check mark from the menu item that is currently checked. The ID of that menu item is stored in *sCurrentBackground*. The program can remove the check mark by sending the menu window a MM_SETITEMATTR message:

```
WinSendMsg (hwndMenu, MM_SETITEMATTR,
            MPFROM2SHORT (sCurrentBackground, TRUE),
            MPFROM2SHORT (MIA_CHECKED, 0)) ;
```

The *mp1* parameter of this message contains two USHORT values. The low USHORT of *mp1* has the ID of the menu item to be changed. However, you're sending this message to the window whose handle is *hwndMenu*. That's the window handle of the top-level window, not the submenu that contains the five color items. The high USHORT of *mp1* must be set to TRUE to tell the window procedure for the top-level menu to search through the submenus for a menu item with an ID equal to *sCurrentBackground*.

The low USHORT of *mp2* contains the attribute bit (or bits) to be changed. In this case, we want to change the MIA_CHECKED attribute bit. The high USHORT of *mp2* is set to the new value of these attribute bits — in this case 0. This removes the MIA_CHECKED attribute from the menu item.

CONVMENU sets *sCurrentBackground* equal to the item the user has chosen from the menu:

```
sCurrentBackground = COMMANDMSG (&msg) -> cmd ;
```

The program then sends the menu another MM_SETITEMATTR message. This is identical to the first message except that the high USHORT of *mp2* is set to MIA_CHECKED:

```
WinSendMsg (hwndMenu, MM_SETITEMATTR,
            MPFROM2SHORT (sCurrentBackground, TRUE),
            MPFROM2SHORT (MIA_CHECKED, MIA_CHECKED)) ;
```

The menu item chosen by the user now has the MIA_CHECKED attribute, and a check mark is drawn to the left of the item.

Most WM_COMMAND processing of mutually exclusive check-marked menu items requires little more than these three statements. Structurally, the code is very similar to that used in the DRAWLINE program in Chapter 11 to check and uncheck radio buttons. In CONVMENU, the only job left is to repaint the client window with the new color. This is accomplished by invalidating the window to generate a WM_PAINT message:

```
WinInvalidateRect (hwnd, NULL, FALSE) ;
```

During the WM_PAINT message, CONVMENU calls *GpiCreateLogColorTable* to use RGB color indices, obtains the dimensions of the client window, and uses *WinFillRect* to color it:

```
WinQueryWindowRect (hwnd, &rcl) ;

WinFillRect (hps, &rcl,
             colBackground [sCurrentBackground - IDM_WHITE]) ;
```

The *colBackground* array is initialized in *ClientWndProc* to contain the five color values corresponding to the five menu items:

```
static COLOR colBackground [] = {
                        0xFFFFFFL, 0xC0C0C0L, 0x808080L,
                        0x404040L, 0x000000L
                        } ;
```

The only assumption the program logic makes is that the five menu item ID numbers are consecutive. The CONVMENU.H file contains a little note to this effect.

```
#define IDM_WHITE      30
#define IDM_LTGRAY     31
#define IDM_GRAY       32    // Program logic assumes these
#define IDM_DKGRAY     33    // five numbers are consecutive
#define IDM_BLACK      34
```

Enabling and Disabling Menu Items

Another useful attribute of menu items is MIA_DISABLED. When a menu item is disabled, it appears in gray text. A disabled menu item doesn't generate a WM_COMMAND message.

CONVMENU uses disabled menu items on its Timer submenu. When the program begins, the Stop item is disabled, as indicated in the menu definition in CONVMENU.RC:

```
SUBMENU "~Timer",        IDM_TIMER
    {
    MENUITEM "~Start",       IDM_START
    MENUITEM "S~top",        IDM_STOP,,   MIA_DISABLED
    }
```

It makes no sense to stop the timer when it hasn't been started yet. When you choose Start from the menu, CONVMENU disables the Start item and enables Stop.

We could handle this enabling and disabling in the same way that we removed and added the check mark, with some additional logic required for starting and stopping the timer. However, in CONVMENU, the processing of WM_COMMAND messages for IDM_START and IDM_STOP doesn't alter the menu item attributes. Instead, IDM_START simply starts the timer, and IDM_STOP stops it:

```
case IDM_START:
    if (WinStartTimer (hab, hwnd, ID_TIMER, 1000))
            fTimerGoing = TRUE ;
    else
        WinMessageBox (HWND_DESKTOP, hwnd,
            "Too many clocks or timers",
            szClientClass, 0,
            MB_OK ¦ MB_ICONEXCLAMATION) ;
    return 0 ;

case IDM_STOP:
    WinStopTimer (hab, hwnd, ID_TIMER) ;
    fTimerGoing = FALSE ;
    return 0 ;
```

CONVMENU enables and disables the menu items while processing the WM_INITMENU message. The Presentation Manager sends a window procedure a WM_INITMENU message when it's about to display a submenu. The low USHORT of *mp1* is the ID of the top-level menu item that invokes the submenu. The program can take this opportunity to change the submenu. CONVMENU processes the WM_INITMENU message as shown on the next page.

```
case WM_INITMENU:
    switch (SHORT1FROMMP (mp1))
        {
        case IDM_TIMER:
            WinSendMsg (hwndMenu, MM_SETITEMATTR,
                    MPFROM2SHORT (IDM_START, TRUE),
                    MPFROM2SHORT (MIA_DISABLED,
                            !fTimerGoing &&
                        WinQuerySysValue (HWND_DESKTOP, SV_CTIMERS) ?
                            0 : MIA_DISABLED)) ;

            WinSendMsg (hwndMenu, MM_SETITEMATTR,
                    MPFROM2SHORT (IDM_STOP, TRUE),
                    MPFROM2SHORT (MIA_DISABLED,
                        fTimerGoing? 0 : MIA_DISABLED)) ;
            return 0 ;
        }
    break ;
```

CONVMENU ignores WM_INITMENU messages unless they involve the Timer submenu.

The first *WinSendMsg* call sets the MIA_DISABLED bit on the Start item if the timer is already active (indicated by a TRUE value of *fTimerGoing*) or if no timers are available (which you can determine from the *WinQuerySys-Value* function). The second *WinSendMsg* call sets the MIA_DISABLED bit on the Stop item if the timer isn't currently active.

Handling the Exit Command

When *ClientWndProc* receives a WM_COMMAND message with the IDM_EXIT menu item ID, it sends itself a WM_CLOSE message:

```
case IDM_EXIT:
    WinSendMsg (hwnd, WM_CLOSE, 0L, 0L) ;
    return 0 ;
```

WM_CLOSE is the same message the system menu sends the window procedure when the user chooses Close from the system menu. Most of the programs I've written so far have not processed the WM_CLOSE message but simply have passed it on to *WinDefWindowProc*. *WinDefWindowProc* responds to the WM_CLOSE message by posting a WM_QUIT message to the program's message queue, which causes the message loop in *main* to end and the program to terminate.

Some programs (those that work with files, for example) will want confirmation that the user really wants to end the program.

A program can be terminated not only from an Exit item on the program's menu or from the Close item on the system menu, but from the Task Manager as well. The user can select the Close option on the Task Manager's Task menu or the Shutdown option. In both of these cases, the Task Manager posts a WM_QUIT message to the program's message queue.

To handle all of these cases, a program that needs to request confirmation from the user before terminating must do so after receiving a WM_QUIT message. This requires that you add some logic to the message loop. Here's how CONVMENU does it:

```
while (TRUE)
    {
    while (WinGetMsg (hab, &qmsg, NULL, 0, 0))
        WinDispatchMsg (hab, &qmsg) ;

    if (MBID_OK == WinMessageBox (HWND_DESKTOP, hwndClient,
                                  "Really want to end program?",
                                  szClientClass, 0,
                                  MB_OKCANCEL | MB_ICONQUESTION))

        break ;
    WinCancelShutdown (hmq, FALSE) ;
    }
WinDestroyWindow (hwndFrame) ;
```

The WM_QUIT message causes *WinGetMsg* to return 0 and drop out of the message loop. CONVMENU then displays a message box with OK and Cancel buttons and asks if the user really wants to end the program. If the user answers by pressing OK, the *break* statement is executed and termination begins with *WinDestroyWindow*.

Otherwise, the program calls *WinCancelShutdown* (which halts any system shutdown that might have been initiated by the Task Manager), ignores the WM_QUIT message, and goes back to the message loop.

In CONVMENU.RC, the Exit menu item is defined like this:

```
MENUITEM "E~xit ConvMenu\tF3",    IDM_EXIT
```

It could have been defined like this:

```
MENUITEM "E~xit ConvMenu\tF3",  SC_CLOSE, MIS_SYSCOMMAND
```

This causes the Exit item to generate a WM_SYSCOMMAND message with the low USHORT of *mp1* equal to SC_CLOSE. This is the same message generated from the system menu when the user selects Close. *WinDef-WindowProc* processes this message by sending the window procedure a WM_CLOSE message. If I had used this, I wouldn't have required the IDM_EXIT identifier or the code to send the window procedure a WM_CLOSE message.

The WM_HELP Message

The menu template in CONVMENU.RC includes this menu item:

```
MENUITEM "F1=Help",    IDM_HELP, MIS_HELP | MIS_BUTTONSEPARATOR
```

The MIS_BUTTONSEPARATOR style puts the text at the far right of the top-level menu. The MIS_HELP style indicates that the menu item generates a WM_HELP message.

The *mp1* and *mp2* parameters that accompany the WM_HELP message are the same as those for WM_COMMAND messages:

WM_HELP Parameters	Description
SHORT1FROMMP (*mp1*)	Menu item ID
SHORT1FROMMP (*mp2*)	CMDSRC_MENU
SHORT2FROMMP (*mp2*)	Nonzero if selected by mouse, 0 if selected by keyboard

A push button can also generate a WM_HELP message if it's given the style BS_HELP. For push buttons, the low USHORT of *mp1* is the child ID, and the low USHORT of *mp2* is CMDSRC_PUSHBUTTON. The WM_HELP message helps you consolidate all your help processing in one place. Regardless of the presence of a menu item for Help, pressing the F1 key always generates a WM_HELP message. F1 is a built-in keyboard accelerator. The *mp1* parameter is 0, and the low USHORT of *mp2* is CMDSRC_ACCELERATOR.

CONVMENU responds to the WM_HELP message by reporting that "Help is not yet implemented." In a real program, you can create a window that reads help text (probably from a programmer-defined resource) and display it.

The Keyboard Accelerator Table

CONVMENU.RC also includes a keyboard accelerator table, which lets the user duplicate menu items from the keyboard. The accelerator table is defined as shown on the next page.

```
ACCELTABLE ID_RESOURCE
    {
    VK_F3, IDM_SAVE,    VIRTUALKEY, SHIFT
    VK_F3, IDM_EXIT,    VIRTUALKEY
    "^W",  IDM_WHITE
    "^L",  IDM_LTGRAY
    "^G",  IDM_GRAY
    "^D",  IDM_DKGRAY
    "^B",  IDM_BLACK
    }
```

Note that the resource name ID of the accelerator table is ID_RESOURCE, which is the same ID as the menu. The resource is loaded by the Presentation Manager because the window frame style bit of FCF_ACCELTABLE is included in the definition of *flFrameFlags*.

The first field in each line is the key, which is either a virtual key code or an ASCII code in quotes. The caret (^) indicates a Ctrl key combination. These keys generate WM_COMMAND messages. The second field specifies the ID that accompanies the WM_COMMAND message. These are the same IDs used in the menu. Following the IDs are some options. The VIRTUALKEY keyword is required if the first field is a virtual key code. SHIFT specifies that the Shift key must be used. Defining this table and including FCF_ACCELTABLE in the definition of *flFrameFlags* frame style is all that's required for keyboard accelerators that duplicate menu items.

Other Approaches to Menus

Now that we've studied the most common form of the Presentation Manager menu, let's look at a few unusual approaches and then complete this chapter with a Presentation Manager version of the famous game of Life.

Altering the System Menu

Small programs often need a menu for only one or two items — an About box and a help screen, perhaps. If you would rather not give such programs their own menu, you can add the required menu items to the system menu. Although this practice isn't recommended, it illustrates some useful concepts involved with menu handling. The ''poor person's menu'' technique is shown in the POORMENU program in Figure 13-2.

The POORMENU File

```
#--------------------
# POORMENU make file
#--------------------

poormenu.obj : poormenu.c
    cl -c -G2sw -W3 poormenu.c

poormenu.exe : poormenu.obj poormenu.def
    link poormenu, /align:16, NUL, os2, poormenu
```

The POORMENU.C File

```c
/*----------------------------------
   POORMENU.C -- Poor Person's Menu
   ------------------------------*/

#define INCL_WIN
#include <os2.h>

#define IDM_ABOUT   10
#define IDM_HELP    11

MRESULT EXPENTRY ClientWndProc (HWND, USHORT, MPARAM, MPARAM) ;

CHAR szCaption [] = "Poor Person\'s Menu" ;

int main (void)
    {
    static CHAR  szClientClass[] = "PoorMenu" ;
    static ULONG flFrameFlags = FCF_TITLEBAR      | FCF_SYSMENU |
                                FCF_SIZEBORDER    | FCF_MINMAX  |
                                FCF_SHELLPOSITION | FCF_TASKLIST ;
    HAB         hab ;
    HMQ         hmq ;
    HWND        hwndFrame, hwndClient ;
    QMSG        qmsg ;

    hab = WinInitialize (0) ;
    hmq = WinCreateMsgQueue (hab, 0) ;

    WinRegisterClass (hab, szClientClass, ClientWndProc, OL, 0) ;

    hwndFrame = WinCreateStdWindow (HWND_DESKTOP, WS_VISIBLE,
                                    &flFrameFlags, szClientClass, NULL,
                                    OL, NULL, 0, &hwndClient) ;
```

(continued)

Figure 13-2. The POORMENU.C File. *continued*

```
        WinSendMsg (hwndFrame, WM_SETICON,
                    WinQuerySysPointer (HWND_DESKTOP, SPTR_APPICON, FALSE),
                    NULL) ;

        while (WinGetMsg (hab, &qmsg, NULL, 0, 0))
            WinDispatchMsg (hab, &qmsg) ;

        WinDestroyWindow (hwndFrame) ;
        WinDestroyMsgQueue (hmq) ;
        WinTerminate (hab) ;
        return 0 ;
        }

MRESULT EXPENTRY ClientWndProc (HWND hwnd, USHORT msg, MPARAM mp1, MPARAM mp2)
        {
        static CHAR     *szMenuText [3] = { NULL,
                                            "A~bout PoorMenu...",
                                            "~Help..." } ;
        static MENUITEM mi [3] = {
                            MIT_END, MIS_SEPARATOR, 0, 0,         NULL, NULL,
                            MIT_END, MIS_TEXT,    0, IDM_ABOUT, NULL, NULL,
                            MIT_END, MIS_TEXT,    0, IDM_HELP,  NULL, NULL
                            } ;
        HWND            hwndSysMenu, hwndSysSubMenu ;
        MENUITEM        miSysMenu ;
        SHORT           sItem, idSysMenu ;

        switch (msg)
            {
            case WM_CREATE:
                hwndSysMenu = WinWindowFromID (
                                WinQueryWindow (hwnd, QW_PARENT, FALSE),
                                FID_SYSMENU) ;

                idSysMenu = SHORT1FROMMR (WinSendMsg (hwndSysMenu,
                                                MM_ITEMIDFROMPOSITION,
                                                NULL, NULL)) ;

                WinSendMsg (hwndSysMenu, MM_QUERYITEM,
                        MPFROM2SHORT (idSysMenu, FALSE),
                        MPFROMP (&miSysMenu)) ;

                hwndSysSubMenu = miSysMenu.hwndSubMenu ;
```

(continued)

Figure 13-2. The POORMENU.C File. *continued*

```
                for (sItem = 0 ; sItem < 3 ; sItem++)
                    WinSendMsg (hwndSysSubMenu, MM_INSERTITEM,
                              MPFROMP (mi + sItem),
                              MPFROMP (szMenuText [sItem])) ;
                return 0 ;

        case WM_COMMAND:
            switch (COMMANDMSG(&msg)->cmd)
                {
                case IDM_ABOUT:
                    WinMessageBox (HWND_DESKTOP, hwnd,
                                "(C) Charles Petzold, 1988",
                                szCaption, 0, MB_OK | MB_ICONASTERISK) ;
                    return 0 ;

                case IDM_HELP:
                    WinMessageBox (HWND_DESKTOP, hwnd,
                                "Help not yet implemented",
                                szCaption, 0, MB_OK | MB_ICONEXCLAMATION) ;
                    return 0 ;
                }
            break ;

        case WM_ERASEBACKGROUND:
            return 1 ;
        }
    return WinDefWindowProc (hwnd, msg, mp1, mp2) ;
    }
```

The POORMENU.DEF File

```
;------------------------------------
; POORMENU.DEF module definition file
;------------------------------------


NAME            POORMENU  WINDOWAPI

DESCRIPTION     'The Poor Person's Menu (C) Charles Petzold, 1988'
PROTMODE
HEAPSIZE        1024
STACKSIZE       8192
EXPORTS         ClientWndProc
```

Figure 13-2. *The POORMENU program.*

During processing of the WM_CREATE message in *ClientWndProc*, POOR-MENU obtains the window handle of the system menu:

```
hwndSysMenu = WinWindowFromID (
              WinQueryWindow (hwnd, QW_PARENT, FALSE),
              FID_SYSMENU) ;
```

This is actually the handle to the top-level system menu — the single bitmap that is displayed to the left of the title bar. What we need is the handle to the system submenu.

Sending the system menu an MM_ITEMIDFROMPOSITION message obtains the menu item ID of the system menu bitmap. Because this bitmap is the only item in the system top-level menu, it's located at position 0:

```
idSysMenu = SHORT1FROMMR (WinSendMsg (hwndSysMenu,
                                      MM_ITEMIDFROMPOSITION,
                                      NULL, NULL)) ;
```

POORMENU then sends the system menu an MM_QUERYITEM message to fill in a MENUITEM structure with the characteristics of this menu item:

```
WinSendMsg (hwndSysMenu, MM_QUERYITEM,
            MPFROM2SHORT (idSysMenu, FALSE),
            MPFROMP (&miSysMenu)) ;
```

The MENUITEM structure is defined in PMWIN.H like this:

```
typedef struct _MENUITEM
    {
    SHORT   iPosition ;
    USHORT  afStyle ;
    USHORT  afAttribute ;
    USHORT  id ;
    HWND    hwndSubMenu ;
    ULONG   hItem ;
    }
    MENUITEM ;
```

This contains all of the information about the particular menu item. The *hwndSubMenu* field has the window handle of the submenu:

```
hwndSysSubMenu = miSysMenu.hwndSubMenu ;
```

POORMENU then sends this submenu three MM_INSERTITEM messages to add three items to the system menu — a separator bar and two text strings:

```
for (sItem = 0 ; sItem < 3 ; sItem++)
    WinSendMsg (hwndSysSubMenu, MM_INSERTITEM,
                MPFROMP (mi + sItem),
                MPFROMP (szMenuText [sItem])) ;
```

The *mi* and *szMenuText* arrays are defined near the top of *ClientWndProc*.

Figure 13-3 shows the new system menu in POORMENU.

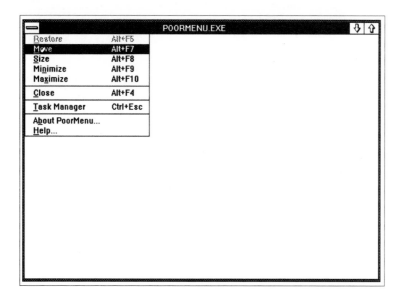

Figure 13-3. *The POORMENU system menu.*

Using Graphics in Menus

You needn't always use text strings in menus; you can also use bitmaps. You either define these bitmaps as resources or create them right in the program. The GRAFMENU program, shown in Figure 13-4 on the following pages, takes the former approach.

The GRAFMENU File

```
#---------------------
# GRAFMENU make file
#---------------------

grafmenu.obj : grafmenu.c grafmenu.h
    cl -c -G2sw -W3 grafmenu.c

grafmenu.res : grafmenu.rc grafmenu.h bighelp.bmp
    rc -r grafmenu

grafmenu.exe : grafmenu.obj grafmenu.def
    link grafmenu, /align:16, NUL, os2, grafmenu
    rc grafmenu.res

grafmenu.exe : grafmenu.res
    rc grafmenu.res
```

The GRAFMENU.C File

```
/*-------------------------------------
   GRAFMENU.C -- A Menu with Graphics
   -------------------------------------*/

#define INCL_WIN
#define INCL_GPI
#include <os2.h>
#include "grafmenu.h"

MRESULT EXPENTRY ClientWndProc (HWND, USHORT, MPARAM, MPARAM) ;

CHAR szClientClass[] = "GrafMenu" ;

int main (void)
    {
    static ULONG flFrameFlags = FCF_TITLEBAR       | FCF_SYSMENU   |
                                FCF_SIZEBORDER     | FCF_MINMAX    |
                                FCF_SHELLPOSITION  | FCF_TASKLIST  |
                                FCF_MENU ;
    HAB          hab ;
    HMQ          hmq ;
    HWND         hwndFrame, hwndClient ;
    QMSG         qmsg ;
```

(continued)

Figure 13-4. The GRAFMENU.C File. *continued*

```
    hab = WinInitialize (0) ;
    hmq = WinCreateMsgQueue (hab, 0) ;

    WinRegisterClass (hab, szClientClass, ClientWndProc, 0L, 0) ;

    hwndFrame = WinCreateStdWindow (HWND_DESKTOP, WS_VISIBLE,
                                    &flFrameFlags, szClientClass, NULL,
                                    0L, NULL, ID_RESOURCE, &hwndClient) ;

    WinSendMsg (hwndFrame, WM_SETICON,
                WinQuerySysPointer (HWND_DESKTOP, SPTR_APPICON, FALSE),
                NULL) ;

    while (WinGetMsg (hab, &qmsg, NULL, 0, 0))
        WinDispatchMsg (hab, &qmsg) ;

    WinDestroyWindow (hwndFrame) ;
    WinDestroyMsgQueue (hmq) ;
    WinTerminate (hab) ;
    return 0 ;
    }

MRESULT EXPENTRY ClientWndProc (HWND hwnd, USHORT msg, MPARAM mp1, MPARAM mp2)
    {
    static MENUITEM miBigHelp = { 0,                      // iPosition
                                  MIS_BITMAP | MIS_HELP,  // afStyle
                                  0,                      // afAttribute
                                  IDM_HELP,               // id
                                  NULL,                   // hwndSubMenu
                                  NULL } ;                // hItem

    FONTMETRICS     fm ;
    HBITMAP         hbm ;
    HPS             hps ;
    HWND            hwndMenu ;

    switch (msg)
        {
        case WM_CREATE:


                    /*-----------------------
                        Load bitmap resource
                       ----------------------*/
```

(continued)

Figure 13-4. The GRAFMENU.C File. *continued*

```
                hps = WinGetPS (hwnd) ;
                GpiQueryFontMetrics (hps, (LONG) sizeof fm, &fm) ;
                hbm = GpiLoadBitmap (hps, NULL, IDB_BIGHELP,
                                    64 * fm.lAveCharWidth / 3,
                                    64 * fm.lMaxBaselineExt / 8) ;
                WinReleasePS (hps) ;


                    /*-----------------------
                      Attach bitmap to menu
                      ---------------------*/


                miBigHelp.hItem = (ULONG) hbm ;


                hwndMenu = WinWindowFromID (
                            WinQueryWindow (hwnd, QW_PARENT, FALSE),
                            FID_MENU) ;


                WinSendMsg (hwndMenu, MM_SETITEM,
                            MPFROM2SHORT (0, TRUE), MPFROMP (&miBigHelp)) ;
                return 0 ;


        case WM_COMMAND:
                switch (COMMANDMSG(&msg)->cmd)
                    {
                    case IDM_NEW:
                    case IDM_OPEN:
                    case IDM_SAVE:
                    case IDM_SAVEAS:
                    case IDM_ABOUT:
                            WinAlarm (HWND_DESKTOP, WA_NOTE) ;
                            return 0 ;
                    }
                break ;


        case WM_HELP:
                WinMessageBox (HWND_DESKTOP, hwnd,
                            "Help not yet implemented",
                            szClientClass, 0, MB_OK | MB_ICONEXCLAMATION) ;
                return 0 ;


        case WM_ERASEBACKGROUND:
                return 1 ;
        }
    return WinDefWindowProc (hwnd, msg, mp1, mp2) ;
    }
```

The GRAFMENU.H File

```
/*-------------------------
   GRAFMENU.H header file
   --------------------------*/

#define ID_RESOURCE      1

#define IDB_BIGHELP      1

#define IDM_FILE         1

#define IDM_NEW         10
#define IDM_OPEN        11
#define IDM_SAVE        12
#define IDM_SAVEAS      13
#define IDM_ABOUT       14
#define IDM_HELP        15
```

The GRAFMENU.RC File

```
/*-----------------------------------
   GRAFMENU.RC resource script file
   ----------------------------------*/

#include <os2.h>
#include "grafmenu.h"

BITMAP IDB_BIGHELP bighelp.bmp

MENU ID_RESOURCE
    {
    SUBMENU "~File",            IDM_FILE
        {
        MENUITEM "~New",                IDM_NEW
        MENUITEM "~Open...",            IDM_OPEN
        MENUITEM "~Save",               IDM_SAVE
        MENUITEM "Save ~As...",         IDM_SAVEAS
        MENUITEM SEPARATOR
        MENUITEM "A~bout GrafMenu...",  IDM_ABOUT
        MENUITEM "",                    IDM_HELP
        }
    }
```

The BIGHELP.BMP File

The GRAFMENU.DEF File

```
;------------------------------------
; GRAFMENU.DEF module definition file
;------------------------------------

NAME            GRAFMENU  WINDOWAPI

DESCRIPTION     'Graphics Menu (C) Charles Petzold, 1988'
PROTMODE
HEAPSIZE        1024
STACKSIZE       8192
EXPORTS         ClientWndProc
```

Figure 13-4. *The GRAFMENU program.*

The BIGHELP.BMP file is a 64-by-64 bitmap created in ICONEDIT. In designing the bitmap, I attempted to capture the frazzled emotions of a person attempting to learn a new program. The bitmap is included as a resource in GRAFMENU.RC and is given the resource name ID of IDB_BIGHELP. The definition of GRAFMENU's menu has an empty string as the last menu item:

```
MENU ID_RESOURCE
    {
    SUBMENU "~File",          IDM_FILE
        {
        MENUITEM "~New",              IDM_NEW
        MENUITEM "~Open...",          IDM_OPEN
        MENUITEM "~Save",             IDM_SAVE
```

(continued)

continued

```
        MENUITEM "Save ~As...",        IDM_SAVEAS
        MENUITEM SEPARATOR
        MENUITEM "A~bout GrafMenu...",IDM_ABOUT
        MENUITEM "",                   IDM_HELP
        }
    }
```

This is the menu item that will use the bitmap.

During the WM_CREATE message, GRAFMENU calls *WinQueryFontMetrics* to obtain the size of a system font character. When the bitmap is loaded into memory, it is stretched in proportion to the character size:

```
hbm = GpiLoadBitmap (hps, NULL, IDB_BIGHELP,
                    64 * fm.lAveCharWidth / 3,
                    64 * fm.lMaxBaselineExt / 8) ;
```

Thus, regardless of the video display resolution, the bitmap will appear in a size relative to the other text in the menu.

GRAFMENU defines a structure named *miBigHelp* of type MENUITEM that is already initialized with everything except the handle of the bitmap. Setting the *hItem* field to the bitmap handle requires an assignment statement:

```
miBigHelp.hItem = (ULONG) hbm ;
```

The program then obtains the window handle of its menu:

```
hwndMenu = WinWindowFromID (
            WinQueryWindow (hwnd, QW_PARENT, FALSE),
            FID_MENU);
```

and sends the menu an MM_SETITEM message:

```
WinSendMsg (hwndMenu, MM_SETITEM,
        MPFROM2SHORT (0, TRUE), MPFROMP (&miBigHelp)) ;
```

When the user now pulls down the File menu, the big bitmapped "Help" offers a comforting beacon of hope, as shown in Figure 13-5 on the next page.

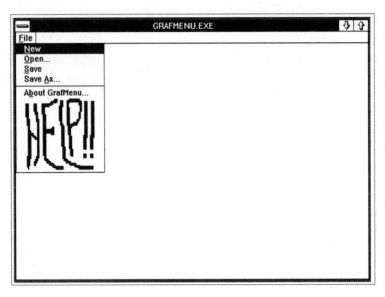

Figure 13-5. *The modified File menu.*

In desperation the user chooses that option, and GRAFMENU responds by displaying the message box: "Help not yet implemented."

A Life Program

It's time for a game. The game of Life was invented by Cambridge mathematician John Conway and popularized by Martin Gardner in his *Scientific American* "Mathematical Games" columns beginning in October 1970. It has been a favorite of programmers ever since. Gardner's columns on Life are collected in his book *Wheels, Life and Other Mathematical Amusements* (W. H. Freeman and Co., 1983). "Some Facts of Life," by David J. Buckingham (*Byte*, December 1978), is one of the best articles on the subject. *Hackers*, by Steven Levy (Anchor Press/Doubleday, 1984), has some good stories on early addictions to Life at MIT.

The Life playing board is a grid. Each cell in the grid can be either "alive" or "empty." You begin by defining a pattern of live cells. Then you take (or rather, the Life program takes) the grid through successive generations. For each new generation, a cell can die (change from alive to empty) or be born (change from empty to alive) based on the contents of the cell's eight immediate neighbors:

- If a live cell has one or no neighbors, it dies from loneliness.

- If a live cell has four or more neighbors, it dies from overpopulation.

- If an empty cell has exactly three neighbors, a new cell is born.

The Presentation Manager version of Life is shown in Figure 13-6.

The LIFE File

```
#----------------
# LIFE make file
#----------------

life.obj : life.c life.h
    cl -c -G2sw -W3 life.c

life.res : life.rc life.h life.ico
    rc -r life

life.exe : life.obj life.def
    link life, /align:16, NUL, os2, life
    rc life.res

life.exe : life.res
    rc life.res
```

The LIFE.C File

```
/*-----------------------------------------
   LIFE.C -- John Conway's Game of Life
   ------------------------------------*/

#define INCL_WIN
#define INCL_GPI
#include <os2.h>
#include <stdlib.h>
#include <string.h>
#include "life.h"

#define ID_TIMER    1

MRESULT EXPENTRY ClientWndProc (HWND, USHORT, MPARAM, MPARAM) ;

CHAR szClientClass [] = "Life" ;
HAB  hab ;

int main (void)
    {
    static ULONG flFrameFlags = FCF_TITLEBAR     | FCF_SYSMENU   |
                                FCF_SIZEBORDER    | FCF_MINMAX    |
                                FCF_SHELLPOSITION | FCF_TASKLIST  |
                                FCF_MENU          | FCF_ICON ;
```

(continued)

Figure 13-6. The LIFE.C File. *continued*

```
    HMQ          hmq ;
    HWND         hwndFrame, hwndClient ;
    QMSG         qmsg ;

    hab = WinInitialize (0) ;
    hmq = WinCreateMsgQueue (hab, 0) ;

    WinRegisterClass (hab, szClientClass, ClientWndProc, CS_SIZEREDRAW, 0) ;

    hwndFrame = WinCreateStdWindow (HWND_DESKTOP, WS_VISIBLE,
                            &flFrameFlags, szClientClass, NULL,
                            OL, NULL, ID_RESOURCE, &hwndClient) ;

    while (WinGetMsg (hab, &qmsg, NULL, 0, 0))
        WinDispatchMsg (hab, &qmsg) ;

    WinDestroyWindow (hwndFrame) ;
    WinDestroyMsgQueue (hmq) ;
    WinTerminate (hab) ;
    return 0 ;
    }

VOID EnableMenuItem (HWND hwndMenu, SHORT idMenuItem, BOOL fEnable)
    {
    WinSendMsg (hwndMenu, MM_SETITEMATTR,
                MPFROM2SHORT (idMenuItem, TRUE),
                MPFROM2SHORT (MIA_DISABLED, fEnable ? 0 : MIA_DISABLED)) ;
    }

VOID ErrorMsg (HWND hwnd, CHAR *szMessage)
    {
    WinMessageBox (HWND_DESKTOP, hwnd, szMessage, szClientClass, 0,
                MB_OK | MB_ICONEXCLAMATION) ;
    }

VOID DrawCell (HPS hps, SHORT x, SHORT y, SHORT cxCell, SHORT cyCell,
            BYTE bCell)
    {
    RECTL rcl ;

    rcl.xLeft   = x * cxCell ;
    rcl.yBottom = y * cyCell ;
    rcl.xRight  = rcl.xLeft   + cxCell - 1 ;
    rcl.yTop    = rcl.yBottom + cyCell - 1 ;

    WinFillRect (hps, &rcl, bCell & 1 ? CLR_NEUTRAL : CLR_BACKGROUND) ;
    }
```

(continued)

Figure 13-6. The LIFE.C File. *continued*

```
VOID DoGeneration (HPS hps, PBYTE pbGrid, SHORT xNumCells, SHORT yNumCells,
                   SHORT cxCell, SHORT cyCell)
     {
     SHORT x, y, sSum ;

     for (y = 0 ; y < yNumCells - 1 ; y++)
          for (x = 0 ; x < xNumCells ; x++)
               {
               if (x == 0 || x == xNumCells - 1 || y == 0)
                    *pbGrid |= *pbGrid << 4 ;
               else
                    {
                    sSum = (*(pbGrid                 - 1) +    // Left
                            *(pbGrid - xNumCells - 1) +    // Lower Left
                            *(pbGrid - xNumCells    ) +    // Lower
                            *(pbGrid - xNumCells + 1))     // Lower Right
                                          >> 4 ;

                    sSum += *(pbGrid                 + 1) +    // Right
                            *(pbGrid + xNumCells + 1) +    // Upper Right
                            *(pbGrid + xNumCells    ) +    // Upper
                            *(pbGrid + xNumCells - 1) ;    // Upper Left

                    sSum = (sSum | *pbGrid) & 0x0F ;

                    *pbGrid <<= 4 ;

                    if (sSum == 3)
                         *pbGrid |= 1 ;

                    if ((*pbGrid & 1) != *pbGrid >> 4)
                         DrawCell (hps, x, y, cxCell, cyCell, *pbGrid) ;
                    }
               pbGrid++ ;
               }
     }

VOID DisplayGenerationNum (HPS hps, SHORT xGen, SHORT yGen, LONG lGeneration)
     {
     static CHAR szBuffer [24] = "Generation " ;
     POINTL      ptl ;

     ptl.x = xGen ;
     ptl.y = yGen ;
```

(continued)

Figure 13-6. The LIFE.C File. *continued*

```
        ltoa (lGeneration, szBuffer + 11, 10) ;

        GpiSavePS (hps) ;

        GpiSetBackMix (hps, BM_OVERPAINT) ;
        GpiCharStringAt (hps, &ptl, (LONG) strlen (szBuffer), szBuffer) ;

        GpiRestorePS (hps, -1L) ;
        }

MRESULT EXPENTRY ClientWndProc (HWND hwnd, USHORT msg, MPARAM mp1, MPARAM mp2)
        {
        static BOOL  fTimerGoing ;
        static HWND  hwndMenu ;
        static LONG  lGeneration ;
        static SEL   selGrid ;
        static SHORT cxChar, cyChar, cyDesc, cxClient, cyClient, xGenNum, yGenNum,
                     cxCell, cyCell, xNumCells, yNumCells, sCellScale = 1 ;
        FONTMETRICS  fm ;
        HPS          hps ;
        PBYTE        pbGrid ;
        POINTL       ptl ;
        SHORT        x, y ;

        switch (msg)
            {
            case WM_CREATE:
                 hps = WinGetPS (hwnd) ;
                 GpiQueryFontMetrics (hps, (LONG) sizeof fm, &fm) ;
                 cxChar = (SHORT) fm.lAveCharWidth ;
                 cyChar = (SHORT) fm.lMaxBaselineExt ;
                 cyDesc = (SHORT) fm.lMaxDescender ;
                 WinReleasePS (hps) ;

                 hwndMenu = WinWindowFromID (
                                WinQueryWindow (hwnd, QW_PARENT, FALSE),
                                FID_MENU) ;
                 return 0 ;

            case WM_SIZE:
                 if (selGrid)
                     {
                     DosFreeSeg (selGrid) ;
                     selGrid = 0 ;
                     }
```

(continued)

Figure 13-6. The LIFE.C File. *continued*

```
if (fTimerGoing)
     {
     WinStopTimer (hab, hwnd, ID_TIMER) ;
     fTimerGoing = FALSE ;
     }

cxClient = SHORT1FROMMP (mp2) ;
cyClient = SHORT2FROMMP (mp2) ;

xGenNum = cxChar ;
yGenNum = cyClient - cyChar + cyDesc ;

cxCell = cxChar * 2 / sCellScale ;
cyCell = cyChar / sCellScale ;

xNumCells = cxClient / cxCell ;
yNumCells = (cyClient - cyChar) / cyCell ;

if (xNumCells <= 0 || yNumCells <= 0)
     {
     ErrorMsg (hwnd, "Not enough room for even one cell.") ;
     }

else if ((LONG) xNumCells * yNumCells > 65536L)
     {
     ErrorMsg (hwnd, "More than 64K cells not supported.") ;
     }

else if (DosAllocSeg (xNumCells * yNumCells, &selGrid, 0))
     {
     ErrorMsg (hwnd, "Not enough memory for this many cells.") ;
     selGrid = 0 ;
     }

else
     {
     pbGrid = MAKEP (selGrid, 0) ;

     for (y = 0 ; y < yNumCells ; y++)
          for (x = 0 ; x < xNumCells ; x++)
               *pbGrid++ = 0 ;
     }

EnableMenuItem (hwndMenu, IDM_SIZE,  TRUE) ;
EnableMenuItem (hwndMenu, IDM_START, selGrid != 0) ;
```

(continued)

Figure 13-6. The LIFE.C File. *continued*

```
            EnableMenuItem (hwndMenu, IDM_STOP,  FALSE) ;
            EnableMenuItem (hwndMenu, IDM_STEP,  selGrid != 0) ;
            EnableMenuItem (hwndMenu, IDM_CLEAR, selGrid != 0) ;

            lGeneration = 0 ;
            return 0 ;

    case WM_BUTTON1DOWN:
        x = MOUSEMSG(&msg)->x / cxCell ;
        y = MOUSEMSG(&msg)->y / cyCell ;

        if (selGrid && !fTimerGoing && x < xNumCells && y < yNumCells)
            {
            pbGrid = MAKEP (selGrid, 0) ;

            hps = WinGetPS (hwnd) ;

            DrawCell (hps, x, y, cxCell, cyCell,
                    *(pbGrid + y * xNumCells + x) ^= 1) ;

            WinReleasePS (hps) ;
            }
        else
            WinAlarm (HWND_DESKTOP, WA_WARNING) ;
        break ;

    case WM_COMMAND:
        switch (COMMANDMSG(&msg)->cmd)
            {
            case IDM_LARGE:
            case IDM_SMALL:
            case IDM_TINY:
                    WinSendMsg (hwndMenu, MM_SETITEMATTR,
                            MPFROM2SHORT (sCellScale, TRUE),
                            MPFROM2SHORT (MIA_CHECKED, 0)) ;

                    sCellScale = COMMANDMSG(&msg)->cmd ;

                    WinSendMsg (hwndMenu, MM_SETITEMATTR,
                            MPFROM2SHORT (sCellScale, TRUE),
                            MPFROM2SHORT (MIA_CHECKED, MIA_CHECKED)) ;

                    WinSendMsg (hwnd, WM_SIZE, NULL,
                            MPFROM2SHORT (cxClient, cyClient)) ;
```

(continued)

Figure 13-6. The LIFE.C File. *continued*

```
                        WinInvalidateRect (hwnd, NULL, FALSE) ;
                        return 0 ;

             case IDM_START:
                        if (!WinStartTimer (hab, hwnd, ID_TIMER, 1))
                             {
                             ErrorMsg (hwnd, "Too many clocks or timers.") ;
                             }
                        else
                             {
                             fTimerGoing = TRUE ;

                             EnableMenuItem (hwndMenu, IDM_SIZE,  FALSE) ;
                             EnableMenuItem (hwndMenu, IDM_START, FALSE) ;
                             EnableMenuItem (hwndMenu, IDM_STOP,  TRUE) ;
                             EnableMenuItem (hwndMenu, IDM_STEP,  FALSE) ;
                             EnableMenuItem (hwndMenu, IDM_CLEAR, FALSE) ;
                             }
                        return 0 ;

             case IDM_STOP:
                        WinStopTimer (hab, hwnd, ID_TIMER) ;
                        fTimerGoing = FALSE ;

                        EnableMenuItem (hwndMenu, IDM_SIZE,  TRUE) ;
                        EnableMenuItem (hwndMenu, IDM_START, TRUE) ;
                        EnableMenuItem (hwndMenu, IDM_STOP,  FALSE) ;
                        EnableMenuItem (hwndMenu, IDM_STEP,  TRUE) ;
                        EnableMenuItem (hwndMenu, IDM_CLEAR, TRUE) ;
                        return 0 ;

             case IDM_STEP:
                        WinSendMsg (hwnd, WM_TIMER, NULL, NULL) ;
                        return 0 ;

             case IDM_CLEAR:
                        lGeneration = 0L ;

                        pbGrid = MAKEP (selGrid, 0) ;

                        for (y = 0 ; y < yNumCells ; y++)
                             for (x = 0 ; x < xNumCells ; x++)
                                  *pbGrid++ = 0 ;
```

(continued)

Figure 13-6. The LIFE.C File. *continued*

```
                            WinInvalidateRect (hwnd, NULL, FALSE) ;
                            return 0 ;
                       }
                  break ;

          case WM_TIMER:
               hps = WinGetPS (hwnd) ;

               DisplayGenerationNum (hps, xGenNum, yGenNum, ++lGeneration) ;

               pbGrid = MAKEP (selGrid, 0) ;

               DoGeneration (hps, pbGrid, xNumCells, yNumCells, cxCell, cyCell);

               WinReleasePS (hps) ;
               return 0 ;

          case WM_PAINT:
               hps = WinBeginPaint (hwnd, NULL, NULL) ;
               GpiErase (hps) ;

               if (selGrid)
                    {
                    for (x = 1 ; x <= xNumCells ; x++)
                         {
                         ptl.x = cxCell * x - 1 ;
                         ptl.y = 0 ;
                         GpiMove (hps, &ptl) ;

                         ptl.y = cyCell * yNumCells - 1 ;
                         GpiLine (hps, &ptl) ;
                         }

                    for (y = 1 ; y <= yNumCells ; y++)
                         {
                         ptl.x = 0 ;
                         ptl.y = cyCell * y - 1 ;
                         GpiMove (hps, &ptl) ;

                         ptl.x = cxCell * xNumCells - 1 ;
                         GpiLine (hps, &ptl) ;
                         }

                    pbGrid = MAKEP (selGrid, 0) ;
```

(continued)

Figure 13-6. The LIFE.C File. *continued*

```
                      for (y = 0 ; y < yNumCells ; y++)
                          for (x = 0 ; x < xNumCells ; x++)
                              if (*pbGrid++)
                                  DrawCell (hps, x, y, cxCell, cyCell,
                                            *(pbGrid - 1)) ;

                      DisplayGenerationNum (hps, xGenNum, yGenNum, lGeneration) ;
                      }
               WinEndPaint (hps) ;
               return 0 ;

          case WM_DESTROY:
               if (fTimerGoing)
                   WinStopTimer (hab, hwnd, ID_TIMER) ;

               if (selGrid)
                   DosFreeSeg (selGrid) ;

               return 0 ;
          }
     return WinDefWindowProc (hwnd, msg, mp1, mp2) ;
     }
```

The LIFE.H File

```
/*--------------------
   LIFE.H header file
   -------------------*/

#define ID_RESOURCE      1

#define IDM_SIZE        10

#define IDM_LARGE        1        /* Values used in    */
#define IDM_SMALL        2        /*   program logic   */
#define IDM_TINY         4        /*    for cell size  */

#define IDM_CLEAR       20
#define IDM_START       21
#define IDM_STOP        22
#define IDM_STEP        23
```

The LIFE.RC File

```
/*-------------------------------
   LIFE.RC resource script file
   -----------------------------*/

#include <os2.h>
#include "life.h"

POINTER ID_RESOURCE life.ico

MENU ID_RESOURCE
    {
    SUBMENU "~Cell-Size",      IDM_SIZE
        {
        MENUITEM "~Large",   IDM_LARGE,, MIA_CHECKED
        MENUITEM "~Small",   IDM_SMALL
        MENUITEM "~Tiny",    IDM_TINY
        }
    MENUITEM "~Start!",        IDM_START
    MENUITEM "S~top!",         IDM_STOP,,  MIA_DISABLED
    MENUITEM "Ste~p!",         IDM_STEP
    MENUITEM "C~lear!",        IDM_CLEAR
    }
```

The LIFE.ICO File

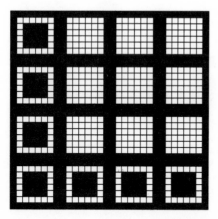

The LIFE.DEF File

```
;----------------------------------
; LIFE.DEF module definition file
;----------------------------------

NAME            LIFE      WINDOWAPI

DESCRIPTION     'Game of Life Program (C) Charles Petzold, 1988'
PROTMODE
HEAPSIZE        1024
STACKSIZE       8192
EXPORTS         ClientWndProc
```

Figure 13-6. *The LIFE program.*

The LIFE.RC resource script defines one submenu that specifies the size of the cells and four top-level items without submenus: Start, Stop, Step, and Clear. I made these items part of the top-level menu so you can more easily choose them with the mouse. By convention, items on the top-level menu that don't invoke submenus are followed by exclamation points.

You can use the mouse to toggle cells between an alive and an empty state. You start the program by choosing Start from the top-level menu. LIFE uses a timer to advance through the generations. You stop the timer by choosing Stop. You can advance through the generations manually with Step. The grid is cleared when you choose Clear from the top-level menu or when you change the cell size. Changing the size of the window also clears the grid.

I won't describe the workings of this program because little of the logic is related to menu processing. However, note that the program often enables and disables some menu items when the user chooses a menu item. The program can then avoid extensive testing during processing of the WM_COMMAND message. For example, when LIFE gets a WM_COMMAND message indicating that Start has been chosen from the menu, it doesn't have to check to see if the timer is already going, because once the timer is going, the Start option is disabled. I think of this technique as an active rather than a passive approach to testing the validity of menu items. At the time a menu item becomes invalid, you send the menu a message to disable the item. You then don't have to worry about getting WM_COMMAND messages for that menu item.

DIALOG BOXES

We have already looked at several ways a Presentation Manager program can obtain input from the user. The most rudimentary is the direct processing of keyboard and mouse input to the program's client window. But we have also seen how a program can create child control windows (such as buttons, scroll bars, and menus) either implicitly as part of the standard window or explicitly with *WinCreateWindow* calls. These control windows provide a layer of processing between user input and the program.

Now we'll go one step further and create dialog boxes. A "dialog box" is a window that contains various child control windows. Programs generally use dialog boxes to obtain user input beyond that which can be easily handled in a menu. A menu item indicates with an ellipsis (...) that it invokes a dialog box.

You define the layout of control windows in a dialog box by creating a dialog box template as part of the resource script file. In your program you create a dialog box window based on this template. You're essentially farming out to the Presentation Manager the job of creating, sizing, and positioning all control windows within the dialog box window.

In Chapter 11 we created control windows on the surface of the program's client window, and we encountered some difficulties in handling the keyboard interface. When you create a dialog box, these problems go away. The dialog box logic within the Presentation Manager implements a keyboard interface that allows the user to move the input focus between controls using the Tab key and the cursor movement keys.

Dialog boxes come in two flavors: modal and modeless. The modal dialog box is the most common. When a program creates a modal dialog box, the user can switch control to another window in the program only after the dialog box is destroyed. A modeless dialog box is more akin to a normal top-level window that you might create in your program (such as those in the

WELCOME2 program in Chapter 3). The user can switch control between the dialog box and the program's client window. With one exception (the HEXCALC program), all of the dialog boxes in this chapter are modal dialog boxes.

The Simple "About" Box

One simple modal dialog box is often called an "About" box. This dialog box is invoked when a user chooses the menu option "About This Program..." The dialog box usually contains a one-line or two-line description of the program, a copyright notice, the program's icon, and a single push button labeled "OK." Pressing the Spacebar or the Enter key destroys the dialog box. The ABOUTBOX program, shown in Figure 14-1, does little but display a standard About box.

The ABOUTBOX File

```
#--------------------
# ABOUTBOX make file
#--------------------

aboutbox.obj : aboutbox.c aboutbox.h
    cl -c -G2sw -W3 aboutbox.c

aboutbox.res : aboutbox.rc aboutbox.h aboutbox.ico
    rc -r aboutbox

aboutbox.exe : aboutbox.obj aboutbox.def
    link aboutbox, /align:16, NUL, os2, aboutbox
    rc aboutbox.res

aboutbox.exe : aboutbox.res
    rc aboutbox.res
```

The ABOUTBOX.C File

```
/*-------------------------------------------------------------
    ABOUTBOX.C -- Demonstration of About Box Dialog Procedure
  -----------------------------------------------------------*/

#define INCL_WIN
#include <os2.h>
#include "aboutbox.h"
```

(continued)

Figure 14-1. The ABOUTBOX.C File. *continued*

```
MRESULT EXPENTRY ClientWndProc (HWND, USHORT, MPARAM, MPARAM) ;
MRESULT EXPENTRY AboutDlgProc  (HWND, USHORT, MPARAM, MPARAM) ;

int main (void)
    {
    static CHAR  szClientClass[] = "AboutBox" ;
    static ULONG flFrameFlags = FCF_TITLEBAR        | FCF_SYSMENU  |
                                FCF_SIZEBORDER      | FCF_MINMAX   |
                                FCF_SHELLPOSITION   | FCF_TASKLIST |
                                FCF_MENU            | FCF_ICON ;

    HAB          hab ;
    HMQ          hmq ;
    HWND         hwndFrame, hwndClient ;
    QMSG         qmsg ;

    hab = WinInitialize (0) ;
    hmq = WinCreateMsgQueue (hab, 0) ;

    WinRegisterClass (hab, szClientClass, ClientWndProc, 0L, 0) ;

    hwndFrame = WinCreateStdWindow (HWND_DESKTOP, WS_VISIBLE,
                                    &flFrameFlags, szClientClass, NULL,
                                    0L, NULL, ID_RESOURCE, &hwndClient) ;

    while (WinGetMsg (hab, &qmsg, NULL, 0, 0))
        WinDispatchMsg (hab, &qmsg) ;

    WinDestroyWindow (hwndFrame) ;
    WinDestroyMsgQueue (hmq) ;
    WinTerminate (hab) ;
    return 0 ;
    }

MRESULT EXPENTRY ClientWndProc (HWND hwnd, USHORT msg, MPARAM mp1, MPARAM mp2)
    {
    switch (msg)
        {
        case WM_COMMAND:
            switch (COMMANDMSG(&msg)->cmd)
                {
                case IDM_NEW:
                case IDM_OPEN:
                case IDM_SAVE:
                case IDM_SAVEAS:
                    WinAlarm (HWND_DESKTOP, WA_NOTE) ;
                    return 0 ;
```

(continued)

Figure 14-1. The ABOUTBOX.C File. *continued*

```
                          case IDM_ABOUT:
                                 WinDlgBox (HWND_DESKTOP, hwnd, AboutDlgProc,
                                           NULL, IDD_ABOUT, NULL) ;
                                 return 0 ;
                          }
                   break ;

            case WM_ERASEBACKGROUND:
                 return 1 ;
            }
      return WinDefWindowProc (hwnd, msg, mp1, mp2) ;
      }

MRESULT EXPENTRY AboutDlgProc (HWND hwnd, USHORT msg, MPARAM mp1, MPARAM mp2)
      {
      switch (msg)
            {
            case WM_COMMAND:
                 switch (COMMANDMSG(&msg)->cmd)
                       {
                       case DID_OK:
                       case DID_CANCEL:
                            WinDismissDlg (hwnd, TRUE) ;
                            return 0 ;
                       }
                 break ;
            }
      return WinDefDlgProc (hwnd, msg, mp1, mp2) ;
      }
```

The ABOUTBOX.H File

```
/*------------------------
   ABOUTBOX.H header file
   ------------------------*/

#define ID_RESOURCE      1

#define IDM_FILE         1

#define IDM_NEW          10
#define IDM_OPEN         11
#define IDM_SAVE         12
#define IDM_SAVEAS       13
```

(continued)

Figure 14-1. The ABOUTBOX.H File. *continued*

```
#define IDM_ABOUT          14

#define IDD_ABOUT          1
```

The ABOUTBOX.RC File

```
/*-----------------------------------
   ABOUTBOX.RC resource script file
   -----------------------------------*/

#include <os2.h>
#include "aboutbox.h"

POINTER ID_RESOURCE aboutbox.ico

MENU ID_RESOURCE
    {
    SUBMENU "~File",           IDM_FILE
        {
        MENUITEM "~New",              IDM_NEW
        MENUITEM "~Open...",          IDM_OPEN
        MENUITEM "~Save",             IDM_SAVE
        MENUITEM "Save ~As...",       IDM_SAVEAS
        MENUITEM SEPARATOR
        MENUITEM "A~bout AboutBox...", IDM_ABOUT
        }
    }

DLGTEMPLATE IDD_ABOUT
  {
  DIALOG "", 0, 32, 32, 200, 88,, FCF_DLGBORDER
    {
    CTEXT "AboutBox"                      -1, 10, 64, 180,  8
    ICON  ID_RESOURCE                     -1,  8, 56,   0,  0
    CTEXT "Sample ""About"" Dialog Box"   -1, 10, 40, 180,  8
    CTEXT "Copyright (C) Charles Petzold, 1988" -1, 10, 32, 180,  8
    DEFPUSHBUTTON "OK"                    DID_OK, 80,  8,  40, 16, WS_GROUP
    }
  }
```

The ABOUTBOX.ICO File

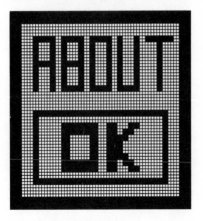

The ABOUTBOX.DEF File

```
;----------------------------------------
; ABOUTBOX.DEF module definition file
;----------------------------------------

NAME            ABOUTBOX   WINDOWAPI

DESCRIPTION     'Sample About Box Dialog Procedure (C) Charles Petzold, 1988'
PROTMODE
HEAPSIZE        1024
STACKSIZE       8192
EXPORTS         ClientWndProc
                AboutDlgProc
```

Figure 14-1. *The ABOUTBOX program.*

Figure 14-2 shows the ABOUTBOX dialog box.

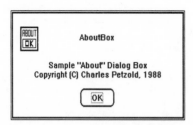

Figure 14-2. *The ABOUTBOX display.*

The Dialog Box Template

The first step in adding a dialog box to a program is to create a template that describes the layout of child control windows within the dialog box window. You create a dialog box template in one of two ways. The easiest way is to use the DLGBOX program supplied as part of the OS/2 Programmer's Toolkit. This program saves a dialog box template as an ASCII file with the extension .DLG. You then include the .DLG file in your .RC resource script file using the following statement:

```
rcinclude mydialog.dlg
```

However, because .DLG file output from DLGBOX is ugly and nearly unreadable, I've taken a more primitive approach in creating the dialog box templates shown in this chapter. I've created them manually, right in the resource script file. The dialog box template in ABOUTBOX.RC looks like this:

```
DLGTEMPLATE IDD_ABOUT
  {
  DIALOG "", 0, 32, 32, 200, 88,, FCF_DLGBORDER
    {
    CTEXT "ABOUTBOX"                            -1, 10, 64, 180,  8
    ICON  ID_RESOURCE                           -1,  8, 56,   0,  0
    CTEXT "Sample ""About"" Dialog Box"         -1, 10, 40, 180,  8
    CTEXT "Copyright (C) Charles Petzold, 1988" -1, 10, 32, 180,  8
    DEFPUSHBUTTON "OK"                      DID_OK, 80,  8,  40, 16, WS_GROUP
    }
  }
```

The keyword DLGTEMPLATE identifies this resource as a dialog box template. (You can use the keyword WINDOWTEMPLATE as a synonym for DLGTEMPLATE.) The resource compiler converts this template to a binary form and stores it in the program's .EXE file with a resource type ID of RT_DIALOG. The IDD_ABOUT identifier, which is defined in ABOUTBOX.H as 1, is the resource name ID.

The definition of the dialog box is enclosed in a pair of curly brackets or between BEGIN and END statements. Within this first set of curly brackets you define one (and only one) main window. In the ABOUTBOX dialog box template, this window is specified by the DIALOG statement. The various child control windows within this dialog box are then nested in another set of curly brackets following the DIALOG statement.

Using the DIALOG statement implies that the dialog box window is to be based on the WC_FRAME window class, the same window class used to create a standard frame window. The general format of the DIALOG statement is as follows:

```
DIALOG "text", ChildID, x, y, width, height [,window style] [,creation flags]
```

The "text" field is the text that would appear in the dialog box's title bar if it had one. (Most modal dialog boxes do not.) Because the dialog box window will be a top-level window, the *ChildID* field isn't important, so in this example it's set to 0.

The next four fields specify the position and size of the dialog box window. The *x* and *y* values are the position of the lower-left corner of the dialog box window relative to the lower-left corner of its owner, which is usually the program's client window. These coordinates and sizes are *not* in units of pixels — they're in special units used only in dialog box templates. I'll describe the dialog box coordinate system in the next section.

The optional *window style* field of the DIALOG statement is a combination of identifiers beginning with WS ("window style"), just like the window style used in the *WinCreateStdWindow* function. WS_VISIBLE is not required for a modal dialog box. This is followed by *creation flags* beginning with FCF, like the *flFrameFlags* parameter passed to the *WinCreateStdWindow* function. The FCF_DLGBORDER flag is normal for a modal dialog box and causes the dialog box to have a normal dialog box border.

Following the DIALOG statement is a set of curly brackets enclosing other statements that define all child control windows to be created on the surface of the dialog box window. In the ABOUTBOX dialog box template, these statements begin with CTEXT, ICON, and DEFPUSHBUTTON, all of which are keywords recognized by the resource compiler. The CTEXT keyword stands for "centered text." CTEXT specifies a control window based on the WC_STATIC window class with the following window style:

```
SS_TEXT | DT_CENTER | WS_GROUP
```

This should look somewhat familiar, because we used the WC_STATIC class and the SS_TEXT window style in the COLORSCR program in Chapter 11. (I'll discuss the WS_GROUP identifier later in this chapter.) Our dialog box template has three CTEXT statements for the dialog box's three lines of centered text.

The CTEXT statement has a format similar to that of the DIALOG statement:

```
CTEXT "text", ChildID, x, y, width, height [, window style]
```

The "text" field is the window's text. In the ABOUTBOX dialog box template, the *ChildID* field for the CTEXT control windows is set to −1 because the child ID isn't used by the program. The *x* and *y* fields specify the position of the lower-left corner of the control window relative to the lower-left corner of the dialog box window. For the optional *window style* field, you can use WS ("window style") or SS ("static style") identifiers to alter the default style of the control window.

The ICON statement specifies another window based on the WC_STATIC class, this one with a window style of

```
SS_ICON ┊ WS_GROUP
```

The ICON statement has a format similar to the CTEXT statement, except that the first field is the resource name ID of an icon. The *height* and *width* fields are ignored because icons have a standard size based on the resolution of the display.

The DEFPUSHBUTTON statement specifies a push button based on the window class WC_BUTTON with the window style

```
BS_PUSHBUTTON ┊ BS_DEFAULT ┊ WS_TABSTOP
```

The BS_DEFAULT style makes this a default push button, which has a wider border than a normal button. I'll discuss the WS_TABSTOP style later in this chapter. The child ID of this push button is set to DID_OK. This is an identifier defined in PMWIN.H that is often used for default push buttons in dialog boxes.

The dialog box template in ABOUTBOX.RC thus defines six windows. The parent is based on the WC_DIALOG window class and has five children. Four of the children are based on the WC_STATIC window class, and the fifth is based on WC_BUTTON.

Dialog Box Coordinates

The coordinates and sizes specified in the DIALOG, CTEXT, ICON, and DEFPUSHBUTTON statements are in special units used only within dialog box templates. The horizontal (*x*) coordinates and sizes are in units of ¼ the average width of a system font character; the vertical (*y*) coordinates and sizes are in units of ⅛ the height of a system font character. Thus the

ABOUTBOX dialog box has a width of 50 characters (200 units) and a height of 11 characters (88 units). These special dialog box coordinates allow you to design dialog box templates that retain the same general appearance regardless of the resolution of the video display. Because a system font character is roughly twice as high as it is wide, the horizontal and vertical coordinates are about the same.

For the dialog box window itself, the position of the window is relative to the lower-left corner of its owner (which is generally the client window in the program that displays the dialog box). The positions of the control windows are relative to the lower-left corner of their parent, which is the dialog box window.

You'll note that the height of the CTEXT window controls in ABOUTBOX is 8 units. That's one character. The height of the push button is 16 units (two characters) because the height must include the border of the button. For static text controls, the minimum width of the window in dialog box units must be 4 times the number of characters. To determine the minimum width of a push button, add 2 to the number of characters and then multiply by 4.

The Dialog Procedure

A program that includes a dialog box must have a dialog procedure that processes messages to the dialog window. This dialog procedure looks a lot like a normal window procedure. The *AboutDlgProc* dialog procedure in ABOUTBOX.C looks like this:

```
MRESULT EXPENTRY AboutDlgProc (HWND hwnd, USHORT msg, MPARAM mp1, MPARAM mp2)
     {
     switch (msg)
          {
          case WM_COMMAND:
               switch (COMMANDMSG(&msg)->cmd)
                    {
                    case DID_OK:
                    case DID_CANCEL:
                         WinDismissDlg (hwnd, TRUE) ;
                         return 0 ;
                    }
               break ;
          }
     return WinDefDlgProc (hwnd, msg, mp1, mp2) ;
     }
```

Within *AboutDlgProc*, the *hwnd* parameter is the window handle of the dialog box window. (Some programmers prefer to use the name *hdlg*.)

Dialog procedures are often much simpler than client window procedures because they needn't worry about painting the window or processing keyboard or mouse input. Aside from possible initialization, a dialog procedure does little but process messages from child window controls on the dialog box window. *AboutDlgProc* processes only the WM_COMMAND message that the push button sends to its owner when the button is clicked.

The dialog procedure calls *WinDefDlgProc* rather than *WinDefWindowProc* for all messages it doesn't process. This is one major difference between a dialog procedure and a window procedure. There are some other differences that I'll discuss in more detail later in this chapter. (For example, a dialog procedure doesn't receive a WM_CREATE message. Instead, you must do initialization during the special WM_INITDLG message.)

The dialog box destroys itself by calling *WinDismissDlg*. In *AboutDlgProc*, it does this when it receives a WM_COMMAND message with the low USHORT of *mp1* (the child window ID or *cmd* field when using the COMMANDMSG macro) equal to DID_OK or DID_CANCEL.

The push button window sends a WM_COMMAND message to its owner (the dialog box window) when the user clicks the push button or presses the Spacebar when the push button has the input focus. The low USHORT of *mp1* is the push button's child ID, which is DID_OK.

AboutDlgProc also calls *WinDismissDlg* when it receives a WM_COMMAND message with the low USHORT of *mp1* equal to DID_CANCEL. This message is generated by *WinDefDlgProc* when the user presses the Escape key. Thus we're also allowing the user to get rid of the dialog box by pressing Escape. When the user presses the Enter key, *WinDefDlgProc* generates a WM_COMMAND message with the low USHORT of *mp1* equal to the child ID of the default push button in the dialog box. This is another part of the keyboard interface that the Presentation Manager adds to control windows organized in a dialog box. When this dialog box is displayed, the user can make it go away by pressing the Spacebar, Enter key, or Escape key or by clicking the button.

Like window procedures, dialog procedures must be listed in the EXPORTS section of the module definition file. This is the EXPORTS section of ABOUTBOX.DEF:

```
EXPORTS ClientWndProc
        AboutDlgProc
```

Creating the Dialog Box Window

A program can create a modal dialog box window by calling *WinDlgBox*. ABOUTBOX calls *WinDlgBox* from *ClientWndProc* when the user selects "About AboutBox…" from the program's menu:

```
WinDlgBox (HWND_DESKTOP, hwnd, AboutDlgProc,
           NULL, IDD_ABOUT, NULL) ;
```

The parameter *AboutDlgProc* is the address of the dialog procedure; IDD_ABOUT is the resource name ID of the dialog box template. The *WinDlgBox* function creates the dialog box window and the child control windows based on the template and displays the dialog box. *AboutDlgProc* then processes messages to the dialog box window. When *AboutDlgProc* calls *WinDismissDlg*, the dialog box window is destroyed. Only then does the *WinDlgBox* function return control to *ClientWndProc*.

The general syntax of the *WinDlgBox* function is

```
usResult = WinDlgBox   (hwndParent, hwndOwner, lpfnDlgProc,
                        hmod, idResource, pCreateParams) ;
```

Dialog boxes are usually top-level windows, so *hwndParent* is set to HWND_DESKTOP. The dialog box is positioned relative to the lower-left corner of the window indicated by the *hwndOwner* parameter; this is usually the client window.

The *hmod* parameter is the module containing the dialog box template resource, and *idResource* is the resource name ID. As with all resources, specifying NULL for *hmod* directs the Presentation Manager to load the resource from the program's .EXE file. The *pCreateParams* parameter is a far (or long) pointer passed to the dialog procedure in the WM_INITDLG message. (I'll explain how this works when we get to the PATTERNS program later in this chapter.)

The value returned from *WinDlgBox* is the second parameter passed to *WinDismissDlg* when the dialog window is destroyed. ABOUTBOX doesn't check this value, but many dialog boxes contain two push buttons labeled OK and Cancel. Customarily, the dialog box procedure passes TRUE to *WinDismissDlg* when OK is clicked and FALSE when Cancel is clicked. Thus the client window procedure can determine from the return value of *WinDlgProc* whether the dialog box was exited with OK or Cancel. (We'll find a use for this in the PATTERNS program.) Note also that the second parameter to *WinDismissDlg* and the return value from *WinDlgBox* are USHORTs, so this value need not be limited to a simple BOOL variable.

The *WinDlgBox* function doesn't return until *WinDismissDlg* is called within the dialog procedure. During the time the dialog box is displayed, the program's other windows are disabled and can't receive user input. However, the client window procedure can still receive other messages such as WM_PAINT or WM_TIMER, so be alert to possible reentrancy problems when you call *WinDlgBox*.

The "Square Button" About Box

You'll recall that in Chapter 11 we created our own window class for a push button control with a square outline and a three-dimensional appearance. Let's use that square push button in a dialog box.

The statements in the ABOUTBOX.RC dialog box template beginning with the words CTEXT, ICON, and DEFPUSHBUTTON are simply convenient ways of defining what classes and styles of child window controls you want in the dialog box. Rather than use these keywords, you can use statements beginning with the keyword CONTROL or WINDOW instead. (The two keywords are synonymous.) The general syntax of a CONTROL statement is

```
CONTROL "text", ChildID, x, y, width, height, class [, style]
```

The second-to-last field is a window class. The last field (which is optional but almost always present) specifies the window style.

For example, rather than use

```
DEFPUSHBUTTON "OK", DID_OK, 80, 8, 40, 16, WS_GROUP
```

you can use

```
CONTROL "OK", DID_OK, 80, 8, 40, 16, WC_BUTTON,
        BS_PUSHBUTTON | BS_DEFAULT | WS_VISIBLE | WS_TABSTOP | WS_GROUP
```

These two statements are equivalent. With the exception of the WS_TABSTOP and WS_GROUP window styles (which I'll explain later in this chapter), the information in the CONTROL statement might clarify what the Presentation Manager does when it creates a dialog box. The various fields of the CONTROL statement translate into parameters used in a *WinCreateWindow* call: WC_BUTTON specifies the window class, BS_PUSHBUTTON and BS_DEFPUSHBUTTON are button styles, and WS_VISIBLE is a window style.

The DEFPUSHBUTTON keyword is recognized only by the resource compiler. The resource compiler constructs an entry in the binary .RES file that contains all information explicitly indicated in the equivalent CONTROL statement. But one advantage of the CONTROL statement is that it lets you go beyond the predefined types of control keywords that the resource compiler recognizes.

For example, suppose you define a window class in your program with the name "SqBtn", just as we did in Chapter 11. In that case you can use a CONTROL statement in a dialog box template like this:

```
CONTROL "OK", DID_OK, 80, 8, 40, 16, "SqBtn",
    WS_VISIBLE | WS_TABSTOP | WS_GROUP
```

Note that the "SqBtn" window class has replaced the WC_BUTTON identifier and that the BS_PUSHBUTTON and BS_DEFAULT identifiers have been removed. The only requirement is that you register the "SqBtn" class in the program before you call *WinDlgBox* for the first time.

To prove that this works, the SQABOUT program shown in Figure 14-3 creates an About box with a square push button.

The SQABOUT File

```
#-------------------
# SQABOUT make file
#-------------------

sqabout.obj : sqabout.c aboutbox.h
    cl -c -G2sw -W3 sqabout.c

sqbtn.obj : sqbtn.c
    cl -c -G2sw -W3 sqbtn.c

sqabout.res : sqabout.rc aboutbox.h aboutbox.ico
    rc -r sqabout

sqabout.exe : sqabout.obj sqbtn.obj sqabout.def
    link sqabout sqbtn, /align:16, NUL, os2, sqabout
    rc sqabout.res

sqabout.exe : sqabout.res
    rc sqabout.res
```

The SQABOUT.C File

```
/*----------------------------------------------------------------
   SQABOUT.C -- Demonstration of About Box with Square 3D Button
   ----------------------------------------------------------------*/

#define INCL_WIN
#include <os2.h>
#include "aboutbox.h"

VOID RegisterSqBtnClass (HAB) ;              // In SQBTN.C

MRESULT EXPENTRY ClientWndProc (HWND, USHORT, MPARAM, MPARAM) ;
MRESULT EXPENTRY AboutDlgProc  (HWND, USHORT, MPARAM, MPARAM) ;

int main (void)
    {
    static CHAR   szClientClass[] = "SqAbout" ;
    static ULONG  flFrameFlags = FCF_TITLEBAR      | FCF_SYSMENU  |
                                 FCF_SIZEBORDER    | FCF_MINMAX   |
                                 FCF_SHELLPOSITION | FCF_TASKLIST |
                                 FCF_MENU          | FCF_ICON ;
    HAB           hab ;
    HMQ           hmq ;
    HWND          hwndFrame, hwndClient ;
    QMSG          qmsg ;

    hab = WinInitialize (0) ;
    hmq = WinCreateMsgQueue (hab, 0) ;

    RegisterSqBtnClass (hab) ;

    WinRegisterClass (hab, szClientClass, ClientWndProc, 0L, 0) ;

    hwndFrame = WinCreateStdWindow (HWND_DESKTOP, WS_VISIBLE,
                                    &flFrameFlags, szClientClass, NULL,
                                    0L, NULL, ID_RESOURCE, &hwndClient) ;

    while (WinGetMsg (hab, &qmsg, NULL, 0, 0))
        WinDispatchMsg (hab, &qmsg) ;

    WinDestroyWindow (hwndFrame) ;
    WinDestroyMsgQueue (hmq) ;
    WinTerminate (hab) ;
    return 0 ;
    }
```

(continued)

Figure 14-3. The SQABOUT.C File. *continued*

```
MRESULT EXPENTRY ClientWndProc (HWND hwnd, USHORT msg, MPARAM mp1, MPARAM mp2)
    {
    switch (msg)
        {
        case WM_COMMAND:
            switch (COMMANDMSG(&msg)->cmd)
                {
                case IDM_NEW:
                case IDM_OPEN:
                case IDM_SAVE:
                case IDM_SAVEAS:
                    WinAlarm (HWND_DESKTOP, WA_NOTE) ;
                    return 0 ;

                case IDM_ABOUT:
                    WinDlgBox (HWND_DESKTOP, hwnd, AboutDlgProc,
                               NULL, IDD_ABOUT, NULL) ;
                    return 0 ;
                }
            break ;

        case WM_ERASEBACKGROUND:
            return 1 ;
        }
    return WinDefWindowProc (hwnd, msg, mp1, mp2) ;
    }

MRESULT EXPENTRY AboutDlgProc (HWND hwnd, USHORT msg, MPARAM mp1, MPARAM mp2)
    {
    switch (msg)
        {
        case WM_COMMAND:
            switch (COMMANDMSG(&msg)->cmd)
                {
                case DID_OK:
                case DID_CANCEL:
                    WinDismissDlg (hwnd, TRUE) ;
                    return 0 ;
                }
            break ;
        }
    return WinDefDlgProc (hwnd, msg, mp1, mp2) ;
    }
```

The SQABOUT.RC File

```
/*-------------------------------------------------
   SQABOUT.RC resource script file
   -------------------------------*/

#include <os2.h>
#include "aboutbox.h"

POINTER ID_RESOURCE aboutbox.ico

MENU ID_RESOURCE
    {
    SUBMENU "~File",            IDM_FILE
        {
        MENUITEM "~New",                IDM_NEW
        MENUITEM "~Open...",            IDM_OPEN
        MENUITEM "~Save",               IDM_SAVE
        MENUITEM "Save ~As...",         IDM_SAVEAS
        MENUITEM SEPARATOR
        MENUITEM "A~bout AboutBox...", IDM_ABOUT
        }
    }

DLGTEMPLATE IDD_ABOUT
  {
  DIALOG "", 0, 32, 32, 200, 88,, FCF_DLGBORDER
    {
    CTEXT   "AboutBox"                          -1, 10, 64, 180,  8
    ICON    ID_RESOURCE                         -1,  8, 56,   0,  0
    CTEXT   "Sample ""About"" Dialog Box"       -1, 10, 40, 180,  8
    CTEXT   "Copyright (C) Charles Petzold, 1988" -1, 10, 32, 180,  8
    CONTROL "OK"                                DID_OK, 80,  8,  40, 16,
                "SqBtn", WS_VISIBLE ¦ WS_TABSTOP ¦ WS_GROUP
    }
  }
```

The SQABOUT.DEF File

```
;-------------------------------------------------
; SQABOUT.DEF module definition file
;-------------------------------------------------

NAME        SQABOUT    WINDOWAPI
```

(continued)

Figure 14-3. The SQABOUT.DEF File. *continued*

```
DESCRIPTION     'About Box with Square Button (C) Charles Petzold, 1988'
PROTMODE
HEAPSIZE        1024
STACKSIZE       8192
EXPORTS         ClientWndProc
                AboutDlgProc
                SqBtnWndProc
```

Figure 14-3. *The SQABOUT program.*

Compiling this program requires the SQBTN.C file from Chapter 11 and the ABOUTBOX.H and ABOUTBOX.ICO files from Figure 14-1.

The SQABOUT.RC resource script file is the same as ABOUTBOX.RC except that a CONTROL statement specifying the ''SqBtn'' window class replaces the DEFPUSHBUTTON statement in ABOUTBOX.RC. The SQABOUT.C program is nearly the same as ABOUTBOX.C except that SQABOUT calls the *RegisterSqBtnClass* function (in SQBTN.C) from *main*. Figure 14-4 shows the dialog box created by SQABOUT.

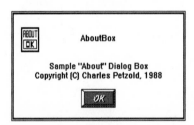

Figure 14-4. *The SQABOUT display.*

A More Complex Dialog Box

Now that you've mastered all the basics, you're ready to create dialog boxes with more than just a single button. In Chapter 11 we wrote a program called DRAWLINE that created some radio buttons on its client window and drew a line based on a specified line pattern and color. The PATTDLG program, shown in Figure 14-5, is similar except that it uses a dialog box.

The PATTDLG File

```
#-------------------
# PATTDLG make file
#-------------------

pattdlg.obj : pattdlg.c pattdlg.h
     cl -c -G2sw -W3 pattdlg.c

pattdlg.res : pattdlg.rc pattdlg.h
     rc -r pattdlg

pattdlg.exe : pattdlg.obj pattdlg.def
     link pattdlg, /align:16, NUL, os2, pattdlg
     rc pattdlg.res

pattdlg.exe : pattdlg.res
     rc pattdlg.res
```

The PATTDLG.C File

```
/*-------------------------------------------------
   PATTDLG.C -- Select GPI Patterns from Dialog Box
   -------------------------------------------------*/

#define INCL_WIN
#define INCL_GPI
#include <os2.h>
#include "pattdlg.h"

typedef struct
     {
     SHORT sPattern ;
     SHORT sColor ;
     BOOL  fBorder ;
     }
     PATTERNSDATA ;

typedef PATTERNSDATA FAR *PPATTERNSDATA ;

MRESULT EXPENTRY ClientWndProc  (HWND, USHORT, MPARAM, MPARAM) ;
MRESULT EXPENTRY AboutDlgProc   (HWND, USHORT, MPARAM, MPARAM) ;
MRESULT EXPENTRY PatternDlgProc (HWND, USHORT, MPARAM, MPARAM) ;

HAB  hab ;
```

(continued)

Figure 14-5. The PATTDLG.C File. *continued*

```
int main (void)
    {
    static CHAR  szClientClass[] = "PattDlg" ;
    static ULONG flFrameFlags = FCF_TITLEBAR      | FCF_SYSMENU  |
                                FCF_SIZEBORDER    | FCF_MINMAX   |
                                FCF_SHELLPOSITION | FCF_TASKLIST |
                                FCF_MENU ;

    HMQ           hmq ;
    HWND          hwndFrame, hwndClient ;
    QMSG          qmsg ;


    hab = WinInitialize (0) ;
    hmq = WinCreateMsgQueue (hab, 0) ;

    WinRegisterClass (hab, szClientClass, ClientWndProc, CS_SIZEREDRAW, 0) ;

    hwndFrame = WinCreateStdWindow (HWND_DESKTOP, WS_VISIBLE,
                                    &flFrameFlags, szClientClass, NULL,
                                    OL, NULL, ID_RESOURCE, &hwndClient) ;

    WinSendMsg (hwndFrame, WM_SETICON,
                WinQuerySysPointer (HWND_DESKTOP, SPTR_APPICON, FALSE),
                NULL) ;

    while (WinGetMsg (hab, &qmsg, NULL, 0, 0))
        WinDispatchMsg (hab, &qmsg) ;

    WinDestroyWindow (hwndFrame) ;
    WinDestroyMsgQueue (hmq) ;
    WinTerminate (hab) ;
    return 0 ;
    }


MRESULT EXPENTRY ClientWndProc (HWND hwnd, USHORT msg, MPARAM mp1, MPARAM mp2)
    {
    static CHAR         szAppName [] = "PATTDLG" ;
    static CHAR         szKeyName [] = "SETTINGS" ;
    static PATTERNSDATA pdCurrent = { IDD_DENSE1, IDD_BKGRND, TRUE } ;
    static SHORT        cxClient, cyClient ;
    HPS                 hps ;
    POINTL              ptl ;
    SHORT               sDataLength ;
```

(continued)

Figure 14-5. The PATTDLG.C File. *continued*

```
switch (msg)
    {
    case WM_CREATE:
        sDataLength = sizeof pdCurrent ;

        WinQueryProfileData (hab, szAppName, szKeyName, &pdCurrent,
                             &sDataLength) ;
        return 0 ;

    case WM_SIZE:
        cxClient = SHORT1FROMMP (mp2) ;
        cyClient = SHORT2FROMMP (mp2) ;
        return 0 ;

    case WM_COMMAND:
        switch (COMMANDMSG(&msg)->cmd)
            {
            case IDM_PATTERNS:
                if (WinDlgBox (HWND_DESKTOP, hwnd, PatternDlgProc,
                               NULL, IDD_PATTERNS, &pdCurrent))

                    WinInvalidateRect (hwnd, NULL, FALSE) ;
                return 0 ;

            case IDM_ABOUT:
                WinDlgBox (HWND_DESKTOP, hwnd, AboutDlgProc,
                           NULL, IDD_ABOUT, NULL) ;
                return 0 ;
            }
        break ;

    case WM_PAINT:
        hps = WinBeginPaint (hwnd, NULL, NULL) ;
        GpiErase (hps) ;

        GpiSetColor (hps, pdCurrent.sColor -
                          IDD_BKGRND + CLR_BACKGROUND) ;

        GpiSetPattern (hps, pdCurrent.sPattern -
                            IDD_DENSE1 + PATSYM_DENSE1) ;

        ptl.x = cxClient / 4 ;
        ptl.y = cyClient / 4 ;
        GpiMove (hps, &ptl) ;
```

(continued)

Figure 14-5. The PATTDLG.C File. *continued*

```
                ptl.x *= 3 ;
                ptl.y *= 3 ;
                GpiBox (hps, pdCurrent.fBorder ? DRO_OUTLINEFILL : DRO_FILL,
                            &ptl, OL, OL) ;

                WinEndPaint (hps) ;
                return 0 ;

        case WM_DESTROY:
                if (MBID_YES == WinMessageBox (HWND_DESKTOP, hwnd,
                                    "Save current settings?", szAppName, 0,
                                    MB_YESNO | MB_ICONQUESTION))

                        WinWriteProfileData (hab, szAppName, szKeyName, &pdCurrent,
                                        sizeof pdCurrent) ;

                break ;
        }
    return WinDefWindowProc (hwnd, msg, mp1, mp2) ;
    }

MRESULT EXPENTRY AboutDlgProc (HWND hwnd, USHORT msg, MPARAM mp1, MPARAM mp2)
    {
    switch (msg)
        {
        case WM_COMMAND:
            switch (COMMANDMSG(&msg)->cmd)
                {
                case DID_OK:
                case DID_CANCEL:
                        WinDismissDlg (hwnd, TRUE) ;
                        return 0 ;
                }
            break ;
        }
    return WinDefDlgProc (hwnd, msg, mp1, mp2) ;
    }

MRESULT EXPENTRY PatternDlgProc (HWND hwnd, USHORT msg, MPARAM mp1, MPARAM mp2)
    {
    static PATTERNSDATA  pdLocal ;
    static PPATTERNSDATA ppdCurrent ;
```

(continued)

Figure 14-5. The PATTDLG.C File. *continued*

```
switch (msg)
    {
    case WM_INITDLG:
        ppdCurrent = MPFROMP (mp2) ;
        pdLocal = *ppdCurrent ;

        WinSendDlgItemMsg (hwnd, pdLocal.sPattern, BM_SETCHECK,
                        MPFROM2SHORT (TRUE, 0), NULL) ;

        WinSendDlgItemMsg (hwnd, pdLocal.sColor, BM_SETCHECK,
                        MPFROM2SHORT (TRUE, 0), NULL) ;

        WinSendDlgItemMsg (hwnd, IDD_BORDER, BM_SETCHECK,
                        MPFROM2SHORT (pdLocal.fBorder, 0), NULL) ;

        WinSetFocus (HWND_DESKTOP,
                    WinWindowFromID (hwnd, pdLocal.sPattern)) ;
        return 1 ;

    case WM_CONTROL:
        if (SHORT1FROMMP (mp1) >= IDD_DENSE1 &&
            SHORT1FROMMP (mp1) <= IDD_HALFTONE)
            {
            WinSendDlgItemMsg (hwnd, pdLocal.sPattern, BM_SETCHECK,
                            MPFROM2SHORT (FALSE, 0), NULL) ;

            pdLocal.sPattern = SHORT1FROMMP (mp1) ;

            WinSendDlgItemMsg (hwnd, pdLocal.sPattern, BM_SETCHECK,
                            MPFROM2SHORT (TRUE, 0), NULL) ;
            }

        else if (SHORT1FROMMP (mp1) >= IDD_BKGRND &&
                SHORT1FROMMP (mp1) <= IDD_PALEGRAY)
            {
            WinSendDlgItemMsg (hwnd, pdLocal.sColor, BM_SETCHECK,
                            MPFROM2SHORT (FALSE, 0), NULL) ;

            pdLocal.sColor = SHORT1FROMMP (mp1) ;

            WinSendDlgItemMsg (hwnd, pdLocal.sColor, BM_SETCHECK,
                            MPFROM2SHORT (TRUE, 0), NULL) ;
            }
        return 0 ;
```

(continued)

Figure 14-5. The PATTDLG.C File. *continued*

```
        case WM_COMMAND:
            switch (COMMANDMSG(&msg)->cmd)
                {
                case DID_OK:
                    pdLocal.fBorder = (BOOL) WinSendDlgItemMsg (hwnd,
                               IDD_BORDER, BM_QUERYCHECK, NULL, NULL) ;

                    *ppdCurrent = pdLocal ;

                    WinDismissDlg (hwnd, TRUE) ;
                    return 0 ;

                case DID_CANCEL:
                    WinDismissDlg (hwnd, FALSE) ;
                    return 0 ;
                }
            break ;
            }
    return WinDefDlgProc (hwnd, msg, mp1, mp2) ;
    }
```

The PATTDLG.H File

```
/*-----------------------
   PATTDLG.H header file
-----------------------*/

#define ID_RESOURCE       1

#define IDM_SELECT        1

#define IDM_PATTERNS      10
#define IDM_ABOUT         11

#define IDD_ABOUT         1
#define IDD_PATTERNS      2

#define IDD_DENSE1        10
#define IDD_HALFTONE      (IDD_DENSE1 + 16)
#define IDD_BKGRND        30
#define IDD_PALEGRAY      (IDD_BKGRND + 15)
#define IDD_BORDER        50
```

The PATTDLG.RC File

```
/*----------------------------------
   PATTDLG.RC resource script file
----------------------------------*/

#include <os2.h>
#include "pattdlg.h"

MENU ID_RESOURCE
    {
    SUBMENU "~Select",              IDM_SELECT
        {
        MENUITEM "~Pattern and Color...",  IDM_PATTERNS
        MENUITEM SEPARATOR
        MENUITEM "A~bout Patterns...",     IDM_ABOUT
        }
    }

DLGTEMPLATE IDD_ABOUT
  {
  DIALOG "", 0, 32, 32, 200, 88,, FCF_DLGBORDER
    {
    CTEXT "PattDlg"                          -1, 10, 64, 180,  8
    CTEXT "Select Patterns from Dialog Box"  -1, 10, 40, 180,  8
    CTEXT "Copyright (C) Charles Petzold, 1988" -1, 10, 32, 180,  8
    DEFPUSHBUTTON "OK"                       DID_OK, 80, 8,  40, 16, WS_GROUP
    }
  }

DLGTEMPLATE IDD_PATTERNS
  {
  DIALOG "", 0, 8, 8, 280, 180,, FCF_DLGBORDER
    {
    GROUPBOX       "Pattern" -1,               8, 30, 128, 144
    RADIOBUTTON    "Dense 1" IDD_DENSE1 +  0, 12, 148,  56,  12, WS_GROUP
    RADIOBUTTON    "Dense 2" IDD_DENSE1 +  1, 12, 134,  56,  12
    RADIOBUTTON    "Dense 3" IDD_DENSE1 +  2, 12, 120,  56,  12
    RADIOBUTTON    "Dense 4" IDD_DENSE1 +  3, 12, 106,  56,  12
    RADIOBUTTON    "Dense 5" IDD_DENSE1 +  4, 12, 92,   56,  12
    RADIOBUTTON    "Dense 6" IDD_DENSE1 +  5, 12, 78,   56,  12
    RADIOBUTTON    "Dense 7" IDD_DENSE1 +  6, 12, 64,   56,  12
    RADIOBUTTON    "Dense 8" IDD_DENSE1 +  7, 12, 50,   56,  12
    RADIOBUTTON    "Vert"    IDD_DENSE1 +  8, 12, 36,   56,  12
    RADIOBUTTON    "Horiz"   IDD_DENSE1 +  9, 76, 148,  56,  12
```

(continued)

Figure 14-5. The PATTDLG.RC File. *continued*

```
        RADIOBUTTON   "Diag 1"   IDD_DENSE1 +  10,  76, 134,  56,  12
        RADIOBUTTON   "Diag 2"   IDD_DENSE1 +  11,  76, 120,  56,  12
        RADIOBUTTON   "Diag 3"   IDD_DENSE1 +  12,  76, 106,  56,  12
        RADIOBUTTON   "Diag 4"   IDD_DENSE1 +  13,  76,  92,  56,  12
        RADIOBUTTON   "No Shade" IDD_DENSE1 +  14,  76,  78,  56,  12
        RADIOBUTTON   "Solid"    IDD_DENSE1 +  15,  76,  64,  56,  12
        RADIOBUTTON   "Halftone" IDD_DENSE1 +  16,  76,  50,  56,  12
        GROUPBOX      "Color"    -1,             144,  44, 128, 130
        RADIOBUTTON   "Backgrnd" IDD_BKGRND +  0, 148, 148,  56,  12, WS_GROUP
        RADIOBUTTON   "Blue"     IDD_BKGRND +  1, 148, 134,  56,  12
        RADIOBUTTON   "Red"      IDD_BKGRND +  2, 148, 120,  56,  12
        RADIOBUTTON   "Pink"     IDD_BKGRND +  3, 148, 106,  56,  12
        RADIOBUTTON   "Green"    IDD_BKGRND +  4, 148,  92,  56,  12
        RADIOBUTTON   "Cyan"     IDD_BKGRND +  5, 148,  78,  56,  12
        RADIOBUTTON   "Yellow"   IDD_BKGRND +  6, 148,  64,  56,  12
        RADIOBUTTON   "Neutral"  IDD_BKGRND +  7, 148,  50,  56,  12
        RADIOBUTTON   "Dk Gray"  IDD_BKGRND +  8, 212, 148,  56,  12
        RADIOBUTTON   "Dk Blue"  IDD_BKGRND +  9, 212, 134,  56,  12
        RADIOBUTTON   "Dk Red"   IDD_BKGRND + 10, 212, 120,  56,  12
        RADIOBUTTON   "Dk Pink"  IDD_BKGRND + 11, 212, 106,  56,  12
        RADIOBUTTON   "Dk Green" IDD_BKGRND + 12, 212,  92,  56,  12
        RADIOBUTTON   "Dk Cyan"  IDD_BKGRND + 13, 212,  78,  56,  12
        RADIOBUTTON   "Brown"    IDD_BKGRND + 14, 212,  64,  56,  12
        RADIOBUTTON   "Pl Gray"  IDD_BKGRND + 15, 212,  50,  56,  12
        AUTOCHECKBOX  "Border"   IDD_BORDER,      148,  30,  56,  12, WS_GROUP
        DEFPUSHBUTTON "OK"       DID_OK,           66,   8,  52,  16, WS_GROUP
        PUSHBUTTON    "Cancel"   DID_CANCEL,      162,   8,  52,  16, WS_GROUP
        }
    }
```

The PATTDLG.DEF File

```
;---------------------------------------
; PATTDLG.DEF module definition file
;---------------------------------------

NAME          PATTDLG   WINDOWAPI

DESCRIPTION   'Select GPI Pattterns from Dialog Box (C) Charles Petzold, 1988'
PROTMODE
HEAPSIZE      1024
STACKSIZE     8192
EXPORTS       ClientWndProc
              PatternDlgProc
              AboutDlgProc
```

Figure 14-5. *The PATTDLG program.*

PATTDLG draws a filled rectangle in its client window using the *GpiBox* function. You use the dialog box to select the fill pattern and color and to choose whether you want a border. The dialog box (shown in Figure 14-6) contains one group of radio buttons for the pattern and another group for the color, one check box for the border, and two push buttons labeled "OK" and "Cancel." Clicking the Cancel button destroys the dialog box without changing PATTERNS's client window.

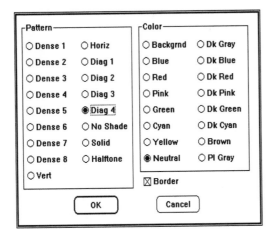

Figure 14-6. *The PATTDLG display.*

Creation Parameters

PATTDLG draws a box within its client window based on a pattern and color you select within the dialog box. Let's examine first how *ClientWndProc* and the *PatternDlgProc* dialog box procedure pass data between each other.

Near the top of PATTDLG.C is the definition of a structure named PAT-TERNSDATA. This structure contains three fields (*sPattern*, *sColor*, and *fBorder*) that provide all the information *ClientWndProc* needs to draw the patterned box in the client window. Within *ClientWndProc*, a static variable of type PATTERNSDATA is defined and initialized:

```
static PATTERNSDATA pdCurrent = { IDD_DENSE1, IDD_BKGRND, TRUE } ;
```

The IDD_DENSE1 and IDD_BKGRND identifiers are defined in PATTDLG.H and used in PATTDLG.RC for child window IDs of the radio buttons. These are the default values when you first run the program. During the WM_PAINT message, *ClientWndProc* uses the three fields of *pdCurrent* to set the color (shown on the next page).

```
GpiSetColor (hps, pdCurrent.sColor -
                IDD_BKGRND + CLR_BACKGROUND) ;
```

and the pattern:

```
GpiSetPattern (hps, pdCurrent.sPattern -
                IDD_DENSE1 + PATSYM_DENSE1) ;
```

and to determine whether a border should be drawn:

```
GpiBox (hps, pdCurrent.fBorder ? DRO_OUTLINEFILL : DRO_FILL,
            &ptl, 0L, 0L) ;
```

When you select the "Pattern and Color" option from the menu, *Client-WndProc* receives a WM_COMMAND message that has a *cmd* field of IDM_PATTERNS. Here's how it's processed:

```
case IDM_PATTERNS:
    if (WinDlgBox (HWND_DESKTOP, hwnd, PatternDlgProc,
                NULL, IDD_PATTERNS, &pdCurrent))

        WinInvalidateRect (hwnd, NULL, FALSE) ;
    return 0 ;
```

A pointer to the *pdCurrent* structure is passed as the last parameter to *WinDlgBox* when you invoke the dialog box. This is the "creation parameters" (*pCreateParams*) field of *WinDlgBox*. You use this field to pass initial data to the dialog box procedure.

Within *PatternDlgProc*, both a structure of type PATTERNSDATA and a pointer to a PATTERNSDATA structure are defined:

```
static PATTERNSDATA pdLocal ;
static PPATTERNSDATA ppdCurrent ;
```

During the WM_INITDLG message, *mp2* is set equal to the last parameter of the *WinDlgBox* call that invoked the dialog box procedure. In *Pattern-DlgProc* the pointer is saved in *ppdCurrent*:

```
ppdCurrent = MPFROMP (mp2) ;
```

The entire structure is also copied to *pdLocal* with a simple assignment statement:

```
pdLocal = *ppdCurrent ;
```

I'll discuss the remainder of the WM_INITDLG message shortly.

As the dialog box is displayed and the user clicks the various radio buttons and so forth, *PatternDlgProc* uses *pdLocal* to store the selected values. However, if the *ClientWndProc* needs to repaint its client window while the dialog box is still displayed, it continues to use the values stored in *pdCurrent*.

You can exit the dialog box by selecting the "OK" or "Cancel" button. When you select the "OK" button, *PatternDlgProc* copies the *pdLocal* structure back to the structure referenced by the pointer it obtained during the WM_INITDLG message:

```
*ppdCurrent = pdLocal ;
```

The *ppdCurrent* pointer points to the *pdCurrent* structure within *ClientWndProc*. *PatternDlgProc* then calls *WinDismissDlg* with a second parameter of TRUE:

```
WinDismissDlg (hwnd, TRUE) ;
```

If you select "Cancel" from the dialog box, the structure is not copied, and the second paramter of *WinDismissDlg* is set to FALSE:

```
WinDismissDlg (hwnd, FALSE) ;
```

In either case, the dialog box is destroyed, and the second parameter of *WinDismissDlg* is returned from the original call to *WinDlgBox* within *ClientWndProc*. If *WinDlgBox* returns TRUE, *ClientWndProc* invalidates the window:

```
if (WinDlgBox (HWND_DESKTOP, hwnd, PatternDlgProc,
        NULL, IDD_PATTERNS, &pdCurrent))

    WinInvalidateRect (hwnd, NULL, FALSE) ;
```

This generates a WM_PAINT message and the client window is repainted with the new fields of *pdCurrent*.

You can simplify some of this logic somewhat by eliminating the PAT-TERNSDATA structure and by using global variables to store the current pattern, color, and border used within *ClientWndProc*. During the WM_INITDLG message, *PatternDlgProc* would copy these variables to local static variables for use within the dialog box procedure. When you select "OK", *PatternDlgProc* then assigns the global variables from the final values of the local variables.

This alternative using global variables may be simpler, but the approach used in PATTDLG is more structured. If you want to use the same dialog box procedure for more than one purpose (for example, if *ClientWndProc* displayed both a box and an ellipse and allowed you to change either from menu options), then using the creation parameters is obviously preferable.

Working with Radio Buttons

Each group of radio buttons in PATTDLG is enclosed in a group box, which is a WC_STATIC window that we also used in the DRAWLINE program in Chapter 11. In the dialog box template, this window style is indicated by the GROUPBOX statements. The first GROUPBOX statement in the dialog box template is followed by 17 RADIOBUTTON statements, which specify control windows based on the WC_BUTTON window class and the BS_RADIOBUTTON button style. The text fields of the 17 radio buttons correspond to the 17 GPI fill patterns.

A radio button width must accommodate the text plus two characters for the button itself. A height of 12 units is adequate for displaying the text and button along with a dotted line that surrounds the radio button text when it has the input focus. I use 14 units for spacing the radio buttons vertically.

The 17 radio buttons have child IDs ranging from IDD_DENSE1 to (IDD_DENSE1 + 16). In PATTERNS.H I've defined identifiers for the first and last child IDs of these 17 controls:

```
#define IDD_DENSE1      10
#define IDD_HALFTONE    (IDD_DENSE1 + 16)
```

Painting logic in *ClientWndProc* requires that the child IDs of the push buttons be consecutive and in the same order as the corresponding PATSYM identifiers.

After *PatternDlgProc* copies the current settings to the *pdLocal* structure in the WM_INITDLG message, it must initialize the radio buttons. Because the *sPattern* field of *pdLocal* is a child ID of one of the radio buttons, *Pattern-DlgProc* can use it to send a BM_SETCHECK message to the radio button to turn the check mark on:

```
WinSendDlgItemMsg (hwnd, pdLocal.sPattern, BM_SETCHECK,
                MPFROM2SHORT (TRUE, 0), NULL) ;
```

The *WinSendDlgItemMsg* sends a message to a child window based on the handle of its parent (*hwnd*) and the child ID of the control (*pdLocal.sPattern*). Normally, if you want to send a message to a child window and you don't know the window handle, you first must call *WinWindowFromID* to get the window handle and then call *WinSendMsg*:

```
hwndChild = WinWindowFromID (hwnd, pdLocal.sPattern) ;

WinSendMsg (hwndChild, BM_SETCHECK,
                    MPFROM2SHORT (TRUE, 0), NULL) ;
```

The *WinSendDlgItemMsg* function does this for you.

This first time the dialog box is displayed, *pdLocal.sPattern* equals IDD_DENSE1, so the first button in the Patterns group is checked. When the user clicks a radio button, the button window sends its owner (in this case, the dialog box window) a WM_CONTROL message. The low USHORT of *mp1* is the child ID.

PatternDlgProc first determines if the child ID is within the range for the first 17 radio buttons:

```
case WM_CONTROL:
    if (SHORT1FROMMP (mp1) >= IDD_DENSE1 &&
        SHORT1FROMMP (mp1) <= IDD_HALFTONE)
        {
```

The function then sends the button a BM_SETCHECK message to uncheck the currently checked button:

```
WinSendDlgItemMsg (hwnd, pdLocal.sPattern, BM_SETCHECK,
                MPFROM2SHORT (FALSE, 0), NULL ;
```

The *pdLocal.sPattern* variable is then set to the child ID of the button just pressed, and that button is sent a BM_SETCHECK message to turn the check on, as shown on the next page.

```
pdLocal.sPattern = SHORT1FROMMP (mp1) ;
WinSendDlgItemMsg (hwnd, pdLocal.sPattern, BM_SETCHECK,
                 MPFROM2SHORT (TRUE, 0), NULL) ;
```

This is similar to the way we handled radio buttons in the DRAWLINE program in Chapter 11.

Thus, *pdLocal.sPattern* always has the ID of the currently checked radio button. But only when the user selects "OK" is this copied to the *pdCurrent* structure in *ClientWndProc*:

```
*ppdCurrent = pdLocal ;
```

The AUTORADIOBUTTON Alternative

The processing of the WM_CONTROL messages from the radio buttons in PATTDLG is quite similar to that shown in the DRAWLINE program in Chapter 11. But for radio buttons in dialog boxes, you have an alternative that makes the processing easier.

First, replace all the RADIOBUTTON keywords in PATTDLG with AUTORADIOBUTTON. The radio buttons in the dialog box are then created with a style of BS_AUTORADIOBUTTON rather than BS_RADIOBUTTON. These buttons check themselves automatically when clicked and also uncheck all other radio buttons in the same group. Thus the processing of the WM_CONTROL message is reduced to this:

```
case WM_CONTROL:
    if (SHORT1FROMMP (mp1) >= IDD_DENSE1 &&
        SHORT1FROMMP (mp1) <= IDD_HALFTONE)
        {
        pdLocal.sPattern = SHORT1FROMMP (mp1) ;
        }

    else if (SHORT1FROMMP (mp1) >= IDD_BKGRND &&
            SHORT1FROMMP (mp1) <= IDD_LIGHTGRAY)
        {
        pdLocal.sColor = SHORT1FROMMP (mp1) ;
        }
    return 0 ;
```

This logic simply keeps track of the most recent button checked.

Working with Check Boxes

In addition to the radio buttons, the dialog box in PATTDLG contains a "check box." This is a style of button that programs use to indicate an option that can be checked on or off. The check box in PATTDLG determines whether the rectangle drawn in the client window should include a border.

The child ID of the check box is IDD_BORDER. During processing of the WN_INITDLG message in *PatternsWndProc*, the state of the button (checked or unchecked) is set based on the value of the *fBorder* field of *pdLocal*:

```
WinSendDlgItemMsg (hwnd, IDD_BORDER, BM_SETCHECK,
                MPFROM2SHORT (pdLocal.fBorder, 0), NULL) ;
```

This check box has the window style BS_AUTOCHECKBOX, which means that the check box window itself toggles the check mark on and off when clicked. Although the check box sends its owner WM_CONTROL messages, *PatternDlgProc* doesn't do anything with them. Instead, when the OK button is clicked, *PatternWndProc* obtains the current state of the check box by sending it a BM_QUERYCHECK message:

```
pdLocal.fBorder = (BOOL) WinSendDlgItemMsg (hwnd,
        IDD_BORDER, BM_QUERYCHECK, NULL, NULL) ;
```

Tab Stops and Groups

The dialog box in PATTDLG has a complete keyboard interface without any apparent effort on our part. You can use the Tab key to jump between the radio buttons, check box, and push buttons. Within each group of radio buttons, you can use the cursor movement keys to change the checked button. These two aspects of the keyboard interface are governed by the window styles called WS_TABSTOP and WS_GROUP. Some of the control windows have these styles by default; some don't. Sometimes it's necessary for you to include one of these window styles in the definition for the control window. For example, in the dialog box template in PATTDLG.RC, the check box and push buttons are explicitly given the WS_GROUP style.

The WS_TABSTOP style determines how the input focus is transferred between control windows when the user presses the Tab key. Initially, the input focus is set to the first control in the dialog box (based on the order in which you define the controls in the template) that has the WS_TABSTOP style. When the user presses the Tab key, the input focus is transferred to the very next control that has the WS_TABSTOP style. After the last

WS_TABSTOP control is reached, pressing the Tab key transfers the input focus to the first WS_TABSTOP control. PUSHBUTTON, DEFPUSHBUTTON, CHECKBOX, and AUTOCHECKBOX control windows all have a WS_TABSTOP style by default, as do the ENTRYFIELD and LISTBOX control windows used in the HEAD program shown later in this chapter.

The WS_GROUP style governs the way the input focus is transferred between controls when the user presses the Up and Down cursor movement keys. A range of controls in which the cursor movement keys transfer the input focus is called a ''group.'' The group ranges from the first control that has a WS_GROUP style up to (but not including) the next control that has a WS_GROUP style. Static control windows defined with CTEXT, LTEXT, RTEXT, ICON, and GROUPBOX have a WS_GROUP style by default. However, these controls can't themselves receive the input focus, so the group really begins with the next control.

This is how the cursor movement keys work in the two groups of radio buttons in PATTDLG. The first radio button after each GROUPBOX window begins a group. The first group of radio buttons ends with the other GROUPBOX window that precedes the second group. The second group of radio buttons ends with the CHECKBOX window, which is explicitly given a WS_GROUP style. The buttons and check boxes in PATTDLG must be explicitly given a WS_GROUP style to prevent the cursor movement keys from doing anything when these windows have the input focus. If you remove the WS_GROUP style from the check box control window, you'll find that you can use the cursor movement keys to move between the check box and the radio buttons in the second group because the check box is no longer functioning as the end of the group.

Although radio buttons don't normally have a WM_TABSTOP style, a checked radio button functions as if it does. Thus, when you press the Tab key, the input focus transfers to the radio button that is currently checked in each group.

The WM_INITDLG Message

The WM_INITDLG message is the first message the dialog procedure receives. You've already seen how the dialog procedure can use *mp1* to reference a pointer passed to *WinDlgBox* and perform initialization during the WM_INITDLG message. However, this message also has another function. The *mp1* parameter that accompanies the WM_INITDLG message contains the window handle of the control window that initially receives the input focus. This is generally the first control in the dialog box that has the WS_TABSTOP style. If this is satisfactory, you can either return 0L from the dialog procedure after processing WM_INITDLG or call *WinDefDlgProc* in lieu of processing WM_INITDLG.

In PATTDLG, the first control that has the WS_TABSTOP style is the check box. But it makes more sense for a radio button in the first group to get the input focus. When you want to set the input focus during WM_INITDLG, call *WinSetFocus* and return 1L from the dialog procedure. In *Pattern-DlgProc* the code looks like this:

```
WinSetFocus (HWND_DESKTOP,
          WinWindowFromID (hwnd, pdLocal.sPattern)) ;
return 1 ;
```

If you don't return 1L after setting the input focus, the Presentation Manager will set the focus to the window indicated by the *mp1* parameter.

Saving the Values

When you end PATTDLG, a message box is displayed that asks "Save current settings?" If you check "Yes" on this message box, PATTDLG will use the last values of the pattern and color that you selected the next time you run the program.

The first question that you might ask is: Where is this information being saved? The Presentation Manager maintains a file named OS2.INI that programs can use for storing configuration data. For example, a user of a Presentation Manager word-processing program might prefer that the program be started with left margins of 1 inch and "insert mode" turned off. OS2.INI is an excellent place to store information like that. The Presentation Manager Control Panel uses OS2.INI to store your color and mouse preferences and your printer setups.

What makes this even better is that programs do not access OS2.INI directly. Instead they use Presentation Manager function calls to write to and read from the file.

Information in OS2.INI is accessed using two text strings: an "application" name, which is generally the same name as the program, and a "key" name, which identifies a particular piece of information that the program stores. For example, suppose the Presentation Manager word-processing program I mentioned is called WORDPROC. To store the user's preference for insert mode and left margins, the program would use an application name of WORDPROC and key names of INSERTMODE and LEFTMARGIN.

For PATTDLG, the application name is PATTDLG, which is stored in the *szAppName* variable in *ClientWndProc*. To store the current settings, the program uses the key name SETTINGS, stored in *szKeyName*.

When you end PATTDLG and answer "Yes" to the message box displayed during the WM_DESTROY message, PATTDLG writes the current settings to OS2.INI by calling

```
WinWriteProfileData (hab, szAppName, szKeyName, &pdCurrent,
                     sizeof pdCurrent) ;
```

You use this function to write binary data of any length to OS2.INI. In this case, PATTDLG writes the entire *pdCurrent* structure to the file. The last parameter is the size of this structure. You can also use *WinWrite-ProfileString* to write a zero-terminated string.

During the WM_CREATE message, PATTDLG attempts to read the data from OS2.INI:

```
WinQueryProfileData (hab, szAppName, szKeyName, &pdCurrent,
                     &sDataLength) ;
```

If the Presentation Manager does not find a matching application and key name in OS2.INI, *WinQueryProfileData* returns FALSE, but PATTDLG doesn't check for this. The *pdCurrent* structure already contains initialized default values, and these will not be altered by the *WinQueryProfileData* function call.

You can read text strings from OS2.INI using *WinQueryProfileString*. If the information you store using *WinWriteProfileData* is a single integer, you can read it using *WinQueryProfileInt*. The *WinQueryProfileSize* function returns the size of the stored data for a particular application and key name.

The File Open Dialog Box

One of the most complex, yet essential, modal dialog boxes is invoked by the menu's File Open option. The HEAD program, shown in Figure 14-7, is a Presentation Manager version of the UNIX *head* utility. The program shows the beginning of the file in its client window. To specify a filename, you can use the HEAD command line or the File Open dialog box.

The HEAD File

```
#----------------
# HEAD make file
#----------------

head.obj : head.c head.h
    cl -c -G2sw -W3 head.c

easyfont.obj : easyfont.c
    cl -c -G2sw -W3 easyfont.c

head.res : head.rc head.h
    rc -r head

head.exe : head.obj easyfont.obj head.def
    link head easyfont, /align:16, NUL, os2, head
    rc head.res

head.exe : head.res
    rc head.res
```

The HEAD.C File

```
/*------------------------------
   HEAD.C -- Displays File Head
   ------------------------------*/

#define INCL_WIN
#define INCL_GPI
#include <os2.h>
#include <malloc.h>
#include <stdio.h>
#include <string.h>
#include "easyfont.h"
#include "head.h"


#define LCID_FIXEDFONT    1L
#define LCID_BOLDFONT     2L


MRESULT EXPENTRY ClientWndProc (HWND, USHORT, MPARAM, MPARAM) ;
MRESULT EXPENTRY AboutDlgProc  (HWND, USHORT, MPARAM, MPARAM) ;
MRESULT EXPENTRY OpenDlgProc   (HWND, USHORT, MPARAM, MPARAM) ;
SHORT            ParseFileName (CHAR *, CHAR *) ;
```

(continued)

Figure 14-7. The HEAD.C File. *continued*

```
CHAR szClientClass [] = "Head" ;
CHAR szFileName [80] ;
HAB  hab ;

int main (int argc, char *argv[])
    {
    static ULONG flFrameFlags = FCF_TITLEBAR       | FCF_SYSMENU   |
                                FCF_SIZEBORDER     | FCF_MINMAX    |
                                FCF_SHELLPOSITION  | FCF_TASKLIST  |
                                FCF_MENU ;
    HMQ         hmq ;
    HWND        hwndFrame, hwndClient ;
    QMSG        qmsg ;

            // Check for filename parameter and copy to szFileName

    if (argc > 1)
        ParseFileName (szFileName, argv [1]) ;

            // Continue normally

    hab = WinInitialize (0) ;
    hmq = WinCreateMsgQueue (hab, 0) ;

    WinRegisterClass (hab, szClientClass, ClientWndProc, CS_SIZEREDRAW, 0) ;

    hwndFrame = WinCreateStdWindow (HWND_DESKTOP, WS_VISIBLE,
                                    &flFrameFlags, szClientClass, NULL,
                                    OL, NULL, ID_RESOURCE, &hwndClient) ;

    if (hwndFrame != NULL)
        {
        WinSendMsg (hwndFrame, WM_SETICON,
                    WinQuerySysPointer (HWND_DESKTOP, SPTR_APPICON, FALSE),
                    NULL) ;

        while (WinGetMsg (hab, &qmsg, NULL, 0, 0))
            WinDispatchMsg (hab, &qmsg) ;

        WinDestroyWindow (hwndFrame) ;
        }
    WinDestroyMsgQueue (hmq) ;
    WinTerminate (hab) ;
    return 0 ;
    }
```

(continued)

Figure 14-7. The HEAD.C File. *continued*

```
MRESULT EXPENTRY ClientWndProc (HWND hwnd, USHORT msg, MPARAM mp1, MPARAM mp2)
    {
    static CHAR   szErrorMsg [] = "File not found or could not be opened" ;
    static SHORT  cxClient, cyClient, cxChar, cyChar, cyDesc ;
    CHAR          *pcReadBuffer ;
    FILE          *fileInput ;
    FONTMETRICS   fm ;
    HPS           hps ;
    POINTL        ptl ;
    SHORT         sLength ;

    switch (msg)
        {
        case WM_CREATE:
             hps = WinGetPS (hwnd) ;
             EzfQueryFonts (hps) ;

             if (!EzfCreateLogFont (hps, LCID_FIXEDFONT, FONTFACE_COUR,
                                                         FONTSIZE_10, 0))

                  {
                  WinReleasePS (hps) ;

                  WinMessageBox (HWND_DESKTOP, HWND_DESKTOP,
                       "Cannot find a fixed-pitch font.  Load the Courier "
                       "fonts from the Control Panel and try again.",
                       szClientClass, 0, MB_OK | MB_ICONEXCLAMATION) ;

                  return 1 ;
                  }
             GpiQueryFontMetrics (hps, (LONG) sizeof fm, &fm) ;
             cxChar = (SHORT) fm.lAveCharWidth ;
             cyChar = (SHORT) fm.lMaxBaselineExt ;
             cyDesc = (SHORT) fm.lMaxDescender ;

             GpiSetCharSet (hps, LCID_DEFAULT) ;
             GpiDeleteSetId (hps, LCID_FIXEDFONT) ;
             WinReleasePS (hps) ;
             return 0 ;

        case WM_SIZE:
             cxClient = SHORT1FROMMP (mp2) ;
             cyClient = SHORT2FROMMP (mp2) ;
             return 0 ;
```

(continued)

Figure 14-7. The HEAD.C File. *continued*

```
        case WM_COMMAND:
            switch (COMMANDMSG(&msg)->cmd)
                {
                case IDM_OPEN:
                    if (WinDlgBox (HWND_DESKTOP, hwnd, OpenDlgProc,
                                    NULL, IDD_OPEN, NULL))
                        WinInvalidateRect (hwnd, NULL, FALSE) ;
                    return 0 ;

                case IDM_ABOUT:
                    WinDlgBox (HWND_DESKTOP, hwnd, AboutDlgProc,
                                NULL, IDD_ABOUT, NULL) ;
                    return 0 ;
                }
            break ;

        case WM_PAINT:
            hps = WinBeginPaint (hwnd, NULL, NULL) ;
            GpiErase (hps) ;

            if (szFileName [0] != '\0')
                {
                EzfCreateLogFont (hps, LCID_FIXEDFONT, FONTFACE_COUR,
                                    FONTSIZE_10,    0) ;
                EzfCreateLogFont (hps, LCID_BOLDFONT,  FONTFACE_COUR,
                                    FONTSIZE_10,    FATTR_SEL_BOLD) ;

                GpiSetCharSet (hps, LCID_BOLDFONT) ;
                ptl.x = cxChar ;
                ptl.y = cyClient - cyChar + cyDesc ;
                GpiCharStringAt (hps, &ptl, (LONG) strlen (szFileName),
                                    szFileName) ;

                ptl.y -= cyChar ;

                if ((fileInput = fopen (szFileName, "r")) != NULL)
                    {
                    GpiSetCharSet (hps, LCID_FIXEDFONT) ;
                    pcReadBuffer = malloc (cxClient / cxChar) ;

                    while ((ptl.y -= cyChar) > 0 &&
                            fgets (pcReadBuffer, cxClient / cxChar - 2,
                                fileInput) != NULL)
                        {
                        sLength = strlen (pcReadBuffer) ;
```

(continued)

Figure 14-7. The HEAD.C File. *continued*

```
                                      if (pcReadBuffer [sLength - 1] == '\n')
                                           sLength-- ;

                                 if (sLength > 0)
                                      GpiCharStringAt (hps, &ptl, (LONG) sLength,
                                                               pcReadBuffer) ;
                                 }
                            free (pcReadBuffer) ;
                            fclose (fileInput) ;
                            }
                       else              // file cannot be opened
                            {
                            ptl.y -= cyChar ;
                            GpiCharStringAt (hps, &ptl,
                                           (LONG) strlen (szErrorMsg),
                                           szErrorMsg) ;
                            }
                       GpiSetCharSet (hps, LCID_DEFAULT) ;
                       GpiDeleteSetId (hps, LCID_FIXEDFONT) ;
                       GpiDeleteSetId (hps, LCID_BOLDFONT) ;
                       }
                  WinEndPaint (hps) ;
                  return 0 ;
             }
        return WinDefWindowProc (hwnd, msg, mp1, mp2) ;
        }


MRESULT EXPENTRY AboutDlgProc (HWND hwnd, USHORT msg, MPARAM mp1, MPARAM mp2)
     {
     switch (msg)
          {
          case WM_COMMAND:
               switch (COMMANDMSG(&msg)->cmd)
                    {
                    case DID_OK:
                    case DID_CANCEL:
                         WinDismissDlg (hwnd, TRUE) ;
                         return 0 ;
                    }
               break ;
          }
     return WinDefDlgProc (hwnd, msg, mp1, mp2) ;
     }
```

(continued)

Figure 14-7. The HEAD.C File. *continued*

```
VOID FillDirListBox (HWND hwnd, CHAR *pcCurrentPath)
    {
    static CHAR szDrive [] = "  :" ;
    FILEFINDBUF findbuf ;
    HDIR        hDir = 1 ;
    SHORT       sDrive ;
    USHORT      usDriveNum, usCurPathLen, usSearchCount = 1 ;
    ULONG       ulDriveMap ;

    DosQCurDisk (&usDriveNum, &ulDriveMap) ;
    pcCurrentPath [0] = (CHAR) usDriveNum + '@' ;
    pcCurrentPath [1] = ':' ;
    pcCurrentPath [2] = '\\' ;
    usCurPathLen = 64 ;
    DosQCurDir (0, pcCurrentPath + 3, &usCurPathLen) ;

    WinSetDlgItemText (hwnd, IDD_PATH, pcCurrentPath) ;
    WinSendDlgItemMsg (hwnd, IDD_DIRLIST, LM_DELETEALL, NULL, NULL) ;

    for (sDrive = 0 ; sDrive < 26 ; sDrive++)
        if (ulDriveMap & 1L << sDrive)
            {
            szDrive [1] = (CHAR) sDrive + 'A' ;

            WinSendDlgItemMsg (hwnd, IDD_DIRLIST, LM_INSERTITEM,
                            MPFROM2SHORT (LIT_END, 0),
                            MPFROMP (szDrive)) ;
            }

    DosFindFirst ("*.*", &hDir, 0x0017, &findbuf, sizeof findbuf,
                            &usSearchCount, 0L) ;
    while (usSearchCount)
        {
        if (findbuf.attrFile & 0x0010 &&
                (findbuf.achName [0] != '.' || findbuf.achName [1]))

            WinSendDlgItemMsg (hwnd, IDD_DIRLIST, LM_INSERTITEM,
                            MPFROM2SHORT (LIT_SORTASCENDING, 0),
                            MPFROMP (findbuf.achName)) ;

        DosFindNext (hDir, &findbuf, sizeof findbuf, &usSearchCount) ;
        }
    }
```

(continued)

Figure 14-7. The HEAD.C File. *continued*

```
VOID FillFileListBox (HWND hwnd)
    {
    FILEFINDBUF findbuf ;
    HDIR        hDir = 1 ;
    USHORT      usSearchCount = 1 ;

    WinSendDlgItemMsg (hwnd, IDD_FILELIST, LM_DELETEALL, NULL, NULL) ;

    DosFindFirst ("*.*", &hDir, 0x0007, &findbuf, sizeof findbuf,
                           &usSearchCount, 0L) ;
    while (usSearchCount)
        {
        WinSendDlgItemMsg (hwnd, IDD_FILELIST, LM_INSERTITEM,
                           MPFROM2SHORT (LIT_SORTASCENDING, 0),
                           MPFROMP (findbuf.achName)) ;

        DosFindNext (hDir, &findbuf, sizeof findbuf, &usSearchCount) ;
        }
    }

MRESULT EXPENTRY OpenDlgProc (HWND hwnd, USHORT msg, MPARAM mp1, MPARAM mp2)
    {
    static CHAR szCurrentPath [80], szBuffer [80] ;
    SHORT       sSelect ;

    switch (msg)
        {
        case WM_INITDLG:
            FillDirListBox (hwnd, szCurrentPath) ;
            FillFileListBox (hwnd) ;

            WinSendDlgItemMsg (hwnd, IDD_FILEEDIT, EM_SETTEXTLIMIT,
                               MPFROM2SHORT (80, 0), NULL) ;
            return 0 ;

        case WM_CONTROL:
            if (SHORT1FROMMP (mp1) == IDD_DIRLIST ||
                SHORT1FROMMP (mp1) == IDD_FILELIST)
                {
                sSelect = (USHORT) WinSendDlgItemMsg (hwnd,
                                          SHORT1FROMMP (mp1),
                                          LM_QUERYSELECTION, 0L, 0L) ;
```

(continued)

Figure 14-7. The HEAD.C File. *continued*

```
                    WinSendDlgItemMsg (hwnd, SHORT1FROMMP (mp1),
                                   LM_QUERYITEMTEXT,
                                   MPFROM2SHORT (sSelect, sizeof szBuffer),
                                   MPFROMP (szBuffer)) ;
               }

          switch (SHORT1FROMMP (mp1))              // Control ID
             {
             case IDD_DIRLIST:
                  switch (SHORT2FROMMP (mp1))    // notification code
                       {
                       case LN_ENTER:
                            if (szBuffer [0] == ' ')
                                 DosSelectDisk (szBuffer [1] - '@') ;
                            else
                    DosChDir (szBuffer, OL) ;

                            FillDirListBox (hwnd, szCurrentPath) ;
                            FillFileListBox (hwnd) ;

                            WinSetDlgItemText (hwnd, IDD_FILEEDIT, "") ;
                            return 0 ;
                       }
                  break ;

             case IDD_FILELIST:
                  switch (SHORT2FROMMP (mp1))    // notification code
                       {
                       case LN_SELECT:
                            WinSetDlgItemText (hwnd, IDD_FILEEDIT,
                                             szBuffer) ;
                            return 0 ;

                       case LN_ENTER:
                            ParseFileName (szFileName, szBuffer) ;
                            WinDismissDlg (hwnd, TRUE) ;
                            return 0 ;
                       }
                  break ;
             }
          break ;
```

(continued)

Figure 14-7. The HEAD.C File. *continued*

```
          case WM_COMMAND:
              switch (COMMANDMSG(&msg)->cmd)
                  {
                  case DID_OK:
                      WinQueryDlgItemText (hwnd, IDD_FILEEDIT,
                                                sizeof szBuffer, szBuffer) ;

                      switch (ParseFileName (szCurrentPath, szBuffer))
                          {
                          case 0:
                              WinAlarm (HWND_DESKTOP, WA_ERROR) ;
                              FillDirListBox (hwnd, szCurrentPath) ;
                              FillFileListBox (hwnd) ;
                              return 0 ;

                          case 1:
                              FillDirListBox (hwnd, szCurrentPath) ;
                              FillFileListBox (hwnd) ;
                              WinSetDlgItemText (hwnd, IDD_FILEEDIT, "") ;
                              return 0 ;

                          case 2:
                              strcpy (szFileName, szCurrentPath) ;
                              WinDismissDlg (hwnd, TRUE) ;
                              return 0 ;
                          }
                      break ;

                  case DID_CANCEL:
                      WinDismissDlg (hwnd, FALSE) ;
                      return 0 ;
                  }
              break ;
          }
      return WinDefDlgProc (hwnd, msg, mp1, mp2) ;
      }

SHORT ParseFileName (CHAR *pcOut, CHAR *pcIn)
    {
      /*------------------------------------------------------------------
          Input:   pcOut -- Pointer to parsed file specification.
                   pcIn  -- Pointer to raw file specification.

          Returns: 0 -- pcIn had invalid drive or directory.
                   1 -- pcIn was empty or had no filename.
                   2 -- pcOut points to drive, full dir, and file name.
```

(continued)

Figure 14-7. The HEAD.C File. *continued*

```
                      Changes current drive and directory per pcIn string.
                 ------------------------------------------------------------------*/

         CHAR   *pcLastSlash, *pcFileOnly ;
         ULONG  ulDriveMap ;
         USHORT usDriveNum, usDirLen = 64 ;

         strupr (pcIn) ;

                      // If input string is empty, return 1

         if (pcIn [0] == '\0')
             return 1 ;

                      // Get drive from input string or current drive

         if (pcIn [1] == ':')
             {
             if (DosSelectDisk (pcIn [0] - '@'))
                 return 0 ;

             pcIn += 2 ;
             }
         DosQCurDisk (&usDriveNum, &ulDriveMap) ;

         *pcOut++ = (CHAR) usDriveNum + '@' ;
         *pcOut++ = ':' ;
         *pcOut++ = '\\' ;

                      // If rest of string is empty, return 1

         if (pcIn [0] == '\0')
             return 1 ;

                      // Search for last backslash.  If none, could be directory.

         if (NULL == (pcLastSlash = strrchr (pcIn, '\\')))
             {
           if (!DosChDir (pcIn, OL))
                 return 1 ;

                          // Otherwise, get current dir & attach input filename

             DosQCurDir (0, pcOut, &usDirLen) ;
```

(continued)

Figure 14-7. The HEAD.C File. *continued*

```
        if (strlen (pcIn) > 12)
             return 0 ;

        if (*(pcOut + strlen (pcOut) - 1) != '\\')
             strcat (pcOut++, "\\") ;

        strcat (pcOut, pcIn) ;
        return 2 ;
        }
             // If the only backslash is at beginning, change to root

if (pcIn == pcLastSlash)
    {
  DosChDir ("\\", 0L) ;

        if (pcIn [1] == '\0')
             return 1 ;

        strcpy (pcOut, pcIn + 1) ;
        return 2 ;
        }
             // Attempt to change directory -- Get current dir if OK

*pcLastSlash = '\0' ;

if (DosChDir (pcIn, 0L))
     return 0 ;

DosQCurDir (0, pcOut, &usDirLen) ;

          // Append input filename, if any

pcFileOnly = pcLastSlash + 1 ;

if (*pcFileOnly == '\0')
     return 1 ;

if (strlen (pcFileOnly) > 12)
     return 0 ;

if (*(pcOut + strlen (pcOut) - 1) != '\\')
     strcat (pcOut++, "\\") ;

strcat (pcOut, pcFileOnly) ;
return 2 ;
}
```

The HEAD.H File

```
/*--------------------
   HEAD.H header file
   --------------------*/

#define ID_RESOURCE      1

#define IDM_FILE         1
#define IDM_OPEN         10
#define IDM_ABOUT        11

#define IDD_OPEN         1
#define IDD_ABOUT        2

#define IDD_PATH         10
#define IDD_FILEEDIT     11
#define IDD_DIRLIST      12
#define IDD_FILELIST     13
```

The HEAD.RC File

```
/*----------------------------
   HEAD.RC resource script file
   ----------------------------*/

#include <os2.h>
#include "head.h"

MENU ID_RESOURCE
    {
    SUBMENU "~File",                IDM_FILE
        {
        MENUITEM "~Open...",            IDM_OPEN
        MENUITEM SEPARATOR
        MENUITEM "A~bout Head...",      IDM_ABOUT
        }
    }

DLGTEMPLATE IDD_ABOUT
  {
  DIALOG "", 0, 32, 32, 200, 88,, FCF_DLGBORDER
    {
    CTEXT "Head"                              -1, 10, 64, 180,  8
    CTEXT "File Head Display"                 -1, 10, 40, 180,  8
    CTEXT "Copyright (C) Charles Petzold, 1988" -1, 10, 32, 180,  8
    DEFPUSHBUTTON "OK"                        DID_OK, 80,  8,  40, 16, WS_GROUP
    }
  }
```

(continued)

Figure 14-7. The HEAD.RC File. *continued*

```
DLGTEMPLATE IDD_OPEN
  {
  DIALOG "", 0, 8, 8, 240, 170,, FCF_DLGBORDER
    {
    CTEXT "Open File"                   -1,             8, 154, 224, 8
    LTEXT "Use mouse to choose file, or type filename." -1, 8, 138, 224, 8
    LTEXT "Current Directory:"          -1,             8, 126, 80, 8
    LTEXT ""                            IDD_PATH,      88, 126, 144, 8
    LTEXT "Filename:"                   -1,             8, 110, 48, 8
    ENTRYFIELD ""                       IDD_FILEEDIT, 56, 110, 176, 8, ES_MARGIN
    CTEXT "Directories"                 -1,            16, 96, 92, 8
    CTEXT "Files"                       -1,           134, 96, 92, 8
    LISTBOX                             IDD_DIRLIST,  16, 32, 92, 64
    LISTBOX                             IDD_FILELIST, 134, 32, 92, 64
    DEFPUSHBUTTON "Open"                DID_OK,       32, 8, 64, 16, WS_GROUP
    PUSHBUTTON "Esc=Cancel"             DID_CANCEL,  144, 8, 64, 16, WS_GROUP
    }
  }
```

The HEAD.DEF File

```
;------------------------------------
; HEAD.DEF module definition file
;------------------------------------

NAME            HEAD      WINDOWAPI

DESCRIPTION     'Displays File Head (C) Charles Petzold, 1988'
PROTMODE
HEAPSIZE        1024
STACKSIZE       8192
EXPORTS         ClientWndProc
                OpenDlgProc
                AboutDlgProc
```

Figure 14-7. *The HEAD program.*

You'll also need the EASYFONT.C and EASYFONT.H files from Chapter 5 to compile HEAD.

As I said, the File Open dialog box is one of the most complex you'll encounter and requires some messy code. To handle the box logic properly, you have to parse file specifications, separating the drive, directory, and filenames. The *ParseFileName* function (the last function in HEAD.C) does a lot of the dirty work. You supply a file specification and *ParseFileName* determines the fully qualified filename with disk drive and directory. It returns a code indicating a possible error.

HEAD must retain this fully qualified filename because the File Open dialog box procedure often changes the current disk drive and directory. If you used HEAD to look at a file and then wanted to look at another file, you would invoke the File Open dialog box. After you changed the drive and directory, you might change your mind and decide to cancel the dialog box. If HEAD did not save the fully qualified filename or the original file, it might not be able to find the file again.

The Overall Structure

One way to use HEAD is to specify a filename parameter when you run the program, like this:

```
HEAD filename
```

The *main* function in HEAD declares the normal *argc* and *argv* parameters. If *argc* is greater than 1, *argv[1]* is passed to the *ParseFileName* function, which creates a fully qualified filename and stores it in the global variable *szFileName*.

During the WM_PAINT message in *ClientWndProc*, HEAD attempts to open this file (using normal C file I/O functions) and display as much of the file as can fit in the window. If this fails, HEAD displays the message "File not found or could not be opened" at the top of the client window. HEAD closes the file at the end of the WM_PAINT message. The file is opened and read only during the WM_PAINT message.

You can also select a file through HEAD's File Open dialog box, which uses the IDD_OPEN template in HEAD.RC and the *OpenDlgProc* function in HEAD.C. The dialog box is shown in Figure 14-8.

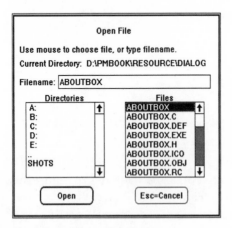

Figure 14-8. *The HEAD display.*

The dialog box contains several static text fields, one of which displays the current drive and directory. You can change the drive or directory — or select a file — by typing directly in a text entry field (the box following the text string "Filename"). The dialog box also contains two list boxes. The first displays all the disk drives and subdirectories of the current directory. You can change the drive or directory using this list box. The second list box lists all the files in the current directory. You can select a file by choosing it from the list box. Much of the complexity of the File Open dialog box stems from the interaction between the list boxes and the text entry field.

Static Text Fields

The File Open dialog box template in HEAD.RC has three static text fields of type CTEXT ("centered text") and four of type LTEXT ("left-justified text"). You'll notice that the third LTEXT statement in the dialog box template has a blank text field and a child ID of IDD_PATH. This is used to display the current disk drive and directory.

The text for this control is set in the *FillDirListBox* function. This function obtains the current disk drive by calling the OS/2 kernel function *DosQCurDisk* and the current directory by calling *DosQCurDir*. The composite drive and directory is stored in the text string *pcCurrentPath*. The *WinSetDlgItemText* function sets the text for the IDD_PATH control:

```
WinSetDlgItemText (hwnd, IDD_PATH, pcCurrentPath) ;
```

This function is similar to the *WinSetWindowText* function we used in the COLORSCR program in Chapter 11 to set the text of a control window.

List Boxes

List boxes list text strings. The File Open dialog box template has two list boxes with child IDs of IDD_DIRLIST and IDD_FILELIST. The first lists disk drives and subdirectories; the second lists files in the current directory.

You can scroll through a list box using the cursor movement keys or a scroll bar. In the File Open dialog box you change the current disk drive or directory by double-clicking an entry in the first list box or by pressing Enter when the list box has the input focus. You can select a file from the second list box in a similar fashion.

The *FillDirListBox* and *FillFileListBox* functions in HEAD.C fill the list boxes with text entries. These functions first delete all entries in the list box by sending the list box an LM_DELETEALL message. Here's the call in *FillDirListBox*:

```
WinSendDlgItemMsg (hwnd, IDD_DIRLIST, LM_DELETEALL, NULL, NULL) ;
```

The first list box is filled with all the valid disk drives and the subdirectories of the current directory. The *FillDirListBox* function uses the *DosQCurDisk* to obtain the valid disk drives and the *DosFindFirst* and *DosFindNext* functions for the directories. To put a text string in a list box, you send the list box an LM_INSERTITEM message. The *mp2* parameter is a pointer to the text string. The *FillDirListBox* function sets the low USHORT of *mp1* to LIT_END to put the disk drives at the end of the list and LIT_SORTASCENDING to put the subdirectories in the list box in alphabetic order.

The *FillFileListBox* function works similarly for the second list box. It finds all the files in the current directory using the OS/2 *DosFindFirst* and *DosFindNext* functions and sends the list box an LM_INSERTITEM message for each file.

OpenDlgProc first calls the *FillDirListBox* and *FillFileListBox* functions during the WM_INITDLG message and then awaits messages from the list boxes. A list box sends its owner a WM_CONTROL message. The low USHORT of *mp1* is the child ID; the high USHORT of *mp1* is a notification code. This notification code is either LN_SELECT (which means that the user has clicked an entry in the list box or moved the cursor to it) or LN_ENTER, which means the user has double-clicked an entry or pressed the Enter key.

OpenDlgProc processes the WM_CONTROL message by first sending the list box an LM_QUERYSELECTION message. This returns a number indicating the current list box selection. Sending the list box an LM_QUERYITEMTEXT message with this selection number obtains the text string of the selection.

For the first list box, an LN_ENTER notification code during a WM_CONTROL message indicates that the user wants to change the current drive or directory. *OpenDlgProc* changes the drive or directory and then calls *FillDirListBox* and *FillFileListBox* again to reflect this new selection. For the second list box, an LN_ENTER notification code indicates that the user is finished. *OpenDlgProc* calls *ParseFileName* for the current selection and ends the dialog box by calling *WinDismissDlg*.

Text Entry Fields

The File Open dialog box template also contains a text entry control in which the user can type a drive, directory, filename, or some combination of the three. The text entry field has a child ID of IDD_FILEEDIT. During the WM_INITDLG message, *OpenDlgProc* sends the text entry control an EM_SETTEXTLIMIT message with the low USHORT of *mp1* set to 80. This limits the amount of text the user can type in the field to 80 characters.

If you simply type something in this field and press Enter, *OpenDlgProc* receives a WM_COMMAND message with the *cmd* field set to DID_OK. This is not a message from the text entry control—when you press Enter, the *WinDefDlgProc* function generates a WM_COMMAND message that contains the child window ID of the default push button in the dialog box.

For a WM_COMMAND message of DID_OK, *OpenDlgProc* obtains the current text in the text entry field by calling *WinQueryDlgItemText* and passes the string to *ParseFileName*. The return value of *ParseFileName* is tested to determine whether the string is invalid (a 0 value), contains a new disk drive or directory (a 1 value), or a valid filename (a 2 value). In the last case, the dialog box is ended by calling *WinDismissDlg*.

The text entry control is also kept updated with the current file selected in the second list box. For a WM_CONTROL message with a child ID of IDD_FILELIST and notification code of LN_SELECT, *OpenDlgProc* calls *WinSetDlgItemText* to set the text in the text entry control.

Modeless Dialog Boxes

So far, the programs shown in this chapter have created "modal" dialog boxes. Although you can switch to other programs while a modal dialog box is displayed, you cannot switch to another window in the same program. However, a "modeless" dialog box works a little differently and is similar to a window that you create with *WinCreateStdWindow*. You can switch between the dialog box and other top-level windows in the program.

To create a modal dialog box, you call *WinDlgBox*. The function does not return until the dialog box destroys itself by calling *WinDismissDlg*. The *WinDlgBox* returns the second parameter passed to *WinDismissDlg*. To create a modeless dialog box, you call *WinLoadDlg*. The function returns after the dialog box is created, returning the handle of the dialog box window.

Perhaps the most interesting application of a modeless dialog box is to create a main window for your program. You create your program's window with *WinLoadDlg* rather than *WinCreateStdWindow*. Why would you want to do this? Simple: If you want to create a lot of child windows on your client, it's much easier to define them in a dialog template than it is to call *WinCreateWindow* in your program.

The HEXCALC Program

To demonstrate this, let's look at the HEXCALC program, which is shown in Figure 14-9 on the following pages.

The HEXCALC File

```
#------------------
# HEXCALC make file
#------------------

hexcalc.obj : hexcalc.c hexcalc.h
    cl -c -G2sw -W3 hexcalc.c

hexcalc.res : hexcalc.rc hexcalc.h
    rc -r hexcalc.rc

hexcalc.exe : hexcalc.obj hexcalc.def
    link hexcalc, /align:16, NUL, os2, hexcalc
    rc hexcalc.res

hexcalc.exe : hexcalc.res
    rc hexcalc.res
```

The HEXCALC.C File

```c
/*------------------------------------
   HEXCALC.C -- Hexadecimal Calculator
   ------------------------------------*/

#define INCL_WIN
#include <os2.h>
#include <ctype.h>
#include <limits.h>
#include <stdlib.h>
#include <string.h>
#include "hexcalc.h"

MRESULT EXPENTRY ClientWndProc (HWND, USHORT, MPARAM, MPARAM) ;

int main (void)
    {
    HAB  hab ;
    HMQ  hmq ;
    HWND hwndFrame ;
    QMSG qmsg ;

    hab = WinInitialize (0) ;
    hmq = WinCreateMsgQueue (hab, 0) ;

    WinRegisterClass (hab, CLIENTCLASS, ClientWndProc, 0L, 0) ;
```

(continued)

Figure 14-9. The HEXCALC.C File. *continued*

```
        hwndFrame = WinLoadDlg (HWND_DESKTOP, HWND_DESKTOP,
                                NULL, NULL, ID_HEXCALC, NULL) ;

        WinSendMsg (hwndFrame, WM_SETICON,
                    WinLoadPointer (HWND_DESKTOP, NULL, ID_ICON), NULL) ;

        WinSetFocus (HWND_DESKTOP, WinWindowFromID (hwndFrame, FID_CLIENT)) ;

        while (WinGetMsg (hab, &qmsg, NULL, 0, 0))
            WinDispatchMsg (hab, &qmsg) ;

        WinDestroyWindow (hwndFrame) ;
        WinDestroyMsgQueue (hmq) ;
        WinTerminate (hab) ;
        return 0 ;
        }

void ShowNumber (HWND hwnd, ULONG ulNumber)
        {
        CHAR szBuffer [20] ;

        WinSetWindowText (WinWindowFromID (hwnd, ESCAPE),
                          strupr (ltoa (ulNumber, szBuffer, 16))) ;
        }

ULONG CalcIt (ULONG ulFirstNum, SHORT sOperation, ULONG ulNum)
        {
        switch (sOperation)
            {
            case '=' : return ulNum ;
            case '+' : return ulFirstNum +  ulNum ;
            case '-' : return ulFirstNum -  ulNum ;
            case '*' : return ulFirstNum *  ulNum ;
            case '&' : return ulFirstNum &  ulNum ;
            case '¦' : return ulFirstNum ¦  ulNum ;
            case '^' : return ulFirstNum ^  ulNum ;
            case '<' : return ulFirstNum << ulNum ;
            case '>' : return ulFirstNum >> ulNum ;
            case '/' : return ulNum ? ulFirstNum / ulNum : ULONG_MAX ;
            case '%' : return ulNum ? ulFirstNum % ulNum : ULONG_MAX ;
            default  : return 0L ;
            }
        }
```

(continued)

Figure 14-9. The HEXCALC.C File. *continued*

```
MRESULT EXPENTRY ClientWndProc (HWND hwnd, USHORT msg, MPARAM mp1, MPARAM mp2)
    {
    static BOOL   fNewNumber = TRUE ;
    static ULONG  ulNumber, ulFirstNum ;
    static SHORT  sOperation = '=' ;
    HWND          hwndButton ;
    SHORT         idButton ;

    switch (msg)
        {
        case WM_CHAR:
            if (CHARMSG(&msg)->fs & KC_KEYUP)
                return 0 ;

            if (CHARMSG(&msg)->fs & KC_VIRTUALKEY)
                switch (CHARMSG(&msg)->vkey)
                    {
                    case VK_LEFT:
                        if (!(CHARMSG(&msg)->fs & KC_CHAR))
                            {
                            CHARMSG(&msg)->chr = '\b' ;
                            CHARMSG(&msg)->fs |= KC_CHAR ;
                            }
                        break ;

                    case VK_ESC:
                        CHARMSG(&msg)->chr = ESCAPE ;
                        CHARMSG(&msg)->fs |= KC_CHAR ;
                        break ;

                    case VK_NEWLINE:
                    case VK_ENTER:
                        CHARMSG(&msg)->chr = '=' ;
                        CHARMSG(&msg)->fs |= KC_CHAR ;
                        break ;
                    }

            if (CHARMSG(&msg)->fs & KC_CHAR)
                {
                CHARMSG(&msg)->chr = toupper (CHARMSG(&msg)->chr) ;

                if (hwndButton = WinWindowFromID (hwnd,CHARMSG(&msg)->chr))
                    WinSendMsg (hwndButton, BM_CLICK, NULL, NULL) ;
                else
                    WinAlarm (HWND_DESKTOP, WA_ERROR) ;
```

(continued)

Figure 14-9. The HEXCALC.C File. *continued*

```
                }
            return 1 ;

        case WM_COMMAND:
            idButton = COMMANDMSG(&msg)->cmd ;

            if (idButton == '\b')                       // backspace
                ShowNumber (hwnd, ulNumber /= 16) ;

            else if (idButton == ESCAPE)                // escape
                ShowNumber (hwnd, ulNumber = 0L) ;

            else if (isxdigit (idButton))               // hex digit
                {
                if (fNewNumber)
                    {
                    ulFirstNum = ulNumber ;
                    ulNumber = 0L ;
                    }
                fNewNumber = FALSE ;

                if (ulNumber <= ULONG_MAX >> 4)
                    ShowNumber (hwnd,
                        ulNumber = 16 * ulNumber + idButton -
                            (isdigit (idButton) ? '0' : 'A' - 10)) ;
                else
                    WinAlarm (HWND_DESKTOP, WA_ERROR) ;
                }
            else                                        // operation
                {
                if (!fNewNumber)
                    ShowNumber (hwnd, ulNumber =
                        CalcIt (ulFirstNum, sOperation, ulNumber)) ;
                fNewNumber = TRUE ;
                sOperation = idButton ;
                }
            return 0 ;

        case WM_BUTTON1DOWN:
            WinAlarm (HWND_DESKTOP, WA_ERROR) ;
            break ;

        case WM_ERASEBACKGROUND:
            return 1 ;
        }
    return WinDefWindowProc (hwnd, msg, mp1, mp2) ;
    }
```

The HEXCALC.H File

```
/*---------------------
    HEXCALC.H header file
    ---------------------*/

#define ID_HEXCALC   1
#define ID_ICON      1

#define CLIENTCLASS "HexCalc"

#define ESCAPE       27
```

The HEXCALC.RC File

```
/*---------------------------
    HEXCALC.RC resource script
    ---------------------------*/

#include <os2.h>
#include "hexcalc.h"

POINTER ID_ICON hexcalc.ico

WINDOWTEMPLATE ID_HEXCALC
    {
    FRAME NULL, 0, 100, 40, 132, 122, WS_VISIBLE,
         FCF_TITLEBAR ¦ FCF_SYSMENU ¦ FCF_MINBUTTON ¦ FCF_BORDER ¦ FCF_TASKLIST
        {
        WINDOW "", FID_CLIENT, 0, 0, 140, 122, CLIENTCLASS, WS_VISIBLE
            {
            PUSHBUTTON "D",      68,   8,  84, 20, 14, BS_NOPOINTERFOCUS
            PUSHBUTTON "A",      65,   8,  68, 20, 14, BS_NOPOINTERFOCUS
            PUSHBUTTON "7",      55,   8,  52, 20, 14, BS_NOPOINTERFOCUS
            PUSHBUTTON "4",      52,   8,  36, 20, 14, BS_NOPOINTERFOCUS
            PUSHBUTTON "1",      49,   8,  20, 20, 14, BS_NOPOINTERFOCUS
            PUSHBUTTON "0",      48,   8,   4, 20, 14, BS_NOPOINTERFOCUS
            PUSHBUTTON "0",   ESCAPE,  32, 104, 68, 14, BS_NOPOINTERFOCUS
            PUSHBUTTON "E",      69,  32,  84, 20, 14, BS_NOPOINTERFOCUS
            PUSHBUTTON "B",      66,  32,  68, 20, 14, BS_NOPOINTERFOCUS
            PUSHBUTTON "8",      56,  32,  52, 20, 14, BS_NOPOINTERFOCUS
            PUSHBUTTON "5",      53,  32,  36, 20, 14, BS_NOPOINTERFOCUS
            PUSHBUTTON "2",      50,  32,  20, 20, 14, BS_NOPOINTERFOCUS
            PUSHBUTTON "Back",    8,  32,   4, 44, 14, BS_NOPOINTERFOCUS
```

(continued)

Figure 14-9. The HEXCALC.RC File. *continued*

```
        PUSHBUTTON "F",      70,  56,  84, 20, 14, BS_NOPOINTERFOCUS
        PUSHBUTTON "C",      67,  56,  68, 20, 14, BS_NOPOINTERFOCUS
        PUSHBUTTON "9",      57,  56,  52, 20, 14, BS_NOPOINTERFOCUS
        PUSHBUTTON "6",      54,  56,  36, 20, 14, BS_NOPOINTERFOCUS
        PUSHBUTTON "3",      51,  56,  20, 20, 14, BS_NOPOINTERFOCUS
        PUSHBUTTON "+",      43,  80,  84, 20, 14, BS_NOPOINTERFOCUS
        PUSHBUTTON "-",      45,  80,  68, 20, 14, BS_NOPOINTERFOCUS
        PUSHBUTTON "*",      42,  80,  52, 20, 14, BS_NOPOINTERFOCUS
        PUSHBUTTON "/",      47,  80,  36, 20, 14, BS_NOPOINTERFOCUS
        PUSHBUTTON "%",      37,  80,  20, 20, 14, BS_NOPOINTERFOCUS
        PUSHBUTTON "Equals", 61,  80,   4, 44, 14, BS_NOPOINTERFOCUS
        PUSHBUTTON "&",      38, 104,  84, 20, 14, BS_NOPOINTERFOCUS
        PUSHBUTTON "¦",     124, 104,  68, 20, 14, BS_NOPOINTERFOCUS
        PUSHBUTTON "^",      94, 104,  52, 20, 14, BS_NOPOINTERFOCUS
        PUSHBUTTON "<",      60, 104,  36, 20, 14, BS_NOPOINTERFOCUS
        PUSHBUTTON ">",      62, 104,  20, 20, 14, BS_NOPOINTERFOCUS
        }
    }
}
```

The HEXCALC.ICO File

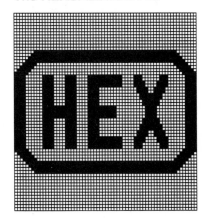

The HEXCALC.DEF File

```
;-----------------------------------
; HEXCALC module definition file
;-----------------------------------

NAME            HEXCALC    WINDOWAPI

DESCRIPTION     'Hexadecimal Calculator (C) Charles Petzold 1988'
PROTMODE
HEAPSIZE        1024
STACKSIZE       8192
EXPORTS         ClientWndProc
```

Figure 14-9. *The HEXCALC program.*

HEXCALC is a hexadecimal calculator with a complete keyboard and mouse interface. You can add, subtract, multiply, and divide 32-bit hexadecimal numbers, as well as perform the C remainder (%), left shift (<<), right shift (>>), and bitwise AND (&), OR (¦), and exclusive-OR (^) operations.

The HEXCALC window is shown in Figure 14-10.

Figure 14-10. *The HEXCALC display.*

To use HEXCALC, type or click in the first number (up to eight hexadecimal digits) followed by the operation and then the second number. You can show the result by clicking the "Equals" button or by pressing either the keyboard equal key or the Enter key. To correct your entries, you can use either the Backspace key, the left arrow cursor movement key, or the "Back" button. Pressing Escape or clicking the result box clears the current entry.

Results are always truncated to 32 bits, just as if you were performing the operation on two unsigned long integers in a C program. The only special handling is a check for division by zero before doing division or a remainder operation. In this case, HEXCALC sets the result to FFFFFFFF.

The client window of HEXCALC contains 29 push button controls, yet the program has not one call to *WinCreateStdWindow* or *WinCreateWindow*. Everything is defined in the dialog box template in HEXCALC.RC. All the windows are created by one call to *WinLoadDlg*.

The HEXCALC Template

The dialog box template shown in the HEXCALC.RC resource script describes the size, appearance, and structure of HEXCALC's main window. The template begins with the WINDOWTEMPLATE keyword, which is equivalent to the DLGTEMPLATE keyword used in the other templates shown in this chapter. The top-level window is denoted by a FRAME statement. The statement contains a window style of WS_VISIBLE and frame creation flags of FCF_TITLEBAR, FCF_SYSMENU, FCF_MIN-BUTTON, FCF_BORDER, and FCF_TASKLIST, such as you might use in a *WinCreateStdWindow* function.

The WINDOW statement that follows specifies a child of the frame window. This is the client window of HEXCALC. The child window ID is set to FID_CLIENT, and the class name is set to the identifier CLIENTCLASS, defined in HEXCALC.H as "HexCalc." This window class is registered in HEXCALC.C before the call to *WinLoadDlg*.

The template then defines 29 children of the client window with 29 PUSHBUTTON statements. The push buttons are given the style of BS_NOPOINTERFOCUS, which causes the push button not to get the input focus when clicked. I'll discuss the push button child window IDs shortly.

Creating the Windows

The *main* function in HEXCALC.C looks as though it's missing something, and it is — it doesn't have a call to *WinCreateStdWindow*. Instead, the *WinLoadDlg* function creates a frame window, client window, and 29 push buttons based on the template in HEXCALC.RC. The frame window also creates a title bar, system menu, and minimize box based on the frame creation flags specified in the template.

Look at the call to *WinLoadDlg*:

```
hwndFrame = WinLoadDlg (HWND_DESKTOP, HWND_DESKTOP,
                    NULL, NULL, ID_HEXCALC, NULL) ;
```

It doesn't even specify a window procedure for the dialog box. The only window procedure in HEXCALC is *ClientWndProc*, which is the window procedure for the "HexCalc" class registered in *main* and specified in the WINDOW statement in the template.

Following the call to *WinLoadDlg*, the windows in HEXCALC function as if they were created with a call to *WinCreateStdWindow* and 29 calls to *WinCreateWindow*. *ClientWndProc* gets WM_COMMAND messages from the push buttons and WM_CHAR messages from the keyboard.

Creative Use of Control IDs

The programs developed so far in this chapter have used identifiers defined in a header file as the child window IDs of controls within a dialog box. The child window IDs of the push buttons in HEXCALC appear to be random, but they're not. The IDs have been set to the ASCII codes of the corresponding number, letter, or symbol that appears inside the push button.

This is an easy way to add a keyboard interface to the calculator. When the user clicks a child window button, the child window sends *ClientWndProc* a WM_COMMAND message with the *cmd* field equal to the control ID. When the user presses a character key on the keyboard, HEXCALC's main window receives a WM_CHAR message with the ASCII code of the character.

When *ClientWndProc* receives a WM_CHAR message, it first makes a few adjustments for the left cursor key, the Escape key, and the two Enter keys. Then it checks to see if a button exists with an ID equal to the typed character. If so, *ClientWndProc* sends the button a BM_CLICK message:

```
if (hwndButton = WinWindowFromID (hwnd, CHARMSG(&msg)->chr))
    WinSendMsg (hwndButton, BM_CLICK, NULL, NULL) ;
```

The BM_CLICK message causes the button to do two things: First, the button inverts itself briefly to appear as if it had been clicked. This gives the user visual feedback. Secondly, the button sends *ClientWndProc* a WM_COMMAND message — again — just as if it had been clicked with the mouse. This allows *ClientWndProc* to process both keyboard and mouse input as WM_COMMAND messages.

Windows and Dialog Boxes

We've come full circle. We began creating standard windows in Chapter 2. Since Chapter 8 we've been looking at different ways that windows get input, first by processing keyboard and mouse input directly, then by using child window controls, and finally by moving to dialog boxes.

Now we've created a dialog box that seems to function just like a standard window! Of course, dialog boxes *are* normal windows, so it shouldn't be *too* surprising that we can do this.

MISCELLANEOUS TOPICS

## CHAPTER FIFTEEN

CUT, COPY, AND PASTE: THE CLIPBOARD

The clipboard is a mechanism for transferring data between Presentation Manager applications. A program that makes use of the clipboard usually has an Edit menu with the options Cut, Copy, and Paste. The Cut and Copy options direct the program to transfer data to the clipboard, and the Paste option directs the program to transfer data from the clipboard to the program.

The clipboard is also useful for some operations that do not involve transferring data between applications. These operations most commonly occur in programs that work with documents — word-processing programs, for example. Such programs use the clipboard as a storage area when moving text from one part of the document to another.

To move text within a word-processing document, the user first selects part of the document to be moved. The user then selects Cut or Copy from the menu. Both commands copy the selection to the clipboard; the Cut command also deletes the selection from the document.

To use the Paste command in a word-processing program, the user first moves the cursor to the point in the document where the text from the clipboard should be inserted. The user then selects the Paste command. The program copies the text from the clipboard to the document. In traditional word-processing terminology, a ''block copy'' is a clipboard Copy command followed by a Paste command. A ''block move'' is a clipboard Cut command followed by a Paste command.

Of course, word-processing programs have included block copy and block move operations for years without any help from a clipboard. But a Presentation Manager program should use the clipboard for these operations rather than its own internal logic: Because all Presentation Manager programs have access to the same clipboard, a user can cut or copy data from one program and paste it into another program. The clipboard makes use of shared memory segments to allow these interprocess transfers.

But the clipboard is really for the convenience of the user. The user controls what is copied to the clipboard by selecting menu commands from Presentation Manager programs. A program should copy data to the clipboard only on a Cut or Copy command; it should not use the clipboard as a form of temporary storage apart from these two commands.

Three standard data formats can be stored in the clipboard: text, bitmaps, and metafiles. (A metafile is a collection of GPI drawing commands.) This chapter discusses the text and bitmap formats.

Transferring Text with the Clipboard

A program that makes use of the clipboard generally has an Edit option on its top-level menu. The standard commands on the Edit submenu (in the order they usually appear) are as follows:

Menu Command	Keyboard Accelerator	Operation
Cut	Shift+Del	Copy selection to clipboard. Delete selection from document.
Copy	Ctrl+Ins	Copy selection to clipboard. Do not delete selection from document.
Paste	Shift+Ins	Copy clipboard contents to document.
Clear	Del	Delete selection from document. Do not copy selection to clipboard.

In some cases, you may not have all of these commands, but you'll probably include at least Copy and Paste. As you can see, the Clear option doesn't involve the clipboard at all. However, you'll want to write your Clear logic at the same time you write your Cut logic because Cut does the same thing as a Copy followed by a Clear.

The most common format of clipboard data is a block of text in normal ASCII format. Each text line is terminated by a carriage return (\r) and linefeed (\n) control characters. The text can contain tab characters (\t). The entire block is terminated by a zero byte.

A block of text that your program copies into the clipboard must be stored in a shared memory segment allocated specifically for this purpose. To allocate this memory segment you use the OS/2 *DosAllocSeg* function with the SEG_GIVEABLE option. This allows the Presentation Manager to call *DosGiveSeg* within its clipboard logic to give access rights to other programs that need to copy the text from the clipboard.

Preparing the Shared Memory Segment

Let's suppose that the user of your program has selected a block of text in a document and selects the Copy or Cut command to copy it to the clipboard. I'll assume your program has two variables named *pchText* (a pointer to the beginning of the character string to be copied to the clipboard) and *usTextLen* (the length of this string). In the general case, *pchText* is a pointer to a text string within a larger document, and the selected block of text will not itself be terminated by a zero byte.

In your program you define variables of type SEL (selector) and PCHAR (a far pointer to a character string):

```
SEL   selClipText ;
PCHAR pchClipText ;
```

You first allocate a block of memory that is the length of the selected text string plus 1 byte (for the terminating zero). To do this, use the *DosAllocSeg* function with a parameter of SEG_GIVEABLE:

```
DosAllocSeg (usTextLen + 1, &selClipText, SEG_GIVEABLE) ;
```

The *DosAllocSeg* function allocates a segment of shareable memory and stores the selector to this segment in *selClipText*. You can convert the selector to a far pointer by using the MAKEP macro:

```
pchClipText = MAKEP (selClipText, 0) ;
```

Now copy the text addressed by *pchText* to the memory block addressed by *pchClipText*. If your program is compiled for compact or large model, you can use the C *memcpy* function for this:

```
memcpy (pchClipText, pchText, usTextLen) ;
pchClipText[usTextLen] = '\0' ;
```

Don't forget to add the zero byte that terminates the text. If you're compiling for small or medium model, it's easy enough to write some code that mimics the *memcpy* function:

```
USHORT usIndex ;
    [other program lines]

for (usIndex = 0 ; usIndex < usTextLen ; usIndex++)
    pchClipText[usIndex] = pchText[usIndex] ;

pchClipText[usTextLen] = '\0' ;
```

Putting Text in the Clipboard

Now that you've prepared the shared memory segment, you're ready to put the text in the clipboard. You use four Presentation Manager clipboard function calls to put text into the clipboard: *WinOpenClipbrd*, *WinEmptyClipbrd*, *WinSetClipbrdData*, and *WinCloseClipbrd*. First you open the clipboard and empty it of all data:

```
WinOpenClipbrd (hab) ;
WinEmptyClipbrd (hab) ;
```

Call *WinSetClipbrdData* to set the text string referenced by *selClipText* into the clipboard:

```
WinSetClipbrdData (hab, (ULONG) selClipText,
                   CF_TEXT, CFI_SELECTOR) ;
```

Note that the second parameter is the selector rather than the far pointer. This parameter is declared as a ULONG in the PMWIN.H header file, so you should cast the selector to a ULONG to prevent compiler warning messages. The third parameter indicates the format of this data. In this case the format is CF_TEXT. (The CF prefix stands for "clipboard format.") The last parameter is the clipboard format information flag. You set this to CFI_SELECTOR to indicate that the second parameter is a selector. Finally, close the clipboard:

```
WinCloseClipbrd (hab) ;
```

You're done.

Do not call *DosFreeSeg* to free the block of memory you allocated using *DosAllocSeg*. (Nothing bad will happen if you do, but the *DosFreeSeg* function will fail because the segment has already been freed for your process by the Presentation Manager.) After you call *WinSetClipbrdData*, do not attempt to reference the text stored in this shared memory block. You allocated this block specifically for transferring the text to the clipboard; once you call *WinSetClipbrdData*, the text no longer belongs to your program.

Getting Text from the Clipboard

When transferring data from the clipboard to your program (the Paste operation), you use three functions: *WinOpenClipbrd*, *WinQueryClipbrdData*, and *WinCloseClipbrd*. The *WinQueryClipbrdData* function gives your program temporary access to the shared memory block containing the data stored by the clipboard. As with the Cut and Copy operations, the most difficult part of a Paste operation is the code involved in using this shared memory segment.

Again, you should define two variables of type SEL and PCHAR:

```
SEL    selClipText ;
PCHAR pchClipText ;
```

You begin by opening the clipboard:

```
WinOpenClipbrd (hab) ;
```

You then obtain a selector to the text block stored in the clipboard by calling *WinQueryClipbrdData*:

```
selClipText = (SEL) WinQueryClipbrdData (hab, CF_TEXT) ;
```

The return value of *WinQueryClipbrdData* is declared as a ULONG. To prevent compiler warning messages, you must cast this value to a SEL before assigning it to *selClipText*. If there is no text in the clipboard, *WinQueryClipbrdData* returns a 0L. In that case, you simply call *WinCloseClipbrd*. If *selClipText* is nonzero, you can continue by converting the selector to a far pointer:

```
pchClipText = MAKEP (selClipText, 0) ;
```

The *pchClipText* pointer points to the shared memory block containing clipboard text contents. During the *WinQueryClipbrdData* call, the Presentation Manager calls *DosGiveSeg* to give your program access to this segment.

You can reference this shared memory block only while the clipboard is still open. Do not alter the text in the clipboard.

The block of text is terminated by a zero byte. If your program is compiled for compact or large model, you can use the *strlen* function to determine the length of the string:

```
usLen = strlen (pchClipText) ;
```

Otherwise, you can use some simple code for this:

```
for (usLen = 0 ; pchClipbrdText[usLen] ; usLen++) ;
```

What you do with this text depends on the program. For example, you may want to allocate a block of local memory using *malloc* and copy the text into that local block:

```
pchText = malloc (usLen + 1) ;

for (usIndex = 0 ; usIndex < usLen + 1 ; usIndex++)
    pchText[usIndex] = pchClipText[usIndex] ;
```

When you finish referencing the clipboard text, you close the clipboard:

```
WinCloseClipbrd (hab) ;
```

Do not attempt to use the *pchClipText* pointer after the clipboard is closed, because the segment is freed for use by your process.

The Open Clipboard

Only one process can have the clipboard open at a time. If one program has the clipboard open and another program calls *WinOpenClipbrd*, the function will not return until the first program calls *WinCloseClipbrd*. For this reason, you should call *WinOpenClipbrd* and *WinCloseClipbrd* within the course of a single message.

You can also obtain information about the current contents of the clipboard without opening the clipboard. The following function call returns TRUE if the clipboard contains data in the CF_TEXT format and FALSE otherwise:

```
WinQueryClipbrdFmtInfo (hab, CF_TEXT, &usf   Info)
```

On return from the function, the *usfInfo* variable is set to CFI_SELECTOR if the clipboard contains data in the CF_TEXT format.

The *WinQueryClipbrdFmtInfo* function is also very handy during processing of the WM_INITMENU message. When the Edit submenu is invoked, the Presentation Manager sends your program a WM_INITMENU message with the low USHORT of *mp1* set to the menu ID of the Edit menu. You can take this opportunity to enable or disable the Cut, Copy, Paste, and Clear options. You disable the Cut, Copy, and Clear options if the user has not selected any text in the document. You disable the Paste option if *WinQueryClipbrdFmtInfo* returns FALSE. However, to be on the safe side, you should still check for a zero return value from *WinQueryClipbrdData* when you carry out the Paste command.

The TYPECLIP Program

The TYPECLIP program shown in Figure 15-1 illustrates the use of the clipboard for text transfer.

The TYPECLIP File

```
#--------------------
# TYPECLIP make file
#--------------------

typeclip.obj : typeclip.c typeclip.h
     cl -c -G2sw -W3 typeclip.c

typeclip.res : typeclip.rc typeclip.h
     rc -r typeclip

typeclip.exe : typeclip.obj typeclip.def
     link typeclip, /align:16, NUL, os2, typeclip
     rc typeclip.res

typeclip.exe : typeclip.res
     rc typeclip.res
```

The TYPECLIP.C File

```
/*------------------------------------------------
   TYPECLIP.C -- Clipboard Text Demonstration
   ------------------------------------------------*/

#define INCL_WIN
#define INCL_VIO
#define INCL_AVIO
#include <os2.h>
```

(continued)

Figure 15-1. The TYPECLIP.C File. *continued*

```
#include <stdlib.h>
#include "typeclip.h"

#define WM_ADJUST_ORG     (WM_USER + 0)
#define WM_SET_BLOCKOUT   (WM_USER + 1)
#define WM_CLEAR_BLOCKOUT (WM_USER + 2)

MRESULT EXPENTRY ClientWndProc (HWND, USHORT, MPARAM, MPARAM) ;

HAB  hab ;

int main (void)
    {
    static CHAR  szClientClass [] = "TypeClip" ;
    static ULONG flFrameFlags = FCF_TITLEBAR      | FCF_SYSMENU   |
                                FCF_SIZEBORDER    | FCF_MINMAX    |
                                FCF_SHELLPOSITION | FCF_TASKLIST  |
                                FCF_MENU          | FCF_ACCELTABLE ;
    HMQ         hmq ;
    HWND        hwndFrame, hwndClient ;
    QMSG        qmsg ;

    hab = WinInitialize (0) ;
    hmq = WinCreateMsgQueue (hab, 0) ;

    WinRegisterClass (hab, szClientClass, ClientWndProc, 0L, 0) ;

    hwndFrame = WinCreateStdWindow (HWND_DESKTOP, WS_VISIBLE,
                                    &flFrameFlags, szClientClass, NULL,
                                    0L, NULL, ID_RESOURCE, &hwndClient) ;

    WinSendMsg (hwndFrame, WM_SETICON,
                WinQuerySysPointer (HWND_DESKTOP, SPTR_APPICON, FALSE),
                NULL) ;

    while (WinGetMsg (hab, &qmsg, NULL, 0, 0))
        WinDispatchMsg (hab, &qmsg) ;

    WinDestroyWindow (hwndFrame) ;
    WinDestroyMsgQueue (hmq) ;
    WinTerminate (hab) ;
    return 0 ;
    }
```

(continued)

Figure 15-1. The TYPECLIP.C File. *continued*

```
MRESULT EXPENTRY ClientWndProc (HWND hwnd, USHORT msg, MPARAM mp1, MPARAM mp2)
     {
     static BOOL  fCapture, fValidBlock ;
     static HPS   hps ;
     static HVPS  hvps ;
     static HWND  hwndMenu ;
     static LONG  cxChar, cyChar ;
     static SHORT cxClient, cyClient, cxVioSize, cyVioSize,
                  xBlockBeg, yBlockBeg, xBlockEnd, yBlockEnd,
                  xBeg, yBeg, xEnd, yEnd ;
     CHAR         *pchText ;
     HDC          hdc ;
     PCHAR        pchClipText ;
     RECTL        rcl ;
     SEL          selClipText ;
     SHORT        sRep, sLen, x, y, s,
                  xCursor, yCursor, xOrigin, yOrigin ;
     SIZEL        sizl ;
     USHORT       usfInfo ;

     switch (msg)
          {
                            /*-------------------------------------------
                              Create, paint, and destroy processing
                            -----------------------------------------*/
          case WM_CREATE:
               hdc = WinOpenWindowDC (hwnd) ;

               DevQueryCaps (hdc, CAPS_CHAR_WIDTH, 1L, &cxChar) ;
               DevQueryCaps (hdc, CAPS_CHAR_HEIGHT, 1L, &cyChar) ;

               cxVioSize = (SHORT) (WinQuerySysValue (HWND_DESKTOP,
                                        SV_CXFULLSCREEN) / cxChar) ;

               cyVioSize = (SHORT) (WinQuerySysValue (HWND_DESKTOP,
                                        SV_CYFULLSCREEN) / cyChar) ;

               sizl.cx = sizl.cy = 0 ;
               hps = GpiCreatePS (hab, hdc, &sizl, PU_PELS  | GPIF_DEFAULT |
                                            GPIT_MICRO | GPIA_ASSOC) ;

               VioCreatePS (&hvps, cyVioSize, cxVioSize, 0, 1, NULL) ;
               VioAssociate (hdc, hvps) ;
```

(continued)

Figure 15-1. The TYPECLIP.C File. *continued*

```
                    hwndMenu = WinWindowFromID (
                                  WinQueryWindow (hwnd, QW_PARENT, FALSE),
                                  FID_MENU) ;
                    return 0 ;

          case WM_PAINT:
               WinBeginPaint (hwnd, hps, NULL) ;

               WinQueryWindowRect (hwnd, &rcl) ;
               WinFillRect (hps, &rcl, CLR_BLACK) ;

               VioShowBuf (0, cxVioSize * cyVioSize * 2, hvps) ;

               WinEndPaint (hps) ;
               return 0 ;

          case WM_DESTROY:
               VioAssociate (NULL, hvps) ;
               VioDestroyPS (hvps) ;
               GpiDestroyPS (hps) ;
               return 0 ;
                              /*----------------------------------------------
                                Window size, keyboard and origin handling
                              ----------------------------------------------*/
          case WM_SIZE:
               WinDefAVioWindowProc (hwnd, msg, mp1, mp2) ;

               cxClient = SHORT1FROMMP (mp2) ;
               cyClient = SHORT2FROMMP (mp2) ;

               VioSetOrg (0, 0, hvps) ;
               WinSendMsg (hwnd, WM_ADJUST_ORG, NULL, NULL) ;
               return 0 ;

          case WM_CHAR:
               if (!(CHARMSG(&msg)->fs & KC_CHAR)         ||
                    (CHARMSG(&msg)->fs & KC_KEYUP)         ||
                    (CHARMSG(&msg)->fs & KC_INVALIDCHAR)  ||
                    (CHARMSG(&msg)->fs & KC_DEADKEY))
                         return 0 ;

               for (sRep = 0 ; sRep < CHARMSG(&msg)->cRepeat ; sRep++)
                    {
                    VioWrtTTY ((PCHAR) & CHARMSG(&msg)->chr, 1, hvps) ;
```

(continued)

Figure 15-1. The TYPECLIP.C File. *continued*

```
            switch (CHARMSG(&msg)->chr)
                {
                case '\b':                          // Backspace
                     VioWrtTTY (" \b", 2, hvps) ;
                     break ;

                case '\r':                          // Return
                     VioWrtTTY ("\n", 1, hvps) ;
                     break ;
                }
            }
        WinSendMsg (hwnd, WM_ADJUST_ORG, NULL, NULL) ;
        return 1 ;

    case WM_ADJUST_ORG:
        VioGetOrg    (&yOrigin, &xOrigin, hvps) ;
        VioGetCurPos (&yCursor, &xCursor, hvps) ;

        if (xCursor < xOrigin)
            xOrigin = xCursor ;

        else if (xCursor >= xOrigin + cxClient / (SHORT) cxChar)
            xOrigin = xCursor - cxClient / (SHORT) cxChar + 1 ;

        if (yCursor < yOrigin)
            yOrigin = yCursor ;

        else if (yCursor >= yOrigin + cyClient / (SHORT) cyChar)
            yOrigin = yCursor - cyClient / (SHORT) cyChar + 1 ;

        VioSetOrg (yOrigin, xOrigin, hvps) ;
        return 0 ;
                        /*-------------------------------
                          Mouse and blockout handling
                        -----------------------------*/
    case WM_BUTTON1DOWN:
        x = MOUSEMSG(&msg)->x / (SHORT) cxChar ;
        y = (cyClient - MOUSEMSG(&msg)->y) / (SHORT) cyChar ;

        WinSendMsg (hwnd, WM_CLEAR_BLOCKOUT, NULL, NULL) ;

        WinSetCapture (HWND_DESKTOP, hwnd) ;
        fCapture = TRUE ;
        fValidBlock = FALSE ;
```

(continued)

Figure 15-1. The TYPECLIP.C File. *continued*

```
            VioGetOrg (&yOrigin, &xOrigin, hvps) ;

            xBlockBeg = xOrigin + x ;
            yBlockBeg = yOrigin + y ;

            WinSendMsg (hwnd, WM_SET_BLOCKOUT, mp1, mp2) ;
            break ;

      case WM_MOUSEMOVE:
            if (fCapture)
                 WinSendMsg (hwnd, WM_SET_BLOCKOUT, mp1, mp2) ;
            break ;

      case WM_BUTTON1UP:
            if (fCapture)
                 {
                 WinSetCapture (HWND_DESKTOP, NULL) ;
                 fCapture = FALSE ;
                 fValidBlock = TRUE ;

                 WinSendMsg (hwnd, WM_SET_BLOCKOUT, mp1, mp2) ;
                 }
            return 1 ;

      case WM_SET_BLOCKOUT:
            x = MOUSEMSG(&msg)->x / (SHORT) cxChar ;
            y = (cyClient - MOUSEMSG(&msg)->y) / (SHORT) cyChar ;

            VioGetOrg (&yOrigin, &xOrigin, hvps) ;

            xBlockEnd = xOrigin + x ;
            yBlockEnd = yOrigin + y ;

            if (cxVioSize * yBlockBeg + xBlockBeg <
                cxVioSize * yBlockEnd + xBlockEnd)
                 {
                 xBeg = xBlockBeg ;
                 yBeg = yBlockBeg ;
                 xEnd = xBlockEnd ;
                 yEnd = yBlockEnd ;
                 }
```

(continued)

Figure 15-1. The TYPECLIP.C File. *continued*

```
      else
          {
          xBeg = xBlockEnd ;
          yBeg = yBlockEnd ;
          xEnd = xBlockBeg ;
          yEnd = yBlockBeg ;
          }

      VioWrtNAttr ("\x07", cxVioSize * yBeg + xBeg, 0, 0, hvps) ;

      VioWrtNAttr ("\x70",  cxVioSize * yEnd + xEnd -
                            (cxVioSize * yBeg + xBeg) + 1,
                            yBeg, xBeg, hvps) ;

      VioWrtNAttr ("\x07",  cxVioSize * cyVioSize -
                            (cxVioSize * yEnd + xEnd) - 1,
                            yEnd, xEnd + 1, hvps) ;
      break ;

case WM_CLEAR_BLOCKOUT:
      VioWrtNAttr ("\x07", cxVioSize * cyVioSize, 0, 0, hvps) ;
      fValidBlock = FALSE ;
      break ;
                      /*--------------------
                        Clipboard handling
                        --------------------*/
case WM_INITMENU:
      switch (SHORT1FROMMP (mp1))
          {
          case IDM_EDIT:
              WinSendMsg (hwndMenu, MM_SETITEMATTR,
                          MPFROM2SHORT (IDM_CUT, TRUE),
                          MPFROM2SHORT (MIA_DISABLED,
                              fValidBlock ? 0 : MIA_DISABLED)) ;

              WinSendMsg (hwndMenu, MM_SETITEMATTR,
                          MPFROM2SHORT (IDM_COPY, TRUE),
                          MPFROM2SHORT (MIA_DISABLED,
                              fValidBlock ? 0 : MIA_DISABLED)) ;

              WinSendMsg (hwndMenu, MM_SETITEMATTR,
                          MPFROM2SHORT (IDM_CLEAR, TRUE),
                          MPFROM2SHORT (MIA_DISABLED,
                              fValidBlock ? 0 : MIA_DISABLED)) ;
```

(continued)

Figure 15-1. The TYPECLIP.C File. *continued*

```
                        WinSendMsg (hwndMenu, MM_SETITEMATTR,
                                 MPFROM2SHORT (IDM_PASTE, TRUE),
                                 MPFROM2SHORT (MIA_DISABLED,
                             WinQueryClipbrdFmtInfo (hab, CF_TEXT, &usfInfo)
                                           ? 0 : MIA_DISABLED)) ;
                    return 0 ;
                }
            break ;

        case WM_COMMAND:
            switch (COMMANDMSG(&msg)->cmd)
                {
                case IDM_CUT:
                case IDM_COPY:
                    if (!fValidBlock)
                        return 0 ;
                                                    // Copy text to
                                                    // malloc'ed memory

                    sLen = (cxVioSize + 2) * (yEnd - yBeg + 1) + 1 ;
                    pchText = malloc (sLen) ;

                    for (s = 0, y = yBeg ; y <= yEnd ; y++)
                        {
                        x    = (y == yBeg ? xBeg : 0) ;
                        sLen = (y == yEnd ? xEnd + 1 : cxVioSize) - x ;

                        VioReadCharStr (pchText + s, &sLen,
                                    y, x, hvps) ;

                        s += sLen ;
                        while (--s >= 0 && pchText[s] == ' ') ;

                        s++ ;
                        pchText[s++] = '\r' ;
                        pchText[s++] = '\n' ;
                        }
                    pchText[s++] = '\0' ;           // s is string length

                                                    // Allocate memory block

                    DosAllocSeg (s, &selClipText, SEG_GIVEABLE) ;
                    pchClipText = MAKEP (selClipText, 0) ;

                                                    // Copy to giveable seg
```

(continued)

Figure 15-1. The TYPECLIP.C File. *continued*

```
                    for (s = 0 ; pchClipText[s] = pchText[s] ; s++) ;
                    free (pchText) ;
                                                   // Set clipboard data
               WinOpenClipbrd (hab) ;
               WinEmptyClipbrd (hab) ;
               WinSetClipbrdData (hab, (ULONG) selClipText,
                                 CF_TEXT, CFI_SELECTOR) ;
               WinCloseClipbrd (hab) ;
                                                   // Clear blockout

               if (COMMANDMSG(&msg)->cmd == IDM_COPY)
                    {
                    WinSendMsg (hwnd, WM_CLEAR_BLOCKOUT, NULL, NULL);
                    return 0 ;
                    }
                                        // fall through for IDM_CUT
          case IDM_CLEAR:
               if (!fValidBlock)
                    return 0 ;
                                                   // Clear selection

               VioWrtNCell (" \x07",  cxVioSize * yEnd + xEnd -
                                     (cxVioSize * yBeg + xBeg) + 1,
                                     yBeg, xBeg, hvps) ;
               fValidBlock = FALSE ;
               return 0 ;

          case IDM_PASTE:
                                        // Get text selector from clipboard

               WinOpenClipbrd (hab) ;
               selClipText = (SEL) WinQueryClipbrdData (hab,
                                                       CF_TEXT) ;
                                        // Display to screen

               if (selClipText != 0)
                    {
                    pchClipText = MAKEP (selClipText, 0) ;

                    for (sLen = 0 ; pchClipText[sLen] ; sLen++) ;

                    VioWrtTTY (pchClipText, sLen, hvps) ;
                    }
               WinCloseClipbrd (hab) ;
```

(continued)

Figure 15-1. The TYPECLIP.C File. *continued*

```
                        WinSendMsg (hwnd, WM_ADJUST_ORG, NULL, NULL) ;
                        return 0 ;
                }
            break ;
        }
    return WinDefWindowProc (hwnd, msg, mp1, mp2) ;
    }
```

The TYPECLIP.H File

```
/*-----------------------
    TYPECLIP.H header file
------------------------*/

#define ID_RESOURCE       1

#define IDM_EDIT         10
#define IDM_CUT          11
#define IDM_COPY         12
#define IDM_PASTE        13
#define IDM_CLEAR        14
```

The TYPECLIP.RC File

```
/*-----------------------------------
    TYPECLIP.RC resource script file
-----------------------------------*/

#include <os2.h>
#include "typeclip.h"

MENU ID_RESOURCE
    {
    SUBMENU "~Edit",            IDM_EDIT
        {
        MENUITEM "Cu~t\tShift+Del",    IDM_CUT
        MENUITEM "~Copy\tCtrl+Ins",    IDM_COPY
        MENUITEM "~Paste\tShift+Ins", IDM_PASTE
        MENUITEM "C~lear\tDel",        IDM_CLEAR
        }
    }
```

(continued)

Figure 15-1. The TYPECLIP.RC File. *continued*

```
ACCELTABLE ID_RESOURCE
    {
    VK_DELETE, IDM_CUT,   VIRTUALKEY, SHIFT
    VK_INSERT, IDM_COPY,  VIRTUALKEY, CONTROL
    VK_INSERT, IDM_PASTE, VIRTUALKEY, SHIFT
    VK_DELETE, IDM_CLEAR, VIRTUALKEY
    }
```

The TYPECLIP.DEF File

```
;------------------------------------
; TYPECLIP.DEF module definition file
;------------------------------------


NAME            TYPECLIP  WINDOWAPI

DESCRIPTION     'Clipboard Text Demonstration (C) Charles Petzold, 1988'
PROTMODE
HEAPSIZE        1024
STACKSIZE       8192
EXPORTS         ClientWndProc
```

Figure 15-1. *The TYPECLIP program.*

To keep the non-clipboard logic of TYPECLIP to a minimum (but still allow the program to do something), the program uses Advanced VIO and displays typed text in a simple teletype manner using *VioWriteTTY*. You can use only character keys, Enter, Backspace, and Tab when typing text. TYPECLIP doesn't interpret the cursor movement keys as the TYPEAWAY program shown in Chapter 8 does.

You use the mouse to select a block of text from the text displayed in the window. Press the mouse button at the beginning of the text you want to select, move the mouse pointer to the end of the text, and release the button. The selected text appears in reverse colors.

You can then select Cut, Copy, or Clear from the Edit menu to perform the standard clipboard options. Cut and Copy copy the selection to the clipboard; Cut and Clear delete the selection from the document. You can also select Paste from the Edit menu to insert the contents of the clipboard at the cursor position.

TYPECLIP's *ClientWndProc* window procedure is divided into four major sections, delimited by comments in TYPECLIP.C. The following text describes each of these four sections.

Handling the VIO Presentation Space

The first section of the program handles the WM_CREATE, WM_PAINT, and WM_DESTROY messages. This section of the program is mostly devoted to creating, maintaining, and destroying the VIO presentation space, as discussed in Chapter 7. TYPECLIP calls *DevQueryCaps* to obtain the size of the Advanced VIO character and creates a VIO presentation space the size of the maximized client window. The WM_PAINT processing simply erases the background to black and updates the window using *VioShowBuf*.

Handling Window Sizing and the Keyboard

The second section of the program handles window sizing and the keyboard. If the window is not maximized, the cursor can be moved outside the visible part of the VIO presentation space. In this case, TYPECLIP uses *VioSetOrg* to set the presentation space origin (the character cell appearing in the upper-left corner of the client window) so that the cursor is always visible. This little job must be done during both the WM_SIZE and WM_CHAR messages.

Rather than use a subroutine for changing the origin, I've defined a new message called WM_ADJUST_ORG. *ClientWndProc* calls *WinSendMsg* during the WM_SIZE and WM_CHAR messages to send itself a WM_ADJUST_ORG message. During the WM_ADJUST_ORG message, *ClientWndProc* checks to see if the cursor is positioned within the visible area of the client window and sets a different origin if it is not.

The keyboard processing is very simple. The program processes only WM_CHAR messages with the KC_CHAR flag set and ignores dead keys. The characters are displayed on the window using the *VioWrtTTY* function. Only for the Enter and Backspace keys does TYPECLIP need a little extra logic: When the Enter key is pressed, a linefeed (\n) character must also be written to the presentation space. Normally, a Backspace (\b) character written through *VioWrtTTY* does not erase characters; it simply moves the cursor back one space. TYPECLIP writes a space and another Backspace (after the first Backspace) to fix this.

Handling the Mouse

The third section of *ClientWndProc* handles the mouse. Two other defined messages — WM_CLEAR_BLOCKOUT and WM_SET_BLOCKOUT — help out with the mouse logic. During the WM_BUTTON1DOWN message the mouse is captured, and the position of the mouse (in terms of the character column and row) is stored in *xBlockBeg* and *yBlockBeg*.

ClientWndProc sends a WM_SET_BLOCKOUT message to itself as part of the WM_MOUSEMOVE and WM_BUTTON1UP messages if the mouse is currently captured. During the WM_SET_BLOCKOUT message, *Client-WndProc* inverts the selected text. This inversion requires three calls to *VioWrtNAttr*. The normal attribute is \x07 (light gray text on a black background). The selected text is displayed with attribute \x70 (black on light gray).

Handling the Clipboard

The fourth section of *ClientWndProc* is responsible for clipboard handling. *ClientWndProc* processes the WM_INITMENU message to enable and disable the menu options when the Edit submenu is displayed. The Cut, Copy, and Clear options are enabled if the variable *fValidBlock* (which indicates that an area of the text has been selected) is TRUE. The Paste option is enabled if *WinQueryClipbrdFmtInfo* with a CF_TEXT parameter returns a value of TRUE.

The WM_COMMAND processing checks for menu IDs of IDM_CUT, IDM_COPY, IDM_PASTE, and IDM_CLEAR. The Cut and Copy commands start out the same. Both of these commands require the program to copy the selected text to the clipboard. TYPECLIP uses *malloc* to get some temporary memory for this job. The program uses *VioReadCharStr* to read each selected line of text from the VIO virtual display buffer into this local memory block. Trailing blanks at the end of each line are discarded, and each line is terminated by a carriage return and linefeed character. The whole block is terminated with a zero byte.

TYPECLIP then allocates a block of shareable memory by calling *Dos-AllocSeg*, copies the prepared block into the shared memory segment, and moves the segment into the clipboard by calling the four standard clipboard functions. The Copy logic is now finished. But the WM_COMMAND message for a Cut continues with the same logic used for a Clear command. This deletes the selection from the virtual display buffer.

The Paste logic is fairly simple. Because TYPECLIP pastes text at the cursor position, it need only find the length of the string and write it to the window by calling *VioWrtTTY*.

The Clipboard and HEXCALC2

Now that we can copy text into the clipboard with TYPECLIP, let's put that clipboard text to use. You'll recall the HEXCALC program from Chapter 14. A revised version, called HEXCALC2 (Figure 15-2 on the following page), uses the clipboard to read a string of hexadecimal numbers and symbols (such as + and −) and calculate the result.

The HEXCALC2 File

```
#-------------------
# HEXCALC2 make file
#-------------------

hexcalc2.obj: hexcalc2.c hexcalc.h
     cl -c -G2sw -W3 hexcalc2.c

hexcalc.res : hexcalc.rc hexcalc.h
     rc -r hexcalc.rc

hexcalc2.exe : hexcalc2.obj hexcalc2.def
     link hexcalc2, /align:16, NUL, os2, hexcalc2
     rc hexcalc.res hexcalc2.exe

hexcalc2.exe : hexcalc.res
     rc hexcalc.res hexcalc2.exe
```

The HEXCALC2.C File

```
/*-------------------------------------------------------------------
   HEXCALC2.C -- Hexadecimal Calculator with Clipboard Cut and Paste
   ----------------------------------------------------------------*/

#define INCL_WIN
#include <os2.h>
#include <ctype.h>
#include <limits.h>
#include <stdlib.h>
#include <string.h>
#include "hexcalc.h"

#define IDM_COPY    256
#define IDM_PASTE   257

MRESULT EXPENTRY ClientWndProc (HWND, USHORT, MPARAM, MPARAM) ;

HAB  hab ;

int main (void)
     {
     HMQ  hmq ;
     HWND hwndFrame ;
     QMSG qmsg ;
```

(continued)

Figure 15-2. The HEXCALC2.C File. *continued*

```
    hab = WinInitialize (0) ;
    hmq = WinCreateMsgQueue (hab, 0) ;

    WinRegisterClass (hab, CLIENTCLASS, ClientWndProc, OL, 0) ;

    hwndFrame = WinLoadDlg (HWND_DESKTOP, HWND_DESKTOP,
                          NULL, NULL, ID_HEXCALC, NULL) ;

    WinSendMsg (hwndFrame, WM_SETICON,
            WinLoadPointer (HWND_DESKTOP, NULL, ID_ICON), NULL) ;

    WinSetFocus (HWND_DESKTOP, WinWindowFromID (hwndFrame, FID_CLIENT)) ;

    while (WinGetMsg (hab, &qmsg, NULL, 0, 0))
        WinDispatchMsg (hab, &qmsg) ;

    WinDestroyWindow (hwndFrame) ;
    WinDestroyMsgQueue (hmq) ;
    WinTerminate (hab) ;
    return 0 ;
    }

HACCEL AddItemsToSysMenu (HWND hwndFrame)
    {
    static CHAR     *szMenuText [3] = { NULL, "~Copy\tCtrl+Ins",
                                            "~Paste\tShift+Ins" } ;
    static MENUITEM mi [3] = {
                        MIT_END, MIS_SEPARATOR, 0, 0,          NULL, NULL,
                        MIT_END, MIS_TEXT,      0, IDM_COPY,   NULL, NULL,
                        MIT_END, MIS_TEXT,      0, IDM_PASTE, NULL, NULL
                        } ;
    ACCELTABLE      *pacct ;
    HACCEL          haccel ;
    HWND            hwndSysMenu, hwndSysSubMenu ;
    MENUITEM        miSysMenu ;
    SHORT           idSysMenu, sItem ;

                        // Add items to system menu

    hwndSysMenu = WinWindowFromID (hwndFrame, FID_SYSMENU) ;
    idSysMenu = SHORT1FROMMR (WinSendMsg (hwndSysMenu,
                                    MM_ITEMIDFROMPOSITION,
                                    NULL, NULL)) ;
```

(continued)

Figure 15-2. The HEXCALC2.C File. *continued*

```
        WinSendMsg (hwndSysMenu, MM_QUERYITEM,
                    MPFROM2SHORT (idSysMenu, FALSE),
                    MPFROMP (&miSysMenu)) ;


        hwndSysSubMenu = miSysMenu.hwndSubMenu ;

        for (sItem = 0 ; sItem < 3 ; sItem++)
             WinSendMsg (hwndSysSubMenu, MM_INSERTITEM,
                         MPFROMP (mi + sItem),
                         MPFROMP (szMenuText [sItem])) ;

                                    // Create and set accelerator table

        pacct = malloc (sizeof (ACCELTABLE) + sizeof (ACCEL)) ;

        pacct->cAccel      = 2 ;     // Number of accelerators
        pacct->codepage    = 0 ;     // Not used

        pacct->aaccel[0].fs  = AF_VIRTUALKEY | AF_CONTROL ;
        pacct->aaccel[0].key = VK_INSERT ;
        pacct->aaccel[0].cmd = IDM_COPY ;

        pacct->aaccel[1].fs  = AF_VIRTUALKEY | AF_SHIFT ;
        pacct->aaccel[1].key = VK_INSERT ;
        pacct->aaccel[1].cmd = IDM_PASTE ;

        haccel = WinCreateAccelTable (hab, pacct) ;
        WinSetAccelTable (hab, haccel, hwndFrame) ;

        free (pacct) ;

        return haccel ;
        }


VOID EnableSysMenuItem (HWND hwnd, USHORT idItem, BOOL fEnable)
        {
        HWND hwndSysMenu ;

        hwndSysMenu = WinWindowFromID (WinQueryWindow (hwnd, QW_PARENT, FALSE),
                                       FID_SYSMENU) ;

        WinSendMsg (hwndSysMenu, MM_SETITEMATTR,
                    MPFROM2SHORT (idItem, TRUE),
                    MPFROM2SHORT (MIA_DISABLED, fEnable ? 0 : MIA_DISABLED)) ;
        }
```

(continued)

Figure 15-2. The HEXCALC2.C File. *continued*

```
void ShowNumber (HWND hwnd, ULONG ulNumber)
    {
    CHAR szBuffer [20] ;

    WinSetWindowText (WinWindowFromID (hwnd, ESCAPE),
                      strupr (ltoa (ulNumber, szBuffer, 16))) ;
    }

ULONG CalcIt (ULONG ulFirstNum, SHORT sOperation, ULONG ulNum)
    {
    switch (sOperation)
        {
        case '=' : return ulNum ;
        case '+' : return ulFirstNum +  ulNum ;
        case '-' : return ulFirstNum -  ulNum ;
        case '*' : return ulFirstNum *  ulNum ;
        case '&' : return ulFirstNum &  ulNum ;
        case '¦' : return ulFirstNum ¦  ulNum ;
        case '^' : return ulFirstNum ^  ulNum ;
        case '<' : return ulFirstNum << ulNum ;
        case '>' : return ulFirstNum >> ulNum ;
        case '/' : return ulNum ? ulFirstNum / ulNum : ULONG_MAX ;
        case '%' : return ulNum ? ulFirstNum % ulNum : ULONG_MAX ;
        default  : return 0L ;
        }
    }

MRESULT EXPENTRY ClientWndProc (HWND hwnd, USHORT msg, MPARAM mp1, MPARAM mp2)
    {
    static BOOL   fNewNumber = TRUE ;
    static HACCEL haccel ;
    static ULONG  ulNumber, ulFirstNum ;
    static SHORT  sOperation = '=' ;
    HWND          hwndButton ;
    PCHAR         pchClipText ;
    QMSG          qmsg ;
    SEL           selClipText ;
    SHORT         s, sLen, idButton ;

    switch (msg)
        {
        case WM_CREATE:
            haccel = AddItemsToSysMenu (
                         WinQueryWindow (hwnd, QW_PARENT, FALSE)) ;
            return 0 ;
```

(continued)

Figure 15-2. The HEXCALC2.C File. *continued*

```
     case WM_CHAR:
          if (CHARMSG(&msg)->fs & KC_KEYUP)
              return 0 ;

          if (CHARMSG(&msg)->fs & KC_VIRTUALKEY)
              switch (CHARMSG(&msg)->vkey)
                  {
                  case VK_LEFT:
                      if (!(CHARMSG(&msg)->fs & KC_CHAR))
                          {
                          CHARMSG(&msg)->chr = '\b' ;
                          CHARMSG(&msg)->fs |= KC_CHAR ;
                          }
                      break ;

                  case VK_ESC:
                      CHARMSG(&msg)->chr = ESCAPE ;
                      CHARMSG(&msg)->fs |= KC_CHAR ;
                      break ;

                  case VK_NEWLINE:
                  case VK_ENTER:
                      CHARMSG(&msg)->chr = '=' ;
                      CHARMSG(&msg)->fs |= KC_CHAR ;
                      break ;
                  }

          if (CHARMSG(&msg)->fs & KC_CHAR)
              {
              CHARMSG(&msg)->chr = toupper (CHARMSG(&msg)->chr) ;

              if (hwndButton = WinWindowFromID (hwnd,CHARMSG(&msg)->chr))
                  WinSendMsg (hwndButton, BM_CLICK, NULL, NULL) ;
              else
                  WinAlarm (HWND_DESKTOP, WA_ERROR) ;
              }
          return 1 ;

     case WM_COMMAND:
          idButton = COMMANDMSG(&msg)->cmd ;

          if (idButton == IDM_COPY)                    // "Copy"
              {
              hwndButton = WinWindowFromID (hwnd, ESCAPE) ;
              sLen = WinQueryWindowTextLength (hwndButton) + 1 ;
```

(continued)

Figure 15-2. The HEXCALC2.C File. *continued*

```
            DosAllocSeg (sLen, &selClipText, SEG_GIVEABLE) ;
            pchClipText = MAKEP (selClipText, 0) ;
            WinQueryWindowText (hwndButton, sLen, pchClipText) ;

            WinOpenClipbrd (hab) ;
            WinEmptyClipbrd (hab) ;
            WinSetClipbrdData (hab, (ULONG) selClipText, CF_TEXT,
                             CFI_SELECTOR) ;
            WinCloseClipbrd (hab) ;
            }

    else if (idButton == IDM_PASTE)                // "Paste"
            {
            EnableSysMenuItem (hwnd, IDM_COPY,  FALSE) ;
            EnableSysMenuItem (hwnd, IDM_PASTE, FALSE) ;

            WinOpenClipbrd (hab) ;

            selClipText = (SEL) WinQueryClipbrdData (hab, CF_TEXT) ;

            if (selClipText != 0)
                {
                pchClipText = MAKEP (selClipText, 0) ;

                for (s = 0 ; pchClipText[s] ; s++)
                    {
                    if (pchClipText[s] == '\r')
                        WinSendMsg (hwnd, WM_CHAR,
                                   MPFROM2SHORT (KC_CHAR, 1),
                                   MPFROM2SHORT ('=', 0)) ;

                    else if (pchClipText[s] != '\n' &&
                            pchClipText[s] != ' ')
                        WinSendMsg (hwnd, WM_CHAR,
                                   MPFROM2SHORT (KC_CHAR, 1),
                                   MPFROM2SHORT (pchClipText[s],
                                                  0)) ;

                    while (WinPeekMsg (hab, &qmsg, NULL, 0, 0,
                                    PM_NOREMOVE))
                        {
                        if (qmsg.msg == WM_QUIT)
                            {
                            WinCloseClipbrd (hab) ;
```

(continued)

Figure 15-2. The HEXCALC2.C File. *continued*

```
                                    return 0 ;
                                    }
                            else
                                    {
                                    WinGetMsg (hab, &qmsg, NULL, 0, 0) ;
                                    WinDispatchMsg (hab, &qmsg) ;
                                    }
                            }
                    }
            }
        WinCloseClipbrd (hab) ;

        EnableSysMenuItem (hwnd, IDM_COPY,  TRUE) ;
        EnableSysMenuItem (hwnd, IDM_PASTE, TRUE) ;
        }

else if (idButton == '\b')                      // backspace
        ShowNumber (hwnd, ulNumber /= 16) ;

else if (idButton == ESCAPE)                    // escape
        ShowNumber (hwnd, ulNumber = 0L) ;

else if (isxdigit (idButton))                   // hex digit
        {
        if (fNewNumber)
            {
            ulFirstNum = ulNumber ;
            ulNumber = 0L ;
            }
        fNewNumber = FALSE ;

        if (ulNumber <= ULONG_MAX >> 4)
                ShowNumber (hwnd,
                    ulNumber = 16 * ulNumber + idButton -
                        (isdigit (idButton) ? '0' : 'A' - 10)) ;
        else
            WinAlarm (HWND_DESKTOP, WA_ERROR) ;
        }
else                                            // operation
        {
        if (!fNewNumber)
                ShowNumber (hwnd, ulNumber =
                    CalcIt (ulFirstNum, sOperation, ulNumber)) ;
        fNewNumber = TRUE ;
```

(continued)

Figure 15-2. The HEXCALC2.C File. *continued*

```
                sOperation = idButton ;
                }
        return 0 ;

    case WM_BUTTON1DOWN:
        WinAlarm (HWND_DESKTOP, WA_ERROR) ;
        break ;

    case WM_ERASEBACKGROUND:
        return 1 ;

    case WM_DESTROY:
        WinDestroyAccelTable (haccel) ;
        return 0 ;
    }
    return WinDefWindowProc (hwnd, msg, mp1, mp2) ;
    }
```

The HEXCALC2.DEF File

```
;------------------------------------
; HEXCALC2 module definition file
;------------------------------------

NAME           HEXCALC2   WINDOWAPI

DESCRIPTION    'Hexadecimal Calculator With Clipboard (C) Charles Petzold 1988'
PROTMODE
HEAPSIZE       1024
STACKSIZE      8192
EXPORTS        ClientWndProc
```

Figure 15-2. *The HEXCALC2 program.*

Compiling HEXCALC2 also requires the HEXCALC.H, HEXCALC.RC, and HEXCALC.ICO files from Chapter 14.

The Copy and Paste options are located on HEXCALC2's System menu. You can copy the current result in HEXCALC2 (the number appearing in the top-most button) to the clipboard using Copy. But it is the Paste command that makes HEXCALC2 most useful. First enter the following text in TYPECLIP:

```
  123
+ 234
* 8
```

Select the text, and use the TYPECLIP Copy command to copy it to the clipboard. Now invoke the Paste command in HEXCALC2. The buttons will quickly flash as the characters are entered. The result then appears: *1AB8*. We've gone from a manual calculator to an automated one.

The *AddItemsToSysMenu* function in HEXCALC2.C adds the Copy and Paste options to the program's System menu using a technique discussed in Chapter 13. As you'll recall, both menus and buttons use WM_COMMAND messages to inform their owner of user input. HEXCALC2 makes use of buttons with IDs set to the ASCII codes of the button text. For this reason, the IDM_COPY and IDM_PASTE commands are given IDs of 256 and 257 — out of the range of the ASCII codes.

The *AddItemsToSysMenu* function also defines an accelerator table for the two new menu items. First, it uses *malloc* to allocate storage for a structure of type ACCELTABLE. One field of the ACCELTABLE structure is an array of structures of type ACCEL. An ACCEL structure exists for each item in the accelerator table. (The definition of ACCELTABLE in PMWIN.H allocates space for an array of only one ACCEL structure; this is why memory for a larger ACCELTABLE structure must be allocated using *malloc*.)

After the fields of the structure are initialized, the accelerator table is created by a call to *WinCreateAccelTable*, which returns a handle to the table. The *WinSetAccelTable* function causes the frame window to use this accelerator table. The handle to the accelerator table is returned from *WinAddItemsToSysMenu* back to *ClientWndProc* so that the accelerator table can be destroyed during processing of the WM_DESTROY message.

The WM_COMMAND processing in HEXCALC2 is expanded to include the Copy and Paste commands; the processing is quite different from that used in the TYPECLIP program.

For Copy, HEXCALC2 needs to retrieve the text displayed in the result button and make a copy for the clipboard. The ID of this button is the ASCII Escape code, so the button handle can be obtained by calling

```
hwndButton = WinWindowFromID (hwnd, ESCAPE) ;
```

HEXCALC2 obtains the length of the button text by calling

```
sLen = WinQueryWindowTextLength (hwndButton) + 1 ;
```

Because this statement adds 1 to the window text length, *sLen* is large enough to accommodate a terminating zero byte. As in TYPECLIP, a block of shareable memory is allocated, and a pointer is obtained:

```
DosAllocSeg (sLen, &selClipText, SEG_GIVEABLE) ;
pchClipText = MAKEP (selClipText, 0) ;
```

But HEXCALC2 need only call *WinQueryWindowText* to copy the button text into the shareable memory:

```
WinQueryWindowText (hwndButton, sLen, pchClipText) ;
```

Finally, HEXCALC2 calls the four standard clipboard functions:

```
WinOpenClipbrd (hab) ;
WinEmptyClipbrd (hab) ;
WinSetClipbrdData (hab, (ULONG) selClipText, CF_TEXT,
                   CFI_SELECTOR) ;
WinCloseClipbrd (hab) ;
```

Processing of the Paste command is also quite different from the earlier examples. It starts out in a fairly normal fashion. HEXCALC2 opens the clipboard and obtains a selector to the clipboard memory:

```
WinOpenClipbrd (hab) ;
selClipText = (SEL) WinQueryClipbrdData (hab, CF_TEXT) ;
```

But *ClientWndProc* doesn't need to store this text in local memory. Instead, the window procedure uses a *for* loop to go through the memory block and send the individual characters as WM_CHAR messages to itself. Any linefeed characters or space characters are ignored (normally HEXCALC2 would beep at these invalid characters), and carriage returns are translated into equal signs, but otherwise the characters are translated directly into WM_CHAR messages:

```
WinSendMsg (hwnd, WM_CHAR,
            MPFROM2SHORT (KC_CHAR, 1),
            MPFROM2SHORT (pchClipText[s], 0)) ;
```

This is why the buttons in HEXCALC2 flash when you paste a numeric calculation from the clipboard into the program: This Paste logic mimics your fingers.

Think about the message traffic for a moment. *ClientWndProc* receives a WM_COMMAND message for IDM_PASTE when you select Paste from the System menu. The window procedure processes this message by sending itself WM_CHAR messages of the characters from the clipboard. The

WM_CHAR processing in *ClientWndProc* obtains the window handle of the button that corresponds to the ASCII code in the WM_CHAR message and sends the button a BM_CLICK message. The button responds by flashing and posting a WM_COMMAND message to *ClientWndProc* with the button ID.

In response to the original WM_COMMAND message, the WM_CHAR and BM_CLICK messages are *sent* directly to the appropriate window procedure. But the WM_COMMAND message from the button (the final result of the Paste operation) is posted to the message queue. This is a problem because the message queue can store only a limited number of messages; it is quite possible that the queue will fill up with unprocessed WM_COMMAND messages from the buttons.

For this reason, the Paste processing in HEXCALC2 contains the following code, which is executed after each WM_CHAR message is sent:

```
while (WinPeekMsg (hab, &qmsg, NULL, 0, 0,
                   PM_NOREMOVE))
     {
     if (qmsg.msg == WM_QUIT)
          {
          WinCloseClipbrd (hab) ;
          return 0 ;
          }
     else
          {
          WinGetMsg (hab, &qmsg, NULL, 0, 0) ;
          WinDispatchMsg (hab, &qmsg) ;
          }
     }
```

The *WinPeekMsg* function is similar to *WinGetMsg* but with two important differences. First, the last parameter to *WinPeekMsg* can be set to either PM_REMOVE or PM_NOREMOVE to remove or not remove the next message from the message queue. Second, if no message exists in the message queue, *WinGetMsg* will wait for one. *WinPeekMsg* returns immediately if there are no pending messages. The return value of *WinPeekMsg* is TRUE if a message was retrieved from the queue and FALSE otherwise.

In HEXCALC2, *WinPeekMsg* uses the PM_NOREMOVE option. If *WinPeekMsg* returns TRUE, then for all messages except WM_QUIT (a case I'll discuss shortly) the message is retrieved from the queue with *WinGetMsg* and dispatched to the window procedure with *WinDispatchMsg*.

The primary purpose of the *WinPeekMsg* function in HEXCALC2 is to retrieve WM_COMMAND messages posted by the buttons and prevent the message queue from overflowing. But this code also has some interesting side effects. If you paste a lengthy calculation into HEXCALC2, you can continue to use the mouse and keyboard with the program. For example, you can use the mouse to move the HEXCALC2 window in the middle of the paste operation. These mouse messages are queued, so *WinPeekMsg* returns TRUE when it encounters one, and the messages are retrieved and dispatched as usual.

You can also select Close from the System menu in the middle of the Paste operation. For this reason, the WM_QUIT command is checked explicitly following the *WinPeekMsg* call. The WM_QUIT message is not removed from the message queue. HEXCALC2 simply closes the clipboard and stops the Paste operation by returning from the window procedure.

Of course, if you can select Close from the System menu while a Paste operation is in progress, you could also select Copy or Paste. For this reason, HEXCALC2 calls the *EnableSysMenuItem* function to disable these two items before the Paste operation. When Paste is finished, HEXCALC2 calls the function again to enable the items.

I'll have more to say about the *WinPeekMsg* function in Chapter 17.

Transferring Bitmaps with the Clipboard

In some ways, transferring bitmaps to and from the clipboard is easier than transferring text. The only hard part is that you generally must make a copy of any bitmap you put in the clipboard if you want to continue using the bitmap in your program. You must also make a copy of a bitmap you get from the clipboard if you want to use the bitmap after the clipboard is closed. In the sample BLOWUP program used in this section, I have a function called *CopyBitmap* that does this.

Transferring from Program to Clipboard

Suppose you have a handle to a bitmap, and it is stored in the variable *hbm* of type HBITMAP. You want to keep this handle, but you want to transfer a copy of the bitmap to the clipboard.

First, you make a copy of the bitmap and store the handle in another variable (named *hbmClip*, for example) of type HBITMAP:

```
hbmClip = CopyBitmap (hbm)
```

If the copy operation is successful, you call the same four functions you use to transfer text into the clipboard:

```
WinOpenClipbrd (hab) ;
WinEmptyClipbrd (hab) ;
WinSetClipbrdData (hab, (ULONG) hbmClip, CF_BITMAP, CFI_HANDLE) ;
WinCloseClipbrd ;
```

Notice that the second parameter to *WinSetClipbrdData* is the handle of the bitmap copy rather than a selector to shareable memory. This parameter is followed by the identifiers CF_BITMAP to indicate bitmap format and CFI_HANDLE to indicate that a handle is being passed as the second parameter.

Following the *WinSetClipbrdData* call, do not use or delete *hbmClip*. This copy of the bitmap is specifically for the clipboard.

Transferring from Clipboard to Program

To transfer a bitmap from the clipboard into your program, first open the clipboard and obtain the bitmap handle:

```
WinOpenClipbrd (hab) ;
hbmClip = WinQueryClipbrdData (hab, CF_BITMAP) ;
```

The *WinQueryClipbrdData* function returns 0L if the clipboard does not contain a bitmap. Thus *hbmClip* will be NULL. The *hbmClip* handle will be valid only when the clipboard is open. You'll probably want to make a copy of the bitmap and then close the clipboard:

```
if (hbmClip != NULL)
    hbm = CopyBitmap (hbmClip) ;

WinCloseClipbrd (hab) ;
```

I told you this was easy. Now all we need is that *CopyBitmap* function.

The BLOWUP Program

The *CopyBitmap* function, as well as some other goodies, is shown in the BLOWUP program in Figure 15-3.

The BLOWUP File

```
#-------------------
# BLOWUP make file
#-------------------

blowup.obj : blowup.c blowup.h
     cl -c -G2sw -W3 blowup.c

blowup.res : blowup.rc blowup.h
     rc -r blowup

blowup.exe : blowup.obj blowup.def
     link blowup, /align:16, NUL, os2, blowup
     rc blowup.res

blowup.exe : blowup.res
     rc blowup.res
```

The BLOWUP.C File

```
/*-------------------------------------
   BLOWUP.C -- Screen Capture Program
   -------------------------------------*/

#define INCL_WIN
#define INCL_GPI
#include <os2.h>
#include "blowup.h"

MRESULT EXPENTRY ClientWndProc (HWND, USHORT, MPARAM, MPARAM) ;

CHAR szClientClass [] = "BlowUp" ;
HAB  hab ;

int main (void)
     {
     static ULONG flFrameFlags = FCF_TITLEBAR      | FCF_SYSMENU   |
                                 FCF_SIZEBORDER    | FCF_MINMAX    |
                                 FCF_SHELLPOSITION | FCF_TASKLIST  |
                                 FCF_MENU          | FCF_ACCELTABLE ;
     HMQ          hmq ;
     HWND         hwndFrame, hwndClient ;
     QMSG         qmsg ;
```

(continued)

Figure 15-3. The BLOWUP.C File. *continued*

```
     hab = WinInitialize (0) ;
     hmq = WinCreateMsgQueue (hab, 0) ;

     WinRegisterClass (hab, szClientClass, ClientWndProc, CS_SIZEREDRAW, 0) ;

     hwndFrame = WinCreateStdWindow (HWND_DESKTOP, WS_VISIBLE,
                                     &flFrameFlags, szClientClass, NULL,
                                     OL, NULL, ID_RESOURCE, &hwndClient) ;

     WinSendMsg (hwndFrame, WM_SETICON,
                 WinQuerySysPointer (HWND_DESKTOP, SPTR_APPICON, FALSE),
                 NULL) ;

     while (WinGetMsg (hab, &qmsg, NULL, 0, 0))
          WinDispatchMsg (hab, &qmsg) ;

     WinDestroyWindow (hwndFrame) ;
     WinDestroyMsgQueue (hmq) ;
     WinTerminate (hab) ;
     return 0 ;
     }

BOOL BeginTracking (RECTL *prclTrack)
     {
     LONG      cxScreen, cyScreen, cxPointer, cyPointer ;
     TRACKINFO ti ;

     cxScreen  = WinQuerySysValue (HWND_DESKTOP, SV_CXSCREEN) ;
     cyScreen  = WinQuerySysValue (HWND_DESKTOP, SV_CYSCREEN) ;
     cxPointer = WinQuerySysValue (HWND_DESKTOP, SV_CXPOINTER) ;
     cyPointer = WinQuerySysValue (HWND_DESKTOP, SV_CYPOINTER) ;

                                   // Set up track rectangle for moving

     ti.cxBorder = 1 ;                      // Border width
     ti.cyBorder = 1 ;
     ti.cxGrid = 0 ;                        // Not used
     ti.cyGrid = 0 ;
     ti.cxKeyboard = 4 ;                    // Pixel increment for keyboard
     ti.cyKeyboard = 4 ;

     ti.rclBoundary.xLeft   = 0 ;           // Area for tracking rectangle
     ti.rclBoundary.yBottom = 0 ;
     ti.rclBoundary.xRight  = cxScreen ;
     ti.rclBoundary.yTop    = cyScreen ;
```

(continued)

Figure 15-3. The BLOWUP.C File. *continued*

```
      ti.ptlMinTrackSize.x = 1 ;                    // Minimum rectangle size
      ti.ptlMinTrackSize.y = 1 ;

      ti.ptlMaxTrackSize.x = cxScreen ;             // Maximum rectangle size
      ti.ptlMaxTrackSize.y = cyScreen ;
                                                    // Initial position

      ti.rclTrack.xLeft   = (cxScreen - cxPointer) / 2 ;
      ti.rclTrack.yBottom = (cyScreen - cyPointer) / 2 ;
      ti.rclTrack.xRight  = (cxScreen + cxPointer) / 2 ;
      ti.rclTrack.yTop    = (cyScreen + cyPointer) / 2 ;

      ti.fs = TF_MOVE | TF_STANDARD | TF_SETPOINTERPOS ;      // Flags

      if (!WinTrackRect (HWND_DESKTOP, NULL, &ti))
          return FALSE ;
                                    // Switch to "sizing" pointer
  WinSetPointer (HWND_DESKTOP,
          WinQuerySysPointer (HWND_DESKTOP, SPTR_SIZENESW, FALSE)) ;

                                    // Track rectangle for sizing

      ti.fs = TF_RIGHT | TF_TOP | TF_STANDARD | TF_SETPOINTERPOS ;

      if (!WinTrackRect (HWND_DESKTOP, NULL, &ti))
          return FALSE ;

      *prclTrack = ti.rclTrack ;    // Final rectangle

      return TRUE ;
      }

HBITMAP CopyScreenToBitmap (RECTL *prclTrack)
      {
      BITMAPINFOHEADER bmp ;
      HBITMAP          hbm ;
      HDC              hdcMemory ;
      HPS              hps, hpsMemory ;
      LONG             alBmpFormats[2] ;
      POINTL           aptl[3] ;
      SIZEL            sizl ;
                                    // Create memory DC and PS

      hdcMemory = DevOpenDC (hab, OD_MEMORY, "*", OL, NULL, NULL) ;
```

(continued)

Figure 15-3. The BLOWUP.C File. *continued*

```
        sizl.cx = sizl.cy = 0 ;
        hpsMemory = GpiCreatePS (hab, hdcMemory, &sizl,
                              PU_PELS   | GPIF_DEFAULT |
                              GPIT_MICRO | GPIA_ASSOC) ;

                                // Create bitmap for destination

        GpiQueryDeviceBitmapFormats (hpsMemory, 2L, alBmpFormats) ;

        bmp.cbFix      = sizeof bmp ;
        bmp.cx         = (USHORT) (prclTrack->xRight - prclTrack->xLeft) ;
        bmp.cy         = (USHORT) (prclTrack->yTop   - prclTrack->yBottom) ;
        bmp.cPlanes    = (USHORT) alBmpFormats[0] ;
        bmp.cBitCount  = (USHORT) alBmpFormats[1] ;

        hbm = GpiCreateBitmap (hpsMemory, &bmp, 0L, NULL, NULL) ;

                                // Copy from screen to bitmap
        if (hbm != NULL)
            {
            GpiSetBitmap (hpsMemory, hbm) ;
            hps = WinGetScreenPS (HWND_DESKTOP) ;

            aptl[0].x = 0 ;
            aptl[0].y = 0 ;
            aptl[1].x = bmp.cx ;
            aptl[1].y = bmp.cy ;
            aptl[2].x = prclTrack->xLeft ;
            aptl[2].y = prclTrack->yBottom ;

            WinLockVisRegions (HWND_DESKTOP, TRUE) ;

            GpiBitBlt (hpsMemory, hps, 3L, aptl, ROP_SRCCOPY, BBO_IGNORE);

            WinLockVisRegions (HWND_DESKTOP, FALSE) ;

            WinReleasePS (hps) ;
            }
                                // Clean up
        GpiDestroyPS (hpsMemory) ;
        DevCloseDC (hdcMemory) ;

        return hbm ;
        }
```

(continued)

Figure 15-3. The BLOWUP.C File. *continued*

```
HBITMAP CopyBitmap (HBITMAP hbmSrc)
    {
    BITMAPINFOHEADER bmp ;
    HBITMAP          hbmDst ;
    HDC              hdcSrc, hdcDst ;
    HPS              hpsSrc, hpsDst ;
    POINTL           aptl[3] ;
    SIZEL            sizl ;

                         // Create memory DC's and PS's

    hdcSrc = DevOpenDC (hab, OD_MEMORY, "*", OL, NULL, NULL) ;
    hdcDst = DevOpenDC (hab, OD_MEMORY, "*", OL, NULL, NULL) ;

    sizl.cx = sizl.cy = 0 ;
    hpsSrc = GpiCreatePS (hab, hdcSrc, &sizl, PU_PELS    | GPIF_DEFAULT |
                                              GPIT_MICRO | GPIA_ASSOC) ;

    hpsDst = GpiCreatePS (hab, hdcDst, &sizl, PU_PELS    | GPIF_DEFAULT |
                                              GPIT_MICRO | GPIA_ASSOC) ;

                         // Create bitmap

    GpiQueryBitmapParameters (hbmSrc, &bmp) ;
    hbmDst = GpiCreateBitmap (hpsDst, &bmp, OL, NULL, NULL) ;

                         // Copy from source to destination

    if (hbmDst != NULL)
        {
        GpiSetBitmap (hpsSrc, hbmSrc) ;
        GpiSetBitmap (hpsDst, hbmDst) ;

        aptl[0].x = aptl[0].y = 0 ;
        aptl[1].x = bmp.cx ;
        aptl[1].y = bmp.cy ;
        aptl[2]   = aptl[0] ;

        GpiBitBlt (hpsDst, hpsSrc, 3L, aptl, ROP_SRCCOPY, BBO_IGNORE) ;
        }
                         // Clean up
    GpiDestroyPS (hpsSrc) ;
    GpiDestroyPS (hpsDst) ;
    DevCloseDC (hdcSrc) ;
    DevCloseDC (hdcDst) ;
```

(continued)

Figure 15-3. The BLOWUP.C File. *continued*

```
    return hbmDst ;
    }


VOID BitmapCreationError (HWND hwnd)
    {
    WinMessageBox (HWND_DESKTOP, hwnd, "Cannot create bitmap.",
                   szClientClass, 0, MB_OK | MB_ICONEXCLAMATION) ;
    }


MRESULT EXPENTRY ClientWndProc (HWND hwnd, USHORT msg, MPARAM mp1, MPARAM mp2)
    {
    static HBITMAP   hbm ;
    static HWND      hwndMenu ;
    static SHORT     sDisplay = IDM_ACTUAL ;
    HBITMAP          hbmClip ;
    HPS              hps ;
    RECTL            rclTrack, rclClient ;
    USHORT           usfInfo ;

    switch (msg)
        {
        case WM_CREATE:
            hwndMenu = WinWindowFromID (
                          WinQueryWindow (hwnd, QW_PARENT, FALSE),
                          FID_MENU) ;
            return 0 ;


        case WM_INITMENU:
            switch (SHORT1FROMMP (mp1))
                {
                case IDM_EDIT:
                    WinSendMsg (hwndMenu, MM_SETITEMATTR,
                              MPFROM2SHORT (IDM_COPY, TRUE),
                              MPFROM2SHORT (MIA_DISABLED,
                                  hbm != NULL ? 0 : MIA_DISABLED)) ;

                    WinSendMsg (hwndMenu, MM_SETITEMATTR,
                              MPFROM2SHORT (IDM_PASTE, TRUE),
                              MPFROM2SHORT (MIA_DISABLED,
                              WinQueryClipbrdFmtInfo (hab, CF_BITMAP, &usfInfo)
                                  ? 0 : MIA_DISABLED)) ;
                    return 0 ;
                }
            break ;
```

(continued)

Figure 15-3. The BLOWUP.C File. *continued*

```
case WM_COMMAND:
     switch (COMMANDMSG(&msg)->cmd)
          {
          case IDM_COPY:
                              // Make copy of stored bitmap

               hbmClip = CopyBitmap (hbm) ;

                              // Set clipboard data to copy of bitmap

               if (hbmClip != NULL)
                    {
                    WinOpenClipbrd (hab) ;
                    WinEmptyClipbrd (hab) ;
                    WinSetClipbrdData (hab, (ULONG) hbmClip,
                                  CF_BITMAP, CFI_HANDLE) ;
                    WinCloseClipbrd (hab) ;
                    }
               else
                    BitmapCreationError (hwnd) ;
               return 0 ;

          case IDM_PASTE:
                              // Get bitmap from clipboard

               WinOpenClipbrd (hab) ;
               hbmClip = WinQueryClipbrdData (hab, CF_BITMAP) ;

               if (hbmClip != NULL)
                    {
                    if (hbm != NULL)
                         GpiDeleteBitmap (hbm) ;

                              // Make copy of it

                    hbm = CopyBitmap (hbmClip) ;

                    if (hbm == NULL)
                         BitmapCreationError (hwnd) ;
                    }
               WinCloseClipbrd (hab) ;
               WinInvalidateRect (hwnd, NULL, FALSE) ;
               return 0 ;
```

(continued)

Figure 15-3. The BLOWUP.C File. *continued*

```
                    case IDM_CAPTURE:
                        if (BeginTracking (&rclTrack))
                            {
                            if (hbm != NULL)
                                GpiDeleteBitmap (hbm) ;

                            hbm = CopyScreenToBitmap (&rclTrack) ;

                            if (hbm == NULL)
                                BitmapCreationError (hwnd) ;

                            WinInvalidateRect (hwnd, NULL, FALSE) ;
                            }
                        return 0 ;

                    case IDM_ACTUAL:
                    case IDM_STRETCH:
                        WinSendMsg (hwndMenu, MM_SETITEMATTR,
                                    MPFROM2SHORT (sDisplay, TRUE),
                                    MPFROM2SHORT (MIA_CHECKED, 0)) ;

                        sDisplay = COMMANDMSG(&msg)->cmd ;

                        WinSendMsg (hwndMenu, MM_SETITEMATTR,
                                    MPFROM2SHORT (sDisplay, TRUE),
                                    MPFROM2SHORT (MIA_CHECKED, MIA_CHECKED)) ;

                        WinInvalidateRect (hwnd, NULL, FALSE) ;
                        return 0 ;
                    }

        case WM_PAINT:
            hps = WinBeginPaint (hwnd, NULL, NULL) ;
            GpiErase (hps) ;

            if (hbm != NULL)
                {
                WinQueryWindowRect (hwnd, &rclClient) ;

                WinDrawBitmap (hps, hbm, NULL, (PPOINTL) &rclClient,
                            CLR_NEUTRAL, CLR_BACKGROUND,
                               sDisplay == IDM_STRETCH ?
                                    DBM_STRETCH : DBM_NORMAL) ;

                }
            WinEndPaint (hps) ;
            return 0 ;
```

(continued)

Figure 15-3. The BLOWUP.C File. *continued*

```
        case WM_DESTROY:
             if (hbm != NULL)
                  GpiDeleteBitmap (hbm) ;
             return 0 ;
        }
    return WinDefWindowProc (hwnd, msg, mp1, mp2) ;
    }
```

The BLOWUP.H File

```
/*----------------------
   BLOWUP.H header file
   ----------------------*/

#define ID_RESOURCE       1

#define IDM_EDIT          10
#define IDM_COPY          11
#define IDM_PASTE         12

#define IDM_CAPTURE       20

#define IDM_DISPLAY       30
#define IDM_ACTUAL        31
#define IDM_STRETCH       32
```

The BLOWUP.RC File

```
/*---------------------------------
   BLOWUP.RC resource script file
   ---------------------------------*/

#include <os2.h>
#include "blowup.h"

MENU ID_RESOURCE
    {
    SUBMENU "~Edit",             IDM_EDIT
        {
        MENUITEM "~Copy\tCtrl+Ins",    IDM_COPY
        MENUITEM "~Paste\tShift+Ins",  IDM_PASTE
        }
```

(continued)

Figure 15-3. The BLOWUP.RC File. *continued*

```
        MENUITEM "~Capture!",         IDM_CAPTURE

        SUBMENU "~Display",           IDM_DISPLAY
            {
            MENUITEM "~Actual size",          IDM_ACTUAL,, MIA_CHECKED
            MENUITEM "~Stretch to window", IDM_STRETCH
            }
        }

ACCELTABLE ID_RESOURCE
    {
    VK_INSERT, IDM_COPY,  VIRTUALKEY, CONTROL
    VK_INSERT, IDM_PASTE, VIRTUALKEY, SHIFT
    }
```

The BLOWUP.DEF File

```
;-----------------------------------
; BLOWUP.DEF module definition file
;-----------------------------------

NAME            BLOWUP          WINDOWAPI

DESCRIPTION     'Bitmap Blowup Clipboard Program (C) Charles Petzold, 1988'
PROTMODE
HEAPSIZE        1024
STACKSIZE       8192
EXPORTS         ClientWndProc
```

Figure 15-3. *The BLOWUP program.*

You can use BLOWUP like a magnifying glass to explore areas of the Presentation Manager screen. First select Capture from the menu. A little rectangle about the size of a mouse pointer appears in the middle of the screen. You can move it around with the mouse or the cursor movement keys. Move it to an area of the screen you want to blow up in size, and press Enter or click the mouse button. You can then use the mouse or keyboard to adjust the upper-right corner of the rectangle. Press Enter or click the mouse button again.

BLOWUP then displays that area of the screen on its client window. By default, it is displayed at actual size. But you can select "Stretch to Window" from BLOWUP's Display menu to stretch the bitmap to the size of the client window. For example, Figure 15-4 shows the results after you use BLOWUP to look at the minimize/maximize menu.

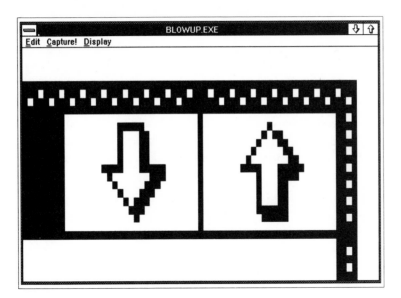

Figure 15-4. *The BLOWUP display.*

BLOWUP has an Edit menu with Copy and Paste options. You can copy the bitmap to the clipboard or paste a bitmap from the clipboard.

BLOWUP maintains a bitmap handle named *hbm* for displaying the bitmap on its client window. The clipboard logic in BLOWUP is almost exactly as I just described it. The only substantial difference is that BLOWUP deletes the *hbm* handle it already has before pasting a bitmap from the clipboard.

```
Case IDM_PASTE:

              // Get bitmap from clipboard

WinOpenClipbrd (hab) ;
hbm = WinQueryClipbrdData (hab, CF_BITMAP) ;

if (hbmClip != NULL)
    {
    if (hbm != NULL)
        GpiDeleteBitmap (hbm) ;

              // Make copy of new bitmap

    hbm = CopyBitmap (hbmClip) ;
```

(continued)

```
      if (hbm == NULL)
          BitmapCreationError (hwnd) ;
      }
WinCloseClipbrd (hab) ;
```

BLOWUP also processes the WM_INITMENU message to enable or disable the Copy and Paste options. The Copy option is enabled only if BLOWUP has a bitmap handle stored in *hbm*. Paste is enabled if the clipboard currently contains a bitmap.

The *CopyBitmap* function is fairly straightforward. The function opens two memory device contexts and creates two presentation spaces associated with these device contexts. *WinQueryBitmapParameters* obtains the BITMAPINFOHEADER structure that describes the original bitmap. This structure is passed to *GpiCreateBitmap* to create a new bitmap of the same size and color organization. The two bitmaps are set into the two presentation spaces, and *GpiBitBlt* copies the contents of the original bitmap to the new bitmap.

In its *BeginTracking* function, BLOWUP uses the powerful *WinTrackRect* function for capturing an area of the screen when you select the Capture option from the menu. *WinTrackRect* is the same function that the title bar window uses when you move a window on the screen and the same function that the frame window uses when you resize a window. The function has its own keyboard and mouse interface.

To use *WinTrackRect*, you need to define a structure of type TRACKINFO:

```
TRACKINFO ti ;
```

The hard part of the job is setting all the fields of this structure. But once they're set, you just pass the structure to *WinTrackRect*:

```
WinTrackRect (HWND_DESKTOP, NULL, &ti) ;
```

The second parameter to *WinTrackRect* is usually a handle to a presentation space, but the function can obtain a presentation space handle using the window handle passed as the first parameter. Because we want to capture anything on the screen, the first parameter is set to HWND_DESKTOP.

WinTrackRect displays a rectangle on the screen and allows it to be moved or sized with the keyboard or mouse. The function has its own message loop and will not return until the user presses the mouse button, presses the Enter key, or presses the Escape key. *WinTrackRect* returns FALSE if the user aborts the tracking operation by pressing Escape and returns TRUE otherwise.

BLOWUP calls *WinTrackRect* twice in its *BeginTracking* function, which is called from *ClientWndProc* when the Capture menu option is selected. The first call to *WinTrackRect* lets you move the tracking rectangle to any area of the screen; the second call lets you change the size of the rectangle.

The TRACKINFO structure contains two fields that are RECTL structures. The first (called *rclBoundary*) indicates the area in which the rectangle can be moved. For BLOWUP, this is the entire screen. The second RECTL structure (called *rclTrack*) specifies the initial position and size of the rectangle when the function is called and specifies the final position and size of the rectangle when the function returns. (For the first call to *WinTrackRect*, BLOWUP makes the rectangle the size of a mouse pointer and places it in the center of the screen.) Two POINTL structures in the TRACKINFO structure specify the minimium and maximum allowable sizes of the rectangle. For BLOWUP, the minimum size is 1 pixel high and 1 pixel wide, and the maximum size is the dimension of the entire screen.

The *fs* field of the TRACKINFO structure specifies how the tracking is to work. For the first call to *WinTrackRect*, the *fs* field is set like this:

```
ti.fs = TF_MOVE | TF_STANDARD | TF_SETPOINTERPOS ;
```

The TF_MOVE flag indicates that the user can move the rectangle. The TF_STANDARD field indicates that the dimensions of the border given in the *cxBorder* and *cyBorder* fields are multiples of the standard border width. The TF_SETPOINTERPOS flag puts the mouse pointer in the center of the rectangle.

On the second call to *WinTrackRect*, the flags are set differently:

```
ti.fs = TF_RIGHT | TF_TOP | TF_STANDARD | TF_SETPOINTERPOS ;
```

The TF_RIGHT and TF_TOP flags allow the user to move the upper-right corner of the rectangle. The mouse pointer is positioned on that corner. Before this second call to *WinTrackRect*, BLOWUP sets the mouse pointer to the system pointer known as SPTR_SIZENESW:

```
WinSetPointer (HWND_DESKTOP, WinQuerySysPointer
          (HWND_DESKTOP, SPTR_SIZENESW, FALSE)) ;
```

The letters "NESW" stand for "north-east south-west." The pointer is a double-headed arrow that points to the upper-right and lower-left corners. This is the mouse pointer that appears when you resize a window by grabbing the upper-right or lower-left corner of the sizing border.

BLOWUP calls its *BeginTracking* function when the user selects Capture from the menu. The *BeginTracking* function returns the final tracking rectangle. BLOWUP then calls *CopyScreenToBitmap* with this rectangle to create a bitmap and to copy the selected area of the screen. In *CopyScreenToBitmap*, the *GpiQueryDeviceBitmapFormats* function obtains the number of color planes and number of color bits per pixel used for the video display. This is required to create the bitmap. The bitmap is selected into a presentation space associated with a memory device context, and *GpiBitBlt* does the copy. Before and after the *GpiBitBlt* call, *CopyScreenToBitmap* makes calls to *WinLockVisRegions* to prevent the screen from changing while the copy is in progress.

If you have the CLOCK or DIGCLOCK program running when you use BLOWUP, you'll notice also that the screen is not updated during the calls to *WinTrackRect*. If the Presentation Manager allowed screen updates, another program might draw over the tracking rectangle or imprint part of the rectangle in its window when drawing in exclusive OR mode. This is one big advantage of using *WinTrackRect* rather than your own logic for tracking areas of the screen outside your window.

## CHAPTER SIXTEEN

DYNAMIC LINK LIBRARIES

Dynamic linking is a process that lets your programs use functions or resources outside of their own .EXE files. Dynamic linking is one of the most interesting features of OS/2 and is very important to the overall structure of the operating system. Its degree of importance is reflected by the number of .DLL files you'll find on your hard disk. These files are "dynamic link libraries" (or DLLs). They contain code, data, and resource segments just as executable files do. However, a dynamic link library is not directly executed but is used by OS/2 executables or other dynamic link libraries.

The Presentation Manager itself is primarily a collection of dynamic link libraries. These libraries extend the functionality of OS/2 to include a windowing user interface and graphics. Every Presentation Manager function your program calls is in a dynamic link library. The two most important Presentation Manager libraries are PMWIN.DLL (which contains most functions with the *Win* prefix) and PMGPI.DLL (which contains most functions with the *Gpi* prefix).

When you use LINK to create a Presentation Manager program, the program's .EXE file contains no code for the various OS/2 and Presentation Manager functions called by the program. Instead, LINK builds tables in the .EXE file that identify these functions and the names of the dynamic link libraries where they are located. In the program itself, the actual calls to these functions contain dummy addresses.

When you run the program, OS/2

- determines from the .EXE file which dynamic link libraries are required by the program

- maps the code and data segments from the dynamic link library into the process's memory space

- replaces the dummy addresses in the program's code segment with the addresses of the functions in the DLL code segment

This is the process known as "dynamic linking."

You can also write your own dynamic link libraries, which is what I'll show you how to do in this chapter.

Code segments, read-only data segments, and resource segments in dynamic link libraries can be shared among all processes running under OS/2. Read-write data segments associated with dynamic link libraries are usually private to each process. However, you can specify that some read-write data segments in a dynamic link library be shared among all processes. This allows dynamic link libraries to assist in interprocess communication (IPC).

Because dynamic linking is a facility of the OS/2 kernel rather than the Presentation Manager, I won't discuss it in detail here. Instead, I'll concentrate on those aspects of dynamic linking that are most important to Presentation Manager programming.

Locating .DLL Files—A Tip

Before we begin, here's a tip to help you more easily develop programs that use dynamic link libraries. When you run a program that requires linking to a dynamic link library, OS/2 uses the directory paths specified in the LIBPATH statement in your CONFIG.SYS file to locate the library files. For example, your LIBPATH statement may look like this:

```
LIBPATH=C:\OS2\DLL;C:\
```

This tells OS/2 that all of the dynamic link libraries are located in the C:\OS2\DLL or C:\ directories. Normally when you create a dynamic link library you must copy it into the C:\OS2\DLL directory or root directory to use it. However, you can add a semicolon and period to the end of the LIBPATH string:

```
LIBPATH=C:\OS2\DLL;C:\;.
```

This causes OS/2 to also search the current directory when a program requires a dynamic link library. This makes developing and testing the library somewhat easier. After you change your CONFIG.SYS file, you'll have to reboot to make the change effective. In the following discussions and examples, I'll assume you've done this.

Dynamic Link Library Basics

The word "library" is used in several different ways in OS/2 programming, so let's take a minute to examine them.

Object and Import Libraries

Normally when you use LINK to link a program, you make use of "object libraries." These are files with a .LIB extension that contain code and data. (For example, SLIBCE.LIB is an object library for the small-model C runtime library functions such as *sprintf* and *strlen*.) Linking with an object library is sometimes known as "static linking" to differentiate it from dynamic linking.

However, some files with a .LIB extension are not object libraries but "import libraries." Import libraries are similar to object libraries because they contain information that LINK uses to construct a program's .EXE file. However, import libraries usually contain no code or data. Instead, LINK uses the import libraries to set up tables within the .EXE file that identify the dynamic link library functions used by the program.

For example, most Presentation Manager programs call the function *WinCreateStdWindow*. When you compile a Presentation Manager program, the .OBJ file produced by the compiler contains an unresolved reference to this function. When LINK links the program to create a .EXE file, it finds the *WinCreateStdWindow* function in OS2.LIB. The OS2.LIB file indicates that this function is located in the PMWIN.DLL dynamic link library module and has an "ordinal number" (a concept discussed later in this chapter) of 140. LINK then stores this information in the program's .EXE file. When OS/2 loads the program into memory, it can then determine both the name of the dynamic link library and the ordinal number within that library of the unresolved call to *WinCreateStdWindow*.

I'll show you how to create your own import libraries later in this chapter.

The object libraries and import libraries need be present on the hard disk only when you link the program. The dynamic link library used by a program must be present when you run the program.

Modules

Both programs (files with a .EXE extension) and dynamic link libraries (files with a .DLL extension) are sometimes called "modules." The .EXE files are "program modules" and the .DLL files are "library modules." Each module has a module name, which you must specify in the NAME statement (for program modules) or the LIBRARY statement (for library modules) of the module definition (.DEF) file.

A library module name *must* be the same as the filename, but without the .DLL extension; a program module name is generally the same as the file-name (without the .EXE extension), but can differ.

Exported Functions

Most dynamic link libraries contain functions that can be called from exe-cutables or other dynamic link libraries. Such functions are said to be ''ex-ported'' from the library. For example, the *WinCreateStdWindow* function is exported from the PMWIN.DLL dynamic link library. A function in a dynamic link library must be exported if it is to be used by another module.

You can get a list of functions exported from a particular dynamic link li-brary by running the EXEHDR program (included with the OS/2 Program-mer's Toolkit) like this:

```
EXEHDR C:\OS2\DLL\PMWIN.DLL
```

After displaying information stored in the .EXE file headers, EXEHDR lists all of the code and data segments in the module, followed by the exported functions. The ''seg'' and ''offset'' columns indicate the segment number and the offset within that segment where the function begins. The ''ord'' column contains the ordinal number of the function. Each exported func-tion has a unique positive ordinal number.

We have been exporting functions since Chapter 2—all window pro-cedures in a program must be exported from the program module. Window procedures are called from the PMWIN dynamic link library. The general rule is this: Any function in a program or library module that can be called from another module must be exported.

Imported Functions

When a program or library module makes use of functions in a library module, the functions are said to be ''imported'' to the module making the function call. You can get a list of the functions imported to a module by running EXEHDR with the -*V* (verbose) switch. This displays a list of all ad-dresses within the module that OS/2 must patch when loading the program into memory. Many of these are calls to functions in dynamic link library modules. You'll notice that imported functions are referred to by the mod-ule name (such as PMWIN and PMGPI) followed by a period and either a function name or an ordinal number. For example, PMWIN.140 refers to the *WinCreateStdWindow* function.

Thus, dynamic linking is the process of connecting calls to functions imported to a program module with the functions exported from a dynamic link library module. Very often a library module imports functions from itself or from another library module, so OS/2 must also be able to dynamically link library modules.

Same Process, Different Module

It's important to remember that a dynamic link library is not a process. Only an OS/2 executable file can become a process. Code that is executed in a dynamic link library (as a result of a call to a function within the library), is executed within the process that makes the call. As you may know, each process running under OS/2 has a "local descriptor table" (or LDT) that the 80286 or 80386 microprocessor uses to reference the process's code and data segments. When a process uses a library module, the code and data segments in that module are also included in the process's LDT.

In this sense, when a program calls a routine in a dynamic link library, it's no different from the program calling a routine in the program itself. The dynamic link library is an extension of the process. Everything the library does is done on behalf of the process. For example, a function in a dynamic link library can open a file or allocate a memory segment. The open file or memory segment belongs to the process that called the function in the library.

This is quite interesting when you think about it. We are accustomed to thinking about operating system code and program code as separate and distinct entities. A function such as *WinCreateStdWindow* is an operating system function call. Yet, when a Presentation Manager program calls *WinCreateStdWindow*, the function really executes as part of the process.

Is PMWIN.DLL an extension of the OS/2 operating system or an extension of a program running under Presentation Manager? It's both. Dynamic link libraries bridge the gap between program and operating system. Under OS/2, the concept of one module calling code located in another module is generalized. There is no real separation between program code and operating system code.

When you write your own dynamic link libraries, you may think of them as extensions of your programs. But you can also view them as extensions of the operating system. This explains why people say that OS/2 is easily and almost infinitely extensible.

Why Use Dynamic Link Libraries?

Of course, the idea of writing an "extension" to OS/2 may be enough of a thrill to induce you to write dynamic link libraries. But there are more practical benefits.

Suppose you were developing an OS/2 accounting package that consisted of several programs. These programs would probably use a lot of the same code. In fact, under DOS you would probably isolate these common routines in separate source code files and put them in object libraries.

But if you did this, each program in the package would contain a copy of these common routines, increasing the total disk space required by the package. Moreover, if someone ran two or more of these programs under OS/2 at the same time, the common routines would also be duplicated in memory.

If you instead put these routines in a dynamic link library, the disk space required by the package would be reduced because only one copy of the routines is required. (And that copy is in the library module.) If two or more of the programs were run at the same time, the code in the library module would be shared among the programs that required it.

Moreover, when compiling and linking the separate programs, link time would be improved because LINK would no longer have to pull the routines from the object library and include them in the program's .EXE file. You could also someday improve the performance of the whole package by upgrading only the routines in the dynamic link library. The programs themselves would not even have to be relinked.

Dynamic link libraries can also be products in themselves. For example, suppose you write a collection of three-dimensional extensions to GPI graphics, put the functions in a dynamic link library, and call it GPI3D.DLL. You might be able to interest other software manufacturers in licensing this library from you for inclusion in their products. Users who own several products that use GPI3D.DLL would need only one copy of the library on their hard disks.

DS != SS and Other DLL Quirks

I mentioned earlier that, in one sense, calling a function in a dynamic link library is no different from calling a function in the program itself. But this is not entirely true. Dynamic link libraries have a few quirks that result from the segmented architecture of the 80286 microprocessor.

The code segments in a program and the code segments in a dynamic link library are different. Any call from a program to a dynamic link library function must be a far call (that is, the call must use both a segment and an offset address). Thus the exported functions in a dynamic link library must be compiled as far functions.

Any pointer passed as a parameter to a function in a dynamic link library must be a far pointer. A dynamic link library usually includes its own data segment, so it requires a far pointer to access data in the program's data segment. Because most DLL functions use the library's data segment, dynamic link libraries must be compiled a little differently than programs. I'll discuss this shortly.

A program includes a segment group called DGROUP. This group contains both the program's default data segment and the program's stack segment. The default data segment is referenced by the DS register, and the stack segment is referenced by the SS register. Because these two segments are grouped in DGROUP, DS and SS are the same. Symbolically,

```
DS == SS
```

Dynamic link libraries usually have their own default data segment, but they have no stack segment. When a program makes a call to a function in a dynamic link library, the function switches to a DS that references its own data segment. But SS still references the calling program's stack segment. In other words,

```
DS != SS
```

By default, the C compiler generates code under the assumption that DS equals SS. When compiling a dynamic link library, you must tell the compiler not to assume this.

The LLIBCDLL Library

The DS != SS quirk of dynamic link libraries is primarily a problem when you compile the library code using small or medium model. Small-model or medium-model modules have only one data segment. By default, references to data use only 16-bit offsets. But if DS is not equal to SS, in some cases the compiler will not know whether a particular pointer to a variable references a variable in the data segment or the stack segment. To make the problem worse, some C library functions assume that DS equals SS.

These problems are greatly alleviated by the inclusion in Microsoft C 5.1 of a C runtime library called LLIBCDLL.LIB. This object library is specifically designed for use in dynamic link libraries. It is a large-model library (and hence uses both segment and offset addresses for referencing code and data), and the C functions do not assume that DS equals SS.

For this reason, we will compile our dynamic link libraries using large model and linking them with LLIBCDLL.LIB. The major disadvantage is that floating-point math functions in LLIBCDLL use the "alternate" math library and will not use a math coprocessor chip if installed. (There is no easy way to prevent a program and a dynamic link library from interfering with each other if each is using the math coprocessor or the same coprocessor emulation routines.)

Another disadvantage of LLIBCDLL is that it cannot be used in dynamic link library functions that are called from separate threads of a single process. (Multithread Presentation Manager programming is discussed in Chapter 17.) To link such functions, you must create a dynamic link library that contains all of the C runtime library functions. Microsoft C 5.1 includes everything you need to do this.

Compile and Link Mechanics

Most of the difficulties in using dynamic link libraries involve the mechanics of compiling and linking. There are several requirements, as well as several possible ways to satisfy each of them:

Requirement One: Use Far Calls and Pointers.

All functions exported from a dynamic link library must be defined as far. In addition, any pointer passed as a parameter to an exported function must also be defined as far.

Compiling the dynamic link library for large model satisfies this requirement. We'll be using the *-Alf* switch to compile dynamic link libraries. (The "l" directs the compiler to "long" code pointers, and the "f" means to use "far" data pointers.)

When you write a program that uses functions in a dynamic link library, you must also write the library function declarations to indicate that they are far functions with far pointers as parameters. You can use the FAR identifier defined in OS2DEF.H for this, and use the PSZ, PSHORT, PLONG, and other data types to indicate far pointers. Use the Presentation Manager header files as a guide in writing the function declarations.

Requirement Two: Decide on a Calling Sequence.

By default, when the C compiler generates code for a function call, the code pushes parameters on the stack from right to left. After the function call returns to the caller, the parameters are removed from the stack. This is the normal C calling sequence.

The Microsoft C compiler also supports a Pascal calling sequence. The parameters are pushed on the stack from left to right and the function itself removes the parameters from the stack before the function returns. The Pascal calling sequence is slightly more efficient when code is generated for the 80286 microprocessor. All OS/2 and Presentation Manager functions use the Pascal calling sequence. However, a function that uses a variable number of parameters must use the C calling sequence.

You can specify a function as using the Pascal calling sequence by specifying the *pascal* keyword or PASCAL identifier. If you use both PASCAL and FAR to define a function, you can use APIENTRY instead. An alternative is to use the *-Gc* switch when compiling the dynamic link library code. This causes the compiler to generate code for the Pascal calling sequence for all functions in the file. In this case, you can use the *cdecl* keyword for functions that must use the C calling sequence.

Requirement Three: Load DS.

Functions in dynamic link libraries most often use the library module's DGROUP for the default data segment. When an exported function is called from a program, however, DS is set to the program's default data segment. The function must save DS and set DS to its own data segment on entry to an exported function and restore DS (the program's DS) on exit from the function.

There are a few ways to do this:

- Use the *-Gw* compiler switch when you compile the dynamic link library. (This is the same switch that we've been using to compile our Presentation Manager programs.) This switch causes the compiler to insert a special "window procedure" prologue and epilogue on all far functions.

- Use the *-Au* compiler switch when compiling the dynamic link library. This adds a "load DS" prologue and epilogue to functions in the module. This prologue and epilogue is slightly simpler than the one you get with the *-Gw* switch, but it's added to all functions in the module rather than just all far functions. (This switch also causes the compiler to assume that DS is not equal to SS.) The *-Au* and *-Gw* switches cannot be used together. When you use the *-Au* switch, you combine it with the *-Alf* switch by using *-Alfu*.

- Use the *_loadds* keyword for the function definitions of all exported functions. This adds the same prologue and epilogue as the *-Au* switch, but only for selected functions.

Requirement Four: Compile for DS != SS.

You can tell the C compiler that DS is not equal to SS in one of two ways:

- Use the *-Aw* switch (which you can combine with *-Alf* by using *-Alfw*).

- Use the *-Au* switch. The *-Au* switch also adds a "load DS" prologue and epilogue to all functions in the module, as previously described.

Requirement Five: Inhibit Stack Checks.

Because the dynamic link library uses the stack of the calling program, you'll want to inhibit stack checks on entry to functions in the library. The easiest way to do this is with the *-Gs* compiler switch. This is the same switch we've used since Chapter 2 to inhibit stack checks in our Presentation Manager programs.

Requirement Six: Export the Functions.

All functions in a dynamic link library that can be called from outside the library module must be exported. You can do this in one of two ways:

- List the functions explicitly in the EXPORTS section of the module definition file. This is the method we've been using for window procedures in our programs.

- Use the *_export* keyword on the function definition.

Requirement Seven: Link with LLIBCDLL.LIB.

When you link the dynamic link library, you must link only with the LLIBCDLL.LIB object library, the OS2.LIB import library, and any other import libraries you may create. You must use the */nod* ("no default library search") switch on LINK when specifying these libraries in the library field.

These requirements pertain to the compilation and linking of the library module only. The program module can be compiled and linked in the normal way. The only requirement for programs using functions from dynamic link libraries is that the library functions must be properly declared within the program.

Creating a Dynamic Link Library

So let's get down to business and write a dynamic link library. Our first library is called HDRLIB ("Handy Drawing Routines Library") and is shown in Figure 16-1.

The HDRLIB File

```
#------------------
# HDRLIB make file
#------------------

hdrlib.obj : hdrlib.c hdrlib.h
     cl -c -Alfu -G2s -W3 hdrlib.c

hdrlib.dll : hdrlib.obj hdrlib.def
     link hdrlib, hdrlib.dll /align:16, NUL, /nod llibcdll os2, hdrlib
```

The HDRLIB.H File

```
/*------------------------------------------------------
     HDRLIB.H -- "Handy Drawing Routines" Header File
   ------------------------------------------------*/

SHORT APIENTRY  HdrPuts    (HPS hps, PPOINTL pptl, PCHAR szText) ;
SHORT cdecl FAR HdrPrintf  (HPS hps, PPOINTL pptl, PCHAR szFormat, ...) ;
LONG  APIENTRY  HdrEllipse (HPS hps, LONG lOption, PPOINTL pptl) ;
```

The HDRLIB.C File

```
/*------------------------------------------------------
     HDRLIB.C -- "Handy Drawing Routines" Dynamic Link Library
   ------------------------------------------------*/

#define INCL_GPI
#include <os2.h>
#include <stdio.h>
#include <stdarg.h>
#include <stdlib.h>
#include <string.h>
#include "hdrlib.h"

SHORT APIENTRY HdrPuts (HPS hps, PPOINTL pptl, PCHAR szText)
     {
     SHORT sLength = strlen (szText) ;

     if (pptl == NULL)
          GpiCharString (hps, (LONG) sLength, szText) ;
     else
          GpiCharStringAt (hps, pptl, (LONG) sLength, szText) ;
```

(continued)

Figure 16-1. The HDRLIB.C File. *continued*

```
    return sLength ;
    }

SHORT cdecl FAR HdrPrintf (HPS hps, PPOINTL pptl, PCHAR szFormat, ...)
    {
    static CHAR chBuffer [1024] ;
    SHORT       sLength ;
    va_list     pArguments ;

    va_start (pArguments, szFormat) ;
    sLength = vsprintf (chBuffer, szFormat, pArguments) ;

    if (pptl == NULL)
        GpiCharString (hps, (LONG) sLength, chBuffer) ;
    else
        GpiCharStringAt (hps, pptl, (LONG) sLength, chBuffer) ;

    va_end (pArguments) ;
    return sLength ;
    }

LONG APIENTRY HdrEllipse (HPS hps, LONG lOption, PPOINTL pptl)
    {
    POINTL ptlCurrent ;

    GpiQueryCurrentPosition (hps, &ptlCurrent) ;

    return GpiBox (hps, lOption, pptl, labs (pptl->x - ptlCurrent.x),
                                       labs (pptl->y - ptlCurrent.y)) ;
    }
```

The HDRLIB.DEF File

```
;------------------------------------
; HDRLIB.DEF module definition file
;------------------------------------


LIBRARY         HDRLIB     INITINSTANCE

DESCRIPTION     '"Handy Drawing Routines" DLL (C) Charles Petzold, 1988'
PROTMODE
DATA            NONSHARED
HEAPSIZE        1024
EXPORTS         HdrPuts
                _HdrPrintf
                HdrEllipse
```

Figure 16-1. *The HDRLIB library.*

This library contains three functions that perform some common GPI tasks that would otherwise take more than one call to complete. *HdrPuts* displays a string starting at a specified position (or starting at the current position if the second parameter is set to NULL). The *HdrPrintf* function uses a technique shown in the *cprintf* function in Chapter 7 to let you write formatted text to your window. The *HdrEllipse* function is a version of the *Ellipse* function shown in Chapter 5. The function uses *GpiBox* to draw an ellipse.

The HDRLIB make file takes care of requirements 1, 3, 4, 5, and 7, as discussed in the Compile and Link Mechanics section:

- The *-Alfu* compiler switch causes the HDRLIB.C source code file to be compiled for large model assuming DS != SS.

- The compiler inserts a "load DS" prologue and epilogue in all functions.

- The *-G2s* switch inhibits stack checks.

- In the LINK step, HDRLIB.OBJ is linked with the LLIBCDLL.LIB object library and the OS2.LIB import library.

The three functions are declared in HDRLIB.H. (This header file will also be used in a program that calls the three functions in HDRLIB.DLL.) The *HdrPuts* and *HdrEllipse* functions are defined as APIENTRY functions. (OS2DEF.H defines APIENTRY as *pascal far*.) The *HdrPrintf* function is defined as *cdecl FAR*. Because *HdrPrintf* has a variable number of parameters, the Pascal calling sequence cannot be used. This satisfies requirement 2. Several parameters to these functions are far pointers. They are specified in HDRLIB.H as using the PPOINTL and PCHAR data types, which are defined in OS2DEF.H as far pointers.

HDRLIB.C contains the three functions. You'll notice that the HDRLIB.C file contains no *main* function. Although dynamic link libraries often do some initialization on the assembly language level, this is taken care of in startup code stored in the LLIBCDLL.LIB that is linked into the .DLL file.

The Module Definition File

The HDRLIB.DEF module definition file is significantly different from module definition files used to create program modules. The first statement is not a NAME statement but a LIBRARY statement:

```
LIBRARY   HDRLIB    INITINSTANCE
```

A NAME statement indicates that the module is a program; a LIBRARY indicates a dynamic link library. This keyword is followed by the module name and INITINSTANCE. The INITINSTANCE keyword means that initialization code in the dynamic link library is executed for each process that links to the library. Use INITINSTANCE when you use the LLIBCDLL.LIB runtime library.

This module definition file also contains a data statement:

```
DATA      NONSHARED
```

This indicates that the data segments in the dynamic link library will not be shared among processes. Every time a process using HDRLIB.DLL begins, OS/2 creates a new set of data segments for the dynamic link library.

There is no STACKSIZE statement. A dynamic link library has no stack.

The EXPORTS list names the three exported functions. This satisfies requirement 6. These are the three functions in HDRLIB.DLL that are available to programs or other dynamic link libraries. The *HdrPrintf* function in HDRLIB.C appears in HDRLIB.DEF with a preceding underline: *_HdrPrintf*. Because the C compiler prepends an underscore to the names of all functions defined as using the C calling sequence, these functions must be specified in the module definition file in this manner as well. The underscore is not used for Pascal functions.

Using the Dynamic Link Library

We can test the dynamic link library with a program that calls the library functions. The HDRTEST program shown in Figure 16-2 does just that.

The HDRTEST File

```
#-------------------
# HDRTEST make file
#-------------------

hdrtest.obj : hdrtest.c hdrlib.h
     cl -c -G2sw -W3 hdrtest.c

hdrtest.exe : hdrtest.obj hdrtest.def
     link hdrtest, /align:16, NUL, os2, hdrtest
```

The HDRTEST.C File

```
/*------------------------------------------------------------------
   HDRTEST.C -- Program to Test HDRLIB.DLL Dynamic Link Library
   ---------------------------------------------------------------*/

#define INCL_WIN
#include <os2.h>
#include "hdrlib.h"

MRESULT EXPENTRY ClientWndProc (HWND, USHORT, MPARAM, MPARAM) ;

int main (void)
    {
    static CHAR  szClientClass [] = "HdrTest" ;
    static ULONG flFrameFlags = FCF_TITLEBAR       | FCF_SYSMENU |
                                FCF_SIZEBORDER      | FCF_MINMAX  |
                                FCF_SHELLPOSITION   | FCF_TASKLIST ;
    HAB          hab ;
    HMQ          hmq ;
    HWND         hwndFrame, hwndClient ;
    QMSG         qmsg ;

    hab = WinInitialize (0) ;
    hmq = WinCreateMsgQueue (hab, 0) ;

    WinRegisterClass (hab, szClientClass, ClientWndProc, CS_SIZEREDRAW, 0) ;

    hwndFrame = WinCreateStdWindow (HWND_DESKTOP, WS_VISIBLE,
                                    &flFrameFlags, szClientClass, NULL,
                                    OL, NULL, 0, &hwndClient) ;

    WinSendMsg (hwndFrame, WM_SETICON,
                WinQuerySysPointer (HWND_DESKTOP, SPTR_APPICON, FALSE),
                NULL) ;

    while (WinGetMsg (hab, &qmsg, NULL, 0, 0))
        WinDispatchMsg (hab, &qmsg) ;

    WinDestroyWindow (hwndFrame) ;
    WinDestroyMsgQueue (hmq) ;
    WinTerminate (hab) ;
    return 0 ;
    }
```

(continued)

Figure 16-2. The HDRTEST.C File. *continued*

```
MRESULT EXPENTRY ClientWndProc (HWND hwnd, USHORT msg, MPARAM mp1, MPARAM mp2)
    {
    static SHORT cxClient, cyClient ;
    HPS        hps;
    POINTL     ptl ;

    switch (msg)
        {
        case WM_SIZE:
             cxClient = SHORT1FROMMP (mp2) ;
             cyClient = SHORT2FROMMP (mp2) ;
             return 0 ;

        case WM_PAINT:
             hps = WinBeginPaint (hwnd, NULL, NULL) ;
             GpiErase (hps) ;

             ptl.x = cxClient / 8 ;
             ptl.y = 3 * cyClient / 4 ;
             HdrPrintf (hps, &ptl, "Welcome to the %s",
                        (PCHAR) "OS/2 Presentation Manager") ;

             ptl.x = cxClient / 8 ;
             ptl.y = cyClient / 4 ;
             HdrPuts (hps, &ptl, "This line was displayed by a ") ;
             HdrPuts (hps, NULL, "routine in a dynamic link library.") ;

             ptl.x = 0 ;
             ptl.y = 0 ;
             GpiMove (hps, &ptl) ;

             ptl.x = cxClient - 1 ;
             ptl.y = cyClient - 1 ;
             HdrEllipse (hps, DRO_OUTLINE, &ptl) ;

             WinEndPaint (hps) ;
             return 0 ;
        }
    return WinDefWindowProc (hwnd, msg, mp1, mp2) ;
    }
```

The HDRTEST.DEF File

```
;-------------------------------------
; HDRTEST.DEF module definition file
;-------------------------------------

NAME            HDRTEST    WINDOWAPI

DESCRIPTION     'Test Program for HDRLIB.DLL (C) Charles Petzold, 1988'
PROTMODE
HEAPSIZE        1024
STACKSIZE       8192
EXPORTS         ClientWndProc
IMPORTS         HDRLIB.HdrPuts
                HDRLIB._HdrPrintf
                HDRLIB.HdrEllipse
```

Figure 16-2. *The HDRTEST program.*

You'll also need the HDRLIB.H header file from Figure 16-1 to compile this program. The function declarations in this header file tell the C compiler that the functions are far and require far pointers as parameters.

And it works! Figure 16-3 shows the HDRTEST program running under the Presentation Manager.

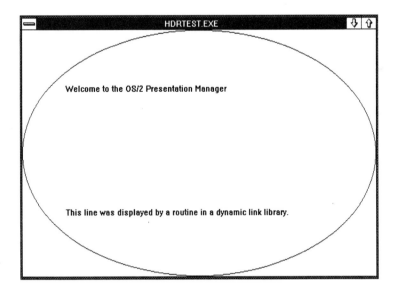

Figure 16-3. *The HDRTEST display.*

One warning when using HDRLIB.DLL: You notice that the call to
HdrPrintf in HDRTEST.C looks like this:

```
HdrPrintf (hps, &ptl, "Welcome to the %s",
           (PCHAR) "0S/2 Presentation Manager") ;
```

The second and third parameters to *HdrPrintf* are declared as far pointers in
HDRLIB.H. However, *HdrPrintf* has a variable number of parameters. Some
of these parameters may also be pointers. Because HDRLIB.C is compiled
using large model, it expects all pointers to be far pointers. Thus the string
passed as a the last parameter to *HdrPrintf* must be cast to a far pointer.
(Functions with a variable number of parameters are rarely used in
dynamic link libraries; this problem is one reason why.)

The HDRTEST.DEF module definition file explicitly lists the three imported
functions in an IMPORTS section:

```
IMPORTS    HDRLIB.HdrPuts
           HDRLIB._HdrPrintf
           HDRLIB.HdrEllipse
```

Once again, *HdrPrintf* must be preceded by an underscore. (If listing the
imported functions in the module definition file annoys you, you'll be
happy to know that we'll eliminate the IMPORTS list shortly.)

Alternate IMPORTS and EXPORTS Lists

The HDRLIB.DEF module definition file lists the functions exported from
HDRLIB.DLL:

```
EXPORTS    HdrPuts
           _HdrPrintf
           HdrEllipse
```

The HDRTEST.DEF module definition file also lists the functions in
HDRLIB.DLL that are imported to HDRTEST:

```
IMPORTS    HDRLIB.HdrPuts
           HDRLIB._HdrPrintf
           HDRLIB.HdrEllipse
```

Notice that each function in the IMPORTS list is identified by a module
name and a function name. LINK uses this information in constructing the
HDRTEST.EXE file.

This is not the only way to specify EXPORTS and IMPORTS. Another approach is to assign "ordinals" to each of the functions. Ordinals are unique positive integers that you assign in the module definition file for the library. You do this by preceding the number with an @ sign. You must change both module definition files. Here's the new EXPORTS list in HDRLIB.DEF:

```
EXPORTS   HdrPuts    @1
          _HdrPrintf @2
          HdrEllipse @3
```

The IMPORTS list in HDRTEST.DEF then references these functions by specifying the ordinal numbers (without the @):

```
IMPORTS   HdrPuts    = HDRLIB.1
          _HdrPrintf = HDRLIB.2
          HdrEllipse = HDRLIB.3
```

The advantage of this approach is that it makes the HDRTEST.EXE file smaller: The .EXE file needs to contain only the ordinal numbers — not the names — of the three imported functions.

The big disadvantage to ordinals is that it's easy to mistakenly use the wrong number in the IMPORTS list. (This problem disappears when you use import libraries, as described in the next section.)

You can also use different function names within HDRTEST.C. For example, suppose you want to refer to these three functions as *Puts*, *Printf*, and *Ellipse*. You'd first have to use these new names to declare the functions when compiling HDRTEST.C. You change HDRLIB.DEF to reference the functions by their real names:

```
IMPORTS   Puts    = HDRLIB.HdrPuts
          _Printf = HDRLIB._HdrPrintf
          Ellipse = HDRLIB.HdrEllipse
```

Or, if you use ordinals in the EXPORTS list of HDRLIB.DEF, you refer to the ordinals:

```
IMPORTS   Puts    = HDRLIB.1
          _Printf = HDRLIB.2
          Ellipse = HDRLIB.3
```

Creating an Import Library

But why do we need an IMPORTS section at all in HDRTEST.DEF? After all, we've been using functions in PMWIN.DLL since Chapter 2, and this is the first time we've had to write an IMPORTS statement.

You can eliminate the need for the IMPORTS section by creating an import library. You'll use this import library in the same way you use OS2.LIB, which is an import library for all the OS/2 and Presentation Manager function calls. The import library provides the same information to LINK as the IMPORTS section of a module definition file.

To create an import library for HDRLIB, you add the following two lines to the HDRLIB make file:

```
hdrlib.lib : hdrlib.def
    implib hdrlib.lib hdrlib.def
```

The IMPLIB.EXE program is included with the Microsoft C compiler. This program reads the module definition file used to create the library. From that file, IMPLIB obtains the module name and the names of the exported functions. (The EXPORTS section of HDRLIB.DEF can use either the names or ordinal numbers.) The IMPLIB.EXE program creates an import library called HDRLIB.LIB. If you want, you can use the LIB program included with the Microsoft C compiler to combine several different import libraries into one. This is how OS2.LIB was created.

To use this import library when creating HDRTEST.EXE, first remove the IMPORTS list from HDRTEST.DEF. Then change the LINK step in the HDRTEST make file to be

```
hdrtest.exe : hdrtest.obj hdrtest.def hdrlib.lib
    link hdrtest, /align:16, NUL, os2 hdrlib, hdrtest
```

Notice the two changes: The HDRLIB.LIB file is now a dependent file for the LINK step. HDRLIB.LIB is also listed in the library field of LINK along with OS2.LIB. (In both cases the .LIB extension is assumed.) You can now create HDRLIB.LIB by running

```
MAKE HDRLIB
```

and remake HDRTEST.EXE by running

```
MAKE HDRTEST
```

For just a few functions, using an explicit IMPORTS list in the program's .DEF file is satisfactory, but for a dynamic link library with lots of functions, the import library is definitely preferable. You'll want to specify ordinal numbers in the EXPORTS section of the library's .DEF file to save space in any .EXE file that uses the library.

Libraries and Window Procedures

What makes Presentation Manager programs different from conventional programs is the messaging system. Window procedures send and receive messages. But is it possible for you to put a window procedure in a dynamic link library?

Of course! All window classes that are predefined by the Presentation Manager (such as those for title bar windows and scroll-bar windows) have window procedures in PMWIN.DLL. There's no reason why we can't also put a window procedure in a library module. Let's try it.

The DLL Version of Square Button

In Chapter 11 we wrote a window procedure for a square 3-D push button and used this button in the BUTTONS2 program. Figure 16-4 shows four source code files to create SQBTNLIB.DLL, a dynamic link library that contains the square button window procedure.

The SQBTNLIB File

```
#-------------------
# SQBTNLIB make file
#-------------------

sqbtnlib.obj : sqbtnlib.c sqbtnlib.h
    cl -c -Alfw -G2sw -W3 sqbtnlib.c

sqbtnlib.dll : sqbtnlib.obj sqbtnlib.def
    link sqbtnlib, sqbtnlib.dll /align:16, NUL, /nod llibcdll os2, sqbtnlib

sqbtnlib.lib : sqbtnlib.def
    implib sqbtnlib.lib sqbtnlib.def
```

The SQBTNLIB.H File

```
/*-----------------------
    SQBTNLIB.H header file
    -----------------------*/


BOOL APIENTRY RegisterSqBtnClass (HAB hab) ;
```

The SQBTNLIB.C File

```
/*--------------------------------------------------------------------
    SQBTNLIB.C -- Dynamic link library version of square 3D push button
    --------------------------------------------------------------------*/

#define INCL_WIN
#define INCL_GPI
#include <os2.h>
#include <malloc.h>
#include <string.h>
#include "sqbtnlib.h"

#define LCID_ITALIC 1L

                    /*-----------------------------------------------------
                        Structure for storing data unique to each window
                        -----------------------------------------------------*/
typedef struct
    {
    PSZ  pszText ;
    BOOL fHaveCapture ;
    BOOL fHaveFocus ;
    BOOL fInsideRect ;
    BOOL fSpaceDown ;
    }
    SQBTN ;

typedef SQBTN *PSQBTN ;

MRESULT EXPENTRY SqBtnWndProc (HWND, USHORT, MPARAM, MPARAM) ;
VOID             DrawButton   (HWND, HPS, PSQBTN) ;

HAB  hab ;
```

(continued)

Figure 16-4. The SQBTNLIB.C File. *continued*

```
                /*------------------------------------------------------------
                   RegisterSqBtnClass function available to other modules
                ------------------------------------------------------------*/

BOOL APIENTRY RegisterSqBtnClass (HAB habIn)
     {
     hab = habIn ;

     return WinRegisterClass (hab, "SqBtn", SqBtnWndProc,
                              CS_SIZEREDRAW, sizeof (PSQBTN)) ;
     }


                /*--------------------------------
                   SqBtnWndProc window procedure
                --------------------------------*/

MRESULT EXPENTRY SqBtnWndProc (HWND hwnd, USHORT msg, MPARAM mp1, MPARAM mp2)
     {
     BOOL          fTestInsideRect ;
     HPS           hps ;
     PCREATESTRUCT pcrst ;
     POINTL        ptl ;
     PSQBTN        pSqBtn ;
     PWNDPARAMS    pwprm ;
     RECTL         rcl ;

     pSqBtn = WinQueryWindowPtr (hwnd, 0) ;

     switch (msg)
          {
          case WM_CREATE:
               pSqBtn = malloc (sizeof (SQBTN)) ;

                    // Initialize structure

               pSqBtn->fHaveCapture = FALSE ;
               pSqBtn->fHaveFocus   = FALSE ;
               pSqBtn->fInsideRect   = FALSE ;
               pSqBtn->fSpaceDown   = FALSE ;

                    // Get window text from creation structure

               pcrst = (PCREATESTRUCT) PVOIDFROMMP (mp2) ;
```

(continued)

Figure 16-4. The SQBTNLIB.C File. *continued*

```
        pSqBtn->pszText = malloc (1 + strlen (pcrst->pszText)) ;
        strcpy (pSqBtn->pszText, pcrst->pszText) ;

        WinSetWindowPtr (hwnd, 0, pSqBtn) ;
        return 0 ;

case WM_SETWINDOWPARAMS:
        pwprm = (PWNDPARAMS) PVOIDFROMMP (mp1) ;

                // Get window text from window parameter structure

        if (pwprm->fsStatus & WPM_TEXT)
            {
            free (pSqBtn->pszText) ;
            pSqBtn->pszText = malloc (1 + pwprm->cchText) ;
            strcpy (pSqBtn->pszText, pwprm->pszText) ;
            }
        return 1 ;

case WM_QUERYWINDOWPARAMS:
        pwprm == (PWNDPARAMS) PVOIDFROMMP (mp1) ;

                // Set window parameter structure fields

        if (pwprm->fsStatus & WPM_CCHTEXT)
            pwprm->cchText = strlen (pSqBtn->pszText) ;

        if (pwprm->fsStatus & WPM_TEXT)
            strcpy (pwprm->pszText, pSqBtn->pszText) ;

        if (pwprm->fsStatus & WPM_CBPRESPARAMS)
            pwprm->cbPresParams = 0 ;

        if (pwprm->fsStatus & WPM_PRESPARAMS)
            pwprm->pPresParams = NULL ;

        if (pwprm->fsStatus & WPM_CBCTLDATA)
            pwprm->cbCtlData = 0 ;

        if (pwprm->fsStatus & WPM_CTLDATA)
            pwprm->pCtlData = NULL ;

        return 1 ;
```

(continued)

Figure 16-4. The SQBTNLIB.C File. *continued*

```
        case WM_BUTTON1DOWN:
             WinSetFocus (HWND_DESKTOP, hwnd) ;
             WinSetCapture (HWND_DESKTOP, hwnd) ;
             pSqBtn->fHaveCapture = TRUE ;
             pSqBtn->fInsideRect  = TRUE ;
             WinInvalidateRect (hwnd, NULL, FALSE) ;
             return 0 ;

        case WM_MOUSEMOVE:
             if (!pSqBtn->fHaveCapture)
                  break ;

             WinQueryWindowRect (hwnd, &rcl) ;
             ptl.x = MOUSEMSG(&msg)->x ;
             ptl.y = MOUSEMSG(&msg)->y ;

                       // Test if mouse pointer is still in window

             fTestInsideRect = WinPtInRect (hab, &rcl, &ptl) ;

             if (pSqBtn->fInsideRect != fTestInsideRect)
                  {
                  pSqBtn->fInsideRect = fTestInsideRect ;
                  WinInvalidateRect (hwnd, NULL, FALSE) ;
                  }
             break ;

        case WM_BUTTON1UP:
             if (!pSqBtn->fHaveCapture)
                  break ;

             WinSetCapture (HWND_DESKTOP, NULL) ;
             pSqBtn->fHaveCapture = FALSE ;
             pSqBtn->fInsideRect  = FALSE ;

             WinQueryWindowRect (hwnd, &rcl) ;
             ptl.x = MOUSEMSG(&msg)->x ;
             ptl.y = MOUSEMSG(&msg)->y ;

                       // Post WM_COMMAND if mouse pointer is in window

             if (WinPtInRect (hab, &rcl, &ptl))
                  WinPostMsg (WinQueryWindow (hwnd, QW_OWNER, FALSE),
                       WM_COMMAND,
                       MPFROMSHORT (WinQueryWindowUShort (hwnd, QWS_ID)),
                       MPFROM2SHORT (CMDSRC_OTHER, TRUE)) ;
```

(continued)

Figure 16-4. The SQBTNLIB.C File. *continued*

```
            WinInvalidateRect (hwnd, NULL, FALSE) ;
            return 0 ;

    case WM_ENABLE:
            WinInvalidateRect (hwnd, NULL, FALSE) ;
            return 0 ;

    case WM_SETFOCUS:
            pSqBtn->fHaveFocus = SHORT1FROMMP (mp2) ;
            WinInvalidateRect (hwnd, NULL, FALSE) ;
            return 0 ;

    case WM_CHAR:
            if (!(CHARMSG(&msg)->fs & KC_VIRTUALKEY) ||
                    CHARMSG(&msg)->vkey != VK_SPACE    ||
                    CHARMSG(&msg)->fs & KC_PREVDOWN)
                break ;

                    // Post WM_COMMAND when space bar is released

            if (!(CHARMSG(&msg)->fs & KC_KEYUP))
                pSqBtn->fSpaceDown = TRUE ;
            else
                {
                pSqBtn->fSpaceDown = FALSE ;
                WinPostMsg (WinQueryWindow (hwnd, QW_OWNER, FALSE),
                    WM_COMMAND,
                    MPFROMSHORT (WinQueryWindowUShort (hwnd, QWS_ID)),
                    MPFROM2SHORT (CMDSRC_OTHER, FALSE)) ;
                }
            WinInvalidateRect (hwnd, NULL, FALSE) ;
            return 0 ;

    case WM_PAINT:
            hps = WinBeginPaint (hwnd, NULL, NULL) ;
            DrawButton (hwnd, hps, pSqBtn) ;
            WinEndPaint (hps) ;
            return 0 ;

    case WM_DESTROY:
            free (pSqBtn->pszText) ;
            free (pSqBtn) ;
            return 0 ;
    }
```

(continued)

Figure 16-4. The SQBTNLIB.C File. *continued*

```
        return WinDefWindowProc (hwnd, msg, mp1, mp2) ;
        }

        /*-----------------------------------------------------------
              Draws filled and outlined polygon (used by DrawButton)
           -------------------------------------------------------*/

VOID Polygon (HPS hps, LONG lPoints, POINTL aptl[], LONG lColor)
        {
                // Draw interior in specified color

        GpiSavePS (hps) ;
        GpiSetColor (hps, lColor) ;

        GpiBeginArea (hps, BA_NOBOUNDARY | BA_ALTERNATE) ;
        GpiMove (hps, aptl) ;
        GpiPolyLine (hps, lPoints - 1, aptl + 1) ;
        GpiEndArea (hps) ;

        GpiRestorePS (hps, -1L) ;

                // Draw boundary in default color

        GpiMove (hps, aptl + lPoints - 1) ;
        GpiPolyLine (hps, lPoints, aptl) ;
        }

        /*---------------------
              Draws Square Button
           -------------------*/

VOID DrawButton (HWND hwnd, HPS hps, PSQBTN pSqBtn)
        {
        FATTRS      fat ;
        FONTMETRICS fm ;
        HDC         hdc ;
        LONG        lColor, lHorzRes, lVertRes, cxEdge, cyEdge ;
        POINTL      aptl[10], aptlTextBox[TXTBOX_COUNT], ptlShadow, ptlText ;
        RECTL       rcl ;

                // Find 2 millimeter edge width in pixels

        hdc = GpiQueryDevice (hps) ;
        DevQueryCaps (hdc, CAPS_HORIZONTAL_RESOLUTION, 1L, &lHorzRes) ;
        DevQueryCaps (hdc, CAPS_VERTICAL_RESOLUTION,   1L, &lVertRes) ;
```

(continued)

Figure 16-4. The SQBTNLIB.C File. *continued*

```
          cxEdge = lHorzRes / 500 ;
          cyEdge = lVertRes / 500 ;

                    // Set up coordinates for drawing the button

     WinQueryWindowRect (hwnd, &rcl) ;

     aptl[0].x = 0 ;                        aptl[0].y = 0 ;
     aptl[1].x = cxEdge ;                   aptl[1].y = cyEdge ;
     aptl[2].x = rcl.xRight - cxEdge ;      aptl[2].y = cyEdge ;
     aptl[3].x = rcl.xRight - 1 ;           aptl[3].y = 0 ;
     aptl[4].x = rcl.xRight - 1 ;           aptl[4].y = rcl.yTop - 1 ;
     aptl[5].x = rcl.xRight - cxEdge ;      aptl[5].y = rcl.yTop - cyEdge ;
     aptl[6].x = cxEdge ;                   aptl[6].y = rcl.yTop - cyEdge ;
     aptl[7].x = 0 ;                        aptl[7].y = rcl.yTop - 1 ;
     aptl[8].x = 0 ;                        aptl[8].y = 0 ;
     aptl[9].x = cxEdge ;                   aptl[9].y = cyEdge ;

                    // Paint edges at bottom and right side

     GpiSetColor (hps, CLR_BLACK) ;
     lColor = (pSqBtn->fInsideRect || pSqBtn->fSpaceDown) ?
                         CLR_PALEGRAY : CLR_DARKGRAY ;
     Polygon (hps, 4L, aptl + 0, lColor) ;
     Polygon (hps, 4L, aptl + 2, lColor) ;

                    // Paint edges at top and left side

     lColor = (pSqBtn->fInsideRect || pSqBtn->fSpaceDown) ?
                         CLR_DARKGRAY : CLR_WHITE ;
     Polygon (hps, 4L, aptl + 4, lColor) ;
     Polygon (hps, 4L, aptl + 6, lColor) ;

                    // Paint interior area

     GpiSavePS (hps) ;
     GpiSetColor (hps, (pSqBtn->fInsideRect || pSqBtn->fSpaceDown) ?
                         CLR_DARKGRAY : CLR_PALEGRAY) ;
     GpiMove (hps, aptl + 1) ;
     GpiBox (hps, DRO_FILL, aptl + 5, 0L, 0L) ;
     GpiRestorePS (hps, -1L) ;
     GpiBox (hps, DRO_OUTLINE, aptl + 5, 0L, 0L) ;

                    // If button has focus, use italic font
```

(continued)

Figure 16-4. The SQBTNLIB.C File. *continued*

```
GpiQueryFontMetrics (hps, (LONG) sizeof fm, &fm) ;

if (pSqBtn->fHaveFocus)
    {
    fat.usRecordLength  = sizeof fat ;
    fat.fsSelection     = FATTR_SEL_ITALIC ;
    fat.lMatch          = 0 ;
    fat.idRegistry      = fm.idRegistry ;
    fat.usCodePage      = fm.usCodePage ;
    fat.lMaxBaselineExt = fm.lMaxBaselineExt ;
    fat.lAveCharWidth   = fm.lAveCharWidth ;
    fat.fsType          = 0 ;
    fat.fsFontUse       = 0 ;
    strcpy (fat.szFacename, fm.szFacename) ;

    GpiCreateLogFont (hps, NULL, LCID_ITALIC, &fat) ;
    GpiSetCharSet (hps, LCID_ITALIC) ;
    }
        // Calculate text position

GpiQueryTextBox (hps, (LONG) strlen (pSqBtn->pszText), pSqBtn->pszText,
                 TXTBOX_COUNT, aptlTextBox) ;

ptlText.x = (rcl.xRight - aptlTextBox[TXTBOX_CONCAT].x) / 2 ;
ptlText.y = (rcl.yTop   - aptlTextBox[TXTBOX_TOPLEFT].y -
                          aptlTextBox[TXTBOX_BOTTOMLEFT].y) / 2 ;

ptlShadow.x = ptlText.x + fm.lAveCharWidth   / 3 ;
ptlShadow.y = ptlText.y - fm.lMaxBaselineExt / 8 ;

        // Display text shadow in black, and text in white

GpiSetColor (hps, CLR_BLACK) ;
GpiCharStringAt (hps, &ptlShadow, (LONG) strlen (pSqBtn->pszText),
                                  pSqBtn->pszText) ;
GpiSetColor (hps, CLR_WHITE) ;
GpiCharStringAt (hps, &ptlText, (LONG) strlen (pSqBtn->pszText),
                                pSqBtn->pszText) ;

        // X out button if the window is not enabled

if (!WinIsWindowEnabled (hwnd))
    {
    GpiMove (hps, aptl + 1) ;
    GpiLine (hps, aptl + 5) ;
```

(continued)

Figure 16-4. The SQBTNLIB.C File. *continued*

```
        GpiMove (hps, aptl + 2) ;
        GpiLine (hps, aptl + 6) ;
        }
            // Clean up

    if (pSqBtn->fHaveFocus)
        {
        GpiSetCharSet (hps, LCID_DEFAULT) ;
        GpiDeleteSetId (hps, LCID_ITALIC) ;
        }
    }
```

The SQBTNLIB.DEF File

```
;-------------------------------------------
; SQBTNLIB.DEF module definition file
;-------------------------------------------


LIBRARY        SQBTNLIB  INITINSTANCE

DESCRIPTION    'Square Button Dynamic Link Library (C) Charles Petzold, 1988'
PROTMODE
DATA           NONSHARED
HEAPSIZE       1024
EXPORTS        RegisterSqBtnClass
               SqBtnWndProc
```

Figure 16-4. *The SQBTNLIB library.*

The SQBTNLIB make file compiles SQBTNLIB.C with the *-Alfw* and *-G2sw* switches. The *-Aw* switch causes the compiler to assume that DS != SS. The *-Gw* switch inserts the "window procedure" prologue and epilogue in all far functions. The EXPORTS section of the SQBTNLIB.DEF file lists both *RegisterSqBtnClass* (which is the function that a program calls to register the window class) and *SqBtnWndProc*, which must be exported because it is a window procedure. The make file reads SQBTNLIB.DEF to create an import library called SQBTNLIB.LIB.

SQBTNLIB.C is mostly the same as the SQBTN.C file shown in Chapter 11. The only changes are as follows:

- *RegisterSqBtnClass* is now defined as an APIENTRY function because it must be called from outside the dynamic link library. The declaration of this function has been moved to SQBNTLIB.H, a header file that will be used in a program that creates a square push button.

- Calls to *_fmalloc* and *_ffree* have been replaced with the more standard *malloc* and *free*. This is not really necessary because the two pairs of functions are identical in large model.

- The *fstrlen* and *fstrcpy* functions have been removed. Calls to these functions have been replaced with *strlen* and *strcpy*. Because we compile the dynamic link library for large model, the normal C library functions can handle far pointers.

The New BUTTONS Program

The BUTTONS3 program is shown in Figure 16-5.

The BUTTONS3 File

```
#-------------------
# BUTTONS3 make file
#-------------------

buttons3.obj : buttons3.c sqbtnlib.h
    cl -c -G2sw -W3 buttons3.c

buttons3.exe : buttons3.obj buttons3.def sqbtnlib.lib
    link buttons3, /align:16, NUL, os2 sqbtnlib, buttons3
```

The BUTTONS3.C File

```
/*-----------------------------------------------------
    BUTTONS3.C -- Square Button Demonstration with DLL
    ---------------------------------------------------*/

#define INCL_WIN
#define INCL_GPI
#include <os2.h>
#include "sqbtnlib.h"

MRESULT EXPENTRY ClientWndProc (HWND, USHORT, MPARAM, MPARAM) ;

HAB  hab ;

int main (void)
    {
    static CHAR  szClientClass[] = "Buttons3" ;
    static ULONG flFrameFlags = FCF_TITLEBAR       | FCF_SYSMENU  |
                                FCF_SIZEBORDER     | FCF_MINMAX   |
                                FCF_SHELLPOSITION  | FCF_TASKLIST ;
```

(continued)

Figure 16-5. The BUTTONS3.C File. *continued*

```
    HMQ          hmq ;
    HWND         hwndFrame, hwndClient ;
    QMSG         qmsg ;

    hab = WinInitialize (0) ;
    hmq = WinCreateMsgQueue (hab, 0) ;

    WinRegisterClass (hab, szClientClass, ClientWndProc, CS_SIZEREDRAW, 0) ;

    hwndFrame = WinCreateStdWindow (HWND_DESKTOP, WS_VISIBLE,
                                    &flFrameFlags, szClientClass, NULL,
                                    0L, NULL, 0, &hwndClient) ;

    WinSendMsg (hwndFrame, WM_SETICON,
                WinQuerySysPointer (HWND_DESKTOP, SPTR_APPICON, FALSE),
                NULL) ;

    while (WinGetMsg (hab, &qmsg, NULL, 0, 0))
        WinDispatchMsg (hab, &qmsg) ;

    WinDestroyWindow (hwndFrame) ;
    WinDestroyMsgQueue (hmq) ;
    WinTerminate (hab) ;
    return 0 ;
    }

MRESULT EXPENTRY ClientWndProc (HWND hwnd, USHORT msg, MPARAM mp1, MPARAM mp2)
    {
    static CHAR   szSqBtnClass [] = "SqBtn",
                  *szButtonLabel [] = { "Smaller", "Larger" } ;
    static HWND   hwndFrame, hwndButton [2] ;
    static SHORT  cxClient, cyClient, cxChar, cyChar ;
    FONTMETRICS   fm ;
    HPS           hps ;
    SHORT         id ;
    RECTL         rcl ;

    switch (msg)
        {
        case WM_CREATE :
            hwndFrame = WinQueryWindow (hwnd, QW_PARENT, FALSE) ;

            hps = WinGetPS (hwnd) ;
            GpiQueryFontMetrics (hps, (LONG) sizeof fm, &fm) ;
```

(continued)

Figure 16-5. The BUTTONS3.C File. *continued*

```
            cxChar = (SHORT) fm.lAveCharWidth ;
            cyChar = (SHORT) fm.lMaxBaselineExt ;
            WinReleasePS (hps) ;

            RegisterSqBtnClass (hab) ;

            for (id = 0 ; id < 2 ; id++)
                hwndButton [id] = WinCreateWindow (
                                    hwnd,                  // Parent
                                    "SqBtn",               // Class
                                    szButtonLabel [id],    // Text
                                    WS_VISIBLE,            // Style
                                    0, 0,                  // Position
                                    12 * cxChar,           // Width
                                    2 * cyChar,            // Height
                                    hwnd,                  // Owner
                                    HWND_BOTTOM,           // Placement
                                    id,                    // ID
                                    NULL,                  // Ctrl data
                                    NULL) ;                // Pres params
            return 0 ;

        case WM_SIZE :
            cxClient = SHORT1FROMMP (mp2) ;
            cyClient = SHORT2FROMMP (mp2) ;

            for (id = 0 ; id < 2 ; id++)
                WinSetWindowPos (hwndButton [id], NULL,
                        cxClient / 2 + (14 * id - 13) * cxChar,
                        (cyClient - 2 * cyChar) / 2,
                        0, 0, SWP_MOVE) ;
            return 0 ;

        case WM_COMMAND:
            WinQueryWindowRect (hwnd, &rcl) ;
            WinMapWindowPoints (hwnd, HWND_DESKTOP, (PPOINTL) &rcl, 2) ;

            switch (COMMANDMSG(&msg)->cmd)                 // Child ID
                {
                case 0:                                    // "Smaller"
                    rcl.xLeft   += cxClient / 20 ;
                    rcl.xRight  -= cxClient / 20 ;
                    rcl.yBottom += cyClient / 20 ;
                    rcl.yTop    -= cyClient / 20 ;
```

(continued)

Figure 16-5. The BUTTONS3.C File. *continued*

```
                      break ;

            case 1:                                    // "Larger"
                rcl.xLeft   -= cxClient / 20 ;
                rcl.xRight  += cxClient / 20 ;
                rcl.yBottom -= cyClient / 20 ;
                rcl.yTop    += cyClient / 20 ;
                break ;
            }
        WinCalcFrameRect (hwndFrame, &rcl, FALSE) ;

        WinSetWindowPos (hwndFrame, NULL,
            (SHORT) rcl.xLeft, (SHORT) rcl.yBottom,
            (SHORT) rcl.xRight - (SHORT) rcl.xLeft,
            (SHORT) rcl.yTop   - (SHORT) rcl.yBottom,
            SWP_MOVE | SWP_SIZE) ;
        return 0 ;

    case WM_ERASEBACKGROUND:
        return 1 ;
    }
return WinDefWindowProc (hwnd, msg, mp1, mp2) ;
}
```

The BUTTONS3.DEF File

```
;----------------------------------------
; BUTTONS3.DEF module definition file
;----------------------------------------

NAME            BUTTONS3  WINDOWAPI

DESCRIPTION     'Square Button Demo with DLL (C) Charles Petzold, 1988'
PROTMODE
HEAPSIZE        1024
STACKSIZE       8192
EXPORTS         ClientWndProc
```

Figure 16-5. *The BUTTONS3 program.*

You'll also need the SQBTNLIB.H header file from Figure 16-4 to compile BUTTONS3.

These three files are nearly identical to those used for the BUTTONS2 program except that the make file lists SQBTNLIB.LIB in the library field of the LINK step, and the declaration of *RegisterSqBtnClass* (which indicates that it's an APIENTRY function) is provided by the SQBTNLIB.H header file.

Resource-only Libraries

You can also store resources in dynamic link libraries and access them from a program. The library module that contains these resources can also contain code and data segments. But it's also possible to create a library module containing nothing but resources.

Why would you want to do this? As we saw in Chapter 12, you can create bitmaps in ICONEDIT and store them as resources in a program. However, bitmaps are very dependent on the resolution of the device for which they are designed. If your program uses bitmaps within its client window, you might want to customize a set of bitmaps for each of the most common video display adapters (for example, the EGA, the VGA, and the IBM 8514/A). Each of these sets of bitmaps would be stored in a different resource-only dynamic link library. You could design an installation routine for your program to copy only the resource library for the user's video adapter to the user's hard disk.

Creating a Bitmap Library

The files shown in Figure 16-6 are used to create a resource-only library called BITLIB.DLL. This dynamic link library contains nine 32-by-32 bitmaps created in ICONEDIT.

The BITLIB File

```
#-------------------
# BITLIB make file
#-------------------

bitlib.obj : bitlib.asm
     masm bitlib ;

bitlib.res : bitlib.rc bitmap1.bmp bitmap2.bmp bitmap3.bmp \
                       bitmap4.bmp bitmap5.bmp bitmap6.bmp \
                       bitmap7.bmp bitmap8.bmp bitmap9.bmp
     rc -r bitlib

bitlib.dll : bitlib.obj bitlib.def
     link bitlib, bitlib.dll /align:16, NUL,, bitlib
     rc bitlib.res bitlib.dll

bitlib.dll : bitlib.res
     rc bitlib.res bitlib.dll
```

The BITLIB.ASM File

```
;-----------------------------------------------------------------
; BITLIB.ASM assembly language module for resource-only library
;-----------------------------------------------------------------

        end
```

The BITLIB.RC File

```
/*-------------------------------------
    BITLIB.RC resource script file
  ---------------------------------*/

BITMAP 1 bitmap1.bmp
BITMAP 2 bitmap2.bmp
BITMAP 3 bitmap3.bmp
BITMAP 4 bitmap4.bmp
BITMAP 5 bitmap5.bmp
BITMAP 6 bitmap6.bmp
BITMAP 7 bitmap7.bmp
BITMAP 8 bitmap8.bmp
BITMAP 9 bitmap9.bmp
```

The BITMAP1.BMP File

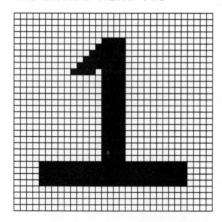

The BITMAP2.BMP File

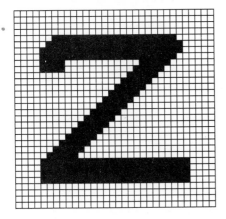

The BITMAP3.BMP File

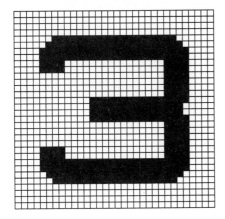

The BITMAP4.BMP File

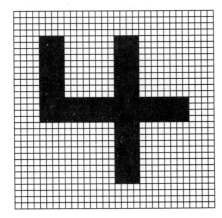

The BITMAP5.BMP File

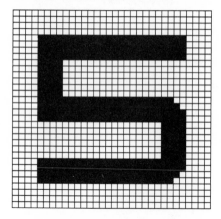

The BITMAP6.BMP File

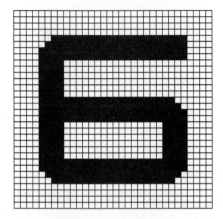

The BITMAP7.BMP File

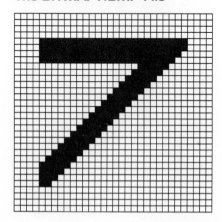

The BITMAP8.BMP File

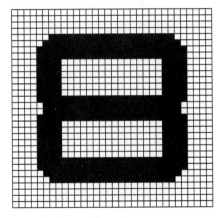

The BITMAP9.BMP File

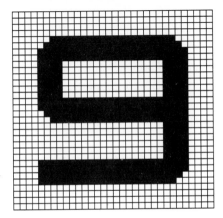

The BITLIB.DEF File

```
;-------------------------------------
; BITLIB.DEF module definition file
;-------------------------------------

LIBRARY        BITLIB

DESCRIPTION    'Bitmap Library for SHOWBIT (C) Charles Petzold, 1988'
```

Figure 16-6. *The BITLIB library.*

The hard part of this job is persuading LINK to create a dynamic link library that contains no code or data segments. But it's actually simpler than it seems. The BITLIB.ASM file is the simplest assembly language source code file possible. It contains only an *end* statement. But this is enough to create BITLIB.OBJ. All LINK needs is BITLIB.OBJ and BITLIB.DEF. The BITLIB.DEF file is equally simple—it contains only LIBRARY and DESCRIPTION statements. The BITLIB.RC resource script file lists the nine bitmap files and assigns them IDs of 1 through 9.

DLLs and Module Handles

After you create BITLIB.DLL, you may wonder again whether loading resources from a library module into a program is possible. When you load a bitmap using *GpiLoadBitmap*, how does OS/2 know whether you want to load the bitmap from your .EXE file or from a library module? And how does OS/2 know *which* library module to load the bitmap from?

If you look again at the various functions that load resources into memory (such as *DosGetResource*, *WinCreateStdWindow*, *WinLoadString*, *WinLoadMessage*, *WinLoadDlg*, *WinDlgBox*, *WinLoadMenu*, *WinLoadAccelTable*, *WinLoadPointer*, and *GpiLoadBitmap*), you'll discover that each function has a parameter called the "module handle." When a program wants to load a resource from its .EXE file, the program sets this parameter to NULL. When the program wants to load a resource from a dynamic link library, the parameter must be set to the module handle of the library.

To obtain a module handle, you first define a variable of type HMODULE:

```
HMODULE hmod ;
```

Then you call *DosLoadModule*:

```
DosLoadModule (NULL, 0, szModuleName, &hmod) ;
```

The first two parameters can be set to a character string and a length of the string to receive information if an error occurs, in which case *DosLoadModule* returns a nonzero value. The third parameter is the name of the dynamic link library file without the .DLL extension.

Besides making the dynamic link library available for use, the *DosLoadModule* function increments the "reference count" of the module. You should free the module before the program terminates:

```
DosFreeModule (hmod) ;
```

This decreases the reference count. When the reference count of a library module is zero, OS/2 can free the module from memory.

Loading Bitmaps from the DLL

With this ability to obtain a module handle, we're ready to load the bitmaps from BITLIB.DLL into memory and display them. The SHOWBIT program in Figure 16-7 shows how this is done.

The SHOWBIT File

```
#-------------------
# SHOWBIT make file
#-------------------

showbit.obj : showbit.c
    cl -c -G2sw -W3 showbit.c

showbit.exe : showbit.obj showbit.def
    link showbit, /align:16, NUL, os2, showbit
```

The SHOWBIT.C File

```
/*-------------------------------------------------------------------
    SHOWBIT.C -- Loads Bitmap Resources from BITLIB.DLL and Draws Them
    ---------------------------------------------------------------*/

#define INCL_DOS
#define INCL_WIN
#include <os2.h>

MRESULT EXPENTRY ClientWndProc (HWND, USHORT, MPARAM, MPARAM) ;

int main (void)
    {
    static CHAR   szClientClass [] = "ShowBit" ;
    static ULONG  flFrameFlags = FCF_TITLEBAR      | FCF_SYSMENU   |
                                 FCF_SIZEBORDER    | FCF_MINMAX    |
                                 FCF_SHELLPOSITION | FCF_TASKLIST ;
    HAB           hab ;
    HMQ           hmq ;
    HWND          hwndFrame, hwndClient ;
    QMSG          qmsg ;

    hab = WinInitialize (0) ;
    hmq = WinCreateMsgQueue (hab, 0) ;
```

(continued)

Figure 16-7. The SHOWBIT.C File. *continued*

```
     WinRegisterClass (hab, szClientClass, ClientWndProc, CS_SIZEREDRAW, 0) ;

     hwndFrame = WinCreateStdWindow (HWND_DESKTOP, WS_VISIBLE,
                                     &flFrameFlags, szClientClass,
                                     " (Space bar or mouse click for next)",
                                     OL, NULL, 0, &hwndClient) ;
     if (hwndFrame != NULL)
         {
         while (WinGetMsg (hab, &qmsg, NULL, 0, 0))
               WinDispatchMsg (hab, &qmsg) ;

         WinDestroyWindow (hwndFrame) ;
         }
     WinDestroyMsgQueue (hmq) ;
     WinTerminate (hab) ;
     return 0 ;
     }

MRESULT EXPENTRY ClientWndProc (HWND hwnd, USHORT msg, MPARAM mp1, MPARAM mp2)
     {
     static HMODULE hmodBitLib ;
     static USHORT  idBitmap = 1 ;
     HBITMAP        hbm ;
     HPS            hps ;
     RECTL          rcl ;

     switch (msg)
         {
         case WM_CREATE:
              if (DosLoadModule (NULL, 0, "BITLIB", &hmodBitLib))
                  {
                  WinMessageBox (HWND_DESKTOP, HWND_DESKTOP,
                                 "Cannot load BITLIB.DLL library",
                                 "ShowBit", 0, MB_OK | MB_ICONEXCLAMATION) ;
                  return 1 ;
                  }
              return 0 ;

         case WM_CHAR:
              if (  CHARMSG(&msg)->fs & KC_KEYUP ||
                   !(CHARMSG(&msg)->fs & KC_VIRTUALKEY) ||
                   !(CHARMSG(&msg)->vkey == VK_SPACE))
                        break ;

              if (++idBitmap == 10)
                   idBitmap = 1 ;
```

(continued)

Figure 16-7. The SHOWBIT.C File. *continued*

```
                  WinInvalidateRect (hwnd, NULL, FALSE) ;
                  return 0 ;

          case WM_BUTTON1DOWN:
                  if (++idBitmap == 10)
                      idBitmap = 1 ;

                  WinInvalidateRect (hwnd, NULL, FALSE) ;
                  break ;

          case WM_PAINT:
                  hps = WinBeginPaint (hwnd, NULL, NULL) ;
                  GpiErase (hps) ;

                  hbm = GpiLoadBitmap (hps, hmodBitLib, idBitmap, 0L, 0L) ;

                  if (hbm != NULL)
                      {
                      WinQueryWindowRect (hwnd, &rcl) ;

                      WinDrawBitmap (hps, hbm, NULL, (PPOINTL) &rcl,
                                          CLR_NEUTRAL, CLR_BACKGROUND, DBM_STRETCH) ;

                      GpiDeleteBitmap (hbm) ;
                      }
                  WinEndPaint (hps) ;
                  return 0 ;

          case WM_DESTROY:
                  DosFreeModule (hmodBitLib) ;
                  return 0 ;
          }
      return WinDefWindowProc (hwnd, msg, mp1, mp2) ;
      }
```

The SHOWBIT.DEF File

```
;------------------------------------
; SHOWBIT.DEF module definition file
;------------------------------------

NAME        SHOWBIT    WINDOWAPI
```

(continued)

Figure 16-7. The SHOWBIT.DEF File. *continued*

```
DESCRIPTION      'Loads bitmap resources from BITLIB (C) Charles Petzold, 1988'
PROTMODE
HEAPSIZE         1024
STACKSIZE        8192
EXPORTS          ClientWndProc
```

Figure 16-7. *The SHOWBIT program.*

SHOWBIT calls *DosLoadModule* during the WM_CREATE message. If the function fails (probably because BITLIB.DLL is not in one of the directories listed in the user's LIBPATH), SHOWBIT displays a message box and returns 1 from the WM_CREATE message, which then causes the program to terminate.

If *DosLoadModule* is successful, *GpiLoadBitmap* loads the bitmap during the WM_PAINT message. The function requires the module handle and the bitmap ID. The module is freed during the WM_DESTROY message.

MULTITHREAD PROGRAMMING TECHNIQUES

OS/2 is a "preemptive multitasking operating system." This means that OS/2 can run multiple programs concurrently and uses a priority-based scheduler to allocate time slices among them. The Presentation Manager is part of OS/2, so the programs running in the Presentation Manager session are also multitasked.

This is probably the most significant difference between the OS/2 Presentation Manager and Microsoft Windows. Windows is a nonpreemptive multitasking environment. It does not perform the preemptive time-slicing we normally associate with a multitasking system. Instead, Windows multitasks programs based on the presence of messages in the programs' message queues.

When a Windows program calls the *GetMessage* function (equivalent to the Presentation Manager *WinGetMsg* function) to retrieve the next message from its message queue, and the message queue is empty, Windows suspends the program. Windows then switches to another program with a non-empty message queue. This causes that other program to return from its own *GetMessage* call to process the message. At any time, only one Windows program is running. The rest are suspended in the *GetMessage* function.

Windows programmers are well aware of the problems associated with this form of nonpreemptive multitasking. If a Windows program requires a long period of time to process a message, other programs running under Windows are effectively halted for the duration. Windows programmers must use special techniques when doing lengthy processing in order to prevent the program from suspending the rest of the system.

At first, the preemptive multitasking of OS/2 would seemingly eliminate the problems associated with the nonpreemptive nature of Windows. You might conclude that Presentation Manager programs can spend as much time as they need processing messages without worrying about suspending other programs.

But this is not so. As you'll see, a Presentation Manager program *cannot* spend a long time processing a message without affecting the environment as a whole. This problem results more from message-based architecture than from the preemptive or nonpreemptive nature of the multitasking system. The real difference between Microsoft Windows and the OS/2 Presentation Manager is that OS/2 provides a better solution to the problem of lengthy processing, specifically through the creation of multiple threads of execution.

Before we attempt to write a multithread Presentation Manager program, we'll examine the problem of lengthy processing jobs and explore some solutions that require only a single execution thread.

The "Big-Job" Problem

Presentation Manager programs can usually process most keyboard and mouse input very quickly. In a word-processing program, for example, a character typed from the keyboard need only be inserted into the stored document and displayed on the screen. But many programs must also carry out commands that require more lengthy processing. Let's call this lengthy processing a "big job."

In a spreadsheet program, the big job is a recalculation of a large spreadsheet or the execution of a long macro. In a database program, the big job is a file sort or indexing. In a word-processing program, it's a pagination or spelling check. In a CAD program, it's redrawing the screen. In a communications program, it's reading the serial port when an incoming character is not immediately available. And in almost any Presentation Manager program, printing is a big job.

The $^1/_{10}$ Second Rule

It is recommended that Presentation Manager programs take no more than $^1/_{10}$ second to process a message. When a message is passed to a window procedure in your program, the window procedure should return control to the Presentation Manager within $^1/_{10}$ second. (You'll see the reason for this shortly.) Hence, the definition of a big job is simple: It is anything your program needs to do that requires more than $^1/_{10}$ second.

I'll be referring to this as the "$^1/_{10}$ second rule," but it's really a guideline rather than a hard-and-fast rule. It is OK if a program violates this rule once in a while. For example, when a word-processing program loads a document file into memory, it's not a serious problem if this requires a few seconds.

In fact, several of the programs shown in this book violate the $^1/_{10}$ second rule. The WELCOME1 program in Chapter 2 spends $^8/_{10}$ second processing the WM_CREATE and WM_DESTROY messages because it plays a little tune by calling the *DosBeep* function. On a 6 or 8 MHz 80286-based machine, the MINMAX2 program in Chapter 6 might take more than $^1/_{10}$ second in the *GpiBitBlt* function. The HEAD program in Chapter 14 might take more than $^1/_{10}$ second to load part of a file into memory if the file is in a large subdirectory on a floppy diskette.

Don't get overly paranoid about violating the $^1/_{10}$ second rule. On the other hand, if your program *frequently* violates this rule, you'll have to do something about it. For example, if a spreadsheet program spends more than $^1/_{10}$ second in recalculations every time the user presses the Enter key, that's a problem. If the violation of the rule is infrequent (for example, if it occurs only when the program begins executing), then you can probably ignore the problem. But if you're spending 30 seconds or so initializing your program, you'll want to seek a solution.

Also keep in mind that it will be apparent when your program has a problem, because it will affect the performance of the entire Presentation Manager environment. Users will not look kindly on this type of behavior.

The Rule Violated

To examine the big-job problem, let's write a Presentation Manager program that does some lengthy processing in response to a WM_COMMAND message from a menu. This program is called BIGJOB1 and is shown in Figure 17-1 on the following pages.

The BIGJOB1 File

```
#------------------
# BIGJOB1 make file
#------------------

bigjob1.obj : bigjob1.c bigjob.h
    cl -c -G2sw -W3 bigjob1.c

bigjob.obj : bigjob.c
    cl -c -G2sw -W3 bigjob.c

bigjob.res : bigjob.rc bigjob.h
    rc -r bigjob

bigjob1.exe : bigjob1.obj bigjob.obj bigjob1.def
    link bigjob1 bigjob, /align:16, NUL, os2, bigjob1
    rc bigjob.res bigjob1.exe

bigjob1.exe : bigjob.res
    rc bigjob.res bigjob1.exe
```

The BIGJOB1.C File

```
/*------------------------------------------------------------
    BIGJOB1.C -- Naive approach to lengthy processing job
  ----------------------------------------------------------*/

#define INCL_WIN
#include <os2.h>
#include "bigjob.h"

HAB  hab ;

int main (void)
    {
    static CHAR  szClientClass [] = "BigJob1" ;
    static ULONG flFrameFlags = FCF_TITLEBAR      | FCF_SYSMENU   |
                                FCF_SIZEBORDER    | FCF_MINMAX    |
                                FCF_SHELLPOSITION | FCF_TASKLIST  |
                                FCF_MENU ;
    HMQ          hmq ;
    HWND         hwndFrame, hwndClient ;
    QMSG         qmsg ;
```

(continued)

Figure 17-1. The BIGJOB1.C File. *continued*

```
      hab = WinInitialize (0) ;
      hmq = WinCreateMsgQueue (hab, 0) ;


      WinRegisterClass (hab, szClientClass, ClientWndProc,
                        CS_SYNCPAINT | CS_SIZEREDRAW, 0) ;


      hwndFrame = WinCreateStdWindow (HWND_DESKTOP, WS_VISIBLE,
                                      &flFrameFlags, szClientClass,
                                      " - The Bad Program",
                                      0L, NULL, ID_RESOURCE, &hwndClient) ;


      WinSendMsg (hwndFrame, WM_SETICON,
                  WinQuerySysPointer (HWND_DESKTOP, SPTR_APPICON, FALSE),
                  NULL) ;


      while (WinGetMsg (hab, &qmsg, NULL, 0, 0))
          WinDispatchMsg (hab, &qmsg) ;


      WinDestroyWindow (hwndFrame) ;
      WinDestroyMsgQueue (hmq) ;
      WinTerminate (hab) ;
      return 0 ;
      }

MRESULT EXPENTRY ClientWndProc (HWND hwnd, USHORT msg, MPARAM mp1, MPARAM mp2)
      {
      static LONG  lCalcRep, lRepAmts [] = { 10, 100, 1000, 10000, 100000 } ;
      static SHORT sCurrentRep = IDM_10 ;
      static SHORT sStatus = STATUS_READY ;
      static ULONG ulElapsedTime ;
      double       A ;
      LONG         lRep ;


      switch (msg)
          {
          case WM_COMMAND:
              switch (COMMANDMSG(&msg)->cmd)
                  {
                  case IDM_10:
                  case IDM_100:
                  case IDM_1000:
                  case IDM_10000:
```

(continued)

Figure 17-1. The BIGJOB1.C File. *continued*

```
              case IDM_100000:
                   CheckMenuItem (hwnd, sCurrentRep, FALSE) ;
                   sCurrentRep = COMMANDMSG(&msg)->cmd ;
                   CheckMenuItem (hwnd, sCurrentRep, TRUE) ;
                   return 0 ;

              case IDM_START:
                   EnableMenuItem (hwnd, IDM_START, FALSE) ;
                   EnableMenuItem (hwnd, IDM_ABORT, TRUE) ;

                   sStatus = STATUS_WORKING ;
                   WinInvalidateRect (hwnd, NULL, FALSE) ;

                   WinSetPointer (HWND_DESKTOP,
                           WinQuerySysPointer (HWND_DESKTOP,
                                            SPTR_WAIT, FALSE)) ;

                   if (WinQuerySysValue (HWND_DESKTOP, SV_MOUSEPRESENT)
                           == 0)
                       WinShowPointer (HWND_DESKTOP, TRUE) ;

                   lCalcRep = lRepAmts [sCurrentRep - IDM_10] ;
                   ulElapsedTime = WinGetCurrentTime (hab) ;

                   for (A = 1.0, lRep = 0 ; lRep < lCalcRep ; lRep++)
                       A = Savage (A) ;

                   ulElapsedTime = WinGetCurrentTime (hab) -
                               ulElapsedTime ;

                   if (WinQuerySysValue (HWND_DESKTOP, SV_MOUSEPRESENT)
                           == 0)
                       WinShowPointer (HWND_DESKTOP, FALSE) ;

                   WinSetPointer (HWND_DESKTOP,
                           WinQuerySysPointer (HWND_DESKTOP,
                                            SPTR_ARROW, FALSE)) ;
                   sStatus = STATUS_DONE ;
                   WinInvalidateRect (hwnd, NULL, FALSE) ;

                   EnableMenuItem (hwnd, IDM_START, TRUE) ;
                   EnableMenuItem (hwnd, IDM_ABORT, FALSE) ;
                   return 0 ;
```

(continued)

Figure 17-1. The BIGJOB1.C File. *continued*

```
                    case IDM_ABORT:        // Not much we can do here
                        return 0 ;
                    }
                break ;

            case WM_PAINT:
                PaintWindow (hwnd, sStatus, lCalcRep, ulElapsedTime) ;
                return 0 ;
            }
        return WinDefWindowProc (hwnd, msg, mp1, mp2) ;
        }
```

The BIGJOB.C File

```
/*-------------------------------------------------------------------
   BIGJOB.C -- Common functions used in BIGJOB1, BIGJOB2, and BIGJOB3
   -----------------------------------------------------------------*/

#define INCL_WIN
#include <os2.h>
#include <math.h>
#include <stdio.h>

double Savage (double A)
    {
    return tan (atan (exp (log (sqrt (A * A))))) + 1.0 ;
    }

VOID CheckMenuItem (HWND hwnd, SHORT sMenuItem, BOOL fCheck)
    {
    HWND   hwndParent = WinQueryWindow (hwnd, QW_PARENT, FALSE) ;
    HWND   hwndMenu   = WinWindowFromID (hwndParent, FID_MENU) ;

    WinSendMsg (hwndMenu, MM_SETITEMATTR,
            MPFROM2SHORT (sMenuItem, TRUE),
            MPFROM2SHORT (MIA_CHECKED, fCheck ? MIA_CHECKED : 0)) ;
    }

VOID EnableMenuItem (HWND hwnd, SHORT sMenuItem, BOOL fEnable)
    {
    HWND   hwndParent = WinQueryWindow (hwnd, QW_PARENT, FALSE) ;
    HWND   hwndMenu   = WinWindowFromID (hwndParent, FID_MENU) ;
```

(continued)

Figure 17-1. The BIGJOB.C File. *continued*

```
      WinSendMsg (hwndMenu, MM_SETITEMATTR,
                 MPFROM2SHORT (sMenuItem, TRUE),
                 MPFROM2SHORT (MIA_DISABLED, fEnable ? 0 : MIA_DISABLED)) ;
      }

VOID PaintWindow (HWND hwnd, SHORT sStatus, LONG lCalcRep, ULONG ulTime)
      {
      static CHAR *szMessage [3] = { "Ready", "Working...",
                                     "%ld repetitions in %lu msec." } ;
      CHAR        szBuffer [60] ;
      HPS         hps ;
      RECTL       rcl ;

      hps = WinBeginPaint (hwnd, NULL, NULL) ;
      WinQueryWindowRect (hwnd, &rcl) ;

      sprintf (szBuffer, szMessage [sStatus], lCalcRep, ulTime) ;
      WinDrawText (hps, -1, szBuffer, &rcl, CLR_NEUTRAL, CLR_BACKGROUND,
                  DT_CENTER ¦ DT_VCENTER ¦ DT_ERASERECT) ;

      WinEndPaint (hps) ;
      }
```

The BIGJOB.H File

```
/*----------------------
   BIGJOB.H header file
   ----------------------*/

#define ID_RESOURCE 1

#define IDM_REPS      1
#define IDM_ACTION    2
#define IDM_10        10
#define IDM_100       11
#define IDM_1000      12
#define IDM_10000     13
#define IDM_100000    14
#define IDM_START     20
#define IDM_ABORT     21

#define STATUS_READY    0
#define STATUS_WORKING  1
```

(continued)

Figure 17-1. The BIGJOB.H File. *continued*

```
#define STATUS_DONE       2

#define WM_CALC_DONE     (WM_USER + 0)  // Used in BIGJOB4 and BIGJOB5
#define WM_CALC_ABORTED  (WM_USER + 1)

#define STACKSIZE   4096                // Used in BIGJOB4 and BIGJOB5

typedef struct                          // Used in BIGJOB4 and BIGJOB5
    {
    HWND   hwnd ;
    LONG   lCalcRep ;
    BOOL   fContinueCalc ;
    ULONG  ulSemTrigger ;               // Used in BIGJOB5
    }
    CALCPARAM ;

typedef CALCPARAM FAR *PCALCPARAM ;

double  Savage (double A) ;
VOID    CheckMenuItem (HWND hwnd, SHORT sMenuItem, BOOL fCheck) ;
VOID    EnableMenuItem (HWND hwnd, SHORT sMenuItem, BOOL fEnable) ;
VOID    PaintWindow (HWND hwnd, SHORT sStatus, LONG lCalcRep, ULONG ulTime) ;
MRESULT EXPENTRY ClientWndProc (HWND, USHORT, MPARAM, MPARAM) ;
```

The BIGJOB.RC File

```
/*---------------------------------
   BIGJOB.RC resource script file
-------------------------------*/

#include <os2.h>
#include "bigjob.h"

MENU ID_RESOURCE
    {
    SUBMENU "~Repetitions",  IDM_REPS
        {
        MENUITEM "~1.\a10",      IDM_10,,       MIA_CHECKED
        MENUITEM "~2.\a100",     IDM_100
        MENUITEM "~3.\a1,000",   IDM_1000
        MENUITEM "~4.\a10,000",  IDM_10000
        MENUITEM "~5.\a100,000", IDM_100000
        }
```

(continued)

Figure 17-1. The BIGJOB.RC File. *continued*

```
SUBMENU "~Action",        IDM_ACTION
    {
    MENUITEM "~Start",        IDM_START
    MENUITEM "~Abort",        IDM_ABORT,,    MIA_DISABLED
    }
}
```

The BIGJOB1.DEF File

```
;-----------------------------------------
; BIGJOB1.DEF module definition file
;-----------------------------------------

NAME            BIGJOB1    WINDOWAPI

DESCRIPTION    'BIGJOB Program No. 1 (C) Charles Petzold, 1988'
PROTMODE
HEAPSIZE        1024
STACKSIZE       8192
EXPORTS         ClientWndProc
```

Figure 17-1. *The BIGJOB1 program.*

I've separated the source code for this program into two files, BIGJOB1.C and BIGJOB.C. The BIGJOB.C file contains subroutines that are used in the next two programs in the BIGJOB series.

The BIGJOB.C file contains a function called *Savage*. This function performs a floating-point calculation called the "savage" benchmark, which is sometimes used to test floating-point speed. The function increments its parameter in a roundabout way: It squares the parameter, then takes the square root, applies the *log* and then *exp* functions (which cancel each other out), then the *atan* and *tan* functions (which do the same), and finally adds 1.

The BIGJOB1 program allows you to repeat this calculation 10, 100, 1000, 10,000, or 100,000 times based on a selection from the program's Repetitions menu. The time required for this job will depend on the speed of your machine and on whether you have a math coprocessor chip installed. An 8 MHz IBM PC/AT with an 80287 math coprocessor requires about three minutes to execute the savage calculation 100,000 times—a clear violation of the $1/10$ second rule.

You start the calculation from the Start option on the Action menu. When the calculation has finished, BIGJOB1 displays the number of repetitions and the calculation time in the client window. The program uses the *WinGetCurrentTime* function to calculate the elapsed time in milliseconds. The Action menu also has an Abort option to abort a calculation before it has finished. (This is not possible in BIGJOB1.)

Most of the code in BIGJOB1's client window procedure handles WM_COMMAND messages from the program's menu. When you select an option from the Repetitions menu, BIGJOB1 unchecks the currently selected option and checks the option you choose. When you select "Start" from the menu, BIGJOB1 disables the Start option, enables the Abort option, and begins the calculation. After *ClientWndProc* is finished with the big job, the program reenables the Start option and exits the window procedure.

BIGJOB1 is a bad program because it spends several minutes processing a single WM_COMMAND message. If you run BIGJOB1 in the Presentation Manager, you'll easily see what's wrong with it.

Stop the World, I'm Working

While doing its big job, BIGJOB1 clogs up the rest of the Presentation Manager. You cannot switch to another program using the keyboard or the mouse. The whole system seemingly ignores all keyboard and mouse input until the calculation is finished. Although the Abort option is present on BIGJOB1's menu, you can't use the keyboard or mouse to select that option. Once you begin the big job, you have to wait until it's finished to do anything else.

At first, this is troubling. Aren't OS/2 and the Presentation Manager supposed to be multitasking? And if so, why does one program apparently cause the whole system to grind to a halt?

OS/2 *is* a multitasking operating system. What is happening with BIGJOB1 is a predictable result of the message-based architecture of the Presentation Manager.

Message-based Architecture: A Review

BIGJOB1 creates a normal collection of windows in its call to *WinCreateStdWindow*. Each window in the collection has a window procedure that processes messages to these windows. The window procedure for BIGJOB1's client window is in the BIGJOB1 program; the other window procedures (such as those for the frame window, the title bar window, and the menu window) are contained in the Presentation Manager PMWIN.DLL dynamic link library.

BIGJOB1 also creates a message queue. Some of the messages for a window are stored in the program's message queue. (These messages are called "queued messages" and are said to be "posted to the queue.") Most of the queued messages report user input from the keyboard and mouse, such as WM_CHAR and WM_MOUSEMOVE. The queued messages are retrieved from the message queue when the program calls *WinGetMsg* and are dispatched to the window procedure by *WinDispatchMsg*.

Other messages are sent directly to the window procedure, bypassing the program's message queue. These "unqueued messages" result from calls to certain Presentation Manager functions. For example, *WinCreateStdWindow* sends WM_CREATE messages to window procedures of the windows it creates; *WinDestroyWindow* sends a WM_DESTROY message. A message can be sent directly to a window procedure by a call to *WinSendMsg*. The menu window uses *WinSendMsg* to send a WM_COMMAND message.

For most of the time that a typical Presentation Manager program is running, the program is suspended in the *WinGetMsg* function awaiting a message. Usually, the *WinGetMsg* function will return with a message that reports keyboard or mouse input. Sometimes the processing of this message will result in other messages being sent to the window procedure. For example, a WM_COMMAND message from a menu is the result of keyboard or mouse input. While a program is awaiting a message in the *WinGetMsg* function, one of its window procedures can also be sent a message. In this case, the Presentation Manager will call the window procedure so that the window procedure can process the message.

Processes and Threads

Multitasking in OS/2 is based on processes and threads within processes. An OS/2 program can consist of one or more processes, although most programs consist of only one process. A process is started by a call to the *DosExecPgm* or *DosStartSession* function. Each process currently running under OS/2 is denoted by a unique process ID number. When a process allocates resources, such as open files and memory blocks, the resources are private to the process; that is, the process owns the resources.

A process running under OS/2 consists of one or more threads of execution. Each thread has a thread ID number that uniquely identifies the thread within the process. The thread that begins execution in the process always has an ID number of 1. A thread can create additional threads in the process by a call to *DosCreateThread*. All threads within a process share the process's resources (such as open files and memory blocks), but each thread has its own stack and its own set of CPU registers, including the instruction pointer. OS/2 multitasks among threads using a priority-based scheduler.

So far, all the programs shown in this book have consisted of a single process with a single execution thread. BIGJOB1 is no exception. When a thread running under the Presentation Manager program creates some windows, the messages for those windows must be processed by the thread that created them. This is true whether a message is posted to a message queue or sent directly to a window procedure, or whether the window's window procedure is contained in the program or in a dynamic link library.

A particular thread of execution can do only one task at a time. A thread cannot be multitasked with itself. While BIGJOB1 is busy doing its big job, no other code in BIGJOB1 can execute.

So here's the problem: When you select "Start" from BIGJOB1's menu, *ClientWndProc* begins the big job on response from the WM_COMMAND message. Now you try to use the Alt-Esc key combination to switch to another program. The window that must process this key combination is BIG-JOB1's frame window. But the window procedure for the frame window runs in the same thread as the client window, and the client window is busy doing the big job. This means the Alt-Esc keyboard message cannot be processed until BIGJOB1 finishes the calculation, exits *ClientWndProc*, and calls *WinGetMsg* to retrieve the message from the queue. This is why the Presentation Manager seemingly ignores keyboard input while BIGJOB1 is calculating.

Serialization of Input

But maybe there's another way to switch programs while BIGJOB1 is doing its big job—a way that doesn't require window procedures in BIGJOB1 to process a message. As you know, you can use the mouse to make another window active. Maybe that will work.

To test this out, you first position the mouse pointer on top of another program's window and then use the keyboard to select "Start" from BIG-JOB1's menu. While BIGJOB1 is calculating, you press the mouse button on this other window and...nothing happens.

Again, this is initially disturbing. Because the Presentation Manager is a true multitasking system, the other program should be able to read that mouse click even while BIGJOB1 is calculating. The Presentation Manager should also be able to change the active window from BIGJOB1 to the other program. But this does not happen.

This behavior results from the serialization of user input: All keyboard and mouse input is stored first in a system message queue. Keyboard and mouse messages are then passed—one message at a time—to an application's message queue. For keyboard messages, the destination of the message depends on which window has the input focus; for mouse messages, it's based on which window is underneath the mouse pointer or which window has captured the mouse.

The serialization of mouse and keyboard input in a system message queue is required to correctly handle "type ahead" and "mouse ahead" input from the user — input that occurs faster than it can be processed. One of the keystrokes or mouse clicks in the system message queue could have the effect of changing the active window and the focus window. Subsequent keyboard input must then go to that new window. Thus a keyboard or mouse message cannot be posted to a particular application's message queue until the previous keyboard or mouse message has been entirely processed.

In this particular example (pressing the mouse button over another window while BIGJOB1 is working), another application cannot read a mouse message until BIGJOB1 processes all of its keyboard input. And BIGJOB1 has not processed the release of the key that caused the menu to send the WM_COMMAND message that started the calculation.

Thus, because BIGJOB1 renders itself resistant to keyboard or mouse input, it also prevents all other programs running under the Presentation Manager from receiving keyboard or mouse input.

But even if another program could read a mouse click, the Presentation Manager cannot change the input focus from BIGJOB1 to another program while BIGJOB1 is busy doing the calculation. To change the input focus, the Presentation Manager must send a WM_SETFOCUS message to the window losing the input focus. That WM_SETFOCUS message is blocked because the window that must receive the message is part of BIGJOB1's thread, and BIGJOB1 is busy doing the big job.

Messages are not like hardware interrupts! Although a window procedure can be sent a message as a result of calling *WinDefWindowProc*, and a window procedure can be sent a message as a result of calling some other Presentation Manager functions, these are examples of recursion in window procedures. Messages do not preemptively interrupt a thread and start execution someplace else in the same thread.

You'll note that BIGJOB1 uses the CS_SYNCPAINT flag when registering its window class. Normally, WM_PAINT messages are posted to the message queue rather than sent directly to the window procedure. This posting allows the Presentation Manager to consolidate multiple WM_PAINT messages into one message that encompasses the entire invalid rectangle of the window. With the CS_SYNCPAINT class style, a WM_PAINT message is sent directly to the window procedure whenever part of the window becomes invalid.

The CS_SYNCPAINT style is necessary in BIGJOB1 because it calls *Win-InvalidateRect* to invalidate the client window before beginning the big job. This enables the *PaintWindow* routine in BIGJOB.C to display the text "Working..." while the big job is executing. Without the CS_SYNCPAINT style, the window would not be updated until the big job was completed. (Alternatively, BIGJOB1 could have called the *WinUpdateWindow* function after *WinInvalidateRect*.)

Now that we've seen how BIGJOB1 effectively disables keyboard and mouse input in the Presentation Manager, the reason for the $1/10$ second rule should be obvious. Presentation Manager programs must continually interact with the system, retrieving and processing their messages promptly.

But Still There Is Multitasking

As bad as BIGJOB1 is, however, OS/2 can still multitask Presentation Manager programs while BIGJOB1 is running. If you have the CLOCK or DIGCLOCK program from Chapter 10 running when you begin the big job, you'll find that these programs continue to update the time every second. The WM_TIMER message is a queued message, but it does not need to be serialized like the keyboard and mouse messages. CLOCK or DIGCLOCK can continue to receive WM_TIMER messages even if BIGJOB1 has clogged up keyboard and mouse input. Threads can also process WM_PAINT messages during this time.

But keep in mind that most messages are user input messages (such as WM_CHAR and WM_MOUSEMOVE), result directly from user input messages (such as WM_COMMAND and WM_CONTROL), or are sent from functions that are called in response to these messages. Most message traffic is initiated by user input. A program doing a big job is a program that's holding up traffic and preventing the user from getting to work.

The Hourglass Pointer

Before BIGJOB1 begins its big job, it calls *WinQuerySysPointer* to obtain a handle to the SPTR_WAIT system mouse pointer and uses this handle in a call to *WinSetPointer*. (The program also displays the pointer by calling *WinShowPointer* if a mouse is not installed.) After the calculation is finished, it calls *WinQuerySysPointer* and *WinSetPointer* to display the normal SPTR_ARROW mouse pointer.

The SPTR_WAIT pointer looks like an hourglass. This signals to the user that a big job is in progress and that the keyboard and mouse are effectively disabled. You should display the SPTR_WAIT pointer whenever you do a big job that requires more than a second or so.

As you probably know, users despise the hourglass pointer. It means they must wait for a piggy program to finish some work. None of the other programs in this chapter will require the hourglass pointer because these programs solve the big-job problem.

Single-Thread Solutions

Before we explore multithread Presentation Manager programs, let's look at two solutions that work with only a single thread: multitasking with the timer and peeking at messages.

Multitasking with the Timer

I noted earlier in this chapter that CLOCK and DIGCLOCK continue to function normally while BIGJOB1 is working. This might have suggested the Presentation Manager timer as a possible solution. The Presentation Manager timer allows a program to break a big job into little pieces that are performed on receipt of a WM_TIMER message. This is the approach taken in the BIGJOB2 program shown in Figure 17-2.

The BIGJOB2 File

```
#-------------------
# BIGJOB2 make file
#-------------------

bigjob2.obj : bigjob2.c bigjob.h
     cl -c -G2sw -W3 bigjob2.c

bigjob.obj : bigjob.c
     cl -c -G2sw -W3 bigjob.c

bigjob.res : bigjob.rc bigjob.h
     rc -r bigjob

bigjob2.exe : bigjob2.obj bigjob.obj bigjob2.def
     link bigjob2 bigjob, /align:16, NUL, os2, bigjob2
     rc bigjob.res bigjob2.exe

bigjob2.exe : bigjob.res
     rc bigjob.res bigjob2.exe
```

The BIGJOB2.C File

```
/*--------------------------------------------------------
   BIGJOB2.C -- Timer approach to lengthy processing job
--------------------------------------------------------*/

#define INCL_WIN
#include <os2.h>
#include "bigjob.h"

#define ID_TIMER 1

HAB  hab ;

int main (void)
    {
    static CHAR  szClientClass [] = "BigJob2" ;
    static ULONG flFrameFlags = FCF_TITLEBAR      | FCF_SYSMENU  |
                                FCF_SIZEBORDER    | FCF_MINMAX   |
                                FCF_SHELLPOSITION | FCF_TASKLIST |
                                FCF_MENU ;
    HMQ          hmq ;
    HWND         hwndFrame, hwndClient ;
    QMSG         qmsg ;

    hab = WinInitialize (0) ;
    hmq = WinCreateMsgQueue (hab, 0) ;

    WinRegisterClass (hab, szClientClass, ClientWndProc,
                      CS_SYNCPAINT | CS_SIZEREDRAW, 0) ;

    hwndFrame = WinCreateStdWindow (HWND_DESKTOP, WS_VISIBLE,
                                    &flFrameFlags, szClientClass,
                                    " - The Timer",
                                    0L, NULL, ID_RESOURCE, &hwndClient) ;

    WinSendMsg (hwndFrame, WM_SETICON,
                WinQuerySysPointer (HWND_DESKTOP, SPTR_APPICON, FALSE),
                NULL) ;

    while (WinGetMsg (hab, &qmsg, NULL, 0, 0))
        WinDispatchMsg (hab, &qmsg) ;

    WinDestroyWindow (hwndFrame) ;
    WinDestroyMsgQueue (hmq) ;
```

(continued)

Figure 17-2. The BIGJOB2.C File. *continued*

```
      WinTerminate (hab) ;
      return 0 ;
      }

MRESULT EXPENTRY ClientWndProc (HWND hwnd, USHORT msg, MPARAM mp1, MPARAM mp2)
      {
      static double A ;
      static LONG    lRep, lCalcRep,
                     lRepAmts [] = { 10, 100, 1000, 10000, 100000 } ;
      static SHORT   sCurrentRep = IDM_10 ;
      static SHORT   sStatus = STATUS_READY ;
      static ULONG   ulElapsedTime ;

      switch (msg)
          {
          case WM_COMMAND:
               switch (COMMANDMSG(&msg)->cmd)
                   {
                   case IDM_10:
                   case IDM_100:
                   case IDM_1000:
                   case IDM_10000:
                   case IDM_100000:
                        CheckMenuItem (hwnd, sCurrentRep, FALSE) ;
                        sCurrentRep = COMMANDMSG(&msg)->cmd ;
                        CheckMenuItem (hwnd, sCurrentRep, TRUE) ;
                        return 0 ;

                   case IDM_START:
                        if (!WinStartTimer (hab, hwnd, ID_TIMER, 0))
                            {
                            WinAlarm (HWND_DESKTOP, WA_ERROR) ;
                            return 0 ;
                            }
                        EnableMenuItem (hwnd, IDM_START, FALSE) ;
                        EnableMenuItem (hwnd, IDM_ABORT, TRUE) ;

                        sStatus = STATUS_WORKING ;
                        WinInvalidateRect (hwnd, NULL, FALSE) ;

                        lCalcRep = lRepAmts [sCurrentRep - IDM_10] ;
                        ulElapsedTime = WinGetCurrentTime (hab) ;
                        A = 1.0 ;
                        lRep = 0 ;
```

(continued)

Figure 17-2. The BIGJOB2.C File. *continued*

```
                              return 0 ;

                  case IDM_ABORT:
                          WinStopTimer (hab, hwnd, ID_TIMER) ;

                          sStatus = STATUS_READY ;
                          WinInvalidateRect (hwnd, NULL, FALSE) ;

                          EnableMenuItem (hwnd, IDM_START, TRUE) ;
                          EnableMenuItem (hwnd, IDM_ABORT, FALSE) ;
                          return 0 ;
                  }
              break ;

         case WM_TIMER:
              A = Savage (A) ;

              if (++lRep == lCalcRep)
                  {
                  ulElapsedTime = WinGetCurrentTime (hab) -
                                          ulElapsedTime ;

                  WinStopTimer (hab, hwnd, ID_TIMER) ;

                  sStatus = STATUS_DONE ;
                  WinInvalidateRect (hwnd, NULL, FALSE) ;

                  EnableMenuItem (hwnd, IDM_START, TRUE) ;
                  EnableMenuItem (hwnd, IDM_ABORT, FALSE) ;
                  }
              return 0 ;

         case WM_PAINT:
              PaintWindow (hwnd, sStatus, lCalcRep, ulElapsedTime) ;
              return 0 ;

         case WM_DESTROY:
              if (sStatus == STATUS_WORKING)
                  WinStopTimer (hab, hwnd, ID_TIMER) ;
              return 0 ;
         }
    return WinDefWindowProc (hwnd, msg, mp1, mp2) ;
    }
```

The BIGJOB2.DEF File

```
;------------------------------------
; BIGJOB2.DEF module definition file
;------------------------------------

NAME            BIGJOB2    WINDOWAPI

DESCRIPTION     'BIGJOB Program No. 2 (C) Charles Petzold, 1988'
PROTMODE
HEAPSIZE        1024
STACKSIZE       8192
EXPORTS         ClientWndProc
```

Figure 17-2. *The BIGJOB2 program.*

Compiling BIGJOB2 also requires the BIGJOB.C, BIGJOB.H, and BIGJOB.RC files shown in Figure 17-1.

When you select the Start option from BIGJOB2's menu, BIGJOB2 calls *WinStartTimer* to start the timer. It disables the Start option, enables the Abort option, and initializes the *A* and *lRep* variables. The *Savage* function is called once for each WM_TIMER message. Thus, for 100 repetitions, the big job is finished after 100 WM_TIMER messages.

WM_TIMER messages are low-priority queued messages: Keyboard or mouse messages are retrieved from the queue and processed before a WM_TIMER message. Thus BIGJOB2 continues to read keyboard and mouse input and allows the user to select "Abort" from BIGJOB2's menu, move or resize BIGJOB2's window, or shift control to another program. The entire system — including BIGJOB2 — continues to function normally while BIG-JOB2 is doing the calculation. The timer is stopped when the calculation is finished or when you select "Abort" from the menu.

Timer Problems

Although the timer approach is feasible for BIGJOB2, it's easy to imagine cases where the timer would be inadequate.

A program using the timer for a big job must enter and exit the processing loop with every WM_TIMER message. This is easy to structure when a single loop is involved (as in BIGJOB2), but it becomes a nightmare for more complex jobs with lots of nested loops.

The timer also slows down the big job. It simply isn't possible to receive WM_TIMER messages at a rate faster than that of the hardware clock. Under OS/2, this means the program receives a WM_TIMER message only once every 31.25 msec. But on most machines that run OS/2, BIGJOB2 spends only a fraction of this time processing the message. Because the calculation is paced by the timer, the calculation won't finish any faster on a faster computer!

Although the Presentation Manager timer can be of help in some big-job problems, as a general solution it must clearly be rejected.

Peeking at Messages

The second solution involves the *WinPeekMsg* function. This function is similar in syntax and functionality to *WinGetMsg*. However, when a program calls *WinGetMsg*, the function does not return until it has a message from the message queue. If the message queue is empty, the *WinGetMsg* function waits. *WinPeekMsg*, on the other hand, always returns immediately. Thus, while doing the big job, a Presentation Manager program can periodically check for messages in the queue. These messages can be removed from the queue and be processed normally.

This approach is used quite often in programs written for Microsoft Windows, where the function is called *PeekMessage*. Windows is entirely a single-thread system — it multitasks among programs only when they call *GetMessage* or *PeekMessage*. Calling *PeekMessage* under Windows effectively yields control to other programs that might have messages in their message queues.

The syntax of *WinPeekMsg* is the same as that of *WinGetMsg* except that it has an options parameter:

```
WinPeekmsg (hab, &qmsg, hwnd, msgFirst, msgLast, fOptions) ;
```

The *fOptions* parameter can be either PM_REMOVE to remove the next message from the queue or PM_NOREMOVE to leave the message in the queue. *WinPeekMsg* returns FALSE if the message queue is empty and TRUE otherwise. (This is where it differs from *WinGetMsg*, which returns FALSE if the message retrieved from the queue is WM_QUIT and returns TRUE otherwise.) Thus *WinPeekMsg* will not wait for a message; if no message is available, the function returns FALSE.

The BIGJOB3 program in Figure 17-3 on the following pages shows how a program can use *WinPeekMsg* to retrieve and process messages while doing a big job.

The BIGJOB3 File

```
#-------------------
# BIGJOB3 make file
#-------------------

bigjob3.obj : bigjob3.c bigjob.h
    cl -c -G2sw -W3 bigjob3.c

bigjob.obj : bigjob.c
    cl -c -G2sw -W3 bigjob.c

bigjob.res : bigjob.rc bigjob.h
    rc -r bigjob

bigjob3.exe : bigjob3.obj bigjob.obj bigjob3.def
    link bigjob3 bigjob, /align:16, NUL, os2, bigjob3
    rc bigjob.res bigjob3.exe

bigjob3.exe : bigjob.res
    rc bigjob.res bigjob3.exe
```

The BIGJOB3.C File

```
/*------------------------------------------------------------------
    BIGJOB3.C -- Peek Message approach to lengthy processing job
   ------------------------------------------------------------------*/

#define INCL_WIN
#include <os2.h>
#include "bigjob.h"

HAB   hab ;

int main (void)
    {
    static CHAR  szClientClass [] = "BigJob3" ;
    static ULONG flFrameFlags = FCF_TITLEBAR       | FCF_SYSMENU   |
                                FCF_SIZEBORDER   | FCF_MINMAX    |
                                FCF_SHELLPOSITION | FCF_TASKLIST |
                                FCF_MENU ;
    HMQ          hmq ;
    HWND         hwndFrame, hwndClient ;
    QMSG         qmsg ;
```

(continued)

Figure 17-3. The BIGJOB3.C File. *continued*

```c
    hab = WinInitialize (0) ;
    hmq = WinCreateMsgQueue (hab, 0) ;

    WinRegisterClass (hab, szClientClass, ClientWndProc, CS_SIZEREDRAW, 0) ;

    hwndFrame = WinCreateStdWindow (HWND_DESKTOP, WS_VISIBLE,
                                    &flFrameFlags, szClientClass,
                                    " - Message Peeking",
                                    0L, NULL, ID_RESOURCE, &hwndClient) ;

    WinSendMsg (hwndFrame, WM_SETICON,
                WinQuerySysPointer (HWND_DESKTOP, SPTR_APPICON, FALSE),
                NULL) ;

    while (WinGetMsg (hab, &qmsg, NULL, 0, 0))
        WinDispatchMsg (hab, &qmsg) ;

    WinDestroyWindow (hwndFrame) ;
    WinDestroyMsgQueue (hmq) ;
    WinTerminate (hab) ;
    return 0 ;
    }

MRESULT EXPENTRY ClientWndProc (HWND hwnd, USHORT msg, MPARAM mp1, MPARAM mp2)
    {
    static BOOL    fContinueCalc = FALSE ;
    static LONG    lCalcRep, lRepAmts [] = { 10, 100, 1000, 10000, 100000 } ;
    static SHORT   sStatus = STATUS_READY ;
    static SHORT   sCurrentRep = IDM_10 ;
    static ULONG   ulElapsedTime ;
    double         A ;
    LONG           lRep ;
    QMSG           qmsg ;

    switch (msg)
        {
        case WM_COMMAND:
            switch (COMMANDMSG(&msg)->cmd)
                {
                case IDM_10:
                case IDM_100:
                case IDM_1000:
                case IDM_10000:
```

(continued)

Figure 17-3. The BIGJOB3.C File. *continued*

```
            case IDM_100000:
                 CheckMenuItem (hwnd, sCurrentRep, FALSE) ;
                 sCurrentRep = COMMANDMSG(&msg)->cmd ;
                 CheckMenuItem (hwnd, sCurrentRep, TRUE) ;
                 return 0 ;

            case IDM_START:
                 EnableMenuItem (hwnd, IDM_START, FALSE) ;
                 EnableMenuItem (hwnd, IDM_ABORT, TRUE) ;

                 sStatus = STATUS_WORKING ;
                 WinInvalidateRect (hwnd, NULL, FALSE) ;

                 lCalcRep = lRepAmts [sCurrentRep - IDM_10] ;
                 fContinueCalc = TRUE ;
                 ulElapsedTime = WinGetCurrentTime (hab) ;

                 qmsg.msg = WM_NULL ;

                 for (A = 1.0, lRep = 0 ; lRep < lCalcRep ; lRep++)
                     {
                     A = Savage (A) ;

                     while (WinPeekMsg (hab, &qmsg, NULL, 0, 0,
                                        PM_NOREMOVE))
                         {
                         if (qmsg.msg == WM_QUIT)
                             break ;

                         WinGetMsg (hab, &qmsg, NULL, 0, 0) ;
                         WinDispatchMsg (hab, &qmsg) ;

                         if (!fContinueCalc)
                             break ;
                         }
                     if (!fContinueCalc || qmsg.msg == WM_QUIT)
                         break ;
                     }
                 ulElapsedTime = WinGetCurrentTime (hab) -
                                            ulElapsedTime ;

                 if (!fContinueCalc || qmsg.msg == WM_QUIT)
                     sStatus = STATUS_READY ;
                 else
                     sStatus = STATUS_DONE ;
```

(continued)

Figure 17-3. The BIGJOB3.C File. *continued*

```
                        WinInvalidateRect (hwnd, NULL, FALSE) ;

                        EnableMenuItem (hwnd, IDM_START, TRUE) ;
                        EnableMenuItem (hwnd, IDM_ABORT, FALSE) ;
                        return 0 ;

                case IDM_ABORT:
                        fContinueCalc = FALSE ;
                        return 0 ;
                }
            break ;

        case WM_PAINT:
            PaintWindow (hwnd, sStatus, lCalcRep, ulElapsedTime) ;
            return 0 ;
        }
    return WinDefWindowProc (hwnd, msg, mp1, mp2) ;
    }
```

The BIGJOB3.DEF File

```
;------------------------------------
; BIGJOB3.DEF module definition file
;------------------------------------


NAME           BIGJOB3    WINDOWAPI

DESCRIPTION    'BigJob Program No. 3 (C) Charles Petzold, 1988'
PROTMODE
HEAPSIZE       1024
STACKSIZE      8192
EXPORTS        ClientWndProc
```

Figure 17-3. *The BIGJOB3 program.*

BIGJOB3 also requires the BIGJOB.C, BIGJOB.H, and BIGJOB.RC files shown in Figure 17-1.

Like BIGJOB1, BIGJOB3 does the entire calculation in response to a WM_COMMAND message. However, within the calculation loop, BIGJOB3 calls *WinPeekMsg* to check for messages in the message queue. BIGJOB3 first removes such messages with *WinGetMsg* and then dispatches them to a window procedure with *WinDispatchMsg*, just as in the normal message loop in *main*.

```
for (A = 1.0, lRep = 0 ; lRep < lCalcRep ; lRep++)
    {
    A = Savage (A) ;

    while (WinPeekMsg (hab, &qmsg, NULL, 0, 0,
                        PM_NOREMOVE))
        {
        if (qmsg.msg == WM_QUIT)
            break ;

        WinGetMsg (hab, &qmsg, NULL, 0, 0) ;
        WinDispatchMsg (hab, &qmsg) ;

        if (!fContinueCalc)
            break ;
        }
    if (!fContinueCalc || qmsg.msg == WM_QUIT)
        break ;
    }
```

Notice that after the *WinGetMsg* and *WinDispatchMsg* calls, the value of
fContinueCalc is checked. BIGJOB3 sets this to FALSE when it receives a
WM_COMMAND message indicating that the user has selected "Abort"
from the menu.

You'll notice that special processing is required for the WM_QUIT message.
This message is posted to the message queue by the Presentation Manager
as a default response when the user selects "Close" from the system menu
or when the program is terminated from the Presentation Manager Task
Manager. The WM_QUIT message should not be removed from the queue
within the window procedure. Instead, BIGJOB3 exits the window procedure so that the WM_QUIT message can be retrieved from the message
queue in the *main* function.

Receiving Unqueued Messages

If you've been thinking about queued and unqueued messages, the preceding code may have seemed incomplete. *WinPeekMsg* returns TRUE only
when the message queue contains a message. Only then does BIGJOB3
retrieve the message from the queue and dispatch it.

But what happens when the user selects "Abort" from the menu? The menu
window sends the WM_COMMAND message by calling *WinSendMsg*. The
message is not posted to the queue. How, then, is BIGJOB3 able to process
this message while doing its big job?

The answer is fairly simple. The WM_COMMAND message is initiated by user input through the keyboard or mouse. The keyboard and mouse messages are queued. *WinPeekMsg* detects their presence and allows *WinGetMsg* to retrieve them and *WinDispatchMsg* to send them to the appropriate window procedure. When the menu window determines that the user has selected the "Abort" option, it sends the WM_COMMAND message that *ClientWndProc* processes. Thus *ClientWndProc* receives this unqueued WM_COMMAND message while calling the *WinDispatchMsg* function for a queued mouse or keyboard message.

Here's a stickier problem: Let's assume you start BIGJOB3 calculating and you move the mouse pointer over the window of another program. You press the mouse button and the active window changes to the other program. The other program is processing this mouse input, not BIGJOB3. Yet, when the Presentation Manager changes the active window and the input focus, it must send BIGJOB3 a WM_SETFOCUS message. BIGJOB3's frame window responds by changing the color of the title bar window. But how can BIGJOB3 process an unqueued message initiated by a queued message outside BIGJOB3's message queue?

Although the purpose of *WinGetMsg* and *WinPeekMsg* is to retrieve messages from the message queue, these functions also allow a window procedure in the thread to process an unqueued message.

If another thread tries to send a message to BIGJOB3 by calling *WinSendMsg* (as happens with the WM_SETFOCUS message), and the recipient of the message is busy (doing a big job, for example), the *WinSendMsg* function is blocked until the recipient thread is free. But when the thread calls *WinGetMsg* or *WinPeekMsg*, the Presentation Manager checks to see if another thread is trying to send that thread a message. If so, the Presentation Manager lets that unqueued message be processed by calling the message procedure with the message. This happens before the Presentation Manager even checks the contents of the thread's message queue.

A window procedure can also receive an unqueued message while calling *WinSendMsg*. This is how the Presentation Manager prevents message deadlocks. For example, suppose a window procedure in thread 1 calls *WinSendMsg* to send a message to a window procedure in thread 2. Thread 2 is doing something in its window procedure, so the *WinSendMsg* function is blocked. But then the window procedure in thread 2 calls *WinSendMsg* to send a message to the window procedure in thread 1. Uh-oh—deadlock. The Presentation Manager resolves the deadlock by letting the message from thread 1 be sent to thread 2 and by then allowing the message from thread 2 to be sent to thread 1.

A Different Message Loop in *main*

In BIGJOB3 I used a normal message loop in *main* but called *WinPeekMsg*, *WinGetMsg*, and *WinDispatchMsg* in the window procedure. You can also alter the message loop in *main*, basing the loop on the *WinPeekMsg* function rather than on *WinGetMsg*. The normal message loop looks like this:

```
while (WinGetMsg (hab, &qmsg, NULL, 0, 0))
    WinDispatchMsg (hab, &qmsg) ;
```

Here's the alternate message loop:

```
#define WM_DO_SOMETHING  WM_USER
    ⋮
while (TRUE)
    {
    if (WinPeekMsg (hab, &qmsg, NULL, 0, 0, PM_REMOVE)) ;
        {
        if (qmsg.msg == WM_QUIT)
            break ;
        else
            WinDispatchMsg (hab, &qmsg) ;
        }
    else
        WinSendMsg (hwndClient, WM_DO_SOMETHING, NULL, NULL) ;
    }
```

Whenever *WinPeekMsg* returns FALSE (indicating that the message queue is empty), *WinSendMsg* is called to send a WM_DO_SOMETHING message to the client window. Note that the WM_QUIT message requires special handling.

This approach is good for demonstration programs that seemingly run "forever." (One example is a program that displays a series of randomly sized and colored rectangles.) The client window procedure handles the WM_DO_SOMETHING message in the same way it handles a WM_TIMER message. The advantage is that the WM_DO_SOMETHING messages come faster than 32 times per second.

This alternate message loop is not quite appropriate for handling the big-job problem in general. Although the client window could ignore the WM_DO_SOMETHING messages when it's not doing the big job, you probably want a normal message loop in that case. This would require making the *sStatus* variable used in the BIGJOB programs (or its equivalent) a global variable and using the alternate message loop only when the value of *sStatus* is STATUS_WORKING.

Peeking Problems

The most serious challenge you face with a program structured like BIG-JOB3 is preventing reentrancy. You don't want to reenter the big-job calculation loop when you call *WinPeekMsg* or *WinDispatchMsg* from within that loop. BIGJOB3 prevents reentrancy by disabling the Start option on the menu before doing the big job.

Although message peeking usually works well in Presentation Manager programs, it's always a little messy for the programmer. Because the *Win-PeekMsg* functions must be called frequently enough to give the system a good response time, an inordinate amount of code is required. If the big job must be aborted, it's sometimes difficult to get out of a calculation loop in a structured manner.

Multithread Solutions

Let's now attack the big-job problem by creating a second thread of execution. When an OS/2 process contains multiple threads of execution, the threads run concurrently. All threads in a process share the program's resources (such as open files, memory, and semaphores), but each thread has its own CPU state, dispatching priority, and stack.

Within a program, the code used by a second thread of execution looks like a function. All local *automatic* variables in the thread function (or functions called from a thread) are private to each thread because they are stored on the thread's stack. Local *static* variables in the thread function (or functions called from each thread) can be shared by all threads that use the function.

The Two Categories of Threads

Threads used in Presentation Manager programs fall into two categories: "message queue threads" and "non-message queue threads." A thread becomes a message queue thread when it calls *WinCreateMsgQueue*. The thread reverts to being a non-message queue thread upon a call to *WinDestroyMsgQueue*.

A Presentation Manager program always creates a message queue in at least one thread. A thread must create a message queue before it can create windows. The message queue is used to store messages for all windows created in the thread. Other threads in a Presentation Manager program need to create message queues only if they create windows.

Although non-message queue threads have some advantages over message queue threads, they also have some disadvantages.

The good news: A non-message queue thread is not bound by the $\frac{1}{10}$ second rule. Because the thread does not receive or process messages, it needn't worry about clogging up the processing of messages in message queue threads. Thus a non-message queue thread is often ideal for doing a big job.

The bad news: Non-message queue threads are restricted in the type of Presentation Manager functions they can call. Non-message queue threads

- Cannot create windows

- Cannot send messages to window procedures in a message queue thread

- Cannot call functions that cause messages to be sent to a window procedure

Some of these restrictions are obvious: A non-message queue thread cannot create a window because it has no queue to store messages for that window. However, a non-message queue thread can call some functions that *affect* windows created in message queue threads. For example, a non-message queue thread can obtain a presentation space handle for a window created in a message queue thread and is able to paint something on the surface of that window.

But non-message queue threads cannot send messages to message queue threads. The *WinSendMsg* function is not allowed. Nor can they call functions that send messages. For example, *WinDestroyWindow* cannot be called from a non-message queue thread because it sends a window procedure a WM_DESTROY message.

Although a non-message queue thread cannot *send* a message using *WinSendMsg*, the thread can *post* a message by calling *WinPostMsg*. The *WinPostMsg* function places the message in a thread's message queue and returns immediately. The non-message queue thread uses the *WinPostMsg* function to signal a message queue thread when it has completed the big job.

The Multithread Run-Time Library

Writing multithread programs in C involves some additional problems caused by the C run-time library. Although many C functions are reentrant (that is, they can be called from multiple threads concurrently), not all of them are. Calling one of the non-reentrant functions from two threads concurrently could cause the threads to interfere with each other.

Fortunately, Microsoft C version 5.1 has a special multithread run-time library called LLIBCMT.LIB. The "L" prefix stands for "large model" (which means that all library functions require far calls and must be passed as far pointers), and the "MT" suffix stands for "multithread." During installation of Microsoft C 5.1, header files that contain templates for these multithread functions are stored in the MT subdirectory of the directory you specify for the normal header files. The *#include* statements in a multithread program can indicate the header files in the MT subdirectory by preceding the file name with MT\. You can link your program with LLIBCMT.LIB by listing it as a parameter to LINK in the make file.

A program that uses this multithread library must use the *_beginthread* function rather than *DosCreateThread* to create a new thread of execution. The code used by the thread looks like a function in the program. The *_beginthread* function allows a far pointer to be passed as a parameter to this function. If this is a far pointer to a structure, the function that creates the thread and the thread function can share nonglobal data.

The BIGJOB4 program in Figure 17-4 uses this multithread run-time library.

The BIGJOB4 File

```
#-------------------
# BIGJOB4 make file
#-------------------

bigjob4.obj : bigjob4.c bigjob.h
     cl -c -Alfw -G2sw -W3 bigjob4.c

bigjobmt.obj : bigjobmt.c
     cl -c -Alfw -G2sw -W3 bigjobmt.c

bigjob.res : bigjob.rc bigjob.h
     rc -r bigjob

bigjob4.exe : bigjob4.obj bigjobmt.obj bigjob4.def
     link bigjob4 bigjobmt, /align:16, NUL, /nod llibcmt os2, bigjob4
     rc bigjob.res bigjob4.exe

bigjob4.exe : bigjob.res
     rc bigjob.res bigjob4.exe
```

The BIGJOB4.C File

```
/*-------------------------------------------------------------------
   BIGJOB4.C -- Second thread approach to lengthy processing job
   -------------------------------------------------------------*/

#define INCL_WIN
#define INCL_DOS
#include <os2.h>
#include <mt\process.h>
#include <mt\stdlib.h>
#include "bigjob.h"

VOID _CDECL FAR CalcThread (PCALCPARAM) ;

HAB  hab ;

int main (void)
     {
     static CHAR  szClientClass [] = "BigJob4" ;
     static ULONG flFrameFlags = FCF_TITLEBAR     | FCF_SYSMENU     |
                                 FCF_SIZEBORDER    | FCF_MINMAX      |
                                 FCF_SHELLPOSITION | FCF_TASKLIST    |
                                 FCF_MENU ;
     HMQ          hmq ;
     HWND         hwndFrame, hwndClient ;
     QMSG         qmsg ;

     hab = WinInitialize (0) ;
     hmq = WinCreateMsgQueue (hab, 0) ;

     WinRegisterClass (hab, szClientClass, ClientWndProc, CS_SIZEREDRAW, 0) ;

     hwndFrame = WinCreateStdWindow (HWND_DESKTOP, WS_VISIBLE,
                                     &flFrameFlags, szClientClass,
                                     " - A Second Thread",
                                     0L, NULL, ID_RESOURCE, &hwndClient) ;

     WinSendMsg (hwndFrame, WM_SETICON,
                 WinQuerySysPointer (HWND_DESKTOP, SPTR_APPICON, FALSE),
                 NULL) ;

     while (WinGetMsg (hab, &qmsg, NULL, 0, 0))
          WinDispatchMsg (hab, &qmsg) ;
```

(continued)

Figure 17-4. The BIGJOB4.C File. *continued*

```
    WinDestroyWindow (hwndFrame) ;
    WinDestroyMsgQueue (hmq) ;
    WinTerminate (hab) ;
    return 0 ;
    }

MRESULT EXPENTRY ClientWndProc (HWND hwnd, USHORT msg, MPARAM mp1, MPARAM mp2)
    {
    static CALCPARAM cp ;
    static LONG     lRepAmts [] = { 10, 100, 1000, 10000, 100000 } ;
    static SHORT    sCurrentRep = IDM_10 ;
    static SHORT    sStatus = STATUS_READY ;
    static TID      tidCalc ;
    static ULONG    ulElapsedTime ;
    static VOID     *pThreadStack ;

    switch (msg)
        {
        case WM_COMMAND:
            switch (COMMANDMSG(&msg)->cmd)
                {
                case IDM_10:
                case IDM_100:
                case IDM_1000:
                case IDM_10000:
                case IDM_100000:
                    CheckMenuItem (hwnd, sCurrentRep, FALSE) ;
                    sCurrentRep = COMMANDMSG(&msg)->cmd ;
                    CheckMenuItem (hwnd, sCurrentRep, TRUE) ;
                    return 0 ;

                case IDM_START:
                    if (NULL == (pThreadStack = malloc (STACKSIZE)))
                        {
                        WinAlarm (HWND_DESKTOP, WA_ERROR) ;
                        return 0 ;
                        }

                    cp.hwnd = hwnd ;
                    cp.lCalcRep = lRepAmts [sCurrentRep - IDM_10] ;
                    cp.fContinueCalc = TRUE ;

                    if (-1 == (tidCalc = _beginthread (CalcThread,
                                    pThreadStack, STACKSIZE, &cp)))
```

(continued)

Figure 17-4. **The BIGJOB4.C File.** *continued*

```
                              {
                              free (pThreadStack) ;
                              WinAlarm (HWND_DESKTOP, WA_ERROR) ;
                              return 0 ;
                              }

                         sStatus = STATUS_WORKING ;
                         WinInvalidateRect (hwnd, NULL, FALSE) ;
                         EnableMenuItem (hwnd, IDM_START, FALSE) ;
                         EnableMenuItem (hwnd, IDM_ABORT, TRUE) ;
                         return 0 ;

                    case IDM_ABORT:
                         cp.fContinueCalc = FALSE ;
                         EnableMenuItem (hwnd, IDM_ABORT, FALSE) ;
                         return 0 ;
                    }
               break ;

          case WM_CALC_DONE:
               sStatus = STATUS_DONE ;
               ulElapsedTime = LONGFROMMP (mp1) ;
               WinInvalidateRect (hwnd, NULL, FALSE) ;
               EnableMenuItem (hwnd, IDM_START, TRUE) ;
               EnableMenuItem (hwnd, IDM_ABORT, FALSE) ;
               free (pThreadStack) ;
               return 0 ;

          case WM_CALC_ABORTED:
               sStatus = STATUS_READY ;
               WinInvalidateRect (hwnd, NULL, FALSE) ;
               EnableMenuItem (hwnd, IDM_START, TRUE) ;
               free (pThreadStack) ;
               return 0 ;

          case WM_PAINT:
               PaintWindow (hwnd, sStatus, cp.lCalcRep, ulElapsedTime) ;
               return 0 ;

          case WM_DESTROY:
               if (sStatus = STATUS_WORKING)
                    DosSuspendThread (tidCalc) ;
               return 0 ;
          }
     return WinDefWindowProc (hwnd, msg, mp1, mp2) ;
     }
```

(continued)

Figure 17-4. The BIGJOB4.C File. *continued*

```
VOID _CDECL FAR CalcThread (PCALCPARAM pcp)
    {
    double A ;
    LONG   lRep, lTime ;

    lTime = WinGetCurrentTime (hab) ;

    for (A = 1.0, lRep = 0 ; lRep < pcp->lCalcRep &&
                             pcp->fContinueCalc ; lRep++)
        A = Savage (A) ;

    DosEnterCritSec () ;     // So thread is dead when message retrieved

    if (pcp->fContinueCalc)
        {
        lTime = WinGetCurrentTime (hab) - lTime ;
        WinPostMsg (pcp->hwnd, WM_CALC_DONE, MPFROMLONG (lTime), NULL) ;
        }
    else
        WinPostMsg (pcp->hwnd, WM_CALC_ABORTED, NULL, NULL) ;

    _endthread () ;
    }
```

The BIGJOBMT.C File

```
/*-------------------------------------------------------------------
    BIGJOBMT.C -- Common functions used in BIGJOB4 and BIGJOB5
    -------------------------------------------------------------*/

#define INCL_WIN
#include <os2.h>
#include <mt\math.h>
#include <mt\stdio.h>

double Savage (double A)
    {
    return tan (atan (exp (log (sqrt (A * A))))) + 1.0 ;
    }

VOID CheckMenuItem (HWND hwnd, SHORT sMenuItem, BOOL fCheck)
    {
    HWND  hwndParent = WinQueryWindow (hwnd, QW_PARENT, FALSE) ;
```

(continued)

Figure 17-4. The BIGJOBMT.C File. *continued*

```
         HWND    hwndMenu   = WinWindowFromID (hwndParent, FID_MENU) ;

     WinSendMsg (hwndMenu, MM_SETITEMATTR,
                 MPFROM2SHORT (sMenuItem, TRUE),
                 MPFROM2SHORT (MIA_CHECKED, fCheck ? MIA_CHECKED : 0)) ;
     }

VOID EnableMenuItem (HWND hwnd, SHORT sMenuItem, BOOL fEnable)
     {
     HWND    hwndParent = WinQueryWindow (hwnd, QW_PARENT, FALSE) ;
     HWND    hwndMenu   = WinWindowFromID (hwndParent, FID_MENU) ;

     WinSendMsg (hwndMenu, MM_SETITEMATTR,
                 MPFROM2SHORT (sMenuItem, TRUE),
                 MPFROM2SHORT (MIA_DISABLED, fEnable ? 0 : MIA_DISABLED)) ;
     }

VOID PaintWindow (HWND hwnd, SHORT sStatus, LONG lCalcRep, ULONG ulTime)
     {
     static CHAR *szMessage [3] = { "Ready", "Working...",
                                    "%ld repetitions in %lu msec." } ;
     CHAR        szBuffer [60] ;
     HPS         hps ;
     RECTL       rcl ;

     hps = WinBeginPaint (hwnd, NULL, NULL) ;
     WinQueryWindowRect (hwnd, &rcl) ;

     sprintf (szBuffer, szMessage [sStatus], lCalcRep, ulTime) ;
     WinDrawText (hps, -1, szBuffer, &rcl, CLR_NEUTRAL, CLR_BACKGROUND,
                  DT_CENTER | DT_VCENTER | DT_ERASERECT) ;

     WinEndPaint (hps) ;
     }
```

The BIGJOB4.DEF File

```
;------------------------------------
; BIGJOB4.DEF module definition file
;------------------------------------


NAME            BIGJOB4    WINDOWAPI

DESCRIPTION     'BigJob Program No. 4 (C) Charles Petzold, 1988'
```

(continued)

Figure 17-4. The BIGJOB4.DEF File. *continued*

```
PROTMODE
HEAPSIZE     1024
STACKSIZE    8192
EXPORTS      ClientWndProc
```

Figure 17-4. *The BIGJOB4 program.*

As you can see, a few changes are required in the make file. First, the source code files are compiled with the *-Alfw* switch. This makes a large-model program ("l" stands for long code pointers and "f" for far data pointers). The *-Aw* switch tells the compiler to assume that the data segment is not the same as the stack segment (or DS != SS). For the main thread, DS will equal SS, but this might not be true for other threads, depending on how you allocate memory for the thread's stack.

The second change to the make file is that LLIBCMT is specified in the library field of the LINK step. The /NOD switch stands for "no default library search."

The BIGJOB.C file used in BIGJOB1, BIGJOB2, and BIGJOB3 is not used with BIGJOB4. The BIGJOBMT.C file takes its place. The functions in BIG-JOBMT.C are identical to those in BIGJOB.C, but the header information is different. The header files must be those in the MT directory. However, the BIGJOB.H and BIGJOB.RC files from Figure 17-1 are required to create BIGJOB4.EXE.

When compiling BIGJOBMT.C, you might receive a warning message from the compiler that says "address of frame variable taken, DS != SS." This message normally indicates a problem, but you can ignore it here, where it's related to how the floating-point functions used in the *Savage* function return values on the stack.

Putting the Thread to Work

The function used for the second thread in BIGJOB4 is called *CalcThread* and is located near the bottom of BIGJOB4.C. The parameter to this function is a pointer of type CALCPARAM, which is defined in BIGJOB.H. This is a structure that *ClientWndProc* uses in order to pass information to the thread function.

When you select "Start" from BIGJOB4's menu, the program first attempts to allocate a stack for the second thread by calling *malloc*. If this fails, the program beeps and exits the window procedure. If the allocation is successful, *ClientWndProc* sets the first three fields of the CALCPARAM structure and creates the thread by calling *_beginthread*. The *_beginthread* call requires the thread function (*CalcThread*), the address of the bottom of the newly created stack, the stack size, and a pointer to a parameter to pass to the thread function. The *_beginthread* function returns the thread ID. If this is −1, the thread could not be created. If *_beginthread* is successful, *ClientWndProc* disables the Start menu option and enables the Abort option.

After the second thread is created, the code in *CalcThread* runs concurrently with the code in the rest of the program. *CalcThread* gets the current time and then enters its calculation loop. Note that the *for* statement checks the *fContinueCalc* field of the CALCPARAM structure before each call to *Savage*. This field was initialized by *ClientWndProc* to TRUE. But when "Abort" is selected from the menu, *ClientWndProc* disables the Abort option and sets *fContinueCalc* to FALSE.

When *CalcThread* drops out of the *for* loop (because the calculation either is finished or has been aborted), it calls *DosEnterCritSec* (more on this shortly) and uses *WinPostMsg* to post either a WM_CALC_DONE or a WM_CALC_ABORTED message to the client window. (These two messages are defined in BIGJOB.H.) *CalcThread* obtains the handle of the client window from the *hwnd* field of the CALCPARAM structure. When *CalcThread* posts a WM_CALC_DONE message, it sets the *mp1* message parameter to the elapsed time. *CalcThread* then calls the *_endthread* function and is terminated.

The *ClientWndProc* function responds to the WM_CALC_DONE and the WM_CALC_ABORTED messages by enabling the Start menu option and freeing the memory allocated for the thread's stack.

A Few Precautions

Threads within a single process must often communicate with each other in various ways. The execution of threads must be coordinated so that the threads don't step on each other's toes. Threads must also often signal each other and pass data among themselves. This requires some handshaking.

The handshaking is important. Don't make any assumptions about one thread being able to execute a certain block of code in its time slice before another thread does something to affect the first thread.

For example, the *CalcThread* function posts a WM_CALC_DONE or a WM_CALC_ABORTED message to *ClientWndProc* and then calls *_endthread*. You can't assume that *CalcThread* will finish processing the *_endthread* function and will be destroyed by the time *ClientWndProc* processes the posted message. *ClientWndProc* responds to either of these two messages by freeing the data allocated for the thread's stack. If the thread is not completely finished when the stack is freed, the entire program will terminate with a protection exception.

This is why *CalcThread* calls *DosEnterCritSec* ("enter critical section") before posting the message. *DosEnterCritSec* causes all other threads in the process to be suspended until the thread calls *DosExitCritSec* or until the thread terminates. *CalcThread* doesn't call *DosExitCritSec*, so the main thread in BIGJOB4 won't execute any code until the thread is terminated. When *ClientWndProc* processes the WM_CALC_DONE or WM_CALC_ABORTED message, it knows that it's safe to free the thread's stack.

During processing of the WM_DESTROY message, *ClientWndProc* suspends the second thread by calling *DosSuspendThread*. *ClientWndProc* receives the WM_DESTROY message when BIGJOB4 calls *WinDestroyWindow* from *main*. The next call, after *WinDestroyWindow*, is to *WinDestroyMsgQueue*. You don't want *CalcThread* attempting to post a message to *ClientWndProc* after the window and the message queue have been destroyed.

Using Semaphores to Trigger Threads

BIGJOB4 creates a thread each time it needs to do the big job. After the thread is finished, the thread terminates itself. This is a good approach for some big jobs, but other big jobs might benefit from a somewhat different structure.

For example, in a spreadsheet program you might want a second thread to perform the spreadsheet recalculation. Because this recalculation occurs quite frequently, it might be best to create the thread initially when the program first begins executing and trigger it whenever you need to do a recalculation.

This is the approach taken in the BIGJOB5 program shown in Figure 17-5.

The BIGJOB5 File

```
#- - - - - - - - - - - - - - - - - - -
# BIGJOB5 make file
#- - - - - - - - - - - - - - - - - - -

bigjob5.obj : bigjob5.c bigjob.h
    cl -c -Alfw -G2sw -W3 bigjob5.c

bigjobmt.obj : bigjobmt.c
    cl -c -Alfw -G2sw -W3 bigjobmt.c
```

(continued)

Figure 17-5. The BIGJOB5 File. *continued*

```
bigjob.res : bigjob.rc bigjob.h
    rc -r bigjob

bigjob5.exe : bigjob5.obj bigjobmt.obj bigjob5.def
    link bigjob5 bigjobmt, /align:16, NUL, /nod llibcmt os2, bigjob5
    rc bigjob.res bigjob5.exe

bigjob5.exe : bigjob.res
    rc bigjob.res bigjob5.exe
```

The BIGJOB5.C File

```c
/*-----------------------------------------------------
    BIGJOB5.C -- Second thread and semaphore trigger
  -----------------------------------------------------*/

#define INCL_WIN
#define INCL_DOS
#include <os2.h>
#include <mt\process.h>
#include <mt\stdlib.h>
#include "bigjob.h"

VOID _CDECL FAR CalcThread (PCALCPARAM) ;

HAB  hab ;

int main (void)
    {
    static CHAR  szClientClass [] = "BigJob5" ;
    static ULONG flFrameFlags = FCF_TITLEBAR       | FCF_SYSMENU  |
                                FCF_SIZEBORDER     | FCF_MINMAX   |
                                FCF_SHELLPOSITION  | FCF_TASKLIST |
                                FCF_MENU ;

    HMQ          hmq ;
    HWND         hwndFrame, hwndClient ;
    QMSG         qmsg ;

    hab = WinInitialize (0) ;
    hmq = WinCreateMsgQueue (hab, 0) ;

    WinRegisterClass (hab, szClientClass, ClientWndProc, CS_SIZEREDRAW, 0) ;
```

(continued)

Figure 17-5. The BIGJOB5.C File. *continued*

```
        hwndFrame = WinCreateStdWindow (HWND_DESKTOP, WS_VISIBLE,
                                        &flFrameFlags, szClientClass,
                                        " - Second Thread with Semaphore",
                                        0L, NULL, ID_RESOURCE, &hwndClient) ;

        WinSendMsg (hwndFrame, WM_SETICON,
                    WinQuerySysPointer (HWND_DESKTOP, SPTR_APPICON, FALSE),
                    NULL) ;

        while (WinGetMsg (hab, &qmsg, NULL, 0, 0))
            WinDispatchMsg (hab, &qmsg) ;

        WinDestroyWindow (hwndFrame) ;
        WinDestroyMsgQueue (hmq) ;
        WinTerminate (hab) ;
        return 0 ;
        }

MRESULT EXPENTRY ClientWndProc (HWND hwnd, USHORT msg, MPARAM mp1, MPARAM mp2)
        {
        static CALCPARAM cp ;
        static INT       iThreadStack [STACKSIZE / 2] ;
        static LONG      lRepAmts [] = { 10, 100, 1000, 10000, 100000 } ;
        static SHORT     sCurrentRep = IDM_10 ;
        static SHORT     sStatus = STATUS_READY ;
        static TID       tidCalc ;
        static ULONG     ulElapsedTime ;

        switch (msg)
            {
            case WM_CREATE:
                cp.hwnd = hwnd ;
                DosSemSet (&cp.ulSemTrigger) ;

                tidCalc = _beginthread (CalcThread, iThreadStack,
                                        STACKSIZE, &cp) ;
                return 0 ;

            case WM_INITMENU:
                if (tidCalc == -1 && SHORT1FROMMP (mp1) == IDM_ACTION)
                    EnableMenuItem (hwnd, IDM_START, FALSE) ;
                return 0 ;
```

(continued)

Figure 17-5. The BIGJOB5.C File. *continued*

```
case WM_COMMAND:
     switch (COMMANDMSG(&msg)->cmd)
          {
          case IDM_10:
          case IDM_100:
          case IDM_1000:
          case IDM_10000:
          case IDM_100000:
               CheckMenuItem (hwnd, sCurrentRep, FALSE) ;
               sCurrentRep = COMMANDMSG(&msg)->cmd ;
               CheckMenuItem (hwnd, sCurrentRep, TRUE) ;
               return 0 ;

          case IDM_START:
               cp.lCalcRep = lRepAmts [sCurrentRep - IDM_10] ;
               cp.fContinueCalc = TRUE ;
               DosSemClear (&cp.ulSemTrigger) ;

               sStatus = STATUS_WORKING ;
               WinInvalidateRect (hwnd, NULL, FALSE) ;
               EnableMenuItem (hwnd, IDM_START, FALSE) ;
               EnableMenuItem (hwnd, IDM_ABORT, TRUE) ;
               return 0 ;

          case IDM_ABORT:
               cp.fContinueCalc = FALSE ;
               EnableMenuItem (hwnd, IDM_ABORT, FALSE) ;
               return 0 ;
          }
     break ;

case WM_CALC_DONE:
     sStatus = STATUS_DONE ;
     ulElapsedTime = LONGFROMMP (mp1) ;
     WinInvalidateRect (hwnd, NULL, FALSE) ;
     EnableMenuItem (hwnd, IDM_START, TRUE) ;
     EnableMenuItem (hwnd, IDM_ABORT, FALSE) ;
     return 0 ;

case WM_CALC_ABORTED:
     sStatus = STATUS_READY ;
     WinInvalidateRect (hwnd, NULL, FALSE) ;
     EnableMenuItem (hwnd, IDM_START, TRUE) ;
     return 0 ;
```

(continued)

Figure 17-5. The BIGJOB5.C File. *continued*

```
        case WM_PAINT:
             PaintWindow (hwnd, sStatus, cp.lCalcRep, ulElapsedTime) ;
             return 0 ;

        case WM_DESTROY:
             if (sStatus = STATUS_WORKING)
                  DosSuspendThread (tidCalc) ;
             return 0 ;
        }
     return WinDefWindowProc (hwnd, msg, mp1, mp2) ;
     }

VOID _CDECL FAR CalcThread (PCALCPARAM pcp)
     {
     double A ;
     LONG   lRep, lTime ;

     while (TRUE)
          {
          DosSemWait (&pcp->ulSemTrigger, SEM_INDEFINITE_WAIT) ;

          lTime = WinGetCurrentTime (hab) ;

          for (A = 1.0, lRep = 0 ; lRep < pcp->lCalcRep &&
                                 pcp->fContinueCalc ; lRep++)
               A = Savage (A) ;

          DosSemSet (&pcp->ulSemTrigger) ;

          if (pcp->fContinueCalc)
               {
               lTime = WinGetCurrentTime (hab) - lTime ;
               WinPostMsg (pcp->hwnd, WM_CALC_DONE, MPFROMLONG (lTime), NULL) ;
               }
          else
               WinPostMsg (pcp->hwnd, WM_CALC_ABORTED, NULL, NULL) ;
          }
     }
```

The BIGJOB5.DEF File

```
;-----------------------------------
; BIGJOB5.DEF module definition file
;-----------------------------------

NAME            BIGJOB5   WINDOWAPI

DESCRIPTION     'BigJob Program No. 5 (C) Charles Petzold, 1988'
PROTMODE
HEAPSIZE        1024
STACKSIZE       8192
EXPORTS         ClientWndProc
```

Figure 17-5. *The BIGJOB5 program.*

This program requires the BIGJOB.H and BIGJOB.RC files from Figure 17-1 and the BIGJOBMT.C file from Figure 17-4.

During the WM_CREATE message, *ClientWndProc* calls *DosSemSet* to set the *ulSemTrigger* field of the CALCPARAM structure. This field is a RAM semaphore used to trigger the calculation thread into action. *ClientWndProc* then calls *_beginthread* to create the thread. In BIGJOB4, memory for the stack thread was allocated using *malloc*; in BIGJOB5, the stack is simply a static array defined in *ClientWndProc*.

BIGJOB5 also processes the WM_INITMENU message. If the Action menu is being displayed, it checks to see if the thread ID originally returned from *_beginthread* is −1. If so, the Start option is disabled.

BIGJOB5 uses the RAM semaphore as a signaling mechanism. The semaphore can be either set (by calling the *DosSemSet* function) or cleared (by calling the *DosSemClear* function). When a thread calls *DosSemWait* and the semaphore is set, the thread is blocked until the semaphore is cleared by another thread. That is, the *DosSemWait* function will not return until the semaphore is cleared. The thread is effectively suspended. If the semaphore is already cleared when *DosSemWait* is called, the thread returns from the function immediately and can continue. Actually, *DosSemWait* has a second parameter that indicates a time-out value. If the semaphore is set, *DosSemWait* can return when the specified time elapses. However, this parameter is set to the identifier SEM_INDEFINITE_WAIT (equal to −1) in BIGJOB5 to indicate an infinite wait.

CalcParam begins by entering an infinite loop. The first function it calls in this loop is *DosSemWait* on the *ulSemTrigger* semaphore. Because *ClientWndProc* set this semaphore before creating the thread, *CalcParam* will be suspended in the *DosSemWait* function until the semaphore is cleared.

When you select "Start" from the menu, *ClientWndProc* sets the *sCalcRep* and *fContinueCalc* fields of the CALCPARAM structure and clears the semaphore. This allows *CalcThread* to start the calculation. As in BIGJOB4, *CalcThread* checks the value of *fContinueCalc* before each call to *Savage*.

After exiting the *for* loop, *CalcThread* calls *DosSemSet* to set the semaphore again and then posts the WM_CALC_DONE or WM_CALC_ABORTED message. It need not suspend the main thread because the main thread doesn't need to free *CalcThread*'s stack. When *CalcThread* returns to the top of the *while* loop, it again calls *DosSemWait*. The semaphore is already set, so *CalcThread* can't proceed with a new calculation until "Start" is chosen again.

Note that the semaphore is used only for blocking and unblocking the non-message queue thread. A message queue thread should not be made to wait on a semaphore because of the possibility of violating the $1/10$ second rule. If absolutely necessary, a non-message queue thread could suspend a message queue thread for very short periods of time by calling *DosSuspendThread* or *DosEnterCritSec*, as in BIGJOB4. This is sometimes helpful when both threads access common variables. (It's not necessary in BIGJOB4 or BIGJOB5 when the threads access *fContinueCalc* because this variable can be accessed in one machine code instruction.)

In general, a message queue thread communicates to a non-message queue thread using semaphores. A non-message queue thread communicates to a message queue thread using posted messages. The two threads can also access common variables.

Message Ordering

The *CalcThread* function in BIGJOB4 and BIGJOB5 used two "user-defined" messages called WM_CALC_DONE and WM_CALC_ABORTED to notify *ClientWndProc* that the job was completed or aborted. User-defined messages can be any value from WM_USER (defined in PMWIN.H as 0x1000 and above).

You might want a little more control over the priority of messages in the message queue. I've mentioned in earlier chapters that WM_PAINT and WM_TIMER messages are low-priority messages: If other messages appear in the message queue, they will be retrieved before WM_PAINT and WM_TIMER.

Four other messages have specific priorities in the message queue. These are WM_SEM1, WM_SEM2, WM_SEM3, and WM_SEM4. The priority of these messages is shown in the table on the next page.

Message	Priority
WM_SEM4	Lowest
WM_PAINT	
WM_SEM3	
WM_TIMER	
WM_SEM2	
All other messages	
WM_SEM1	Highest

For example, if you post a WM_SEM1 message to a message queue, it will be retrieved before any other message in the queue.

Only one of each of the four WM_SEM messages is allowed in the message queue at any time. If you post another, the Presentation Manager will perform a bitwise OR of the *mp1* parameter of the message already in the queue with the *mp1* parameter of the message you're posting. You can thus use the *mp1* parameter as a series of flags that combine messages in whatever way you want.

Thinking Threads

A non-message queue thread is almost essential in Presentation Manager programs that must read input other than keyboard and mouse input.

For example, a communications program might have a client window in the message queue thread that processes keyboard messages, writes the characters to the communications port using *DosWrite*, and (if local echo is in effect) also writes the characters to the surface of the window.

The non-message queue thread reads the communications port with the *DosRead* function. Used most efficiently, this function returns only if a character has been read from the serial port. A message queue thread should not call *DosRead* to get input from the serial port because it might violate the $1/10$ second rule. When the non-message queue thread reads a character, it can post either a user-defined message to the window containing that character or a pointer to a string of characters. The client window processes the message by displaying the character to the window.

A Presentation Manager program using queues (not Presentation Manager message queues, but the queues supported by the OS/2 kernel) for interprocess communication should also create a non-message queue thread for reading the queue. The non-message queue thread calls the *DosRead-Queue* function with the "no wait" flag set to 0, thus blocking the thread until something is in the queue.

No More Hourglasses!

We started out looking at BIGJOB1, a program that did the job it was meant to do but did it in a way that was not advantageous for the user. Our immediate rejection of this program and our search for better ways of doing big jobs indicate some major changes in our perception of proper behavior in application programs.

In a traditional single-tasking, non-windowed environment, you accept the fact that you have to wait while your database program is sorting a file. When you start a file sort, it's time to take a coffee break.

In a traditional multitasking operating environment, you might be able to run the database program sort in the background while you work on another program.

However, in a multitasking windowing environment like the Presentation Manager, we are satisfied only when the user can continue to interact with a program even when it's doing a big job. Obviously, the complexities involved with structuring a program in this way require some extra work on the part of the programmer. But that makes the program better for the user.

Just as we can no longer tolerate programs that require the user to memorize scores of commands, we can no longer tolerate programs that display an hourglass pointer and require a user to wait until the program has finished its big job.

Index

Note: *Italicized page numbers refer to figures and illustrations.*

Insert key 337, 350
interline spacing of text output 114–15
inverse screen 550
IOPL segments, accessing hardware with, in
    ORGAN program 385–86
IRGB (Intensity-Red-Green-Blue) color
    encoding 206, 207 (table), 254
    AVIO attribute byte color values *302*

K

KbdCharIn function 31
Kbd functions 10
KbdStringIn function 375
KC_ALT identifier 354
KC_CHAR identifier 348, 374
KC_COMPOSITE identifier 354, 373, 374
KC_CTRL identifier 354
KC_DEADKEY identifier 354, 373, 374
KC_identifiers 339, *340*
KC_INVALIDCOMP identifier 354,
    373, 374
KC_KEYUP identifier 352, 353
KC_LOANKEY identifier 354
KC_PREVDOWN identifier 353
KC_SCANCODE identifier 347
KC_SHIFT identifier 354
KC_TOGGLE identifier 354
KC_VIRTUALKEY identifier 348
keyboard
    codes identifying keys/characters 347–49
    emulating mouse with 405–12
    examining specific keys 340–47
    functions not provided in OS/2 kernel 31
keyboard accelerator 582, 593–94, 712
keyboard input 335–86
    active windows and focus windows 354–55
    cursor use 356–58
    dead keys and foreign language keyboards
        372–75
    foreign keyboards 335–36
    getting keyboard states 355–56
    input focus (*see* input focus)
    keyboard numeric codes 336–37
    ORGAN program using scan code 375–86
    OS/2 kernel and 338
    pre-OS/2 processing of 337–38
    Presentation Manager processing of 338
    reading character strings 375
    sample processing (TYPEAWAY program)
        358–72
    serialization of 787–89

keyboard input *(continued)*
    WM_CHAR message and 339–54
        key-up, key-down‚processing 352–54
        looking at keys when calling 340–47
        processing virtual keys and characters in
            349–51
        shift status 354
        three parameter codes accompanying
            347–49
keyboard interface
    with calculator 680
    with dialog box 651–52
    scrolling with keyboard keys 144–51
KEYLOOK program 340–47
    code *341–45*
    display *346*
    information abbreviated in display *346–47*

L

laser printer 235
LCID_BRICKS_BITMAP identifier 287
LCID_DEFAULT identifier 288
LHANDLE data type 20
LIBPATH statement, locating .DLL files
    with 732
LIBRARY statement, .DEF files 743–44
LIFE game program 606, *607–17*
line(s), drawing with GPI primitives 154–77
    boxes and simple ellipses 173–74
    curves 162–67
    line type attributes 168–72
    multiple lines 157–61
    POINTL structure for 154–55
    simple straight lines 155–57
LINETYPE program 168–72
LINK 15, 16
linking files 16
    window procedures while 50
list boxes 668, 669–70
LLIBCDLL library 737–38
    linking with 740
LLIBCMT.LIB library 805
LM_DELETEALL message 669
LM_INSERTITEM message 670
LM_QUERYSELECTION message 670
LN_ENTER message 670
LOADBMP1 program 539–44
    code *539–42*
    display *544*
LOADBMP2 program *544–47,* 548
_loadds keyword 739

T

tab(s)
  as keyboard interface with dialog box
    651–52
  in submenu text 582
Tab key 337, 351
target file 15
template(s), dialog box 625–27
text
  color 206, 217
  dialog box entry fields 670–71
  entry window field 92
  right-justified 140–41
  static text fields 669
text, transferring with Clipboard 686–715
  Edit submenu standard commands 686–87
  getting text from Clipboard 689–90
  open Clipboard 690–91
  putting text in Clipboard 688–89
  reading hexadecimal number and symbol
    strings with Clipboard in HEXCALC2
    703–15
  shared memory segment preparation
    687–88
  TYPECLIP demonstration program
    691–703
text output 99–151. *See also* Advanced VIO
    (video input/output) functions
  AVIO and VIO functions for 314–16
  device-independent programming and
    105–19
    coordinate system 111–15
    GpiChar function 115–17
    numeric formatting 117–19
    presentation space 108–11
    size of client window 106–8
    WM_PAINT message and 115
  displaying on client windows 99–105
    different types of 76
  GPI primitives and 215–28
    color 217
    EASYFONT system program 219–23
    font files 217–18
    FONTS program 223–27
    output functions 215–17
  keyboard interface added in SYSVALS4
    144–51
  scroll bars
    adding to text output 119–23
    keyboard controlled 144–51
    optimizing 134–44

text output *(continued)*
  SYSVALS1 program 101–104
  SYSVALS2 program 126–33
  SYSVALS3 program 134–44
  SYSVALS program 144–51
  in title bar windows 68
text string resource. *See* string resources
TF_MOVE flag 729
TF_RIGHT flag 729
TF_SETPOINTERPOS flag 729
TF_STANDARD flag 729
TF_TOP flag 729
thread(s)
  coordinated execution of 812–13
  creating windows using message loop
    37–38
  execution of 811–12
  message ordering and 819–20
  message queues within multiple 26
  non-message queue thread 803–4, 821–21
  within processes 786–87
  two categories of 803–4
  using semaphores to trigger 813–19
TID_CURSOR identifier 447
TID_FLASHWINDOW identifier 447
TID_SCROLL identifier 447
timer 437–72
  analog clock in CLOCK program 464–72
  common method of using, in BEEPER1
    program *438–40*
  digital clock in DIGCLOCK program
    457–64
  free memory display in FREEMEM
    program 451–57
  immediate processing of timer message in
    BEEPER2 program 447–51
  imprecision in 442
  intervals over 65½ seconds 444–45
  limited availability of 443
  multiple 445–46
  multitasking with 790–95
  one-time message from 443–44
  resetting timer 445
  timers not set by the user 446–47
  WinStartTimer syntax 441–42
TIMES.FON font file 218
title bar window(s) 34, 38, 59
  as control window 77
  text in 68
Tms Rmn italic font 228, *229*
toggle keys 336

Charles Petzold

Charles Petzold is a full-time freelance writer and a contributing editor to *PC Magazine*, in which he writes about OS/2 in the "Environments" column. He has written articles about Microsoft Windows and OS/2 programming for the *Microsoft Systems Journal* and is the author of *Programming Windows*, also from Microsoft Press.

The manuscript for this book was prepared and submitted to Microsoft Press in electronic form. Text files were processed and formatted using Microsoft Word.

Cover design by Thomas A. Draper
Interior text design by Darcie S. Furlan
Illustrations by Becky Geisler-Johnson
Principal typography by Ruth Pettis

Text composition by Microsoft Press in Times Roman with display in Eurostile Demi, using the Magna composition system and the Linotronic 300 laser imagesetter.

Invest in CD-ROM Technology!

Microsoft Programmer's Library is the ultimate programmer's reference on a single CD-ROM disc. It contains full text of the MS-DOS Encyclopedia, the OS/2 Software Development Kit (SDK) manuals, the Windows SDK manuals, most Microsoft Language manuals, and several Microsoft Press books written for the serious programmer. Plus 20 floppies' worth of "clip art" sample code. Navigate through this mass of programming knowledge with boolean searches and hypertextual links between related data. The price is $395 suggested retail - a fraction of the price for this material in print form.

CD-ROM Demo Disc: This CD Disc contains the self running demo of Programmer's Library, as well as a full interactive demo with three portions of the actual Programmer's Library database.

1.2 MB floppy Demo Disk: Contains the self running demo as well as self-guided and interactive demos of the features of Programmer's Library. Also includes a portion of the actual Programmer's Library database.

360K floppy Demo Disk: The self running demo showing the impressive features of Programmer's Library.

Print your name and address:

Name

Company Name (*if applicable*)

Street Address

City   State   ZIP

Daytime telephone (*in case we have questions about your order*)

Check the appropriate box:

[ ]	CD-ROM disc.	098-078-201	$ 5 per disc X ____ordered	$ _____
[ ]	1.2 MB disk.	098-125-611	$ 3 per disk X ____ordered	$ _____
[ ]	360K disk.	098-125-203	$ 3 per disk X ____ordered	$ _____

Subtotal $ _____

Shipping and handling $ 2.50

TOTAL $ _____

Please send this card with check or money order to the following address:

Microsoft Programmer's Library
Demo Disk Offer
Box 3011
Bothell, WA 98041-3011

(Programming Presentation Manager by Charles Petzold   Feb '89)